Teaching Science as Inquiry

JOEL E. BASS
Late of Sam Houston State University

TERRY L. CONTANT
Science Curriculum and Instruction Specialist, LEARN

ARTHUR A. CARIN
Late of Queens College

Vice President and Executive Publisher: Jeffery W. Johnston
Publisher: Kevin M. Davis
Editor: Meredith D. Fossel
Development Editor: Bryce Bell
Editorial Assistant: Maren Vigilante
Senior Managing Editor: Pamela D. Bennett
Project Manager: Mary Harlan
Production Coordination: S4Carlisle Publishing Services

Design Coordinator: Diane C. Lorenzo
Photo Coordinator: Valerie Schultz
Cover Design: Candace Rowley
Cover Image: Fotosearch
Operations Specialist: Susan W. Hannahs
Director of Marketing: Quinn Perkson
Marketing Manager: Erica M. DeLuca
Marketing Coordinator: Brian Mounts

For related titles and support materials, visit our online catalog at www.pearsonhighered.com.

Copyright © 2009, 2005, 2001, 1997, 1993, 1989, 1985, 1980, 1975, 1970, 1964 by Pearson Education, Inc.

All rights reserved. No part of the material protected by this copyright notice may be reproduced or utilized in any form or by any means, electronic or mechanical, including photocopying, recording, or by any information storage and retrieval system, without written permission from the copyright owner.

To obtain permission(s) to use material from this work, please submit a written request to Pearson/Allyn & Bacon, 501 Boylston Street, Suite 900, Boston, MA 02116 or fax your request to 617-671-2290.

Between the time website information is gathered and then published, it is not unusual for some sites to have closed. Also, the transcription of URLs can result in typographical errors. The publisher would appreciate notification where these errors occur so that they may be corrected in subsequent editions.

Library of Congress Cataloging-in-Publication Data
Bass, Joel E.
   Teaching science as inquiry / Joel E. Bass, Terry L. Contant, Arthur A. Carin. -- 11th ed.
     p. cm.
   Rev. ed. of: Teaching science as inquiry / Arthur A. Carin. 10th ed. 2005.
   Includes bibliographical references and index.
   ISBN 978-0-13-159949-9
  1. Science--study and teaching (Elementary) I. Contant, Terry L. II. Carin, Arthur A.
III. Carin, Arthur A. Teaching science as inquiry. IV. Title.
   LB1585.C28 2009
   372.3'5044--dc22.

                         2008002463

Photo Credits: EyeWire Collection/Getty Images–Photodisc, p. 2; Arthur A. Carin, pp. 7, 80 (*top*); Thinkstock, p. 9; Anthony Magnacca/Merrill, pp. 28, 45 (*both*), 86, 89, 119, 190, 208 (*both*), 236, 244; Barbara Schwartz/Merrill, p. 60; Scott Cunningham/Merrill, p. 80 (*center, bottom*), 92, 252, 262; Valerie Schultz/Merrill, p. 96; Laura Bolesta/Merrill, p. 110; Getty Images–Stockbyte, p. 136; Krista Greco/Merrill, p. 139; Richard T. Nowitz/Photo Researchers, Inc., p. 184; Getty Images, Inc., p. 206; David Buffington/Getty Images, Inc.–Photodisc, p. 209; © Ellen B. Senisi/Ellen Senisi, p. 230; Richard Haynes/Prentice Hall School Division, p. 263; Helen Bass, p. A-213. All color insert photos by Helen Bass.

Printed in the United States of America

10 9 8 7 6 5 4 3 2 1   EB   12 11 10 09 08

**Allyn & Bacon
is an imprint of**

Dedication

THIS BOOK IS DEDICATED to the memory of Dr. Joel E. Bass, who passed away after completing the eleventh edition. Dr. Bass inspired many science educators during his 35 years at Sam Houston State University, and he touched thousands more through his work on the ninth, tenth, and eleventh editions of *Teaching Science as Inquiry*. Joel, your passion for teaching science lives on in our memories, and in this book.

THIS BOOK IS ALSO DEDICATED to the memory of Dr. Arthur A. Carin, author of the first eight editions of the book (then called *Teaching Science as Discovery*). Through five decades of exemplary writing, teaching, research, and service, Dr. Carin had a significant, positive impact on science education. Art, you are remembered and honored.

Preface

THE RAPID ADVANCE of cognitive learning theories in the past few years has led educators to realize the need for students to be more actively engaged in their own construction of knowledge. This research tells us that an inquiry approach to science teaching motivates and engages all types of students, helping them understand the relevance of science to their lives, as well as the nature of science itself.

Inquiry is both a way for scientists and students to investigate the world and a way to teach. In this instructional environment, teachers act as facilitators of learning, guiding students in asking simple but thoughtful questions about the world and finding ways to engage them in answering their questions.

Inquiry incorporates the use of hands-on and process-oriented activities for the benefit of knowledge construction while building investigation skills and habits of mind in students. Inquiry encourages students to connect their prior knowledge to observations and to use their observations as evidence to increase personal scientific knowledge and explain how the world works.

But is there a manageable way for new and experienced teachers to bring inquiry into their science classrooms?

Drawing on a solid understanding of inquiry with a teaching framework that builds in accountability for science content learning, and using inquiry-based activities, teachers can create and manage an engaging, productive science classroom. By integrating an inquiry approach, science content, teaching methods, standards, and a bank of inquiry activities, the eleventh edition of *Teaching Science as Inquiry* demonstrates a manageable way for new and experienced teachers to bring inquiry successfully into the science classroom.

The Inquiry Framework

In this edition we have used the National Science Education Standards (NSES) and the 5-E Learning Cycle model of instruction to create an inquiry framework for science teaching. *Teaching Science as Inquiry* models this effective approach to science teaching with a two-part structure. *Part 1: Methods for Teaching Science as Inquiry* lays the foundation for teaching standards-based elementary science, scaffolding an understanding of an inquiry lesson model and how to use it to teach science.

Part 2: Activities for Teaching Science as Inquiry uses the 5-E instructional model, clarified in Part 1 of the text, as a framework for all inquiry activities. By keying each activity to the National Science Education Standards, the text further provides new and experienced teachers with a solid foundation for science teaching.

NSES
STANDARDS ABOUT ORGANISMS AND CONCEPTS AND
PRINCIPLES THAT SUPPORT THE STANDARDS FOR GRADES K–4

NSES Standards

Students should understand:

- Characteristics of Organisms (K–4)
- Life Cycles of Organisms (K–4)

Concepts and Principles That Support the Standards

- Organisms have basic needs. For example, animals need air, water, and food; plants require air, water, nutrients, and light. Organisms can survive only in environments in which their needs can be met.
- Each plant or animal has different structures that serve different functions in growth, survival, and reproduction.
- Plants and animals have life cycles that include being born, developing into adults, reproducing, and eventually dying. The details of this life cycle are different for different organisms.

Source: Reprinted from *National Science Education Standards* by The National Academy of Sciences, with permission courtesy of the National Academies Press, Washington DC.

National Science Education Standards

Many years of work and research in the science education community have provided a coherent, research-based vision for a new era of science education. As a result, the *National Science Education Standards* (NSES) were created to coordinate the goals and objectives for science instruction.

Throughout this edition, you will have an opportunity to become familiar with the *National Science Education Standards* through margin notes and lengthier features quoting from the *Standards* document, showing the *Standards'* relationship to chapter content and specifically connecting activities to the *Standards*. This integrated coverage in all chapters and activities highlights the importance of using the *National Science Education Standards* to inform instruction.

5-E Model

The *Activities* portion of the text follows the 5-E model of instruction, which frames each activity in terms of engaging, exploring, explaining, elaborating, and evaluating. This learning cycle model, introduced early in the text, reflects the NSES *Science as Inquiry Standards,* seamlessly integrating inquiry and the *Standards* to create a science teaching framework best suited for engaging students in meaningful science learning while providing accountability opportunities for teachers.

3. How do the seeds in the two bags compare?
4. What do you think is the effect of temperature on germination (sprouting)? Why do you think so? What is your evidence?

10. WHAT SEEDS DO WE EAT? (K–4)

ENGAGE

a. Ask: *What seeds or seed products do we eat?*

EXPLORE

b. Hold a classroom "seed feast." Provide a variety of seeds for children to eat. Consider some of the seeds and seed products in the accompanying chart for the seed feast.

Safety Precautions

Make sure children are not allergic to any food you provide for them to eat, such as peanuts.

EXPLAIN

c. Using the chart, conduct a discussion of the various seeds and seed products we eat. Emphasize that rather than the cotyledons providing food for the seeds to germinate and begin growth, they are providing food energy for our survival and growth.

SEEDS AND SEED PRODUCTS WE EAT

Food	Seed or Seed Product
Peas	seeds (and fruit)
Beans	seeds (and fruit)
Corn	seeds
Rice	seeds
Peanuts	seeds
Sunflower seeds	seeds
Chocolate	made from seeds of cacao plant
Coffee	made from seeds of coffee plant
Vanilla	made from seeds of orchid
Cumin (spice)	made from cumin seeds
Flour	made from wheat, barley, or other grass seeds
Pretzels	made from flour
Bread	made from flour
Tortillas	made from flour or corn
Breakfast cereals	made from the seeds of grasses including wheat, rye, oats, and barley

Source: Adapted from National Gardening Association, 1990. *GrowLab.* National Gardening Association, Burlington, VT.

ELABORATE

d. As a take-home activity, have the students keep a mini-journal about the seeds they eat for a week. Have a discussion with the class to identify the kinds of information that should be included in their journal. Draft a letter to parents describing the project.

EVALUATE

e. Create a checklist, to be included with the parent letter, that students can use to self-evaluate their work. Use the same checklist to assist in your evaluation of the final products.
f. Post the mini-journals so students can view and have discussions about the different kinds of seeds their classmates eat. This is a form of informal peer assessment.

Methods for Teaching Science as Inquiry

The *Methods* portion of this edition scaffolds the understanding of science concepts; investigation procedures; concepts of teaching, learning, and assessment; and the 5-E and other instructional models to help readers understand the inquiry approach to teaching. Among the many highlights of this revision, you will find

- attention given to strategies for teaching with inquiry methods in a high-stakes testing environment;
- a revised assessment chapter, based on Bloom's taxonomy of educational objectives, including the interpretation of high-stakes testing results and linking standards to both learning objectives and assessment items;
- updated, research-based coverage on meeting the needs of English Language Learners (ELLs) and strategies for diverse learners;
- full integration with additional online material found on MyEducationLab (www.myeducationlab.com) to complement chapter content;
- a strong focus throughout the book on the 5-E model of instruction;
- a comprehensive discussion of conceptual change and how to use conceptual change strategies within the 5-E model of instruction;
- margin notes that link readers to activities that model standards-based inquiry and developmentally appropriate science content;
- suggestions on how to construct and use performance assessments and how to use traditional assessments in new ways;
- the presentation of exciting new advancements and trends in educational technology and how they apply to the science classroom;
- clarification of various ideas important to inquiry, including aspects of the nature of science and constructivist principles of learning;
- classroom scenarios that illustrate strategies of inquiry instruction and introduce readers to important science concepts; and
- a look at descriptive investigations, classificatory investigations, and experimental investigations, three main ways children can learn to investigate the world.

Activities for Teaching Science as Inquiry

An important change in the eleventh edition is an update of *Part 2: Activities for Teaching Science as Inquiry*. The activities continue to follow the NSES *Content Standards*, further developing new and experienced teachers' fluency with a *Standards*-based science classroom. In addition, these activities have been revised to follow, even more closely, the 5-E instructional model, creating a manageable way to engage students in inquiry activities.

Using Activities for Teaching Science as Inquiry

The *Activities for Teaching Science as Inquiry*

- can be used to illustrate and expand on the science content, and model the 5-E lesson procedures, engaging students in constructivist inquiry;
- provide a comprehensive view of how the NSES *Science Content Standards* can be used to organize curriculum and inform instruction in elementary and middle school science;

EXPLORE

b. Arrange students in groups. Provide two lenses of different magnifying power to each group. Show students how to support a lens vertically by taping it to the bottom of a Styrofoam cup. Remove the shade from the lamp and place the lamp in the room so that all groups have an unobstructed view of it.

Provide these instructions to students:
1. Tape each of the two lenses to the bottom of cups. Label the cups and lenses A and B.
2. Place lens A, supported by a cup, on the table so that it faces the lamp.
3. Fold a white sheet of paper along two opposite edges so it will stand up.
4. Place the sheet of paper behind the lens and move it back and forth until you see an image of the lamp on the paper.

5. Measure and record the distance from the lens to the image on the paper.
6. Ask: *Is the image inverted or right side up?* (Inverted) *Is the image of the lamp larger or smaller than the lamp itself?* (Smaller) Record your answers on a record sheet or in your science journal.
7. Repeat the procedures for lens B. Is the image formed on the paper inverted or right side up? Is the image larger or smaller than the lamp?
8. Which lens, A or B, formed a larger image? For which lens, A or B, was the lens closer to the paper screen?

- provide an interesting way for readers to learn significant science content that will be important for them to know in teaching science;
- provide a way for readers to prepare for the science portion of state certification exams; and
- become a bank of activities readers can draw on in developing lesson plans to teach during their science methods courses when they move into the schools as professional teachers.

The changes made to this edition help to build a clearer understanding of teaching science as inquiry and practical methods for implementing an inquiry approach to science education.

Instructor Supplements

Instructor's Manual

Free to adopters, this manual provides chapter-by-chapter supplements to enrich each class meeting. You will find an extensive test bank, as well as suggested activities, objectives and overviews, suggested readings, and other tools for teaching.

myeducationlab

"Teacher educators who are developing pedagogies for the analysis of teaching and learning contend that analyzing teaching artifacts has three advantages: it enables new teachers time for reflection while still using the real materials of practice; it provides new teachers with experience thinking about and approaching the complexity of the classroom; and in some cases, it can help new teachers and teacher educators develop a shared understanding and common language about teaching. . . ." [1]

As Linda Darling-Hammond and her colleagues point out, grounding teacher education in real classrooms—among real teachers and students and among actual examples of students' and teachers' work—is an important, and perhaps even an essential, part of training teachers for the complexities of teaching today's students in today's classrooms. For a number of years, we have heard the same message from many of you as we sat in your offices learning about the goals of your courses and the challenges you face in teaching the next generation of educators. Working with a number of our authors and with many of you, we have created a website that provides you and your students with the context of real classrooms and artifacts that research on teacher education tells us is so important. Through authentic in-class video footage, interactive simulations, rich case studies, examples of authentic teacher and student work, and more, **MyEducationLab** offers you and your students a uniquely valuable teacher education tool.

MyEducationLab is easy to use! Wherever the MyEducationLab logo appears in the margins or elsewhere in the text, you and your students can follow the simple link instructions to access the MyEducationLab resource that corresponds with the chapter content.

Go to the Homework and Exercises section in Chapter 1 of MyEducationLab to view the five part set of videos called "Water Wheels." These videos provide a view of a third grade class as they investigate, construct, and test water wheels. These videos provide a good example of the application of both the technological design cycle and the science as inquiry tasks. A video guide for this video is included in the *Online Professional Development* section at the end of this chapter.

[1]Darling-Hammond, L., & Bransford, J., Eds. (2005). *Preparing Teachers for a Changing World.* San Francisco: John Wiley & Sons.

These include:

Videos: Authentic classroom videos show how real teachers handle actual classroom situations.

Homework & Exercises: These assignable activities give students opportunities to understand content more deeply and to practice applying content.

Building Teaching Skills: These assignments help students practice and strengthen skills that are essential to quality teaching. By analyzing and responding to real student and teacher artifacts and/or authentic classroom videos, students practice important teaching skills they will need when they enter real classrooms.

Case Studies: A diverse set of robust cases drawn from some of our best-selling books further expose students to the realities of teaching and offer valuable perspectives on common issues and challenges in education.

⟨ONLINE PROFESSIONAL DEVELOPMENT

Pretests and Posttests to assess your knowledge of chapter content, along with exercises to enhance your understanding, can be found on MyEducationLab at www.myeducationlab.com.

Video Guides

Video clips on MyEducationLab selected for this chapter include *Teacher Discussion of Moon Phase Lessons* and *Investigating Goldfish—Parts 1, 2, 3,* and *4*.

Accessing the Videos

1. Go to the Homework and Exercises section in Chapter 4 of MyEducationLab to select and view videos for this chapter.
2. Videos might be viewed individually, by small groups of colleagues, or by the whole class.
3. As you watch each video, use the **Questions for Reflection** to guide your thoughts and note taking for personal use and group discussion.
4. Discuss your answers to the questions about each video with classmates.

Video: Teacher Discussion of Moon Phase Lessons

Overview

In this video we listen to the two fourth- and fifth-grade teachers we saw in the moon phase videos of Chapter 3 as they reflect on what they were trying to accomplish in the moon phase lessons.

Questions for Reflection

1. What examples of student records of observations do you see in the investigations of moon phases?

2. What evidence do you see that the 5-E model (or a similar model) forms the structure for the moon phase lessons?

Videos: Investigating Goldfish, Parts 1, 2, 3, and 4

The first three videos in the *Investigating Goldfish* video set follow kindergarten students as they investigate goldfish. In the fourth part, the classroom teacher reflects on her purposes for the lesson and the children's investigations. In this part, the teacher also discusses how the goldfish lesson followed the 5-E model of inquiry instruction.

Questions for Reflection

1. What Connecticut standards does the kindergarten teacher say the science lessons emphasize?
2. What questions did the teacher ask to engage the children in inquiry?
3. During the explore phase, what observations of the goldfish were made in response to the questions from the engage phase?
4. What conclusions about goldfish did the children reach in the explain phase of the lesson? What was the basis for the children's explanations?
5. How well do you think the teacher followed the 5-E model in designing and implementing the goldfish lesson?

Annenberg Videos

Video Series: Science K–6: Investigating Classrooms

Video: Completing the Circuit

To access Annenberg videos, follow the instructions given in the Online Professional Development section in Chapter 1 on page 26.

Simulations: Created by the IRIS Center at Vanderbilt University, these interactive simulations give hands-on practice at adapting instruction for a full spectrum of learners.

Student & Teacher Artifacts: Authentic student and teacher classroom artifacts are tied to course topics and offer practice in working with the actual types of materials encountered every day by teachers.

Individualized Study Plan: Your students have the opportunity to take pre- and post-tests before and after reading each chapter of the text. Their test results automatically generate a personalized study plan, identifying areas of the chapter they must reread to fully understand chapter concepts. They are also presented with interactive multimedia exercises to help ensure learning. The study plan is designed to help your students perform well on exams and to promote deep understanding of chapter content.

Readings: Specially selected, topically relevant articles from ASCD's renowned *Educational Leadership* journal expand and enrich students' perspectives on key issues and topics.

Other Resources

Lesson & Portfolio Builders: With this effective and easy-to-use tool, you can create, update, and share standards-based lesson plans and portfolios.

MyEducationLab is easy to assign, which is essential to providing the greatest benefit to your student. Visit www.myeducationlab.com for a demonstration of this exciting new online teaching resource.

Acknowledgments

Science education is a dynamic field. Application of new research findings, technological advances, and state and national initiatives result in a gradual evolution of learning theories, instructional and assessment strategies, state content, and inquiry standards. Application of these current ideas in practice occurs most directly in the classrooms of our nation's schools. Our goal in writing and revising this textbook is to provide you an accurate view of contemporary science education, with specific suggestions, guidelines, and examples as you prepare to teach science to children and early adolescents so they become scientifically literate citizens of the future.

The revisions and modifications incorporated in the eleventh edition would not have been possible without insightful reviews of the tenth edition and suggestions for improvement from our colleagues. We acknowledge and express our gratitude to the following reviewers: James D. Ellis, The University of Kansas; Wendy Frazier, George Mason University; Violetta Lien, Texas State University, San Marcos; Leann Steinmetz, University of Texas, San Antonio; and Senay Yasar, Arizona State University.

We want to thank the many editors at Pearson who have helped make this edition possible, especially Meredith Sarver Fossel and Bryce Bell, whose amiable advice and support has enriched the efficacy of this text. The creation of classroom video segments to illustrate the content of the text would have been impossible without Meredith's support and the talents of videographer Carl Harris. We are also grateful for our collaboration with Autumn Benson, which led to the on-line components of the text through MyEducationLab. We also wish to thank Mary Harlan, our supportive project manager at Pearson. For their help in bringing the book to production, we appreciate the assistance of Mary Tindle and Amy Gehl at S4Carlisle Publishing Services.

Contents

Methods for Teaching Science as Inquiry

"Messing About in Science"

An Introduction

SCIENCE IS FUN! *The geneticist Barbara McClintock was one of the few women in American science in the 1930s. When asked 40 years later why she chose science as a career, she said: "I did it because it was fun! I couldn't wait to get up in the morning. I never thought of it as 'science.'" (Judson, 1980, p.4). Expressions of the sheer enjoyment of science appear again and again in scientists' reflections on their work. In doing science, the excitement of pursuing the unknown, the joy of discovery, the achievement of elegance in an explanation, and the satisfaction of accomplishment are almost what matters most.*

The developers of the Elementary Science Study (ESS) program drew on the adventures of Rat and Mole in The Wind in the Willows *to express the spirit of "fun" they wanted to incorporate into science for children. Rat and Mole found pure joy in "messing about in boats." The ESS developers sought to design science activities that would create similar feelings in young learners. Thus, they adopted "messing about in science" as a metaphor for their program activities. Written by Kenneth Grahame in the early 1900s,* The Wind in the Willows *still enchants young readers today. Read this delightful excerpt from Mole's first river adventure and see how Rat and Mole can serve as models for you and your students as you freely engage in scientific inquiry and encounter, once again, the wonders of science.*

As the narrative begins, Mole and Water Rat are eyeing each other cautiously across a great river.

"Hullo, Mole!" said the Water Rat.

"Hullo, Rat!" said the Mole.

"Would you like to come over?" inquired the Rat presently.

"Oh, it's all very well to *talk*," said the Mole, rather pettishly, he being new to a river and riverside life and its ways.

The Rat said nothing, but stooped and unfastened a rope and hauled on it; then lightly stepped into a little boat which the Mole had not observed. It was painted blue outside and white within, and was just the size for the two animals; and the Mole's whole heart went out to it at once, even though he did not yet fully understand its uses.

The Rat sculled smartly across and made fast. Then he held up his fore-paw as the Mole stepped gingerly down. "Lean on that!" he said. "Now then, step lively!" and the Mole to his surprise and rapture found himself actually seated in the stern of a real boat.

"This has been a wonderful day!" said he, as the Rat shoved off and took to the sculls again. "Do you know, I've never been in a boat before in all my life."

"What?" cried the Rat, open-mouthed. "Never been in a—you never—well I—what have you been doing, then?"

"Is it so nice as all that?" asked the Mole shyly, though he was quite prepared to believe it as he leant back in his seat and surveyed the cushions, the oars, the rowlocks, and all the fascinating fittings, and felt the boat sway lightly under him.

"Nice? It's the *only* thing," said the Water Rat solemnly, as he leant forward for his stroke. "Believe me, my young friend, there is *nothing*—absolutely *nothing*—half so much worth doing as simply messing about in boats. Simply messing," he went on dreamily: "messing—about—in—boats: messing—"

"Look ahead, Rat!" cried the Mole suddenly.

It was too late. The boat struck the bank full tilt. The dreamer, the joyous oarsman, lay on his back at the bottom of the boat, his heels in the air.

"—about in boats—or *with* boats," the Rat went on composedly, picking himself up with a pleasant laugh. "In or out of 'em, it doesn't matter. Nothing seems to matter, that's the charm of it. Whether you get away, or whether you don't, whether you arrive at your destination or whether you reach somewhere else, or whether you never get anywhere at all, you're always busy, and you never do anything in particular; and when you've done it there's always something else to do, and you can do it if you like, but you'd much better not. Look here! If you've really nothing else on hand this morning, supposing we drop down the river together, and have a long day of it?"

The Mole waggled his toes from sheer happiness, spread his chest with a sigh of full contentment, and leaned back blissfully into the soft cushions. "What a day I'm having!" he said. "Let us start at once!"

In the words of the Mole, "Let us start at once" to explore the *whats*, *whys*, and *hows* of teaching children science as inquiry and see for ourselves why children find such joy in messing about in science.

Source: From *The Wind in the Willows* (pp. 3–5), by Kenneth Grahame, 1908/1981, E. Shepard, illus. New York: Charles Scribner's Sons.

1

F*rom the earliest grades, students should experience science in a form that engages them in the active construction of ideas and explanations and enhances their opportunities to develop the abilities of doing science. Teaching science as inquiry provides teachers with the opportunity to develop student abilities and to enrich student understanding of science.*

(*National Science Education Standards,* National Research Council, 1996, p. 121)
(Emphasis added.)

Children, Science, and Inquiry: Some Preliminary Questions

CHILDREN ARE NATURALLY CURIOUS. Their curiosity shows itself as they watch and wonder about the world around them. If we are careful to listen to them, we can hear young children ask such questions as: *Do ants make tunnels under the ground? Where does the rain come from? Where does the puddle go after the rain?* As children grow and mature, their questions become more complex: *Why can astronauts go to the moon but not to the sun? Why does the moon look different every night but the sun always looks the same?*

A childlike curiosity remains in adult scientists, but it has erupted into a passion, an urge—even rage—to know and understand the universe (Judson, 1980). A lone scientist, driven primarily by an intense desire to know, might spend years researching different aspects of mosquitos: *How do mosquitos sense their prey? Do they smell it? If so, how does the olfactory sense work?* It may take a large team of scientists to answer some questions: *What is the moon's surface like? What are the causes of different cancers?*

How we as teachers view science and the learning of science is critical to the ways we build on and nurture our students' inborn curiosity. If the meaning teachers attach to science is "finding the right answer," they will probably focus on providing factual answers to children through a direct instruction and reading approach to science (Rowe, 1996, p. 164). Taught in this way, however, students are not likely to remain interested in questioning, collecting information, and generating explanations, because that is not the approach to science they encounter. On the other hand, if teachers view science as inquiry and children as constructive learners, they will want to teach science in ways that engage students in the active construction of ideas and explanations and enhance their abilities to inquire.

The vision of science education we present in this book is one in which all children have the opportunity to engage in science as inquiry—to explore and construct ideas and explanations of the natural world within a supportive community of learners (Loucks-Horsley, Hewson, Love, & Stiles, 1998). The realization of this vision for each of your students depends on what you choose to teach in science, how you teach and assess it, and how you arrange your classroom environment for learning. Solid scientific knowledge is necessary, but you don't need to be a science major to teach science effectively through an inquiry approach. What you do need is contagious curiosity, a willingness to explore with your students, and a commitment to personal excellence and continued learning. Your own science knowledge will grow as you teach.

This chapter provides background and guidance as you begin to explore teaching science as inquiry to children and adolescents. When you have finished studying this chapter, you should be able to answer these questions:

- *What do scientist do when they inquire? What should students learn to do when they inquire? What does it mean to teach science as inquiry?*

- *Why should children learn science from the earliest grades? What does it mean to be scientifically literate? What is the NCLB Act, and why is early science education important for this federal law?*

- *What are the National Science Education Standards? How are standards connected to curriculum, instruction, and assessment? What approach to science teaching and learning do national and state standards recommend?*

- *What is meant by conceptual understanding in science? How are facts, scientific concepts, principles, and theories interconnected?*

- *What are the tasks of scientific inquiry? What can we do to help students develop inquiry abilities?*

- *Why is it important for students to understand the nature of science and scientific inquiry? What are some specific understandings about science and inquiry that chilldren and adolescents should learn?*

- *How does technology differ from science? What are the steps in the technological design cycle? How can the tasks of inquiry and the technological design cycle be used together in classroom investigations?*

Science is a way of knowing the natural world. As a way of knowing, "science is both a body of knowledge that represents current understanding of [the natural world] and the process whereby that body of knowledge has been established and is being continually extended, refined, and revised" (Duschl, Schweingruber, & Shouse, 2007, p. 2). Understanding science requires an understanding of both elements.

Inquiry instruction is a method of teaching that parallels what scientists do when they do science. *What do scientists do when they do science?* No single "scientific method" invariably works for scientists. Rather, there are many methods. But scientists typically ask questions, find ways to investigate the questions through observations and experiments, collect and organize data, and construct models, theories, and explanations based on observational evidence, existing knowledge, and clear arguments. Scientists' imagination also plays a critical role in this process. Through participating in inquiry like scientists, students learn to raise questions, gather data through observation and investigation, acquire scientific knowledge, and use the knowledge in making sense of and explaining observational data.

Constructive Learning

Inquiry instruction supports a *constructivist* approach to learning science. According to this approach, learning is a construction based on the learner's prior knowledge. Students take in information from many sources, including personal discoveries and acquisition from teachers, books, videos, and other resources. But in constructing understanding, students must connect new information to their existing knowledge and experiences, reorganize

> Scientific knowledge is always tentative; if a prediction fails, theories must be modified to fit new evidence.

their knowledge structures and assimilate new information to them, and construct meaning for themselves (Loucks-Horsley et al., 1998).

Although learners are the ones who construct knowledge, in inquiry instruction teachers are active in the process. Teachers provide for new experiences of the natural world, encourage wonder, help students form questions that can be investigated, help them plan investigation strategies, provide materials for investigations, interact with students as they investigate, assist them in organizing and making sense of the data, provide direct instruction on concepts, principles, and theories, and guide them in constructing scientific explanations.

Consider this example of an inquiry lesson in science in first grade.

An Invitation to Inquiry Science: Leaves

To begin an inquiry lesson on leaves, Debbie Wu talked with her first graders about trees, leaves, and the seasons. She pointed out that since this was the fall season, the trees were losing their leaves and the leaves were accumulating on the ground. She also discussed what season would come next and asked the children what the trees would look like when winter came, what the weather would be like then, and how they would dress for it. Through this dialogue, Ms. Wu helped the children begin to focus their curiosity and attention on particular aspects of the world. It also helped her to assess the children's prior knowledge and to adjust her instructional plans accordingly.

At the next science time Ms. Wu gave each child a small basket containing about 10 leaves. She arranged the class into pairs and instructed the children in each pair to place leaves from their baskets together into a pile on their table. "What do you notice about the leaves? What do you wonder about? What would you like to *investigate* about leaves?" Ms. Wu asked. The children observed the leaves and talked with each other and Ms. Wu about what they saw. Most children were first drawn to the different colors of the leaves. One child said, "Leaves are usually green. Why are these leaves brown and red?" A second child wondered why one part of a leaf was white and another part red. Another child noticed the "spines" of the leaves (the stem). "It's straight," the child exclaimed, feeling a stem, "with little bumps on it." This little observer also commented on the "bones" of the leaves (the veins) sticking out from the spines.

Acknowledging the children's questions and comments, Ms. Wu guided them to explore the questions: *Which leaves are alike? How are they alike? How do they differ from the other leaves?* After a discusson of how the children might investigate this question, the children sorted their piles of leaves into groups based on likenesses. As the children worked on sorting the leaves, Ms. Wu went around the classroom, observing the children, discussing the similarities and differences of the leaves with them, and providing assistance as needed. Since there were four different kinds of trees in the yard where the teacher gathered the leaves, most groups of children ended up with four piles of leaves (see Figure 1-1).

Back in a whole-class configuration, Ms. Wu reminded the children of the initial question, *How are leaves alike and different?* The students then discussed what they noticed about the leaves in the different piles and what their observations made them wonder. Building on their observations of leaves, Ms. Wu helped the children begin to recognize that leaves from the same tree are alike; they have similar properties such as similar shapes and structures of veins and points along their edges. Extending their generalization that leaves from the same tree are alike, the children also concluded that leaves from different trees have different shapes and structures of veins and edges.

Go to the Homework and Exercises section in Chapter 1 of MyEducationLab to read "A Conversation on Leaves," an interesting report on the observations and reflections of pre-school learners about leaves.

A variety of additional activities on leaves can be found on pages A-138 and A-139 of *Activities for Teaching Science as Inquiry,* the activities volume that accompanies this book.

Many topics in elementary school science can be addressed at any grade level, K–6. In early grades, emphasis is primarily on observaton and classification, as in the leaves lesson. In upper grades, emphasis on observation and classification continues, but activities that lead children to use their data as evidence in constructing complex explanations are typically added.

Figure 1-1 Leaves of different kinds have different attributes. What are some of the ways the leaves illustrated here differ?

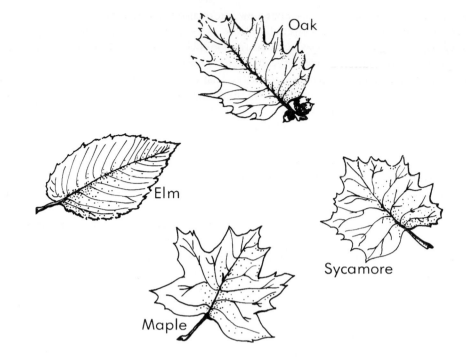

Features of the leaves lesson are found in most inquiry lessons in science. These features include:

* A question about some aspect of the natural world that could be investigated was asked.
* The children, aided by the teacher, found ways to gather observational data relevant to the question.
* The observations were then used as evidence to form generalizations, interpretations, and explanations to answer the question.

Through their own inquiry, the children were beginning to learn an approach to observing and understanding that would serve them well as they watched and wondered about the world. Teachers of science in grades K–8 should make a coordinated effort to teach science concepts and inquiry processes simultaneously.

Are you beginning to see the importance of inquiry experiences for children? Can you see yourself incorporating genuine inquiry into your own science lessons?

* What were the questions investigated by the children in the lessons on leaves?
* What did they do to gather data relevant to these questions?
* What generalization did they develop?
* How were the generalizations connected to the children's observational evidence?
* How did the children use the new generalization to answer the questions raised?

Why Should Science Be Taught in Elementary School?

In the modern world, some knowledge of science is essential for everyone (Duschl et al., 2007). But, why should students begin to learn science in the elementary grades? There are several reasons to support early science education.

Learning to Think and Understand

Developing understanding in science involves various processes of inquiry, including observing, raising questions, engaging in meaningful investigations, combining, comparing, and reflecting on data, and using existing knowledge to make sense of what is seen. Jean

Piaget has shown that such processes of thinking develop gradually over a long period of time from infancy through adolescence. Piaget was concerned with the spontaneous development of thought. Contemporary research by educators and psychologists highlights the important contribution that interactions with peers, teachers, and others can make in the development of thinking. Learning to think scientifically and to understand the scientific view of the natural world takes time. Science experiences from the earliest grades are essential for helping students learn to think and understand.

Scientific Literacy

A second reason to teach science in elementary school is to begin early to build *scientific literacy*. Some of your students will likely choose to work in a scientific, technical, or health-care profession, but *all* of them will need to be scientifically literate to take an active role in recognizing problems, contributing to solutions, and making informed decisions about local, state, national, and global issues.

The *National Science Education Standards* (National Research Council, 1996) define **scientific literacy** as

> the knowledge and understanding of scientific concepts and processes required for personal decision-making, participation in civic and cultural affairs, and economic productivity. (p. 22)

According to the *National Science Education Standards* (National Research Council 1996, p. 114), "Lifelong scientific literacy begins with understandings, attitudes, and values established in the earliest years."

Science Education and National Concerns

Many people believe that what happens in elementary science today can have potentially dramatic effects, not only on the lives of children, but also on the economic future of our

Go to the Homework and Exercises section in Chapter 1 of MyEducationLab to read the "Science Literacy for All in the 21st Century" article detailing why science literacy is such an important goal for our nation.

"Lifelong scientific literacy begins with understandings, attitudes, and values established in the earliest years." (National Science Education Standards, National Research Council, 1996, p. 114)

nation. A prestigious panel sponsored by the National Academies of Science produced a report, *Rising Above the Gathering Storm* (National Academies of Science, 2006), that details some of the global issues our nation faces.

The report noted that the "high quality of life" in the United States, "our national security, and our hope that our children and grandchildren will inherit ever-greater opportunities" is derived, in large part, from "the steady stream of scientific and technological innovations" produced in this country since World War II. But there are indications that our global leadership position in science and technology is changing. Among the findings of the committee are these:

- Since the early 1990s, the United States has become a net importer of high-technology products.
- Other nations are graduating considerably more engineers, computer scientists, and information technologists than the United States.
- Lower labor costs and the availability of highly trained scientists and engineers have led to the location of factories by U.S. companies in foreign countries and the outsourcing of many jobs.
- International assessments in math and science indicate that U.S. K–12 students lag behind students from other countries.

In response to such findings, the committee recommended, among other things, that the United States vastly improve science and math education to increase the pool of students prepared to choose science as a career. Improving science and math education must begin in the early grades.

Language Literacy and Mathematics Competency

Science provides a rich context for children to apply and further develop their language and mathematics skills. In the process of acquiring information, students have opportunities to improve the skills needed in reading expository texts. For example, children learn to apply their skills of reading expository texts as they read about the many interesting treatments of science in trade books and children's literature (see Figure 1-2). Skills of reading in the content area are not only necessary in acquiring new information, they are essential in preparing for and taking standardized tests in reading, science, and other content areas.

Writing on prepared observations sheets and in science journals, editing collaboratively, refining procedures, and rewriting at each stage of the inquiry process can be an effective ways to enhance inquiry and to improve writing skills (Champagne & Kouba, 2000).

Science can also provide a context in which children can apply and practice their math skills, such as counting, estimating, measuring, putting data into tables, and constructing and interpreting graphs.

Early Science and the NCLB Legislation

Responding to growing concerns about the quality of education for all students in our nation, Congress passed the *No Child Left Behind* (NCLB) Act in 2001. Science education was an important part of this legislation. According to the NCLB Act, by the 2007–2008 school year, every state had to administer annual assessments of reading, math, and science at elementary, middle school, and high school levels. Results of these assessments provide information for determinations of whether schools are demonstrating adequate

---

Teachers of science at all grades, K–8, need to make a coordinated push—with teachers of mathematics and literacy—to connect science, math, and language arts instruction at all grades.

Currently, only the results of reading and math tests are used in the adequate yearly progress determinations at the federal level, but congressional leaders periodically present addendums to the NCLB Act that would include science in demonstrations of AYP. However, some states already include the results of the science tests in high-stakes evaluations of students and teachers.

Children's Literature and Science

There are many wonderful books that connect science and literacy. For example, when studying *astronomy* in science, read some of the following books during language arts time.

A cricket looks for another insect that is just like himself. This and other Eric Carle books, The Very Hungry Caterpillar, The Very Busy Spider, *and* The Very Clumsy Click Beetle, *delight children with surprising interactive elements. All of these stories launch children into wanting to find out more about insects, patterns, and the natural environments where survival is dependent on interdependency.*

- *Follow the Drinking Gourd* by Jeanette Winter (Grades K–6). Runaway slaves followed the "Drinking Gourd," another name for the Big Dipper, north to Canada and freedom. In science, children can learn how to use the Big Dipper to tell time and find the North Star.

- *The Magic School Bus Lost in the Solar System* by Joanna Cole (Grades K–6). A fantasy trip to the moon, sun, and planets, noting their colors, sizes, and unique features. In science, construct scale models of the solar system and charts of planetary features.

- *Sky Songs* by Myra Cohn Livingston (Grades 5–12). Poems about various aspects of the sky.

- *To Space and Back* by Sally Ride with Susan Okie (Grades 4–7). An astronaut's fascinating description of what it's like to travel in space—to live and work in conditions unlike anything we know on earth. In science, students can access and study NASA's website, including real-time data.

- *The Way to Start a Day* by Byrd Baylor (Grades 3–7). The many ways people of the world have celebrated the dawn. In science, construct models of the earth-sun system that explain why the sun rises each morning. Also, observe the changing positions of sunrise and sunset throughout the seasons.

Figure 1-2   Children's literature connections to science.

Source: "Children's literature connections to science" is based on material in the Great Explorations in Math and Science (GEMS) teacher's handbook entitled *Once Upon a GEMS Guide: Connecting Young People's Literature to Great Explorations in Math and Science,* copyright by The Regents of the University of California, and is used with permission. The GEMS series includes more than 70 teacher's guides and handbooks for preschool through eighth grade, available from: LHS GEMS, Lawrence Hall of Science, University of California, Berkeley, CA 94720-5200. (510) 642-7771. For more information, visit our website at www.lhsgems.org

yearly progress (AYP) toward the goal of 100% proficiency for all students. Schools that do not maintain adequate yearly progress are subject to severe sanctions. Many believe that the best way to prepare elementary and middle school students for the science portion of these statewide examinations is a coordinated K–8 effort built around inquiry approaches to science.

You will likely have some students with disabilities and students who are English Language Learners (ELLs) in your inclusion classroom. Although different learning pathways may be necessary for some individuals, the goals of science instruction are the same for all students. With the exception that about 30% of students with special needs take an alternative form of the test, according to the NCLB, most students with special needs must take the same statewide assessments as regular education students. Assisting all learners to achieve proficiency in science, as well as in language, mathematics, and other subjects, is a national challenge.

What do you think? Do you agree that early experiences in science are essential for children today?

Ways to modify science activities and instruction for students with disabilities and for ELL students are discussed in Chapter 10.

U.S. Science Education: Where Have We Been, Where Are We Now, Where Are We Going?

Where Have We Been in Science Education?

Off and on since at least the 1950s, national concern has focused on the quality of U.S. science education. An early stimulus to these concerns was the successful launching of an earth-orbiting satellite, *Sputnik*, by the Russians in 1957. In response to *Sputnik*, the federal government began to commit more and more tax money to the development of exemplary science programs in the United States.

Most of the newly developed science programs were widely known by acronyms. At the elementary school level, the most successful programs funded by the National Science Foundation (NSF) were SAPA (Science—A Process Approach), SCIS (Science Curriculum Improvement Study), and ESS (Elementary Science Study). These programs, which were developed beginning in the 1960s, represent three very different approaches to science education. SAPA focused on the processes involved in doing science, SCIS on broad concepts for organizing scientific ideas, and ESS on investigation as a way to develop science knowledge.

The various "alphabet soup" programs were widely used in school districts across the nation. But it was the common, hands-on spirit of these new approaches to learning science that most influenced science education in the 1960s, 1970s, and 1980s. In these federally funded elementary science programs students did not just read about science, they did science. Science was more than a noun; it was also a verb—*sciencing*.

The late 1980s saw national movements toward establishing common goals and standards of excellence for science education and other subjects. The American Association for the Advancement of Science (AAAS) established Project 2061 to begin to explore what all U.S. students should know and be able to do in science in the 21st century. The year 2061 marks the next return of Halley's comet to our region of the solar system. By including this distant date in the project title, AAAS implied that it intended to take a very long view indeed in determining what students will need to know and be able to do to be scientifically literate throughout a new century.

Project 2061 published a number of pivotal documents, including *Science for All Americans* (Rutherford & Ahlgren, 1990), *Benchmarks for Science Literacy* (AAAS, 1993), and the *Atlas of Science Literacy, Volume 1* (AAAS, 2001) Volume 2 (2007). These documents have effectively expressed and clarified ideas about the nature and importance of science and science teaching. They have also laid the foundation for the development of national standards for science education.

Where Are We Now in Science Education?

Building on the work of Project 2061 and other groups, a distinguished panel coordinated by the National Research Council (NRC) worked on standards for science education throughout the early 1990s. In 1996, the *National Science Education Standards* (NSES) were published. The NSES offer the U.S. public a coherent vision of what it means to be scientifically literate.

There are six categories of standards in the *National Science Education Standards,* including Science Content Standards, Assessment Standards, Teaching Standards, Professional Development Standards, Science Education Program Standards, and Science Education System Standards. For teachers, the heart of the standards is the Science Content Standards, which include (1) standards related to conceptual knowledge and under-

You can read the *National Science Education Standards* on the website of the National Academies Press. For the URL to access the standards, see Table 1-1.

standing in physical science, life science, and earth and space science; (2) specific abilities of scientific inquiry; and (3) understandings about the nature of scientific inquiry.

The *National Science Education Standards* do not prescribe curriculum; that is a state and local responsibility. Rather, they describe what all students must understand and be able to do in science as a result of their cumulative learning experiences.

The central message that the NSES content standards convey, and the other types of standards support, is that students should be engaged in an *inquiry* approach to learning science that basically parallels the procedures scientists use and the attitudes they display in doing science. The standards emphasize that inquiry can involve many different approaches to science instruction, including hands-on–minds-on investigations, reading books, using Internet resources, talking and listening to scientists and teachers, and direct teacher instruction on the concepts, principles, and procedures of science. A common feature of all inquiry methods of instruction is a shift from a teacher-centered to a student-centered classroom. Through engaging in the many forms of inquiry, students learn how to investigate on their own and to work cooperatively with others. They learn important science knowledge and the process of generating science knowledge. And, they learn to use science knowledge in understanding the objects, organisms, and events in their environments. It is clear why the *National Science Education Standards* have declared, "inquiry into authentic questions generated from student experience is the central strategy for teaching science" (National Research Council, 1996, p. 31).

Where Are We Going in Science Education?

Although much has been accomplished in science education, much remains to be done. Recently, the National Research Council commissioned a distinguished panel chaired by science educator Richard Duschl to examine the state of science education in elementary and middle schools in our nation. In the report, *Taking Science to School: Learning and Teaching Science in Grades K–8* (Duschl et al., 2007), the panel critiqued and evaluated the standards movement and made recommendations about science education for the future. The panel also reviewed contemporary studies from psychologists and educators about how children develop understanding in science. Among the recommendations of the committee was the call to reduce the K–12 science content taught and to emphasize fewer well-chosen core concepts to focus more on understanding rather than just accumulating knowledge.

The National Science Teachers Association (NSTA) has recently initiated a new project, *Science Anchors*, that focuses on reducing the broad range of science topics and skills taught in the schools. Science Anchors seeks to help bolster student achievement in science by emphasizing the essential skills and topics in science that must be taught, given the limited amount of time teachers have with students. Achieving this objective will aid all of our nation's education stakeholders in the alignment of curriculum, instruction, and assessment practices and help teachers better manage their instruction, making teaching and learning more effective and efficient.

Research and best practices clearly show the importance of an inquiry approach to science teaching and learning. Yet many teachers are more comfortable with traditional approaches to science instruction that rely largely on telling and reading about science. The implementation of new approaches to science depends now on teachers like you. Will you join the growing body of teachers who are committed to the idea that children are constructive learners and learn best through approaches that involve them in doing science?

The No Child Left Behind Act requires states to have high-quality state standards in science. The statewide tests administered in each state are based on that state's standards. In most cases, state science standards reflect the *National Science Education Standards,* but go well beyond them in specificity and detail. You will be expected to use the standards in your state in planning instruction, guiding learning, and preparing students for statewide tests.

TABLE 1-1 NATIONAL SCIENCE EDUCATION REFORM PROJECTS

Documents	Description
Science for All Americans Project 2061 http://www.project2061.org/	• describes the nature of science and technology, including historical perspectives and their impact on society • describes understandings and ways of thinking that are essential for all citizens
Benchmarks for Science Literacy Project 2061 http://www.project2061.org/	• builds on *Science for All Americans* • states what all students should know and be able to do in science by the end of grades 2, 5, 8, and 12
Atlas of Science Literacy, Volumes 1 and 2 Project 2061 http://www.project2061.org/	• presents conceptual strand maps that show how K–12 students' understanding at the ideas and skills that lead to scientific literacy interconnect
National Science Education Standards National Research Council http://www.nap.edu/catalog.php?record_id=4962	• defines science education standards for science content, teaching, professional development, assessment, programs, and systems • emphasizes scientific literacy • focuses on inquiry approaches to teaching
Inquiry and the National Science Education Standards National Research Council http://www.nap.edu/catalog.php?record_id=9596	• provides a learning research foundation for the science standards • serves as a companion volume to the science standards
Federal No Child Left Behind Act of 2001 http://www.ed.gov/nclb/landing.jhtml	• requires that states must have their own standards and statewide assessments
Rising Above the Gathering Storm (2006) National Academies of Science http://www.nap.edu/catalog/11463.html	• provides a view of science in the national economy and the growing precariousness of our nation's leadership in the global economy • recommends that U.S. K–12 science and math education be vastly improved
For state standards and released tests, see state education agencies or departments. You can access links to many state standards and released tests through the Chapter 1 Resources for this text at http://www.prenhall.com/bass	• provides access to state standards • provides access to released tests from different states
Duschl, R. S., Schweingruber, H. A., & Shouse A. W. (2007). *Taking Science to School: Learning and Teaching Science in Grades K-8.* Washington, DC: National Academies Press, http://www.nap.edu/catalog/11625.html	• provides a critique and evaluation of the science standards movement • presents new research on how children learn science • suggests that science content should be further reduced to concentrate only on core conceptualizations in science

Direct links to the URLs in Table 1-1 are given in Chapter 1 of MyEducationLab.

Table 1-1 briefly describes several reform programs and documents that can impact the "whats and hows" of your science education program. For additional information, you are invited to access the Internet sites listed in Table 1-1.

What Shall We Teach in Science?

A synthesis of recommendations by science education leaders (Bybee et al., 1989; Duschl et al., 2007; National Research Council, 1996; National Research Council, 2000) suggests that major outcomes of science instruction should include the following goals or proficiencies:

- *Proficiency 1: Conceptual knowledge and understanding in science.* Students should acquire facts, build organized and meaningful conceptual structures, and use these conceptual structures in interpreting observations and constructing theories and explanations (Duschl et al., 2007, p. 37).
- *Proficiency 2: Abilities to carry out scientific inquiries.* Students should learn to gather, organize, and communicate observational data and use the data in developing knowledge, forming explanations, and answering questions.
- *Proficiency 3: Understandings about the nature of science and scientific inquiry.* Students should understand science as a way of knowing, the nature of scientific knowledge, and the connections between theory and evidence in science (Duschl et al., 2007, p. 37).

Duschl and his colleagues have emphasized that these proficiencies are not independent but should always be interconnected in learning science. We will examine each of these major science proficiencies in the following sections.

Proficiency 1: Conceptual Knowledge and Understanding in Science

As they engage in inquiry, students develop conceptual knowledge and understanding in science. The specific knowledge and understandings in physical science, life science, and earth and space science that elementary and middle school students should achieve are identified in national and state science standards.

Knowledge and understanding in science are composed of facts, concepts, principles or laws, models, theories, and explanations (National Research Council, 1996; Duschl et al., 2007).

Facts. A **fact,** in science, is a statement about an observation that has been repeatedly confirmed. Facts are not mere collections of random observations of the world. We make observations and generate facts selectively, based on prior knowledge and assumptions about what is valuable and what might be disregarded.

Concepts. **Concepts** are abstract ideas derived from experience around which new experiences may be organized. Concepts go beyond observations and facts and reflect the larger *ideas* of science. By reducing many observations to fewer categories, concepts bring a measure of coherence and simplicity to the world. Concepts are developed gradually, from many experiences and reflections on them.

Examples of concepts encountered in elementary science include stems and veins of leaves, magnets, magnetic poles, birds, minerals, cotyledons, and light reflection. Each of these concepts is a class in which the members of the class have some common attributes. Birds, for example, have two legs, wings, and feathers. Some birds lay eggs in nests and live in trees. Some birds, but not all, fly. Concepts enable us to interconnect past experiences so that we can better use them to begin to make sense of new experiences.

From the constructivist viewpoint, concepts are not simply passed from teachers or books to students; in order to *understand* a concept, children must be actively engaged in making sense of their experiences. Understanding of concepts begins to take place as students actively learn and use them to guide their own observations and extend their prior knowledge.

Investigations will sometimes show that there are exceptions to a principle. For example, contrary to the general principle that materials expand when heated and contract when cooled, water expands rather than contracts when it is cooled to its freezing point. That is why automobile radiators must have antifreeze added—to prevent damage that would be caused by expansion if water in the radiator froze.

 A glossary containing definitions of important terms used in this chapter can be found on MyEducationLab.

Seven-year old Rick stared out the car window for mile after mile as his family traveled across the endless plains of the American southwest. Finally he said, "The earth really is round, isn't it?" He was attempting to accommodate his own perceptions that the earth is flat with the theory of a round earth presented to him in school.

Principles. **Principles** are ideas about relationships among concepts. They are formed from investigations and observations of a few situations and generalized through inductive reasoning to other similar events and situations. In reasoning inductively, learners move from particular instances to generalizations about all cases.

As an example of principles, consider a science principle related to how things change with heat. Expanding (getting larger), contracting (getting smaller), hot (having a high temperature), and cold (having a low temperature) are all concepts in science (Vitale & Romance, 2000). These concepts are related to one another in the principle "objects expand when heated and contract when cooled." This relationship might be found in individual investigations and then generalized to a universal principle that holds in all cases. This principle can be used to explain, for instance, why concrete sidewalks are poured in sections with "expansion gaps" between the sections.

Well-established principles in science are sometimes referred to as *laws*, though there are no clear-cut guidelines in science for elevating principles to the status of laws. Examples of laws in science include the laws of reflection and refraction of light, the laws of motion, and the law of gravity.

Students should be guided to organize facts, concepts, and principles into conceptual structures or networks. Conceptual structures are important to students in developing theories and explanations of what is seen in the natural world.

Theories. In everyday language, people sometimes say, "I have a theory about that," or "Well, that's only a theory, not a fact." In the language of science and science education, the term **theory** has two, more precise, meanings. First, a scientific theory is an explanation of some aspect of the natural world that has undergone considerable testing and refinement. Examples of theories in this sense include Newton's theory of motion, the theory of light, and the theory of plate tectonics. Scientific theories generally use existing conceptual structures. But sometimes, new theories require the construction of new concepts and principles.

In the second meaning, theories are tentative explanations that serve to make observations of the world meaningful. Children of all ages watch the world, wonder about what they see, and form "theories" that help them make sense of what they encounter.

For example, in the leaves lesson described earlier in this chapter, young children theorized that leaves are like animals and have spines and bones. As another example, many, if not most, early grade children observe the earth around them, perceive that it is flat, and theorize that they live on a flat earth. It will take careful instruction, with evidence from various sources, such as photographs from space, to convince them that their flat-earth theory is unsatisfactory and that the earth is spherical, with plains, hills, valleys, mountains, and canyons scattered about on its surface.

Models. Scientists find that the use of models often makes it easier to think about physical reality. A **model** is a representation of objects and interactions in a physical system. Types of models include *physical models* (such as a model airplane or a model of the arrangement of planets and the sun in our solar system), *mathematical models* (such as an equation for principles of levers and balances), and *propositional models* (such as a set of rules for how magnets interact with other magnets and with different kinds of materials).

Through science instruction, teachers help students develop understanding by integrating facts, concepts, principles, models, and theories into coherent conceptual structures. An example of an inquiry approach to helping students construct integrated networks of the properties of water is given next.

Activity 1-1: Observations of Water Phenomena

1. Fill a 30 ml medicine cup all the way to the top with water. Use a dropper to add water drop by drop to the cup until it is heaping full and starts to overflow. How many drops of water from a dropper do you think you can add to the medicine cup before it overflows? Make a prediction. Try it and see. What does the surface of the water look like as drops are added? What happens to each drop of water as it is added to the cup? What do you observe happening when the water overflows the rim?

2. Use the dropper to add some water back into the cup so that it is almost ready to overflow again. How many paper clips do you think you can add to the filled medicine cup before it overflows? Make a prediction. Now, gently slide paper clips into the cup, one at a time down the edge of the cup. How many paper clips could you put in the water?

3. How do you explain your observations of the behavior of water in these two cases?

Building Conceptual Understanding: Properties of Water. Scientific understanding begins with observations of the real world. Through engaging in activities with water, children have opportunities to make many new observations and learn many new facts, as well as to raise questions, generate new conceptual knowledge, and form some explanations to answer their questions. Activity 1-1 provides an example of an investigation of the properties of water. This investigation may be new to you. Before reading on, obtain the necessary materials and try this activity for yourself.

The water drop investigation supports NSES standards about properties of objects and materials, as is shown in the accompanying NSES box.

Hands-on investigations like these arouse our curiosity, raise our interest level, and increase our motivation to learn. What did you observe and what *facts* did you learn about water from Activity 1-1? It is a fact, for example, that when water is added drop by drop to a small plastic medicine cup, the water will tend to heap up a surprising amount before it starts to spill over the edge of the cup. It is also a fact that as many as 30 paper clips can be

See *Activities for Teaching Science as Inquiry*, pages A-19–A-27 for a variety of additional activities for children on properties of water.

NSES **Science Standards**

Students should develop an understanding of

- properties of objects and materials (K–4).

Concepts and Principles That Support the Standards

- Objects have many observable properties (K–4).
- Materials can exist in different states—solids, liquids, and gases (K–4).

gently slid along the edge into a filled cup without the water overflowing. Such facts are the data or products of our observations that we organize and attempt to explain. How would you explain this puzzling behavior of water?

Children spontaneously form theories to explain what they see in the world. In a field test of an ESS unit called Kitchen Physics, some sixth-grade children explained the heaping effect of water by theorizing that water is "grabby" or "sticky." According to the grabbiness model of heaping, drops of water added to a cup *grab* on to or *stick* to water already in the cup, thus allowing the water to "heap."

Educational research indicates that teachers should recognize children's explanations and treat them with respect but go beyond them by providing learners with scientific explanations (Duschl et al., 2007). The scientific explanation for heaping is not so very different from the children's grabbiness explanation, but it is more powerful. Scientists model water as tiny particles (molecules) that attract or bond to one another. The attractive bonds between water particles account for heaping. Water heaps up in a cup until the gravitational forces pulling on the water that is above the rim of the cup overcome the attractive forces of the water particles for one another.

Since the children's concept of "grabbiness" comes close to capturing the essence of the bond theory, teachers can build on the children's conception when teaching them the scientific theory of attractive bonds between particles of the liquid.

Many other activities about the properties of water can be used to deepen and extend the knowledge and understanding of children about the properties of liquids. Activity 1-2 illustrates some additional facts about the properties of water. Before reading on, obtain the necessary materials, do this activity for yourself, and generate a possible explanation for what you observe.

To explain why water drops bead up on wax paper and spread out on aluminum foil, two concepts—cohesive bonds and adhesive bonds—are needed. *Cohesive bonds* bind water drops to one another; *adhesive bonds* bind water drops to different surfaces, such as wax paper or aluminum foil. Applying these new principles of cohesive and adhesive bonds, we might theorize that water beads up on wax paper because the cohesive forces within drops are greater than the adhesive forces between the drops and the wax paper. In contrast, water spreads out on aluminum foil because the adhesive forces between water drops and the aluminum are greater than the cohesive forces within the drops. Children might come up with this theory on their own. However, children's theories need to be refined and extended through instruction, including instruction on scientific terms. Just remember to build on concepts already developed and stay close to the observations of the real world made in investigations.

"Inventing hypotheses or theories to imagine how the world works and then figuring out how they can be put to the test of reality is as creative as writing poetry, composing music, or designing skyscrapers."

Science for All Americans, Rutherford and Ahlgren, 1989

Water drop phenomena may also be modeled in terms of *the skinlike* effect at the surface of a container or drop of water. Water acts as if it has a skin across its surface. Water heaps up in a medicine cup until the skin of the water becomes stretched too much and breaks. This skin like effect has been called *surface tension;* the term *tension* is a British term for force. Surface tension is a force acting at the surface of a container or drop of water.

Activity 1-2: Water Drops on Different Surfaces

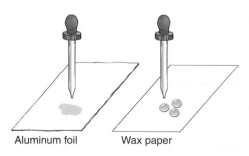
Aluminum foil   Wax paper

Using a dropper, put drops of water on wax paper and aluminum foil, as in the illustration. Make large drops and small drops. How do drops of water on wax paper compare with those on aluminum foil? What do the drops look like? Can you lead a drop around with a toothpick on each surface? What happens to small drops of water when led to interact with other drops of water on wax paper? What happens when you try to combine small drops of water on aluminum foil?

How can you explain your observations of what happens to water drops on the different surfaces?

TABLE 1-2 ANALYZING SCIENCE TOPICS IN TERMS OF FACTS, CONCEPTS, PRINCIPLES, AND THEORIES		
Knowledge Component	**Definition**	**Examples Related to Water**
Facts	objectively confirmed statements about observable objects or events	water heaps in medicine cups and beads up on wax paper
Concepts	classes of things or ideas that serve in the organization of experiences	bonds between particles, adhesion, cohesion
Principles	generalizations about the relationships among concepts	the closer the water particles, the stronger the bonds
Theories	networks of terms, assumptions, concepts, principles, and inferences that can be used to form tentative explanations of observations	at the surface of water the particles bond, forming a skinlike effect that can be applied to explain heaping and beading

Table 1-2 summarizes how scientific knowledge about water can be analyzed in terms of facts, concepts, principles, and theories.

Proficiency 2: Abilities to Carry Out Scientific Inquiry

Science is both a body of knowledge and a way of knowing (Duschl et al., 2007). Scientific inquiry—asking questions, gathering and analyzing observational data, and using the data as evidence in forming theories and building explanations—provides the basis for scientific knowledge. Thus, scientific inquiry and conceptual knowledge in science are intimately linked.

The *National Science Education Standards* (National Research Council, 1996) have captured the way that scientists inquire in a set of inquiry tasks that students should learn. Through engaging in scientific inquiry, students should learn to:

- *Ask a question about objects, organisms, and events in the environment.* In elementary and middle school science, questions should come (in so far as possible) from the experiences and activities of learners. Children need ample time to simply watch and wonder about the world around them—to observe and compare leaves, tend to mealworms, watch ants in their underground homes, find out about air, observe weather changes, and on and on. It is from such experiences that interesting and productive questions about the natural world can be generated.
- *Plan and conduct a simple investigation.* When inquiring scientifically, children investigate to gather evidence to use in answering their questions. In their investigations, children might observe what things are like or what is happening within a system, collect specimens for analysis, or do experiments (American Association for the Advancement of Science, 1993).
- *Use appropriate tools and techniques to gather data.* As students investigate, they use simple tools, such as thermometers, rulers and meter sticks, and hand lenses, and practice simple skills, such as observing, measuring, recording data, graphing, inferring, and predicting.
- *Use evidence and scientific knowledge to develop explanations.* As they develop explanations to answer their questions, children should reflect on the evidence they obtained and draw on existing and developing scientific knowledge to support their thinking. Most children have personal theories and explanations of objects, organisms, and

Chapter 2 describes and provides examples of three types of investigations—descriptive, classificatory, and experimental investigations—that students should understand and be able to carry out.

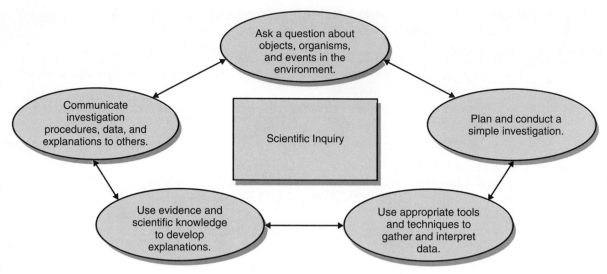

Figure 1-3 Tasks of scientific inquiry.

events but will need some degree of assistance from teachers in constructing scientific explanations.

- *Communicate investigations, data, and explanations to others.* Throughout the inquiry process, students engage in discourse with one another and their teachers about questions, investigations, findings, and explanations. Students should use different means, including speaking, writing, and drawing to represent and communicate their procedures, observations and data, and explanations to others.

Figure 1-3 graphically depicts the tasks of scientific inquiry.

The NSES (National Research Council, 1996, p. 121) emphasize that the inquiry tasks of Figure 1-3 should not be interpreted as the "scientific method." The tasks suggest some common characteristics of scientific investigations and a logical progression, but they do not imply a rigid approach to solving problems. Like inquiry in scientists' studies of the natural world, inquiry in elementary and middle school science classes can take many forms, but each form generally involves some level of use of each of these inquiry tasks.

In the various chapters of this book and in the video series that accompanies the book, we will be examining what you can do to help children and adolescents develop these tasks of inquiry. What you can do to help them form questions for inquiry is treated in the following section.

Questions for Investigations

The very first task in inquiry, according to the *National Science Education Standards*, is to ask a simple question about objects, living things, and events in the environment. In this stage, inquiry can be initiated from a wide range of activities (National Research Council, 1996, p. 33):

- Something puzzling that children may notice in their everyday experiences may trigger inquiry.
- Some questions for inquiry grow out of hands-on activities involving observations, data collection, data organization, and reflection.

"Full inquiry involves asking a simple question, completing an investigation, answering the question, and presenting the results to others."

(*National Science Education Standards*, National Research Council, 1996, p. 122)

"Scientific inquiry is not easily described apart from the context of particular investigations. There simply is no fixed set of steps that scientists always follow, no one path that leads them unerringly to scientific knowledge."

(Rutherford and Ahlgren, 1990, p. 5)

- Questions may come from the critical analysis of information gathered from books, CD-ROMs, the Internet, and other sources.
- Novel or discrepant events demonstrated by the teacher or presented through pictures and videos may also generate questions for inquiry.
- Questions might even be raised in lecture, if they are authentic and relate to the students' own experiences.

Children wonder about many things, and they can ask many questions. But which questions can be investigated through their own activities? A teacher brings several hundred earthworms into his fourth-grade classroom. He places them in some soil on paper plates and distributes the plates to each small group in the class. Some students let the earthworms crawl on a finger, while some others find the earthworms "yucky" and will not touch them. But all are curious and thoughtful. Wondering about how they move, one child says, "I think they are made up of two parts. One part moves forward and then pulls the second part up to it." The teacher asks, *"Which part has the head, and which part has the tail?"* Another child observes that the earthworms use their "legs" to move forward. *"Are they really legs? How could we find out?"* asks the teacher. "We could look in a book," one child suggests. "Yes, but how else could we find out? *What could we do on our own to find out if earthworms have legs?"* A child says, "We could use a hand lens to watch them move and see how they use their legs."

In this classroom episode, curiosity grows into *wonder*, wonder results in *thinking*, and, with the teacher's assistance, thinking *produces new questions* that can be investigated. Children can learn to improve their questioning skills. As you emphasize the importance of questions for investigations, ask the students how they could investigate the questions they ask. Also guide them to reformulate some of the questions they ask, and provide them many good models of scientific questions.

Figure 1-4 describes some characteristics of good questions for initiating scientific inquiry.

Following is an example of an inquiry lesson in which children use the tasks of scientific inquiry as they discover facts and build concepts and principles about magnets and how they interact with different materials

Teaching for scientific literacy includes helping students "ask, find, or determine answers to questions derived from curiosity about everyday experiences."

(National Research Council, 1996, p. 22)

An Invitation to Inquiry Science: Magnetic Interactions

To begin a lesson on magnets, Julie Clark arranged her second-grade class in cooperative learning groups and gave each group sets of materials consisting of magnets and an assortment of

---

Good questions for initiating inquiry:

- lead to interesting new knowledge about the world
- lead to a deeper understanding of the nature of science and scientific inquiry
- require students to gather observable evidence and use it with developing knowledge to generate answers
- require a variety of science processes to answer them
- may require students to observe, compare, and classify objects and organisms
- may require students to infer and predict
- may require students to identify and measure variables
- may require controlled experiments

Figure 1-4 Characteristics of good questions for initiating inquiry.

metal and nonmetal objects. She challenged the students to find out how magnets interact with each other and with the various objects.

The curious children eagerly explored the magnets and materials. Holding up two magnets, one surprised child said, "Look, Ms. Clark, these push apart and they are not even touching." Another child noted, "Put them like this and they come together." "It won't pick this thing up," a third child observed. Going beyond the materials given to them, several children found that the magnets would stick to the metal filing cabinet, but not to the teacher's wooden desk. One surprised child observed that the magnets did not attract a cola can. Another child explained, "The cola can is not made of iron." Through their observations and descriptions, the children were learning many new *facts* about magnets and magnetic interactions.

Ms. Clark then asked the children what they wondered about magnets and what they wanted to find out about them. Among the things the children wanted to know were: *What are magnets? Why do they stick to some things?* From the children's watching and wondering, Ms. Clark helped them form a question that they could investigate: *How do magnets interact with one another and with other materials?*

To address this question, the children decided they should test all of their various materials to find out if they were attracted to a magnet. While the children worked on this question, Ms. Clark circulated among the small groups, asking and answering questions, supplying terms, and suggesting some procedures. To help the students organize their findings and communicate them to others, she challenged them to sort their materials into groups according to how they interacted with magnets. As she went about the room, she asked each group of students to explain how they had sorted the objects. Some children had grouped the objects by color or size. After some prompting, these children began to understand how to classify the objects, not by their more obvious attributes but by the ways they interacted with the magnets. Most children ended up with two piles: things that were attracted to a magnet and things that were not attracted to a magnet.

In a whole-class discussion, Ms. Clark asked the children to report what they had found out. Collectively, the children's knowledge from their explorations of magnets and magnetic interactions was quite complete. To summarize the children's observations and discussion about how magnets interact with other magnets and with various materials, Ms. Clark wrote these "magnet rules" on the chalkboard.

1. Two magnets can *attract* (pull) one another, but they can also be made to *repel* one another (push one another apart).
2. Magnets will not attract nonmetal objects.
3. Magnets attract some metal objects but not all.

Each of the magnet rules was based on observational evidence the children had discovered as they investigated. Through the magnet rules, the teacher introduced some new *concepts*, including *attract* and *repel*. The rules themselves were *principles*, because they showed how concepts were related to one another.

To help the children remember and understand the rules, Ms. Clark pointed to each rule in turn and asked the teams to search for and hold overhead one example of objects that fit each rule. In each case, the class decided whether the objects selected were correct examples. This "game" continued until every object of every team had been held aloft. To further help children to understand and apply the rules of magnetism, children went about the room making predictions and then testing them with different materials.

Many interesting activities on magnetism that you can use to involve your students in inquiry can be found on pages A-97–A-105 in *Activities for Teaching Science as Inquiry*, the companion volume to this text.

Why are the rules of magnetic interaction rightfully considered to be scientific principles?

Because magnets can damage computer monitors and TV screens, before this activity the teacher put stickers announcing "NO MAGNETS HERE!" on all the classroom computers and the TV.

This inquiry lesson on magnetism incorporates each of the tasks of inquiry identified previously in Figure 1-3. First, a question about magnetism was asked (Inquiry Task 1). Then, an investigation plan was formulated to address the question, and the students followed the plan to gather observational data relevant to the question (Inquiry Tasks 2 and 3). Observations were then used as evidence in formulating rules and generating explanations to answer the initiating question (Inquiry Task 4). In the course of the investigation, the students discussed their investigation results and conclusions with the teacher and other class members (Inquiry Task 5).

In inquiry teaching, assessment is a continuing process, occurring during a lesson series (formative assessment), as well as at the end of the lessons (summative assessment). Assessment is directed toward determining how well students are attaining lesson objectives. Information on student achievement is used to modify instruction and improve learning approaches.

Successful inquiry teaching depends on a host of additional teaching variables. Successful teachers establish communities of learners focused on understanding and provide instructions to students about working together in groups. They apply planned classroom management procedures strategically and fairly. They emphasize safety rules, provide opportunities for practice, rehearsal, and review, and attend to various other classroom variables. We will discuss many of these in the different chapters of this book.

Are you beginning to see the importance of inquiry experiences for children? Can you see yourself incorporating genuine inquiry into your own science lessons?

Proficiency 3: *Understandings About the Nature of Science and Scientific Inquiry*

Understanding the nature of science and scientific inquiry is also an important goal of science education (National Research Council, 1996; National Research Council, 2000). Emerging research suggests that children's abilities to engage in inquiry and form new conceptual understandings are enhanced when they grasp the nature and construction of scientific knowledge. Following is a discussion of some of the specific aspects of the nature of science and scientific inquiry that elementary and middle school students should begin to understand.

Science Is Something People Do and Create. From this idea follows the understanding that scientific knowledge is not based on the authority of scientists, teachers, or books, nor is it simply a copy of reality. Science is a product of the activity of knowing. Science knowledge is based in scientists' investigations, observations, and explanations (Duschl et al., 2007).

Further, virtually all people are involved in science in some way. Scientists generate new knowledge through their investigations. All of us are consumers of products developed from scientific knowledge. We are all affected by issues involving science and technology, such as issues related to pollution, global warming, and other environmental changes that result from decisions about how to use scientific and technological knowledge.

Many people find science to be a rewarding career. Scientists are involved with fascinating puzzles to be solved, innovative methods and instruments to be developed, contacts with colleagues around the world to keep up, reports to write, and scientific meetings to attend. The pursuit of science is, for most scientists, sheer *fun* (Judson, 1980). "And," as the science writer Gary Zukav (1979) observed, "the clever rascals get paid for doing it" (p. 3).

- What question about magnetism was asked to initiate the magnets investigation?
- What investigation plan was formulated to address the question?
- What did the students do to gather observational data relevant to the question?
- How were observations used as evidence in formulating principles and generating explanations to answer the initiating question?

Science Is a Way of Answering Questions About the Natural World. Science is a special way of thinking in the modern world, but students should understand that science is only one way humans seek understanding. Knowing what types of questions science can investigate and those it cannot is important in the inquiry process.

Science deals only with questions about the natural world that can be answered, even if tentatively, through data gathering, logical reasoning, the use of scientific knowledge, and the formation and testing of explanations. Consider, for example, the question: *Why did the boy speak up in the story of the Emperor's New Clothes?* Providing satisfying answers to this question may require personal interpretation and empathy. Reflecting on the question may yield valuable new understandings of people and new self-knowledge. But the question simply cannot be answered through scientific investigation, description, and explanation.

As another example, science cannot answer questions involving religious beliefs, such as: *Does God exist?* We must answer questions about things we simply cannot see, but hope for, through personal faith, not through scientific investigations. Similarly, questions about beauty, ethics, and moral choices generally involve personal interpretations and beliefs and cannot be answered through scientific data taking and analysis.

Sometimes teachers can help children reformulate their questions so they can be investigated scientifically. The question *Why do birds fly?*, which is a question of motivation and purpose, might be revised so it can be investigated scientifically. For example, *How do bird bones differ from mammal bones?* can be a productive scientific question. A follow-up question might ask: *How do birds' bones make it easier for them to fly?*

Scientific Knowledge Is Generated Through Questions, Investigations, Observations, and Explanations. As portrayed in the five tasks of scientific inquiry (Figure 1-3), in generating science knowledge, scientists and students ask questions about the natural world and plan and conduct investigations to provide evidence to be used in answering the questions. Logical reasoning, scientific knowledge, and imagination must be used in the construction of explanations of observational evidence. The interplay among the *evidence of investigations, scientific knowledge,* and *explanations* provides the basis for scientific advances. Figure 1-5 provides a model of how observation, scientific knowledge, and explanations are linked in scientific inquiry.

Scientific Knowledge Is Tentative. Because science is a human construction and depends on limited observations and incomplete explanations, scientific knowledge is subject to change as new evidence becomes available (National Research Council, 1996). Even in the best of circumstances, the theories and explanations of children and scientists must be considered tentative. No matter how well a widely accepted theory fits observations, a new theory might fit them just as well or better or might fit a wider range of observations (American Association for the Advancement of Science, 1993). Thus, science knowledge is never fixed, never complete, always tentative, and subject to revision or even rejection with new evidence.

Scientists Present Their Investigations and Explanations to the Scientific Community for Critical Evaluation. Establishing science knowledge is a social process involving the community of scientists (Duschl et al., 2007). Scientists make the results of their investigations public. To evaluate scientific studies, other scientists review experimental procedures, examine evidence, identify faulty reasoning, point out statements that go beyond the evidence, try out investigations for themselves, and suggest alternative explanations. Children also should present their procedures and findings to their classmates and teachers for evaluation.

The many videos in the Homework and Exercises section at www.myeducationlab.com, directed by Dr. Terry Contant, can help illustrate and extend the concepts presented in each chapter. Now would be a good time for you to watch the first video, *What Do Scientists Do?* A video guide is provided in the section on Online Professional Development at the end of this chapter.

The *Benchmarks for Science Literacy* (American Association for the Advancement of Science, 1993) remind us that even though science knowledge is subject to change, students should understand that it also has an enduring quality. Some science knowledge is several hundred years old and remains applicable today.

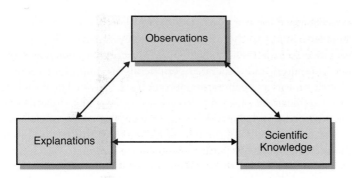

Figure 1-5 In understanding the natural world, scientists and students link obervations, scientific knowledge, and scientific explanations.

Scientists Display Certain Attitudes and Habits of Mind in Doing Science. Doing science with integrity requires that scientists display certain attitudes as they engage in science. Children should also acquire and display scientific attitudes and habits of mind as they do science. Some of these attitudes are (National Center for Improving Science Education, 1989, pp. 18–19):

1. *Curiosity.* an enduring interest and fascination about the natural and human-constructed worlds.
2. *Desire for Knowledge*—an urge, even "rage" (Judson, 1980), to know and understand the world.
3. *Placing a Priority on Evidence*—using data as the basis for testing ideas and respecting the facts as they accrue.
4. *Willingness to Modify Explanations*—changing initial conceptions and explanations when the evidence suggests different ones.
5. *Cooperation in Investigating Questions and Solving Problems*—working in collaboration with others is fundamental to the scientific enterprise.
6. *Honesty*—presenting data as they are observed, not as the investigator expects or wishes them to be.

The nature of science and scientific inquiry is *implicit* in the inquiry activities of students but must be made *explicit* to them. To teach students about how scientific knowledge is generated, for example, teachers can involve students in inquiry and discuss with them how what they have done is like what scientists do. In small group and whole class discussion of students' investigations, teachers can emphasize the importance of observation and data gathering, how simple instruments such as magnifiers and thermometers extend observations, how data is used as evidence in forming explanations of what is observed and why results are communicated to others for evaluation.

Especially good problems for investigation can be found from applications of science in technology. Application opens up the opportunity for students to explore the natural and technological world more deeply and to realize how extensively science and technology are interactive and affect people.

"Experiences in which students actually engage in scientific investigation provide the background for developing an understanding of the nature of scientific inquiry."

(*National Science Education Standards*, National Research Council, 1996, p. 179)

Science and Technology

As stressed in the *National Science Education Standards*, science and technology are closely related, but they differ in goals. The goal of *science* is to understand the natural world; the goal of *technology* is to make modifications in the world to meet human needs (National Research Council, 1996, p. 24).

The term *technology* refers not just to instructional technology, but also to innovations that enable people to adjust to the world better. Pulleys, levers, telescopes, bridges of different designs, modern medicines, medical imaging techniques (such as x-rays, MRIs, and CT-scans), and computers and associated peripherals are important technologies, as are light bulbs, electric motors and generators, automobiles, and the latest high-tech products.

Investigating applications of science in technology provides students opportunities to connect to the designed world, offers them experiences in making models of useful things, and extends their understanding of the laws of nature through their investigations of how technological devices and systems work.

Tasks of Technological Design. Paralleling the five tasks of scientific inquiry given in Figure 1-3, the *National Science Education Standards* (National Research Council, 1996, p. 137) identify five *tasks of technological design* that students should learn to do:

* *Identify a simple problem.* Students identify a specific need, problem, or task and explain it in their own words.
* *Propose a solution.* Students should make proposals to build something or to make something work better.
* *Implement a proposed solution.* Children should work individually and collaboratively and use simple materials, tools, techniques, and appropriate quantitative measurements when solving the problem.
* *Evaluate a product or a design.* Students should evaluate their own results or solutions as well as those of other children by considering how well a product or design met the challenge to solve a problem.
* *Communicate a problem design and solution.* Students should prepare oral, written, and pictorial communication of the design process and products. The communication might involve show-and-tell, group discussions, short written reports, pictures, or multimedia computer presentations.

Implementing the technological design cycle requires that students observe, measure, draw inferences, make hypotheses and predictions, conduct controlled investigations, and apply scientific knowledge. A graphic illustration of the tasks of technological design is provided in Figure 1-6.

Here is an example of applying science concepts and principles in the course of the technological design cycle. In a unit on water quality, students in one Florida middle school studied local water resource issues and created public service announcements (PSAs) to convey the message of water conservation to their community. In creating the PSAs, student teams had to clearly identify a simple problem, propose a solution to the problem in terms of the intended PSA, create a PSA and evaluate it, and show their PSA to their teacher, peers, and public for their examination and comments. It is clear from the ways students engaged in this project and their reactions to it that they were beginning to understand, appreciate, and care about the real-world interactions of science, technology, and society. Read about this innovative approach to studying issues involving science, technology, and people in an article by Stokes and Hull (2002) in *The Science Teacher*.

Teachers and Inquiry

Teachers have preferred styles of instruction. Some prefer more student-centered classrooms. Others want more control of activities and prefer teacher-centered activities, such as is the

Go to the Homework and Exercises section in Chapter 1 of MyEducationLab to view the five part set of videos called "Water Wheels." These videos provide a view of a third grade class as they investigate, construct, and test water wheels. These videos provide a good example of the application of both the technological design cycle and the science as inquiry tasks. A video guide for this video is included in the *Online Professional Development* section at the end of this chapter.

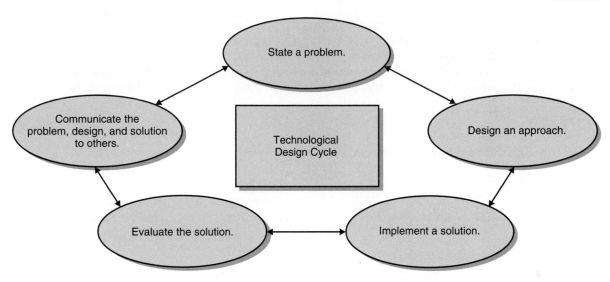

Figure 1-6 Tasks in designing a technological solution to a problem.

case in most direct instruction models. Some see the overriding goal of instruction in subject matter as the development of language literacy and thus prefer a reading approach to science.

In this text we take the position that inquiry-constructivist approaches to science best enable students to develop the three main goals of science education—conceptual understanding, abilities to inquire, and understanding of science and scientific inquiry. Although we emphasize inquiry approaches, we show you in Chapter 4 how to use inquiry as a framework in which direct instruction and reading approaches to science can fit together with inquiry.

Teaching science as inquiry provides many opportunities for you to interact with each of your students, to guide and challenge them to acquire and understand a scientific view of the world, and to develop the abilities and attitudes they need to inquire on their own.

Are you beginning to understand why inquiry approaches are so important for teaching science?

SUMMARY

• Inquiry instruction is an approach to science teaching focusing on understanding the world by questioning, investigating, observing, and explaining the order of the world around us.

• There are several advantages to science being a part of the school day at the elementary level. Science in the elementary school lays a foundation for children to develop abilities to understand the world scientifically; it can help ensure that students can successfully engage in scientific, technological, and medical careers and participate in a scientific society; it can support the learning of reading, writing, and math skills; and it is important for student success on statewide assessments required by the NCLB Act.

• According to the *National Science Education Standards*, all students should be engaged in an inquiry approach to science that basically parallels the procedures scientists use and the attitudes they display in doing science.

• Inquiry involves asking questions, planning investigations, gathering data, learning and using scientific knowledge to make sense of observational data, and communicating results to others.

• Scientific understanding is based in observations of the natural world and involves abilities to construct and apply concepts, principles, and theories.

• Through engaging in inquiry, students can begin to understand the nature of science and scientific inquiry. Scientific knowledge should always be considered tentative. Scientists must adjust their ideas when investigations produce new evidence that no longer supports previous conclusions. The study of science can build and reinforce important attitudes and habits of mind. Curiosity—the urge, even rage, to know—is the driving force for science. Scientists are skeptical of new ideas; they always insist on examining evidence offered in support of conclusions.

• Technological design seeks to apply science knowledge to the design of technological innovations.

ONLINE PROFESSIONAL DEVELOPMENT

Pre- and post-tests to assess your knowledge of chapter content, along with exercises to enhance your understanding, can be found on MyEducationLab at www.myeducationlab.com.

Throughout this book, you will be provided opportunities through MyEducationLab to view videos that show children engaged in inquiry in classrooms. Watching and reflecting on these videos can extend your understanding of chapter concepts and ideas and confront some of the issues and decisions facing science teachers. The process of observing and reflecting on teachers' actions and on students' learning and thinking can lead to changes in the knowledge, beliefs, attitudes, and ultimately the practice of pre-service and in-service teachers.

Video Guides

Video clips on MyEducationLab selected for this chapter include "What Do Scientists Do?" and "Water Wheels"—Parts 1, 2, 3, 4, and 5.

Accessing the Videos

1. Go to the Homework and Exercises section in Chapter 1 of MyEducationLab to select and view videos for this chapter and compute the questions.
2. Videos might be viewed individually, by small groups of colleagues, or by the whole class.
3. As you watch each video, use the **Questions for Reflection** to guide your thoughts and note taking for personal use and group discussion. Also, go beyond the Questions for Reflection, and reflect on the many different aspects of instruction and learning that interest you.

Video: What Do Scientists Do?

Overview

In this video excerpt, we watch fifth-grade students as they investigate pin-hole cameras. We also hear from second-, third-, and fifth-grade teachers about how the implementing of inquiry in classrooms can help students understand what scientists do.

Questions for Reflection

1. What do scientists do when they do science?
2. What do the teachers say about how classroom inquiry investigations can help children learn what scientists do?
3. What activities do the fifth-grade students do in investigating pin-hole cameras? How do the activities relate to what scientists do?

Video: Water Wheels: Parts 1, 2, 3, 4, and 5.

Overview

In this five-part series of videos, we watch as a third-grade class investigates water wheels. As the students design, construct, and test their own water wheels, we can see application of science in the technological design cycle (Figure 1-6).

Questions for Reflection

1. What do the children say that water wheels do? How do they describe how water wheels work?
2. What examples do you see in the videos that are related to the five tasks of technological design? What examples do you notice that show the students using the five tasks of scientific inquiry?
3. What does the teacher do to facilitate the investigations by the children?

Annenberg Videos

The Annenberg/CPB Foundation has made a wealth of 30- to 90-minute professional development videos on science learning and teaching available to you on the Web. We have selected a number of these for you to view in connection with various chapters in this book. This chapter features a video entitled, *What Is Inquiry and Why Do It?* This video is part of the Annenberg series called **Learning Science Through Inquiry.**

Websites change periodically, and we cannot guarantee that the selected video will be available on the Annenberg website when you wish to see it. Because of the potential importance to your professional development, we recommend that, if available, you take advantage of the invitation to view the Annenberg videos and learn about the Annenberg website.

Instructions for Accessing and Watching Annenberg Videos

1. Access the Annenberg website at http://learner.org/. Follow the instructions for registering the first time you access the Annenberg videos.

2. Go to *Browse Teacher Resources: Science*. Click on *Go*.
3. Click on the video series of interest.
4. Go to *Individual Program Descriptions*. Click the *Videos on Demand (VoD)* icon for the video you wish to watch.

2

I n the vision presented by the Standards, inquiry is a step beyond "science as process," in which students learn skills, such as observation, inference, and experimentation. The new vision includes the "processes of science" and requires that students combine processes and scientific knowledge as they use scientific reasoning and critical thinking to develop their understanding of science.

(*National Science Education Standards*, National Research Council, 1996, p. 105)

Processes and Strategies for Inquiring

ONCE STUDENTS (AND SCIENTISTS) have formed questions that can be investigated scientifically, they collect data, decide on ways to record and report the data, and interpret the data using logical reasoning and prior scientific knowledge. In investigating the natural world, children use simple tools such as thermometers, meter sticks, and hand lenses and practice simple skills such as observing, measuring, recording data, graphing, inferring, and predicting. The skills used in investigating are called *processes of science*.

Elementary and middle school teachers have traditionally taught specific processes of science in isolation from other processes and science content. However, the *National Science Education Standards* emphasize that the real value of a process approach to science comes as students learn to incorporate them into scientific investigations.

In this chapter, we focus on both processes of science and strategies of investigation. First, we describe individual processes and show you some examples of their use in elementary and middle school science. Then, we describe and provide examples of three particular investigational strategies—descriptive, classificatory, and experimental investigations. These special ways of investigating incorporate various processes of science. As you work your way through this chapter, reflect on these questions:

- *What specific processes of science are featured in elementary and middle school classrooms?*

- *What activities might be useful in teaching children how to apply specific processes of science?*

- *How can teachers help children use their natural curiosity to develop questions to investigate?*

- *What are the main features of descriptive, classificatory, and experimental investigations?*

- *How can you help students learn to apply these investigational strategies?*

- *How are different processes of science used in these three ways of investigating?*

- *At what grade level or grade span might each of the three kinds of investigations best be introduced?*

Processes of Science

Although the processes of science are especially characteristic of the work of professional scientists, everyone can exercise them in thinking about various matters of interest in everyday life (Rutherford & Ahlgren, 1990). They are the same skills that will serve children as

Teaching science processes parallels a well-known proverb: Give a man a fish and he eats for a day. Teach him how to fish and he eats for a lifetime.

Many good activities for teaching science process skills can be found in Rezba, Sprague, Fiel, and Funk (2003) and Ostlund and Mercier (1999).

adults, "when they measure their floor for a carpet, try to figure out why their automobile didn't start, or decide which presidential candidate to vote for. These are the thinking skills they will use when separating evidence from opinion while listening to someone's side of a story, or when looking for evidence and contradictions in written or spoken opinions" (Mechling & Oliver, 1983, p. 8).

A variety of science processes that are emphasized in elementary and middle school science classes are described in Table 2-1 and in the following sections.

Observing

Observation is the process of gathering information using all appropriate senses and instruments that extend the senses, such as hand lenses and microscopes. Children use their senses

TABLE 2-1   SOME PROCESSES OF SCIENCE EMPHASIZED IN ELEMENTARY AND MIDDLE SCHOOLS

Process of Science	Procedure	Example
Observing	Gather information using all appropriate senses and instruments that extend the senses.	Visually observe a melting ice cube as it changes phase, feel the water to determine its coldness, or use a hand lens to watch a snowflake melt.
Classifying	Group objects or organisms according to one or more common properties.	Classify rocks as igneous, sedimentary, or metamorphic.
Inferring	Draw a tentative conclusion about objects, organisms, or events based on observations and prior knowledge.	Infer that when water evaporates, it goes into the air; infer that heat caused the ice cube to change to water.
Measuring	Quantify variables using a variety of instruments and standard or nonstandard units.	Measure the length, width, thickness, and weight of bean seeds before and after they soak in water; use a clock to determine the number of minutes for an ice cube to melt; weigh ice cubes and water before and after melting.
Communicating	Record observations, measurements, inferences, experiments, etc., in multiple ways, and present them to others.	Draw pictures of, write about, and give an oral report on observations of amphibians; use a data table and a graph to display the number of children in a group who are wearing each of several different color shoes; use a data table and a graph to display the temperature of water every 5 minutes as it cools.
Predicting	Make a forecast of a possible outcome of an investigation based on known patterns in data.	Based on this investigation data, I predict that a 30-gram ice cube placed in 300 ml of water will melt in 50 minutes.
Hypothesizing	Make a statement to guide an investigation of a question.	The greater the amount of water in which an ice cube is placed the more time it will take to melt.
Experimenting: Controlled Investigating	Investigate by deliberately manipulating one variable at a time and observing the effect on a responding variable, while holding all other variables constant.	Conduct an experiment to determine the effect of the amount of water on the time it takes an ice cube to melt in water while keeping the size and shape of the ice cube and the initial temperature of the water the same.

to explore the world from the day they are born—or perhaps earlier. In preschool and kindergarten, they begin to discover the part each of their senses plays in making observations.

"What can you tell me about this?" a kindergarten teacher asks her class as she holds up a flower. "Yes, it is a flower. But can you tell me more about it? What color is it? What part of your body tells you that?" Then she asks the children to touch and smell the flower and to identify which sense they use to acquire their information (Minnesota Mathematics and Science Teaching Project, 1970).

Young children tend to observe globally and, thus, to miss potentially relevant details. They often see what they expect to see, and they may focus more on differences than similarities. As they develop skills in observing, children learn to observe for detail, to see what is actually there, and to pay attention to both similarities and differences (Harlen & Jelly, 1990).

Science provides children many opportunities to observe, to wonder, and to seek their own answers to questions through discovery and testing. Almost any objects, organisms, or events are suitable as a base for developing observing skills. For example, observing popcorn—including observing characteristics of the uncooked kernels, observing the popcorn as it is being popped, and observing the cooked popcorn—provides an excellent context for children to consider how each of their senses provides different information.

Take a moment to examine Activity 2-1. This activity can be used to test your own observation skills or as an activity to help your students develop their observation skills while learning some significant science knowledge. Do this activity on observing candy before reading further.

Did you make a variety of observations about the candy in Activity 2-1? Use the components of good scientific observing shown in Table 2-2 as a checklist to see how comprehensive your list of observations is.

- Did you use all appropriate *senses*, and perhaps a hand lens, in observing your candy?
- Did you make quantitative observations? For example, did you measure the size and the weight of the pieces of candy in standard or nonstandard units?

A glossary containing definitions of important terms used in this chapter can be found on MyEducationLab.

Many good activities using a variety of materials to teach and assess different processes of science are available on the PALS (Performance Assessment Links in Science) website at http://pals.sri.com.

Using a Magnifier

To observe an object through a magnifier or magnifying lens, hold the magnifier close to the object, look through the magnifier at the object, then lift the magnifier toward your eye, stopping when the object begins to blur.

Many science classrooms have magnifiers with three lenses. The large lens usually provides a twofold magnification, the medium-sized lens provides a sixfold magnification, and the small lens an eightfold magnification. To provide increased magnification, two or even three magnifiers can be fitted together and used as a single magnifier.

Activity 2-1: Observing Candy

Obtain several pieces of hard candy, such as sour balls or M&Ms of different colors. Write down all of the qualitative and quantitative observations of the candy you can make.

Safety Precaution: Stress the importance to students of their not tasting anything that has not been approved by an adult!

TABLE 2-2 COMPONENTS OF GOOD SCIENTIFIC OBSERVING

Component	Description
Senses	Use all appropriate senses as well as instruments that extend the senses in gathering extensive and clear information.
Measurements	Make quantitative observations—that is, measurements—to supplement qualitative observations when it matters.
Questions	Ask questions about the objects that can lead to new investigations and observations.
Changes	Make deliberate alterations in the objects that can help answer new questions and observe the responding changes.
Communication	Report your observations clearly, using verbal descriptions, charts, diagrams, drawings, and other methods as appropriate.

- Did you ask *questions* about the candy that might be investigated through further observations or experiments? For example, did you raise questions about what happens to the candy when you crush it?
- What *changes* did you make to the candy? For example, did you crush a piece or place it in water?
- How did you *communicate* your observations? Did you make a written list or perhaps a chart that might facilitate comparisons? Did you include drawings?

Learning to be a good observer is a lifelong task. Under your guidance as a sensitive teacher, students can begin to develop effective observation skills.

Classifying

In **classifying**, people sort objects according to their common properties (characteristics, attributes, or features). Classifying is an important process in science. Why do we classify objects or organisms?

Classifying things requires not only that we observe properties but also that we look for relationships among the properties. This enhances our understanding of the structure and function of the things. Also, placing an object or organism within a group means you already know something about it, if you are familiar with the characteristics of the group. Additionally, grouping things with other things gives us an added way to search for information about them, by direct observation, in the library, or through the Internet (National Aquarium in Baltimore, 1997).

In an article titled "Unlocking the Power of Observation," Anderson, Martin, and Faszewski present a useful set of criteria for good observations and provide a checklist and rubric for evaluating them. You can find the article in the September 2006 issue of *Science and Children* (pp. 32–35).

In the magnets lesson described in Chapter 1, children learned more about magnetism by classifying or sorting objects into piles based on whether or not they were attracted to magnets.

Special ways of classifying often introduced in elementary science are binary and multistage classification. In a *binary classification system*, a set of objects is divided into two groups on the basis of whether each object has a particular property. For example, a set of buttons might be classified into two groups based on the number of holes they have. One group might consist of all the buttons that have four holes; the other group would be made up of all buttons that do not have four holes.

In a *multistage classification system*, the objects in the original set are sorted again and again so that a hierarchy of sets and subsets is formed. For example, the four-hole buttons in our example of binary classification might be further classified as being round or not round. Four-hole, round buttons might then be classified as being plastic or not plastic.

Figure 2-1 shows an example of a multistage classification of button properties. What might a multistage classification of living things in a terrarium look like?

As another example of multistage classification, organisms might be described and classified based on similar characteristics. At a first level, the organisms might be classified as plants or animals. Animals might then be classified according to number of body parts. At a third level, animals with three main body parts might be further classified according to number of legs. Animals with three main body parts (head, thorax, and abdomen), six legs attached to the thorax, and two antennae attached to the head are classified as "insects."

Focusing on similar properties in classifying can lead to understandings about the most significant properties of objects and their functions. For example, a focus on the four-hole property of buttons might lead to a question about why some buttons have holes and others do not. What is the function of the holes? Do buttons without holes have some characteristic that substitutes for the holes (such as another means to attach them to garments)?

A variety of activities about observing, describing, and classifying buttons are provided in the activity titled "How Are Buttons Alike and Different" on pages A-16 through A-19 in *Activities for Teaching Science as Inquiry*.

Classifying according to only a few properties can lead to classification problems. For example, lobsters also have three main body parts, six legs, and two antennae. Why are they not classified as insects? What are some of the other critical properties of insects and lobsters that exclude lobsters from the insect class?

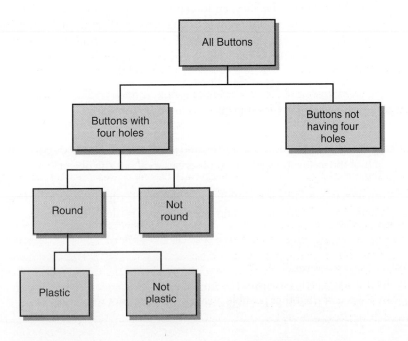

Figure 2-1 A multistage classification of button properties.

Inferring

Observations are statements about information that is available directly through the five senses; inferences are interpretations of these observations. In inferring, we use experiences and knowledge to fill in gaps about observed events and information. An **inference,** then, is an *interpretation* of observations based on prior knowledge and experiences.

Children often experience difficulties in distinguishing between their observations and their inferences (Duschl et al., 2007). Students should be especially encouraged to make explicit the observations and prior knowledge on which their inferences are based. When they claim that a statement is an observaton, you might ask, "What sense did you use in making that observaton?" When they draw inferences, you might ask: "What is your evidence?" and "Why do you think so?" Helping children distinguish between observations (evidence of the senses) and inferences (conclusions based on evidence) is important to their understanding of science.

In one popular activity designed to teach the skill of inferring, students are supplied with closed boxes in which mystery objects have been placed. They lift, shake, and tilt the boxes to gain information about the mystery objects. A student might observe, for instance, that the object rolls when the box is tilted one way and slides when it is tilted differently. What is the shape of the object? A good inference is that the object is cylindrical. The goal of this activity is not just for children to find out what is in the box, but to help them learn to distinguish between observations and inferences.

Activity 2-2 shows a sample test item to assess student understanding of the differences between observations and inferences. The item is similar to ones that might appear on statewide tests of science. Work through the activity and discuss it with a group of colleagues.

What answer did you choose for the item? Choices A, B, and C are all observations based on the sense of hearing or the sense of smell. Choice D is an inference based on observations of the content of the box and prior experience with rolling and sliding cylinders.

Moisture sometimes appears on the outside of a glass full of ice water, as is illustrated in Figure 2-2. Some people might say, "The glass is sweating." Is this statement an observation or an inference? It is, of course, an inference. Did the moisture on the glass come from inside the glass (sweating) or from outside the glass (perhaps from water vapor in the air)? What investigations might be carried out to help students decide between the two inferences about the source of the water on the outside of the glass?

One way to gather evidence about where the moisture on the outside of the glass of ice water came from is to put red food dye in the water and, when moisture forms, check it carefully for any hint of red. The observation that the moisture contains no sign of red supports the inference that it likely came from the air surrounding the glass, rather than from the water in the glass.

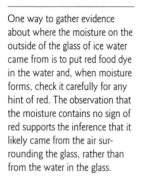

Figure 2-2   Where does the moisture on the outside of a glass of ice water come from? What is your evidence?

Activity 2-2: Observation and Inference

Sample Test Item.   Four children tilt, rattle, and smell a small box to discover the object inside. Which of the following is NOT an observation about the object?

A.   "It makes a sound like it is sliding when the box is tilted in one direction."
B.   "It makes a sound like it is rolling when the box is tilted the other way."
C.   "It smells like peppermint."
D.   "I think it is candy."

- What is your answer choice?
- Why did you select that answer?
- Why is each of the other possible answers not a correct response?

Measuring

It is often important in science to quantify observations through measurement. For example, knowing the length of the roots and stems of developing plants and how these variables change from day to day can be important for understanding plant growth. Accurate measurements not only enhance descriptions, they can improve the quality of predictions and explanations of natural phenomena.

Measuring is founded on processes of observing and comparing. "Children naturally make comparisons" (National Science Resources Center, 1996, p. 3). They stand back to back to see who is taller, line up their feet to see whose are longer, and match their bodies to different size clothing to see what will fit.

The need to make comparisons leads to the notion of units of measure. At first, children may use nonstandard units to make comparisons. For example, they stretch out their own arms, use their own bodies, or use handy objects like pencils or plastic spoons as nonstandard units to measure length. However, nonstandard units have a main disadvantage. Because spoons and pencils, as well as children's arm spans and bodies, vary in length, it is difficult to use them to consistently compare objects that cannot be held side by side.

Science lessons at different grade levels can help students learn different aspects of the measuring process. First-grade lessons on measuring should be designed to enable children to understand (National Science Resources Center, 1996):

- Comparing involves observing similarities and differences.
- One way to make comparisons is by matching.
- A common starting line is required to make fair comparisons.
- Using beginning and ending points and placing units end to end are important factors when measuring.
- Nonstandard units of measure can be used in comparing.
- Standard units of measure produce more consistent results than nonstandard units.

By second grade, children should use standard units—centimeters, grams, and degrees Celsius or Fahrenheit—marked on rulers, balance scales, and thermometers to measure objects and events. Standard units enable consistent descriptions and comparisons of measured objects that are not side by side and cannot be directly compared.

Through activities in grade 3–6 science *and* mathematics classes, students should begin to understand:

- the meaning of each property that is being measured, such as volume or temperature;
- how to use a variety of measuring instruments;
- the meaning and use of a variety of standard units of measurement;
- the meaning and relationships among the various prefixes used with metric measurement units, such as *milli-, centi-,* and *kilo-;*
- how to interpolate between numbers in reading thermometers, rulers, and other instruments;
- how to express measurements in terms of decimals when appropriate; and
- how to estimate measurements and determine when estimation is appropriate.

In elementary and middle school science, children should be afforded a great deal of practice in using and reading metric rulers, metersticks, thermometers, balances, spring scales, timers of various kinds, graduated cylinders, measuring cups, and other measuring instruments.

Appendix B describes some important tools and skills for measuring length, area, volume, mass, weight, and temperature at the elementary and middle school level. Take a few minutes to read through this appendix.

Communicating

Recording, organizing, and reporting observations, measurements, experiments, findings, and conclusions is also an essential process of science. According to the *Benchmarks for Science Literacy* (American Association for the Advancement of Science, 1993, p. 10), "An important part of students' explorations is telling others what they see, what they think, and what it makes them wonder about. Children should have lots of time to talk about what they observe and to compare their observations with others." In addition to oral discourse, communications might take the form of drawings, written reports, journal entries, data tables, and graphs. Children might even use music, art, and role playing to communicate their understanding.

In science activities, once data have been obtained, they must be organized and interpreted. Data tables and graphs are common means of displaying data. Data tables display data in column form and facilitate the discovery of patterns within the data. Table 2-5 shows an example of a data table used in an investigation of white powders. Putting measurement data into graphs better enables students to discover relationships and patterns that help them make sense of the data. Graphs also facilitate the construction of precise predictions.

The types of graphs most often used in scientific applications in elementary and middle schools are bar graphs, histograms, and line graphs.

Bar Graphs. Bar graphs visually show *differences* in data collected. Bar graphs can be used, for example, to show the number of children with each different type of eye color. Data about how many students in a class have blue eyes, brown eyes, green eyes, and so on, may be displayed visually in bar graphs.

An example of a bar graph is shown in Figure 2-3. This graph depicts the number of children in a group wearing shoes of different colors. The bottom line, or *horizontal axis*, shows different shoe colors worn by the children. The left side, or *vertical axis* of the graph, shows the number of children wearing a particular color shoe. Four children in the group wear black shoes, six children wear white shoes, three children wear red shoes, and two children wear blue shoes.

Histograms. Histograms display the *number of times* a *number event* occurs in a large set. Histograms differ from bar graphs in that the *x*-axis on a bar graph simply names a category, while the *x*-axis on a histogram is a number line representing a continuous variable. A familiar example of data that might be displayed in a histogram is how many students made each score on a test. Here, all possible scores are arranged in a number line on the *x*-axis;

Some good examples of bar graph activities may be found in a *Science and Children* article by Susan Pearlman and Kathleen Pericak-Spector (1995) called "Graph That Data!"

Figure 2-3 Bar graph of number of children with different color shoes.

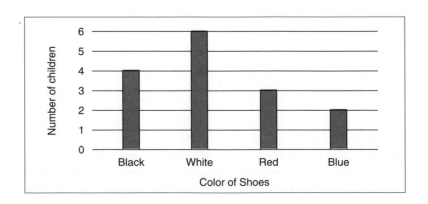

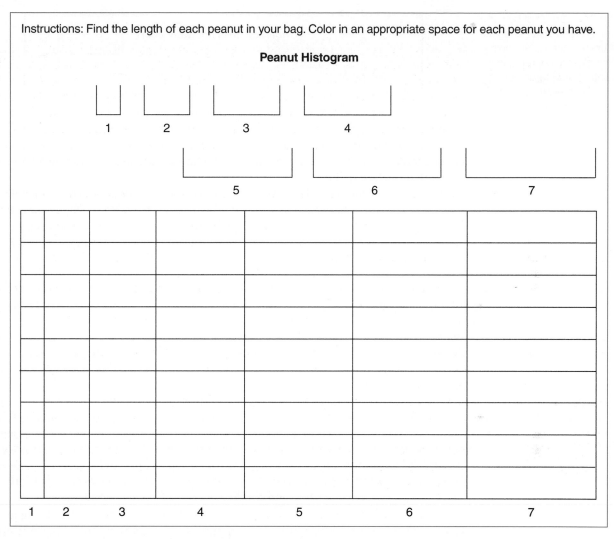

Figure 2-4   A histogram for graphing the lengths of unshelled peanuts.
Source: Used with permission from Larry Malone, Lawrence Hall of Science, University of California, Berkeley.

the frequencies, or number of occurrences, of scores are arranged in a number line on the y-axis. As an example, Figure 2-4 shows how many unshelled peanuts in a large bag there are of each designated length (or small range of lengths).

Line Graphs. Line graphs are more advanced; students from about fourth grade can learn to construct and interpret them. With line graphs, your students can graphically show numerical data about variables that are continuous. A line graph displays visually the changes in a *responding or dependent variable* in an investigation corresponding to changes in the values of a *manipulated or independent variable*.

As an example, suppose students wished to investigate the rate of cooling of a sample of hot water contained in an uncovered Styrofoam cup. Specifically, how does the temperature of the water vary with time? In gathering data to answer this question, students

A discussion of how measurement and graphing might be used to connect science and mathematics in the classroom is included in Chapter 9.

Figure 2-5 Graph of how the temperature of water changes with time as the water cools. The small squares represent the water temperature each time it was measured, then a best-fit curve was drawn to show the cooling trend over time.

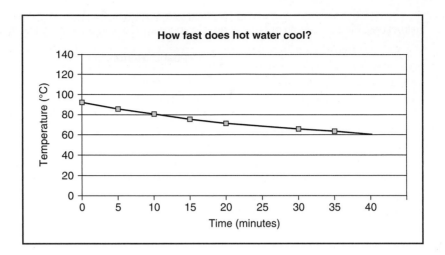

might begin with a cup of hot water. They might measure the initial temperature of the water and then measure the temperature every 5 minutes as the water cools. Figure 2-5 shows a graph for an investigation of temperature versus time for water as it cools. The graph indicates that the temperature decreases in a regular (predictable) way with time. Using the graph, students can predict the temperature of the water at different times.

Keeping Records in Science. One useful format for record keeping is the *"I Notice / I Wonder"* chart. The left column of this two-column chart should be labeled "I Notice." In this column students write their observations and discoveries as they explore objects, organisms, and events. The right column should be labeled "I Wonder." In this column students write questions that come to mind as they are exploring. These questions often begin with *What, Why,* or *How.* Such questions can lead to further inquiry investigations.

As you view the many classroom videos of children's investigations provided with this book, notice how often teachers and children use the I Notice/I Wonder chart.

I Notice	I Wonder
The cat's fur is black and white.	Are most cats black and white? Were this cat's parents black and white? What percent of this cat's fur is each color?
The pupils of the cat's eyes change shape as the brightness of the room changes.	Why the cat's eyes look different than human eyes?
The cat purrs when I pet him.	Does petting make the cat happy or angry?

Teachers help students turn their "I Wonder" questions into questions that they can investigate. For example, in lessons on light, such as the one seen in the video *What Do Scientists Do?*, featured in Chapter 1, students might ask, *Why does light travel in straight lines?*

It would be difficult, if not impossible, for children to answer this *why* question from their own investigations. Teachers can help them form this question that can be investigated: *What happens to the image of an arrow when seen in a pinhole camera?* Writing this focus question in their science notebooks or journals helps the students to clarify their purposes and keep those purposes in mind as they continue to investigate.

Scientists keep accurate records of data collected, so they are prepared to recall data taken, make comparisons of the data, draw inferences, make predictions, and generate explanations. For similar reasons, students should also keep accurate records.

During an activity, provide time for students to record their findings. Recording data will be a natural part of the work of some students; other students will need encouragement to stop and record their findings. Initially allow the students to use their own methods of recording data. Many will use sentences in making records. If so, encourage them to use labeled drawings and lists (Fulton & Campbell, 2003).

After discussions with the class about which of their observations are likely to be useful in answering the focus question and which are likely to be less useful, you might prepare a data sheet for students to fill in. An example of a class discussion about data is given in the Annenberg video *Bring It All Together: Processing for Meaning.* This video is featured in the Online Professional Development section of Chapter 3. An example of a prepared data sheet for white powder investigations can be seen in Figure 2-11 later in this chapter.

In making the transition from observational data to explanations, students might first reflect on their data and write about any patterns they see. For example, students might use writing and drawings to indicate that both vertical and horizontal arrows are inverted when seen in pin-hole viewers.

At the explanation phase of inquiry, students might be asked to explain why they think an arrow appears inverted when observed through a pin-hole viewer. With appropriate scaffolding, including introduction to some new concepts and principles through direct instruction, students can succeed with this task. In developing explanations, students should use writing and drawing to connect their observations with new conceptions and explanations that are developed through discussion or introduced by the teacher.

Through writing, students make their thinking visible, both to themselves and to teachers (Fulton & Campbell, 2003). Writing helps students to reflect on their data, offer their own interpretations of it, and better understand the new conceptions and explanation given by teachers. Further, writing gives teachers an important performance product to use in formative assessment.

Predicting

It is often important in science to predict future occurrences. A **prediction** is a forecast of a future outcome based on knowledge of patterns and relationships in data. Predictions look forward to what might happen. Inferences, in contrast, look backward; inferences are types of explanations of what has already happened.

Predictions are greatly enhanced when measurement data is organized into graphs to illustrate a trend. As an example, use the graph in Figure 2-5 to predict the temperature of the water after 25 minutes. What do you predict would be the temperature after 40 minutes? To make these predictions, determine what temperature would continue the trend already established by the data. A good prediction for the first case (after 25 minutes) is about 104°F, while a good prediction for the second case (after 40 minutes) is about 90°F. Some estimation from the graph is necessary in both cases. The first prediction in the water temperature example is called an *interpolation* because it is between (*inter-*) available

Go to the Homework and Exercises section in Chapter 2 of MyEducationLab to watch the video *Keeping Observation Records.* In this video we observe kindergarten and fifth-grade children involved in activities that help build the process skills of observation and record keeping.

See Hand and Keys (1999) for a well-designed science writing heuristic for developing reports on inquiry investigations in science. A discussion of inquiry reports is also included in our discussion of seed germination and plant growth later in this chapter.

Go to the Homework and Exercises section in Chapter 2 of MyEducationLab to watch the *Identifying Variables* video, highlighting the process skills of observation and record keeping. Each activity also helps students to attain writing standards for the state and introduces children to important science concepts.

Activity 2-3: Predicting

Sample Test Item. It is a cloudless, sunny day. A student measures the temperature of the air outside every hour. She collects the following data.

Time	Air Temperature
8:00 a.m.	18°C
9:00 a.m.	19°C
10:00 a.m.	21°C
11:00 a.m.	23°C

What will the air temperature outside most likely be at noon?

A. 18°C
B. 21°C
C. 25°C
D. 32°C

Source: National Assessment of Educational Progess (NAEP) released test item, grade 4, 2005.

data points; the second prediction is called an *extrapolation* because it is outside (*extra-*) the collected data points.

Activity 2-3 contains a sample test item involving predicting. The item is from the National Assessment of Educational Progress but is like those that might appear on statewide tests. Take some time to work through the activity.

What is your answer to the question in the activity? How did you arrive at it? To answer the item, students would first have to determine the trend of the data from the data table. They should determine that the air temperature increases about 1° or 2°C every hour. From this pattern, they could then predict that the temperature at 12:00 noon would be closest to 25°C, which is answer choice C.

Hypothesizing

The process of formulating and testing hypotheses is one of the core activities of scientific investigations. A **hypothesis** is a statement about a possible answer to a question that might be found through investigating. Hypotheses are often stated in an *if . . . then* form. For example,

> *If* more magnets are added to the magnets stack, *then* more washers will stick to the stack.
> *If* more weights are added to the bottom of the string, *then* the pendulum will make more cycles in 15 seconds.

Hypotheses guide scientists in choosing what data to collect, what available data to pay attention to, what additional data to seek, and possible ways to interpret the data in an investigation. To be useful, a hypothesis should suggest what observational evidence would support it and what evidence would refute it.

To test a hypothesis, students will typically need to conduct an experiment. For example, suppose children asked how the temperature of water affects the time for an effervescent tablet to dissolve in it. They might hypothesize, "If the water is warmer, a tablet will dissolve in it more quickly." To test this hypothesis, the children could conduct an in-

See the April 2001 *Science and Children* article by Louise Baxter and Martha Kurtz titled "When a Hypothesis Is Not an Educated Guess" for an interesting perspective on teaching children the similarities and differences among predictions, hypotheses, and theories.

vestigation in which the temperature of the water is systematically varied. For example, water temperatures of 40°F, 60°F, and 80°F might be used. Then, the time for the tablet to completely dissolve would be measured for each temperature. All other variables, such as the type of container, the volume of water, and the size and type of tablet, remain fixed. The data would be examined to see whether or not the hypothesis is supported.

Experimenting

Sometimes scientists or students can control circumstances deliberately and precisely in an experiment to obtain evidence to test hypotheses and arrive at explanations. Scientists may, for example, control the temperature while changing the concentration of chemicals in an experiment. In a variation of the experiment on water cooling, students may keep the room temperature and size and type of the container the same, while varying the volume of water to see if volume affects the rate of cooling. By controlling all other conditions and varying just one condition in the experiment, they can hope to identify its effects on what happens, uncomplicated by changes in other conditions (Rutherford & Ahlgren, 1990).

Controlled experiments involve (1) deliberately changing one variable at a time, (2) observing the effect on another variable, while (3) holding all other variables constant. A controlled investigation might be used to answer questions such as these:

- What factors affect the rate of swing of a pendulum?
- How does milk in a hamster's diet affect its health and growth?
- Which brand of paper towel is the best buy, considering such factors as absorbency, wet strength, quality, and cost per sheet?

Elementary and middle school students seem to understand controlled experiments better when they think of them as **fair tests**. If a test of a hypothesis is a fair one, then all variables are kept exactly the same except that one variable is changed intentionally. For example, if you wanted to conduct a "fair test" to find out how water temperature affects how quickly an ice cube melts, all of the following variables (the controlled variables) should be kept exactly the same (held constant): volume of water, size and shape of container, size of the ice cube, and air temperature. The water temperature is the variable that is changed intentionally on (the manipulated variable). You might use water at 35 degrees, 45 degrees, and 55 degrees. You would measure how long it takes each ice cube to completely melt, since melting time is the responding variable.

How would you design a fair test to determine which boy in your fourth-grade class is the fastest? What conditions would make this investigation a fair test? Would it be fair to give smaller children a headstart in determining who is fastest?

Working with variables is a particularly important part of controlled investigations. A **variable** is a property of objects or events that can change, has variations, or has differing amounts. The changing height and weight of a growing child, the time a candle can burn under a glass jar, and the amount of rainfall in a day are all examples of variables. The different colors of children's shoes is also an example of a variable.

Three types of variables are important in scientific investigations:

- A **manipulated variable** (also called an **independent variable**) is a variable that the experimenter deliberately changes or manipulates in an investigation.
- A **responding variable** (also called a **dependent variable**) is a variable that changes in an investigation in response to changes in the manipulated variable.
- **Controlled variables** are variables that are deliberately kept constant or unchanged in an investigation in order not to confound the results—that is, so the investigation is a fair test.

Here is an example to illustrate experimenting and the three types of variables. The students in a fifth-grade class wondered why NASA chose white as the color for astronauts' space suits. Several students thought the reason might relate to the sunlight absorbed by the space suit. Challenged by the teacher, the students reformulated their question to: "Do different colored materials absorb sunlight differently?" The teacher then guided the students as they designed and carried out a controlled experiment to help answer their question.

Working in cooperative groups, each team took two identical, empty vegetable cans and wrapped one with black construction paper and the other with white construction paper, filled the cans with equal amounts of water, and placed them side by side in sunlight for a period of time. What were the manipulated, responding, and controlled variables in the sunlight absorption investigation? The manipulated variable in the investigation was the color (light or dark) of the can; the color of the can was the variable that the investigators deliberately changed. The responding variable was the change in temperature of the water in the cans; the change in temperature was the outcome variable the investigators measured for each trial. To make the temperature test a fair one, in each investigation trial the teams would have to control such variables as the size of the cans and materials they were made from, the amount of water in each can, and the time the cans were left in sunlight.

Noting that the water in the dark can got warmer in the investigation of each team, the children, with the teacher's scaffolding assistance, concluded that it had absorbed more sunlight. In answer to their original question, the color of a material does make a difference in the absorption of sunlight. Generalizing from their observations, the children stated this principle: *Darker colored materials absorb more heat from sunlight than lighter colored materials.*

Returning to their initial question, the fifth graders reasoned that NASA chose white for astronauts' suits because white suits absorb less heat in sunlight than darker-colored suits. Follow-up reading activities and direct instruction from the teacher confirmed this inference.

Table 2-3 gives the meaning and examples of each of the three types of variables in the sunlight absorption experiment.

Children can learn to observe, measure, classify, infer, predict, and perform fair tests as part of isolated exercises, but these science processes become more meaningful when used together as intellectual tools in the context of full scientific inquiry. In the following sections, we will look more closely at how children learn processes of science through inquiry activities.

State tests typically include questions involving responding, manipulated, and controlled variables. Often students taking these high-stakes tests are called on to go beyond a multiple-choice format and provide written responses to questions.

How would you find out how stirring affects the time for the complete dissolving in water of three white powders—salt, sugar, and corn starch? What would be your manipulated and responding variables, and what variables would you control? (National Aquarium in Baltimore, 1997)

Go to the Homework and Exercises section in Chapter 2 of MyEducationLab to watch the *Identifying Variables* video. In this video, we see students in a dual-language classroom participating in a study of the variables associated with the most effective design of sails for "skimmers."

TABLE 2-3   DEFINITIONS AND EXAMPLES OF MANIPULATED, RESPONDING, AND CONTROLLED VARIABLES

Variable Type	Definition	Example
Manipulated or independent variable	Variable that is deliberately changed	Color of paper wrapped around the cans in color and sunlight absorption investigation
Responding or dependent variable	Variable that responds to manipulated changes	Change in temperature of the water in each can
Controlled variable	Variable that remains unchanged in an experiment	Type of container; amount of water in each can; time each can was left in sunlight

Investigation Strategies

Although recognizing the value of students knowing how to use individual processes of science, the authors of the *National Science Education Standards* called for "more than 'science as process'" (p. 2). The *Standards* stress that children should learn to use science processes within a framework of inquiry.

Consider, for example, how observation is used in inquiry in the process of generating scientific understanding. Kathleen Roth (1993), an educational researcher who has drawn much of her research data from teaching fifth graders in science and social studies, has suggested that:

> A scientist who observes well . . . is not one who spends endless hours documenting and describing every possible detail that can be observed about a particular phenomenon. . . . In contrast, good scientific observation focuses on key features in ways that will contribute new knowledge, increase the explanatory power of a particular conceptual framework, generate new understandings of relationships among concepts, or raise significant questions about accepted conceptual frameworks. . . . The importance of the observations is not how accurately the scientists can detail and describe all facets of the observed phenomenon, but how the scientists use the observed phenomenon to develop more powerful and complete explanations. (pp. 31–32)

Types of Investigations

There is no fixed set of steps that scientists always follow in doing science, no one path that leads them unerringly to scientific knowledge (Rutherford & Ahlgren, 1990). However, there are some specific types of investigations that children should experience. According to the *National Science Education Standards*, *three* types of investigations children should learn to conduct include:

- descriptive investigations;
- classificatory investigations; and
- experimental investigations.

In *descriptive investigations*, students gather observational and measurement data to answer questions about the properties and actions of objects, organisms, events, and systems. *Classificatory investigations* focus on using classification processes to organize collected information by sorting and grouping it according to one or more properties. Organizing data through classification and other procedures is an important step in identifying the defining properties of the objects and organisms of interest and in answering questions. *Experimental investigations* use experimental procedures, including controlled experiments, to provide evidence needed in forming and testing hypotheses and generating explanations.

Table 2-4 identifies the main characteristics and provides examples of each of these ways of investigating.

These three main approaches to investigating involve the application of processes of observing, measuring, classifying, inferring, predicting, experimenting, and communicating. When you make processes of science explicit to students during scientific investigations, you help them to develop skills for doing science, better understand how science is done, and appreciate more fully the real-world basis of all scientific knowledge.

Each of these three ways of investigating—descriptive, classificatory, and experimental—involve the five tasks of inquiry identified in Figure 1-3. In each type of investigation, students identify a queston or problem to investigate, conduct investigations, collect relevant data, analyze the data, form conclusions and explanations, and communicate their investigations and findings to others for review.

"Scientists use different kinds of investigations, depending on the questions they are trying to answer. Types of investigations include describing objects, events, and organisms; classifying them; and conducting a fair test (experimenting)."

(*National Science Education Standards*, National Research Council, 1996, p. 123)

TABLE 2-4   TYPES OF INVESTIGATIONS

Types of Investigations	Investigative Procedures	Example Science Topics	Example Engagement Questions
Descriptive Investigations	Gather observational and measurement data to answer questions about the properties and actions of objects, organisms, events, and systems.	White powders Seeds and plants	What are the visual properties of different kinds of white powders? What is the sequence of germination and growth for a bean seed?
Classificatory Investigations	Organize collected information by sorting and grouping it according to one or more properties in order to identify relationships and better define properties.	Rocks and minerals	Which mineral is hardest? How can you tell the difference between igneous and sedimentary rocks?
Experimental Investigations	Conduct experiments, including controlled experiments, to determine how variables are related and to isolate causal factors in natural phenomena.	Color and sunlight absorption Seeds and plants	Do different colored materials absorb sunlight differently? Do plants take in water through their leaves or their roots?

Go to the Homework and Exercises section in Chapter 2 of MyEducationLab to watch two videos, *Designing Experiments* and *Controlling Variables*. Together, the videos reveal the difficulties that even older students have with controlled experiments and how students can remarkably improve their understanding of a control of variables task through discovery activities and teacher instruction.

The theoretical and practical foundations for the grade placement of different types of investigation are considered in Chapter 3. Many activities in elementary science can be adapted to different grade levels. This is true for the many different activities provided in this chapter. In general, grade 1–3 children can readily carry out simple descriptive and classificatory investigations with moderate teacher assistance. With greater teacher assistance, children at this level might also carry out simple experimental investigations. Grade 4–6 students continue to conduct descriptive and classificatory investigations. They can also conduct more complex experimental investigations. However, they will likely need considerable teacher assistance to identify variables, plan and conduct controlled investigations, and interpret the results of investigations.

Sometimes statewide tests in science include items in which students are required to formulate and write out their answers. Activity 2-4 provides a sample item related to fair tests that might appear on a statewide test. Take some time to work through this activity. Follow the directions given. Compare your answers with those from a group of your colleagues.

Following are some examples of classroom inquiry involving the three types of investigations.

Activity 2-4: Experimenting with Soils: A Fair Test

Sample Test Item. James and Maria noticed three different types of soil, black soil, sand, and clay, were found in their neighborhood. They decided to investigate the question, "How does the type of soil (black soil, sand, and clay) under *grass sod* affect the height of grass?"

Plan an investigation the students could use to answer their question.

In your plan, be sure to:

1. Identify the manipulated, responding, and controlled variables for the investigation.
2. Describe the steps to do in the investigation.
3. Tell how often measurements are to be taken and recorded.

Mealworms are the larval stage of various beetles. They can usually be purchased from a local pet store. Talk to your pet store about how to feed, care for, and humanely dispose of mealworms. A bed of oatmeal on newspaper provides a good environment for students to observe mealworms.

To observe mealworms, student groups will need newspaper, oatmeal, crackers, plastic forceps, petri dish (for water), hand lenses, and their journals.

Investigating Mealworms: Descriptive, Classificatory, and Experimental Inquiries

The *National Science Education Standards* emphasize that "different kinds of questions suggest different kinds of scientific investigations" (National Research Council, 1996, p. 148). An investigation of mealworms can involve all three types of investigation strategies, depending on the question asked. Figure 2-6 provides a number of questions for mealworm investigations. Study the questions given in the figure and decide which type of investigation—descriptive, classificatory, or experimental—is most suitable for investigating each one.

What kind of investigation strategy is called for by the different questions for investigating mealworms? Questions 1 and 2 call for descriptive investigations about the body characteristics

Mealworms are the larval stage of beetles. They go through complete metamorphosis, with four different life stages: egg, larva, pupa, and adult.

1. What are the main body characteristics of mealworms?
2. How many legs does your mealworm have? Where on the body are the legs located?
3. Do mealworms have the general characteristics of insects? What are the similarities and differences between mealworms and other insects?
4. How does a mealworm move? How do its legs work together when it moves? How does it turn corners?
5. What kinds of food do mealworms prefer to eat?

Figure 2-6 Questions for investigating mealworms.

Figure 2-7   What are the main body parts of a mealworm?

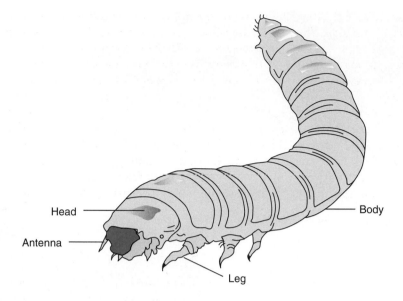

Head

Antenna

Body

Leg

of mealworms. To answer the question, students must observe the mealworms carefully, including observation with a magnifying lens. They can observe that mealworms have a segmented body with six legs attached to the body. Two antennae are attached to the head. Children might communicate this information through labeled drawings (see Figure 2-7).

Question 3 calls for a classificatory investigation. In response to question 3, for example, students can find out from their teachers, or through their textbook, a trade book, or the Internet that insects have three main body parts, six legs, and two antennae. By comparing their observations of the characteristics of mealworms with their findings from outside sources, they can conclude that mealworms should be classified as insects.

Question 4 calls for a descriptive investigation with an experimental component. In the experiment, students might work together to discover different ways the six legs of a mealworm might be used in moving (see Figure 2-8). Through observing whether meal-

Figure 2-8   How do mealworms use their legs when they walk and turn corners?

worms actually use their legs in the proposed way, students can test the different models of mealworm movement. The psychomotor involvement of the students helps them to understand the complexity and appreciate the wonder of mealworm movement.

Question 5 calls for an experimental investigation. One way to investigate question 5 is for student teams to draw a small circle (about 5 cm in diameter) in the center of a paper plate and draw four equally spaced lines straight from the edge of the inner circle to the edge of the plate. Different foods, including bran, sugar, lettuce, and potato are then placed equidistant from the center within the four segments created by the four lines. A number of mealworms are then placed in the inner circle. Students can observe how many mealworms move to each segment, note whether they eat the foods in the segments, and infer which foods they prefer. What is the manipulated variable in this experiment? What is the responding variable? What variables should be controlled?

Mystery Powders: A Descriptive and Classificatory Investigation

In classificatory investigations, students find out more about objects and organisms by discovering ways of grouping them according to their properties or traits. By focusing on properties, classificatory investigations tend to incorporate descriptive inquiry procedures. Investigating the properties of white powders forms the basis for an exciting descriptive and classificatory inquiry for children in about grade 3.

In this series of activities, children investigate common white powders, including sugar, table salt, baking soda, and cornstarch (see the accompanying Lesson Activities: Investigating White Powders). The powders are similar in color but differ in other properties. Through investigation, the children learn several indicator tests they can use to identify properties of the powders. For example, they learn that salt dissolves in water and baking soda fizzes in vinegar. Table 2-5 shows a chart of the properties of some common white powders.

Once children learn to identify each white powder through tests, they are given "mystery powders" consisting of mixtures of *two* powders.

A comprehensive set of activities on the properties of white powders can be found on pages A-30–A-33 in *Activities for Teaching Science as Inquiry*.

To connect science and social studies, you might ask children in social studies to investigate which white powders pioneer settlers would have carried with them on wagon trains and why they would need them.

TABLE 2-5 PROPERTIES OF WHITE POWDERS				
Observations	**Powder 1 Granulated Sugar**	**Powder 2 Table Salt**	**Powder 3 Baking Soda**	**Powder 4 Cornstarch**
Visual (Magnifying Glass)	White crystals	White box-shaped crystals	Fine white powder	Fine yellowish white powder
Water Test	Dissolves in water	Dissolves in water	Forms milky mix	Makes water cloudy
Vinegar Test	Dissolves in vinegar	Has no reaction with vinegar	Fizzes with vinegar	Gets thick, then hard with vinegar
Iodine Test	Turns yellow with iodine	Has no reaction with iodine	Turns yellow-orange with iodine	Turns red, then black with iodine

Lesson Activities: Investigating White Powders

Materials

Salt, sugar, baking soda, and cornstarch; containers of water, vinegar, and iodine; medicine droppers; plastic spoons; toothpicks; blank data table for recording data; laminated blank data table to use as an investigation tray; magnifying lenses; safety goggles.

Safety Precautions

- Wear safety goggles for these investigations with powders.
- Do not taste any of the powders or liquids.
- Wash your hands after you test each powder.

Initiating Question

What are the identifying properties of some common white powders?

Preparation

Laminate copies of the blank data table shown and use one as an investigation tray for each group. Prepare an additional, unlaminated data table for each team to use for recording data.

Investigation Procedures

1. *Visual Observations:* Use a plastic spoon to place a small amount of each powder in the appropriate cells of your investigation tray. Use a magnifying glass to observe each powder. Write down your observations on a paper copy of the data table.
2. *Water Test:* Use a clean plastic spoon to place a small amount of each powder in a row on your investigation tray. Add several drops of water and mix with a toothpick to see what happens. Record your observations in your data table.
3. *Iodine Test:* Use a clean plastic spoon to place a small amount of each powder in a row on your tray. Add a drop or two of iodine to each powder. Write down the results in your data table. Be careful! Iodine can stain your hands and clothing.
4. *Vinegar Test:* Use a clean plastic spoon to place a small amount of each powder in a row on your tray. Add several drops of vinegar to each powder. Write down the results in your data table.

Explanations

Write your answers to these questions on your data record sheet.

5. What do the rows in your data table indicate?
6. What do the columns indicate?
7. How are the four powders alike?
8. How are the powders different? What is the best test for identifying each powder?

Communication

Throughout the activity, keep accurate written records of the array of data collected. Also, be prepared to present and discuss your investigation procedures, your data, and your explanations of the data with the whole class.

Clean Up

Throw away toothpicks. Return powders, test supplies, and the cleaned laminated data table to teacher-designated spot. Clean and dry anything dirty, including your hands. Do not put powders in the sink as they might harden and clog the drain.

DATA TABLE FOR INVESTIGATING WHITE POWDERS

	Powder 1 Granulated Sugar	Powder 2 Table Salt	Powder 3 Baking Soda	Powder 4 Cornstarch
Visual Observations				
Water Test				
Iodine Test				
Vinegar Test				

Useful commercial guides to this activity can be found at: http://www.csulb.edu/~lhenriqu/mysterypowder.htm.

Scientists keep accurate records of data collected, so they are prepared to recall data taken, make comparisons of the data, draw inferences, make predictions, and generate explanations. For similar reasons, students should also keep accurate records. You can use the student records to assess understanding and decide next steps in instruction.

During this activity on white powders, provide time for students to record their findings. Recording data will be a natural part of the work of some students; other students will need encouragement to stop and record their findings.

Take some time to discuss with students the design of data record sheets. For example, column 1 of the data sheet used in the white powders investigation shows the types of investigation tests carried out. These include visual examination, water tests, and so on. The rows describe the results of each test with each of the white powders. Seen together, the columns and rows provide a display of data that allows patterns to be found and used in further investigations.

The teacher gives each pair of students a mixture of two powders. Working together, each pair uses visual and tactile observations to form hypotheses about their mixture. They then perform the various tests on the mixture to test their hypotheses. Here is what some of the children do and say during their mystery powders investigations:

Student 1: Put a little bit here.

Student 2: (Student 2 pours some of the mystery powder on a piece of white paper, and the pair look at it and feel it.)

Student 3: You do the water (test); I'll do the vinegar. (One of the partners in this pair drops water from a small bottle on a bit of the mystery powder. The other one puts a few drops of vinegar on another small amount of the powder. The children observe the resulting reactions.)

Student 4: It's fizzing a little!

Student 3: Fizzing, yeah! Try one more time. (The partner puts more drops of vinegar on the powder.)

Student 4: There's definitely baking soda in there.

Student 3: Big time!

Student 5: I think it's not salt.

Student 6: I don't know. What would be the best way to find out if it is not salt? (Pauses and ponders for a moment.) All right, let's try water.

Student 7: We thought it was cornstarch. We did the iodine test and we're positive that it is cornstarch. We want to move on to a really, really, hard one, a challenge. We want to put four (powders) in.

Teacher: Do you think you can solve that?

Students: Yes!

(Annenberg/CPB Foundation, 1997)

Go to the Homework and Exercises section in Chapter 2 of MyEducationLab to view the video, *Investigating Particles: Parts 1 and 2*. This video features second-grade children investigating a variety of particles, including different kinds of beans, rice, and cornmeal.

In performing the various tests on their mystery powders, the children take their role as scientists very seriously. They are thoughtful, respectful of one another, but excited.

Through these lessons, the child-scientists develop well-structured and grade-level-appropriate knowledge about matter. These lessons on matter align well with the *National Science Education Standards* for grades K–4 (see the NSES box on standards and concepts and principles related to matter). The children also have many opportunities to practice and extend their science process skills—but always within a context of inquiry and significant concepts and principles.

In the white powders lesson, the inquiries are primarily descriptive and classificatory. Next, let us look at a classroom investigation involving descriptive and experimental investigation procedures.

NSES   **STANDARDS ON MATTER AND CONCEPTS AND PRINCIPLES THAT SUPPORT THE STANDARDS**

NSES Standards

Students should understand:

- Properties of objects and materials (K–4).

Concepts and Principles That Support the Standards

- Objects have many observable properties, including size, weight, shape, color, temperature, and the ability to react with other substances.
- Some properties can be measured using tools, such as rulers, balances, and thermometers.
- Objects are made of one or more materials, such as paper, wood, and metal. Objects can be described by the properties of the materials from which they are made, and those properties can be used to separate or sort a group of objects or materials.
- Materials can exist in different states—solids, liquids, and gases. Some common materials, such as water, can be changed from one state to another by heating or cooling.

Activity 2-5: What Are the Parts of a Seed?

1. Obtain several lima bean seeds. Make as many observations and measurements as you can about the bean seeds.
2. Soak some of the bean seeds for at least 48 hours.
3. Gently break a soaked lima bean seed open into its two halves. Observe the two halves carefully, including with a magnifying lens.
4. Communicate your observations to others using writing, charts, and drawings.

Germinating Seeds and Growing Plants: A Descriptive amd Experimental Inquiry Project

There is nothing like being around children to rekindle our own interest in the natural world. Children love to study living things. They especially enjoy planting seeds and watching and caring for plants as they grow. Forming good questions that can be empirically investigated and that lead to significant knowledge is the first step in scientific inquiry. Some questions children ask are not easily investigated, for example, *Why do plants develop from seeds?* and *How do plants grow? What* questions (questions about *what* might happen in an investigation) are more easily investigated in the classroom than *why* or *how* questions. If students ask *why* or *how* questions, teachers can help them rework the questions into forms that can be investigated. In this series of lessons on seeds and plants, the teacher helped the students formulate this question: *What happens to the seeds and plants during plant growth?* As the children began to investigate and collect data related to this question, through group discussion the teacher helped them focus on these additional questions:

- What are the parts of a seed?
- What happens to the different parts of the seed as the plants grow?
- What is the sequence of germination and growth for a bean seed?

These questions fit investigations that can be carried out at almost any grade level, K–6. Investigating questions such as these can be instrumental in helping children attain the K–4 NSES Content Standards related to organisms (see accompanying NSES box).

What Are the Parts of a Seed? Activity 2-5 is directed toward the first question, concerning the parts of the seed. Do this activity before continuing.

This activity reveals that once bean seeds are soaked and broken into two halves, three main parts can be observed. Through instruction, students can learn that the three parts are called a *seed coat*, the *cotyledon* (the pulpy mass in a seed), and a small plantlike structure—the *embryo plant*. The beginnings of a leaf and root are clearly observable in the embryo plant (see Figure 2-9).

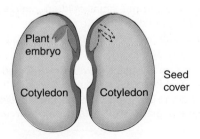

Figure 2-9 A bean seed has three main parts: a seed covering, the cotyledon, and an embryo plant.

NSES STANDARDS ABOUT ORGANISMS AND CONCEPTS AND PRINCIPLES THAT SUPPORT THE STANDARDS FOR GRADES K–4

NSES Standards

Students should understand:

- Characteristics of Organisms (K–4)
- Life Cycles of Organisms (K–4)

Concepts and Principles That Support the Standards

- Organisms have basic needs. For example, animals need air, water, and food; plants require air, water, nutrients, and light. Organisms can survive only in environments in which their needs can be met.
- Each plant or animal has different structures that serve different functions in growth, survival, and reproduction.
- Plants and animals have life cycles that include being born, developing into adults, reproducing, and eventually dying. The details of this life cycle are different for different organisms.

Source: Reprinted from *National Science Education Standards* by The National Academy of Sciences, with permission courtesy of the National Academies Press, Washington DC.

In inquiry, children must plan investigations carefully and use their science process skills selectively in collecting data. The investigation procedures and the science processes used depend on the inquiry questions asked. What types of investigations—descriptive, classificatory, or experimental—are called for by the questions in the seed and plant study?

Once children identify the parts of a seed, they might engage in brainstorming and raise their own questions about the functions of the seed parts, such as *What is the seed coat for?* or *What does the cotyledon do?*

These and other questions lead to more investigation and research.

What Is the Sequence of Germination and Growth of Bean Seeds? This question calls for a descriptive investigation. Children cannot just place the seeds underground in moist soil, because then they would not be able to see them germinate. However, they can use a transparent germination bag like the one shown in Figure 2-10. The germination bags should be attached to a bulletin board or some other flat, vertical surface.

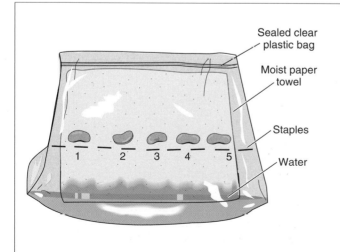

Sealed clear plastic bag

Moist paper towel

Staples

Water

- Line a 7 inch × 8 inch (quart size) sealable, transparent storage bag with a moist paper towel.
- Place nine staples across the bag about 4 to 5 cm from the bottom, as shown in the diagram.
- Position the seeds to be germinated above the line of staples.
- The seeds may be presoaked for about 24 hours.
- Gently pour water from a small container into the bag, being careful not to dislodge the seeds (the water should bulge slightly at the bottom of the bag to about a finger's thickness).

The water will soak the paper towel and keep the seeds moist. The staples keep the seeds from lying in the water at the bottom of the bag. The transparent bag allows the seeds, developing plant, and roots to be observed.

Figure 2-10   How to construct a seed germination bag.

| Date | Descriptions | | | Measurements | | |
	Changes in seeds	Changes in roots	Changes in stems	Length of roots	Length of stems	Drawing
Monday March 5						
Wednesday March 7						
Friday March 9						
Monday March 12						

Figure 2-11 Sample data sheet for recording seed germination data.

Children should observe their germinating seeds and developing plants regularly for 2 or 3 weeks. What should they observe? Initially, in this investigation children recorded their observations of a wide variety of changes through words and drawings in their journals and on data sheets. As the children *reflected* on their question and data through class discussion, they found that they needed some additional observations. They also found that there were some observations that they would likely not use in drawing conclusions. The children decided to use a new data sheet like the one in Figure 2-11. The data sheet provides for recording data on changes in color, size, and apprearance that might occur in the seeds and in the emerging roots, stems, and leaves.

In investigating the process of germination, children might observe that first the seed becomes moist and softens. Early in the process, a "sprout" begins to emerge from the bean seed near where the embryo plant is located. As children observe further, they can see that the tip of the sprout becomes the root. The stem grows upward from the root carrying the cotyledon with it. Because the root has emerged from near the location of the embryo plant, children might infer that the growing plant develops from the embryo.

During the germination process, the seed coat comes off. Although they cannot know for sure from observation alone, children might infer that the seed coat protected the seed to ensure that it did not become moist earlier than desired. Instruction and reading can confirm this inference.

As the plant develops, the cotyledon shrivels and sometimes falls off the stem. Building on this observation, children might learn from instruction that the cotyledon is an energy or food source that is used by the young plant as it is germinating, before the leaves develop and the process of photosynthesis begins to take place. Your students can investigate further by trying to germinate each of the two halves of a cotyledon, one with the embryo plant and one without.

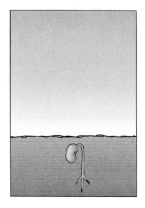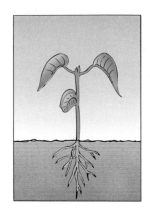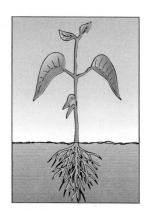

Figure 2-12 The developmental sequence from a bean seed to a young bean plant.

Eventually as the bean plant develops, green leaves begin to grow. Figure 2-12 summarizes the developmental sequence of a bean seed into a young bean plant.

Observation of the seeds and developing plants in the baggie suggest that the plant takes in and uses the water in some way. The children wanted to know, *How does the plant take in water?* The teacher helped the children reformulate this question to, *Do plants take in water through roots or leaves?*

Do Plants Take in Water Through Roots or Leaves? To gather evidence to use in answering this question, children might carry out an experimental investigation like the one illustrated in Figure 2-13. This investigation involves two plants. The manipulated variable is how the plants are watered. The responding variable is the resulting condition of each plant. The variables that are controlled or kept constant are the amount of water each plant gets and environmental conditions such as temperature and light exposure. In the investigation, water is added to the soil of one plant so that it can reach the roots. The same amount of water is sprinkled on the leaves of the second plant, with a plastic bib keeping the water from reaching the soil and roots (National Gardening Association, 1992).

Children should keep daily records of their observations. Teachers might prepare data sheets for chldren to use, or students might be required to construct their own record

 Additional activities about seeds and plants can be found on pages A-124–A-150 in *Activities for Teaching Science as Inquiry*. Also, see the delightful resource, *GrowLab: Activities for Growing Minds* (1992), published by the National Gardening Association (see Appendix B for address).

Figure 2-13 Do plants get water through their roots or their leaves?

plastic "bib"

dish

Pot A
Water soil

Pot B
Water leaves

sheets. After about 2 weeks, the teacher might guide the children as they use the data sheets to remember and review their observations as a basis for any discussions of their findings. In guiding discussion, the teacher might ask:

- What did you do in the investigation?
- What did you observe? How did your findings compare with your predictions?
- What can you infer about the role of leaves and roots in taking in water? What makes you confident in your inference that water is taken in by roots?
- Did you actually see roots taking in water? (National Gardening Association, 1992)

Through this investigation the children were able to conclude that water was taken into the plant by the roots, rather than through the leaves. This finding led to an additional question, *Is water carried to the leaves through the stem?*

Is Water Carried to the Leaves Through the Stem? Answering this question requires an experiment, though it is different somewhat from a true controlled investigation. Here are the investigation procedures:

- Obtain two clear drinking glasses.
- Fill the glasses about two-thirds full of water.
- Add blue food coloring to the water in one glass.
- Cut a small slice off the bottom of a celery stalk. Set the stem into the glass of colored water as in the left side of Figure 2-14(a).
- Cut a small slice off the bottom of a second celery stalk. Set the stem into the glass of plain water as in the right side of Figure 2-14(a).
- Allow both glasses with celery stalks to sit in a sunny area for 2 hours. At the end of this period, cut across both stalks as in Figure 2-14(b).
- To help the children organize and make sense of their observational data, teachers might ask: *Do both stalks look the same? What has happened to the celery stem? What parts of the stem appear to contain the colored water? How do you know? What can you conclude about the function of a stem? How is water carried to different parts of the plant?*

Through instruction, media, textbooks, or other means, teachers can provide the following information that will help students organize their developing knowledge:

- All organisms have basic needs. Plants need light, air, water, and nutrients. Animals need air, water, and nutrients.
- Plants and animals can survive only in environments in which their needs are met.

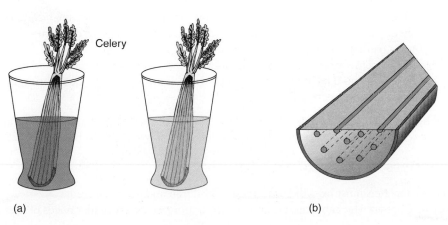

Celery

(a)　(b)

Figure 2-14 "What is the function of the stem of a plant? Why do you think so?"

- Roots absorb water and nutrients through small root hairs. Water and nutrients are carried from the roots to the leaves through small tubes, called capillaries, that are inside the stem.
- Plants get their energy for survival and growth directly from sunlight through a process called photosynthesis.
- Animals live by consuming the energy-rich foods initially synthesized by plants (*National Science Education Standards*, National Research Council, 1996).

Through inquiries like these—asking questions, conducting investigations, collecting and recording observational data, and using the data and science knowledge to generate theories and explanations—students build integrated conceptual structures that can be used in further descriptive, classificatory, and explanatory studies.

Communicating Investigation Results. Full inquiry involves asking a simple question, completing an investigation, answering the question, and communicating the results to others. In one kindergarten class, at the conclusion of a unit in which they planted seeds and investigated plant growth, the children communicated what they learned by acting out seed germination and plant growth. As the teacher read aloud from a children's book about seeds and life, the children solemnly played the roles of seeds, moisture, and sunlight. At first, each seed-child rolled into a tight ball close to the floor. The water-child then went about, sprinkling blue crepe-paper "rainwater" on the seed-children, and they began, one by one, to shake themselves and gradually spring to life. When the seed-children popped up through the "ground," they looked around for the sun-child, who held a large yellow circle with rays drawn on it. With the warming rays of the sun, the seed-children began to stretch and grow to their full heights. The children's understanding of seed germination and plant growth could be inferred from the seriousness of their role playing, the ways their actions paralleled the teacher's reading, and the connections between each seed-child's actions and the actions of the growth factors of moisture and sunlight.

Questions, investigations, observations, and explanations/conclusions might be communicated through a science journal or notebook, or orally to the class. The written records should be developed as the investigation unfolds, with questions, data, and conclusions recorded. The presentation might include the following components:

A. *Questions. What I want to find out.* (The focus question for investigation is expressed in writing.)
B. *Investigation Plans: What I will do to answer my questions* (Investigation procedures are described.)
C. *Observations: What I found out from my observations and measurements.* (Data sheets, verbal information, measurement data, graphs, labeled diagrams, and pictures, perhaps from digital cameras, would be included here.)
D. *Conclusions: What I concluded.* (In drawing conclusions, children should use their observational data as evidence to support their answers to the questions raised in the Questions section of the journal.)

The use of written records not only improves conceptual understanding and inquiry skills in science, it also contributes to the development of writing skills (Klentschy, 2005).

Teachers, Children, and Inquiry

Effective teachers must be skilled observers of children and effective guides of the inquiry process. Teachers who can match their teaching actions to the particular needs of students are essential in inquiry learning: deciding when and how to guide; when to encourage more exploration; how to scaffold learning through prompts, hints, questions, and other means; when to demand more rigorous grappling by the students; when to provide information; and when to connect students to other sources (National Research Council, 1996).

Teaching and learning science through an inquiry approach is challenging but well worth the effort!

SUMMARY

- Processes of science are skills that scientists and children apply in collecting, organizing, and using data to interpret and make sense of the world. Specific processes emphasized in elementary and middle school science include observing, measuring, classifying, inferring, hypothesizing, conducting controlled investigations, predicting, explaining, and communicating. These science processes are much like the mental processes we all use in solving everyday problems.

- Sometimes processes of science are taught in elementary classrooms primarily through isolated activities. But the *National Science Education Standards* have called for more than science as process, emphasizing that processes should be embedded and integrated in inquiry.

- Elementary and middle school students can be expected to engage in descriptive, classificatory, and experimental inquiries. In grades K–4, investigations are largely based on systematic description and classification of material objects and organisms.

- By grade 5 or 6, and even earlier with a great deal of teacher guidance, children begin to engage in experimental inquiries. In controlled investigations, students work to understand some phenomenon by determining the effect of a manipulated variable on a responding variable, while controlling all other relevant variables.

- Participating in investigations that incorporate processes of science is essential to the science learning and cognitive development of elementary and middle grade students. All of these ways of investigating involve the application of the various processes of science. By making processes of science explicit to students during scientific investigations, you help them to develop skills for doing science, to better understand the nature of scientific inquiry, and to appreciate more fully the real-world basis of all scientific knowledge.

ONLINE PROFESSIONAL DEVELOPMENT

Pre- and post-tests to assess your knowledge of chapter content, along with exercises to enhance your understanding, can be found on MyEducationLab at www.myeducationlab.com.

Video Guides

Video clips on MyEducationLab for this chapter include: *Keeping Observation Records, Identifying Variables,* and *Investigating Particles—Parts 1 and 2*.

Accessing the Videos

1. Go to the Homework and Exercises section in Chapter 2 of MyEducationLab to select and view videos for this chapter and answer the questions.

2. Videos might be viewed individually, by small groups of colleagues, or by the whole class.

3. As you watch each video, use the **Questions for Reflection** to guide your thoughts and note taking for personal use and group discussion.

4. Discuss your answers to the questions about each video with classmates.

Video: Keeping Observation Records

Overview

In this video we watch kindergarten and fifth-grade children involved in activities that help build the process skills of observation and record keeping. Each activity also helps students to attain state writing standards and introduces children to important science concepts.

Questions for Reflection

1. What does the kindergarten teacher say about the gold-fish lesson and the Connecticut Science Standards? On what specific standards does the lesson focus?
2. What examples of observation do you see in the gold-fish, pin-hole viewer, and moon phases lessons? What kinds of observation records do the children make in the different lessons?
3. How do the different observation records represent a means of developing the process skill of communicating? How do you think the different records also relate to the state writing standards?

Video: Identifying Variables

Overview

In this video, students watch a demonstration by two teachers, aided by students, of the variables associated with the most effective design of sails for "skimmers." Students respond excitedly to the demonstration and to the teachers' questions.

Questions for Reflection

1. What differences do you see in the two sails being tested?
2. What are the manipulated and responding variables in the investigation, and what variables are controlled?

What examples do you find of children naming or discussing the various variables?
3. What do the teachers do to help make sure the children are thinking about the different variables as they watch the demonstration?

Video: Investigating Particles, Parts 1 and 2

Overview

In these two videos, we watch as second-grade children investigate a variety of particles, including lima beans, mung beans, pinto beans, rice, and corn meal. For example, they investigate how the size of particles affects the size of the hills that can be made from them.

Questions for Reflection

1. What questions about particles do the children investigate in these videos?
2. How are observation skills used in investigating the different questions?

Annenberg Videos

Case Studies in Science Education: Jean

To access Annenberg videos, follow the instructions given in the Online Professional Development section in Chapter 1 on page 26.

3

L earning science is something students do, not something that is done to them.

(*National Science Education Standards*, National Research Council, 1996, p. 20)

Learning Science with Understanding

ONCE STUDENTS INVOLVED in inquiry have formulated questions that can be investigated and collected and organized data, they face the challenge of using the data as evidence in generating new knowledge, forming theories, and constructing explanations that can be used in answering their initial question. In learning science with understanding, most students will need considerable assistance from their teachers.

Fortunately, there is a growing body of research available on teaching and learning science with understanding. Teachers who know and use this research can greatly enhance the learning of science by their students. Consider how such research might be used in the following lesson scenario.

During a series of investigations on properties of light, Don Roach's fifth grade students pointed out one morning that they could see their "reflections" in a plate-glass door. Mr. Roach had studied children's theories about light in an in-service workshop and knew that his students would have a variety of conceptions and misconceptions about mirrors and images.

Through class discussion, Mr. Roach guided his students to think about what an image is and where it appears to be in mirrors and other reflecting surfaces. Most of the students knew that the image was just a copy of the real thing, but thought that it was on the surface of a mirror or just behind it (Shapiro, 1994). A few thought it might be deeper in the mirror. Drawing on their ideas and their knowledge of light reflection gained in previous lessons, Don helped the students form a simple question that might be investigated scientifically: *Where is my image in a mirror?*

The children decided to search for evidence to answer the question by investigating their own images in a glass door near the classroom. In the investigation, students worked in small, cooperative groups. One student, called the *object partner*, stood on one side of the glass door so she could see her image in it (see Figure 3-1). Another student, the *image partner*, went to the other side of the door, and after some direction stood right on top of the image of the partner's shoes.

One group decided to use the classroom meter sticks to measure each partner's distance from the door. Soon other groups were also measuring the distance from the door of the object and image partners. Mr. Roach suggested that the groups combine their data into a class data table (see Figure 3-2). When each group had entered its measurements in the data table, Mr. Roach asked the groups if they could discover a pattern in the data. Some of the students noted that in the data table the object distance and image distance were always

Figure 3-1 A child examines the image of herself formed in a glass door.

Figure 3-2 Data table for mirror images activity. What are some things you might conclude from the data?

Group	Distance of Image from Door (cm)	Distance of Object from Door (cm)
A.	200	190
B.	350	365
C.	250	238
D.	225	225
E.	300	320

about the same. Based on this discovery, the class generalized that an image appears to be just as far inside a mirror as the real object is in front of the mirror.

The teacher in this lesson used a number of research findings on how children learn, including findings related to knowledge construction, prior knowledge, knowledge organization, scaffolding assistance, learning communities, and naive theories. As a teacher, you need to know how children learn and develop so you can adjust instruction to meet the needs of all your students. This chapter describes some of the abundant research on learning and development that can provide a strong theory base for you as you guide children's learning of science with understanding.

As you study the chapter, keep these questions in mind:

- *What is meant by constructivism? What is the role of prior knowledge in new learning? What does it mean to learn science with understanding?*

- *How do various internal and external factors, including access to prior knowledge, knowledge organization, scaffolding, and learning communities affect science learning?*

- *What is meant by transfer? How can you help students learn to transfer their knowledge to new situations?*

- *How do students' naive theories and alternative conceptions affect their science learning? How can you use inquiry instruction to promote conceptual change and deeper understanding of science?*

- *What is meant by development? How does development differ from learning? How does development affect learning?*

- *What are some of Piaget's findings on the development of thinking that are relevant to science teaching?*

- *How do cognitive development, prior knowledge, and the availability of teacher scaffolding affect the learning of science with understanding?*

The New View of Learning

Contemporary research findings and theories on learning are well summarized by Bransford, Brown, and Cocking (1999) in *How People Learn* and by Duschl, Schweingruber, and

Shouse (2007) in *Taking Science to School: Learning and Teaching Science in Grades K–8.* Both of these important reports were sponsored by the National Research Council, the group that also sponsored the *National Science Education Standards.*

The traditional view of learning is that knowledge is discovered through the manipulation of objects or acquired from others when learners listen to what they say. However, we now accept that learning is more complex than that. Knowledge cannot be passed intact from a teacher or book to a learner, nor is it simply discovered in the real world. Students must *construct* new knowledge for themselves.

This view of learning is called *constructivism.* In the constructivist perspective, new knowledge is always based on the prior or existing knowledge that learners bring to learning situations. Students take in information from many sources, but in building their own knowledge, they connect information to prior knowledge and experiences, organize it, and construct meaning for themselves (Loucks-Horsley et al., 1998). Without an adequate level of prior knowledge, new learning and its transfer to new situations cannot be expected (Bransford et al., 1999). What learners already know influences what they attend to, how they organize input, and how they are able to integrate new constructions to expand their knowledge bases.

Constructing Knowledge with Understanding in Science

To *know* something implies to be able to remember or recall it so that it can be accessed and used when needed. *Understanding* is based in knowledge, yet it involves more than mere recall. What does it mean for a student to understand an idea? Contemporary researchers insist that when students truly understand an idea, they can do something with it. They can:

- interpret questions for investigation and express them in their own words;
- interpret what they learn and express it in their own words;
- relate concepts to real-world experiences;
- plan and conduct investigations to answer investigation questions;
- interpret data collected, relate it to real-world activities, find patterns in the data, compare and contrast their data with that of others; and
- apply their knowledge and their investigation findings in drawing inferences, making predictions, constructing explanations, and solving novel problems (Bransford et al., 1999; Wiggins & McTighe, 1998; Wiske, 1998).

As an example of the differences between knowledge and understanding, if students have knowledge of the facts, concepts, and principles of water introduced in Chapter 1, they should be able to describe what happens in heaping and other water phenomena, define important terms, such as cohesive bonds, and recall what they learned about the role of cohesive bonds in explaining why water heaps up in cups. On the other hand, if students truly *understand* the nature of water, when they encounter a new event, such as the beading of drops on wax paper or the spreading of drops on aluminum foil, they should be able to apply the concept of cohesion and the concept of adhesion between water and different types of materials to explain why the drops bead up on one surface and spread out on another.

Students often have limited opportunity to develop understanding because the curriculum, textbooks, and tests emphasize memory and recall. Too much emphasis on memory results in knowledge that is fragmented, incomplete, and tied to specific situations. In contrast, understanding in science must be based in knowledge that is integrated rather than fragmented, that is growing in completeness, and that can be transferred to a wide

> *"The new view of learning is that people construct new knowledge and understanding based on what they already know and believe."*
>
> (Bransford, Brown, and Cocking. 1999, p. 10)

Figure 3-3 Levels of student understanding.

1. *Proficient understanding.* Students use the knowledge, methods, evidence, and arguments involved in a topic as powerful tools in new problem situations.
2. *Satisfactory understanding.* Learners' understanding enables them to succeed with new tasks with only minimum amounts of teacher scaffolding support.
3. *Limited understanding.* Students succeed on new tasks, but only with considerable support from teachers and peers in the form of prompts, hints, series of questions, and direct instruction.
4. *No understanding.* Students fail to succeed on new tasks, even with a great deal of assistance from teachers and peers.

range of contexts and situations. Through its emphasis on investigations, such as the investigations of water, magnets, mealworms, common white powders, and seeds and plants described in previous chapters, inquiry instruction provides an excellent context in which to foster children's science understanding.

Levels of Understanding

Understanding is not an all or nothing proposition; rather, it develops gradually through different levels of understanding (Wiggins & McTighe, 1998). The rubric in Figure 3-3 suggests a continuum for thinking about the different levels of student understanding.

In the following sections we consider ways teachers can assist learners to develop higher levels of understanding.

Enhancing the Understanding of Science

Bransford, Brown, and Cocking (1999) have emphasized a variety of internal and external factors that affect children's learning with understanding. Each of the factors suggests something specific you can do in teaching to influence your students' understanding.

One important way to enhance learning with understanding is to provide for student access to previously acquired knowledge.

Provide for Access to Prior Knowledge

Students may have learned particular knowledge of concepts, principles, and strategies in the past but fail to access and use this knowledge when needed. Teachers can use a number of strategies to enhance access to prior knowledge. One thing teachers can do is to help students recall what they already know.

Another way to enhance access to prior knowledge is through frequent review in the form of rehearsal. *Rehearsal* is often contrasted with *practice*. Practice means to do something over and over again the same way to improve a performance (Ormrod, 2004). What is learned in practice is an item of knowledge or a specific skill applicable in a specific context. Rehearsal, in contrast, takes place "when people do something again in similar but not identical ways to reinforce what they have learned while adding something new" (Lowery, 1998a, p. 28). When the focus is on rehearsal rather than just practice, children's knowledge is less likely to be bound to specific tasks and more likely to be transferable and useful in a variety of ways (Lowery, 1998a).

Research on learning indicates that abstract representations of knowledge, in terms of concepts and principles rather than facts, promote access and transfer (Bransford et al., 1999). In the chapter-opening lesson scenario on light reflection, Mr. Roach was careful to guide his students to go beyond observations and data and to develop an abstract principle about image formation: *An image in a mirror appears to be just as far inside the mirror as the object is outside the mirror.* Stated in this form, the principle can promote both access to and transfer of knowledge about images and reflection.

Sometimes the problem with learning with understanding is not that children cannot access knowledge they already have, but that they simply have never had opportunity or occasion to acquire the knowledge needed in a task. In that case, teachers must provide learning activities that enable students to develop needed knowledge. The construction of new knowledge may come from a preliminary sequence of investigations or through direct instruction and reading, provided the new knowledge is firmly anchored in real-world activities and students are given opportunities to make the new knowledge their own.

Provide for Transfer of New Knowledge

An important way to enhance understanding is to include transfer tasks as part of science lessons. **Transfer** refers to the use of previously learned knowledge in new situations. As an example, in a follow-up to the lesson on reflection and images described in the chapter introduction, Don Roach guided his students to transfer their newly constructed principle on images to predict where a candle should be placed inside an empty aquarium so that the candle appeared lit when a burning candle was placed a few centimeters away outside the aquarium (see Figure 3-4). Transferring the principle on images to a new situation, each group of children correctly predicted and then empirically verified that the first candle had to be just as far inside the aquarium as the second candle was outside the aquarium.

Assessment tasks provide an excellent framework for students to use what they know to solve new problems. Such an assessment item is given in Activity 3-1. It pertains to the second-grade lesson on magnetism described in Chapter 1. Do Activity 3-1 for yourself before reading on.

Did you decide that the object in the item must be another magnet because it was repelled by a test magnet? Iron is attracted to magnets, but is not repelled by them. Copper and glass are neither attracted to nor repelled by a magnet.

> *"Knowledge that is overly contextualized can reduce transfer; abstract representations of knowledge can promote transfer."*
>
> (Bransford et al., 1999, p. 41)

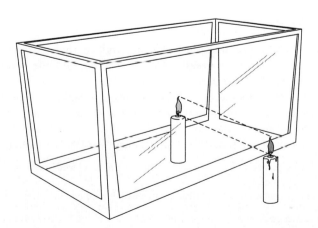

Figure 3-4 Although the candle inside the aquarium is not lit, it appears to be burning.

Activity 3-1: An Assessment Item about Magnetism

An object is placed on a table. A magnet is slowly moved toward it. The object moves away from the magnet. The object is most likely

A. another magnet.
B. a piece of glass. — *glass would not move away*
C. a copper coin. — *copper would not move*
D. a piece of iron. — *iron would move toward the magnet*

- Select an appropriate answer for the item.
- Using the rules for magnetic interactions, briefly explain why you chose the answer you did and why the other choices are not suitable.

"Tests of transfer that use graduated prompting provide more fine-grained analysis of learning and its effects on transfer than simple one-shot assessments of whether or not transfer occurs."

(Bransford et al., 1999, p. 54)

This item requires the transfer of the magnet rules learned in the magnets lesson—that is, their application in a new context. In individual interviews, children might be asked to select an answer and then to talk about why they chose that answer rather than one of the other choices. If their answer choice was incorrect, they might be given a prompt, hint, question, or information to help them solve the problem. For example, asking children to remember the rules of magnetism they had learned helps some children to use knowledge they already have but fail to access. Simply clarifying terms used in the item helps some other children to access needed knowledge and solve the problem. Further, to help children apply their knowledge in problem solving, they might be asked how the magnet rules could be applied to determine if an object found on the school campus contained iron (Rowe, 1973).

Some second graders are able to solve problems like these spontaneously. Other children succeed on the item with some level of teacher assistance. But, some children will have a hard time solving this problem even with a great deal of prompting. These results illustrate that teaching and learning science for recall and understanding so that "no child is left behind" is a challenging task.

Providing students opportunities to encounter concepts and principles in diverse circumstances not only results in more useful knowledge that can be transferred to new situations, it enhances the recall of knowledge.

A glossary containing definitions of important terms used in this chapter can be found on MyEducationLab.

Enhance Knowledge Organization

Another way to enhance understanding is to assist students in organizing new knowledge. Psychologists today theorize that useful knowledge is organized into connected networks called *knowledge structures*. According to Rosenshine (1997), "The size of these structures, the number of connections between items of knowledge, and the organization and richness of the connections are all important for processing knowledge, constructing meanings, and solving problems" (p.1).

From his review of research on learning, Rosenshine (1997) concluded:

"Education is a process of developing, enlarging, expanding, and refining our students' knowledge structures."

(Rosenshine, 1997, p. 1)

When the knowledge structure on a particlar topic is large and well-connected, new information is more readily acquired and prior knowledge is more readily available for use . . . (S)tudents have more points in their knowledge structures to which they can attach new information. (p.1)

One way you can enhance the organization of knowledge is through using and teaching your students to use graphic organizers. A variety of graphic organizers have been proposed

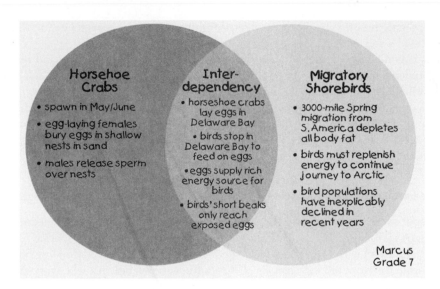

Figure 3-5 Graphic organizers such as Venn diagrams help students to organize their developing knowledge.

to portray and facilitate the organization of knowledge in memory, such as outlines, spider maps, webs, and Venn diagrams. Figure 3-5 shows how a Venn diagram can help learners organize information about animals.

Joseph Novak (1995) and his colleagues (Mintzes, Wandersee, & Novak, 1998) have advocated the use of *concept maps* to enhance the knowledge organization and science understanding of students. A **concept map** is a visual representation of a major concept and its relations to subsidiary concepts.

In constructing concept maps, teachers and students enclose specific concepts in circles or boxes. They draw lines between these concepts to indicate connections and hierarchical relationships. Words or phrases written on or near the connecting lines specify the type of relationship that might exist between two concepts. Main ideas are generally placed near the top of the concept map and subsidiary concepts below. Figure 3-6 provides

"Concepts, principles, and generalizations are the markers on a conceptual map. These markers become connected into a complex network of mental highways over which the student travels during problem solving."

(Rowe, 1973, p. 305)

To learn more about how to construct and use concept maps, go to http://cmap.ihmc.us. This site provides access to software you can download and use to make your own concept maps. An informative article about concept maps by Joseph Novak is available on the site.

Figure 3-6 To be useful, scientific knowledge must be well structured and interconnected.

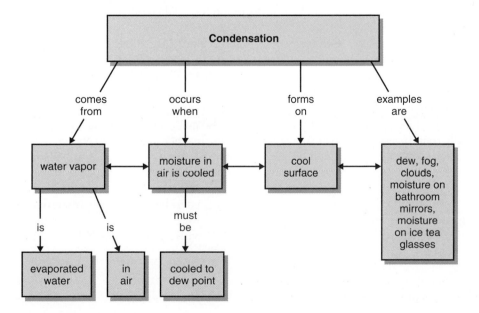

Nancy Gallenstein has written an interesting article titled "Never Too Young for a Concept Map" that suggests a variation for young children. Rather than using only words, young learners can create concrete concept maps by using objects or pictures. Connections between concepts are made through the use of paper arrows, string, yarn, pipe cleaners, etc. Read this article in the September 2005 issue of *Science and Children*.

a concept map that shows concepts and relationships among concepts related to the condensation of water.

Teachers might construct concept maps to highlight specific concepts and relationships. Students might construct concept maps to express and enhance their understanding. By using concept maps and other graphic organizers in instruction, teachers can help students organize their developing knowledge. Through examining students' graphic organizers during instruction, teachers can discover and provide feedback to students on their conceptual understandings, their misconceptions, and the kinds of links in cognitive structure they are building.

Provide Scaffolding Support

Contemporary research supports the value of the deliberate scaffolding of learning by teachers. In **scaffolding** student learning, teachers supply external support that helps learners to be successful with the various learning tasks. The rationale for scaffolding has been derived from the work of Lev Vygotsky (1962), a Russian psychologist who worked in the early years of the twentieth century. Vygotsky translated Jean Piaget's works on intellectual development into Russian. He accepted the developmental nature of knowledge as proposed by Piaget, but, whereas Piaget focused on constructing a general theory of intellectual development, Vygotsky was concerned mainly with how schooling affects cognitive development.

In investigations of the relationship between learning assistance and level of cognitive development, Vygotsky (1962) gave two children of the same age (say, 8 years) problems that were harder than they could manage on their own. The investigator also gave some assistance to the children, such as the first step in a solution, a leading question, or some other form of help. Vygotsky discovered "that one child could, with cooperation, solve problems designed for twelve-year olds, while the other could not go beyond problems intended for nine-year olds" (p. 103).

Vygotsky referred to the difference in what children can do with assistance and what they can do on their own without assistance as the *zone of proximal development*. For Vygotsky, the goal of instruction is to assist all children to reach their potential as defined by this zone. "What the child can do in cooperation today," he concluded, "he can do alone tomorrow" (p. 104).

"Ideally, an individual spontaneously transfers appropriate knowledge without a need for prompting. Sometimes, however, prompting is necessary. With prompting, transfer can improve quite dramatically."

(Bransford et al., 1999, p. 54)

Thus, for Vygotsky, instruction needs to be challenging, running ahead of the actual level of knowledge of the learner. If students are to learn with understanding when instruction runs ahead of their level of knowledge, they will need varying degrees of teacher and peer assistance, or *scaffolding*.

To scaffold the learning process for students, inquiry teachers might provide suggestions, questions, prompts, or hints. They might also guide students to clarify, elaborate, or justify their investigation procedures and findings. Teachers might even choose to provide necessary terms, concepts, and principles to students through formal, direct instruction. Textbooks, videos, the Internet, and other means might also be used to help students develop knowledge needed to support understanding.

Just as scaffolds in a building project are designed to be taken down when the building walls are strong, scaffolding support in teaching should be gradually removed or "faded" (Ormrod, 2004) as students gain facility with science knowledge and inquiry processes.

Information from ongoing informal and formal assessments provides the basis for decisions about who, when, and how to scaffold. Inquiry teaching provides teachers with many opportunities to gather assessment data. Teachers can gather information on students' learning and understanding through listening carefully to their discourse, asking students questions and listening to their responses, watching children as they work, and examining their work products. Through such means, teachers seek information from students about what they know and can do, including information related to such questions as:

- What do students already know about activities before they begin?
- Do students connect data they have collected to real-world activities?
- Are students using science knowledge to provide plausible explanations for their observations? Are the students' reasons becoming more detailed? Do students provide more than one reason for their explanations?
- Do students use their data to make inferences and predictions? How well are students able to provide reasons for their inferences and predictions? Are the reasons plausible?
- What do students do to test their inferences, predictions, and explanations?

Teachers use assessment data related to such questions as a basis for decisions related to scaffolding assistance.

More information, including examples, related to ongoing, formative assessments are provided in Chapters 5 and 6.

Build Learning Communities

Vygotsky found that students can learn at higher levels in cooperation with others than occurs when they work alone. Thus, learning is enhanced when teachers work to establish a shared understanding of a learning task among a community of learners (Hogan & Pressley, 1997). According to Brown and Campione (1998),

> A community of learners reflects a classroom ethos different from that found in traditional classrooms. In the traditional classroom, students are perceived as relatively passive learners who receive wisdom from teachers, textbooks, or other media. In the community of learners classroom, students are encouraged to engage in self-reflective learning and critical inquiry. (p. 153)

One role of a teacher within a community of inquirers is to organize the learning environment to encourage an underlying cooperative culture that centers on thinking. Just as communication among scientists is central in the construction of scientific knowledge, students learn by talking among themselves and writing about and formally presenting their ideas. Teachers, as part of the classroom community of learners, make students' ideas more meaningful by commenting and elaborating on them and asking students to clarify, expand, and justify their own emerging conceptions and those of others. Conversational partnerships with the teacher allow students to build on and use the teacher's thinking processes to support their efforts to think in more flexible and mature ways. In addition, the give and take among learners in a learning community enables them to scaffold one another's learning.

Forming cooperative teams and assigning job functions (Principal Investigator, Recorder, Maintenance Manager, etc.) to each team member is discussed in Chapter 5.

Table 3-1 provides a summary of factors that affect learning with understanding.

Children's prior knowledge not only facilitates understanding, it can also interfere with it. In the next section, we will examine the effect of children's existing alternative conceptions on their understanding of new concepts.

TABLE 3-1 ENHANCING THE LEARNING OF SCIENCE WITH UNDERSTANDING

Teaching Actions That Enhance Learning	Description and Rationale
Provide for access to prior knowledge.	• Students take in information from many sources. In building new knowledge, they connect information to relevant *prior knowledge*, organize their developing knowledge, and construct meaning for themselves. • Failure to access prior knowledge interferes with new learning. Reminding students of what they already know is one way to provide for access to prior knowledge.
Provide for the transfer of new knowledge to new situations.	• Using new knowledge in new situations enhances its transferability and access. • Constructed knowledge is refined, expanded, and elaborated as learners transfer it to new situations in trying to understand the world. • Teachers should provide many opportunities for students to transfer their developing knowledge to new situations.
Provide for knowledge organization.	• The size of cognitive structures, the number of connections between items in the structures, and the organization and richness of the connections are important for accessing prior knowledge, processing information, constructing meanings, and solving problems. • Using and teaching students to use graphic organizers, such as spider maps, Venn diagrams, and concept maps, promotes knowledge organization.
Provide scaffolding support.	• Scaffolding the learning process for students effectively reduces the complexity of knowledge construction and enables students to learn at higher levels. • In scaffolding, teachers might provide suggestions, questions, prompts, or hints; guide students to clarify, elaborate, or justify their investigation procedures and findings; or provide necessary terms, concepts, and principles to students through formal, direct instruction or the use of textbooks, videos, the Internet, and other means.
Build learning communities.	• Being a member of a collaborative community allows students to cooperatively work and think together and to scaffold one another's learning. • You can support learning communities by encouraging cooperative learning and teaching students how to work cooperatively. • Arranging for students to investigate in small groups is another way to promote learning communities.

Children's Alternative Conceptions and Science Learning

Children are busy learning every day, processing and organizing information from many sources (Rutherford & Ahlgren, 1990). Consequently, when they come to science classes, children already have formed many ideas about the world from their daily experiences. The prior knowledge children bring to new learning situations is often fragmented, incomplete, and naive, and their ideas are typically not congruent with accepted scientific views. Children's partial understandings, naive theories, and alternative conceptions must be recognized and dealt with by teachers if students are to learn science with understanding.

Children's ideas about the world have received a great deal of attention by researchers. Here are two humorous examples of students' spontaneous notions (Paulu & Martin, 1991):

- "Fossils are bones that animals are through wearing."
- "Some people can tell what time it is by looking at the sun, but I have never been able to make out the numbers."

Table 3-2 presents other example of children's alternative conceptions of science topics. Roth (1991) described an interesting example of children's alternative conceptions from her research with fifth-grade students. Children may know the word *photosynthesis*, but they

TABLE 3-2 ALTERNATIVE CONCEPTIONS OF CHILDREN RELATED TO SCIENTIFIC TOPICS

Science Content Area	Students' Naïve Conceptions	Scientific Conceptions
Biology	• Animals are living because they move, but plants are nonliving.	• Living things are composed of cells that carry out life processes such as the extraction of energy from nutrients and energy release. • Plants and animals are living organisms, composed of living cells.
Physical Science	• Anything that pours is a liquid, including powders. • When liquids evaporate, they just disappear. • Electric current is used up in bulbs and there is less current going back to a battery than coming out of it. • Light rays move out from the eye in order to illuminate objects. • Loudness and pitch are the same thing. • Suction causes liquids to be pulled upward in a soda straw.	• Powders are solids, composed of individual solid particles. • In evaporation, molecules in a liquid break free from molecular bonds and go into the surrounding air. • Electric current is the same throughout a continuous series circuit. • Light from other sources reflects off objects to our eyes, enabling us to see them. • Loudness and pitch are different variables associated with sound. • When the air pressure in a soda straw is reduced, atmospheric pressure pushes liquid up into the straw.
Earth and Space Science	• The earth is flat, like a pancake. • The phases of the moon are caused by shadows of the earth falling on the moon. • Seasons are caused by the changing distance of the earth from the sun (closer in the summer, more distant in the winter).	• The earth is spherical, as is shown by lunar eclipses and photographs from space. • The sun illuminates half of the moon at all times. Phases of the moon result from the way light from the sun reflects off the moon to the earth. • We experience seasons because light from the sun reaches the earth at a steeper angle in the summer than in the winter.

Source: Compiled by the authors from different sources.

have a lot of alternative ideas about where plants get their energy for life processes and growth. They may have the conception, for instance, that plants get their food from the soil through their roots. Plants do absorb nutrients from the soil, but this alternative conception conflicts in critical ways with the scientific view that plants use sunlight to make food from carbon dioxide and water. Students have arrived at their explanations through their own experience with plants, and the explanations work for them. Furthermore, common language usage about "plant food" that is mixed with the soil to "feed" plants reinforces erroneous beliefs. Personal theories are not easy to give up, especially when they are so commonly reinforced.

For conceptual change to occur, students must be challenged to recognize that their personal theories and explanations are in conflict with accepted scientific views. As Roth (1991) explained,

> They need to be convinced that their own theories are inadequate, incomplete, or inconsistent with experimental evidence, and that the scientific explanations provide a more convincing alternative to their own notions. (p. 49)

Convincing children that they should change their conceptions does not come from "telling" or threats. Roth proposed that to change their beliefs, students need repeated opportunities to struggle with the inconsistencies between their own ideas and scientific explanations, to reorganize their ways of thinking, and to make appropriate links between their own ideas and scientific concepts.

A Strategy for Conceptual Change: Moon Watching

Anderson (1987) proposed a strategy for conceptual change. According to Anderson, for conceptual change to occur, teachers must

- identify students' alternative conceptions,
- promote student dissatisfaction with them,
- introduce scientific conceptions, and
- provide for application and integration of the new conceptions.

An inquiry approach to science is especially compatible with this *conceptual change strategy*. Inquiry teachers have many opportunities to interact with students, observe and listen to them, and recognize their conceptions that are incomplete and inadequate and need further development. Understanding students' misconceptions and naive theories, teachers are then better prepared to "structure learning experiences that assist the reconstruction of core concepts. New constructions can then be applied to different situations and tested against other conceptions of the world" (Trowbridge & Bybee, 1996, p. 214).

As an example, consider a conceptual change emphasis in an inquiry lesson on moon watching. In the moon watching lesson, students observe and record the appearance and position of the moon each day or night for one month. They organize their observations in a table, on a calendar, through narrative descriptions, using drawings, or in some other way. Then they attempt to discover and explain the pattern of the phases of the moon they observe (see Figure 3-7). The first step in a conceptual change strategy is for the teacher to identify students' misconceptions.

Identify Alternative Conceptions. One advantage of an inquiry approach to science teaching is that it allows teachers to uncover what students already know or think about a topic. In inquiry lessons, students are encouraged to talk and frequently write about their understandings of the natural world and to illustrate them through drawing pictures and diagrams. As discussed previously, by paying close attention to student ideas, you can begin to gain some insight into their prior knowledge, including their misconceptions (Anderson, 1987).

Figure 3-7 The moon displays a pattern of phases in its monthly cycle.

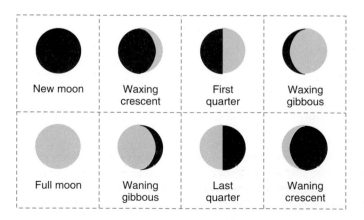

New moon Waxing crescent First quarter Waxing gibbous

Full moon Waning gibbous Last quarter Waning crescent

For example, when asked to explain why the moon shows phases, research and experience suggest that children and adolescents ages 9–16 are likely to give these explanations about why lunar phases appear:

- Clouds cover part of the moon so that we cannot see all of it (cloud viewpoint).
- The shadow of the earth falls on the moon so that we cannot see all of the moon (eclipse viewpoint).
- The shadow of the sun falls on the moon.
- Planets cast shadows on the moon.
- Only a portion of the sunlight illuminating the moon is reflected to earth (scientific viewpoint) (Stahly, Krockover, & Shepardson, 1999).

Up to 70% of subjects in research studies explain the phases of the moon from the "eclipse viewpoint."

The second step in the conceptual change strategy is to promote dissatisfaction with alternative concepts.

Promote Dissatisfaction with Alternative Conceptions. In teaching for conceptual change, it is not enough to just discredit misconceptions, nor is it sufficient to merely provide correct explanations. Rather, teachers should encourage students to test their own ideas through observation and investigation.

If children think that lunar phases are caused by clouds, for instance, you might lead them to add information on "cloud conditions" to the daily and weekly moon-watching charts they keep. Students can then examine their data and see if there is evidence to support the theory of a connection between clouds and moon phases. This process can help students develop awareness of and dissatisfaction with their own inaccurate and incomplete explanations.

Sometimes students have inadequate conceptions simply because they lack relevant information. For example, students may have difficulty in explaining lunar phases due to their lack of knowledge about earth-moon-sun distance relationships. On the National Assessment of Educational Progress (NAEP) for 2000, only about one-half of eighth-grade students tested knew that the moon is always much closer to the earth than it is to the sun. One-third of the eighth-grade students thought the earth's moon is sometimes closer to the sun than it is to the earth and sometimes closer to the earth than it is to the sun.

Most models of the sun-earth-moon system that are illustrated in science texts or assembled by students for science projects do not show relative sizes and distances on the same scale. One way for students to begin to understand the size and distance relationships of the earth, moon, and sun is to do the math involved in the relationships and build a scale model. If a basketball were used to represent the earth, the moon would be a softball placed about 10 meters (30 feet) away. On this scale, the diameter of the sun would be represented by a 10-story building about 2 miles away from the basketball and softball. Such a model can help students realize that the earth and moon are near neighbors that orbit the distant sun together.

When students' misconceptions have been identified, and they have been guided to become dissatisfied with their own explanations, you are ready to introduce scientific conceptions.

Introduce Scientific Conceptions. According to Anderson (1987), exploratory and discovery activities are useful but do not in themselves lead to conceptual change. Left to their own devices, children may discover many interesting things about the world, but they will develop scientific ideas "about as rapidly as the human race: in other words, not in a single lifetime . . . Therefore," Anderson (1987) asserted, "scientific concepts need to be explicitly introduced and taught to students" (p. 86).

When students have become dissatisfied with their own conceptions about the causes of the moon's phases and have collected a great deal of data and information at the descriptive level, it is time to formally teach key scientific concepts, principles, and explanations related to the topic. You should build on observational activities in ways that can be meaningfully understood by students. Guide students to examine and contrast misconceptions with scientific conceptions. At each point in instruction, assist students to modify, restructure, or abandon their existing conceptions in favor of new understandings of scientific concepts and explanations.

Realizing that clouds and eclipses are not satisfactory explanations for moon phases and that the earth and moon are near neighbors that are a great distance from the sun can help prepare children for a scientific explanation. Then, through expository instruction, diagrams, physical models, computer planetarium displays, and discussion, the scientific explanation for phases is presented. According to this explanation, light from the distant sun strikes the moon, but only a portion of that sunlight is reflected to the earth, resulting in the appearance of moon phases.

It is through applying new conceptions in new situations that students integrate and make sense of the new conceptions.

Provide for Transfer of New Conceptions. A physical model of the sun-earth-moon system provides an excellent approach to understanding phases of the moon. Provide each student with a Styrofoam ball. Instruct students to stand facing a central light source, but caution them not to look directly at the light. Give these instructions:

1. Imagine that the Styrofoam ball is the moon, that the light source is the sun, and that your head is the earth.
2. Place your Styrofoam ball on a stick or pencil. Hold your Styrofoam ball away from you at arm's length, slightly above your head, with the ball between you and the light. Look at the ball. Notice how much of the ball is lighted from where you are standing. Does the visible lit part of the ball look like any of the phases of the moon you have observed? (See Figure 3-8.)

Figure 3-8 How can different phases of the moon be illustrated in this model?

3. Stay in one spot. With your arm extended, slowly move your arm and the ball 90 degrees to your left. Look at the ball again. How much of the ball's visible surface is lighted from where you stand? Is this like another phase of the moon you have seen?

4. Rotate another 90 degrees to the left and look at the ball. How much of the visible surface of the ball is lighted now? Is this like another phase of the moon you have observed?

5. Rotate your arm 90 degrees more to the left and look at the ball. Compare what you see to the phases of the moon you have seen in the sky.

6. Can you see some of the phases of the moon? When is the Styrofoam "moon" full? What position creates the new moon? Why can't you see the new moon? (The new moon occurs when the lighted side of the moon is turned away from the earth.)

7. Try to identify the positions of the moon relative to the earth and sun when you see the waxing crescent moon, the first quarter moon, the waxing gibbous moon, the full moon, and the waning phases.

For all students to attain real understanding of scientific conceptions remains a challenging ideal. Nevertheless, as Anderson (1987) reported from his studies, when teachers use conceptual change approaches with inquiry methods, the percentage of students attaining real understanding jumps from the 0 to 20% range to the 50 to 80% range. This is clearly a great improvement, helping to close the performance gap that so often exists among groups of learners.

Next, we examine cognitive development and its effect on science understanding.

Go to the Homework and Exercises section in Chapter 3 of MyEducationLab to watch the videos, *Investigating Moon Phases: Parts 1, 2, 3, 4,* and 5, and follow fourth- and fifth-grade students through a set of activities on moon phases.

Development, Learning, and Science Teaching

The growth of understanding of the natural world by children and adolescents is a product of both learning and development. The term **learning** refers to the construction of knowledge in specific situations. **Development**, in contrast, refers to the general growth and change of cognitive structures that allow knowledge to be extended from particular to general cases (Brown, Bransford, Ferrara, & Campione, 1983). Development occurs over time and requires abundant learning experiences.

The period of time from age 5 to 13, encompassing grades K–8, is marked by very dramatic developments in children's cognitive capabilities. These changes greatly affect what is appropriate to teach in science at the various grade levels. Piaget's theory of cognitive development is a rich source of details about children's cognitive development and their theories of the world. Consequently, this theory provides a basis for helping teachers make decisions about developmentally appropriate science.

Piaget's Theory of Cognitive Development

Through investigations carried out over nearly 60 years, Jean Piaget and his colleagues found that the understanding of science tasks grows and develops across the childhood and adolescent years. Piaget (Inhelder & Piaget, 1958) proposed that the development of understanding takes place across four age-related stages called the sensorimotor, preoperational, concrete operational, and formal operational stages. The characteristics of children's and adolescents' thinking at the preoperational, concrete operational, and formal operational stages greatly influence what is appropriate to teach in science at different grade levels.

The age spans given here in the descriptions of each stage are based on research studies, but should be considered approximations. Individual children may show characteristics of a given developmental phase at earlier or later ages than their peers.

Go to the Homework and Exercises section in Chapter 3 of MyEducationLab to watch the video, *Conservation of Matter, Volume X*. As you watch the video, reflect on the differences in the ways younger learners and older learners approach tasks. Also consider how effective you think teacher scaffolding and direct instruction would be in helping young learners develop higher-order reasoning skills needed for the tasks.

Preoperational Stage. Piaget found that children from about age 2 to age 7 display characteristics of *preoperational* thinking. At this stage, children tend to make judgments on the basis of perceptions rather than conceptions. Furthermore, they tend to focus on one, main perception of a situation and do not tend to shift back and forth *reversibly* or flexibly from one aspect of a situation to another. Because of their difficulties with reversible thinking, children at this level of development do not tend to mentally group elements into coherent wholes. This is shown, for example, through various *conservation* tasks.

Conservation. **Conservation** refers to the recognition that if an object or situation is transformed in some way, there may still be aspects of the object or situation that remain the same. Piaget and others have investigated the thinking of children and adolescents across a number of different conservation tasks. In a conservation of liquid amount task (see Figure 3-9), subjects are presented with two identical glasses filled with equal amounts of liquid. The liquid from one of the glasses is poured into a taller, narrower container. Subjects are then asked if there is now more, less, or the same amount of liquid in the new container.

In the conservation of liquid amount task, children at the preoperational stage tend to focus on only one aspect of the situation—the heights of the original and new containers. Noting that the level of liquid in the new container is higher, they conclude that there is more liquid in it. While focusing on the heights of the liquid in the two containers, they fail to simultaneously consider the widths.

In a conservation of length task, subjects are presented with two strings of the same length. One of the two strings is transformed into a curving, snakelike form. Learners classed as preoperational do not coordinate perceptions about the two end points of the strings and the pathways joining the end points (whether straight or curved). Thus, they fail to reason that the transformed piece of string has a constant length, regardless of how it is configured.

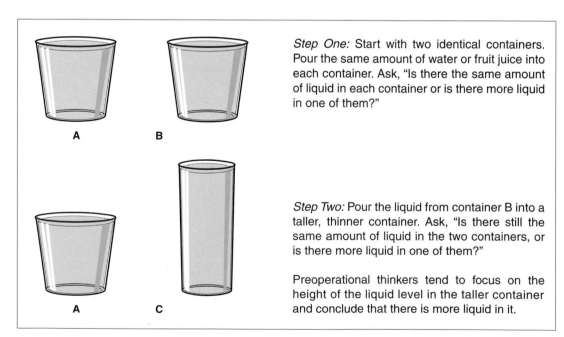

Step One: Start with two identical containers. Pour the same amount of water or fruit juice into each container. Ask, "Is there the same amount of liquid in each container or is there more liquid in one of them?"

Step Two: Pour the liquid from container B into a taller, thinner container. Ask, "Is there still the same amount of liquid in the two containers, or is there more liquid in one of them?"

Preoperational thinkers tend to focus on the height of the liquid level in the taller container and conclude that there is more liquid in it.

Figure 3-9 Task for assessing conservation of liquid volume.

Children's failure to consistently conserve variables, such as length, leads to difficulty in their conception of different variables and in their learning to measure them with understanding. For instance, in measuring length, young learners fail to correctly align the end point of a ruler with the end point of the object being measured; they do not understand the importance of units of measurement and the meaning of the numbers associated with measuring length; and they fail to count accurately the number of units, (such as centimeters or inches) in a measured length.

Because considering multiple aspects of a situation and forming holistic combinations is hard for young children, they have difficulty in science with such essential processes as identifying variables, measuring, classifying, inferring, and predicting. They also have difficulty forming and understanding principles.

Concrete Operational Stage. The gradual development of reversible thinking enables children in grades 3, 4, and 5 to form some new types of knowledge, including *series*, *classes*, and *relationships*. These three special ways of combining information are critical tools for the construction of knowledge in elementary science. The ability to form serially ordered groups, coupled with conservation, enables students to identify variables and measure them with understanding. The development of class logic enables students to organize their perceptions so they can think about them more clearly. The ability to form relationships enables an understanding of simple scientific principles and cause-and-effect relationships.

Piaget investigated the order of children's success across three different conservation tasks, including the conservation of substance, the conservation of weight, and the conservation of displacement volume. The conservation of substance task involves comparisons between the amount of clay in an original lump and the amount when an equivalent lump is transformed into a pancake, sausage, or hot dog. Conservation of weight involves comparions between the weight of an original lump of clay and its weight when it is transfomed into a different shape. Conservation of displacement volume involves judgment of the water level rise for an original lump of clay when it is placed in water compared with the water level rise when the lump is transformed into a new shape and immersed in water.

Piaget found that the age level for success is about 7 for the conservation of substance task, about 9 for the conservation of weight task, and about 11 for the *conservation of displacement volume* task (Piaget, in Gruber and Voneche, 1997). The order of these findings has been supported by other investigators, though the age ranges found in these investigations show some differences with Piaget's findings.

The realization that a variable may be conserved is essential to understanding the variable, measuring it with understanding, forming relationships involving the variable, identifying manipulated and responding variables, and carrying out controlled investigations.

Given the chance through hands-on, minds-on inquiry activities and teacher guidance, concrete operational thinkers begin to organize investigations in terms of concepts and variables, measure variables meaningfully, and arrange data in tables and graphs. They can also form and understand simple principles, use what they know to make inferences and predictions, and generalize from common experiences. The concrete operational years can be especially exciting times in science for children and their teachers.

Formal Operational Stage. The formal operational level is characterized by higher-order thinking with the concepts, variables, and principles formed at the concrete operational level. The cognitive advances at the formal operational level are revealed as adolescents engage more independently in thinking tasks such as

- planning and conducting controlled experiments or fair tests that involve *responding* (dependent), *manipulated* (independent), and *controlled* variables, as described in Chapter 2;
- organizing and thinking about complex numerical data sets in terms of ratios, proportions, and equations;
- constructing theories and models that coordinate facts, concepts, and principles; and
- coordinating evidence and knowledge in forming complex explanations of puzzling phenomena.

These formal operational advances better prepare learners to seek answers to their questions through designing and carrying out more complicated investigations.

As a word of caution, Duschl and colleagues (2007) report studies of cognitive psychologists and educational researchers that indicate that through continual assessment, proper scaffolding, and judicious direct instruction, students can learn much more about science than previously suspected. Nevertheless, instruction should take place within the context of development of children and adolescents.

Table 3-3 presents a summary of children's developmental characteristics that affect science learning.

TABLE 3-3 CHARACTERISTICS OF CHILDREN'S THINKING IN PIAGET'S FOUR COGNITIVE STAGES

Cognitive Stages and Approximate Age Spans	The Child at This Stage
Sensorimotor (0–2 years)	- adapts to the external world through actions - coordinates actions related to substance, space, time, and causality
Preoperational (2–7 years)	- maintains sensorimotor capabilities - develops extensive physical knowledge of objects, organisms, and events - begins to represent objects and actions with words and sentences - does not think "reversibly" - makes judgments on the basis of perceptions, not conceptual considerations
Concrete Operational (5–11 years)	- maintains capabilities of previous stages - thinks reversibly - groups elements into coherent wholes - conserves substance, liquid, volume, length, and area - identifies *variables* and measures them - forms *classes* and uses them to organize perceptions and experiences - forms and uses *relationships*, including simple scientific principles and cause-and-effect relationships
Formal Operational (12 + years)	- maintains capabilities of previous stages - engages in higher-order thinking - forms hypotheses, carries out controlled experiments, and relates evidence to theories - deals with ratios, proportions, and probabilities - constructs and understands complex explanations

Next, as an example, we look at children's development related to their understanding of floating and sinking.

Children's Theories of Floating and Sinking

When young children are given an array of objects and asked to predict whether the objects will float or sink, they rely primarily on past experiences. When asked why they think something will float or sink, they tend to focus on salient characteristics of the objects. Their answers are generally inconsistent. For instance, they may say one object floats because it is large and a second thing floats because it is small.

As children mature, their thinking about floating and sinking becomes more consistent. By grades 3–5, many children begin to realize (with appropriate scaffolding from their teachers) that weight (mass) and size (volume) are not the same thing and that both variables make a difference in whether an object floats or sinks. Applying the logic of serial ordering, the children can describe the weight of objects as heavy or light; they also describe the volume or size of objects as large or small. Applying the logic of relationships allows children to understand (with scaffolding) the concrete operational principle that *objects sink in water if they are too heavy for their size.*

It is not until adolescence that students typically add numerical considerations about weight and volume to their judgments and explanations. Some adolescents, but by no means all, begin to use proportions and ratios to think of floating and sinking in terms of the density of the object. **Density** is the mass per unit volume of a substance; that is, it is the ratio of the mass to the volume. Quantitatively, the dividing line for whether an object sinks or floats in fresh water is the density of water, which is 1 gram per cubic centimeter (1 g/cc). Thus, *objects float in fresh water if their density is less than that of water.*

Centimeter-gram cubes—small cubes that are 1 cm on each side and have a mass of 1 g—are often used in elementary and middle school math and science. The volume of each of these cubes is exactly 1 cc; the density of the cubes is then 1 g/cc. The density of fresh water is also 1 g/cc. Thus, these cubes float just under the surface of fresh water because their density is exactly the same as the density of water. If a small bit of clay is added to a cube, its density goes above 1 g/cc and the cube sinks in fresh water.

A lesson plan on floating and sinking is included in Chapter 5 (pages 122–126).

Developmentally Appropriate Science

As we have seen, the period of time spanning ages 5 to 13, which encompasses grades K–8, is marked by very dramatic developments in children's cognitive capabilities. These changes greatly affect what is appropriate to teach in science at the various grade levels.

According to the *Benchmarks for Science Literacy* (American Association for the Advancement of Science, 1993),

> Overestimation of what students can learn at a given age results in student frustration, lack of confidence, and unproductive learning strategies, such as memorization without understanding. Underestimation of what students can learn results in boredom, overconfidence, and poor study habits, and a needlessly diluted education. So it is important to make decisions about what to expect of students and when on the basis of as much good information as possible. (p. 327)

It is essential, then, for teachers to select types of science investigations, as well as concepts, principles, theories, and explanations, that are *developmentally appropriate* for their students.

Table 3-4 provides a summary of some characteristics of learners that affect inquiry learning in different grade spans. The items in this list are derived from the experience of

TABLE 3-4 CHARACTERISTICS OF LEARNERS IN DIFFERENT GRADE SPANS

Grade K–2 Learners

- Have a natural interest in almost everything around them.
- Work best with common objects, living things, and events within familiar contexts.
- Observe the world using all of their senses, but do not construct consistent explanations of it.
- Push, pull, and transform objects by acting on them.
- Observe, sort, group, and order objects.
- Carry out simple descriptive and classificatory investigations.
- Form concrete concepts based on their own observations.
- Make judgments and explanations primarily from perceptions and descriptions rather than conceptions.
- Make simple inferences with assistance.
- Can solve problems through trial and error, if guided to work step by step.

Grade 3–4 Learners

- Tend to create larger, more complex organizations, instead of being satisfied with grouping and ordering objects by limited attributes.
- Discover and understand simple rules of classification.
- Carry out simple classificatory investigations.
- Design simple comparative tests, carry out the tests, analyze the results, and communicate their findings.
- Carry out simple controlled investigations, with considerable teacher scaffolding.
- Record data and keep simple journals.
- Use data and knowledge to make inferences and predictions.
- Develop and use more abstract concepts and simple cause-and-effect principles in constructing explanations.
- Understand cycles (life cycles, seasons, water cycles) as continuous, repeatable chains of events.

Grade 5–6 Learners

- Effectively use cause-and-effect relationships in constructing more complex explanations.
- Engage in experimental inquiries that are more advanced than simple descriptive and classificatory investigations.
- Generate simple hypotheses, conduct "fair" tests, and record and analyze data to find evidence to support or not support the original hypotheses.
- Have difficulty controlling all the variables in an experiment.
- Can keep extensive journals, diaries, records of information over time, and prepare written reports based on these records.
- Have preconceptions and expectations that can influence interpretation of data, even in a fair test.
- Generate, interpret, and make predictions from graphs; understand that graphs describe two variables at the same time.

teachers, the cognitive development research of Jean Piaget and others, and the NSTA publication, *Pathways to the Science Standards: Elementary School Edition* (Lowery, 1997).

With teacher scaffolding, students are enabled to think in more complex ways and carry out the different investigations at earlier ages. The guidelines in Table 3-4 are useful whatever the science topic investigated, whether leaves, magnets, ants, pillbugs, seeds and plants, floating and sinking, or other topics.

Grade Placement of the Cartesian Diver

As an example of appropriate grade placement, consider the Cartesian diver. Explaining the *Cartesian diver* involves the principles of floating and sinking, along with principles related to air pressure. This fun phenomenon has been introduced in elementary science to children as young as second grade. However, as shown in the following discussion, it is more appropriate for older learners.

The Cartesian diver (see Figure 3-10) consists of a 1-liter clear, plastic bottle filled with water nearly to the top. A medicine dropper, partially filled with water so that it floats at the surface of a container of water, is placed in the bottle. A cap is screwed tightly on the bottle. When the bottle is squeezed, the dropper descends. When it is released, the dropper ascends to the surface.

You can learn a great deal for yourself about observation, evidence, and explanation by building and trying out a Cartesian diver.

Explaining the Cartesian diver requires two main principles. One principle is related to objects floating and sinking in water: *objects sink in water if they are too heavy for their size (volume)*. The other principle is related to air pressure: *if a space containing air is decreased, the pressure of the air will increase*.

Here are explanations of the Cartesian diver given by some second graders:

Student 1: It's like a parachute going up and down.
Student 2: I think when the water goes in, then the air pushes it up with the metal thing.
Student 3: When you squeeze it, the water goes in the eyedropper and when you let it go, some water goes out of it.
Student 4: It gets heavier when it goes down and then it gets lighter and then it goes up.

As teachers, we need to listen carefully to what children say, filter their ideas through theories of learning and development and our own experiences, and decide how we should respond. Let's use the theories introduced in this chapter to analyze these second-grade children's thinking about the diving dropper.

Student 1 provides a *description* of the actions of the dropper. Focusing on observations and descriptions in the absence of concepts that bind them together is a general learning characteristic of K–2 students.

Student 2 gives a somewhat confused explanation of the event. He mentions air and the water going into the dropper, but focuses on his observation of the "metal thing" (the cap screwed on the bottle.)

Student 3 observes the event more closely, noting that water goes into and then comes out of the dropper. Thus, evidence for part of the explanation is present, but the child does not use these ideas further in forming an explanation of the event, nor does he propose a principle that might govern it.

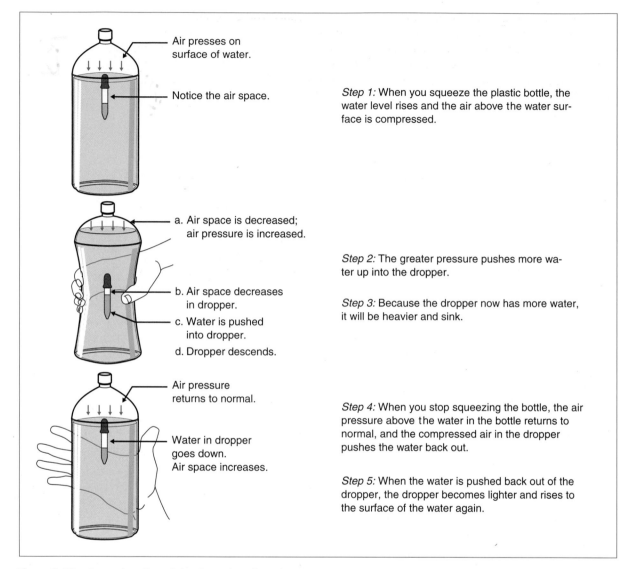

Air presses on surface of water.

Notice the air space.

Step 1: When you squeeze the plastic bottle, the water level rises and the air above the water surface is compressed.

a. Air space is decreased; air pressure is increased.

Step 2: The greater pressure pushes more water up into the dropper.

b. Air space decreases in dropper.

c. Water is pushed into dropper.

d. Dropper descends.

Step 3: Because the dropper now has more water, it will be heavier and sink.

Air pressure returns to normal.

Step 4: When you stop squeezing the bottle, the air pressure above the water in the bottle returns to normal, and the compressed air in the dropper pushes the water back out.

Water in dropper goes down. Air space increases.

Step 5: When the water is pushed back out of the dropper, the dropper becomes lighter and rises to the surface of the water again.

Figure 3-10   An explanation of the Cartesian diver demonstration.

Student 4 explains the phenomenon by stating that the dropper gets heavier and then gets lighter. But, she does not mention why the weight of the dropper changes or what the effect of the weight changes might be.

The thinking of students 3 and 4 is somewhat advanced for second graders, but they still do not recognize and connect: (1) their actions on the bottle, (2) the resulting changes in the air pressure in the bottle, (3) the changes in the amount of water in the dropper that is caused by the air pressure changes, and (4) the consequent change in weight of the dropper. In brief, these second graders deal with the descriptive aspects of the Cartesian diver, but fail to deal adequately with the explanatory aspects of the task.

Consider how you might provide scaffolding to advance the children's explanations. You could, for example, provide assistance through questioning. Hearing student 3's explanation, you might ask what causes the dropper to get heavier and then get lighter. Hearing student 4's explanation, you might ask why the water goes into the dropper and what happens to the dropper when the water goes into it. Even if students do not form complete scientific explanations initially, you can help them to make better connections between the various elements of the task and to think about them more flexibly.

From a Piagetian perspective, difficulties that young learners have in trying to explain the Cartesian diver are a result of their having not yet developed the cognitive structures required by the task. According to Vygotsky (1962), a primary distinguishing characteristic of children's spontaneous concepts learned through discovery is the absence of a system that holds the concepts together. Similarly, Ebenezer and Connor (1998) describe children's initial knowledge about the world as fragmented, made up not of organized theories but of a large number of fragments.

Because second-grade children generally have difficulties in constructing consistent explanations, the Cartesian diver is not a grade-level appropriate activity for most learners at this grade level. In Vygotskian terms, the explanation of the Cartesian diver is not one within the zone of proximal development for most second graders. It is not a phenomenon that children at this level are likely to understand well, even with good scaffolding assistance. Thus, it would be more appropriate to provide second graders with other experiences on the properties of air and floating and sinking and wait until about grade 4 to introduce the Cartesian diver. Further, at grade 4, to simplify the process, the teacher might decide to focus more on the qualitative principle of floating and sinking, without emphasizing the role of air pressure in the investigation.

SUMMARY

• Learning is a constructive process. In the process of constructing new knowledge, learners use prior knowledge to *organize* incoming information in various ways to form new knowledge, and they *integrate* new knowledge with prior knowledge to expand the knowledge base.

• Contemporary learning theorists emphasize the importance of enhancing learning through providing students ways to access prior knowledge, promoting the organization of knowledge, providing opportunities for transfer, providing scaffolding support, providing for formative assessment of student understanding, and establishing communities of inquirers.

• To scaffold student learning, set challenging and interesting learning tasks; simplify tasks for students; facilitate student talk in different settings; ask meaningful questions; lead students to clarify, elaborate, or justify their responses; and supply necessary information, concepts, and principles for learners.

• Students often come to science classes with pervasive alternative conceptions about how the world works. If students are to learn with understanding, teachers must help them recognize and deal with their incomplete and erroneous ideas.

• The term *learning* refers to the construction of knowledge or performance capabilities in specific situations. *Cognitive development*, in contrast, refers to the general growth and change of cognitive structures that allow knowledge and performance capabilities to be extended from particular to general cases.

• By looking closely at Piaget's theory, science teachers can get an idea of how scientific conceptions develop.

• Piaget's findings are important for science education, but they should not place a limit on what is appropriate for children to learn at each grade level. With prior knowledge and appropriate scaffolding assistance from their teachers, they can do more than previously expected.

ONLINE PROFESSIONAL DEVELOPMENT

Pre- and post-tests to assess your knowledge of chapter content, along with exercises to enhance your understanding, can be found on MyEducationLab at www.myeducationlab.com.

Video Guides

Video clips on MyEducationLab selected for this chapter include *Investigating Moon Phases—Parts 1, 2, 3, 4,* and *5.*

Accessing the Videos

1. Go to the Homework and Exercises section in Chapter 3 of MyEducationLab to select and view videos for this chapter and answer the questions.
2. Videos might be viewed individually, by small groups of colleagues, or by the whole class.
3. As you watch each video, use the **Questions for Reflection** to guide your thoughts and note taking for personal use and group discussion.
4. Discuss your answers to the questions about each video with classmates.

Video: Investigating Moon Phases: Parts 1, 2, 3, 4, and 5.

Overview

The first three videos in the five-part set of videos on Moon Phases, shows fourth- and fifth-grade children discussing their observations of moon phases and the different types of records they choose and learn to use. The fourth and fifth videos in the set show Terry Contant leading the children in using a physical model of the earth-moon-sun system to illustrate and explain the appearance of moon phases.

Questions for Reflection

1. What were some of the observations of the children of the moon phases?
2. What kinds of records did they keep? What was the purpose of the long record strip?
3. How did the activity with balls illustrate the connection between the positions of the sun, the moon, and the earth and the effect of these positions on the phases of the moon observed? How did the Internet pictures of moon phases on any date, past, present, or future, help to connect the 3-D model to the children's observations?
4. What did the teachers think was important for the children in the moon phase activities? What do you think the children were learning about observation, record keeping, and explanations? What do you think they learned about moon phases?

Annenberg Videos

Video Series. *Learning Science Through Inquiry Video.* Bring It All Together: *Processing for Meaning During Inquiry*

To access Annenberg videos, follow the instructions given in the Online Professional Development section in Chapter 1 on page 26.

4

O*ver the years, educators have developed many teaching and learning models relevant to classroom science teaching. Knowing the strengths and weaknesses of these models, teachers examine the relationship between the science content and how that content is to be taught. Teachers of science integrate a sound model of teaching and learning, a practical structure for the segment, and the content to be learned.*

(National Research Council, 1996, p. 31)

Teaching Science for Understanding: The 5-E Model of Instruction

THE MAJOR PROFICIENCIES or goals of science instruction emphasized in the *National Science Education Standards* are conceptual understandings in science, abilities to carry out scientific inquiries, and understandings about the nature of science and scientific inquiry (National Research Council, 1996). These proficiencies are also reflected in the science standards developed by most states. A number of different instructional approaches are available to you for teaching science, including an inquiry approach, a textbook-based approach, direct instruction, and guided discovery. These approaches to science instruction differ in the opportunities they afford students to achieve each of the major proficiencies.

Textbook and direct instruction approaches have typically focused on students acquiring science knowledge. But they do not usually provide students with opportunities to develop the broad range of abilities necessary to inquire scientifically, nor do they deliberately provide opportunities for students to understand the nature of scientific inquiry. Further, they often fail to go beyond knowledge to understanding.

Discovery approaches have been very popular among science teachers. In carrying out discovery activities, students have opportunities to experience the processes and procedures of inquiry. Discovery activities provide students abundant opportunities for manipulating materials and observing what happens in the world, but they often do not focus on specific science knowledge and conceptual understanding that enable students to make sense of what they see and do.

On the other hand, inquiry methods of teaching science are designed to enable students to achieve each of the three main goals of science instruction. By providing opportunities for students to ask questions, gather, record, and reflect on data, and form their own theories and explanations, inquiry approaches help students to develop inquiry abilities and, at the same time, construct scientific knowledge and understanding. Further, the involvement of students in inquiring into the natural world provides a strong basis for them to develop understandings of the nature of science and scientific inquiry.

Just as the different teaching approaches vary in their treatment of the central goals of science education, they also differ in their attention to research on learning. Again, of these four approaches to instruction, inquiry is the only one especially designed to enable teachers to use a wide range of instructional factors that promote learning with understanding. In teaching science through inquiry methods, teachers enhance access to and transfer of science knowledge. By building in opportunities to transfer knowledge to new situations, inquiry teaching assists learners to go beyond knowledge and develop understanding.

Similarly, inquiry teaching provides many opportunities for teachers to assess and scaffold learning to assist students to develop understanding. Additionally, learning communities are a natural part of inquiry teaching approaches.

Teaching science through inquiry can be effective and rewarding, but it can also be complex. To help you simplify the process, we present in this chapter the 5-E model of inquiry instruction. We also examine the special features, advantages, and disadvantages of other approaches to science learning and how you can expand these approaches by setting them in the context of inquiry and the 5-E model.

As you study this chapter, consider these questions:

- *What are the main features of inquiry instruction?*

- *What are the phases of the 5-E model of instruction? How are they related to the the tasks of scientific inquiry? How do they relate to contemporary research on learning with understanding?*

- *What is the discovery approach to teaching science? What are the advantages and disadvantages of this method?*

- *What are the main features of textbook and direct instruction approaches to teaching science? What are the advantages and disadvantages of each of these approaches to science instruction?*

- *How can guided discovery, textbook-based instruction, and direct instruction be incorporated into the 5-E model for teaching science?*

Inquiry Instruction

 A glossary containing definitions of important terms used in this chapter can be found on MyEducationLab.

In inquiry instruction, students build conceptual understandings, investigation skills, and understandings of the nature of science through inquiry procedures that mirror methods used by scientists. As inquirers, learners assume major responsibility for constructing their own knowledge and understanding. Teachers share in and facilitate this process, guiding children as they ask questions, conduct investigations, and use observational evidence and scientific knowledge to develop explanations and answer their questions.

Features of Inquiry Instruction

A number of special features characterize inquiry instruction and learning (National Research Council, 2000). These features include:

1. *Learners Are Engaged by Scientific Questions.* At every stage of inquiry, students are connected to objects, organisms, and events in the real world. An early stage in inquiry

---

NSES TEACHING STANDARD B

To *guide and facilitate learning, teachers should*

- focus and support inquiries while interacting with students;
- orchestrate discourse among students about scientific ideas;
- challenge students to accept and share responsibility for their own learning;
- recognize and respond to student diversity and encourage all students to participate fully in science learning; and
- encourage and model the skills of scientific inquiry, as well as the curiosity, openness to new ideas and data, and skepticism that characterize science.

Encourage students to collect, organize, and interpret data.

is the formulation of questions for investigation. Ideally, students would generate questions from their own real-world experiences. Many students, however, will need considerable assistance in learning to form questions that can be investigated scientifically. In many cases, the focus question or problem is formulated by the teacher.

2. *Learners Give Priority to Evidence as They Plan and Conduct Investigations.* In inquiry approaches, students devise ways to gather evidence to answer their questions. With varying degrees of assistance, students determine what data might be relevant, decide how to collect the data, how to represent it, and how to organize it in useful ways. Students use a variety of investigational approaches to gather evidence, including descriptive, classificatory, and experimental investigations and other approaches.

3. *Learners Connect Evidence and Scientific Knowlege in Generating Explanations.* Continuing in inquiry, students describe, classify, and explain their observations, and clarify and justify their work to themselves and to one another. Children gradually learn that explanations must involve scientific knowledge and always be based on observational evidence gathered through investigations. Students should reflect on their observations often, reexamining them, using prior and developing knowledge to draw inferences from their observations, and collecting more data if necessary. As they develop cognitive skills, students should learn to distinguish between explanations, which are ideas about *why* something happens, and descriptions, which are based on observations of *what* has happened.

4. *Learners Apply Their Knowledge to New Scientific Problems.* To develop and extend understanding, learners must have the opportunity to apply their new science knowledge to new circumstances. For example, in the magnets lesson of Chapter 1, students learned fundamental rules of magnetic interaction. To help them be able to access and apply the new rules in new circumstances, the children might be asked to apply the rules to interactions between magnets and other objects in new classsroom activities.

5. Learners Engage in Critical Discourse with Others About Procedures, Evidence, and Explanations. Children love to talk about their experiences. Inquiry science provides a rich context for all students to develop language and thought (Rowe, 1973), including students with special needs and English Language Learners (ELL). Communicating and justifying scientific procedures, collecting, recording, reporting, and reflecting on evidence, and generating interpretations focus the students on *what* they know, *how* they know it, and *how* their knowledge connects to the knowledge of other people, to other subjects, and to the world beyond the classroom (National Research Council, 1996).

The complex process of tending to these five features of inquiry while teaching a classroom of students can be a daunting task. However, inquiry instruction can be considerably simplified through use of the 5-E model of instruction.

Models of Instruction

Models of instruction involve some arrangement of phases, steps, actions, or decision points for teaching and learning. Different instructional models in science build on different points of view about the nature of inquiry, processes of science, scientific knowledge and understanding, and goals of science learning. They also incorporate different principles from research on learning and development.

According to Brown and Campione (1994), teachers cannot just import an instructional model, follow prescribed procedures, and expect to attain student understanding of complex subject matter. A teacher's use of a model must reflect the viewpoints and principles on which it is based.

One of the earliest models of inquiry instruction in science is called the *learning cycle*. The learning cycle was developed in the 1960s by Robert Karplus (Karplus & Thier, 1974) and his colleagues for the Science Curriculum Improvement Study (SCIS) program. The model has been widely used by science teachers since that time. As is shown in Figure 4-1, the learning cycle consists of three phases of instruction:

* *Discovery*, in which children explore materials and discover new knowledge
* *Concept invention*, in which teachers build on student ideas in formally teaching information, concepts, and principles that help students make sense of their discoveries
* *Concept application*, in which students construct new understandings by applying their discovered and acquired knowledge to new situations

Figure 4-1 The Karplus and Thier SCIS Learning Cycle.
Source: Modified with permission from Charles R. Barman, "An Expanded View of the Learning Cycle: New Ideas About an Effective Teaching Strategy." Monograph and Occasional Paper Series, no. 4 (Washington, DC: Council for Elementary Science International, 1990), 5.

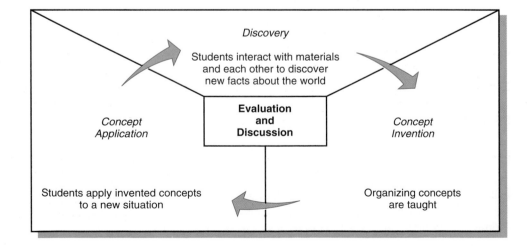

More recently, a model of instruction called the 5-E model has been designed to facilitate inquiry teaching.

The 5-E Model of Science Instruction

The 5-E model, which was developed by the Biological Sciences Curriculum Study (1989) group, builds on the learning cycle model. This model of instruction consists of five teaching phases: *engage, explore, explain, elaborate,* and *evaluate.* The five phases of the 5-E model and their functions are summarized in Table 4-1. One special value of the 5-E model in inquiry teaching is that the different phases of the model parallel the five tasks of inquiry identified in the *National Science Education Standards* (see Figure 1-3). Thus, Table 4-1 also shows how the different phases of the model are related to the tasks of scientific inquiry.

Notice that the middle three phases of the 5-E model—explore, explain, and elaborate—parallel the three phases of the learning cycle.

The 5-E model also facilitates the implementation of the research-based factors that influence learning with understanding presented in Chapter 3 (see Table 3-1), including accessing prior knowledge (at the engage phase), scaffolding (at every phase), building learning communities (in preparation for lessons and throughout the 5-E lesson phases), transfer (especially at the elaborate phase), and continual assessment (at every phase).

Let us examine each of the 5-E phases in more detail.

Phases of the 5-E Model

Engage. The first component in the 5-E instructional model, engage, is intended to pique curiosity and provide focus for the ensuing activities. It also provides an opportunity for teachers to identify the prior conceptions students have about the topic of study. Most important, at this stage, the question for investigation is formulated.

Chapters 1 and 2 provided many examples of questions that might be used in engaging students in inquiry.

Explore. At this phase of the 5-E model, teachers guide students as they devise ways to gather evidence to answer their questions. Students use a variety of observational and experimental investigational procedures to gather data. In planning investigations, they may

TABLE 4-1 THE FIVE PHASES IN THE 5-E MODEL OF INSTRUCTION, STUDENT ACTIONS IN EACH PHASE, AND THE TASKS OF SCIENTIFIC INQUIRY CORRESPONDING TO EACH PHASE		
5-E Phase	**Student Actions in Each Phase**	**Corresponding Tasks of Inquiry**
Engage	Ask a question about objects, organisms, or events in the environment.	Ask a question about objects, organisms, and events in the environment.
Explore	Plan and conduct simple investigations to collect relevant data.	Plan and conduct a simple investigation. Use appropriate tools and techniques to gather data.
Explain	Use data and scientific knowledge to generate explanations.	Use evidence and scientific knowledge to develop explanations.
Elaborate	Extend strategies, concepts, principles, and explanations to new problems and questions.	Apply knowledge and skills in new situations.
Evaluate	Demonstrate knowledge, understanding, and ability to use inquiry strategies through formal and informal formative assessments.	Communicate investigations, data, and explanations to others. (Formative assessment helps to provide a basis for decisions about scaffolding and improving instruction. Helps to provide a basis for scaffolding.)

Encourage children to discover new knowledge through exploration.

consider whether descriptive, classificatory, experimental, or some other approach to investigations would be most appropriate. In the process of gathering data, students develop simple process skills such as how to observe, measure, infer, and predict. They also learn how to cut, connect, switch, pour, tie, hold, and hook. Beginning with simple instruments, students learn to use rulers, thermometers, watches, spring scales, and balance scales to measure important variables. They learn to use magnifiers and microscopes to see finer details of objects and organisms (National Research Council, 1996).

Students should be encouraged to record their discoveries during the explore phase. One useful format for accomplishing this task and supporting future inquiry is the *I Notice/ I Wonder* chart. The left column of this two-column chart should be labeled "I Notice." In this column students write their observations and discoveries as they explore with the materials. The right column should be labeled "I Wonder." In this column students write questions that come to mind as they are exploring. These questions can lead to further inquiry investigations. Keeping records helps children to organize their findings and to remember them when they are needed in reflection, or during the explain and elaborate phases.

The explore phase of inquiry involves largely guided discovery by the students. It is in the explain and elaborate phases of inquiry that the 5-E model goes beyond discovery approaches to learning with understanding.

Explain. In the explain phase of the 5-E model, first, the teacher asks children to describe what they have noticed during the explore phase, reflect on their observations, and give their own theories and explanations that make sense of the observational data. Building on the activities and discussion of students, the teacher may use direct instruction, textbooks, and other means to formally introduce scientific knowledge (terms, facts, concepts, and principles) needed to make sense of the event. In presenting science knowledge, teachers should place an emphasis on students' understanding the natural world rather than just acquiring terminology and facts.

The teacher then assists students to use the new knowledge and the evidence from investigations during the explore phase to examine their initial conceptions and then to build accurate scientific explanations that help to answer the initiating question. At some point in the explain phase, the teacher may provide an explanation for the students.

Elaborate. It is not enough just to have knowledge. In developing understanding, learners must be able to access their knowledge and use it in new learning and problem solving. Failure to access knowledge at the appropriate time can severely constrain new learning and transfer (Bransford, Brown, & Cocking, 1999).

Mary Budd Rowe (1973), a distinguished science educator, has suggested that concept application is too often the neglected ingredient in science teaching. It is through concept application that understanding is generated. Rowe emphasized that children need to learn to view knowledge as procedures to be applied rather than just as information to be memorized and recalled.

Concept application takes place at the elaborate phase of 5-E instruction. At this phase, learners are presented with new learning tasks and called on to use their developing knowlege to negotiate the new task.

Evaluate. Assessment and evaluation always go hand in hand. *Assessment* is the process of gathering data on learning. *Evaluation* involves making decisions based on the assessment data. Assessment and evaluation in inquiry instruction are based on the objectives of the lesson taught. They provide a basis for decisions related to how to improve teaching and learning and are designed for the purpose of continual improvement of learning and teaching. In the 5-E model, assessment information is gathered through *formative* (ongoing) and *summative* (end of lesson or unit) assessments.

Self-assessment is an important aspect of the evaluation process. Brown and Campione (1994) argued that students should be taught metacognition strategies for planning, executing, monitoring, and adjusting their processes and products of learning.

As a summary view of the 5-E instructional model, Table 4-2 provides a chart that identifies teacher actions and student behaviors consistent with each phase of the model.

Teaching Electrical Concepts Through the 5-E Model of Instruction

Joyce Jackson used the 5-E approach to guide her fourth-grade class in a series of inquiry activities on electricity (see the accompanying 5-E lesson plan). When children learn about batteries and bulbs through the 5-E approach, they formulate initiating questions, explore electrical circuits, form generalizations about them, use the generalizations to explain why bulbs in different circuit arrangements do or do not light, and transfer the generalizations to new types of circuits.

Go to the Homework and Exercises section in Chapter 4 of MyEducationLab to watch the video clip *Teacher Discussion of Moon Phase Lessons*. In this video, we listen to two fourth- and fifth-grade teachers reflect on what they were trying to accomplish in the moon phase lessons, which appear to follow the 5-E (or a similar) model.

TABLE 4-2 APPLYING THE 5-E INSTRUCTIONAL MODEL

Stage of the Instructional Model	What the TEACHER Does	
	That Is Consistent with This Model	That Is Inconsistent with This Model
Engage	• Creates interest • Generates curiosity • Raises questions • Elicits responses that uncover what the students know or think about the concept/topic	• Explains concepts • Provides definitions and answers • States conclusions • Provides closure • Lectures
Explore	• Encourages students to work together without direct instruction from the teacher • Observes and listens to students as they interact • Asks probing questions to redirect students' investigations when necessary • Provides time for students to puzzle through problems • Acts as a consultant for students	• Provides answers • Tells or explains how to work through the problem • Provides closure • Tells students that they are wrong • Gives information or facts that solve the problem • Leads students step-by-step to a solution
Explain	• Encourages students to explain concepts and definitions in their own words • Asks for justification (evidence) and clarification from students • Formally provides definitions, explanations, and new labels • Uses students' previous experiences as the basis for explaining concepts	• Accepts explanations that have no justification • Neglects to solicit students' explanations • Introduces unrelated concepts or skills
Elaborate	• Expects students to use formal labels, definitions, and explanations provided previously • Encourages students to apply or extend the concepts and skills in new situations • Reminds students of alternative explanations • Refers students to existing data and evidence and asks: "What do you already know?" "Why do you think . . . ?" (Strategies from explore stage apply here also.)	• Provides definitive answers • Tells students they are wrong • Lectures • Leads students step-by-step to a solution • Explains how to work through the problem
Evaluate	• Observes students as they apply new concepts and skills • Assesses students' knowledge and/or skills • Looks for evidence that students have changed their thinking or behaviors • Allows students to assess their own learning and group-process skills • Asks open-ended questions, such as: "Why do you think . . . ?" "What evidence do you have?" "What do you know about x?" "How would you explain x?"	• Tests vocabulary words, terms, and isolated facts • Introduces new ideas or concepts • Creates ambiguity • Promotes open-ended discussion unrelated to the concept or skill

TABLE 4-2   APPLYING THE 5-E INSTRUCTIONAL MODEL

Stage of the Instructional Model	What the STUDENT Does	
	That Is Consistent with This Model	That Is Inconsistent with This Model
Engage	• Asks questions, such as: "Why did this happen?" "What do I already know about this?" "What can I find out about this?" • Shows interest in the topic	• Asks for the "right" answer • Offers the "right" answer • Insists on answers or explanations • Seeks one solution
Explore	• Thinks freely, but within the limits of the activity • Tests predictions and hypotheses • Forms new predictions and hypotheses • Tries alternatives and discusses them with others • Records observations and ideas • Suspends judgment	• Lets others do the thinking and exploring (passive involvement) • Works quietly with little or no interaction with others (only appropriate when exploring ideas or feelings) • Plays around indiscriminately with no goal in mind • Stops with one solution
Explain	• Explains possible solutions or answers to others • Listens critically to one another's explanations • Questions one another's explanations • Listens to and tries to comprehend explanations offered by the teacher • Refers to previous activities • Uses recorded observations in explanations	• Proposes explanations from thin air with no relationship to previous experiences • Brings up irrelevant experiences and examples • Accepts explanations without justification • Does not attend to other plausible explanations
Elaborates	• Applies new labels, definitions, explanations, and skills in new, but similar, situations • Uses previous information to ask questions, propose solutions, make decisions, and design experiments • Draws reasonable conclusions from evidence • Records observations and explanations • Checks for understanding among peers	• Plays around with no goal in mind • Ignores previous information or evidence • Draws conclusions from thin air • Uses in discussions only those labels that the teacher provided
Evaluate	• Answers open-ended questions by using observations, evidence, and previously accepted explanations • Demonstrates an understanding or knowledge of the concept or skill • Evaluates his or her own progress and knowledge • Asks related questions that would encourage future investigations	• Draws conclusions, not using evidence or previously accepted explanations • Offers only yes-or-no answers, memorized definitions, or explanation and answers • Fails to express satisfactory explanations in own words • Introduces new, irrelevant topics

Source: Teaching Secondary School Science, 6th ed. (pp. 218–219), by Leslie Trowbridge and Rodger Bybee, 1996, © Reprinted by permission of Pearson Education, Inc., Upper Saddle River, NJ.

5-E Lesson Plan for Batteries and Bulbs

All students should develop an understanding of:

- Light, heat, electricity, and magnetism (Grades K–4)

- Electricity in circuits can produce light, heat, sound, and mechanical motion (Grades K–4)
- Electrical circuits require a complete conducting loop through which an electric circuit can pass (Grades K–4)

National Science Education Standards

Concepts and Principles that Support the Standards

Young girls are as curious as boys about science and inquiry. Sensitive teachers nurture that interest.

Objectives

Through these lesson activities, students should be able to,

1. Demonstrate and explain through words and drawings how to make a bulb light in various ways, given one or two batteries, one or two bulbs, and one or two wires.

2. State, explain, and demonstrate the complete circuit rule. For a bulb to light:
   - the base of the bulb must be touched on the side and the bottom;
   - the battery must be touched on both ends; and
   - there must be a complete circuit or continuous path along the wires and through the battery and bulb.

3. Explain in their own words what a conductor is and demonstrate how to test a material to determine if it is an electrical conductor.

4. Identify and construct series circuits and use the complete circuit rule to explain why the other bulbs in a series circuit go out when one bulb is removed from its holder.

5. Identify and construct parallel circuits and use the complete circuit rule to explain why the other bulbs in a parallel circuit stay lit when one bulb is removed from its holder.

6. Understand, appreciate, and apply safety rules and procedures related to electricity.

Safety

- Respect electricity! Do not touch or go near frayed or broken wires. Do not insert anything but an electrical plug into an electrical outlet.
- Never try these activities with any battery larger than a 1.5 volt D cell (flashlight battery).
- Always wear goggles when you work with batteries, bulbs, and wires to protect your eyes from the sharp points of wires.
- If wires get hot, immediately disconnect them from the battery. This arrangement of the parts of the circuit will not light the bulb, so try a different arrangement.

Learning Activities	5-E Phases	Procedures

Learning Activities

Engage

Explore

5-E Phases

- Engage students in the learning task
- Discover what happens

- Show What You Observe

- Predict and test

Procedures

1. Tell a story of three campers lost in the dark. They have batteries, bulbs, and wires, but do not know how to light a bulb. Ask: Can you help the campers light the bulb?
2. Students work individually to light a bulb using one wire and one battery.
3. Find several ways to light the bulb (students may work individually or with team members on this and subsequent tasks).
4. Light a bulb using two wires, without the bulb touching the battery.
5. Draw pictures to represent the bulb-battery-wire arrangements for tasks 2 and 3.
6. Draw a picture to represent the arrangement of the bulb, wires, and battery in task 4.
7. Complete Prediction Sheet 1. Work frame by frame, going from one frame to the next using what you learn to move from one to another.
   - Make a prediction.
   - Test your prediction.
   - Learn from your test.
   - Apply what you have learned.

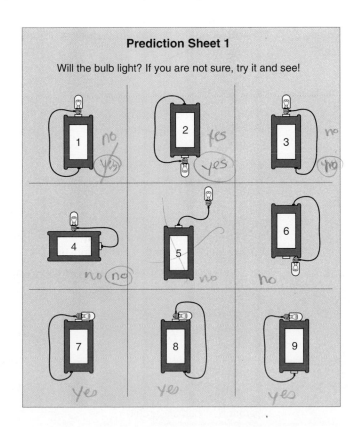

Explain
- Generalize
- Apply
- Use knowledge to infer and explain

8. Where must a bulb be touched in order for it to light? Where must a battery be touched? Write a general rule for what must be done to make a bulb light.

9. Apply your generalizations or rule to explain each frame in Prediction Sheet 1.

10. Examine a bulb with a magnifying lens. The coiled wire across the top of the bulb is called a *filament*. That is what uses electrical energy to produce light. Do you see the two wires that disappear into the base of the bulb? How do you think they are connected internally within the base of the bulb? Use your rule from task 8 in making your inference.

11. Examine a bulb holder. What are its parts? How is a bulb holder designed to touch the tip and metal side of the base of a bulb?

Elaborate
- Apply knowledge to new situations

12. Make the circuit shown in diagram A.
    - How many wires are needed?
    - Remove one of the bulbs from its holder. What happens? Why?
    - Replace the bulb. Remove another bulb. What happens? Why?
    - Add one or two more batteries. What happens? Why?
    - What would the label "series circuit" describe about the circuit in diagram A?

13. Make the circuit shown in diagram B.
    - How many wires are needed?
    - Remove one of the bulbs from its holder. What happens? Why?
    - Replace the bulb. Remove another bulb. What happens? Why?
    - Add one or two more batteries. What happens? Why?
    - What would the label "parallel circuit" describe about the circuit in diagram B?

Evaluate
- Formative assessment
- Summative assessment

- Through informal and formal assessments, the teacher should continually monitor understanding and adjust individual and group instruction accordingly.

- Develop a test card with new illustrations of battery and bulbs arrangements similar to those on Prediction Sheet 1. Give the test card to students. Have them work alone to answer the test card items.

- Use the test card as a basis for one-on-one interviews with students to assess their understanding of complete circuit ideas.

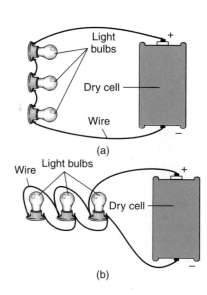

(a)

(b)

Diagram A. A series circuit.
Diagram B. A parallel circuit.
Source: Adapted from discovery activities in *Batteries and Bulbs*, Elementary Science Study, 1968, Cambridge, MA: Educational Development Center.

Engage. Ms. Jackson arranged her class in cooperative learning groups and assigned jobs, such as Principal Investigator, Materials Manager, Recorder, and Reporter, to different team members within each group. To *engage* the students in the learning task, she began with an improbable little story:

> Three campers had strayed deep into the woods, far from their campsite. Night had fallen and they had no flashlight to find their way back in the darkness. However, one camper had a spare battery in his backpack, another had a flashlight bulb, and a third had a few pieces of copper wire. Unfortunately, they did not know how to connect the battery, bulb, and wire to light the bulb.

Then, while interest was high, Ms. Jackson asked the class: "Can you use the materials in front of you to light a bulb and help the campers get back to their campsite safely?"

Explore. As she talked, Ms. Jackson had quietly given each group a box containing several 1.5-volt D-cell batteries, small flashlight bulbs, and pieces of wire. Now, she asked the Materials Manager in each group to place one battery, one bulb, and one piece of wire before each child. She had planned the engagement activities so that once the problem had been introduced and curiosity was high, students could begin to *explore* immediately, manipulating materials and making observations. The story helped the students comprehend and maintain focus on the task.

Initially, the students worked individually to light the bulb (see task 2 in the batteries and bulbs lesson). Many students lit the bulb within a few minutes; others took considerably longer. During the explore phase, Ms. Jackson resisted the temptation to give too much help. As students successfully lit a bulb, she acknowledged their success with a little cheer, a word or two, or a smile or gesture. But she cautioned those who had succeeded not to reveal to others what they had done to light a bulb and rob them of the joy and feeling of accomplishment of discovery and the opportunity to develop real understanding.

As students succeeded in the discovery task, she directed their attention to two additional tasks she had written on the chalkboard:

- Find several ways to light a bulb using only one battery and one wire.
- Light a bulb using two wires, without the bulb touching the battery.

These were tasks 3 and 4 from the lesson plan. Students either worked individually or with their team members on these tasks. Children freely exchanged information and ideas as they worked in their groups, but Ms. Jackson always noted whether each child could succeed on a task. She invited those who were content to learn from others to show her with their own materials how to do each task.

In the process of exploration, most students used trial and error. Some students thought about possibilities, made hypotheses and predictions, and tried out their ideas. Each cooperative group moved through the exploration activities at their own pace, with the teacher giving hints, adding information, posing questions, or providing additional activities and material as needed. Most of the groups were able to complete tasks 2 through 4 on the first day.

To start the next science time, Ms. Jackson turned out the lights in the classroom and asked the children to individually make a bulb light and hold it aloft to light the room. As she walked about the room watching what the children were doing, she was able to quickly assess the knowledge and skills of each child, to note who needed help, and to either supply assistance or ask someone in a cooperative group to help.

Back in a large group, she asked the children to talk about what they had done. Then, she directed the children, working individually, to draw pictures of the different ways they

You may need to study circuit ideas yourself before teaching batteries and bulbs activities. Good presentations on electricity and electrical circuits at an elementary level are available in many curriculum resources. Especially good treatments can be found in the STC (Science and Technology for Children) *Teachers' Guide for Electric Circuits,* and the FOSS (Full Option Science System) *Teachers' Guide for Magnetism and Electricity.*

Through the Annenberg video *Completing the Circuit,* which is recommended in the Online Professional Development section of this chapter, you can learn a great deal about electrical circuits as you watch a class of fourth-grade students learning electrical concepts and principles through their own investigations and teacher scaffolding. A study guide and instructions for accessing this video are given in the Online Professional Development section.

had found to light a bulb (tasks 5 and 6 of the lesson plan). This activity was designed to lift thought from a kinesthetic, hands-on level to a more abstract, iconic, or imaging level. As she went about the room assessing each child's drawings, she noted that some had not perceived exactly what it was they did to light a bulb. Again, she either provided assistance or asked another child to assist. Thus, the children's understanding was continually assessed and enhanced.

Ms. Jackson passed out Prediction Sheet 1 and gave directions for it (task 7). Circulating among the students as they worked in their groups, she encouraged them and supplied assistance as needed.

Explain. When all groups had finished the prediction sheet, Ms. Jackson led the students to shift from exploration to explanation. She began the third day with task 8 from the lesson plan. She posed the question for this activity by saying,

> "Suppose one of the campers lost in the woods had a cell phone and called you to find out how to light a bulb. What would you tell her? Write out your answer."

This task was intended to raise the children's level of thought from kinesthetic and imaging levels to a higher semantic level. Children worked individually, then as groups, to answer the question. Noting that the children had considerable difficulty with this more abstract task, Ms. Jackson decided to provide some direct instruction on the concept of circuits.

In formally presenting the new concept, Ms. Jackson followed these simple guidelines:

- First, she grouped her students near her so they could all hear what she said and see what she demonstrated or wrote on the chalkboard.
- She referred to tasks 2 through 6 that the students had done themselves during exploration.
- As she discussed the activities, she defined the circuit concept that she wanted to develop. Referring through gestures to the complete circuit in front of her, she said,

  A *circuit* is an arrangement of bulbs, batteries, and wires. A circuit is a complete circuit if the bulb lights. If the circuit is complete, there is an unbroken pathway around the circuit from one terminal of a battery, along the wires, through the bulb, and back to the other terminal of the battery.

- She wrote the word *circuit* on the board for all the children to see. (Writing the word gives visual as well as oral introduction of the new word.) Through questioning and verbal instruction, she led the students to apply their new knowledge of circuits to the circuit arrangements they had already encountered in tasks 2 through 6.

This instructional sequence referred to activities the students had already done or observed but added a new concept, *circuit*. With this new information, the children went back to the task of writing out a general rule for lighting a bulb. The class-as-a-whole, under Ms. Jackson's assistance, decided on these rules:

To light a bulb with one wire:

1. *Touch the tip of the bulb to one terminal of the battery.*
2. *Touch the wire to the metal on the side of the bulb.*
3. *Make a complete pathway for the electricity to flow by touching the other end of the wire to the other end of the battery.*

The children, working in their groups, then applied their new rule to each frame in Prediction Sheet 1, noting which circuits must be complete ones and identifying why other circuits pictured might not provide complete paths for the electricity (task 9).

Elaborate. Once they have been introduced, concepts, principles, and explanation must be applied or transferred to new situations to be understood. Through tasks 10–13 from the lesson plan, circuit concepts and principles were refined, extended, and linked to one another and to real-world experiences. Although all of the children enjoyed these activities and were able to learn a good deal more factual and conceptual information about electrical circuits from them, many of the children were not able to spontaneously apply the new circuit rules to understand what happened in each case. Because of their complexity and novelty, the new problem situations were challenging for the students. Yet, for many students, the challenges yielded to the application of complete circuit concepts developed through earlier activities.

Evaluate. Ms. Jackson used a combination of *formative* and *summative* assessments as a basis for evaluating student performance and understanding. She conducted formative assessments primarily through student responses to the various questions featured in the lesson plan. Teachers monitor students' performances during investigations, examine their products, such as drawings and notebook entries, and listen to discourse. The goal of formative assessment in this case was to determine and improve student understanding of electrical circuits. Ms. Jackson used the results of formative assessments to adjust instruction in order to improve learning.

Summative assessment was undertaken through a teacher-made test card that parallels Prediction Sheet 1. The teacher used the test card for whole-group assessment and as the basis of one-on-one interviews with students to assess their understanding of complete circuit ideas. The teacher also used the performance task and rubric shown in Chapter 6 in Figures 6-12 and 6-13 to assess understanding. Decisions about next steps in the teaching sequence were determined from these results.

Using the 5-E Model to Sequence Science Activities

In the previous example on electrical circuits, the teacher used the 5-E model to plan and implement an entire lesson. The 5-E model might also be used to sequence individual science activities within a lesson or unit.

Here are some important guidelines for using the 5-E model with individual activities.

- Plan each individual activity so that it involves the first three phases in the 5-E model—engage, explore, and explain. This means that explanation is implemented within each activity, rather than letting the data from exploration accumulate across different activities before the explain phase is introduced (as in the previously presented lesson sequence).
- Use the engage, explore, and explain phases of the 5-E model, with each succeeding activity to develop additional concepts, principles, and explanations.
- Also, use succeeding activities in a sequence as elaborations of previously learned concepts, principles, explanations, and procedures. Thus, succeeding activities require the transfer/application of previously learned ideas to new situations.
- Use formative assessment procedures within each activity to obtain information for improving learning and instruction.

Go to the Homework and Exercises section in Chapter 4 of MyEducationLab to watch the video *Investigating Goldfish: Parts 1, 2, 3, and 4*. In this set of videos, we watch kindergarten children as they raise questions about goldfish and observe live goldfish to answer their questions.

An Annenberg video entitled *Completing the Circuit* illustrates the engage, explore, and explain phases within each activity. This video is featured in the Online Professional Development section at the end of this chapter. In addition, each activity in the companion volume for this book, *Activities for Teaching Science as Inquiry*, uses the engage, explore, and explain phases of the 5-E model.

- Use summative assessment after the last activity as a basis for evaluating the students' conceptual understanding, use of inquiry abilities, and understandings of the nature of science and scientific inquiry.
- Keep in mind that summative assessments can serve as evidence for decisions about grades and for reports to students and parents.

Guided Discovery, Textbook, and Direct Instruction Approaches to Teaching Science

So far in this book, we have focused on using inquiry instruction to help students construct conceptual understanding in science, develop their abilities to do science, and further understand the nature of scientific inquiry. The emphasis on inquiry, however, does not mean that all science lessons should be inquiry oriented, nor does it imply that teachers should pursue a single approach to teaching. According to the *National Science Education Standards* (National Research Council, 1996), "Just as inquiry has many different facets, so teachers need to use many different strategies to develop the understandings and abilities described in the *Standards*" (p. 2).

Let us examine first the guided discovery approach to teaching science.

Guided Discovery

In guided discovery learning, children begin with interesting questions and concrete materials. Learners work individually or in small groups to explore materials, make observations, and discover answers to their questions about the natural world. The teacher serves as a facilitator and guide through the discovery process.

Discovery lessons are highly motivational. There is joy for children in probing into and finding out about the unknown. As children start to explore, they seem to suddenly awaken to exciting possibilities in the natural world and in themselves. Discovery allows students to find their own meanings and organize their own ideas. In discovery learning, children's imagination, hunches, and insight precede proof and instruction by teachers (Wiggins & McTighe, 1998). As young students engage in probing interesting questions, much open inquiry can take place if teachers allow students to explore. Students do not have to be scientifically mature, merely curious.

The Elementary Science Study (ESS) program developed in the 1960s with federal funds was one of the pioneers in the use of discovery approaches to learning science. The ESS group devised many activities and units and tested them in classrooms across the nation. Dozens of lessons from ESS modules such as *Kitchen Physics, Batteries and Bulbs, Bones, Mealworms, Gases and Airs, Rocks and Minerals, Mystery Powders,* and *Small Things* were developed.

The ESS philosophy was captured in the phrase "messing about in science," which was based on an expression in Kenneth Grahame's (1981) children's book *The Wind in the Willows*. In this delightful tale, Water Rat explained to Mole the joys of simply "messing about in boats" on a lazy afternoon. If you have not already done so, read the account of Mole and Water Rat's river adventure in the introduction to this book (page 2) and think about why it inspired the developers of ESS. As you read, consider how Water Rat's little speech at the end of the selection can also fit some of the purposes of discovery learning.

Through discovery learning, children enjoy simply messing about in science. But well-planned discovery materials and activities also give children opportunities and time to observe, investigate, and appreciate the order and diversity of the world.

Preparing for Guided Discovery. Although it is the students who engage in the discovery work, careful teacher planning is necessary for successful discovery lessons. Teachers must consider the kinds of introductory questions that can effectively set the stage for exploration. Here are some sample questions:

- What are some things you notice about butterflies? What colors are they and what patterns do you see? How might different color patterns serve to protect butterflies?
- How do mealworms respond to environmental conditions, such as moisture, light, and heat? What foods do mealworms prefer?
- What things live on the edge of the pond? How do they interact with one another? Why do they live on the edge of the pond and not in it?

Strategies for Guided Discovery. To teach by guided discovery, you should introduce the problem, distribute materials in an orderly way, and let the discoveries begin as soon as possible. Circulate among the children as they engage in discovery activities, spending no more than about 30 to 60 seconds with each student or small group. You should give only enough assistance to ensure that students do not become overly frustrated, experience undue failure, and give up.

Rather than telling the students what to do while investigating, teachers can scaffold children's discoveries by asking questions or giving hints that help them sense the direction for solving problems. You must be careful to respect the discovery process and not to supply too much information. Do not rob children of opportunities for thought and creativity in their investigations. Thus, in discovery lessons, you might choose to answer children's questions with "What do you think?" or "What are your ideas?" Deciding when to give assistance and when to withhold it is an important part of the art of discovery teaching.

At different points in the discovery process, you will want to hear from and talk with the class as a whole about their procedures and discoveries. You will be tempted to give students the "right" answer. However, a skilled discovery teacher listens to and uses the ideas of children in questioning and discussion to help them organize their thoughts and build more scientifically accurate understandings of the world (see Chapter 7).

Guided Discovery in a Nutshell. We can summarize the teaching approach to discovery learning in the following way:

- Engage children in activities.
- Encourage them to explore concrete materials and reflect on what they find out.
- Engage children in conversations, listen to their ideas, and provide guidance to help them build and test their own explanations of what is happening (Koch, 1999).

Guided discovery is a wonderful approach to learning science that students and teachers have enjoyed for many years. Nothing raises the sense of wonder and joy of learning about the natural world like discovery. In teaching science, you should provide your students a variety of opportunities to experience the joy of discovery.

Discovery approaches to science instruction share several features of inquiry instruction. Yet, often missing in guided discovery teaching are careful attention to constructing and applying specific scientific knowledge, opportunities for students to develop conceptual understanding by attempting to transfer what they have learned to new problems, and a planned development of specific abilities of inquiry. Adding explain and elaborate phases to guided discovery can greatly enhance the science learning of students.

As you probably have noticed, guided discovery is essentially the approach students and teachers should take in the explore phase of the 5-E model.

Go to the Homework and Exercises section in Chapter 4 of MyEducationLab to read an interesting and informative article, "Inquiring Scientists Want to Know." The article contrasts three approaches to science teaching: a laboratory verification method, a discovery approach, and an inquiry approach. This article extends and refines the comparisons of different teaching approaches to science discussed in this chapter.

Direct Instruction

Direct instruction is an approach to science instruction in which teachers present to learners the primary information to be learned. It emphasizes learning from being told. Hunter (1984) incorporated some behavioral principles of S-R learning into a direct instruction model called *lesson design*. Behavioral learning principles in Hunter's model focus on teacher stimulus (S), student response (R), teacher reinforcement of responses, and student practice.

Following are the instructional steps in Hunter's lesson design model of direct instruction. Note especially that learning input does not come from student activities but from teachers and other sources.

- *Anticipatory set.* In this phase, focusing activities are carried out that orient students to the lesson and lead them to access relevant prior knowledge.
- *Objectives and purpose.* Here, the students are informed of the objectives for the day. The teacher also explains how and why the ideas of the lesson are useful and important.
- *Instructional input.* The teacher uses a wide variety of methods—including lecture, media presentations, role playing, simulations, demonstrations, and even laboratory investigations—to help the students achieve the objectives. The specific content and processes to be learned are contained explicitly in the instructional input.
- *Modeling.* Through modeling, the teacher provides examples of the content knowledge and procedures to be learned.
- *Monitoring understanding and adjusting instruction.* The teacher elicits an active response from each student and assesses the response for evidence of understanding. The teacher adjusts instruction as necessary to improve understanding.
- *Independent and guided practice.* Because practice is essential to learning and retention, ample opportunity is afforded for students to practice the new content and processes.

Considerable content in elementary and middle school science is well suited to direct instruction, and you will want to use this method when appropriate. Direct instruction methods can be useful and effective for teaching well-defined performance skills or specific facts, concepts, and information to be remembered. Arbitrary conventions such as stoplight colors, measurement equivalencies, and vocabulary labels that cannot be logically deduced, as well as concepts and procedures that may be invented by some students but not by others, can be taught by direct methods. Also, direct instruction is more appropriate for content that we do not want students to learn by trial and error, such as safety precautions or how to focus a microscope.

Within inquiry contexts expository methods can be important, such as for providing background knowledge, giving directions, teaching specific skills, inventing concepts and principles in the explain phase of the 5-E model, applying them to new situations in the elaborate phase of the model, and summarizing inquiries (Wolfinger, 2000). You might recognize that in the classroom example of teaching science by the 5-E model, Ms. Jackson used direct instruction in the explain phase to teach the concept of complete circuits.

Yet, in light of the *National Science Education Standards* and contemporary learning research, there are several problems with the direct instruction approach to science teaching. It typically fails to provide opportunities for students to ask their own questions about the natural world, explore and collect data, and use the evidence of their own explorations and their prior or new scientific knowledge as the basis for their own theories and explanations. It does not provide the experiential base needed for learning processes of science and investigational strategies. Further, it does not typically build in discourse among students and teachers that promotes learning with understanding. Finally, direct instruction does not usually provide authentic opportunities for teachers to assess student understanding formatively and provide scaffolding assistance.

A Textbook Approach to Science Teaching

The textbook approach has traditionally consisted of textbooks and worksheets as the major instructional materials, supplemented with teacher lecture, class discussion, demonstrations, videotape presentations, or other short activities. Students may also read about and conduct some hands-on activities to provide a basis for science knowledge and explanations. Typically, teachers present information, students read text materials and examine pictures (such as pictures of circuits, switches, or electromagnets), and engage in independent and guided practice activities using worksheets. This approach generally places high demands on students' reading, language, and memory skills and presents large amounts of vocabulary to learn (Scruggs, Mastropieri, Bakken, & Brigham, 1993). As with other approaches, textbook methods should be well structured and involve daily review, active engagement by students, formative and summative evaluation of student products, and questioning.

In the past, because of an emphasis on reading about science rather than doing science, textbook series did not usually provide opportunity for children to investigate and to learn investigative procedures. Further, science textbooks tended to focus more on presenting specific concepts and principles to be learned.

However, contemporary textbook series are increasingly placing emphasis on inquiry. Inquiry lessons in textbook series typically include initiating questions, data gathering, and data interpretation, but investigations are largely directed or guided by the textbook, with little opportunity for student inquiry.

With the changing emphasis of textbooks, the question to be considered is not whether textbooks should be used in teaching science, but how the texts should be used. Lowery (1998) has explained that new, meaningful knowledge acquired from text materials is actually a construction based on prior knowledge and linguistic input. With something to work with, an author can help readers understand abstract ideas and make difficult connections. But if readers have inadequate prior knowledge related to the content, they will gain little from reading. Thus, *reading is more powerful in science when it follows experience and is based on prior knowledge.* Following this principle, the FOSS (Full Option Science System) has designed reading materials to be used after hands-on instruction.

An approach in which text reading is introduced only after inquiry would seem to work well with most textbook series. In that case, topics might be introduced through inquiry approaches, such as the 5-E approach, with textbook materials being read and text activities conducted after the 5-E lessons or during the explain phase of the model. The texts would then serve to supplement previous learning by filling in gaps, providing new information and concepts, reinforcing definitions, and summarizing what has been constructed through earlier inquiry lessons. Since readers would have some prior knowledge of a topic through their own activities, when they encounter textbook presentations, they should be able to read them with more comprehension.

For example, in the inquiry lesson plan on electrical circuits presented previously, students built series and parallel circuits. They predicted on the basis of the complete circuit rule what would happen to the other bulbs in the circuit if one of the bulbs were removed. Figure 4-2 shows a reading selection on series and parallel circuits that appears in a fourth-grade science textbook. In an *inquiry first, reading later* approach, children would carry out

Some specific suggestions on connecting reading and science instruction are given in Chapter 9.

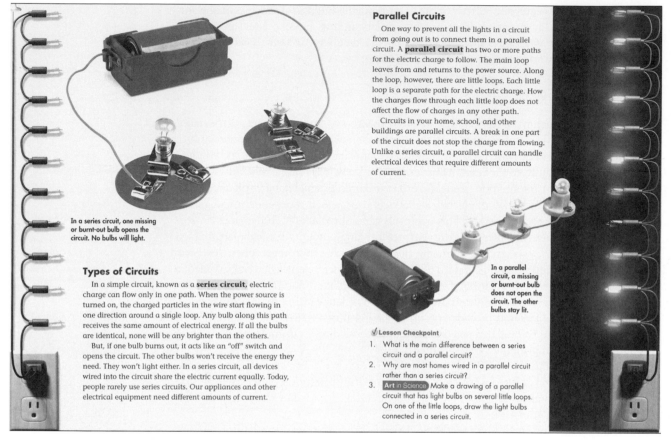

Figure 4-2   In an *inquiry first, reading later* approach, children carry out activities on series and parallel circuits before they read about them in their textbooks.

inquiry activities on series and parallel circuits before they read about them in their textbooks. Because the students would have some prior knowledge of series and parallel circuits and complete circuit paths, they should be able to read the text selection with more comprehension and understanding.

Research on the Effectiveness of Different Approaches to Science Instruction

A key question asked in many research studies on learning and instruction in science has been: *What is the relative effectiveness of different approaches to teaching science?* Haury (1993), the National Research Council (2001), and Duschl and colleagues (2007) have reviewed a large number of research studies on the effectiveness of different approaches to teaching science. Although definitions of inquiry vary from study to study, research data indicate that inquiry instruction is effective in fostering problem solving, creativity, and independent learning and in improving reasoning, observing, and logical analysis. Research indicates further that students exposed to inquiry methods in science typically perform better than their peers in more traditional classes on measures of general science achievement, process skills, analytical skills, and related skills such as language arts and mathematics.

Studies consistently found that, when compared with students in more traditional, textbook-oriented science programs, students engaged in inquiry activities

- found science more exciting and interesting,
- had greater feelings of success, and
- had a more positive view of science and scientists.

Studies indicate that the advantages of inquiry-oriented instruction also extend to special student populations (Duschl et al., 2007). Research indicates that students with learning disabilities and English Language Learners (ELL) can successfully engage in inquiry and learn science concepts through inquiry instruction.

Research data on measurable cognitive and affective variables support the advantages of inquiry instruction over other methods. Yet, intangible achievements may outweigh tangible ones, as students learn through an inquiry approach to ask questions, place a priority on evidence, and use observable data, knowledge, and clear reasoning to arrive at explanations and evaluate claims.

Klahr and Nigam (2004) compared discovery and direct instruction models of instruction, although the researchers used somewhat unconventional definitions of discovery and direct instruction. Discovery instruction was defined in terms of pure discovery, with essentially no teacher guidance, rather than the guided instruction model presented in this chapter. Also, in contrast to the direct instruction approach described here, direct instruction as defined in Klahr and Nigam's study involved considerable hands-on activities, with appropriate teacher scaffolding.

The science topic treated in both methods was designing and constructing controlled investigations for problems involving balls rolling down ramps. Tests assessed *near transfer* (transfer to the design of experiments related to the balls and ramps problem, but requiring the testing of different variables) and *far transfer* (transfer to the evaluation of the design of totally new experiments). Results of the study by Klahr and Nigam strongly favored direct instruction (with hands-on activities) over discovery (with no teacher input).

The critical importance of teacher input in instruction can be shown through the Klahr and Nigam study. In the discovery approach tested, there was little if any scaffolding and no direct instruction on how to design and set up controlled investigations. In contrast, teacher scaffolding, including teacher instructions about controlled experiments, was a critical part of the researchers' direct instruction approach. Further, tasks involving the transfer of knowledge of experimental design were included in the direct instruction condition.

From one perspective, the discovery condition in the Klahr and Nigam study omitted the critically important 5-E phases of explain and elaborate. In contrast, the direct instruction approach emphasized the importance of teaching explicit concepts and skill in the explain phase of the model. Thus, the study by Klahr and Nigam indirectly demonstrates the value of the 5-E approach in learning and instruction.

Selecting Instructional Approaches for Teaching Science

In addition to inquiry, discovery, textbook, and direct instruction methods, a variety of other strategies available for use in science are presented in this book. The questioning strategies of Chapter 7 work well with teacher demonstration approaches to science. Learning centers are discussed in Chapter 5. Field trips to large public science institutions, such as aquariums, are treated in Chapter 5. Reading as a strategy for learning science is discussed in Chapter 9. Writing to learn science is discussed in Chapters 2 and 9. Web-based lessons are presented in Chapter 8. Computer simulations and virtual field trips as teaching methods are also introduced in Chapter 8.

There is no one best way to teach all science concepts to all children all the time. You cannot guarantee how effective any individual method will be. Students differ in prior knowledge, experiences, learning abilities, preferred learning approaches, and the amount of structure they need in learning. Classroom and environmental factors vary and can affect teaching and learning. Some science lessons might be planned to prepare students for future science learning. Other lessons might be intended to provide for reinforcement, practice, and review of topics. Lessons focusing on application of science concepts and principles are also important. That is why you need to use a variety of teaching techniques throughout the school year.

Regardless of the approach selected, it should involve knowledge of objectives, daily review, active engagement by students, a variety of practice activities, opportunities for transfer learning, teacher scaffolding, and regular evaluation of student products. When direct input is called for, effective teachers should also pay attention to such presentation variables as structure, clarity, redundancy, enthusiasm, appropriate rate of presentation, and maximum engagement through questioning and feedback. "If these variables are considered along with the specific needs of students during instruction," conclude Mastropieri and Scruggs (2004, p. 181), ". . . overall achievement will improve."

What conclusions are you beginning to form about science teaching models and strategies? Although there are many valuable methods for teaching science, all children should experience, at least two or more times a year, the joy and satisfaction of asking questions about the natural world, finding ways to investigate and gather evidence, and using their evidence and science knowledge to arrive at explanations that provide answers to their questions. In short, all children should have the opportunity to learn science through inquiry.

SUMMARY

- Inquiry instruction refers to teaching procedures focused on student investigations of the natural world. Through inquiry activities, students have opportunities to develop conceptual knowledge and understanding, inquiry abilities, and understandings about the nature of science and scientific inquiry.

- Throughout the inquiry process, teachers guide, focus, challenge, and encourage student learning, using their knowledge of students as well as their knowledge of science and how it is learned.

- The 5-E model of instruction is a second-generation version of the learning cycle model.

- The five Es in the model are engage, explore, explain, elaborate, and evaluate. The 5-E model provides a specific focus on the NSES tasks of inquiry.

- The 5-E model also provides opportunities for teachers to use the different factors that enhance learning with understanding, such as providing access to prior knowledge,

providing for scaffolding assistance, and building learning communities.

- Several different instructional strategies have been developed for teaching science. In guided discovery approaches, children are presented with interesting questions and concrete materials. They work individually or in small groups to explore materials, make observations, and discover answers to their questions about the natural world. The teacher serves as facilitator and guide of the discovery process.

- Direct instruction and textbook instruction strategies are teacher-directed methods in which teachers and textbooks present to learners the main information to be learned.

- The 5-E model incorporates guided discovery strategies in the explore phase. Building on student explorations and ideas can include the use of direct teaching of core concepts in the explain phase. In science, textbook reading should follow experiences with the concepts. This order enables students to build prior knowledge useful in comprehending science texts. Science textbooks would then be used to supplement and summarize inquiry activities.

• No one method of teaching science is best for all teachers and all students, all the time, under all circumstances.

Inquiry models of instruction mirror inquiry procedures of science, are consistent with constructivist approaches to learning, and are motivational and effective in teaching science to children. All children should have the opportunity to learn science through inquiry.

ONLINE PROFESSIONAL DEVELOPMENT

Pre- and post-tests to assess your knowledge of chapter content, along with exercises to enhance your understanding, can be found on MyEducationLab at www.myeducationlab.com.

Video Guides

Video clips on MyEducationLab selected for this chapter include *Teacher Discussion of Moon Phase Lessons* and *Investigating Goldfish—Parts 1, 2, 3,* and 4.

Accessing the Videos

1. Go to the Homework and Exercises section in Chapter 4 of MyEducationLab to select and view videos for this chapter.
2. Videos might be viewed individually, by small groups of colleagues, or by the whole class.
3. As you watch each video, use the **Questions for Reflection** to guide your thoughts and note taking for personal use and group discussion.
4. Discuss your answers to the questions about each video with classmates.

Video: Teacher Discussion of Moon Phase Lessons

Overview

In this video we listen to the two fourth- and fifth-grade teachers we saw in the moon phase videos of Chapter 3 as they reflect on what they were trying to accomplish in the moon phase lessons.

Questions for Reflection

1. What examples of student records of observations do you see in the investigations of moon phases?

2. What evidence do you see that the 5-E model (or a similar model) forms the structure for the moon phase lessons?

Videos: Investigating Goldfish, Parts 1, 2, 3, and 4

The first three videos in the *Investigating Goldfish* video set follow kindergarten students as they investigate goldfish. In the fourth part, the classroom teacher reflects on her purposes for the lesson and the children's investigations. In this part, the teacher also discusses how the goldfish lesson followed the 5-E model of inquiry instruction.

Questions for Reflection

1. What Connecticut standards does the kindergarten teacher say the science lessons emphasize?
2. What questions did the teacher ask to engage the children in inquiry?
3. During the explore phase, what observations of the goldfish were made in response to the questions from the engage phase?
4. What conclusions about goldfish did the children reach in the explain phase of the lesson? What was the basis for the children's explanations?
5. How well do you think the teacher followed the 5-E model in designing and implementing the goldfish lesson?

Annenberg Videos

Video Series: Science K–6: Investigating Classrooms

Video: Completing the Circuit

To access Annenberg videos, follow the instructions given in the Online Professional Development section in Chapter 1 on page 26.

5

Teachers are designers. An essential act of our profession is the design of curriculum and learning experiences to meet specified purposes. . . . We are not free to teach any topic we choose. Rather, we are guided by national, state, district, or institutional standards that specify what students should know and be able to do. These standards provide a framework to help us identify teaching and learning priorities and guide our design of curriculum and assessments.

(Wiggins & McTighe, 1998, pp. 7–8)

Planning and Managing Inquiry Instruction

BY DESCRIBING THE CONCEPTUAL knowledge and understandings, inquiry abilities, and understandings about the nature of science and science inquiry that children at different grade levels should learn, national and state standards provide a framework for instruction. Teachers, then, are responsible for selecting science content to be learned, developing lesson plans, and implementing them effectively to help students attain goals specified in the standards. Further, teachers plan how to group students for instruction, establish safety rules, and plan and implement fair and effective behavior management procedures that will help establish positive learning environments for students.

In Chapter 4, we showed you a 5-E lesson plan on electrical circuits. This chapter explores how you can develop your own instructional plans. We also discuss ways of organizing your class for instruction, deciding on safety rules and practices to emphasize, and managing student activities during instruction.

As you study this chapter and continue to build your background for teaching science, think about the following questions:

* *How can you select science content topics that are aligned with national and state standards?*

* *How can you develop and write learning objectives?*

* *How can you create and sequence activities that engage students in meaningful learning? How will you design the introductory activities so they initiate the lesson, establish focus questions, and pique the interest of children? How will you design activities for the body of the lesson that enable students to attain learning objectives?*

* *What will you attend to in designing assessments of student understanding?*

* *How can you effectively design the learning environment and group students for learning?*

* *What safety precautions should you and your students take in doing science?*

* *What strategies will you use to manage student behavior?*

* *How can you bring it all together to implement effective science instruction in your own classroom?*

Planning Science Lessons

In this chapter we emphasize these generic steps in planning well-designed science lessons:

- Select science content to be learned that is consistent with state or national content standards.
- Write learning objectives.
- Develop learning activities that enable students to achieve the objectives. Describe these activities in writing.
- Plan assessment tasks and procedures.

The accompanying NSES box summarizes some of the program standards related to planning and implementing science lessons.

Select Science Content to Be Taught and Learned

You can review the *National Science Education Standards* online. Go to http://www.nap.edu/readingroom/books/nses/html. Click on Chapter 6: Science Content Standards. A synopsis of content standards is available on the PALS (Performance Assessment Links in Science) website at http://pals.sri.com.

National standards in science are designed to specify broad goals but do not inform teachers specifically of what to teach. Usually specific content to be learned will be presented in state frameworks or district curriculum guides. These documents are typically developed based on the national standards and other resources, such as the *Benchmarks for Science Literacy* (American Association for the Advancement of Science, 1993) and scope and sequence charts of nationally developed science programs and textbook series. Classroom teachers must determine the teaching strategies and sometimes instructional materials suitable for enabling their students to master the required content.

As an example of how standards can guide the selection of science topics, consider Figure 5-1. This figure provides a list of NSES content standards and related concepts and principles on the topic of sound. The concepts and principles on sound are much more specific than is usually the case for other science topics. State standards are often more detailed than national standards. For example, many states include indicators that give specific concepts and principles to be learned and assessed relative to each science topic.

The FOSS (Full Option Science System) teachers' guide for *The Physics of Sound* (Full Option Science System, 2000) provides an excellent model to follow in selecting your own

 NSES

According to the program standards of the *National Science Education Standards*:

- All students, regardless of gender, cultural or ethnic background, physical or learning disabilities, or future aspirations, should have the opportunity to experience the richness and excitement of knowing about and understanding the natural world.
- Clear goals and expectations for students must be used to guide the design, implementation, and assessment of all elements of the science program.
- Science content should be embedded in curriculum patterns and activities that are developmentally appropriate, interesting, and relevant to students' lives.
- The science program must emphasize inquiring into and understanding natural phenomena and science-related social issues.
- The science program should connect to other subjects.

NSES SCIENCE CONTENT STANDARDS

Science Content Knowledge Standards: Sound

As a result of their science activities, all students should develop an understanding of:

- Position and motion of objects (sound) (K–4)
- Sound as a form of energy (5–8)
- Transfer of energy (5–8)

Fundamental Concepts and Principles on Sound

As a result of their science activities, all students should develop an understanding of fundamental concepts and principles underlying the knowledge standards:

- Sound is produced by vibrating objects (K–4)
- The pitch of a sound can be varied by changing the rate of vibration (K–4)
- Vibrations in materials set up wavelike disturbances that spread away from the source. Sound waves and earthquake waves are examples. These and other waves move at different speeds in different materials. (*Benchmarks for Science Literacy,* 6–8)

Scientific Inquiry Standards

As a result of their science activities, all students should develop abilities to:

- Ask a question about objects, organisms, and events in the environment.
- Plan and conduct a simple investigation.
- Use appropriate tools and techniques to gather data.
- Use evidence and scientific knowledge to develop explanations.
- Communicate investigations, data, and explanations to others.

Figure 5-1 What students are expected to learn about sound in grades K–4 and 5–8, according to the *National Science Education Standards.*

content that fits state and national standards. This module is designed for grades 3 and 4. It focuses on this content:

- What the characteristics of sound are;
- What causes sound: vibrating sources;
- How sound travels;
- Where sound comes from, how it is transferred through various materials, and how it is received;
- How we hear sounds.

These topics of sound can be expanded into content descriptions, objectives, and lesson activities.

The Physics of Sound Module includes lessons with content descriptions, objectives, and instructional plans. Even if teachers are not using the commercial module, these topics provide a good outline of concepts that should be included.

Developing Teachers' Knowledge of Science. Teachers often feel that their science background is inadequate. But you do not need to be a science major to teach science effectively. Truth be known, many experienced teachers of science began to really understand science topics only after teaching them.

To develop your own background knowledge on a science topic you will be teaching, you should:

The federal government often funds programs at universities and colleges for teachers of science and mathematics at every level. A typical program focuses on a narrow range of content and uses hands-on approaches. Funds for tuition, fees, and books, abundant teaching materials, stipends, and expenses to a state science conference are often provided for teacher participants. We urge you to take advantage of these professional development opportunities. They are not only educational— they are great fun.

- Read widely, including textbook chapters, teachers' guides for nationally funded science projects, and especially books written for children; but be aware that children's books sometimes provide inaccurate information.
- Use an Internet search engine such as Google or Yahoo! to locate appropriate science content discussions.
- Talk to other teachers and science education specialists.
- Attend college courses and institutes for teachers.
- Attend relevant sessions at national, regional, and state conferences for science teachers.
- Visit websites of science education professional organizations such as http://www.nsta.org.

When you have selected standards-based science content to be learned and understand that content yourself, you are ready to begin to develop and write objectives.

Write Appropriate Objectives

In planning for instruction, you must translate content descriptions into instructional objectives. Instructional objectives are specific intended learning outcomes. Clear objectives aid teachers in planning instructional activities and choosing instructional approaches. They serve as a guide in the process of teaching and facilitate the assessment of student learning. They also make clear to students the specific performances you will expect from them.

The ABCs of Objectives. An instructional objective typically contains three main components: the audience, the behavior, and the conditions. In these ABCs of objectives, the *audience* identifies who will be expected to achieve the objective, such as learners or students. The audience is often specified in a phrase placed before a list of objectives, such as, "Through the experiences of this lesson, the students will be able to." Here, the audience is "the students."

The *behavior* identifies the specific type of performance that will be expected of students and what actions they will be expected to take. Action words such as *compute, compare, identify, demonstrate,* and *predict* identify specific behaviors to be demonstrated by students. Table 5-1 defines several action words denoting different types of performances that are particularly useful for science instruction. Although objectives might be described in terms of specific behaviors, collectively they are intended to indicate understanding.

The *conditions* for an instructional objective specify the "givens"—that is, what the learner will have access to, if anything, in demonstrating the expected performance. For example, in the objective "*Given an array of boxes, cans, strings, rubber bands, etc., construct a simple stringed instrument,*" the material supplies available are the conditions.

The quality of performance that will be expected of students is sometimes stated within the objective, but more often today it is given in the assessment plan for the lesson. How to design assessment plans is considered later in this chapter.

As an example for your use, Figure 5-2 provides a list of instructional objectives for a third grade lesson on sound.

A glossary of definitions for important terms used in this chapter can be found on MyEducationLab.

TABLE 5-1   SOME ACTION WORDS ESPECIALLY USEFUL IN WRITING COGNITIVE OBJECTIVES FOR SCIENCE LESSONS

Cognitive Processes	Action Words
Remembering	**Identify.** To select (by pointing to, touching, or picking up) the correct object or designating the object property, in response to its name.
	Name. To supply the correct name for an object, property, or event.
	Define. To state the meaning of a term.
	State. To make a verbal statement that conveys a fact, concept, principle, or procedure.
Doing	**Distinguish.** To show how objects or events that might be confused are different.
	Describe. To give details of objects' properties, sequences of events, or relationships in a situation.
	Compare. To note similarities and differences among two or more things.
Understanding	**Classify.** To place objects into groups based on common properties.
	Interpret. To express the meaning, in one's own words, of a concept, principle, or model; or to find and express patterns and relationships in data.
	Explain. To draw conclusions about relationships involved in an event, giving special attention to links between observational evidence and prior knowledge that serve to support the conclusions.
	Apply. To use a concept, principle, or procedure to derive an answer to a question or problem.
	Demonstrate. To perform the operations involved in a given procedure, such as using instruments, collecting and organizing data, or carrying out a controlled investigation.

At the conclusion of the activities on sound, students will be able to:

1. *Ask* questions about sound, *plan* investigations, *collect* data, *record* data, *form* simple explanations, and *report* investigations and findings to the class.
2. *State, explain, and demonstrate* that all sound originates in vibrating sources.
3. *Given an array of boxes, cans, strings, rubber bands, etc., construct* a simple stringed instrument.
4. *Identify* the vibrating source of sound in each constructed musical instrument.
5. Given different sounds, *distinguish* between the pitch and loudness of the sounds.
6. *Demonstrate* and *explain* the production of different pitches of sound using the instrument.
7. *State* and *explain* that pitch is related to how fast or slow a sound source vibrates.
8. *Describe* the outer ear and *explain* its role in receiving sounds.
9. *Demonstrate appreciation* of the importance of safety rules related to hearing and sound through consistently *practicing* them.
10. *Show respect* for partners when working in cooperative groups by taking turns and by listening attentively and responding courteously to their ideas and suggestions.

Figure 5-2 Sample instructional objectives for lessons on sound at about grades 3–5.

Activity 5-1: Selecting and Writing Appropriate Objectives

1. Study the following lesson activity.
2. Write a set of learning objectives that fit the activity. Follow the guidelines for writing objectives given in this chapter. Be sure to include objectives related to conceptual understanding, inquiry abilities, and safety where appropriate.
3. Share and discuss your instructional objectives with a group of your classmates.

Sample Lesson Activity

Fourth graders constructed electromagnets by wrapping many turns of wire around a large iron core consisting of a nail or bolt. They connected the bare ends of the wire to a battery. The teacher cautioned the children not to leave the connection in place for very long as there were no bulbs or motors in the circuit, and the battery would run down within a few seconds.

The children learned to test the strength of their electromagnets by counting how many paper clips they could pick up. Noticing that some electromagnets picked up more paper clips than others, the children asked why was this so?

Through discussion, teacher guidance, and some direct instruction, the students theorized that the type of iron core, the number of turns of wire, and the number of batteries used determined an electromagnet's strength. The children designed and conducted a controlled investigation to test their theories. They concluded that all three of the variables made a difference in the strength of the electromagnet.

Activity 5-1 is designed to help you improve your ability to write learning objectives related to an inquiry science lesson. Spend some time with this activity before reading on.

Select and Design Lesson Activities

When you have selected content to be learned, checked its alignment with standards, and written clear instructional objectives, you are ready to develop lesson activities. In designing lesson activities, teachers determine what specific learning experiences relate to the content, lead to the attainment of specified objectives, and promote interest and understanding. Many good examples of science learning activities have been provided in the lessons and lesson plans described in previous chapters. Table 5-2 describes the content description, objectives, and synopsis of activities for the FOSS unit on sound.

Good lessons begin with good introductions.

Introduction to the Lessons. Introductory activities should be designed to engage the students in an activity or lesson. Consistent with the engage phase of the 5-E model, introductory activities should be designed to:

- create a "hook" that draws in the students,
- relate abstract academic knowledge to familiar experiences,
- motivate students,
- assess prior knowledge and identify current conceptions, and most importantly,
- engage students in a question that can be investigated.

TABLE 5-2   CONTENT, OBJECTIVES, AND ACTIVITIES FOR THE FOSS (FULL OPTION SCIENCE SYSTEM) MODULE ON THE PHYSICS OF SOUND

Science Content Description	Science Objectives	Synopsis of Activities
1. Characteristics and Causes of Sound • Objects can be identified by the sounds they make when dropped. • Sounds have identifiable characteristics. • Sounds can convey information. • Sound is caused by vibrations. • A sound source is an object that is vibrating. • A sound receiver detects sound vibrations.	Students should be able to: • *Describe* sounds made by objects when dropped. • *Communicate* with others using a code. • *Compare* sounds to develop discrimination.	**Dropping In** Students explore their ability to discriminate between sounds, by dropping objects into a drop chamber and identifying each object by the property of its sound. They develop a code by assigning letters to objects and send messages to one another by using their drop code.
2. Pitch and Vibrating Sources • Sound originates from vibrating sources. • Pitch is how high or low a sound is. • Differences in pitch are caused by differences in the rate at which objects vibrate. • Several variables affect pitch, including size (length) and tension of the source material.	Students should be able to: • *Demonstrate* that sound originates from a vibrating source. • *Compare* high-, low-, and medium-pitched sounds. • *Record* observations on sound. • *Relate* the pitch of a sound to the physical properties of the sound source.	**Good Vibrations** Students explore sound generators and musical instruments in mini-activities to find out what causes sound and what changes the pitch. They investigate variables that affect changes in pitch: the length of vibrating objects and the tension on vibrating strings.
3. How Sound Travels • Sound vibrations need a medium to travel. • Sound travels through solids, water, and air. • Sound that is directed travels better through air. • Our outer ears are designed to receive, focus, and amplify sounds.	Students should be able to: • *Describe* evidence that sound travels through solids, water, and air. • *Compare* how sound travels through different mediums. • *Record* observations on sound.	**How Sound Travels** Students work in collaborative groups on mini-activities that introduce a sound source and a medium of sound travel. They observe and compare how sound travels through solids, water, and air.
4. Sources, Mediums, and Receivers of Sound • Several variables affect pitch, including size (length), tension, and thickness of the source material. • Sound can be directed through air, water, or solids to the sound receivers. • The medium that sound passes through affects its volume and the distance at which it can be heard.	Students should be able to: • *Describe* the outer ear and *explain* that it is designed to receive sounds. • *Compare* different ways of amplifying sounds and making them travel longer distances. • *Record* observations of how sound travels. • *Report* findings in a class presentation.	**Sound Challenges** Students investigate the nature of our sound receivers, ears. They are challenged to put their knowledge of sound sources, sound travel, and sound receivers to work. They take one of the instruments they used earlier and change its pitch, make its sound travel farther, or make it louder.

Source: Adapted from FOSS® (Full Option Science System®) Physics of Sound, Overview. © The Regents of the University of California and published by Delta Education. Adapted with permission.

Introductory activities should be brief. Your goal is to open a door to learning. As soon as possible, escort your students through the door by moving on to the next sequence of activities. In the electric circuits lesson of Chapter 4, for example, the teacher told a story to engage the students. The story served as a good focus, but it was the hands-on investigations of batteries and bulbs that really served as the "hook."

A variety of introductory activities can be designed for science lessons. For example, to introduce lessons on weather, you might show brief segments of videos illustrating different weather conditions, including rain, snow, and violent winds. Include a video segment of a person measuring and recording weather factors and conditions and a segment of a TV weathercast. One purpose of the video segments is to bring the abstract topic of a school lesson into the familiar and interesting world of the student.

To stimulate discussion, ask such questions as: *What is weather? What factors are important in producing weather? How are these various factors measured? How are they used in predicting the weather?* In guiding discussion, be generally accepting of students' answers, recording them in your own notes and/or on the chalkboard. Remember that the purposes of the introductory activities are to engage the students in the content and skills to be learned, to create interest, to motivate, to determine prior knowledge, and to establish a question for investigation. There will be plenty of opportunities in later activities for students to confront and clear up misconceptions and construct new knowledge and understandings.

As another example, to introduce a series of lessons on food chemistry, you might ask: *What is healthy eating? Do foods that are good for you have to taste "yucky"?* (Wiggins & McTighe, 1998).

Because they usually fascinate students and enable you to probe what students already know and what they think, *discrepant events* make excellent introductory activities.

Discrepant Events. A discrepant event is some scientific phenomenon that has a surprising or unusual outcome for students to consider. Discrepant events may be demonstrated by the teacher, presented by video, or embedded within student activities. As an example, Activity 5-2 shows a puzzling discrepant-event, *The Floating Coin*, that can serve as an activity for lessons on light refraction. Try this activity for yourself before reading on. Why do you think the coin appears to float into view?

Activity 5-2: The Floating Coin

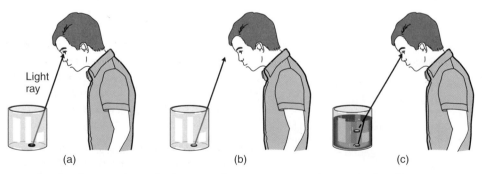

Light ray

(a)   (b)   (c)

1. Anchor a coin to the bottom of an opaque container as in the illustrations.
2. Stand directly above the coin so that you can see it from above.
3. Step back gradually so the coin is just out of sight.
4. Ask another person to slowly pour water into the container. What do you see happening? (The coin will slowly appear to float into view.)
5. Why do you think this happens?

INVESTIGATING AQUATIC LIFE

Structure and Function

When you visit a public aquarium, observe the wide diversity of aquatic life. Notice how the different aquatic animals move, such as fish, jellies, and sea turtles. For example, sea turtles use their flippers to move forward, backward, and turn. Fish have caudal fins, dorsal fins, pelvic or ventral fins, and pectoral fins. Many fish swim forward by moving their *caudal fins* back and forth. They maneuver up and down by moving their *dorsal fins* and *pelvic* or *ventral fins*. They turn to the right or left by using their *pectoral* fins. Watch the fish closely to see how they use their fins in swimming.

Fish are adapted to living in water. Aquatic animals still need oxygen. Fish obtain oxygen through their *gills*, which take in water and filter out oxygen trapped in the water. Sea turtles are actually reptiles; they have no gills and must surface from time to time to obtain oxygen from the atmosphere.

A large school of multicolored fish swims by in an exhibit at Georgia Aquarium, Atlanta.

What do you observe in this photo about the fin structure of a fish?

How do you think jellies propel themselves in water?

Aquatic animals, such as this octopus at the South Carolina Aquarium in Charleston, seek protection in the nooks and crannies of corals.

Habitats

Aquariums provide habitats for a wide variety of aquatic life. A *habitat* is a place where animals or plants live. Aquatic habitats must provide food, shelter, and protection. Aquariums offer many examples of aquatic habitats and the animals or plants that are at home in them. With the wide variety of aquatic life and habitats available for you and your students to study, aquariums make wonderful places for field trips for science classes.

Coral Reefs. Many aquariums display coral reef habitats and the array of life in and around them. Corals are tiny animals that live in colonies that create complex structures resembling branching antlers, brains, knobby fingers, dinner plates, or giant fans. Reef animals find food and shelter within the nooks, crevices, crannies, and caves of the complicated coral structures. Sponges, anemones, and clams attach themselves to the coral surfaces and rocks they need to survive. Snails, shrimp, lobsters, sea stars, and crabs travel over and through the reef searching for food or shelter. Colorful fish swirl over and around the more sedentary inhabitants. The coral reef is a fragile world susceptible to destructive natural and human-made forces.

An Oil Platform Habitat. The Texas State Aquarium on the Texas Gulf Coast displays a model of a habitat formed from the bare steel legs of an abandoned oil platform. This habitat supports an amazing variety of life.

Preserving Biodiversity

Through different activities, people often cause permanent disruption or destruction of oceanic animal and plant communities and their habitats. Some important activities contributing to these changes are pollution, commercial fishing, physical alterations to the coasts, introduction of nonnative species, and human factors contributing to global climate change. The result is a serious decline in the abundance of most species of preferred edible fish and shellfish, reductions (or the total loss) of species, reduced aesthetic and recreational value of coastal habitats, unpredictable and serious changes to the structures and functions of ecosystems, and potentially harmful effects on human health and well-being.

What can you do to help reserve the biodiversity of our oceans, lakes, ponds, rivers, and streams?

An abandoned oil platform serves as a dynamic habitat for diverse aquatic life, Texas State Aquarium, Corpus Christi.

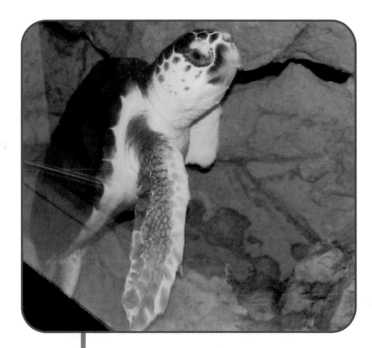

What are some differences you notice between sea turtles and land turtles?

How does coloration, as shown in an exhibit at the Texas State Aquarium, Corpus Christi, help preserve the life of aquatic animals?

Some Questions to Guide Student Observations

- Can you find fish seeking protection through their coloration?
- Can you find fish seeking protection in the nooks, crannies, and caves of coral habitats in the aquarium tanks?
- How are the "models" of ocean habitats displayed in the large aquarium like the real thing? How are they different?

An abundance of colorful life forms is found in the world's oceans and in the exhibits at public aquariums, such as this at Georgia Aquarium.

A few raisins placed in a glass of clear, carbonated soda water create a "raisin elevator."

Here is an explanaton of the floating coin phenomenon.

- Light ordinarily travels in straight lines.
- In refraction, light rays bend as they go from one medium, such as water, to another medium, such as air.
- Light refracts or bends outward when it goes from water into air.
- As the light rays reflected from the coin emerge from the water, they bend outward and follow a new path that carries them to your eyes.
- The illusion created is that the light rays followed a straight-line path and came directly from a coin floating high in the water.

After doing the activity and observing the phenomenon, ask students to discuss what they saw and their theories and explanations of why the coin floated into view. Use the discrepant event activity to assess students' prior knowledge. In the activities that follow in the explore and explain phases of inquiry, you can build on student ideas, investigations, and developing concepts and principles to construct an explanation of the floating coin phenomenon.

Activity 5-3 shows another example of a discrepant event, *The Raisin Elevator*. This novel event is sure to be interesting and puzzling to children. Try this activity yourself before reading further.

Activity 5-3: The Raisin Elevator

- Place a few raisins in a glass of clear, carbonated soda water. Shelled peanuts also work fine for this activity.
- Wait a minute or so.
- What do you observe?
- How would you explain the "raisin elevator" phenomenon?
- What scientific concepts and principles did you use in your explanation?

Have you formed an explanation about the phenomenon in Activity 5-3? Did you observe that the raisins initially sink to the bottom and then rise to the top of the liquid, stay a moment, then descend once more, only to rise again? How did you explain this phenomenon? If you had appropriate prior experiences and scientific knowledge about floating and sinking, you might have inferred that the raisins were initially too heavy for their size to float and, thus, sank. As the raisins sank, air bubbles became attached to them. The air bubbles served to buoy up the raisins.

Explanations in science need to be checked out through further observations and investigations. By looking very carefully, perhaps with a magnifying lens, children can watch the bubbles attaching themselves to the raisins when they are at the bottom of the carbonated drink and popping when the raisins reach the surface.

Use a Variety of Lesson Activities. Activities are learning experiences that enable students to attain the specified instructional objectives. Activities are at the core of science lessons. If you are using the 5-E model, activities appropriate for explore (data gathering), explain (interpretation), and elaborate (extension and transfer) phases should be selected here. Look again at Table 5-2 for an example of good lesson activities from the FOSS module on sound. Note especially how the lesson activities are aligned with instructional objectives.

A wide variety of activities you can include in your lesson plan are given in various science activity sources. *Activities for Teaching Science as Inquiry,* the companion volume to this book, contains about 140 activities related to more than 30 science topics. Elementary textbook series, kit-based science programs, and other books and documents provide access to a wide range of activities.

There are hundreds, if not thousands, of activities available on the Internet. But a word of caution is in order. Many of the Internet science activities, and some published traditionally, are merely "show and tell" or "vocabulary drill" activities. They are not designed to lead students to develop conceptual understanding and inquiry abilities. However, you can modify almost any science activity to make it more inquiry and constructivist oriented.

Although hands-on inquiry activities are essential in science learning, this does not mean that every science lesson activity must have students handle science materials and generate new data. Your lesson activities should include a variety of teaching and learning approaches, including listening and speaking, reading and writing, research in books and the Internet, and watching as well as doing. Films and videos, books, research reports, use of Internet sources, existing data sets, and field trips, including virtual field trips presented through websites, can also provide excellent learning opportunities for students.

But over the long term be sure that your lesson plans provide opportunities for students to learn inquiry skills through their own activities and better understand the nature of science and scientific inquiry.

Activities to Develop Inquiry Abilities. Exploration activities that incorporate *descriptive, classificatory,* and/or *experimental investigations* are ideal for developing inquiry abilities. But almost any activity that follows an inquiry or 5-E teaching approach can build inquiry abilities as well as conceptual understanding. For example, the electricity lessons of Chapter 4 do not use the investigational strategies introduced in Chapter 2, but they help students build inquiry abilities and understandings.

Open inquiries represent another type of activity that might be included in a lesson.

Open Inquiry Activities. In open inquiry, the teacher may provide the problem and materials for students but then allow them time and freedom to simply "mess about." In the 5-E

Many of the nearly 150 science activities in *Activities for Teaching Science as Inquiry* feature discrepant events, especially at the engage phase of inquiry. More examples of discrepant events for elementary science are given at:
http://tiger.coe.missouri.edu/ ~pgermann/DiscEvent/
http://physics.unco.edu/ sced441/demos99.pdf
Enter "discrepant events science" into a search engine for more examples of discrepant events.

model of instruction, this typically occurs in the explore stage. For example, you might give cooperative groups of students soft drink bottles and pitchers of water (and newspapers and plenty of paper towels to mop up spills). You might then ask the groups to discover what they can do to change the pitch of the sounds produced with the bottles. In producing sounds, some groups might try to strike the bottles with a wooden object. Others might blow across the open ends of the bottles. As they try different things, students may discover that putting different amounts of water in the bottles changes the pitch produced by their actions on the bottles.

After allowing students to explore for some time, collect the equipment and discuss with the students what they discovered. Students might also write in their journals and read about wind instruments, such as horns and flutes.

In classrooms where students actively engage in inquiry, learning centers can be a good way to present activities.

Science Learning Centers. Learning centers are created and directed by the teacher for independent activities of students. They can motivate, guide, and support the learning of individuals and small groups. Science learning centers will better enable you to meet individual needs and provide students with self-directed learning opportunities. They can also encourage student responsibility.

There are various types of science learning centers. A guided discovery learning center involves students in developing a better understanding of specific science concepts. For example, place materials in shoe boxes with a series of guiding questions on cards for students to read. An example of a question to guide activities on light at the learning center is: "How can you use a flashlight and the cards in the box to show that light appears to travel in a straight line?" Include a flashlight and a number of blank index cards with 1 cm holes punched in the center of each card. Children should discover that light from the flashlight will pass through the holes in the center of the cards only if they are all aligned as in Figure 5-3. This provides evidence that light travels in straight lines.

Field Trips. Field trips to zoos, discovery centers, museums, public aquariums, planetariums, natural areas, and even the school playground provide wonderful opportunities to create interest and serve as rich learning experiences for students. An important part of any field trip is the advance preparation that takes place in the classroom before the trip. Teachers should plan in advance for field trips, developing instructional objectives, well-planned learning activities for students before, during, and after the trip, and relevant assessments. Often discovery institutions have science educators on staff who can provide materials and assist in planning.

The accompanying photo essay on investigating aquatic life provides some examples of how students can get the most out of a field trip.

See Chapter 8 for a discussion of virtual field trips presented through Internet websites.

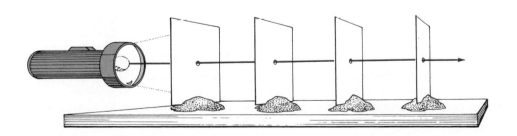

Figure 5-3 How does this activity show that light travels in straight lines?

Designing Assessment Experiences

In developing lesson plans, teachers should use both formative (ongoing assessments) and summative (end of lesson) assessments. As introduced in Chapter 4, *formative assessment* involves gathering assessment information during the process of instruction. A main function of formative assessment is to serve as a basis for adjusting instructional strategies to improve learning. For example, information from formative assessment is important for teachers in determining what kinds of scaffolding assistance to provide for students.

Summative assessment is assessment at the end of lessons or instructional units that provides important information for determining what the students learned and did not learn as a result of instructional activities. Summative assessment provides a basis for feedback to students and for grades and accountability.

Rubrics are often used in assessment of inquiry learning.

Rubrics. A rubric defines several different levels of knowledge and understanding in specific terms. Thus, teachers can use rubrics to specify the ideal levels of learning performance on lesson objectives and assess the actual level of student attainment. The number of levels in a rubric should be based on the needs of your class and your observations of what your students are actually doing in science activities. Four-level rubrics are frequently used.

- Level 3: Advanced, Excellent, Exceeds Expectations
- Level 2: Proficient, Satisfactory, Meets Expectations
- Level 1: Basic, Below Expectations
- Level 0: Unacceptable

Many examples of rubrics are treated in Chapter 6 on assessing science learning. Figure 5-4 shows a sample rubric related to two of the objectives for the sound lesson given in Figure 5-2. This rubric defines the level of expected performance of students on the two objectives.

In the next section, we will see how the different parts of a lesson plan fit together by examining how two preservice teachers developed a lesson plan for teaching a series of activities on floating and sinking to fourth-grade students.

A Lesson Plan on Floating and Sinking

In preparing a series of lessons for fourth graders, one pair of preservice teachers in a science methods class chose to focus on the properties of matter related to whether objects float or sink in a liquid. They were assigned to teach science in a fourth grade class in a rural elementary school. Each of the preservice teachers would be teaching the topic to one-half of the class for 5 days. They had already formed some ideas about the children's prior knowledge and developmental levels based on their experiences observing, assisting, and formatively assessing students in the classroom. They chose to prepare a series of lessons related to whether objects float or sink in a liquid.

In planning, the teachers considered Piaget's work on children's theories of floating and sinking as described in Chapter 3. Although students in grades 3–5 can understand the concrete, qualitative aspects of floating and sinking, it is not until adolescence that they can add numerical considerations about mass, volume, and density to their judgments and explanations. Thus, the preservice teachers chose to focus on the qualitative

Rubric Related to Objectives 3 and 6 of the Sound Unit

Objectives

Objective 3. Given an array of boxes, cans, strings, rubber bands, etc., construct a simple stringed instrument.

Objective 6. Demonstrate and explain the production of different pitches of sound using the instrument.

Criteria	3 Points Advanced	2 Points Meets Expections	1 Point Below Expectations	0 Points Unacceptable
Construction of instrument (Objective 3)	Instrument is sturdy, well constructed with attention to detail.	Instrument is sturdy and neatly constructed.	Instrument is not well constructed, but can be played.	Instrument is not sturdy, falls apart when played.
Demonstration of instrument (Objective 6)	Student plays a recognizable tune on instrument consisting of at least 4 different pitches.	Student plays instrument producing at least 4 different pitches.	Student plays instrument producing 2 or 3 different pitches.	Student plays instrument, but only 1 pitch is demonstrated, or no sound is produced.
Explanation (Objective 6)	Student explains what is vibrating and the relationship between the properties (length, width, tension) of the rubber band and the pitch produced.	Student explains what is vibrating and how the different pitches were produced.	Student attempts to explain how instrument works, but explanation is incomplete.	Student does not explain how different pitches are produced or explanation is incorrect.

Figure 5-4 Rubrics can be used to define the level of expected performance of students.

rule: *Objects float in fresh water if they are not too heavy for their size; objects sink in water if they are too heavy for their size.*

Figure 5-5 provides an outline of the content knowledge and understandings to be developed in the lesson on floating and sinking. Before creating this outline, the preservice teachers consulted a variety of sources, including state frameworks and local curriculum guides, chapters within the science textbook adopted by the local district, the activities sections of science methods textbooks, and lessons developed by national curriculum groups.

They noted in their reading that any explanation of floating and sinking that uses the numerical concept of density (ratio of mass to volume) is generally beyond elementary and middle school children and should be introduced only in grades 8–12.

The preservice teachers focused on grade-level appropriate concepts of weight and volume (size) and the relationship between weight and volume for floating and sinking

Figure 5-5 Content knowledge outline for floating and sinking unit.

I. Floating and sinking
   A. Several variable factors contribute to whether an object floats or sinks:
      1. Volume (size)
      2. Weight
      3. Design
II. Some characteristics that affect floating and sinking can be measured and compared
   A. Volume (size)
   B. Weight
III. Theory/rules for floating and sinking in fresh water
   A. The weight and volume (size) of objects are compared in predicting whether they will float or sink.
   B. Objects float if they are light enough for their size.
   C. Objects sink if they are too heavy for their size.
IV. Investigating boat designs
   A. The buoyant force on a boat is increased when the amount of space of the boat underwater is increased.
   B. Boats can weigh the same but be designed so that they occupy different amounts of space underwater.
   C. Boats that occupy more space underwater can carry the largest cargo.

objects. By considering the design of boats, the content knowledge is expanded, related to technology, and applied to the children's real-world experiences.

Using the outline of content knowledge and understandings as a guide, the preservice teachers could then develop a lesson plan, complete with relevant standards, learning objectives, activities, and assessments. The lesson plan is shown in Figure 5-6. This lesson plan is appropriate for students in about grades 3–5.

Assessment and Evaluation Plan for the Floating and Sinking Lesson

The preservice teachers used a combination of formative and summative strategies to assess conceptual understanding and inquiry abilities of students during the floating and sinking lessons.

In formative assessment of student attainment of the learning objectives on floating and sinking, the teachers listened carefully to student responses to the various questions given in the lesson plan. They noted student performance during hands-on activities and demonstrations and checked students' written work and notebooks.

In summative assessment, the teachers used a rubric (see Figure 5-7) related to the objectives of the clay boat activity. Information gathered through formative assessment was used to provide a basis for scaffolding or feedback to students and to monitor and adjust instruction to improve learning.

As a part of summative assessment, the teachers demonstrated another discrepant event. They placed a can of regular Coke and a can of Diet Coke in a large container of water. The regular Coke sank, but, surprisingly, the Diet Coke can floated.

Before the Coke float demonstration was discussed, the children wrote their explanations for the activity on an assessment sheet. The teachers used a rubric similar to the one in Figure 5-7 to evaluate the children's explanations in terms of how they used concepts of *weight* and *size* to explain why one can floated and the other can sank. After the written explanations were collected, the group discussed the demonstration and how the floating and sinking rules applied. The can of Diet Coke floated because it was lighter, although

Details of the Coke float activity are given on pages A-186 and A-187 in *Activities for Teaching Science as Inquiry*. The emphasis of the activity in that section is on the sugar content of diet and regular soft drinks.

Instructional Objectives

As a result of the lessons on floating and sinking, students should be able to:

1. Demonstrate inquiry abilities, including asking questions, conducting investigations, and using observational evidence and science knowledge to construct logical explanations and communicate their findings.
2. Design and construct a clay boat that floats and holds as much cargo as possible.
3. Distinguish between size and weight.
4. Identify size and weight as variables related to the floating and sinking of clay boats.
5. Demonstrate ability to coordinate size and weight of floating and sinking objects by stating and applying the following rules.
   - Objects sink in water if they are too heavy for their size.
   - Objects float in water if they are light enough for their size.
6. Explain how the floating and sinking rules apply to clay boats and golf ball "floaters."

Activities and Procedures

1. **Engage.** Introduce the lesson by demonstrating the raisin elevator discrepant event.

   Ask: *Why do you think the raisin descended in the bottle and then rose to the surface again?* Ask more generally: *What factors do you think determine whether or not an object floats in water? How could we find out?* Note explanations, ideas, and prior knowledge of students, but do not provide any explanation at this point.

2. **Explore.** Arrange class in teams of two. Set up stations around the room, with objects that float and objects that sink at each station. Place a container of water at each station. Direct students to move in orderly fashion from station to station. Also, tell them to make predictions about whether objects will float or sink and give a reasonable basis for the predictions in each case. Provide a record sheet for students to record their predictions, explanations, and test results. Encourage students to go beyond experience to consider the variable attributes of the objects.
   - Place a different array of objects at each station.
   - At one station, include a number of centimeter-gram cubes, cubes that have a mass of 1 gram and are 1 cm on a side and thus have a volume of 1 cc.
   - At another station include two golf balls, one that floats and one that sinks in fresh water.

3. **Explain.** Ask: *What observations did you make at each station? In general, how did you decide whether an object would float or sink? Why did the cubes float just under the surface of the liquid? What would happen to a cube if you added a bit of clay to it and placed it in the container of water?* (Try it and see.) *Why did one golf ball float and the other one sink?*
   - Solicit student ideas and discuss them. Ask students to compare results and to give their own theories/ideas about why objects float or sink.
   - At some point, teach the two qualitative rules for floating and sinking by direct instruction. Write the rules on the chalkboard. Discuss with the students how the rules apply in each case they encountered.
   - Lead the children to suggest that one golf ball may have been lighter than the other. Ask: *How can we test this idea?* The explanation might be tested by comparing the weight of the two golf balls with a balance scale. Carry out the test.

4. **Elaborate.** Give each group two same size lumps of clay about 3 or 4 cm in diameter. Ask: *How can you design and construct a clay boat that floats and holds a large cargo of pennies?*
   - Each team designs and constructs two clay boats and tests them in the classroom "lake." If a boat floats, load it with pennies one by one until the boat sinks. Promote a competition in which the winning boat supports the largest number of pennies.
   - Guide students to talk about their boat designs and results. Note particularly any mention of the size or weight of the boat. Ask: *How do the floating and sinking rules apply to the clay boats?* Lead the students to recognize that the boats that supported the most cargo were those with the greatest effective size—that is, boats that floated with more of their volume under water.

5. **Evaluate.** See the accompanying assessment plan.

Figure 5-6 A lesson plan on floating and sinking.

Objectives

Students should be able to:

2. Design and construct a clay boat that floats and holds as much cargo as possible.

5. Explain how floating and sinking rules apply to clay boats of different designs.

Criteria	3 Points	2 Points	1 Point	0 Points
Design and Construction (Objective 2)	Boat is well designed and constructed and holds at least 25 pennies	Boat is well designed and holds at least 15 pennies, but has some flaws that limit cargo	Boat has major flaws	No boat constructed
Explanation (Objective 5)	Student clearly explains that the boat floats until the weight of the cargo becomes too heavy in relation to the size of the boat	Student uses notion of the size of the boat and the weight of the cargo in explaining floating and sinking, but explanation has some flaws	Unsatisfactory explanation of the role of size and weight in whether the boat floats or sinks	No attempt to explain floating and sinking of the clay boat

Figure 5-7   Rubric for assessing student performance and understanding on clay boats objectives.

Go to the Homework and Exercises section in Chapter 5 of MyEducationLab to watch the set of videos entitled *Pinhole Cameras: Parts 1, 2,* and *3.* In this series of videos we see fifth-grade children constructing pinhole viewers. We also see how the children used the pin-hole viewers to observe, then generalizing about images seen when the viewers are pointed at illuminated arrows. Further, you can examine how the structure of the pin-hole viewer lessons is consistent with the principles presented in this chapter. A video guide for these videos is provided in the Online Professional Development section at the end of the chapter.

the two cans had the same volume. Regular Coke contains sugar, making it heavier than an equal volume of Diet Coke. The students compared the weights of the two cans on a balance scale. If children wished to, they were allowed to write revised explanations.

Throughout the lessons, the teachers took opportunities to read to the children about and discuss boats, submarines, life preservers, and other real-world experiences related to floating and sinking.

The preservice teachers' lesson plans were well designed and assisted them immensely as they taught. Keep in mind, however, that lesson plans are not scripts, and even the very best set of activities must be adjusted to your own objectives, the needs of the children, and classroom facilities.

Now let's turn to how you can best manage your classroom for inquiry learning and teaching.

Managing Inquiry Instruction and Learning

Establishing a classroom learning environment focused on learning with understanding is a critical factor for effective inquiry instruction. Research indicates that learning with understanding is enhanced when students are grouped in ways that provide them opportunities to discuss their investigations, findings, and conclusions with one another and with the teacher (Duschl et al., 2007).

Grouping Students for Learning

Expert teachers use a variety of classroom arrangements for science and other subjects. These include (Lowery, 1998):

- *Whole class structure* (e.g., the teacher lectures, demonstrates, or guides the whole class in discussion),
- *Cooperative group structure* (e.g., students in small groups cooperatively collect data, organize it, exchange ideas, and arrive at collaborative conclusions),
- *Pair structure* (e.g., two students work together to construct an explanation of some action in a demonstration), and
- *Individual structure* (e.g., each student works individually on an investigation, collecting data, recording it in a science journal, and answering relevant questions).

Cooperative groups—small groups of students working cooperatively—are especially important in contemporary upper elementary and middle school science classrooms. At the primary level, pairs often are more appropriate than small groups.

Whether working cooperatively or in small groups, students consider problems and assignments together, verbalize what they know, consider the multiple viewpoints of group members, collect data together, learn from one another, and come up with group solutions to problems. These group processes are the kinds of student interactions that help establish *communities of learners* in which students have opportunities to learn from and teach each other. The concept and rationale for communities of learners was discussed in Chapter 3.

Cooperative groups might be formed from children who sit near one another. More strategically, heterogeneous grouping strategies are often used. Heterogeneous grouping is used to maximize variety within groups. Factors considered in heterogeneous grouping include achievement or ability, interests, learning styles, ethnic or cultural background, age, attitude toward subject matter, and leadership ability (Watson & Marshall, 1995).

In addition to encouraging cooperative learning, using cooperative teams can facilitate classroom management by providing for group sharing of limited science materials and giving students responsibility to manage materials.

Pair structures often provide for more interaction between students. Some teachers use a *think-pair-share* strategy to lead students to express their own ideas and learn from one another, Jones and Carter (1997) described a verbal interaction between a pair of fifth- grade boys, in which one of the boys assisted the other in understanding written directions about a lever activity. The goal of the activity was to formulate a generalization about how to get a crossbar to balance. Larry was confused about the task:

> Larry: Do we place the three blocks on the same side of this thing?
> Billy: No, we are supposed to figure out how to balance these two blocks using this other block.
> Larry: How do we know when it is balanced?
> Billy: The lever will be straight out. Neither side of the lever will be touching the table. That means it's balanced. (p. 265)

In this exchange, Billy provided Larry with an interpretation of the problem and the meaning of the term *balance*, which enabled Larry to proceed toward constructing generalizations.

Figure 5-8 Possible cooperative learning group job assignments and functions.

- **Principal Investigator.** In charge of team operations including checking assignments, seeing that all team members participate in activities, and leading group discussions.
- **Materials Manager.** Gets and inventories materials and distributes them to the team.
- **Recorder/Reporter.** Collects and records data on lab sheets and reports results to whole class orally or in writing on class summary chart posted on chalkboard.
- **Maintenance Director.** With the assistance of other team members, cleans up and returns materials and equipment to their appropriate storage space or container. Directs the disposal of used materials and is responsible for team members' safety.

Source: Richard M. Jones. (1990, December). *Teaming Up! The Inquiry Task Group Management System User's Guide.* LaPorte, Texas: ITGROUP.

A cooperative group structure might involve specific roles for group members, such as Principal Investigator (PI), Recorder/Reporter, Materials Manager, and Maintenance Director (see Figure 5-8). However groups are organized, students should share responsibilities within a small group. Throughout the year, each student should have an opportunity to take the responsibilities required of each of the cooperative learning jobs. The various small group structures described here are typically used during the explore and/or elaborate phases of the 5-E instructional model.

Teachers can also enhance student learning by bringing the whole class back together and giving groups opportunities to make presentations of their work. Deeper understanding is attained when students explain, clarify, and justify what they have learned (National Research Council, 1996, p. 30). As the students communicate their findings and explanations, they should be encouraged to accept and react to the constructive criticism of others. Communication of investigations and findings to others typically occur during the explanation and/or the evaluation phases of the 5-E instructional model.

Used thoughtfully and strategically, different types of grouping arrangements can be effective tools for promoting cooperation, discourse, and improving learning and instruction.

Safety in the Science Classroom

Safety in the science classroom is critical. Teachers are legally responsible for the safety of students in their classroom (Gerlovich, 1996). But the law does not require teachers to be superhuman in their efforts. It is only expected that teachers be reasonable and prudent in their judgment when performing their duties with students. Teachers must attempt to anticipate hazards, then eliminate or address them.

You can read NSTA's recommendations about the shared teacher–school district responsibility by visiting http://www.nsta.org/about/positions/safety.aspx.

According to NSTA's current position statement on safety and school science instruction (2000), "Inherent in many instructional settings including science is the potential for injury and possible litigation. These issues can be avoided or reduced by the proper application of a safety plan." NSTA recommends that the responsibilities for the establishment and maintenance of safety standards be shared between school district authorities and teachers.

Safety in the science classroom is often closely tied to the room's size and arrangement. As you arrange your room, think out patterns of student movements and avoid overcrowding any area.

At the onset of the school year, you should generate and post a list of safety rules that students should always follow. Review these rules as appropriate throughout the year especially targeting rules that apply to the current lab activity. Here are some general classroom safety rules you might provide to students (Full Option Science System, 2000).

1. Always follow the safety procedures outlined by your teacher.
2. Never put any materials in your mouth.
3. Avoid touching your face, mouth, ears, or eyes while working with chemicals, plants, or animals.
4. Always wash your hands immediately after using materials, especially chemicals or animals.
5. Be careful when using sharp or pointed tools. Always make sure that you protect your eyes and those of your neighbors.
6. Wear American National Standards Institute approved safety goggles (with Z87 printed on the goggles) whenever activities are done in which there is a potential risk to eye safety.
7. Behave responsibly during science investigations.

As emphasized in the safety precautions, live animals in the classroom require special care and cautions.

Live Animals in the Classroom. In its 2005 position statement on Responsible Use of Live Animals and Dissection in the Science Classroom, NSTA supports including live animals as part of instruction in the K–12 science classroom because observing and working with animals firsthand can spark students' interest in science as well as a general respect for life while reinforcing key concepts as outlined in the NSES. NSTA encourages districts to ensure that animals are properly cared for and treated humanely, responsibly, and ethically. Ultimately, decisions to incorporate organisms in the classroom should balance the ethical and responsible care of animals with their educational value.

Teachers and students must be aware of their responsibilities and use precaution when keeping and caring for live animals in the classroom. Here are some directions to help students care for and adopt a humane attitude toward the living things they are observing.

Small animals, such as insects, frogs, and fish, may be kept for short periods of time, from 24 hours to several weeks, if the habitat in which they were found is simulated as closely as possible in captivity. Teachers should be aware that diseases such as salmonellosis can be transmitted to students who handle classroom animals. The small painted turtles that are frequently kept in elementary classrooms have been found to carry salmonella (Texas Safety Standards, 2002). Keeping the cages clean of fecal remains will reduce the presence of bacteria that may cause an illness.

Always insist that students wash their hands before feeding the animals and after they have handled the animals or touched materials from the animals' cage. They should research information about identification, characteristics, feeding habits, and values. The animals should eventually be released unharmed in their natural habitat or as prescribed in safety guidelines.

Managing Classroom Behavior

Maintaining an orderly learning environment is crucial in inquiry classrooms. During inquiry, students are naturally active—getting materials, performing investigations, discussing procedures and results with one another and with you, and moving into different group structures. Still, you must establish rules for behavior, monitor students' activities, and enforce disciplinary consequences when necessary.

Additional safety precautions for elementary and middle school science classrooms are given in Appendix A and in safety manuals produced by your district or state.

You can read NSTA's recommendations to teachers about including live animals in the classroom by visiting http://www.nsta.org/about/positions/animals.aspx.

Safety guidelines for keeping a variety of animals such as earthworms, mealworms, crickets, guppies, and butterflies can be also found in the FOSS (Full Option Science System), STC (Science and Technology for Children) and AIMS (Activities that Integrate Math and Science) teachers' guides.

Also consult the Science Store offerings on the NSTA website (http://www.nsta.org) for various helpful how-to publications on living things in the classroom.

Go to the Homework and Exercises section in Chapter 5 of MyEducationLab to watch the set of videos, *Managing Classroom Instruction, Parts 1, 2, 3, and 4*. These videos illustrate and expand the discussion of classroom management strategies presented in this chapter. A video guide to these videos is provided in the Online Professional Development section at the end of this chapter.

Keep in mind that all misbehavior is not equal. Classify misbehavior as *off-task* (attention wandering, failing to attend to the task at hand), *inappropriate* (doing something that is against the agreed-on rules), or *disruptive* (inappropriate behavior that prevents learning or is potentially dangerous). Deal with each case in an appropriate way, such as regaining attention indirectly or stopping inappropriate behavior and cautioning the student.

Monitor the behavior of individuals or groups during science lessons to see if you need to address any of these obstacles:

- Some students may be too immature for group work. You may have to work with them individually while the rest of the class works in groups. The goal is to help each student develop strategies for following class rules and participating in activities effectively. Don't just give up on a student and stop trying to help him or her.
- If there is a chronic offender in your class, you might
  1. talk with the student;
  2. ask for the student's perceptions of the problem and schedule a student-parent-teacher conference to develop a plan; and
  3. if necessary, invite the principal, school psychologist, social worker, or other professional to attend the conference or observe the behavior of the student in the classroom.

Dealing strongly and consistently with disruptive students is essential if they and their neighbors are going to learn science effectively in inquiry settings. Here are some special actions you might consider:

- Prepare contingency plans for problem situations, for example, deliberate damage to science supplies or explosive student behavior (fighting and pushing).
- Consider beforehand the pros and cons of various methods of discipline, such as removing a student from the situation, so you can use the methods effectively if necessary. Consider developing routine procedures for handling improper actions so students understand beforehand the consequences of bad behavior. If it fits within your school/district policy, you might review the following policy with students and then display it in the classroom:

  First offense: warning addressed to student by name in clear, calm voice.

  Second offense: student given 10-minute time-out in an isolated part of the classroom, another teacher's classroom, or school office. Never use learning centers for time-out.

  Third offense: 15-minute time-out in isolation.

  Fourth offense: phone call to student's parents or guardian.

  Fifth offense: conference with student, parent or guardian, school principal, and/or school psychologist or counselor. (Baron, 1992)

If you feel the lesson is getting away from you, don't hesitate to end it. Assess what went wrong and plan the next lesson to eliminate the problem.

Despite your best efforts, some students may exhibit disruptive or asocial behaviors or be diagnosed as having serious emotional disorders. Because students with disorders may be included in your classroom, a few suggestions may be helpful.

As you work with students who have emotional or behavioral disorders, remember that your utmost concern is to provide a safe and supportive learning environment for all of your students. To work successfully with students whose conduct is often disorderly, try viewing their deficit in appropriate social behaviors just as you would academic deficits—skills that need to be taught. Don't condone inappropriate behaviors; teach alternative, appropriate ways to interact. With patience and guidance some students can learn to "correct" social behaviors just as they can learn to be more successful academically. One way to teach "correct" behavior is to use behaviorist principles.

Behavior modification is one technique that is often effective when other techniques are not, because (1) students know exactly what is expected of them; (2) through the gradual process of shaping, students attempt to learn new behaviors only when they are truly ready to acquire them, and (3) students find learning new behaviors usually leads to success.

These four steps are routinely used in behavioral modification:

1. Identify the problem behavior to be modified.
2. Log behavior with regard to how often and under what conditions it occurs.
3. Reinforce desired behavior(s) by initiating a system that reinforces or rewards appropriate, positive behavior.
4. Determine the type of positive reward to use: manipulatives (computer games, interactive videos, games); visuals (videos, CD-ROMs); physical (extra gym or recess privileges, dance); social (praise, attention, status); tactile (art time); edibles (food and drink); auditory (music as choices of audiotapes or CDs); and others selected by students. Positive (or negative) reinforcers can vary.

The use of behavior modification with children diagnosed as emotionally disturbed is discussed in detail in Chapter 10.

Remember, the special education teachers in your building are prepared, available, and desiring to assist you with students identified as emotionally disturbed.

Implementing Learning Activities

In preparing to implement learning activities, an ounce of prevention is worth a pound of cure. Thinking and planning can help you spot many, though never all, potential challenges. Here are some things to keep in mind as you plan lessons, make teaching preparations, and move into that most important phase of teaching—implementing your lessons with students in the classroom.

Phase A: Teacher Preparation

- Formulate your objectives, activities, and assessment design into a lesson plan.
- Collect supplies and equipment you and the students will need.
- If possible, place materials into separate kits in sacks, baggies, or boxes, or on trays for each group. The organization and distribution of materials and the transition from one activity to another can make or break your science lesson.
- Practice all activities in advance to identify and then problem-solve to eliminate or reduce potential problems.
- Plan grouping structures for the lesson.

Phase B: Pre-Activity Teacher/Student Activities

- Establish with students a minimum set of rules and working directions that cover classroom and cooperative group behavior that is fair and courteous. Wherever possible, give students a reason for the rule. Post the rules so all students can see them.
- Establish beforehand a signal calling for quiet (e.g., putting lights out for a moment, ringing a bell, raising a hand in the air).
- Establish and consistently use a system for distributing and collecting science supplies and equipment, as well as cleanup procedures.

- Working within the framework of inquiry instruction, lead the students to pose questions that can be investigated and to suggest procedures for investigating them.
- Organize the class into learning groups.
- Before students move into groups, give them time to ask questions, discuss what will be done, and exchange ideas. It is important for students to internalize what will be done and to form working relationships with other students.

Phase C: Distribution and Collection of Science Materials

- Once students are in their groups, make sure each group knows exactly what is needed. Then ask the Materials Manager from each group to go to the supply stations, two or three at a time, and get the needed items (which you have prepackaged for each group).
- Work efficiently and quickly in all pre-activity tasks. Remember, time is of the essence. Students should be working in their cooperative groups within a few minutes after the start of the science period.

Phase D: Beginning the Activity

- With all the groups in place with their supplies, move quickly from group to group, checking once more to see that each group knows what to do. Sometimes it helps to check by asking the students on a team who have the most difficulty, so that you can be sure all team members understand the directions.

Phase E: During the Activity

- As your students engage in their group work, move about the room. Do not plant yourself in the front of the room, but move quietly to each group.
- Encourage communication among the students in each group.
- Be sure to spend only a brief time—less than a minute—with each group. When working with one group, keep an eye and ear on the other groups in the classroom. Remember, as a teacher you must have eyes in the back of your head.
- Assess the student behavior in each group and see if it's appropriate for the specific activity. If it's not, you might try these solutions:
  1. Use the preestablished signal for quiet. When everyone becomes quiet and attentive, remind the class that it was too noisy. Ask the students to work more quietly.
  2. Move to the offenders and quietly remind them to lower their voices.
  3. Temporarily remove individual students from their groups if they are displaying disruptive behavior and ask them to watch groups that are working well together. In a few minutes you might say, "Jason, I know you want to work with your group. Do you think you are ready to cooperate with your group, work quietly, and share your materials properly?" If Jason answers, "Yes," have him return to his group to work.
  4. Conclude the lesson if you feel the class is out of control or is not responding to your directions. Do this only as a last resort.
- Praise students who are working well instead of criticizing those who are not working well. Be specific so students know exactly the behavior you are praising, such as, "Notice how quietly Ann's group is discussing what effect the length of the pendulum string has on its swings."
- Show respect for students by speaking politely and listening to each student in an unhurried manner.

- Do not add to class noise by shouting above students' voices. Calm and quiet the students with a firm but soft voice.

Phase F: After the Activity

- At the conclusion of the hands-on phase of the activity, ask Materials Managers to inventory equipment and materials and return them to the collection stations. Remind students to clean up their group work area. This helps teach students to share responsibility in caring for equipment, materials, and the classroom environment.
- Assemble the whole group to share data, examine different ways data has been organized, discuss conclusions, and review what they have learned.
- Throughout the class discussion, focus deliberately on observations, the data students collect, things they notice, and things they wonder about before shifting the level of thought to interpretations. Accept, extend, and probe student responses, building toward understandable explanations. As an alternative or supplement to questioning, promote higher-level thinking through group presentations of their investigations, findings, and conclusions. Students from other groups should be encouraged to ask questions and make suggestions to the presenting group.
- Use the conceptual change strategies of Chapter 6 to deal with misconceptions and encourage conceptual change. Identify misconceptions and alternative theories; lead students to be dissatisfied with their alternate ideas; and use discrepant events that challenge alternative theories.
- Use direct instruction to teach terms and concepts. Guide students in using prior and acquired knowledge, along with observational data, in constructing explanations that help them make sense of the problems posed.
- Use science textbooks as resources after students have engaged in hands-on, minds-on activities that have helped them develop the knowledge base necessary for comprehending text materials.

School, district, or regional in-service sessions are often available to help beginning teachers handle classroom management; to guide them in choosing lessons and activities; to show them how to modify activities to meet their students' needs; and to show them how to manage science classrooms safely. If your district does not offer this kind of support, you might suggest it, along with a hands-on learning day that involves teachers in inquiry, making science discoveries just like students.

SUMMARY

- Working within a framework of national, state, and local district expectations for science learning, teachers are responsible for planning effective science lessons and managing learning environments.
- Designing science lessons is a complex task requiring professional knowledge and skills. In lesson planning, you must make decisions related to four generic lesson components: science content, instructional objectives, learning activities, and assessment procedures.
- Science content outlines specify and organize the science facts, concepts, principles, models and theories, and inquiry procedures to be taught.
- Objectives state what students will do to demonstrate the attainment of skills, knowledge, understandings, attitudes,

and values related to the content. Learning activities describe the opportunities you will provide for students to attain the objectives.

* Science learning centers can be an important part of lesson plan activities. Centers allow your students to explore, discover, and experiment on their own in structured or less-structured situations.

* Well-planned field trips can add to the quality experiences you provide for students in your classroom.

* Inquiry-oriented lessons can include a variety of types of teaching and learning methods, such as listening-speaking, reading-writing, and watching-doing. Examples are included in the chapter and other chapters to serve as models as you design your own lessons.

* Assessment procedures detail how you will use specific performances of students and the products they will develop to determine what they are learning during lessons and to adjust your instruction to improve learning.

* Building an effective learning environment centered on learning with understanding is an important task in preparing to teach. The way you group your students for learning is important to the success of cooperative learning in your classroom.

* Attention to safety standards and the safety of individual and groups of students is a must in science classrooms.

* How you manage your science classroom, including managing materials and student behavior, can make or break your science teaching. The main purposes of classroom management are to ensure safety and to facilitate learning. Specific practical examples of classroom management and discipline guidelines are highlighted in the chapter.

ONLINE PROFESSIONAL DEVELOPMENT

Pre- and post-tests to assess your knowledge of chapter content, along with exercises to enhance your understanding, can be found on MyEducationLab at www.myeducationlab.com.

Video Guides

Video clips on MyEducationLab selected for this chapter include: *Investigating Pin-hole Viewers: Parts 1, 2, and 3* and *Managing Classroom Instruction—Parts 1, 2, 3, and 4.*

Accessing the Videos

1. Go to the Homework and Exercises section in Chapter 5 of MyEducationLab to select and view videos for this chapter.
2. Videos might be viewed individually, by small groups of colleagues, or by the whole class.
3. As you watch each video, use the **Questions for Reflection** to guide your thoughts and note taking for personal use and group discussion.
4. Discuss your answers to the questions about each video with classmates.

Video: Pin-hole Cameras: Parts 1, 2, and 3

Overview

In this series of videos we see fifth-grade children constructing pin-hole viewers. We also see how the children used the pin-hole viewers in observing and generalizing about images seen when the viewers are pointed at illuminated arrows.

Questions for Reflection

1. How did the teacher assess the children's prior knowledge about light?
2. How were the pin-hole viewers constructed?
3. What questions did the teacher ask the children to engage them in the investigation task?
4. At the explore phase of the lesson, what observation records did the children make to describe what they noticed about the arrows when the viewer was pointed at them?
5. What patterns did the childen notice in their observaton records of the orientation of the arrow when seen through the viewer? How did the pattern-finding part of the activity fit the explain phase of the 5-E model?

6. What additional tasks did the teacher introduce for the children to investigate?
7. What did the teacher say about the objectives of pinhole viewer lessons, the Connecticut science standards, the process skills of science, and the ways in which the lesson follows what scientists do?

Video: Managing Classroom Instruction

Part 1: Grouping

Part 2: Clear Directions, Grade 5

Part 3: Clear Directions, Kindergarten

Part 4: Time Management

Overview

In Part 1 of this four-part video, we have a chance to observe different grouping structures and how grouping students can affect inquiry learning. In Parts 2 and 3, we see examples of clear directions for children as they prepare to carry out inquiry tasks. In Part 4, we see some ways that teachers at kindergarten and grade 5 manage time in science lessons.

Questions for Reflection

1. What do the children in Part 1 say is the importance of working in teams?
2. What task assignments did the teacher use in building the teams? What did the children say about the role of each designated task in working together in teams?
3. In what different ways did the teacher in the Part 1 video group the children for learning?
4. How effective do you think the chosen grouping structures were in promoting dialogue among the children and in enhancing understanding?
5. How would you change the grouping structure in your own classroom?
6. In Parts 2 and 3, what do you think is the importance of clear directions for students in their successfully carrying out the different activities?
7. In Part 4, what did the teachers do in managing time effectively in the different lesson activities?

6

Assessment and learning are two sides of the same coin. The methods used to collect educational data define in measurable terms what teachers should teach and what students should learn. And, when students engage in an assessment exercise, they should learn from it.

(National Research Council, 1996, p. 76)

Assessing Science Learning

LEARNING AND ASSESSMENT ARE CLOSELY linked in inquiry teaching. Consider how learning and assessment interact in these scenarios.

- *Students observe as a boy grasps a piece of paper and blows steadily across the top of it. Unexpectedly, the paper moves up rather than down. The students each draw a line down the middle of a page in their science logs. On one side, they list questions pertaining to the event that might be investigated; on the other side they propose explanations about why the paper went up rather than down. The teacher uses the results to assess the students' prior knowledge about Bernoulli's principle and the effect of rushing air.*

- *During a period of watching and keeping records on the moon every night for 2 weeks, students respond to their teacher's oral questions about any patterns they may have discovered in the data. The teacher recognizes the students' responses and decides what kinds of scaffolding assistance might help them improve their understanding.*

- *Later in the moon-watching lessons, students respond to multiple-choice questions about moon phases and their causes and justify their answers through drawings and in writing. Their teacher studies the answers and explanations to determine students' levels of understanding and misconceptions that might interfere with their continued learning about lunar phases. The teacher also uses the students' responses in making decisions about changes in instruction that might be needed.*

- *After a lesson in which students learned the investigation strategy of controlling variables, a teacher displays rolls of three different brands of paper towels to the class. She says: "Your job is to test these paper towel brands for a consumer magazine. What factors will you test? How will you determine which brand is the best buy?" Students work together in small groups to formulate and carry out a plan for investigation, write a brief report, and present their results to the rest of the class. As the students work, the teacher circulates among the groups, keeping notes and marking a check sheet.*

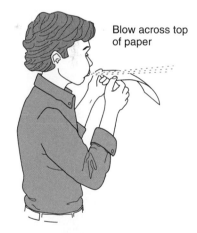

Blow across top of paper

What happens when the boy blows across the top of the paper?

What do these four situations have in common? All of them are examples of assessments used in the service of science learning. Assessment takes place at the beginning of instruction (the first case), during instruction (the second and third situations), and at the end of instruction (the fourth case). In the first situation, students' prior conceptions and misconceptions are being assessed. In the second and third situations, students' conceptual understanding is assessed through oral and written responses of students to teacher questions.

Inquiry skills and understandings about inquiry are being assessed with a performance task in the fourth situation. The first three assessments provide the teacher feedback for modifications in instruction to improve learning. The fourth situation provides for a summing up after the lesson on what students have learned. As these examples demonstrate, asessment is an ongoing process, not one that occurs just on tests given at the end of a period of instruction.

In the past, concern with assessment techniques took a back seat to learning theory and instructional reforms. Today, as is shown in the chapter opening quote, the assessment scenarios, and the discussion of formative and summative assessment in Chapters 3, 4, and 5, assessment is an integral part of the teaching-learning process. To participate in the assessment transformation, you will need to develop new assessment techniques and use traditional techniques in more creative ways.

In this chapter, we place the notions of assessment and evaluation into a broad framework and show how information from assessment is used in making evaluative decisions. We also provide many examples of informal assessments, performance tasks, and traditional assessments that you can use in formulating your own assessment plans.

As you study this chapter, reflect on the following questions:

- *How do assessment and evaluation differ? What are the purposes of assessment in science classrooms?*

- *What are the characteristics of diagnostic, formative, and summative assessments? How are formative and summative assessment linked to inquiry instruction?*

- *What are the characteristics of informal and formal assessments?*

- *What is performance assessment, and how does it differ from traditional assessment techniques?*

- *What are the components of an effective performance assessment task?*

- *What specific informal assessments, performance tasks, and traditional test items can be used to assess science knowledge, understanding, and inquiry procedures as described in national and state science standards.*

- *What are the characteristics of test items used on statewide tests of science?*

Assessment and Evaluation

Assessment is a process of gathering information about student learning for decision making. Teachers gather information on the learning of students through oral questioning, watching and listening to students, student entries in journals and record sheets, performance tasks, and formal tests. By emphasizing multiple means of collecting student data on a variety of variables, assessment goes beyond mere testing.

Assessment and evaluation are closely related concepts, but they are not the same. Assessment involves collecting data, while **evaluation** involves using that data in judging student performance and making decisions about learning and instruction. Teachers, students, parents, administrators, and legislators need different kinds of assessment information for different purposes (see Table 6-1).

Each of the assessment procedures and evaluation purposes listed in Table 6-1 is important. Our focus in this chapter is on the role of assessment and evaluation by the classroom teacher in the teaching-learning process.

A glossary containing definitions of important terms used in this chapter can be found at MyEducationLab.

TABLE 6-1   DIFFERENT AUDIENCES USE DIFFERENT TYPES OF ASSESSMENT RESULTS FOR DIFFERENT PURPOSES

Users of Assessment Data	Purposes	Frequency	Results	Assessment Types
Teachers	planning, monitoring, evaluating, and adjusting instruction; assisting students in learning; assigning grades	daily	immediate; gained through classroom observation of student performance and products	variety of assessment types, formal and informal performance assessment tasks, traditional tests
Students	feedback about learning performance and progress	daily	communicated directly from teacher or personally developed	traditional tests, performance tasks, teacher observation, self-assessment
Administrators and Legislators	accountability; budget, policy, and personnel decisions; student placement, promotion, and graduation	once each year	delayed; calculated outside of schools; made available at a later date	standardized tests; multiple-choice and short-answer items so many objectives can be assessed in a short period of time
Parents	feedback about their children's learning performance and progress	as needed; at least once each grading period	immediate or delayed; communicated directly from teachers or students	traditional tests; performance tasks; informal assessments

Assessment should help make students' work and progress understandable to students and parents. It should also guide further instruction.

Assessment and Inquiry Science

The interactive approach to teaching science as inquiry provides teachers with unique opportunities to teach science for understanding, to assess student learning in ongoing ways, and to make reflective judgments based on concrete evidence of students' accomplishments.

Think of classroom assessment as a tool used in the service of learning and instruction. By observing students while they work, asking key questions, examining the performance and products of students, and administering assessment tasks of various designs, teachers can ascertain the quality of students' conceptual understanding and ability to use inquiry strategies.

Student participation is a key component of successful assessment. If students are to participate successfully in the process, they need to be clear about the objectives and criteria for good work, to assess their own efforts in light of the criteria, and to share responsibility in taking action (National Research Council, 2001).

Key Questions to Guide Assessment in Inquiry Science

Assessment in inquiry science should be based on three guiding questions (National Research Council, 2001):

1. Where are students trying to go?
2. Where are students now?
3. How are students going to get there?

The first question leads to a consideration of standards and objectives. The second question involves assessing students' learning. The third question leads to the critical step of teachers using assessment results in making decisions about scaffolding, learning strategies, and instruction.

Where Are Students Trying to Go? There is growing consensus that the *National Science Education Standards* and the standards of the various states define the goals that should be achieved in science at different grade levels. As discussed in Chapter 5, it is the responsibility of district curriculum personnel and classroom teachers to determine the specific objectives that will lead to the attainment of the goals set forth in the science standards.

NSES **Assessment Standard A**

Assessments must be consistent with the decision they are designed to inform.

- Assessments are deliberately designed.
- Assessments have explicitly stated purposes.
- The relationship between the decision and data is clear.

Assessment Standard B

Achievement and opportunity to learn science must be assessed.

- Achievement data should focus on the science content that is most important for students to learn.
- Equal attention must be given to the assessment of opportunity to learn and to the assessment of student achievement.

Teachers and districts develop specific objectives designed to guide the learning process. Then, teachers should provide students opportunities to attain the objectives and learn standards-based science in active ways.

Where Are Students Now? Students should be required to show evidence of their learning through formal and informal assessments. Assessment in the past centered too often on what was easy to measure with multiple-choice items: the recall of facts, concepts, principles, and theories. State and national science standards have not lost sight of the importance of a strong knowledge base, but they go beyond knowledge and place emphasis on students' understanding and applying science concepts and principles, as well as on their being able to use a variety of science processes and investigative procedures.

How Are Students Going to Get There? Assessments of any kind must always be related to standards and lesson objectives and have a clear purpose. The purpose of classroom assessment is to improve learning and instruction. Assessment results can be used to guide decisions about how modifications in instruction can help learners achieve agreed-on objectives. Classroom assessments can also be used to provide summative information on what students have actually learned through instruction.

Diagnostic, Formative, and Summative Assessment

Assessments can be diagnostic (before starting teaching), formative (during teaching), or summative (after instruction).

Diagnostic Assessment

Diagnostic assessment, sometimes called *preassessment,* is used before you start teaching to discover needed information about your students' knowledge, interests, abilities, and preferences. Diagnostic questions asked and observations made at the beginning of a lesson (in the engage phase of the 5-E instructional model, for example) can help you identify what students already know about a topic, what misconceptions and alternative theories they carry, and what they are interested in learning. By using informal assessments, performance assessments, paper-and-pencil tests, and inventories diagnostically before you begin teaching, you can decide what specific experiences will best encourage students' learning progress. Diagnostic data will help you adjust instructional strategies to students' individual differences.

Formative Assessment

Formative assessment is integral to inquiry learning and instruction. Formative assessment involves collecting data on student learning during a lesson. A combination of informal and formal assessment methods should be used in formative assessment.

Duschl and colleagues (2007) have emphasized the importance of linking formative assessment to scaffolding. A central theme in scaffolding is to make a process, concept, or principle more explicit for learners by enabling them to do something they could not do without some crucial element. For example, the crucial elements in the process of using evidence to formulate explanations include the claim, the empirical evidence in support of the claim, and the reasoning that connects the evidence and the claim (Duschl et al., 2007). Assessment of what students understand and can do provides support for further instruction, including scaffolding.

Go to the Homework and Exercises section in Chapter 6 of MyEducationLab, to read "Seven Practices for Effective Learning," an informative article on the uses of diagnostc (preassessment), formative, and summative assessment to measure student understanding. Read this article to extend your own understanding of these three forms of assessment.

Scaffolding of these crucial elements might come through teachers, instructional materials, or other students. Sometimes, explicit or direct instruction of concepts, principles, and strategies might be needed to improve learning. Remember from Chapter 4 that explicit teaching of concepts and strategies is a part of the explain phase of the learning cycle and the 5-E model of instruction.

Summative Assessment

Summative assessments are assessments that come after instruction. Formative assessments are key elements of inquiry instruction, but they are usually informal and insufficiently documented to answer many of the hard questions posed by teachers, parents, district administrators, and legislators, such as:

* What have students actually learned?
* What evidence demonstrates that they are learning?
* How well are they learning it and at what level of understanding? (National Research Council, 2000, p. 76).

Summative assessments call for more standardized instruments than are typically used in formative assessment. They also require systematic ways of recording, analyzing, and reporting student responses. Decisions about grades typically require high-quality summative assessments.

Large-scale assessments administered at district, state, national, or international levels provide evidence needed to make fair, high-stakes decisions about students, teachers, and a district's need to redesign professional development opportunities for teachers (National Research Council, 2000). Large-scale assessments are usually not classified as formative or summative, because they do not apply directly to what has just been taught in the classroom.

Informal, Traditional, and Performance Assessments

Three types of assessment measures are available to teachers in science, including informal assessments, traditional assessments, and performance assessments.

Informal Assessment

Assessments are generally characterized as informal if they are administered "on the fly" (Duschl et al., 2007) rather than at planned intervals, do not provide for standardized procedures of administration, and do not involve systematic ways to record, analyze, and report student responses. Formal assessments typically involve using traditional items and performative tasks to determine where students are in the learning process.

Informal assessments may involve teachers asking students questions, listening to what they say, watching what they do in learning performance, and examining the products from their performances. Teachers also gather informal assessment data through reading and analyzing what students have written on their record sheets and in their science notebooks. Checklists can be used as a guide in systematically watching and assessing students as they work.

Traditional Assessment

Traditional assessments may be used before, during, or after instruction, but they are most often used after instruction as summative assessments. Traditional assessments typically use multiple-choice, true-false, short-answer, and essay items. Multiple-choice and true-false items are

How to formulate effective questions for inquiry is the subject of Chapter 7.

sometimes called *forced-choice* or *selected-response items*, while short-answer and essay items are referred to as *constructed-response items*. These types of assessments offer teachers a number of advantages, but they also have some disadvantages.

Multiple-choice and short-answer items are easy to administer and score. They enable teachers to measure a wide range of knowledge over a short period of time. However, multiple-choice and short-answer items do not usually require students to show their reasoning. Further, traditional multiple-choice items measure more than just knowledge; the reading level, language ability, and vocabulary of students can also affect their choices of answers.

Carefully constructed essay items can assess both the knowledge and understanding of students. Essay items have the advantage of requiring students to generate information in their own words, rather than to just recognize correct answers. Such items can also provide teachers with knowledge about how the student arrived at the answers. A disadvantage of essay items is that poor writing skills can mask the student's science understanding.

Traditional assessments can be used if teachers are careful to follow through and give feedback to students on learning. However, more powerful methods of assessment have been developed to fit the expanded formative and summative purposes of classroom assessment. In recent years, there has been an increasing emphasis on this new type of assessment, called *performance assessment*.

Performance Assessment

Performance tasks provide students opportunities to demonstrate what they know and understand. Sometimes, performance tasks are a natural part of the science lesson. At other times, teachers design special performance tasks that require students to demonstrate their understanding.

When compared with traditional assessment measures, performance assessment offers students a wider range of options for communicating what they know in science and what they are able to do with their knowledge. Students are generally more comfortable with performance assessments, because they are typically set in authentic contexts and often have the look and feel of regular, hands-on learning situations.

Performance tasks can be used to assess conceptual understanding and inquiry abilities. All performance assessment tasks have a performance that can be observed and/or a product that can be examined. Student performances in science assessment tasks might include such tasks as measuring, observing, collecting and organizing data, constructing a graph, making a visual or audio presentation, presenting an oral defense of work, interpreting data, or presenting a how-to explanation of a procedure. Products presented for assessment could include such tangible things as data tables, graphs, models, reports, and written explanations and problem solutions.

Creating a good performance task involves determining the *focus* of the task, setting the *context* for the task, writing *directions*, and developing a *scoring guide* (Kentucky Department of Education, n.d.).

 Assessment Standard C

- Assessment tasks are authentic.
- Students have adequate opportunity to demonstrate their achievement.

Focus. The first step in developing a performance assessment is to decide what students are expected to learn and how they can demonstrate that they have learned it. This becomes the *focus* of the performance task. Focus is closely related to learning objectives. In determining the focus, state precisely what you expect your students to know, understand, and be able to do. Once you have determined a focus for the assessment task, a context should be created.

Context. The context of a performance assessment usually includes a background and a question related to the focus objective. The background may be presented in a variety of ways, including in written form and through hands-on activities. The focus question should center on a problem to which students will want to find an answer or solution. The background scenario and focus question represent the "hook" that draws students in and engages them in the task.

The scenario should be made as authentic, or as close to the "real thing," as classroom conditions will allow (Jarolimek & Foster, 1997). Authentic contexts better portray the nature of science, relate classroom learning to the real world, are more intrinsically motivating to students, and serve not only as assessments but also as interesting learning situations.

Directions. Directions for performance tasks should explain what students are expected to do and should describe the final performance or product to be assessed. It is very important to make sure that the directions are clear. You should ask other teachers and some students to review the directions for clarity.

Scoring Guides. The scoring guide provides a means for judging the quality of the assessment performance or product. Begin creating the scoring guide by describing what a high-quality performance or product will look like. The next step is to decide how many performance criteria and performance levels are needed. Descriptions of each criterion and level can then be written.

Scoring of performance assessment typically involves the use of rubrics.

Rubrics. As introduced in Chapter 5, a rubric is a type of scoring guide consisting of a number of evaluative criteria that are precisely described according to level of quality, usually with points assigned to each level. The number of levels should be based on the needs of your class and your observations of what your students are actually doing in science activities. Four-level rubrics are frequently used.

Examples of rubrics for assessing students' mastery of sound and floating and sinking concepts appear in Chapter 5 in Figures 5-5 and 5-8. Figure 6-1 provides examples of criteria and scoring levels for rubrics related to four types of science tasks. You must provide enough information about each performance level to communicate expectations to students and for scorers to distinguish differences in the quality of the students' performances and products.

Include your students in creating rubrics and in the process of scoring task performance. When students are involved in the assessment process, they become more aware of learning expectations and are enabled to take more responsibility for their own learning. Performance assessments have been criticized as being too subjective, but when good scoring guides are used, consistent scoring can be obtained.

Fitting Assessment Methods to Learning Objectives

Your choice of whether to use informal or formal assessments and traditional or performance assessment methods in science will depend largely on the type of objectives you wish to assess.

If you wish to make a quick assessment of where students are in science understanding, informal strategies might be used.

Knowing Science Information

1. Responds only in terms of specific examples experienced in class or presented in instructional materials.
2. Responds in terms of generalizations of these experiences but is unable to show relationships or to go beyond that which was experienced.
3. Demonstrates thorough understanding by applying information in a new context or by explaining relationships, implications, or consequences.

Using Science Concepts and Generalizations

1. Rarely connects previous learning with new situations in which it could be applied unless told what skill or idea is relevant.
2. Uses previous experiences in new situations once the relationship between the new and previous situation has been pointed out.
3. Works out what earlier learning could be applied in a new context by using relationships between one situation and another.

Doing Written Reports and Projects

1. What he writes or says is disorganized and difficult to follow; takes time to understand information in books or verbal directions.
2. Seems to have a clear idea of what he wants to express but does not always find the word to put it precisely or concisely; prefers to seek information orally than to use books.
3. Expresses himself clearly, using words appropriately and economically and at a level which can be understood by whomever receives the message; expands his knowledge through reading.

Experimenting/Investigating

1. Is unable to progress from one point to another in a practical investigation or inquiry without help, failing to grasp the overall plan.
2. Tries things out somewhat unsystematically unless the various steps in a practical inquiry are planned out for him, in which case he uses materials and collects results satisfactorily.
3. Has a clear idea of the reason for the various steps in an investigation; can work through them systematically, making reasonable decisions with only occasional guidance.

Figure 6-1 Criteria and scoring levels for rubric on major science categories. *Source:* From Elizabeth Meng and Rodney L. Doran, *Improving Instruction and Learning Through Evaluation: Elementary School Science* (Columbus, OH: ERIC Clearinghouse for Science, Mathematics, and Environmental Education, 1993), 162–163.

If you wish to assess recall of factual or conceptual knowledge, traditional multiple-choice or short-answer items are often suitable. Traditional assessments might also be appropriate to assess student attainment of objectives related to understanding of science knowledge, particularly if you use essay items or combine multiple-choice responses with written explanations of why a particular response was chosen.

You might be able to probe deeper into student understanding and assess inquiry abilities more completely when you use performance assessments that enable students to demonstrate their understanding and investigative abilities during or after a learning task. Finally, performance methods are much more appropriate than traditional assessments when you wish to assess how well students can apply knowledge and plan and carry out inquiry procedures.

Examples of informal assessments, performance assessments, and traditional assessments are given in the following sections. Table 6-2 presents a guide to the assessment examples to help you sort through and keep up with the various assessment procedures illustrated in the chapter. You should begin now to build up a bank of assessment items and sources for each subject you teach. You can find many good assessment examples on the

TABLE 6-2   SCIENCE ASSESSMENT EXAMPLES

Assessment Purpose	Informal Assessment Examples	Performance Tasks Assessment Examples	Traditional Items Assessment Examples
Accessing Recall of Science Knowledge	Teacher questioning: Chapter 7 Student experience charts: Figure 6-2 Science record pages: Figure 6-3 Science notebooks: Figure 6-4 Using a checklist to assess microscope skills: Figure 6-5 Using checklists to assess use of science processes: Figure 6-6 Using checklists to assess investigative procedures: Figure 6-7 Using checklists as a tool for assessing attitudes: Figure 6-8	Oral/written pictorial interpretations: Figures 6-9 and 6-10	Multiple choice: Items 1–3 Short answer: Item 4
Assessing Science Understanding		Concept mapping: Figure 6-11 Electrical circuits performance task: Figure 6-12 Holistic scoring of a performance task: Figure 6-13	Essay: Item 6, 7, 8 Justified multiple choice: Figure 6-22 Essay with investigation data: Items 9, 10, 11 Figure 6-23
Assessing Investigative Procedures and Inquiry Strategies	Watching students as they investigate Examining student products developed in investigation	A leaves task for assessing data-gathering processes: Figures 6-14 and 6-15 Rubric for performance task on growing plants task: Figure 6-16 Scientific processes—Mealworms task: Figures 6-17 and 6-18 Hands-on practical assessment–TIMSS task: Figures 6-19 and 6-20	Multiple choice, short answer: Items 12, 13 Cluster of multiple-choice and essay items with investigation data: Items 14, 15, 16 Essay with application: Item 17
Assessing Multiple Objectives		Models: pp. 165–166 Demonstratons: p. 166 Student Projects: p. 166 Science Fair Projects: pp. 167–168, Figure 6-21	

Internet, in teachers' guides, and in the education literature. In most cases, it is necessary to modify examples from outside sources so that they fit your own learning objectives and classroom situation. And of course, you should begin to create, try out, and revise your own performance and traditional assessments.

Examples of Informal Assessments

Informal methods for assessing students' conceptual knowledge and understanding and their abilities to use inquiry procedures include teacher questioning, student experience charts, student records, student notebooks, and checklists.

Assessing Students' Conceptual Knowledge and Understanding

Teacher Questioning. Teachers' questions are crucial in helping students make connections and learn important science concepts. As an example of how teachers' questions can facilitate understanding, consider the electrical circuits lesson described in Chapter 4. A simple question like "Can you use these materials to make a bulb light?" engages the children in practical activities. By watching the children and listening to them, teachers can begin to assess the students' prior knowledge and current understanding. A follow-up question like "Can you draw a picture of the circuit you made to light the bulb?" reveals the extent to which students understand what they did to light the bulb. As students work on Prediction Sheet 1 in the circuits lessons, the guiding question "In which of these circuits will the bulb light?" discloses how the students conceptualize and generalize what they did to light a bulb. Such questions help to make students' thinking and understanding visible and provide a basis for the continual adjustment and improvement of learning and instruction.

Teacher questioning is treated in more detail in Chapter 7, Effective Questioning.

Experience Charts. At first, you may want students to use a group activity such as the experience chart illustrated in Figure 6-2. When assessing experience charts, consider the following questions (Shepardson & Britsch, 2001):

- Does the drawing or writing relate to and accurately correspond with what was observed or done?
- Does the child label or name the objects used?

Our Trip to the Park

Things We Saw	Things We Heard	Things We Smelled
Sally: Branches moving in wind	Birds singing	
Greg: Little bugs crawling		Fresh air
Tom: A bird's nest	An airplane	Flowers
Amy: Yellow flowers in grass	Dog barking	
Juan: Squirrel running	Twigs snapping	Dirt (soil)
Jill: Water drops on grass	Our class laughing	Wet grass

Figure 6-2 Science experience chart.

- Does the drawing or writing elaborate on the details of what was observed or done?
- Does the drawing or writing provide a context of people, materials, and processes from the science activity in which the child was engaged?
- Does the child relate the materials or activity to contexts that might be encountered outside the classroom?

Provide scaffolding to improve learning whenever it is warranted by your assessment data.

Student Record Pages. Record keeping for all students may involve the use of simple data sheets formulated by students or teachers. Record keeping for older students can include brief descriptions of what they did, what they observed, and what they concluded. Prompts to guide investigation and thinking might be included on data sheets.

When your students learn how to give brief descriptions of what they did in groups, they are ready to start their own individual record keeping. You can design a page, such as the one in Figure 6-3, on which your students record their observations and thinking. An example of a more complex data record sheet for organizing data related to activities on white powders is given in Chaper 2, p. 49.

You have been working with things that sink or float. What did you do to find out which objects sink or float? Write a description and draw a picture.

We put objects in the bowl of water. If the object floated, we put it in box with the Float label. If it sank, we put it in box Sink. Then we tried all the objects in the Float box to check if they all floated. We did the same with the objects in the Sink box.

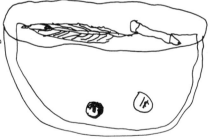

What did you find about which objects sink or float? Record your observations on the chart below.

OBJECT	SPECIAL FEATURES	LARGE OR SMALL	HEAVY OR LIGHT	SINK OR FLOAT
Penny		small	heavy	sink
Styrofoam ball		large	light	float

Figure 6-3 Science record page.

To show their understanding, students might:

* *write* a description of what they did,
* *draw* a picture of the activity, and/or
* *record written observations* in the chart supplied.

Once students become familiar with this strategy, encourage them to devise their own observation formats.

Science Notebooks.   Science notebooks are tools for students to grapple with scientific questions and help them make sense of what they have observed through using meaningful recording and organizing strategies. As an example, students often keep notes of their observations. Your examination of observation notebooks can reveal the students' developing knowledge about a topic. Student notes can take many forms, such as drawings, narratives, charts, and graphs.

* *Technical drawings and diagrams with labels.* These are drawings based on careful observations of objects and organisms.
* *Notes and lists.* These are reports of observations used to record information quickly.
* *Charts, tables, and graphs.* These represent different ways to display and view data.
* *Written observations.* These are more detailed accounts of investigations and observations.
* *Additional questions about which students wonder.*
* *Personal judgments and feelings related to activities.*

An example of a student's entry in her science notebook is given in Figure 6-4.

As you assess notebooks, keep your objectives in mind. Content learning may be your main goal, but for students to learn to use different reporting and organizational strategies can also be important. You might teach reporting and organizational strategies in mini-lessons, perhaps in language arts classes, and use later lessons to assess student use of these. Provide feedback to improve reporting strategies whenever appropriate.

More suggestions related to student science notebooks are given in Chapter 9.

Several good articles related to writing to learn science are published in the November/December 2004 issue of *Science and Children*. This topic is also addressed in Chapter 9.

Today we used one wire and one battery to make a bulb light. At first, I didn't think I could do it, but I did! I made the bulb light on my own! I can't wait for more activities on electricity tomorrow. I feel really confident now and like this way of learning.

Figure 6-4   Student science notebook entry.

The *National Science Education Standards* emphasize that students must be provided opportunity to develop both conceptual understandings and abilities of scientific inquiry (National Research Council, 1996; 2000). Assessing inquiry abilities formatively through informal assessment is an important part of science learning.

Checklists. A checklist is simply a list of the specific key elements that a teacher wishes to consider in judging a student performance or product. Scorers observe student performances and examine products and check *yes* or *no* for each element on the checklist. The check mark typically shows only whether the element is observed; no effort is made on a checklist to assess how well the skill is performed. However, space might be added to a checklist for teacher notes or comments. Checklists are easy, quick, and handy to use. They help keep teacher observations focused.

Figure 6-5 is a sample checklist for observing and assessing students' skills in using a microscope. Student results determined with checklists might be used both to provide feedback on learning and to adjust instruction. Be sure to keep a separate record for each student. Review it with students periodically to assess their progress in specific skills.

Hands-on inquiry activities provide an authentic setting for assessing children's developing abilities to do scientific inquiry. Figure 6-6 displays a checklist that can be used to judge students' use of specific science processes. Figure 6-7 shows a checklist for use in assessing investigation procedures. The checklists are best used in informal assessment, since there are no standardized procedures for collecting and reporting this type of student information.

Think about using the checklists over the course of a year. You might

* keep a checklist record for processes and procedures on each student,
* consider each student's performance in a variety of science activities,
* note whether or when each student exhibits the indicated task or behavior,

Student's Name _____									
Behavior/Skills	Date	Yes	No	Date	Yes	No	Date	Yes	No
Is careful in handling microscope									
Cleans lenses properly									
Focuses instrument properly									
Prepares slides correctly									
Orients mirror for correct amount of light									

Figure 6-5   Checklist for observing microscope skills.

Student Name: _____			
Process or Skill	**Task or Behavior**	**Task Observed?**	
		Date	**Comment**
Observing	Uses several senses in exploring objects		
	Uses magnifying glasses and other instruments to extend the senses		
	Identifies details in objects, organisms, and events		
	Notice patterns, relationships, or sequences in events		
Inferring	Uses evidence and scientific knowledge in making inferences		
	Explains basis for inferences		
	Makes reasonable inferences that fit the evidence and scientific knowledge		
	Suggests how to test inferences		
Predicting	Uses evidence in making a prediction		
	Explains basis for predictions		
	Makes reasonable predictions that fit the evidence, whether accurate or not		
	Makes interpolations and extrapolations from patterns in information or observation		
	Suggests how to test predictions		
Communicating	Talks freely with others about activities and ideas		
	Listens to others' ideas and looks at their results		
	Reports observations coherently in drawings, writing, and charts		
	Uses tables, graphs, and charts to report investigation results		

Figure 6-6 Checklist for assessing science processes.

- add comments to guide learning and instruction, and
- work with all students to help them improve in their abilities to use each process or inquiry procedure.

A critical part of understanding the nature of science and scientific inquiry is a knowledge of scientific habits of mind, the attitudes that characterize scientists. Although students

Figure 6-7 Checklist for assessing investigation procedures.

Student Name: _____

Procedure	Task or Behavior	Task Observed?	
		Date	Comment
Questions	Asks a variety of questions, focusing on questions that can be investigated		
	Recognizes differences between questions that can be investigated and questions that cannot be investigated		
Places Priority on Evidence	Has some idea of what evidence to look for to answer the question		
Plans Investigations to Obtain Needed Data or Information	Chooses a realistic way of investigating, measuring, or comparing to obtain results		
	Plans descriptive, classificatory, experimental, and other investigation procedures		
Conducts Planned Investigation	Carries out investigation procedures carefully		
	Works cooperatively with teammates		
	Takes steps to ensure that the results obtained are accurate		
Explains, Interprets, or Make Sense of Data	Gives explanation consistent with evidence and scientific knowledge		
	Explains basis for explanations		
	Shows awareness that other explanations may fit the evidence		
	Asks questions about ways to test predictions and explanations made in activities		
	Suggests how explanations and predictions can be checked		
	Shows awareness that explanations are tentative and subject to change		

should attain many affective goals in science, five main attitudes, values, and habits of mind are especially relevant to successful inquiry in elementary and middle school classrooms:

1. being curious,
2. insisting on evidence,
3. seeking to apply science knowledge,
4. being willing to critically evaluate ideas, and
5. working cooperatively.

It is difficult to measure attitudes reliably, but attitudes cannot be improved without an understanding of students' existing attitudes (Shepardson & Britsch, 2001). Figure 6-8 shows a

Student Name: _____

Attitude	Component Behavior	Behavior Observed	
		Date	Comment
Curiosity	Notices and attends to new things and situations		
	Shows interest through careful observation of details		
	Asks questions		
	Uses resources to find out about new or unusual situations		
Respect for Evidence	Searches for evidence to answer questions posed		
	Checks evidence that does not fit the pattern of other findings		
	Challenges conclusions or interpretations where there does not seem to be sufficient evidence		
Predisposition to Apply Knowledge in Problem Solving	Searches for available scientific knowledge to apply in problem solving		
	Uses available knowledge to guide exploration of problem situation		
	Uses available knowledge and evidence in generating explanations and problem solutions		
Willingness to Critically Evaluate Ideas	Changes existing ideas when there is sufficient evidence		
	Considers alternative ideas to her own		
	Willing to examine positive and negative aspects of his own investigations		
	Seeks alternative ideas rather than just the first idea		
	Realizes that it may be necessary to change an existing idea		
Working Cooperatively	Talks freely with other students about topic-related ideas in small group and whole group settings		
	Shows respect for others in groups		
	Considers multiple viewpoints within groups		
	Readily assumes and fulfills assigned role in inquiry group		
	Assists others in investigation and learning tasks when appropriate		

Figure 6-8 Checklist for assessing science attitudes.

Source: From *Assessment in Science: A Guide to Professional Development and Classroom Practice* (pp. 119–147), by D. P. Shepardson, and S. J. Britsch, 2001, Boston: Kluwer. Adapted with permission.

checklist that can be used to gain some understanding of students' science attitudes. The checklist draws on a number of sources, including the work of Shepardson and Britsch (2001). By categorizing attitudes into a number of different components, the checklist allows teachers to watch for specific indicators of these important science attitudes.

As with the science processes and investigation procedures checklists, you might keep an assessment checklist for each student throughout the year, noting when you judge that the child has displayed the attitude or failed to display the attitude when it mattered. Information gained via the checklist should be used formatively to praise and improve attitudes, rather than summatively for grading purposes.

Examine your science program to see where you can use these suggestions to develop informal assessment measures suited to your immediate needs.

Examples of Performance Assessment Items

The PALS (Performance Assessment Links in Science) website has collected many excellent performance assessment examples. Peruse the PALS website at http://pals.sri.com/index.html.

In this section, we provide a large bank of assessment examples that you can draw on in developing your own performance assessment tasks for use in science.

Performance tasks can be a part of the regular learning activity. The focus, context, and direction of the performance tasks are then derived directly from the learning activities.

Using Performance Tasks to Assess Science Knowledge

Conceptual understanding of the natural world is a key goal of elementary and middle school science. When students understand, they are able to do something with their knowledge. They can interpret concepts and principles and use them along with observational evidence in inferring, predicting, analyzing, and explaining. Performance tasks are particularly suited to assessing understanding.

Oral/Written Pictorial Interpretations. Teachers can gain insights into their students' understanding of concepts and principles by using assessments that ask them to respond to pictorial situations. Look for more than mere observations. Assess for hidden meanings, underlying patterns, and explanatory schemas that bring coherence to the students' observations. Such an assessment is intended to determine students' abilities to communicate the trends and sequences of the pictorial situation.

In developing pictorial assessments, decide on the learning objective (the *focus* of the performance task). You might show a science pictorial situation (the *context*), then give *directions* for how to respond to the questions. This can be done orally for younger students or those with limited reading skills, or in written form for others. Figure 6-9 illustrates such an activity.

An example of a *scoring guide* to assess students' responses to the snowman item in Figure 6-9 is given in Figure 6-10. The scoring guide relates to each of the three questions in the pictorial assessment. This scoring guide is similar to a checklist in that the teacher is to examine students' responses for specific criteria. However, points are to be assigned for each relevant response. Teachers must use their own experience to judge the quality of the response and to assign points.

The assessment in Figures 6-9 and 6-10 could be used formatively to guide teachers to improve student understanding or summatively in assigning student grades.

Using Performance Tasks to Assess Science Understanding

Concept maps are useful tools to assess science understanding. Assessing performance on performance tasks through holistic rubrics is another useful tool to assess understanding.

Teacher shows pictures and says to children:

What differences do you see in these three pictures?
Which do you think will happen first? Second?
 Last?
Why do you think the snowman is changing?

Figure 6-9 Pictorial interpretation assessment.
Source: From *Material Objects Student Manual,* Section 5, Chapter 18, SCIS3, 1992, Hudson, NH: Delta Education, Inc. Copyright 1992 by Delta Education, Inc. Reprinted with permission.

Figure 6-10 Scoring guide for pictorial interpretation assessment.

Element	0–8 Points
Differences among pictures	At least three key differences are clearly stated. Differences might relate to the snowman's height, size, position of arms, depiction of eyes. (0–3 points)
Ordering of pictures	Pictures arranged in correct order (picture 1, picture 2, picture 3). (0–1 point)
Reasons for changes	Judge how well the reasons for changes relate to the *evidence* in the pictures and to *knowledge* of heating and melting. Examples: The sun came out and melted the snowman; the longer the sun was out, the more the snowman melted. The snowman melted because he got hot. The snow changed to water because of the sun. (0–4 points)
Scoring	Outstanding 7–8 points Satisfactory 5–6 points Needs improvement 3–4 points Unsatisfactory 0–2 points

Concept Maps. Psychologists theorize that learners organize their knowledge into connected networks called *knowledge structures.* The size of these structures, the number of connections between items of knowledge, and the organization and richness of the connections are all important for processing knowledge, constructing meanings, and solving problems (Rosenshine, 1997).

As discussed in Chapter 3, a **concept map** is a visual representation of a major concept and its connections to subsidiary concepts. Joseph Novak and others (Edmondson, 1999; Mintzes, Wandersee, & Novak, 1998; Novak, 1995) have advocated the use of concept maps in assessing the science understanding of students.

By examining student concept maps before or during instruction, teachers can discover learners' conceptual understandings and their misconceptions. Students' concept maps can then be used by the teacher to provide feedback to students and as a guide to improve instruction.

The concept maps shown in Figure 6-11 provide a means to compare the conceptual understanding of two students on blood circulation. We might judge that the first student

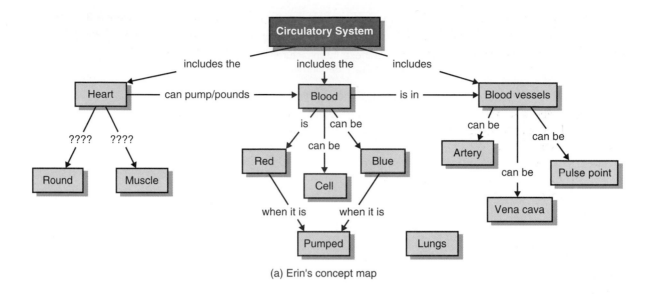

(a) Erin's concept map

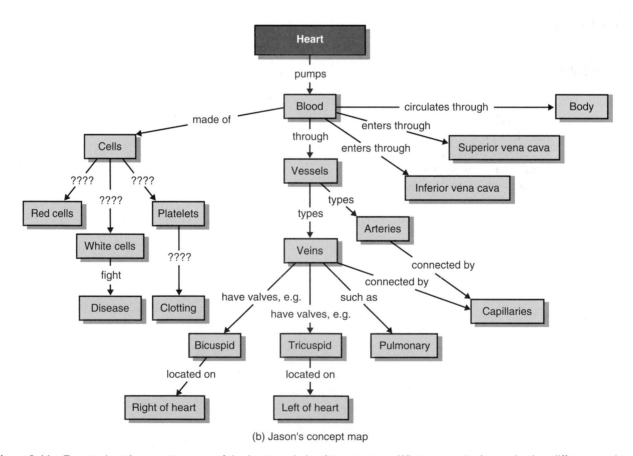

(b) Jason's concept map

Figure 6-11 Two students' concepts maps of the heart and circulatory system. What conceptual organization differences do you note between Erin and Jason?

Source: Figures from Joel J. Mintzes, James H. Wandersee, and Joseph D. Novak, in J. Mintzes, J. Wandersee, and J. Novak (Eds.), *Teaching Science for Understanding: A Human Constructivist View,* copyright © 1998 by Academic Press. Used with permission from Elsvier.

focused more on descriptive aspects of the heart and circulatory system, whereas the second student showed more understanding by focusing on interactions. The concept map assessments in this case might serve as a basis of feedback to students and scaffolding to improve learning.

Performance Tasks and Rubrics. In the performance task shown in Figure 6-12, students make predictions about what happens in an illustrated circuit when switches are either open or closed. Then they construct the circuit and use it to test predictions. Finally, they write explanations of what happens to each of the bulbs in the test. This performance task gauges how well students solve a real-world scientific problem in a laboratory setting. It is appropriate for students in about grade 4 or above. Using what you learned from the 5-E lesson on electrical circuits in Chapter 4, do the performance task in Figure 6-12 for yourself before reading on.

Rubrics could be used in assessing levels of understanding. Two rubrics might be appropriate for the electrical circuits task. One of the rubrics could assess understandings and abilities needed in constructing the circuit. A second rubric could be used to assess students' explanations.

Holistic rubrics might be used with performance tasks, such as an electrical circuits task. Scoring guides are holistic if teachers make judgments about task performance by considering simultaneously all of the criteria that go into a high-quality product or performance. Teachers observe, assess, and evaluate the student's written responses to the questions. The teachers also assess and evaluate the student's performance in constructing and using the test circuit. A holistic scoring guide for the electrical circuits task is shown in Figure 6-13.

Using Performance Tasks to Assess the Application of Inquiry Procedures and Science Processes. A distinctive element of the *National Science Education Standards* is the dual focus on students attaining science understanding and, at the same time, improving their abilities to inquire. Assessing inquiry procedures and science processes, both formatively for learning improvement and summatively for accountability and grading, is an important part of elementary and middle school science programs.

In an inquiry-oriented classroom, there are many opportunities to extend learning activities by making them the centerpiece of performance tasks for assessing science processes and procedures.

Assessing Data-Gathering Processes with a Leaves Task. *Data-gathering* refers to the process of students making observations and recording data about objects, organisms, and events. Figure 6-14 shows a data-gathering task about leaves that can provide teachers with knowledge of students' observing and communicating skills. Figure 6-15 shows a leaves data sheet for use with the leaves task. The leaves task is suitable for use with students from K–8, depending on their prior experiences and developmental levels. It may be adapted for a variety of science topics.

When assessing data-gathering, consider the following questions:

* Does the child use all appropriate senses and instruments such as a hand lens in main observations?
* Are observations reported in writing, labeled drawings, and charts or data tables?
* How well do the written communication and drawings relate to and accurately correspond with what was observed with each sense?
* Does the communication provide details of what was observed?

Performance Task:

A. PREDICT: Study the diagram of the electric circuit. Make a prediction about what will happen to each light bulb if switch 1 is closed and switch 2 is open.

My Predictions:

Bulb 1: Lit   Not Lit   (Circle Lit or Not Lit)
Bulb 2: Lit   Not Lit   (Circle Lit or Not Lit)
Bulb 3: Lit   Not Lit   (Circle Lit or Not Lit)

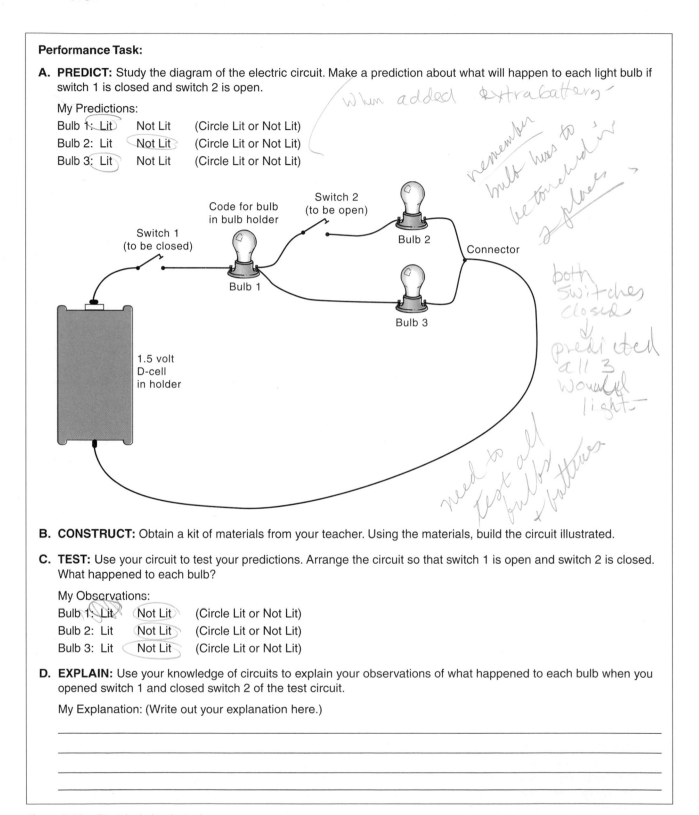

When added extra battery —

remember bulb has to be touched in 2 places →

both switches closed
↓
predicted all 3 would light —

need to test all bulbs + batteries

B. CONSTRUCT: Obtain a kit of materials from your teacher. Using the materials, build the circuit illustrated.

C. TEST: Use your circuit to test your predictions. Arrange the circuit so that switch 1 is open and switch 2 is closed. What happened to each bulb?

My Observations:

Bulb 1: Lit   Not Lit   (Circle Lit or Not Lit)
Bulb 2: Lit   Not Lit   (Circle Lit or Not Lit)
Bulb 3: Lit   Not Lit   (Circle Lit or Not Lit)

D. EXPLAIN: Use your knowledge of circuits to explain your observations of what happened to each bulb when you opened switch 1 and closed switch 2 of the test circuit.

My Explanation: (Write out your explanation here.)

_____
_____
_____
_____

Figure 6-12 Electrical circuits task.

Score: 0 Points

The student does not attempt to solve the problem. A 0-point score is characterized by most of the following:

- No predictions are given.
- There is no attempt to build the circuit.
- No observations are made.
- No explanations are given.

Score: 1 point

The overall responses are inconsistent with sound scientific thinking and investigation procedures. The responses indicate the student has little or no understanding of the problem and of circuit ideas. A 1-point response is characterized by most of the following:

- Predictions are inaccurate or missing.
- The student makes a limited attempt to build the test circuit; the circuit, if constructed, has many faults.
- The student's attempts to test the predictions are unsuccessful; the observations are missing.
- Explanations are missing or they are illogical and cannot be supported; understanding of circuit concepts is not demonstrated.

Score: 2 points

The responses represent a limited attempt at applying a sound scientific approach to the problem. Although the responses exhibit errors, incompleteness, and/or omissions, the student demonstrates some understanding of how to predict, how to construct a test circuit, and how to use the circuit to test predictions. Little understanding of the concept of circuits is demonstrated. A 2-point response is characterized by most of the following:

- The student makes two or more inaccurate predictions.
- The student attempts to build a test circuit but it is faulty.
- The students uses the constructed circuit to test the predictions.
- Observations of what happens to the bulbs in the test are inaccurate.
- Explanations are illogical and cannot be supported; clear understanding of the circuit concepts is not demonstrated.

Score: 3 points

The overall response is largely consistent with a sound scientific approach to design. The response indicates that the student has a general understanding of the problem, of how to make predictions, how to construct a circuit, and how to use it to test predictions. The quality of the explanation is good, although minor errors may be present. A 3-point response is characterized by most of the following:

- The student makes generally accurate predictions, with no more than one error.
- The student's test circuit is well constructed with only minor faults.
- The student uses the circuit to test predictions; one or two observations may be inaccurate.
- The explanation is logical and, for the most part, is consistent with observations and shows understanding of circuit ideas.

Score: 4 points

The responses are consistent with a sound scientific approach. The responses indicate that the student has a clear understanding of the problem and of how to predict, construct circuits, and use the circuits to test predictions. The explanation may, in some cases, define additional aspects of the problem or include extensions beyond the requirements of the task. Some inconsistencies may be present, but they are overwhelmed by the superior quality of the responses. A 4-point score is characterized by most of the following:

- The student makes accurate predictions.
- The circuit is well constructed, with no flaws.
- The circuit is successfully used to test the predictions; all observations in the test are accurate.
- The explanation is clear and detailed, and is convincingly supported with the data collected and an accurate presentation of circuit concepts.

Figure 6-13 Holistic scoring guide for an electrical circuits task.

Figure 6-14 Data capture assessment.
Source "Leaves" An Investigation" and "Leaves Data Capture Sheet" (pp. 67–68) in *TCM771 Science Assessment,* 1994 Westminster, CA: Teacher Created Materials, Inc. Copyright 1994 by Teacher Created Materials, Inc. Reprinted with permission.

Observing Leaves

NSES

Science Standards

All students should develop understanding of:

- Characteristics of organisms (K–4).

Investigation

- Collect different kinds of leaves. If possible, allow children to gather their own leaves around their homes and the school.

- Give each group of students a small collection of leaves. Instruct the students to observe the different characteristics (properties, attributes) of the leaves. Ask: *What do you notice about the leaves in your collection? How are they alike? In what ways are they different?* Provide rulers and magnifying glasses for the children to use in observing the leaves. Encourage the children in each group to discuss with one another the similarities and differences among their leaves.

- Let each child choose two leaves to observe and describe. Instruct the students to work individually to compare the leaves according to each of these characteristics: size, color, number of points, and number of veins. Give them the "Leaves Data Sheet" to record their observations.

Assessing Data-Gathering Processes with a Plant Growth Task. One performance task uses a plant growth project to assess ability to apply processes of science. The performance task requires students to observe pairs of growing plants over time and to answer questions about them. During this task, students measure, record data, and determine patterns and trends from the data. The products to be judged are the students' oral or written answers to the questions.

The scorer judges the quality of students' performance in measuring plant heights using a four-point rubric as a scoring guide. The rubric is shown in Figure 6-16. Because the rubric is detailed, teachers will need to adapt it to their particular situations.

A mealworm activity similar to this one was discussed in Chapter 2 as an example of an investigation involving descriptive, classificatory, and experimental procedures.

Assessing Scientific Processes and Investigative Procedures with a Mealworms Task. The assessment of scientific processes and investigation procedures in practical activities can be structured or formalized to guide teacher observations. In one performance task, students are introduced to mealworms, provided necessary materials, including mealworms and different foods, and directed to find out the food preferences of the mealworms.

A student record page, such as the one in Figure 6-17, can be used by students to list observational notes and results on the mealworms task. The teacher may provide a cue, prompt, or question if students are stuck and cannot continue or if the teacher seeks students' thinking or reason for some action.

Leaves Data Sheet

Name _____ Date _____

- Draw a picture of Leaf #1

- Draw a picture of Leaf #2

Look at Leaf #1.

- What is its color or colors?

  _____

  _____

- How many centimeters long is Leaf #1?

  _____

  _____

- How many points does Leaf #1 have?

  _____

  _____

- Describe the veins in Leaf #1.

  _____

  _____

Look at Leaf #2.

- What is its color or colors?

  _____

  _____

- How many centimeters long is Leaf #2?

  _____

  _____

- How many points does Leaf #2 have?

  _____

  _____

- Describe the veins in Leaf #2.

  _____

  _____

Figure 6-15 Data sheet for leaves task.

The teacher might, for example, make this suggestion: "One way you can try to find the food preference is to make a mark in the middle of the paper. Take some of each food and place it at the same distance from the mark and then put some mealworms on the mark" (Meng & Doran, 1993).

The student inquiry behaviors checklist in Figure 6-18 lists problem-solving skills for the observer to focus on during the mealworms task. If cues or prompts are given, the observer should make a record of them. The checklist spotlights specific behaviors to look for as students progress toward finding answers to the question. Emphasis is placed on observable behaviors such as: "places approximately equal quantities of food on the sections of the paper."

Figure 6-16 Rubric for performance assessment in a unit on plants.
Source From "Scoring Active Assessments: Setting Clear Criteria and Adapting Them to Your Students Are the Key to Scoring Classroom Performance," by Sabra Price and George E. Hein, October 1994; *Science and Children 32*, no. 2 p. 29. Copyright 1994, National Science Teachers Association, 1840 Wilson Blvd., Arlington, VA 22201-3000.

Sample Scoring System

Question One. Students are asked to measure the height of two seedlings and to record their results.

Scoring Rubric for Question One

0 =   The student either did not record results or reported measurements that were inaccurate by more than a certain percentage determined by the teacher.

1 =   The student did not record results, but did report approximate measurements. The teacher needs to determine the meaning of "approximate." This will depend on such things as the markings on students' rulers and students' classroom experiences.

2 =   The student recorded approximate measurements.

3 =   The student recorded accurate measurements. The teacher needs to determine the meaning of "accurate."

Question Two. Students are asked to explain their recorded measurements to their teacher.

Scoring Rubric for Question Two

0 =   The student provided either no explanation or one that makes no sense to the teacher or is unrelated to any unit activities.

1 =   The student's explanation related to unit activities but did not explain the growth pattern.

2 =   The student provided an explanation for the growth pattern.

3 =   The student gave more than one reasonable explanation for the growth pattern.

Figure 6-17 Example of student record page for mealworms activity.
Source: From Elizabeth Meng and Rodney L. Doran, *Improving Instruction and Learning Through Evaluation: Elementary School Science* (Columbus, OH: ERIC Clearinghouse for Science, Mathematics, and Environmental Education, 1993), p. 93.

Mealworms

> Find out if the mealworms prefer some of these foods to others. If they do, which ones do they prefer?

a)   Record notes and results as you go along here:

b)   Write down what you found about the foods the mealworms prefer here:

☐ Uses hand lens correctly

☐ Hint given for using hand lens

☐ Deliberately provides mealworm with choice; i.e., at least 2 foods at once

☐ Employs an effective strategy such as:
  (i)   uses 6 or more mealworms if all 4 foods compared at once
  (ii) compares foods in all possible pairs with 1 mealworm
  (iii) tries at least 4 mealworms with one food at a time

☐ Attempts to provide equal quantities of different foods

☐ Places approximately equal quantities of food on the sections of the paper

☐ Attempts to release mealworms at equal distance from all foods *or* arranges mealworms to be randomly distributed around food

☐ Arranges to release mealworms from points equidistant from foods, *or* places mealworms randomly around foods

☐ Arranges for all mealworms to have same time to choose (i.e., puts them all down together or uses a clock)

☐ Uses clock to time definite events

☐ Allows about 4–7 minutes for mealworms to make choice (not necessarily timed)

☐ Examines behavior carefully (to see if food is being eaten)

☐ Counts mealworms near each pile after a certain time (or notes which food the mealworm is on for strategy [ii] above)

☐ Makes notes at (a) on record page (however brief)

☐ Records details such as time of choice and numbers near each food

☐ Can read stop clock correctly (to nearest second)

☐ Makes a record of finding at (b) on record page without prompting

☐ Results at (a) and (b) consistent with evidence (even if only rough)

☐ Results based on and consistent with quantitative evidence

Figure 6-18 Laboratory student behavior checklist. *Source:* From Elizabeth Meng and Rodney L. Doran, *Improving Instruction and Learning Through Evaluation: Elementary School Science* (Columbus, OH: ERIC Clearinghouse for Science, Mathematics, and Environmental Education, 1993), p. 124.

When the checklist is used formatively, scaffolding instruction is provided as needed related to specific checklist criteria to individuals, small groups, or the class as a whole. Consider the checklist as an example that shows how to construct an assessment checklist that uses content (the behavior of mealworms) as the vehicle to gather data on the skills and processes used by students in scientific investigation or problem solving.

Which of your science activities lend themselves to this type of assessment?

Assessing Inquiry Procedures in Science with Performance Tasks: The TIMSS Test. Performance assessments are especially useful for assessing the planning and implementing of inquiry procedures in science. Since the 1980s, assessment data have been collected in the United States and other countries from students in elementary and middle school grades on a series of practical hands-on science activities (Chan, Doran, & Lenhardt, 1999). The 1995–1996 Third International Mathematics and Science Study TIMSS—now The International Mathematics and Science Study—collected data on a

Although interpretations of data from the TIMSS and the earlier international comparisons vary, information from these studies is important for the development of educational policies at national and state levels.

Task	Description	Task	Integrated Tasks (Science and Mathematics)
Pulse	Student investigates changes in pulse rate during exercise, records and analyzes data, and explains results.	Shadows	Student manipulates the position of light source and object to find three positions at which a shadow is twice the width of an object and expresses the relationship of distance of the light and object to the screen as a general rule.
Magnets	Student determines the stronger of two magnets and describes strategies to support the conclusion.		
Batteries	Student determines which of four batteries is worn out, describes strategies, and uses concept knowledge to explain proper arrangement of batteries in a flashlight.	Plasticine	Given only two standard masses, student develops and describes strategies to determine the masses of lumps of various specified masses.
Rubber Band	Student attaches increasing numbers of masses to a rubber band, investigates the effect on the length, and explains results.		
Solutions	Student investigates the effect of different temperatures on rate of tablet disintegration; collects, records, and analyzes data; and explains results.		

Figure 6-19 Description of eighth-grade performance assessment tasks from the Third International Mathematics and Science Study (TIMSS).
Source: From "Learning from the TIMSS," by Alfred Chan, Rodney Doran, and Carol Lenhardt, 1999, *The Science Teacher, 66*(1), p. 20. Copyright 1999 by National Science Teachers Association. Reprinted with permission.

half-million students from 41 nations. U.S. students were well above the average science performance of students worldwide at the fourth-grade level, surpassed only by students from Korea (U.S. Department of Education, 1997). U.S. eighth graders were slightly above the international average in science but trailed the average performance of students in 16 other countries (U.S. Department of Education, 1996).

Figure 6-19 shows seven performance tasks that were included on the TIMSS tests at the eighth-grade level in science (Chan, Doran, & Lenhardt, 1999). These tests used science content and equipment from physics, chemistry, and biology. Students completed the tasks at tables where the necessary materials were provided. Students were asked to manipulate equipment and materials; observe, reason, and record data in test booklets; and interpret data.

Figure 6-20 provides the directions and questions for a TIMSS task called the Solutions Task. In this task, students first planned procedures to determine what effect different water temperatures have on the speed with which effervescent antacid tablets dissolve. The students then carried out tests, measuring water temperatures and corresponding times for the tablets to dissolve. Students were asked to use the evidence from their tests to draw conclusions about the effect of different water temperatures on the speed with which a tablet dissolves. Finally, the students were instructed to explain why different temperatures have different effects. Student activities in this performance assessment closely parallel the tasks of inquiry identified by the writers of the *National Science Education Standards*.

Materials:
Hot and cold water
Several beakers
Effervescent antacid tablets
Stirrer
Clock or watch with a second hand
Thermometer
30 centimeter ruler

Task: Plan an experiment to find out what effect different water temperatures have on the speed with which the tablets dissolve.
    Part one. Write down a plan that includes what will be measured, how many measurements will be taken, and how the measurements will be presented in a table.
    Part two. Carry out the test(s). Make a table and record all measurements.
    Part three. According to the investigation, what effect do different water temperatures have on the speed with which a tablet dissolves?
    Part four. Explain why different water temperatures have different effects.
    Part five. If the plan must be changed, describe the changes and explain why they will be made. If there are no changes, write "no change." Empty all beakers into the waste container, dry them, and leave everything the way it was found.

Figure 6-20 Directions and questions for the TIMSS solutions task.
Source: From "Learning from the TIMSS," by Alfred Chan, Rodney Doran, and Carol Lenhardt, 1999, *The Science Teacher, 66*(1), p. 20. Copyright 1999 by National Science Teachers Association. Reprinted with permission.

Table 6-3 shows the average percentage scores on each question for the solutions performance assessment. How do U.S. eighth-graders' average percentage scores compare with the international average? On what tasks are they above average? On what tasks are they below average? Why do you think these trends exist? For example, why do U.S. students lag behind in planning investigations but exceed international averages in drawing and explaining conclusions?

Assessing Multiple Objectives Through Performance Assessments

Students can use previously acquired science knowledge and understanding to solve problems and create products in situations that are new or different from those to which they were exposed.

Model Building. Physical models that illustrate students' understanding of natural objects, organisms, structures, and phenomena and that require abilities to use science inquiry processes and procedures are excellent products for assessment. In building models,

TABLE 6-3   AVERAGE PERCENTAGE SCORES ON EACH PERFORMANCE CRITERION FOR THE TIMSS SOLUTIONS TASK

Sample	Overall Task Average	Q1 Plan Investigation	Q2 Conduct Investigation		Q3 Draw Conclusions	Q4 Explain Conclusion	Q5 Evaluate Design
			Presentation	Data Quality			
International	49	44	62	59	77	22	30
United States	48	33	64	59	82	27	24

Source: From "Learning from the TIMSS," by Alfred Chan, Rodney Doran, and Carol Lenhardt, 1999, *The Science Teacher, 66*(1), p. 21. Copyright 1999 by National Science Teachers Association. Reprinted with permission.

students are required to research relevant information, discover what kind of models illustrate the scientific concept(s) to be shown, collect needed scientific supplies and equipment, plan and build the model, and explain it to the class and teacher. Students have successfully accomplished these things for models of the solar system, geological structures, physiological systems of the human body, and so forth.

Student Demonstrations. Students can demonstrate much of what they know and understand about scientific concepts and their interrelationships through planning, manipulating, and demonstrating with scientific supplies and equipment. The audience may be their own classmates and teacher, other classes, their parents, or other persons. Individual students or groups may give the demonstrations, such as showing how electrical circuits work, exhibiting static electricity in everyday situations, or demonstrating what happens when colored lights are mixed.

Student Projects. Student projects may uncover much about students' understanding and thinking. Project assessments provide the teacher with insight into how well students have learned, recorded, and put their knowledge into practical use. The teacher and students should work out expectations of what the projects will encompass *before* students start their projects. Primary grade students often make something as part of their science learning.

In the example of project assessment that follows, groups of students worked together to design an aquarium. The project is built around a "WebQuest" in which students use the Internet to gather information about the habitat and animals selected. A description of the performance task, the detailed rubric, and the WebQuest for the project was originally found online. Websites change and the aquarium project is no longer available on the Internet.

Here is the students' task.

> **Performance Task: You are a zoologist at a city zoo. Many people have suggested adding aquariums to the zoo. Your task as a zoologist is to (a) choose a type of water habitat; (b) choose three animals that can coexist in the water habitat; and (c) design an aquarium so that it is an appropriate habitat for the three animals.**

The students would need to have explored the habitat and food needs of organisms in previous activities. In this activity, they use reference books and the Internet to gather information on the habitat and animals selected. They will need to find information concerning the different components of the habitat, such as plants and rocks, the food that should be available for their animals, and what enables each of the animals to live in a water habitat.

Their aquarium design can be presented to the teacher and the class in the form of a Kid Pix or PowerPoint display or as an actual aquarium. As the teacher, you will be there to assess learning and provide scaffolding and instruction as needed. But do not give too much assistance—this is a student project.

A rubric is used to assess the students' aquarium designs and their performance in oral discussions. The rubric might include these three main criteria:

1. The student identifies and distinguishes between freshwater and saltwater habitats.
2. The student lists at least three animals that live in the chosen water habitat and gives information about each, including the food, shelter, and parts of the body that enable them to live in the environment.
3. The aquarium design includes an appropriate habitat for each of the three animals, including shelter and a source of food for each.

Take some time to develop the aquarium task rubric by writing quality descriptions for three levels: high, medium, and low quality. How does the project call for the development of knowledge and understanding and of science processes and procedures?

Science Fair Projects. Students in many elementary and middle schools are required to develop science fair projects. Projects are usually evaluated by external judges, using a common set of judging criteria. Figure 6-21 shows a composite of the judging criteria used in many science fairs.

The first step in creating a good science fair project is for the student to select an interesting, sufficiently narrow question to investigate. In Chapter 2 we identified and gave examples of three types of scientific investigations: descriptive, classificatory, and experimental. Judging criteria often favor experimental investigations, with hypotheses, responding and manipulated variables, and adequate controls designed into the investigation. Because true experiments are difficult for younger learners, we suggest that school and district science fairs be for students from the fourth or fifth grade up. Younger students might be involved in descriptive and classificatory investigations and the construction of models and demonstrations. These might be displayed in their own classrooms.

Judging Criteria	Indicators
Creativity	• Creativity is shown in the selection of a problem to investigate. • Ingenuity in the design and development of the project is shown.
Scientific Thought	• The problem selected is appropriate. • The question and hypothesis are clear, well formulated, and sufficiently narrow to be investigated empirically. • Experimental variables are clearly defined and appropriate controls are used. • Data are well organized and accurate graphs are shown. • Data collected serve as adequate evidence to support the conclusions formed.
Thoroughness	• The project shows thorough planning. • Review of background information is thorough. • All data are accurate. • All data collected were used in drawing conclusions. • A project notebook sufficiently documents the student's work from beginning to end.
Skill	• The project clearly represents the student's work. • The project is sturdy and well constructed. • The student clearly understands the equipment used. • The project shows continual attention to safety standards.
Clarity	• The student kept and displayed an original, bound logbook. • The project report was well done and easily understandable, with appropriate documentation. • The project display was eye-appealing, with appropriate materials, posters, charts, and graphs. • Lettering, signs, and diagrams are neat and accurate. • Visual aids assist the reader or judge in understanding the project.

Figure 6-21 Science fair judging criteria.
Source: Multiple science fair judging sheets found on the Internet.

In carrying out experimental investigations, students must perform a test to answer their research questions. If they are interested in earthworms, for example, they might perform a test to see if temperature has an effect on how earthworms move. Students would have to get some earthworms, find a way to vary the temperature of the soil in the earthworm container, and measure what happens, related to earthworm movement, at different temperatures.

The question or hypothesis, background information, experiment design, and results might be recorded in a bound notebook. The data collected would be used as evidence to answer the question posed. Students would need to carry out the project with only a little help from parents, teachers, or friends.

The project should be clearly and dramatically displayed, perhaps using show boards. Finally, the students would explain the project in detail through an interview with a judge or team of judges.

For elementary and middle school students, downplay the competitive nature of projects. The goal is for students to improve in their abilities and understanding of science, not necessarily to "win." Thus, you should use the project assessment formatively to improve student learning, rather than summatively for grades. Science fair projects are fun. Students will learn a great deal, and they will display to others what students know and have learned.

Examples of Traditional Assessment Items

Traditional assessment items are useful for assessing students' knowledge, understanding, and abilities to inquire. They have the advantage that they are quicker to construct, administer, and score than performance assessments.

Assessing Science Knowledge with Traditional Items

Traditional multiple-choice, short-answer, completion, and essay items can be useful and effective for assessing science knowledge, understanding, and abilities.

Multiple-Choice Items. You will probably use multiple-choice items frequently in your assessment program to measure the attainment of science knowledge. Multiple-choice items have three parts:

- *Stem:* presents the task or question to your students
- *Distractors:* incorrect responses
- *Correct response*

Item 1. Goal: Students should know that

- water circulates through the atmosphere in what is known as the *water cycle*.

Which of the following is *not* a form of precipitation?
A. hail
B. wind
C. rain
D. snow

Source: 2000 National Assessment of Educational Progress (NAEP), fourth-grade level.

Go to the Homework and Exercises section in Chapter 6 of MyEducationLab and view the video *Science Fair Projects*. In this video clip, students explain projects they have planned and carried out. Through student discussions of their projects, such as Cleaning Golf Balls, Amount of Water Held by Different Kinds of Diapers, and Electrical Conductors, teachers have an opportunity to assess how well students understand and are able to use the tasks of inquiry emphasized earlier in the text (Figure 1-3).

A number of items in this section are from released tests from the National Assessment of Educational Progress (NAEP), a government-sponsored program. Access more NAEP released tests items at http://nces.ed.gov/nationsreportcard/ITMRLS/searchresults.asp.

Item 2. Goal: Students should know that

* the earth is the third planet from the sun in a system that includes the moon, the sun, and the planets.

The moon is
A. always closer to the sun than it is to the earth.
B. always much closer to the earth than it is to the sun.
C. about the same distance from the sun as it is from the earth.
D. sometimes closer to the sun than it is to the earth and sometimes closer to the earth than it is to the sun.

Reference: Stahly, Krockover, & Shepardson (1999).

Item 3. Goal: Students should develop knowledge of scientific inquiry.

Which task would you undertake first in scientific inquiry?
A. collect relevant data
B. ask a question that can be investigated
C. report your investigation and findings to others
D. use data in forming explanations

Source: Released test item from National Assessment of Educational Progress (NAEP), fourth-grade level.

Completion and Short-Answer Items. Short-answer and completion items require students to generate, not just recognize, correct answers, as is shown in the following example. Note that item 4 is a modification of item 1.

Item 4. Name three forms of precipitation.

_____

_____

_____

Score all assessments as quickly as possible, give feedback to students on their results, and use the assessment results to provide feedback to learners and to modify your own instruction to improve student learning.

Assessing Science Understanding with Traditional Items

Traditional assessments can be used to go beyond simple recall to assess student understanding of science concepts and principles. Standard multiple-choice items and justified multiple-choice items can be designed that require students to integrate information and to use knowledge in thinking and problem solving.

Using Standard Multiple-Choice Items to Assess Understanding. Here is an example of a multiple-choice item that measures understanding rather than mere recall.

Item 5. Goal: Students should understand that

* energy is a property of many substances and is associated with heat, light, electricity, mechanical motion, sound, nuclei, and the nature of a chemical.

Go to the Homework and Exercises section in Chapter 6 of MyEducationLab, and select the artifact *Rocks* (6–8) to see an item assessing students' knowledge of the rock cycle. In the item, nine stages of the rock cycle are given out of order. Students are asked to number the stages 1 to 9 to indicate the order in which they occur.

Beans and coal both have stored energy. Where did the energy come from that is stored in beans and coal?

    A. from the earth's gravity
    B. from the sun's light
    C. from the heat in the earth's core
    D. from the airs in carbon dioxide

Source: 2000 National Assessment of Educational Progress (NAEP), fourth-grade level.

This item assesses understanding because it requires students to think about two different examples of stored energy and then to examine each possible source of energy to find one that fits both samples. The item was designed by the NAEP (National Assessment of Educational Progress) project to be used on a national assessment, but it can be used formatively if teachers score it quickly, give immediate feedback, provide opportunity for students to learn from their mistakes, and use the assessment results to modify instruction.

Assessing Understanding with Justified Multiple-Choice Items. In justified multiple-choice questions, students first mark the best answer and then explain in several sentences why they chose that answer. A rubric might be used to assess students' explanations of their answers. An example of a justified multiple-choice item is shown in Figure 6-22.

Figure 6-22 Justified multiple-choice assessment.

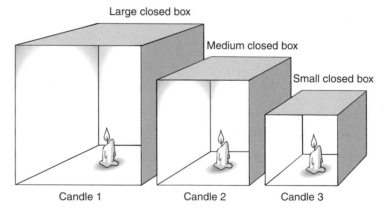

Directions

Three candles, exactly the same size, were put in different boxes like those in the drawing below and lit at the same time. Then the boxes were closed.

Large closed box

Medium closed box

Small closed box

Candle 1   Candle 2   Candle 3

Circle the letter that shows the order in which the candle flames most likely will go out.

    A. 1, 2, 3   C. 3, 1, 2
    B. 2, 3, 1   D. 3, 2, 1

Explain (in two or three sentences) why you think the answer you selected is correct.

Assessing Understanding from Written Responses. Essays, which involve written responses, represent an important way for students to demonstrate understanding. Through an essay, a student might interpret data, describe and explain an event, or show relationships among facts, generalizations, definitions, values, and skills. Like all assessment devices, the written response or essay has disadvantages as well as advantages:

1. Written response (essays) show how well the student is able to organize and present ideas, but scoring may be subjective without firm answers unless you have a clear scoring guide.
2. Written responses show varying degrees of correctness, because there is often not just one right or wrong answer, but scoring requires excessive time.
3. Written responses assess abilities to analyze problems using pertinent information and to arrive at generalizations or conclusions, but scoring is influenced by spelling, handwriting, sentence structure, and other extraneous items.
4. Written responses assess deeper meanings, reasoning, and interrelationships rather than isolated bits of factual materials, but questions may be either ambiguous or obvious unless you carefully construct them.

To offset the disadvantages of essays, you must carefully construct each essay question. Word the question so students will be limited, as much as possible, to the concepts being tested.

Item 6. Goal: Students should develop

* abilities necessary to do scientific inquiry (NSES K–4, 5–8).

A science fair judge asks you, "What is a controlled investigation?" Write out your answer.

_____

_____

_____

Scoring criteria for item 6: The student's answer must show clearly that

* a responding variable and manipulated variable are selected;
* what is investigated is how the responding variable changes in response to changes in a manipulated variable; and
* all other variables are controlled or held constant.

From these three scoring criteria, the teacher might develop a rubric to use as a scoring guide. The rubric would show the quality of the responses relative to each criterion necessary for the student to receive full, partial, or no credit.

Here are two related essay questions to assess your students' ability to interpret scientific concepts in their own words. Item 7 calls for an explanation of a physical phenomenon. Item 8 requires students to describe a test of the explanation given in item 7.

Item 7. Goal: Students should understand that

* unbalanced forces will cause changes in the speed or direction of an object's motion (NSES 5–8).

In the floating and sinking of golf balls task, explain why one golf ball floated and one sank in fresh water.

_____

_____

Items 7 and 8 would fit a
fourth- or fifth-grade lesson on
floating and sinking similar to
the one developed in Chapter 5.

Item 8. How could you test your explanation?

_____

_____

_____

The following set of related items shows written response questions used with an investigation. Items 9 and 10 ask students to interpret data from an investigation. Item 11 requires students to apply the concepts and relationships from items 9 and 10 in a novel situation.

Items 9, 10, and 11. Goals:

a. Students should understand that energy is transferred in many ways (NSES 5–8).
b. Students should develop abilities necessary to do scientific inquiry (NSES K–4, 5–8).

One hot, sunny day Sally left two buckets of water out in the sun. The two buckets were the same except that one was black and the other was white. She made certain that there was the same amount of water in each bucket. She carefully measured the temperature of the water in both buckets at the beginning and end of the day. The following pictures show what Sally found.

Look at the pictures of Sally's experiment.

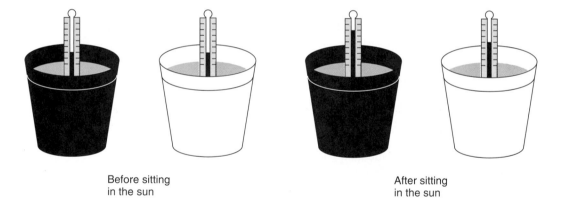

Before sitting
in the sun

After sitting
in the sun

Item 9. What can Sally conclude from her experiment?

_____

_____

Item 10. What is the evidence for Sally's conclusion?

_____

_____

Item 11. How does the experiment help explain why people often choose to wear white clothes in hot weather?

_____

_____

Source: Adapted from released test items, National Assessment of Educational Progress, grade 4, 2000.

Score and Description

Complete
 Student explains that white clothes reflect more heat from the sun than black clothes, or that black clothes absorb more heat from the sun than white clothes.
   a. Black clothes soak up the heat from the sun.
   b. The sun's rays bounce off white clothes.

Partial   Student explains that black clothes attract more heat or that white clothes do not attract as much heat.

Unsatisfactory/Incorrect
 Student provides little or no explanation that is related to the heat-absorbing proper- ties of dark-colored clothes and light-colored clothes, or gives unrelated answers.
   a. They stay cooler in white clothes.
   b. The sun likes dark clothes better.

Figure 6-23 NAEP scoring guide for essay item 11.

You will be able to overcome or minimize subjectivity in scoring answers to written questions by preparing a rubric beforehand and scoring each question separately. If a list of the important ideas you expect is made before scoring, there is less chance for ambiguity while scoring. This list can be developed with your students or at least shared with them when they get the assignment.

Figure 6-23 shows the scoring guide used by NAEP to evaluate responses to item 11. This item proved to be quite difficult for the national sample of fourth-grade students who took the NAEP tests. Only 12% of the national sample wrote complete explanations and 15% supplied partial explanations, while 73% gave unsatisfactory, incorrect, or off-task answers.

Assessing the Application of Science Processes and Inquiry Procedures with Traditional Items

Adding traditional items to your plan for assessing the application of science processes and inquiry procedures can help to achieve balance in assessment. Such items are often easy to construct, are quick to score, and can provide the basis for immediate feedback for the im- provement of learning.

Assessing Investigative Procedures with Justified Multiple-Choice Items. Ability to ap- ply scientific procedures can be assessed with standard multiple-choice items, especially if they are combined with essays as is shown in the following examples.

Item 12. Goal: Students should develop abilities to do scientific inquiry.

John cuts grass for several different neighbors. Each week he makes the rounds with his lawn mower. The grass is usually different in the lawns. It is tall in some lawns, but not in others. Which of the following is a suitable hypothesis he could investigate related to this situation?
    A. Lawn mowing is more difficult when the weather is warm.
    B. The amount of fertilizer a lawn receives is important.
    C. Lawns that receive more water have longer grass.
    D. The more hills there are in a lawn, the harder it is to cut.

Item 13. Explain in a few sentences why you think your answer choice in item 12 is better than the other choices.

Complete answers to item 13 should note that

- the variable of interest (responding variable) in the item stem is *length of grass;*
- length of grass is a variable only in answer choice C; and
- answer choice C implies a hypothesis/question that can be investigated: *What effect does the amount of watering have on grass length?*

Items 14, 15, and 16. Goal: Students should develop abilities necessary to do scientific inquiry (NSES K–4, 5–8).

Context: Shannon decided to compare different kinds of popcorn to find out which was the best buy. She bought three kinds of popcorn: regular white popcorn, regular yellow popcorn, and gourmet yellow popcorn. She put 50 kernels of each kind in the popper. She kept the popper running for each batch until the popcorn stopped popping. Then she counted the number of kernels of each kind that popped. She repeated the procedure two more times and averaged the results for each kind of popcorn. Next, she put 25 popped kernels of each kind into a measuring cup to find out which kernels popped the biggest. Then she tasted some of each kind of popcorn. Her results are shown in the following chart.

Kind of popcorn	Average number of kernels that popped	Volume of 25 popped kernels	Price for a 16-ounce bag	Shannon's taste test
Regular white	38	60 ml	$1.19	OK
Regular yellow	46	60 ml	$1.19	BEST
Gourmet yellow	45	80 ml	$1.50	OK

Item 14. Shannon's brother looked at her results and decided that the gourmet popcorn was the best buy. What evidence from the chart supports his decision?
   A. There is no evidence from the chart to support his decision.
   B. More of the gourmet popcorn popped.
   C. There is more popcorn in the bag of gourmet popcorn.
   D. The gourmet popcorn kernels popped the biggest.

Item 15. If Shannon's brother repeated the popcorn test, which results would have the greatest probability of being different for the new test?
   A. the average number of kernels that popped
   B. the volume of 25 popped kernels
   C. the price for a 16-ounce bag
   D. the results of the taste test

Item 16. Shannon decided that the regular yellow popcorn was the best popcorn to buy. Identify two pieces of evidence from the chart that support her decision.

_____

_____

Scoring guide for item 16:

2 points for two acceptable reasons

1 point for one acceptable reason

0 points for no acceptable reasons

Acceptable reasons include:
- Yellow popcorn had the largest number of popped kernels (46 out of 50 popped).
- Yellow popcorn had the best taste.
- Yellow popcorn is one of the cheaper kinds/is cheap.

Source: Adapted from released test items from the National Assessment of Educational Progress (NAEP), fourth-grade level.

Assessing Application of Scientific Procedures with Essay Items.

Item 17. Goal: Students should develop

- abilities of technological design (NSES 5–8).
- understanding that perfectly designed solutions do not exist; all technological solutions have trade-offs, such as safety, cost, efficiency, and appearance (NSES 5–8).

We have just come back from a field trip to our city's landfill. We were told that there was too much trash being discarded and placed in the landfill. How would you gather information about the amount of different types of trash coming from your school cafeteria? Gather the information and use it to set up a trash management and reduction plan for your school cafeteria.

In developing a scoring guide for this assessment, analyze the problem situation, planning techniques, and communication skills to identify specific things you think should be evident in the students' answers, such as ideas about reducing, reusing, and recycling waste. Use either a rubric or a checklist to guide you in scoring the answers.

What are some topics of interest to you, your students, and the community that might lend themselves to this type of assessment?

Characteristics of Items on State Tests of Science

According to the NCLB legislation, all states had to begin administering statewide assessments in science at the elementary, middle school, and high school levels by the 2007–2008 school year. Although they are ultimately based on similar standards, tests of science differ widely from state to state. It is hardly possible to generalize from such an array of tests and items. State education agencies and local school districts typically provide inservice workshops to familiarize teachers with the tests designed for use in their states. Additionally, many states release test items from previous tests to assist teachers as they work with students to improve performance on the tests.

State assessments of science are designed, administered, and scored outside the specific context of classrooms. Results of these assessments are typically not available to teachers until near the end of the school year. Thus, statewide tests of science learning do not typically provide formative information to be used immediately in improving science learning and instruction. Nor are the statewide tests suitable as summative assessments to determine overall levels of understanding at the end of instruction. Rather, as emphasized in Table 6-1, state measures of student understanding and performance are intended to provide a basis for policy makers to judge accountability and formulate new regulations. Statewide tests have standardized administration procedures and ways of using assessment results to reliably and fairly judge the levels of understanding of students.

At the elementary and middle school levels, statewide tests are typically administered at grades 4 or 5 and at grade 8. However, helping students prepare for these high-stakes assessments is an imporant task at every grade level, not just the grade at whch the tests are administered.

One of the first steps in understanding test items used for statewide assessment is to examine the specific standards on which they are based.

Science Standards and Statewide Tests

According to Wilson and Berthenthal (2006):

> Standards are the most important element in the science education system because they make explicit the goals around which the system is organized. . . . They guide the development of curriculum, and the choices of teachers in setting instructional priorities and planning lessons. They are the basis for developing assessments, setting performance standards, and judging student and school performance. (p. 54)

As you read the following standards and examine the test items, take some time to complete Activity 6-1.

Activity 6-1: Matching Science Standards and Test Items

Directions

1. Examine the following sample state standards. Note that the standards include *indicators*. These are the evaluation criteria that teachers will use along with standards in lesson planning and test developers will use in writing tests.
2. Examine each of the first four sample test items. Determine which standard each test item is designed to assess.

Sample State Standards

Standard 1.   Ask questions that can be investigated scientifically.

Sample Indicators

a. The student identifies appropriate questions that can be answered through scientific evidence and knowledge.
b. The student recognizes the question being investigated by observing the investigation procedures.

Standard 2.   Design and conduct a scientific investigation to collect and interpret data about a question.

Sample Indicators

a. The student compares strategies or methods for collecting data.
b. The student selects appropriate method or strategy to collect data.
c. The student determines if an investigation strategy fits the question asked.
d. The student identifies and demonstrates appropriate steps to collect data.
e. The student interprets data collected in an investigation.

Standard 3. Use appropriate tools and techniques to make observations and gather data.

Sample Indicators

    a. Student uses tools (e.g., hand lens, camera) to extend the senses.

    b. Student accurately uses different measuring instruments, such as rulers, balance scales, graduated cylinders, and thermometers, to collect data.

Standard 4. Investigate and understand natural phenomena commonly encountered in daily life, including phenomena related to light, heat, sound, electricity, magnetism, life science processes, and earth and space science concepts and models.

Sample Indicators

    a. The student investigates and understands that natural and artificial magnets have certain characteristics and attract specific types of metals.

    b. Student understands that the sun supplies heat and light to the earth and the moon.

Item ST-1

The following chart shows the results of an experiment designed to study how exercise affects heart rate.

Activity Stage	Heart Rate of Person A (Beats per minute)	Heart Rate of Person B (Beats per minute)	Heart Rate of Person C (Beats per minute)
Before Exercise	75	62	70
After Exercise	100	110	130

Which of these statements is the best conclusion for this experiment?

    A. Exercise triples a person's heart rate.
    B. Exercise decreases a person's heart rate.
    C. Heart rate is not affected by exercise.
    D. Heart rate is increased by exercise.

Source: Released test item, California Standards Test, grade 5.

Item ST-2

Which of the following systems breaks food into nutrients that can be used by the body?

    A. circulatory system
    B. digestive system
    C. respiratory system
    D. reproductive system

Source: Released test item, California Standards Test, grade 5.

Item ST-3

Julie conducted an investigation about seed germination. She kept one group of seeds in a light place. She placed another group of seeds of the same kind in a dark environment.

She kept the seeds moist and observed them for five days. What question was she investigating?

A. Will seeds germinate in the dark?
B. Do seeds need soil for germination?
C. Will seeds germinate better with more moisture?
D. Do seeds need air for germination?

Source: Constructed by the authors.

You might want to check your answers to the standards-items matches against ours. Our answers are:

Standard 1 – Item ST-3
Standard 2 – Item ST-1, Item ST-4
Standard 3 – Item ST-4

Items often assess more than one standard, so that matching standards and items is not an easy task; you may have good reasons for matching them differently than we have.

Examples of Different Types of State Test Items

Test items on state assessments typically include stand-alone multiple-choice items, items requiring written responses, and clusters of items based on a given scenario.

Stand-Alone Test Items. Many released test items are stand alone, multiple-choice items.

Item ST-4

Which best describes a parallel circuit?

A. Electricity flows along one pathway.
B. The flow of electricity comes from one source.
C. Electricity flows along more than one pathway.
D. The flow of electricity comes from more than one source.

Source: Released test items for grade 5, 2003–2006, California Board of Education.

Item ST-5

Which of the following is the **BEST** way to investigate the effect of fertilizers on tomato plants?

A. Put several plants outdoors and several indoors.
B. Add fertilizer to several plants and change the amount of water given to each.
C. Grow several plants under the same conditions, but change the amount of fertilizer added to each.
D. Grow several plants under various temperature conditions, but keep the amount of fertilizer the same for each.

Source: Released test item from California.

Item ST-6

After a rainstorm, Jolanda saw a lot of soil on the sidewalks. Sidewalks next to grassy areas stayed much cleaner. Sidewalks next to areas without grass were covered with soil. Jolanda hypothesized that grass would help protect soil from being washed away. In the classroom, she set up two boxes. She placed grass sod in one box with its roots in the soil. She placed only soil in the second box. Following are some steps (scrambled) that Jolanda carried out.

A. Tilt the boxes the same amount.
B. Draw conclusions from her data.
C. Add moisture to the soil.
D. Observe and measure the amount of erosion of soil in each box.

What should be the order of steps in this investigation?

A. a, c, d, b
B. b, c, a, d
C. c, d, b, a
D. d, b, c, a

Source: Adapted from a series of released test items from the Washington State Assessment Program, 2006.

Items Requiring Written Responses. States also include many written response items in which students might write descriptions and explanations or plan investigations to answer questions. Detailed rubrics are typically provided to facilitate and standardize scoring.

Item ST-7

While observing birds in the neighborhood, James noticed that the birds pecking in the grassy areas had different beaks than the birds feeding at the bird feeder in a tree. Explain why birds have different beaks.

In your description, be sure to:

- Identify **two** different types of bird beaks.
- Describe **why** birds need these different types of beaks.

Use words, labeled pictures, and/or labeled diagrams in your answer.

(Source: Based on released test item from the Washington State Assessment Program, 2006.

Clusters of Related Test Items. Some states use clusters of items related to a scenario. Both multiple-choice and written responses are used with the clusters.

Information for Items ST- 8-12

Jose and Maria noticed the grass in one part of the yard was growing better than in other areas. They thought this happened because parts of the yard received more light than other parts. They did the following investigation with *grass sod* (a layer of grass with its roots in soil).

Hypothesis:
Grass that receives more light will grow taller.

Materials:
grass sod cut into three equal pieces
meter stick
water
200 ml beaker
three trays of the same size
three grow lights connected to timers

Procedure:
1. Set the three pieces of grass sod into the three trays and put the trays in a dark place with the lights above them.
2. Measure the average height of the grass in each tray and record as starting heights.
3. Set the timers to turn the lights on daily: one light for 2 hours, one light for 6 hours, and one light for 12 hours.
4. Water each tray with 200 ml of water every 4 days.
5. Measure the average height of the grass at the end of each week.
6. Record the average heights in the data table for 3 weeks.

Item ST-8

What question were Jose and Maria asking in their investigation?

    A. How does the amount of light affect the color of grass?
    B. How does the amount of light affect the thickness of grass?
    C. How does the amount of light affect the height of grass?

Item ST-9

Why is soil important to the plant in Jose and Maria's investigation?

    A. The soil prevents dust from getting to the leaves.
    B. The soil provides support and nutrients for the grass.
    C. The soil provides a place for insects and worms to live.

Item ST-10

Which variable did Jose and Maria change (manipulate) in their investigation?

    A. The amount of light
    B. The amount of water
    C. The amount of grass sod

Item ST-11

Name **two** needs besides sunlight that Jose and Maria must provide for the grass so that it can grow healthy and tall. Explain why grass needs these things.

Item ST-12

Jose and Maria noticed that three different types of soil—black soil, sand, and clay—were found in their neighborhood. They decided to investigate the question, "How does the type of soil (black soil, sand, and clay) under grass sod affect the height of grass?"

Plan an investigation that could answer their new question.

In your plan, be sure to include:

- Hypothesis about the outcome of the investigation

- Materials needed to do the investigation

- Procedure that describes:

  - logical steps to do the investigation

  - the variables kept the same (controlled variables)

  - the variable that was changed (manipulated variable)

  - the variable that responds to the changes (responding variable)

  - any variables being measured, and recorded

  - how often measurements are taken and recorded

Source: Items 8–12 are from 2004 test items released by Washington State.

Using Released Tests to Help Students Prepare for State Tests

Preparing students for tests at a specific grade level, say fifth grade, is a responsibility of K–5 teachers, not just fifth-grade teachers. An examination of the sample items given shows that items measuring inquiry procedures also measure conceptual knowledge and understanding. Thus, science lessons from the earliest grades should be designed to build conceptual knowledge and understanding as well as inquiry procedures.

A group of teachers from the same district might work together to study items released from their own state tests. The information gained through this process can then be used to plan instruction.

Released test items from your own or other states can be directly used to help your students prepare for future statewide tests. One way to use the items is to break the test up into four- or five-item mini-tests, and administer the mini-tests to your students periodically (only after the concepts or inquiry abilities to be assessed have been taught and mastery expected). Have your students complete the mini-tests individually and turn in their answer sheets to you. Students keep a copy of their answer sheets. While you score answer sheets, students should work together in small groups to develop a "key" for the test. Record student scores on the mini-tests. Ask them to keep a copy of their answer sheets and compare their answers with yours. When students have developed answer keys that are satisfactory to them, go over the items one by one with them. Through this procedure, students have an opportunity to receive immediate feedback on their work, to think through their answers more completely, to learn from one another, and to better prepare for the high-stakes statewide examinations.

Effective assessments in science require thorough planning, skillful execution, and careful, constant review and modification. Learning to use assessment effectively will help you become a better teacher and your students better learners. It is clearly worth the effort.

SUMMARY

- Various principles form the foundation for assessment; they critically affect the *what*, *how*, and *how well* of your science teaching/learning. Assessments can be *diagnostic* (before starting teaching), *summative* (after teaching), and *formative* (during teaching).
- Assessment is focused on two questions: *Where are learners going?* and *Where are they now?* In answer to the first question, local, state, and national standards define the science facts, concepts, and principles, and the inquiry processes and procedures students should know, understand, and be able to apply. A wide variety of traditional assessment items and performance assessment tasks can be used to determine where learners are now. The results of assessments can then guide teachers as they work with individual students to help them reach learning goals.
- Authentic performance assessments are particularly relevant for inquiry science. Performance assessment tasks are authentic whenever they simulate tasks that scientists, students, or other citizens might be called on to perform in real-world contexts. Developing performance assessment tasks involves determining the focus, context, directions, and scoring guides for the tasks. Types of scoring guides discussed included holistic scoring guides, checklists, and rubrics. Rubrics are particularly important in performance assessment. Keep these things in mind as you write your own rubrics:

  - Set clear assessment standards to interpret the specifics of your students' work.
  - Determine levels of rubric scoring—often on a four-point scale—that are applicable to the unique scientific processes, skills, content, and attitudes you are assessing.

- A large bank of traditional items, performance assessment tasks and techniques, checklists, and rubrics have been provided as resources for you to draw on in developing your own assessment program.
- Assessment is a critical component of inquiry learning and instruction. The assessment revolution is here to stay.

ONLINE PROFESSIONAL DEVELOPMENT

Pre- and post-tests to assess your knowledge of chapter content, along with exercises to enhance your understanding, can be found on MyEducationLab at www.myeducationlab.com.

Video Guides

The video clip on MyEducationLab selected for this chapter is *Science Fair Projects.*

Accessing the Video

1. Go to the Homework and Exercises section in Chapter 6 of MyEducationLab to select and view videos for this chapter.
2. The video might be viewed individually, by small groups of colleagues, or by the whole class.

3. As you watch the video, use the **Questions for Reflection** to guide your thoughts and note taking for personal use and group discussion.
4. Discuss your answers to the questions about the video with classmates.

Video: Science Fair Projects

Overview

In this video excerpt, we watch as students explain projects they have planned and carried out. Through student discussions of science fair projects, such as Cleaning Golf Balls, Amount of Water Held by Different Kinds of Diapers, and Electrical Conductors, teachers have an opportunity to assess how well students understand and are able to use the tasks of inquiry (Figure 1-3) emphasized earlier in the text.

Questions for Reflection

1. What examples of students asking questions and planning and conducting investigations do we see in the video?
2. What different kinds of records that students have made do we see in the video?
3. How do students communicate their investigations and results to teachers and others?
4. How could science fair projects be used for summative assessment?

Annenberg Videos

Video Series: Learning Science Through Inquiry

Video: Assessing Inquiry

To access Annenberg videos, follow the instructions given in the Online Professional Development section in Chapter 1 on page 26.

7

Teachers' questions are crucial in helping students make connections and learn important mathematics and science concepts. Effective questioning—the kind that monitors students' understanding of new ideas and encourages students to think more deeply—was relatively rare in the mathematics and science classes we observed. . . . Unfortunately, teachers more often used low-level, "fill in the blank" questions asked in rapid-fire fashion with an emphasis on getting the right answer and moving on rather than helping students make sense of the concepts.

(Weiss and Pasley, 2004, pp. 24–25)

Effective Questioning

ASKING THE RIGHT QUESTION is at the heart of doing science. It is also at the heart of learning and teaching science as inquiry. Science teachers who use inquiry methods ask questions to focus investigations, probe prior knowledge, stimulate reflective thinking, shift the focus from observation to explanation, encourage creativity, and develop student understanding.

Just as important as asking the right question at the right time is the way you respond to and promote student discourse. *Discourse*—expressing one's own questions, observations, and meaning making and listening to and reflecting on the ideas of others—is a normal part of science. It is also an essential part of children's inquiry. Making meaning from investigations and experience requires that you guide student dialogue, encouraging your students to make connections, draw conclusions, and ask new questions.

Does the way you respond to students open a discussion up, or does it close it down? Do your responses acknowledge student ideas, probe for deeper understanding, and serve to scaffold inquiry?

This chapter is intended to provide some guidelines as you use questioning strategically, respond to student ideas, and promote understanding.

Here are some questions to guide you as you study the chapter:

- *What is meant by open-ended and closed questions, and what are their functions in teaching science?*

- *How can you help children formulate productive questions to initiate investigation?*

- *What types of questions can teachers ask to facilitate children's inquiry and promote understanding?*

- *How can you respond to children to promote deeper thinking and improved science learning?*

Questioning: An Essential Tool for Teachers

Questions are among the most important tools teachers have. Teachers use questions for many purposes: to manage classroom activities, discourage inattentiveness, and cut down on disruptive behavior; to initiate inquiry; to guide student organization of data; and to encourage students to reflect on their data and use it as evidence in constructing explanations.

Go to the Homework and Exercises section in Chapter 7 of MyEducationLab and select the article, "What Is High Quality Instruction?" In this interesting article, Weiss and Pasley (2004) observed and analyzed 364 science and mathematics lessons to assess the quality of science and math instruction in schools. Factors that distinguished more effective lessons related to student engagement with content, culture conducive to learning, equal access by all students, effective questioning, scaffolding assistance to help students make sense of content, and teacher decision making.

Teachers' questions are widely accepted as crucial in helping students make connections and learn important science concepts. However, as is indicated in the chapter-opening quote, in a series of classrooms observations of science teachers' questionng behavior, Weiss and Pasley (2004) found that effective questioning was relatively rare. Teachers must learn to use questions strategically and be committed to using strategic questioning.

Strategic questioning involves selecting and using specific types of questions with well-defined functions. A specific questioning skill, such as asking open-ended questions, is like a tool used by a master carpenter. Tools have unique purposes. Carpenters use different tools to drive a nail, cut a board, or square off the end of a piece of lumber. The master carpenter plans ahead by keeping a well-stocked toolbox and becoming proficient in using each tool. Similarly, master teachers need different questioning tools for specific educational tasks, such as setting the cognitive level of inquiry, promoting discussion by class members, stimulating deeper thought on the part of students, and building meaningful explanations that connect investigative evidence to what students already know. Teachers, like carpenters, need well-honed tools that they know when and how to use.

Closed and Open-Ended Questions

One important tool in your questioning toolbox is the skill of knowing how and when to ask open-ended and closed questions. Both types of questions are important for assessing prior knowledge and promoting new learning, but in very different ways. A **closed question** has a single correct answer, while **open-ended questions** can be answered in a number of ways (Texas A&M Center for Mathematics and Science Education, 2005, 2006).

Closed questions require students to think *convergently*—that is, to focus on a single fact, define a particular term, or attend to specific objects or specific aspects of events. Children's responses to closed questions help you assess their factual recall and observation skills and allow you to adjust your teaching accordingly.

In contrast, open-ended questions enable all students to make useful contributions to a discussion. Open-ended questions require children to engage broad portions of their schemas. They also trigger *divergent* thinking. In thinking divergently, children consider a wide array of possibilities.

Figure 7-1 provides a series of closed and open-ended questions about a pictorial riddle. The closed questions in Figure 7-1 focus on specific observations and recall of prior knowledge and experience. The open-ended questions are broader questions that can engage students reflectively and build toward understanding.

In typical classrooms in every subject, the large majority of teachers' questions are closed, calling for factual knowledge and convergent thinking. Research indicates that even a slight increase in the percentage of open-ended questions by teachers yields a significant increase in divergent productivity by students; that is, a larger number of students respond, and their responses are more thoughtful and exhibit higher levels of thinking. These types of responses, in turn, stimulate further discussion among students (Carin & Sund, 1978).

Students learn from teachers how to ask good questions. If teachers' questions are open-ended, with no one right answer, students can learn to ask open-ended questions. Teachers should ask and encourage questions such as *What would happen if . . . ?*, *What will happen next?*, and *Why did that happen?*

In the following sections we describe some questioning strategies for inquiry discussions.

A glossary containing definitions of important terms used in this chapter can be found on MyEducationLab.

Questioning to Guide Inquiry Discussions

Duschl and colleagues (2007) described a *formative assessment scaffolding* "feedback loop" proposed by Furtak and Ruiz-Primo (2005). In this loop:

1. Teachers ask questions to elicit levels of student understanding.
2. Students respond to the questions orally, in writing, or through diagrams and drawings.
3. Teachers recognize and acknowledge student responses.
4. Teachers provide scaffolds to improve learning and understanding.

According to Duschl et al. (2007), when the strategies of formative assessment and scaffolding are applied together, continuous improvement in student understanding, as well as modifications in teaching approaches, can be achieved.

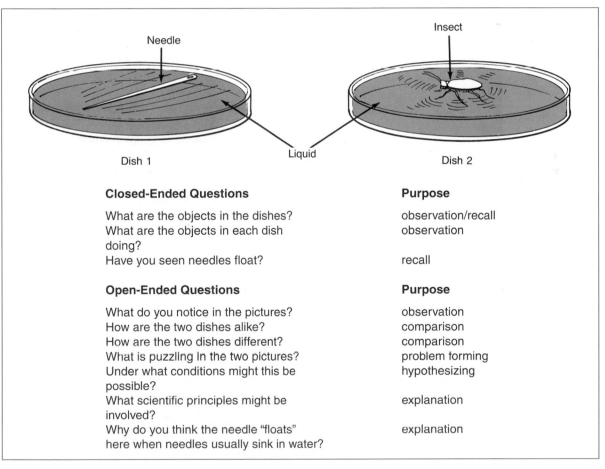

Closed-Ended Questions	Purpose
What are the objects in the dishes?	observation/recall
What are the objects in each dish doing?	observation
Have you seen needles float?	recall

Open-Ended Questions	Purpose
What do you notice in the pictures?	observation
How are the two dishes alike?	comparison
How are the two dishes different?	comparison
What is puzzling In the two pictures?	problem forming
Under what conditions might this be possible?	hypothesizing
What scientific principles might be involved?	explanation
Why do you think the needle "floats" here when needles usually sink in water?	explanation

Figure 7-1 Pictorial riddle using closed and open-ended questions.

TABLE 7-1 TEACHER QUESTIONS FOR GUIDING SCIENCE DISCUSSIONS	
Phases of 5-E Model	**Descriptions and Purpose of Question**
1.1 Engage	**1.1.1. Building Intrinsic Interest.** Ask questions to focus thought on puzzling events and to build intrinsic motivation.
	1.1.2. Prior Knowledge. Ask questions to assess students' prior knowledge and conceptions.
	1.1.3. Focusing Questions. Ask questions to initiate and focus inquiry.
1.2 Explore	**1.2.1. Observing.** Ask questions to focus students' thoughts on investigations, observations, and data.
	1.2.2. Reflecting on Data. Ask questions to guide students in reflecting on data.
	1.2.3. Patterns and Relationships. Ask questions that require students to identify patterns and relationships in their data.
1.3 Explain	**1.3.1. Student Theories.** Ask questions that invite students to offer their theories and explanations of why an event took place.
	1.3.2. Reflecting on Personal Ideas. Ask questions that encourage students to examine and reflect on their theories.
	1.3.3. Scientific Knowledge. Ask questions that invite students to relate evidence to prior and existing knowledge.
	1.3.4. Developing New Knowledge. Ask questions that prepare the way for instruction on new scientific knowledge.
	1.3.5. Scientific Explanations. Ask questions that guide students to build on their theories, use prior and new knowledge, and construct new scientific explanations that relate to observational evidence.
1.4 Elaborate	**1.4.1. Apply.** Ask questions that require students to apply new knowledge in new situations.

Tables 7-1 and 7-2 provide a strategy for such a formative assessment scaffolding loop. Table 7-1 focuses on asking questions strategically. The strategy follows the 5-E model of instruction. It involves asking questions that can initiate inquiry discussion (engage), guiding discussions of information and data obtained through observation and experiments (explore), assisting students to make the transition from observaton to explanation (explain), and applying new ideas in new situations (elaborate).

Consider first how to use questioning to engage students in inquiry.

1.1. Engage: Using Questioning to Initiate Inquiry

In science inquiry, we want students to be intrinsically motivated to pursue a learning task and to engage in it for intrinsic reasons, rather than because of grades or teacher approval. Nothing creates intrinsic motivation in students more than presenting them with novel events.

Novel or discrepant events, such as the ones presented in Chapter 5, can be presented through hands-on student investigations or through a teacher demonstration using science materials. If time and resources are constrained, you could show a film segment or use a pictorial riddle instead.

Here is an example of a discrepant event that might build interest and initiate inquiry about the earth's magnetic field.

Place a needle on a styrofoam chip floating in a container of water. What do you see happening? (Nothing special.) Stroke the needle several times in one direction with a bar magnet. Lay the needle on the styrofoam chip again. Regardless of how you orient the needle, it always swings around and points in the same direction.

Ask, *What do you see happening?*

After a discussion of what is observed, refocus the discussion on what was puzzling here. Ask, *What is unexpected or puzzling in the event observed?*

If you had appropriate prior experiences and scientific knowledge about magnetism, you might have inferred that the needle was not initially a magnet. (*What observations support this inference?*) However, stroking it with a bar magnet served to magnetize the needle. When the magnetized needle was placed on the styrofoam chip, it swung around until it was oriented along the direction of the earth's magnetic field. The needle pointed along a magnetic north-south direction.

Demonstrating discrepant events is certainly a good way to arouse curiosity and promote interest in the topic you plan for them to investigate.

For students to construct understanding of a discrepant event, they must have relevant prior knowledge. To help your students build and strengthen their scientific concepts, you must be aware of what they know or do not know at the start of any study. You might assess children's prior knowledge by simply asking them what they already know about a topic. However, discrepant events, such as the magnetized needle demonstration, provide a natural context for you to discover what they already know.

In the needle demonstration, children display their prior knowledge of magnetism as they talk about the event and respond to your questions:

- What is happening to the needle?
- What have you seen that is like this?
- What is puzzling here? What needs explaining?
- What might cause the needle to point in a particular direction?

When building toward understanding of descrepant events, students are called on to observe objects and events, form a question about why something happens, and recall relevant knowledge to be used in explaining the event. As children conduct an investigation or watch a demonstration, they typically talk about what they observe and think. By listening and interacting with the students, you will be better able to assess their prior knowledge and conceptions.

When students are ready, ask questions or lead them to ask questions to initiate and focus inquiry. Of course, the questions asked should be ones that students are able to investigate through their own inquiries.

In Chapter 1, we discussed and gave examples of a variety of kinds of investigation questions that can initiate and focus inquiry.

1.2. *Explore: Using Questioning to Guide Discussions of Observations*

One way children seek answers to their questions is through using the senses or instruments that extend the senses to observe what happens in an investigation or demonstration activity.

Through questioning, students try to infer the contents of the mystery box.

Observing what happens familiarizes children with the natural world and provides evidence for understanding it.

An important key to inquiry teaching is to lead children to think about their observations. You can guide children in thinking about their observations through the questions you ask. In general, observation questions should be open-ended. An open-ended question such as *What are some of the things you noticed during the demonstration?* allows many students to contribute useful information during inquiry.

When working with small groups or the class as a whole, do not seek closure on a question until a number of responses have accumulated. Such a strategy not only gives more students a chance to enter into the discussion but also ensures that all students will have a variety of descriptive information from which to later build explanations. Observational information from students might be recorded on the chalkboard or through electronic media.

When getting responses from several students on the same question, it is generally not necessary to repeat or rephrase the question. After one student has supplied an answer, you may redirect the question to another student by asking a question such as, *Juan, would you like to add anything else?*

Following are some suggestions you might follow and some sample questions you might ask or train students to ask to focus their attention on observing and describing.

A. If you seek descriptions of objects in a discrepant event or investigation, ask such questions as:
   • *What objects were involved in the investigation (demonstration)?*
B. If you seek *descriptions of events* in an investigation or demonstration, ask such questions as:
   • *What did you do?* (or, *What did I do?*)
   • *What happened in the experiment (demonstration)?*
   • *What are some of the changes you noticed in the . . . ?*
   • *What did you see that surprised you?* (*that you liked? that startled you?*)

By focusing on the aspect of an event that is puzzling, the last question begins to lay the groundwork for explanations.

Often discussion about observations occurs when children report their observations and data to the class. When groups report, train them to consider two kinds of questions about observational information (Rowe, 1973, p. 347):

- *What was observed?*
- *In what sequence did events happen?*

Then, ask students to compare their observations:

- *Were the observations of all groups the same? Are the reported sequences the same? How are they alike? How are the observations different?*

Differences among groups in reports of what they observed or the sequence of events observed can lead to disagreements. To resolve these disagreements, students must think more carefully about their data and sometimes repeat an activity. If students are unclear about what happened in an investigation, they will not have adequate evidence for constructing explanations for why it happened.

If the observations reported by groups represent numerical data and you want children to make and compare measurements (quantitative observations), you might ask:

- *Which of the reported measurements is highest? Which is lowest?*
- *Why do you think there is variation (differences) in the class's measurements?*

Discussing differences in the data reported by groups gives you an opportunity to discuss the nature of science with your students. According to the *Benchmarks for Science Literacy* (American Association for the Advancement of Science, 1993, pp. 6, 10), by the end of second grade, students should know that

- science investigations generally work the same way in different places; and
- when people give different descriptions of the same thing, it is usually a good idea to make some fresh observations instead of just arguing who is right.

Sometimes you want children to compare measurements and notice changes that occurred:

- *What changes in the temperature of the water did you notice?*

It is important that children spend considerable time at the *observation* level before beginning to search for problem *explanations*. Unless sufficient time is spent in developing an adequate foundation at the lower cognitive level, students are often not able to sustain discussion at higher levels of thought.

1.3. Explain: Using Questioning to Guide Discussions of Explanations

At some point in the discussion, you should shift the thinking of students from *observation* to *explanation*. Explaining is the counterpart of observing. In observing, students are directly involved with objects and events. Explanations require students to go beyond observations, to reason about their experiences, and to make up and test interpretations of them. Careful observations determine *what* happens. Explanation is concerned with *why* it happened.

When you are ready to shift instruction from an observation or exploration phase to explanation, let children help you decide which aspects of an investigation might need explaining. Find out what *they* want to know about the results of an investigation or why a

Go to the Homework and Exercises section in Chapter 7 of MyEducationLab to read the article "Helping Students Ask the Right Questions" by Richetti and Sheerin. They have developed a questioning strategy to help students integrate their thinking and produce a logical, well-considered conclusion or point of view that builds on previous thinking.

puzzling event occurred. List the children's questions where they can see and think about them. Make sure that all children have a chance to frame their own questions.

In leading students to identify problems, you might ask:

- What do you think needs explaining here?
- What surprised you?
- What is most puzzling to you?

When attempting to focus thought on interpreting and explaining, a good approach is to start with the simpler problems that have been identified, gradually gather interpretative ideas, and build toward the more difficult problems.

The transition from observation to explanation can be a difficult process for students. One of your jobs in inquiry teaching is to facilitate the process of *making meaning* from data. To facilitate the meaning-making process, you might begin by asking students, *Do you notice any pattern in your data (in your moon observations)?*

At some point, you will want to shift the thinking of students to making sense of the data and patterns in the data. You might begin to facilitate the process of explaining by asking: *What ideas do you have about why this happened?*

The *National Science Education Standards* (National Research Council, 1996, p. 145) emphasize that in constructing explanations, students must think critically about evidence, considering which of their observations constitute evidence and which are irrelevant. They must also have adequate subject matter knowledge. Finally, they must be able to link their evidence with their knowledge in a reasonable way to explain why something happened.

Learners in grades K–2 observe the world using all of their senses and offer their theories about why an event happened. Typically, grade 1 and 2 learners do not construct consistent explanations of events in the world. It is not until late second grade or third or fourth grade that children begin to distinguish between observations and interpretations (or inferences) and to construct simple explanations involving effects and their causes. Complex explanations involving chains of causes and effects are not formed until about grades 5 or 6. Yet learners at every grade level can profit from considering why an event happened and how the world works.

A first step in developing explanations is for students to organize their data or observations in some way. To *organize* means to fit individual parts into a whole. Discussion of data and organization might take place as groups build data tables or report their findings to the class or perhaps in a whole class discussion.

Research suggests that understanding is enhanced when students actively integrate information in various ways. To help students see their data holistically rather than as fragmented parts, teachers might ask them to

- describe to others what they did and what they found out,
- summarize their data,
- organize their data/information into tables and graphs,
- elaborate information by adding details,
- generate relationships between the new material and information already in memory, and
- recognize patterns in observational data.

For example, in developing ideas about relationships, ask such questions as:

- *How is this situation like (different from) the other one?*
- *What similarities (differences) do you see in these situations?*

Viewing data holistically is not enough, however. According to Duschl and colleagues (2007), research evidence indicates that children and adolescents had particular problems in coordinating evidence and theories. Through strategic use of questions, science teachers can help children reflect on and represent evidence more completely, think at deeper levels, and connect evidence and knowledge more logically in explaining events in the natural world.

Students may need considerable scaffolding assistance in accessing prior knowledge to make sense of observations. Sometimes, as is emphasized in the 5-E model of instruction, relevant scientific knowledge must be taught to students.

Here are some sample questions that focus on accessing knowledge and constructing explanation.

A. If you seek suggestions about scientific knowledge that might be involved in an explanation, ask such questions as:
  * *What principles that we have learned do you think may come into play here?*
  * *What do we already know that might help us here?*
  * *What principles (rules, laws, concepts) do you think are needed in solving this problem?*
  * *How do you think that the principles of floating and sinking apply to this problem?*
B. If you seek ideas about the possible cause of an event, ask questions such as:
  * *Why do you think the raisins sank (the puzzling event happened)?*
  * *What ideas do you have about why this happened?*
  * *What suggestions (theories) do you have about the cause of this?*
  * *Can you explain why it might have happened?*
  * *What do you think is the cause of . . . ?*

Questions that focus on interpretation and explanation should be open-ended and divergent and should be pursued for a sufficient time to get responses from several students. This strategy helps to ensure that ideas and explanations at a variety of levels of abstractness are at hand for students of different abilities to consider.

Note the use of the personal pronoun *you* in the examples of explanation questions. Framing questions in this way helps to make them more open-ended, allowing children to respond at their own level of thought. An explanation question such as *What ideas do you have about why . . . ?* (rather than *Why did this happen?*) focuses more on the act of thinking than on correct answers. This questioning approach frees children from the burden of knowing in advance why something took place. It encourages them to think about possible reasons for the cause of a puzzling event and to offer suggestions or theories to build on. Their initial responses need not be absolutely correct. The teacher, through sensitive listening, careful and caring questioning, and appropriate scaffolding, can help the class as a whole formulate a satisfying response that is age and grade level appropriate. Practical experience demonstrates that children can learn to go beyond their observations and construct scientific explanations for why things happen.

"We really want children to be explorers and investigators and we want them to try to dictate for themselves what is the problem they should be exploring and what ways they are going to go about exploring that problem."

Dr. Thomas M. Dana, Pennsylvania State University, *Annenberg Video Case Study, Erien (Year One)* (Annenberg Foundation,1997)

1.4. Elaborate: Questioning to Guide Discussions of Applications to New Situations

In building understanding, children need opportunities to apply or transfer new knowledge and understanding in many problem-solving situations (Bransford, Brown, & Cocking, 1999). Problems can be generated in various ways. For example, you may plan the problem situations, or they may arise from students' creative ideas and interests. As they work on fresh problems, students try out their recently learned ideas by transferring them to the new situations, thereby refining and extending their developing understanding. In a 5-E model of instruction, the elaborate (application) phase of a lesson allows students to make new connections and construct more useful schemas from the knowledge they gained in previous activities.

To elicit thinking about how new knowledge and understanding might be extended to different phenomena, ask such questions as:

- *How do you think . . . applies to . . . ?*
- *In what ways does this idea compare/contrast with . . . ?*
- *How can we use this principle to explain . . . ?*
- *What new problems does this suggest?*
- *What might happen if . . . ?*

Especially good problems for the elaborate phase can be found from applications of science in technology. Application opens up the opportunity for students to explore the natural and technological world more deeply and to realize how extensively science and technology affect people.

In an Annenberg video entitled *Case Studies in Science Education: Greg*, Greg challenged his sixth-grade students to design and constuct a bridge that was tall enough for a radio-controlled car to pass under it and sturdy enough for the car to ascend to the top of the bridge and cross over on it.

In constructing their bridges, the students followed the design cycle. As a test of their bridges, the class watched as each group successfully passed the robot car under the bridges. However, in all cases, the approach to the bridge was too steep for the robot cart to climb. By applying what they had learned previously about inclined planes, the student groups decided they needed longer approaches to the bridges that were not too steep for the robot car.

Next we look at how teachers use strategic responding to encourage and guide discourse.

You can find the video Case Studies in Science Education: Greg on the Annenberg website. Instructions for accessing this website are provided in the Online Professional Development section of Chapter 1.

Responding to Student Ideas

By responding strategically, teachers encourage critical discourse and communication of procedures, data, and explanations. Instructional research indicates that student growth is influenced by teacher actions that involve students in the development and extension of ideas (King, 1994).

There are three main ways you can respond strategically to nurture and extend children's ideas during inquiry. You can *accept* or recognize student responses without judging them; you can *extend* student responses by adding something new to what was said; and you can *probe* student responses by asking questions based on their responses. Extending and probing represent two different ways to scaffold student understanding. Table 7-2 shows what is involved in applying these three teacher responses strategically. (Note that Table 7-2 extends the taxonomic numbering system of Table 7-1.)

2.1. Accept Student Responses

Your inquiry teaching repertoire should incorporate an attitude of initial *acceptance* of student ideas, even when they contain errors, mistakes, and alternative conceptions. Students should feel that they have the "right to be wrong." Because the very process of inquiry involves the challenge of trying the unknown, it necessarily must result in mistakes. The need to be always right, whether imposed by teachers, peers, or self, is a limiting and threatening position. Teachers have a major responsibility to help students explore new experi-

TABLE 7-2	TEACHER RESPONSES THAT ACCEPT, EXTEND, AND PROBE STUDENT IDEAS
Teaching Purpose	**Description of Response**
2.1 Accepting	**To accept student responses, teachers:**
	2.1.1. Acknowledge. Teacher statements or actions that acknowledge or recognize student responses.
	2.1.2. Reinforce. Teacher statements that reinforce or praise student responses.
	2.1.3. Repeat. Teacher statements that repeat, restate, or paraphrase student responses.
2.2 Extending	**To extend student responses, teachers:**
	2.2.1. Build on Student Ideas. Teacher statements that add to and build on student ideas.
	2.2.2. Compare Ideas of Students. Teacher statements that compare and contrast student responses.
	2.2.3. Apply Student Ideas. Teacher statements that apply or relate student ideas to explanations or problem solving.
	2.2.4. Summarize Student Responses. Teacher statements that summarize or review what a student or class has arrived at so far through thinking and discussion.
2.3 Probing	**Teacher questions that ask students to:**
	2.3.1. Build on Ideas. Ask questions that call for students to build on and follow up on their own and other students' ideas.
	2.3.2. Clarify. Teacher questions that call for students to clarify or explain their ideas.
	2.3.3. Justify. Teacher questions that ask students to justify or give reasons for their ideas.
	2.3.4. Verify. Teacher questions that ask students to test their ideas or to give evidence to support their ideas.

ences and new meanings without penalizing the mistakes and wrong turns that are certain to accompany the process of inquiring. By accepting children's ideas without initially judging or evaluating them, the teacher helps establish a climate in which students feel they can risk their ideas.

Teachers can show acceptance of student ideas by acknowledging, repeating, and reinforcing them. When *acknowledging,* you should refrain from evaluating students' responses. This leaves the door open for further discussion. For example:

- *OK.*
- *All right.*
- *Let's list your idea on the board.*
- *Let's keep your idea in mind.*

You might also use nonverbal behaviors such as a nod to tell students that their responses have been heard and accepted.

Simply repeating a student idea is another way to acknowledge and accept it. You can show that you accept a student's idea by repeating it almost verbatim or by paraphrasing the idea, without changing or adding to it significantly. For example:

Student: Maybe it's the air leaking.
Teacher: OK. You think it may be the air leaking. (Repeating); or,
Teacher: OK. You think the bubbles may be caused by escaping air. (Paraphrasing)

Blosser (1991) cautioned against the overreliance on repeating student responses. If students know you are going to repeat responses, they may tend not to listen to one another but wait for your repetition. If you think the whole class has not heard a response, you might say something like:

Teacher: That's an interesting idea. I don't think the whole class heard it, though. Would you say it again so everybody can hear?

Another type of accepting behavior is *reinforcing* student ideas. It is an established principle of behavioral psychology that a person's tendency to display an action is dependent on events that follow the action (Ormrod, 2004). These special events are called *reinforcements*. In order to encourage student participation in discussion, a teacher may need to reinforce the act of responding. Teachers may also wish to reinforce both good thinking and good ideas.

One way of reinforcing student responses is with praise. For example:

* *Good!*
* *Fine!*
* *Excellent!*

A stronger way of reinforcing children's responses is through praise followed by an explanation of the reason for the praise:

* *Great! I like the way you are contributing.*
* *Good job! Your idea is particularly good because it relates your theory to your observations.*
* *Fine! I like the way you compared your idea to Celeste's idea.*

Praise is important, but it should not be given in such a way that students think the idea praised is the only possible one. Other children might thus give up on their own lines of thought. Even when the idea you are seeking is voiced by a student, reinforce the child but let the class know there is more to be done. For example,

Teacher: Great thinking! Your idea is one we will have to consider. (Then, to the class) What other ideas do you have on why this happened?

Reinforcement is more effective if it follows an unpredictable schedule. If students can predict that the teacher will say "very good" after every response, this form of praise loses its effectiveness. For best results, the teacher should vary the type of reinforcements.

Reinforcement is, of course, more than a matter of what the teacher says. Both research and practice show that students are less inhibited about making responses and show more productivity and achievement when their teachers tend to be approving, to provide emotional support, to express sympathetic attitudes, and to accept their feelings.

2.2. Extend Student Responses

When students give vague, incomplete, unorganized, or partially correct responses or when they are on the right track but need assistance, the teacher may act to nurture and extend their ideas. Perhaps the best reinforcement for students comes when they see their own ideas used by the teacher. Several techniques for extending student responses are described next.

To help move the discussion along it is sometimes appropriate to focus on an idea suggested by one or more students and to build on it. For example.

- *All right! I believe we are on the right track here. We might also consider what we learned last week in science. Remember . . .*

To help clarify a student idea, a teacher may restate the idea in simpler terms, reorganize the idea, or perhaps summarize it. For example, suppose a student has given an unclear and unorganized response. The teacher may reply:

- *In other words, the air takes up more space when heated.*
- *If I understand you correctly, you are saying that the air takes up more space when it is heated.*

When two or more students make suggestions that have significant similarities or differences, the teacher may wish to extend the ideas by comparing or contrasting them:

- *Your idea is similar to Jamal's in that . . .*
- *Notice the difference in Kenesha's suggestion and Sean's suggestion. Kenesha said the wire would expand when it was heated; Sean said it would expand when it cooled. Both are good suggestions. How could we test these two hypotheses?*

There is uncertainty among teachers about how to handle incorrect ideas and misconceptions held by students. On the one hand, a student who is told that his idea is all wrong may be reluctant to participate in discussions again. On the other hand, misconceptions left unchallenged can cause confusion and interfere with understanding. Teachers need tactful ways of helping students confront and change wrong notions. One possibility is to plan lessons to lead students to challenge their own misconceptions, as is illustrated in Chapter 3 with the moon-watching lesson.

Sometimes a teacher wishes to directly correct an incorrect notion and move on. In that case, the teacher might determine if part of the student's answer is correct and reinforce this part. For example:

Teacher: Yes, heat does play a part in the expansion of the copper rod, but melting does not take place. Remember, in melting, the solid rod would become a liquid. Can you make another suggestion?

Applying an idea suggested by a student in building an explanation is an excellent method of extending student ideas. However, teachers should be careful not to shift from extending student ideas to simply giving the desired information through lecture.

To move the inquiry along, occasionally summarize the group's discussion and assess the various suggestions. This will not only extend students' ideas but also promote further inquiry. When the concepts involved are abstract or vague, when there are many responses, when student answers have been lengthy, or when some investigations have taken a great deal of time, you might briefly summarize what has been said or identify and restate the main ideas discussed.

2.3. *Probe Student Responses*

After a student has contributed an idea to a discussion, the teacher may attempt to produce greater critical awareness by *probing*. Probing is a strategy in which the teacher reacts to student responses by asking penetrating questions that require students to go beyond superficial, first-answer responses.

Extending and probing student ideas represent important ways to scaffold their understanding.

Probing differs from extending. In *extending*, the teacher does the clarifying, comparing, and contrasting of student ideas; in *probing*, the teacher asks students to look deeper at their own ideas or those of others. Let's consider a variety of probing techniques.

A good way to probe student ideas is to ask questions that build on those ideas. Here the teacher builds on a student response by asking a question based on it. For example:

- *You have said that the bubbles are caused by escaping air. What do you think happens to the air pressure in the tube when some of the air escapes?*

A teacher may probe students' responses by asking them to clarify the response by giving more information, explaining a term used, or restating the response in other words. For example:

- *What do you mean by melting?*
- *Was the wicked witch who claimed "I'm melting . . ." actually melting, or was she dissolving? What do you think?*
- *How could you restate that to make clearer what you mean?*
- *How could you explain that further?*
- *What do you mean by the term . . . ?*

The following interaction illustrates the clarification technique:

Teacher: What do you think is the relationship between the pressure of the air and its volume?
Student: The pressure got more and the gas condensed?
Teacher: What do you mean by condensed? (Or) How would you restate that in terms of volume?

You can also probe to seek justification of student ideas. In asking a student to justify a response rationally, you might say:

- *What are you assuming here?*
- *Why do you think that is so?*
- *I'm not sure I follow your reasoning. Tell us how you arrived at that answer.*
- *What evidence supports your idea?*

Sometimes you might probe by asking students how they would test and verify ideas or confirm a theory. For example, you may say:

- *You have suggested that the heaping effect might involve both adhesive and cohesive forces. Can you think of a way to test your idea?*
- *What would you do to test your idea?*
- *What would it take for that to be true?*
- *What evidence (additional information, data) would we need to support your explanation (suggestion)?*
- *What experiment could we do to test your idea?*

Questioning Strategies in the Classroom: Properties of Air in First Grade

Go to the Homework and Exercises section in Chapter 7 of MyEducationLab to watch the video *Properties of Air in First Grade Science*, excerpts from which appear on the next page. Spend some time watching and listening to this delightful example of first graders' ideas about air.

In a video of first-grade science produced by Merrill Education, Ms. Newhall is preparing to teach her students that "air" is a real material substance. In front of her, she has a fish bowl about three-quarters full of water and a small, transparent glass. She plans to push the small glass, open-end down, all the way under the water, as in Figure 7-2, and asks the chil-

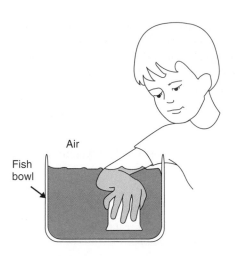

Figure 7-2 What happens when a glass is pushed open-end down into a container of water?

Air

Fish bowl

dren what they saw and why they think it happened. Before beginning the actual demonstration, Ms. Newhall questioned the children to ascertain their prior knowledge.

> *Teacher: I'm going to push this glass into the water until it is all the way under the water. What will happen? Terry, what do you think?*
> *Terry: It's going to stay at the bottom . . . sink.*

Ms. Newhall wanted the children to focus on the air and the water rather than the glass. So, with a nod acknowledging Terry's answer, she turned to another student who had her hand up.

> *Teacher: Samantha.*
> *Samantha: Me and my dad took a glass into the pool one time. We put the glass under the water. We kept it straight, and if you keep it straight, no water will come in. The air will stay in there, but if you tip it up, the water will come in.*
> *Teacher: Interesting.*

Samantha's answer revealed that she had significant prior experience and knowledge about what would happen in the demonstration. Some of her knowledge came from personal discoveries. She had also acquired some knowledge from discussions with her father. Samantha used the term *air* appropriately, but Ms. Newhall was not sure what she really *understood* about the concept.

Ms. Newhall acknowledged Samantha's answer and filed it away for later use. But she wanted to know what the other children knew about air and what they thought would happen in the demonstration. So she turned to the class again.

> *Teacher: Is there anybody else who thinks if you put this whole glass under the water, nothing is going into the glass? What do you think, Michelle?*
> *Michelle: Water may go in the glass.*

After giving the rest of the class time to offer opinions, Ms. Newhall polled the students to see which of the two ideas they supported. There was about equal support for Samantha's idea that water would not come into the glass and Michelle's idea that the glass may fill up with water. Then the teacher continued with the demonstration.

> *Teacher: OK. We have two ideas. Let's test these ideas.*

Ms. Newhall called on a student to help her with the demonstration. First, she asked the student to check to make sure the glass was dry. To encourage careful observation, she told the students to "watch with your eyes." Then she pushed the glass open end down all the way under the water. Most students noted that the water did not get into the glass, but one student was not sure.

Ms. Newhall then dried the glass carefully, took a paper towel, and crumpled it into the bottom of the dry glass. She pushed the glass with its open end down under the water again. When she removed the glass from the water, she asked a child to examine the paper towel, and the child observed that it was dry. The teacher then attempted to lift the children's thoughts from a level of observation and description to the higher cognitive level of explanation.

> *Teacher: Why did it stay dry? What do you think, Jessica?*
> *Jessica: Because it was inside that glass and the rest is outside.*
> *Teacher: But what kept the water out? Anthony?*
> *Anthony: A water seal. It was pooled up. There was water on the bottom, but not on the inside.*
> *Teacher: But if there's all that water around the outside, why didn't it go in here (pointing to the inside of the glass)?*
> *Student: Because the air was in there.*
> *Teacher: The air. . . . Oh . . . Is that what kept the water out?*

The initial answers to Ms. Newhall's question about why the paper towel stayed dry indicated that the children did not yet have a good understanding of air. Although they knew the term *air* and had connected it to some physical situations such as wind and breathing, they had difficulty applying the concept in interpreting the demonstration. When one child said that the air kept the water out, Ms. Newhall decided to extend Samantha's earlier contribution.

> *Teacher: Samantha said something earlier. When she put the glass down straight, the glass stayed dry, but when she pushed it down and tipped it, the glass got wet.*

Ms. Newhall then demonstrated that when she tilted the glass, bubbles came from the glass and rose in the water. She tried to get the children to describe the bubbles as bubbles of air. However, the children described the bubbles as "water bubbles" and in other ways, but no one used the term "air bubbles." So, the teacher attempted to extend the children's thinking by giving them a hint.

> *Teacher: In the bottom half of the glass is water; in the top half of the glass is . . .*
> *Student: Dry.*
> *Teacher: What is in there?*

No answers were forthcoming, so the teacher further extended the dialogue by giving an explanation.

> *Teacher: When I tip it (a small amount), the water keeps the air in. When I tilt it far enough, the air can come out.*

There is much for you to learn about questioning from the teacher in this lesson. She strategically used some exceptional science questioning techniques.

* First, she asked questions to ascertain the students' prior knowledge.
* Then, she asked observation questions to get the children to focus on what happened and to help them improve their observational skills.

- Only after sufficient evidence had been introduced into the discussion did she ask explanation questions, focusing on why the events happened.
- She did not immediately acknowledge that Samantha's initial answer was correct but kept the discussion open so that all children could enter in and possibly construct knowledge about air for themselves.
- Also, she asked her questions before calling on a student by name, thus helping to ensure that all students would have to listen to and think about their answers to the questions.
- She kept the discussion orderly, asking students to raise their hands when they wished to volunteer an answer.
- She called on a diversity of students, making sure she included both boys and girls and children of all ability levels.

Despite the teacher's use of model teaching techniques, the children had difficulty constructing notions about air and its properties that would be useful in *understanding* why the paper in the glass remained dry. That is, the children still had problems in *applying* their knowledge to *explain* or make sense of the demonstrations involving air.

From the perspective of child development theory presented in Chapter 3, most of these young students have simply not yet developed the conceptual structures and types of relational thinking that will support the construction of complex explanations. Nevertheless, through their discoveries and discussion, the children are building knowledge to apply in future knowledge construction experiences when they are more developmentally ready.

Some Considerations in Questioning

Through your questioning, your body language, your treatment of students, and your general demeanor, you are establishing the climate of your classroom. Here are some general considerations to think about as you guide students in questioning, listening to them, and responding.

Increase Your Wait-Time

Elementary and middle school teachers often feel pressured to cover everything in the few hours that students are in the classroom each day. So it is no surprise that teachers try to rush through many of the things they do, even question-and-answer times. Rowe (1973, 1987) found that most teachers usually wait less than a second for a response after asking a question! These very brief intervals, or **wait-times**, encourage rote, verbatim recall, usually of textbook or teacher-made information. In contrast, inquiry requires time for students to reflect, make connections, and construct inferences and explanations.

What differences in student responses do you think were found with longer teacher wait-times? Rowe found that when teachers waited 3 seconds or longer student responses included greater speculation, conversation, and argument than when wait-times were shorter. She also found that when teachers are trained to wait an average of more than 3 seconds before responding, the following positive student behaviors happen:

- The length of student response increases by 400 to 800%.
- The number of unsolicited but appropriate responses increases.
- Failure to respond decreases.
- Confidence increases.
- The number of questions asked by students increases.
- Academically challenged students contribute more.

- The variety of types of responses increases. There is more reacting to each other, structuring of procedures, and soliciting.
- Speculative thinking increases by as much as 700%.
- Discipline problems decrease.
- Achievement improves in cognitively complex items on written tests.

Rowe also found that teachers trained to prolong wait-time changed their teaching behavior in the following ways:

- The number of teacher questions decreased, because more students responded and the responses of students became longer.
- The number of teacher questions that called for reflection and clarification increased.
- Teacher expectations for student performance were modified. (Teachers were less likely to expect only the brighter students to reply and viewed their class as having fewer academically challenged students.)
- Teachers changed the direction of discussion from teacher-dominated to teacher-student discussion.

There are two types of wait-time. **Wait-time 1** is the pause that follows a question by the teacher. The students may answer quickly, but if they do not, the teacher waits. **Wait-time 2** is the pause that follows a burst of responses by the students. The teacher waits before responding or asking another question to see if the students will continue to talk.

Of the two, Rowe (1987) indicated that wait-time 2 is more important for a teacher to develop. She found an increase of 500 to 700% in student responses when teachers used it. Furthermore, the responses from the academically challenged students increased significantly when teachers increased their wait-time after student talk.

Instructors need to increase their wait-time tolerance so learners have more opportunities to think, create, and fully demonstrate their potential.

Gradually Fade Your Questioning Support

Teachers model, coach, and scaffold thinking behaviors through their questions. But gradually, students should come to ask self-regulatory questions themselves as teachers fade their support (Bransford et al., 1999). This approach highlights the importance of students' **metacognition** in planning, monitoring, and adjusting their own learning and inquiry behaviors. Thus, as teachers use questioning strategies, they are not just scaffolding student understanding, they are teaching students how to formulate productive inquiry questions for themselves.

Listen to One Another

Listening carefully and sensitively—not only to the answer but to the thinking behind the answer—provides you with much information about your students. The way teachers perceive their roles is undoubtedly related to their listening skills. If you see your function as mainly to develop or achieve some subject matter concept or principle, you naturally will focus on its achievement. However, if you perceive your role as helping students develop cognitively and construct their own concepts and understanding, you will tend to focus on the students, as well as on the students' thinking processes.

To help students make discoveries and use their own developing thought processes, listen intently to what they have to say. Formulate questions and responses only when they have finished. There is no substitute for a teacher who is primarily interested in people and really listens to them.

Try not to analyze, evaluate, or judge what students are saying until after they have completed their thoughts about the questions. Unfortunately, some teachers start to dissect what students say before they have had a chance to finish. Many students' ideas are good, but they suffer from poor verbalization. If you wait until students finish their answers before reacting, you will grasp their ideas better and be more likely to convey in nonverbal ways that you are sincerely interested in their ideas. If you are not clear about what the children are saying, you can engage them in discussion to clarify their meanings by asking a probing question.

Students often do not learn and achieve as well as they could because they have not developed their own listening skills. By modeling good listening yourself, you can help your students become better listeners.

Consider Cultural Implications of Your Questions

Because of students' diverse backgrounds, questions may take on different meanings for different students (Bransford et al., 1999). For example, research indicates that many African American parents engage in different patterns of questioning with their children than do their white counterparts. African American parents are likely to emphasize metaphorical questions ("What is that like?") rather than fact-gathering questions ("What is that?"). Thus, African American students may not understand the purposes of white teachers' inquiry questions. According to Bransford and colleagues (1999), the answer to cultural mismatch between schools and communities "is not to concentrate exclusively on changing children or changing schools, but to encourage adaptive flexibility in both directions" (p. 99).

Some Native American students are averse to responding when called on in class. It may be that they perceive the traditional classroom, where teachers control all activities and interactions, as very different from their community social events, where there are no clear leaders and no clear separation between performers and audience. These students usually perform better one-on-one with the teacher or in cooperative settings with small groups of classmates (Vasquez, 1990).

You must know your students well so that your manner of questioning and presentation does not conflict with their cultural backgrounds.

Remember, We All Need Strokes!

Research indicates that teachers should use praise judiciously when they guide discussions. Praise can provide a signal to students that their contributions to discussion are appropriate. But praise of one student's answer might also tend to stop discussion. Other students may think that the purpose of the inquiry discussion is to find the right answer, not to probe more deeply into nature. Students look to their teacher for guidance and approval.

However, it is important to recognize students during individual work and group work for specific things they have done well. Teachers who try to look for good in every student and who inform them specifically and privately about these things are effective. They also are more likely to enjoy teaching. It is possible to look for something good to say to each individual, when they come into class or in private discussions, for example. As Abraham Maslow indicated in his theory of human needs, we all need to be recognized as valuable persons so our self-concepts continue to grow positively (Maslow, 1987).

SUMMARY

- Questioning is at the heart of inquiry teaching. By questioning effectively, you can ascertain what students already know, guide them in establishing questions for inquiry and collecting relevant data, help them construct explanations, and lead them to apply their new knowledge in different situations.
- Open-ended questions are more likely to promote inquiry than closed questions.
- Questions can be used to assess the prior knowledge and conceptions of students. Questions can also be used to engage the interest and motivation of students, to guide them in exploring systems, and to lead them in building explanations. Questions are also important in leading students to apply what they are learning to new situations, including societal issues and concerns.
- How you respond to students' answers is important in ongoing inquiry discussion. To keep students involved, be accepting of all their (relevant) answers; to keep them on target and supply needed information, extend their answers by adding to them; to lead them to think about their own ideas more deeply, probe their responses by building additional questions on them.
- After asking a question and calling on a student, teachers often wait only a second or two for students to compose and state their answer. When teachers wait just a little longer, 3 seconds or more, students tend to think more deeply, give longer answers, provide a wider variety of answers, and respond to one another more often.
- Learning to use questions effectively and productively in inquiry teaching takes practice, feedback, and reflection. Keep honing your questioning and responding tools to better guide children's inquiry.

 ONLINE PROFESSIONAL DEVELOPMENT

Pre- and post-tests to assess your knowledge of chapter content, along with exercises to enhance your understanding, can be found on MyEducationLab at www.myeducationlab.com.

Video Guides

Video clips on MyEducationLab selected for this chapter include: *Effective Questioning* and *Investigating Recycling—Parts 1, 2,* and *3.*

Accessing the Videos

1. Go to the Homework and Exercises section in Chapter 7 of MyEducationLab to select and view videos for this chapter.
2. Videos might be viewed individually, by small groups of colleagues, or by the whole class.
3. As you watch each video, use the **Questions for Reflection** to guide your thoughts and note taking for personal use and group discussion.
4. Discuss your answers to the questions about each video with classmates.

Video: Effective Questioning

Overview

In this video we return to three lessons we saw previously: goldfish at kindergarten, water wheels at third grade, and moon phase observations at fifth grade. This time around, the focus is on how teachers use questions to guide children in engagement and exploration tasks.

Questions for Reflection

1. Open-ended questions invite students to think more deeply about observations, observation records, and activities. Do you think the teachers' questions are primarily open-ended or closed in these three lessons?
2. What questions did the teacher use to guide students in engagement and exploration in each of the three lessons?
3. How did the teacher respond to children's answers to her questions in the different lessons?

Video: Investigating Recycling—Parts 1, 2, and 3

Overview

In this video we see how a teacher uses questions with third graders in activities on recycling.

Questions for Reflection

1. How did the teacher use questions to engage students in this unit and guide them through it?
2. What did the teacher do to *redirect* questions from one student to other students?
3. What were some of the things the teacher did to *acknowledge* the children's responses to a question?
4. How did the teacher use questions to guide the activity on classifying the materials of the different packages?

8

New technological developments can help transform schools if these developments are used to support new models of teaching and learning, models that characterize sustained community-centered, constructivist classrooms for learner investigation, collaboration, and construction. The Internet and educational software can support a collaborative culture in "doing science."

(Ebenezer and Lau, 1999, p. 17)

Technology Tools
and Resources
for Inquiry Science

ADVANCES IN EDUCATIONAL TECHNOLOGY certainly have much to offer science students and teachers. The Internet offers a gold mine of opportunities for classroom use, such as pictures, videos, and animations to pique curiosity, online data sources, web-based lessons, and worldwide connectivity. Software, ranging from simple instructional programs to sophisticated interactive, multimedia learning environments, present endless possibilities for learning. Data sensors connected to your computer enable the collection of data about temperature, motion, light intensity, air pressure, and more that can be displayed in real time through tables or graphs. Application programs from desktop publishing to multimedia presentation packages enhance the art of communication. Spreadsheets and graphing software facilitate the organization and display of data. Digital cameras and image processing software expand opportunities for observations and measurements of scientific phenomena. These imaginative products of the information technology age provide innovative ways to expand the classroom walls to encompass the universe.

This chapter provides a framework and some suggestions for using technology tools and resources to support science teaching and learning. Because technology changes rapidly, however, you will need to continue to take advantage of professional development opportunities to keep up with the latest innovations.

As you study the chapter, consider these questions:

- *How does educational technology fit within the broader context of inquiry and constructivist learning of science?*

- *What Internet sites, telecommunications resources, commercial instructional software, and data collection and analysis tools are available to enhance the teaching and learning of inquiry science in your classroom?*

- *How should the hardware and software available in your classroom be managed?*

- *How can you stay on the cutting edge of learning technology throughout your teaching career?*

Are you prepared to use educational technology in the most effective way in your science instruction? This chapter will help you see possibilities of incorporating educational technology into hands-on, inquiry science programs in your classroom.

Educational Technology

Educational technology is a prime example of technology in general. As discussed in Chapter 1, technology refers to any process or product that has been invented to assist humans in adapting to their natural, constructed, and social environments. Technological advances have certainly changed the way people do science, handle personal affairs, and run businesses, and they have the potential to enhance the way schooling takes place.

Innovative technology can facilitate science teaching and learning. The technology shown here allows the teacher to place a slide on a microscope so the whole class can view it at once by video.

NSES

Content Standards

Children in grades K–4 should develop skills in the use of computers and calculators for conducting investigations (National Research Council, 1996, p. 122).

Students in grades 5–8 should be able to use computers to access, gather, store, retrieve, and organize data using hardware and software designed for these purposes (National Research Council, 1996, p. 145).

In 1999, the National Science Teachers Association adopted a position statement about the use of computers in science education. The position statement presents the following rationale:

> Just as computers play a central role in developing and applying scientific knowledge, they can also facilitate learning of science. . . . Computers have become an essential classroom tool for the acquisition, analysis, presentation, and communication of data in ways which allow students to become more active participants in research and learning. In the classroom the computer offers the teacher more flexibility in presentation, better management of instructional techniques, and easier record keeping. It offers students a very important resource for learning the concepts and processes of science through simulations, graphics, sound, data manipulation, and model building. . . .These capabilities can improve scientific learning and facilitate communication of ideas and concepts.

Using educational technology tools, such as the Internet, DVDs and CD-ROMs, data sensors, digital microscopes, and digital cameras, enables students to practice science and technology in ways similar to professionals in the field, leading to a deeper understanding of concepts and improved thinking and problem-solving capabilities (see Figure 8-1).

Let us examine in more detail how these technology tools and resources can enhance learning at the various phases of inquiry.

You can read the complete NSTA Position Statement on "The Use of Computers in Science Education" at http://www. nsta.org/about/positions.aspx.

The *National Educational Technology Standards* describe what it means for students and teachers to be technology literate. You can learn more about these standards at http://cnets.iste.org/. On the website, look especially at *NETS-S: The Next Generation*.

Technology Tools and Resources

The Internet
CD-ROMs
DVDs
Digital Images
Databases
Computer- or Calculator-Based
    Laboratory Systems
Virtual Field Trips
Simulations
Computer-Enhanced Instruction
Spreadsheets
Graphing Software
Presentation Software
Global Information Systems
Global Positioning Systems

Figure 8-1 Technology resources and tools for inquiry science.

The Internet as a Technology Resource for Inquiry Science

The Internet is an important resource for teaching and learning in all subject areas. It consists of a vast connection of computers that was initially developed for communication among scientists and now is used by businesses, governments, homes, and schools around the globe (Stull, 1998). If your computer is connected to the Internet, you can access and exchange information with millions of computers worldwide. The World Wide Web, which was developed in 1989, allows users to access text, visual images, video, and audio presentations. Web browsers, such as Internet Explorer and Safari, enable users to navigate along the electronic superhighways that crisscross the Internet.

Suppose you wish to find out what is available on the Internet about a specific topic. You can use a search engine, such as Google, to find hundreds of sites related to the topic. To use a search engine, type in a descriptor of the topic in the appropriate space and begin.

Following are some suggestions of Internet sources for science lessons and how to use them.

A glossary containing definitions of important terms used in this chapter can be found on MyEducationLab.

Use Internet Images to Engage Students in Inquiry into Volcanoes

The best way for elementary or middle school students to learn something is through firsthand experiences. However, this is not always practical, cost-effective, or safe. Simulating the experience by computer can be an effective substitute. Simulation follows the constructivist idea that learners construct their own unique concepts through active participation.

High-speed Internet access makes downloading of still and video images from the World Wide Web a practical approach to supplementing teaching with visual material. Picture yourself teaching elementary or middle school students about volcanic action. To engage students in the investigation of volcanoes, you would love to have them experience the sights, sounds, and other sensory aspects of these dramatic forces of nature. But how will you do that? Take them to a volcano? That is not practical for most of us, and it is potentially dangerous.

Fortunately, you can take students via the Internet to the sights and sounds of an erupting volcano. Go on the Internet to http://mam.ngdigitalmotion.com/SearchRes.aspx. This site, sponsored by *National Geographic,* shows actual motion picture footage of active volcanoes at different stages of eruption.

Using a search engine, you will be able to find many different pictures and videos of other exciting natural phenomena, including earthquakes, tornadoes, and hurricanes and exotic animals such as whales and sharks. By investing a little bit of time in Internet searches, you can enable your students to observe not just the immediate world around them, but exciting things that happen far away in both distance and time.

Use Archived Data on Whale Movements in 5-E Lessons

Whales never cease to fascinate children and adults alike. Judith Hodge (n.d.) writes:

> Whales are monarchs among the animals of the ocean. They are some of the most enormous—and most intellgent—animals on earth. The blue whale, for example, is the largest animal that has ever lived. Full grown, it can be nearly one hundred feet long and weigh one hundred and fifty tons.

> Although they live in the oceans, whales are not fishes. They are mammals, like humans. As mammals, whales must come to the surface to take in air, they are warm-blooded, and they give birth to their young.

Due to the whaling industry in the 19th and early 20th centuries, whales of virtually all species are scarce today (Hodge, 1997). For example, there are fewer than 300 right whales living today. Right whales inhabit the Atlantic Ocean along the eastern seaboard of the United States. Despite their great size, right whales are very slow swimmers, averaging less than 4 miles per hour. Consequently they are often hit by boats and become entangled in fishing gear.

Preserving whales from danger and extinction is a global problem. One way to preserve right whales is to warn fishermen and boat captains when right whales are likely to be in their area. Thus, scientists are intent on finding patterns in the movements of right whales. By tagging several right whales with radio transmitters, marine biologists can collect data on the movement of these whales.

The following 5-E lesson is designed to introduce students to the right whale named *Metompkin* and to find patterns in Metompkin's movements.

An Internet-Based Lesson Plan on Right Whales

* Access the Internet and go to: http://whale.wheelock.edu/whalenet-stuff/metompkin. html.
* There you will find the exciting story called *Metompkin: Entangled and Heading for Home*. To engage students in the plight of Metompkin, read this brief story aloud.
* Ask: *Why would scientists want to attach a radio tag to Metompkin? Why would they wish to use the radio tag to track her movements?*
* Ask your class: *What questions might you ask about the pattern of Metompkin's movements?* Here are some suggested questions about Metompkin's movements that students might investigate:
  1. How far does Metompkin travel in a day? (Average)
  2. How far did Metompkin travel between Jan. 6, 1996, and March 10, 1996?
  3. Why do you think Metompkin is traveling from a south to north direction?
  4. Why do whales migrate?
  5. What is Metompkin's average rate of travel per hour? Per day?

* Ask: *What data would you need to collect to answer your selected question?*
* Show students the resources on the website so they are able to use the map of Metompkin's route north. The map is at http://whale.wheelock.edu/whalenet-stuff/ images/GOES_map6.GIF.
* Allow the students to work in small groups to use the Metompkin data and map to collect data to answer the questions they are investigating.

Use the data the students bring from the explore phase of the lesson, the WhaleNet site, and other Internet sites to answer these questions:

* Why was Metompkin in the coastal waters off of Florida in January 1996?
* Does Metompkin tend to move day after day in one main direction? Why do you think this is so?
* What do you think Metompkin did in April and May 1996? Why do you think this is so?

Engage

An Annenberg video entitled *The Journey North* is available for viewing on the Internet. The video documents and explains the movement of different animal species from south to north. To access the Annenberg Internet site and this video, follow the instructions given in the Online Professional Development section in Chapter 1.

Explore

Explain

Elaborate

Use the WhaleNet site and other related sites to answer these additional questions:

- What is a whale? How large are whales? What are some varieties of whales? Are whales fish or mammals?
- What are the distinguishing characteristics of right whales? How many of these endangered right whales are there now in the Atlantic?

Explore Space Through the Internet

To see a collection of space–science related games, projects, animations, and amazing facts, visit The Space Place (http://spaceplace.jpl.nasa.gov/do.htm). There you will find a variety of memory and matching games, puzzles of images, crosswords, word finds, and so on. Go to Space Place Live to hear what NASA scientists say about their jobs, how they became scientists, and what they do from day to day. Participate in the Space Place Quiz Show and assess your own knowledge of space.

Earth Observing 1 (EO-1 for short) is a satellite with some great instruments for taking images and gathering other information about Earth. It can take such a clear picture you can make out an airplane sitting on a runway from 430 miles away! Satellite data can help scientists and others understand and deal with all sorts of problems, such as

> Volcanoes
> Earthquakes
> Floods
> Droughts
> Forest fires
> Forest diseases
> Erosion of beaches
> Melting of polar ice sheets
> Oil spills
> Planning cities
> Farming (agriculture)
> Making maps

The possibilities for data taking to support investigations are almost limitless.

Come to Space Place and check out the games, animations, projects, and fun facts and images about Earth, space, and technology. The site is maintained by NASA.

Take a Virtual Field Trip

Consider what you do when you organize a traditional field trip. You pick a location, plan the day's schedule, and guide the group from one spot to the next (Dockterman, 1997). You are creating an educational experience that supports your curriculum objectives and classroom activities. On a real field trip—whether to a local pond, aquarium, wetlands area, museum, zoo, planetarium, or any one of dozens of other exciting places—students experience new things and relate the experiences to concepts previously encountered in the classroom. Taking an electronic field trip can offer many of the same advantages as real field trips. Additionally, virtual field trips can enhance students' skills in using word processors, spreadsheets, databases, presentation programs, and the Internet (Bitner, Wadlington, Austin, Partridge, & Bitner, 1999).

Visit Science Exhibits Online

The Internet provides opportunities for children to take virtual field trips to museums, zoos, or science centers without ever leaving the classroom (Ebenezer & Lau, 1999). For example, visit the Exploratorium, a San Francisco–based interactive science museum, at http://www.exploratorium.edu. An "exhibit cam" captures live views of Exploratorium visitors interacting with featured exhibits in the hall. The "roof cam" provides real-time images of the surrounding area, and you can select the direction it points. It is almost like being there. Additionally, "on-line exhibits" featuring optical illusions let students try out some of the museum's exhibits through interactions with their computer.

Take a Factory Tour via the Internet

How Everyday Things Are Made, published online by Alliance for Innovative Manufacturing (AIM) in cooperation with Stanford University, provides links to narrative video clips and collections of still images of manufacturing processes ranging from the production of airplanes and golf clubs to jellybeans and denim (http://manufacturing.Stanford.edu/). The links on this page can take you to forty different virtual factory tours. Students interested in engineering and how familiar products are made will be impressed with the diversity of products included. Those with a sweet tooth will be satisfied, too, since eight of the links are to candy factories.

Successful electronic field trips that support your curriculum need to be well planned (Dockterman, 1997). You can choose what your students will visit and what you expect them to learn, or you can let your students plan their own pathways through the software. Alternatively, you can let the Internet serve as a guide through the virtual landscape.

Use Commercially Available Multimedia Packages to Enhance Science Inquiry

CD-ROMs and DVDs can provide some of the same types of sensory experiences found on the Internet. A single CD can store more than 600 MB of data, the equivalent of about 250,000 pages of text or 20,000 images.

CD-ROMs embellish science teaching and learning by dispensing instant individual illustrations and sound for hard-to-grasp material. They invite creativity for teachers and students. Best of all, they are easy to use. It is little wonder they are among the most popular teaching and learning technologies. For example, to use CD-ROMs to explain the concept of phototropism, select time-lapse shots and slides of plants growing toward the light to make the learning more dramatic and meaningful. These technological tools allow you to pause at critical points, show entire sequences in slow motion, speed up action that is very slow, and review important concepts quickly and easily.

CD-ROMs provide a library of images and text for students as they research, study, and present reports. Your students can use the materials stored on CD-ROMs just as they would an encyclopedia. When they are ready to present their reports, they can display pertinent images to dramatically illustrate their understanding.

Many computers also have DVD (digital video disk) drives allowing direct access to digital information stored on this even more powerful medium. DVD players can be connected to a television to enable viewing of a DVD without a computer. DVDs enable students and teachers to use menus to quickly select certain topics or segments of the presentation to view.

To find current links to virtual field trips on the Internet, just search for "virtual field trips" using Google or another search engine. You will discover many sites that provide links to places to visit.

Computer simulations have great potential as a teaching tool. NSTA's position statement about the use of computers in science education states,

> Simulation software should provide opportunities to explore concepts and methods which are not readily accessible in the laboratory, e.g., those that require: expensive or unavailable materials or equipment; hazardous materials or procedures; levels of skills not yet achieved by the students; and more time than is possible or appropriate in a real-time classroom.

Simulated activities that are difficult or impossible to do in your classroom include visits to the planets of our solar system, investigations of ocean wave properties, studies of population growth of various organisms in an ecosystem, dissections, and monitoring of the inheritance of traits. Students enjoy engaging with the colorful, animated displays. While engaging with colorful, animated displays, students are placed in a situation where they control an environment by interacting with the computer. They collect data, correlate results, and learn skills, attitudes, and concepts. Your job is to help your students understand the relationship of the simulation to reality.

The Great Solar System Rescue: A Simulation for Science Classes

Tom Snyder Productions has developed a space simulation in which students search for a probe lost somewere in space:

Mi and her three teammates watch the monitor closely as the lost space probe sends back images of the planet where it has crashed. They can see craters, so they know the planet is terrestrial rather than gaseous. But which one is it?

"Temperatures here range from very mild to −135° Celsius," the probe informs them.

Mi, the meteorology expert on the team, quickly searches her data to learn more about the weather on the terrestrial planets. "Only Earth and Mars have mild weather," she tells her teammates, "and only Mars has temperatures as low as −135°C. The probe must be on Mars!"

After listening to information from the probe in their areas and consulting their own expert data, they concur: The lost probe crashed on Mars.

"I'm going to check it out," Cassie says. She clicks the mouse on the Mars symbol on the screen to test her team's hypothesis. The screen confirms their inference: The probe is on Mars!

"But," Gerald says, "where on Mars?" Gerald and Cassie decide from their collective historical data that there are only four possible locations where the probe could have landed. Angelo, the team's geology expert, clicks the mouse on the probe's elevation detector. The probe informs the team that its location is 4 km deep. Angelo quickly searches through his geological database. "The probe must be either in Valles Marineris or Argyre Basin," he tells his teammates. "The other two locations aren't that deep." Then Angelo tries a rock analysis. He clicks on the rock analysis label on the probe. The probe tells the team that it senses violent activity within Mars's crust.

"It has to be Valles Marineris!" Angelo tells them. "That's where there's folding and faulting of the surface due to Marsquakes!"

Take Your Case to Science Court

Science Court (for grades 4–6) and *Science Court Explorations* (for grades 2–4) are innovative series of programs developed by Tom Snyder Productions (http://tomsnyder.com) on such topics as friction, sound, work and simple machines, flight, electrical current, and the water cycle. Each episode engages students in a scientific question presented in a humorous, animated video. The case ends up in Science Court, where lawyers and expert witnesses seek the answer to the question. Before the case is decided, students form hypotheses and test them through hands-on activities. They then use their findings to predict the verdict in the Science Court trial.

For example, in the case of the electric circuit, I. M. Richman refuses to relinquish his ping-pong trophy to the new champion, Mary Murphy. But he does agree to let her look at it. On the way into Richman's mansion, Mary trips and breaks the wire for Richman's alarm system. He repairs the break by inserting his dog's leash in the circuit, but later discovers that his alarm system is not working. Did Mary attempt to steal the trophy, or does the broken alarm system have to do with the way the wiring was repaired? The case is argued before the Science Court. Before the answer is revealed on the CD-ROM, students discuss the case, form hypotheses, and test them through hands-on activities with electric circuits.

Many other good simulation programs are available that let your students explore an unknown universe.

Explore the Skies with Planetarium Programs

Voyager 4 by Carina Software (2006) is a planetarium simulation that displays the sun, moon, planets, and stars in their correct spatial positions for any day of the year, from the distant past, through the present, to the future. As a dynamic simulation, *Voyager 4* allows students to do compressed time studies of motions of objects in the sky. In a few seconds, students can watch the circumpolar constellations as they revolve about the North Star throughout a 24-hour period, follow the moon on its cycle around the earth, or keep track of a planet as it moves through the night sky.

Planetarium programs can be used to understand sky relationships. For example, the positions of sunrise along the horizon for different days throughout the year might be measured using *Voyager 4*. Students would note that the sun rises along the northeastern horizon around June 21, due east around September 21, along the southeastern horizon around December 21, and due east again around March 21. Through studying the sun's movements, students can construct a better understanding of the causes of the seasons. Further, students can better understand and appreciate the annual movements of the sun along the horizon, a means people thousands of years ago used to establish a solar calendar. *Voyager Stargazer* even allows students to map the changing areas of day and night on the earth's surface at different times and dates to help them explore the reasons for seasons.

Another quality computer planetarium simulation appropriate for the classroom is *Starry Night EDU* by Space Holding Corp. This program has many of the same features as *Voyager Stargazer* and is packaged with a printed teacher's manual with reproducibles. Visit http://www.starrynight.com to learn more about this program's features.

Use Virtual Laboratories

Some simulation programs allow learners to conduct experiments in a virtual setting. *Virtual Labs: Light* allows students to use virtual lasers and optical tools to safely investigate the nature of light, reflection, refraction, and color, rather than setting up light beams, mirrors, and lenses in a laboratory. *Virtual Labs: Electricity* enables students to construct virtual circuits by clicking and dragging labeled icons that specify electrical components, including batteries, bulbs, motors, resistors, and wires. Students can discover the basic properties of a circuit and the purpose of devices such as switches and fuses without the expense or potential safety issues of exploring with electrical components in the laboratory. The school version of this program includes structured learning activities, opportunities for open exploration, thinking questions and challenges, and embedded assessment activities. For example, "Broken? Fix It!" requires students to alter two circuits that do not work to make them functional.

A wonderful library of online simulations that power inquiry and understanding can be accessed at http://www.explorelearning.com. Here you will find nearly 400 *Gizmos* designed to develop lasting conceptual understanding in science and mathematics at the middle and high school levels. All Gizmos have certain things in common. They are visual and interactive, have greath depth, and encourage student inquiry. Gizmos appropriate for grades 3 through 5 are being added to the collection. One allows users to investigate the growth of three common garden plants: tomatoes, beans, and turnips. The amount of light, the amount of water, and the type of soil in which the seed is planted can be varied. The plants' height, mass, leaf color, and leaf size can be observed. Tables and graphs of height and mass data can be displayed. Investigators can use this simulated greenhouse to answer such questions as: *What type of soil will produce the best tomato plant? Or How much should we water a turnip planted in garden soil?* A thirty-day free-trial enables users to explore this award-winning site, read research articles about the effectiveness of this approach to teaching and learning, and try out Gizmos that correlate with their instructional standards.

Use Instructional Software Packages

A variety of innovative instructional packages, often incorporating interactive multimedia activities and presentations, are currently available to schools from commercial sources.

Learn with Computer-Assisted Instruction Packages

Computer-assisted instruction (CAI) packages may range from text-based drill and practice or tutorial software to open-ended multimedia environments that support student's exploration of information (Reynolds & Barba, 1996). Tutorials present information to students, often like an electronic textbook. Drill and practice, or review and reinforcement, programs provide opportunities for students to rehearse their knowledge and get immediate feedback about the accuracy of their answers. Though both of these approaches have developed negative connotations over the years, they can be effective learning tools when used in conjunction with other learning approaches.

In their book *Technology for the Teaching and Learning of Science*, Reynolds and Barba (1996) present a concise review of the research into the effectiveness of CAI, then summarize the research-based implications for computer-assisted instruction as follows:

> From the research of the past two decades, we have learned that computer-assisted instruction is a powerful learning tool for improving students' knowledge of science concepts at the knowledge and comprehension levels. Drill-and-practice packages help students decrease learning time, while increasing their achievement levels. Students enjoy working in electronic environments and enjoy learning in electronic microworlds. Computer-assisted instruction provides science teachers with supplementary resources to enrich basic science instruction. (p. 41)

Computer presentations can enhance the learning of science topics such as the circulatory system, the organs in the respiratory system of a fish, the parts of a microscope, and constellations and star names.

Explore the World with Global Information Systems

ArcView is a global information systems (GIS) software package that is being used in middle and secondary schools. A license and training for using this software tool are available for purchase through the Internet. The book *Mapping Our World: GIS Lessons for Educators* by Malone, Palmer, and Voigt (2002) provides a 1-year license for ArcView, a teacher

An example of a program that explores human anatomy (basic organization and terminology, bones and body organs, and body systems and how they relate to each other) is *A.D.A.M. The Inside Story* from A.D.A.M. Software (http://www.adam.com).

resource CD, and lesson plans for a variety of science and geography investigations. For example, "The Earth Moves: A Global Perspective," can engage students in investigating patterns of earthquake and volcanic activity on the earth's surface and the relationship of those patterns to the location of diverse landforms, plate boundaries, and the distribution of population. Based on their exploration of these relationships, students will form a hypothesis about the earth's distribution of earthquake and volcanic activity and identify world cities that face the greatest risk from those phenomena (p. 49).

Explore the Potential of Digital Cameras and Digital Microscopes

Digital and video cameras are now affordable tools for schools. Their availability makes it possible for teachers and students to electronically record images of objects and events in their environment. This capability adds a real-world connection to science learning. Visual and written and drawn observational records can be stored for future analysis. A photographic record of the seasonal changes in the school yard, the growth of plants in a classroom investigation, or the position of shadows at different times during the day can provide familiar visual data for students to observe, sequence, and analyze.

In a Mississippi elementary school, students worked with a partner in a parklike setting to collect digital photographs of at least 10 different leaves and the bark of the trees from which the leaves came (Carter, Sumrall, & Curry, 2006). The students downloaded the photographs onto computers and used a special program to edit the images. They were encouraged to explore and edit the pictures using the color, contrast, brightness, and cropping features of the program.

> A simple editing program for digital photos, Microsoft Office Picture Manager, is part of the Microsoft Office suite of programs.

The students used a variety of sources to identify the trees from which the leaves and bark came. The URLs of Internet sites they used in the identification process included:

http://www.fw.vt.edu/dendro/forsite/key/intro.htm
http://www.uwsp.edu/cnr/leaf/treeid.htm

You should be able to find other identification keys through Internet and literature searches and visiting bookstores.

Digital microscopes are also useful tools in elementary and middle school classrooms. They make it possible to display magnified images of objects and organisms on a computer monitor, television screen, or video projection device. A huge advantage of displaying the image for the whole class to see is that the teacher knows that all students are looking at the same thing, so questions can be asked, observations can be discussed, and parts of the object or organism can be pointed out, described, and identified. Digital microsopes eliminate a common problem that occurs when students are each looking through their own microscopes, that the teacher doesn't know for sure whether each student is observing the object being investigated or simply seeing their eyelashes as they gaze through the microscope's tube.

Some digital microscopes are simply small digital video cameras that magnify the image when positioned close to an object because the image is displayed on a screen with a greater area than the object being imaged. These can be placed at the end of a traditional microscope tube, where your eye would normally be, to display what is on the microscope's stage for all to see. Other digital microscopes have a variety of lenses that can be attached to change the magnification of the displayed image. Computer software can enable students to capture images they see on the computer screen and save them for future use in written or oral reports.

Contribute to and Use Computer Databases

Useful data collected over long periods of time are available to students and scientists today on the Internet and CD-ROMs. Your science classroom computer can be used to search through database materials from throughout the United States and other parts of the world. **Databases** (electronically stored information) exist in all curricular areas, including science. For instance, if your students are studying the interrelationships between wind direction, speed, and weather conditions, they can instantly gather information from a variety of geographic locations without leaving your classroom. This not only motivates students and encourages them to use higher-thinking processes but also helps students learn how to effectively select and secure information.

Students can use a computer to:

- access commercial databases and information services;
- do collaborative research with other teachers and students locally or around the world;
- get up-to-the-minute weather and other science-related data;
- use computer based laboratories to collect and process data for addition to databases; and
- communicate with other investigators using e-mail.

Contribute to and Use Regional Databases

Dotty is a participating teacher in the Tennessee Valley Project, which was designed and funded to improve science education in eight rural school districts in eastern Tennessee. In an Annenberg video entitled *Case Studies in Science Education: Dotty*, we see Dotty's students collecting and testing water samples for pH and dissolved oxygen. They use the one computer in their classroom and telecommunications to exchange data with students from other schools in their area. In this way, they both contribute to and use a common database of water quality in the eastern Tennessee region. The students also send e-mail messages to students in all 50 states asking for water samples.

Telecommunications allow these students from rural Tennessee to feel connected to students in other parts of the state, the nation, and the world. The video *Case Studies in Science Education: Dotty is* available to view on the Annenberg website. Take some time to view the video on Dotty and her students and learn more about the potential for using computers in school science.

Participate in the GLOBE Project

Global Learning and Observations to Benefit the Environment (GLOBE) is a model for international cooperation in monitoring the environment. GLOBE is an Internet-based research program involving scientists, students, and teachers worldwide (Ebenezer & Lau, 1999; Rock, Blackwell, Miller, & Hardison, 1997). GLOBE students learn to observe the environment by taking scientific data, such as the maximum and minimum temperature of the atmosphere, precipitation, cloud cover, cloud type, and the temperature, pH, dissolved oxygen, and alkalinity of bodies of water. Protocols for data collection are specified by GLOBE and some require specific instruments to be purchased by the participating school. Students send their data via the Internet to the GLOBE, student data archive. Environmental and earth scientists use the data to accurately map such features as rivers, lakes, reservoirs, forest types, wetlands, and urban areas. The data are then available for students to use in their own research projects.

Though many projects are designed for middle and high school participation, there are several designed specifically for elementary students to contribute to and learn from

You can access the GLOBE website at http://www.globe.gov.

worldwide data. One GLOBE research project that requires no special equipment, focuses on light pollution and its effect on viewing stars in the night sky. Known as *GLOBE at Night,* this investigation, which happens each spring during a period when the moon is not in the night sky, challenges observers to match a card showing the part of the sky where the constellation Orion is found with the way this region of their sky appears. In areas with a lot of light pollution, only the brightest stars are visible; when there is little light pollution, many stars both bright and dim are visible in the sky. Observers input their location (longitude and latitude), time and date of viewing, and indicate the which card is the closest match for their sky. Data from around the world is assembed and displayed at the GLOBE website so that patterns of light pollution can be analyzed geographically and from year to year.

Collect Observational Data on Clouds

NASA's S'COOL (Students' Cloud Observations On-Line) project provides another opportunity for students to contribute to real scientific research by making and sharing their observations. Classes provide *ground truth* measurements to assist in the validation of the CERES (Clouds and the Earth's Radiant Energy System) instrument. Students make visual cloud observations at the same time the satellite does and share their findings electronically with NASA. Then the two observations are compared to validate the analysis of the satellite data. Students can also compare the surface- and space-based observations to learn more about clouds and climate.

The S'COOL project is suggested for students in fourth grade or above, but classes of younger students have also participated successfully. Instructional materials and all materials necessary for participating in S'COOL are free. If you are teaching about clouds and weather, consider using the S'COOL materials.

The S'COOL Project has recently been revised for classrooms. For more information, visit the S'COOL website at http://asd-www.larc.nasa.gov/SCOOL.

Use Archived Data to Discover Weather Patterns

Scientific databases are also available on CD-ROMs. Michael Passow (1996) and his eighth grade science students have used a CD-ROM called the *Global Tropical/Extratropical Cyclone Climatic Atlas* to study historic storms. The *Climatic Atlas* CD-ROM was produced by the National Climatic Data Center of the National Oceanic and Atmospheric Administration (NOAA).

In one activity, Passow's class (1996) studied storms along the East Coast of the United States. Selecting a North Atlantic option on the CD-ROM allowed them to view a list of storms that occurred between 1871 and 1992. From the list, they found that most of the storms (21) in the North Atlantic occurred in 1933. They chose a particular 1933 storm and used the CD-ROM data to map its path from its beginning to its ending dates. The storm formed in the Atlantic Ocean, moved along the East Coast, and struck land in North Carolina on August 23, 1933.

Another CD-ROM in the NOAA series allowed students to study historical climatic data from more than 2,000 stations worldwide. Thus, they could select a station near their city and determine such things as annual temperature and wind patterns.

Passow (1996) concluded that CD-ROMs and other technologies

To find more information on the Internet about weather and weather patterns over long periods of time, type "Weather Data" into Google or another search engine and begin your search.

> lie at the heart of the Standards' vision of "Science as Inquiry," where students sharpen observing, inferring, and experimenting skills while increasing their knowledge and using scientific reasoning and critical thinking. (p. 23)

Use Computer-Based Laboratories to Collect and Process Data

Nothing adds to student excitement and links to real-world science like **computer-based laboratory (CBL)** systems. These electronic systems use data sensors and software programs to collect, organize, display, and process real-world data automatically. Data sensors need not replace direct measurements of temperature, time, force, air pressure, and so on. The direct measurement of variables in your classroom science program is still very important. However, the use of electronic data taking can help shift the focus from mechanical procedures to higher-level and more creative scientific processes, such as analyzing and hypothesizing. CBLs allow students to focus on thinking about data, not merely gathering it (Nachmias & Linn, 1987; Price, 1989).

The website of Vernier, a CLB supplier, features a lesson plan for using a temperature probe to investigate temperature. In the investigation, students use temperature sensors and computers to compare temperature readings from two different cups when hot or cold water is added to them. Through these data-taking and analysis procedures, students determine which material is a better conductor and which is a better insulator.

Caniglia (1997) has pointed out that the exchange of ideas and results is just as important in science as collecting and analyzing data. When engaging in CBL activities, students do more than just look for patterns in graphs. They also argue about experimental procedures, discuss inconsistencies, draw conclusions, and make connections to the physical processes underlying the data. These are core activities in both science and mathematics. CBL investigations offer exciting opportunities for students to model real-world events and make needed connections between science, mathematics, and engineering design.

TERC (formerly, Technical Education Research Center, now simply TERC) has been a leader in developing the potential of computer-based laboratories since 1984. The *Hands-On Elementary Science Project Leader's Manual* developed by TERC (1993) states that a computer-based laboratory provides

> more opportunity for learners to pay attention to the data—to interpret it, redisplay it, and analyze it to inform their understanding of the phenomenon. Since the time span between changing a variable in their investigation and seeing the results is shortened, learners can ask more 'what if' questions and are more likely to revise their test design and try it again. (p. A-21)

TERC (1993) suggests that CBL systems also introduce learners to some standard representations of science data, including bar graphs and line graphs, and assists them in acquiring the "language of graphing" (p. A-22). This instructional technology is especially applicable when trying to measure events that happen very slowly or very quickly, that change over a very small range, or that must be measured indirectly.

A variety of computer-based lab packages is available commercially (see Table 8-1).

Here is a sample lesson using CBL activities. As part of their study of measurement, a third-grade class was monitoring the temperature of their room every school day. Each hour, a student read the thermometer and posted the temperature on the class chart. At the end of each day, Ms. Winter worked with the class to construct a graph showing how the temperature changed during the school day. After a week or so, during a discussion of that day's graph, Suzy wondered, "But what does the temperature do while we are at lunch?" Then Ben said, "You know, we really don't know how it changes between the times we check it." Yelana added, "Sometimes the heater comes on and it gets hot in here but we aren't measuring then." Ms. Winter asked, "Would that show up on the graph?" "No, we don't have data for it," replied Heather.

Teachers are continually searching for ways to help students make connections among subject areas. Using data sensors and computers can be a critical way to help students tie mathematics and science together.

Several lessons using the GO! Temp probe are available online at the Vernier website. Go to http://www.vernier.com/cmat/cmatdnld.html and select an indented title from the drop-down menu under "Elementary Science."

TABLE 8-1 SOME COMPUTER-BASED LAB SUPPLIERS	
Company	**Website**
Acculab Products	http://www.sensornet.com
Data Harvest Company	http://www.dataharvest.com
EyeThink Station Probeware System	http://www.eyethinkcorp.com/
Pasco	http://www.pasco.com/probeware/
Vernier Go! Lab	http://elementary.vernier.com/

The next day, Ms. Winter attached the GO! Temp probe to her computer and set it up to collect temperature data all day long. Meanwhile, the students didn't really notice the metallic rod attached to a wire that was near the thermometer they continued to read each hour. In the afternoon, after the hourly data was graphed as usual, Ms. Winter turned on the projector attached to her computer, and a graph appeared on the screen. She asked the class to compare the two graphs, then do an "I Notice/I Wonder" chart in their science journals before they left for the day. As she looked over the journals after school, she discovered that most students noticed that both displayed time on the X axis and temperature in degrees Celsius on the Y axis. A few of the students noticed that the graph on the screen was shaped somewhat like the class graph, but was smoother. Several of the children commented that the starting temperature and the ending temperatures on both graphs were the same.

The next day, Ms. Winter showed the class the GO! Temp probe and explained that it was a temperature sensor connected to the computer, basically a digital thermometer. Joey said, "You mean like the barbeque fork that tells you when the meat is done?" Ms. Winter agreed, then went on to say that the data from the Go! Temp probe was stored in the computer and displayed as a graph as it was collected. She told the class, "Today when we check the thermometer, we'll also check the thermometer shown on the computer screen. Then in the afternoon, we'll compare graphs again."

During the afternoon discussion, connections between the graphs were made. The students were all excited about what else they could do with this new tool. They discussed what the GO! Temp probe would let them do that would be hard to do with just the thermometer. Ben said, "We don't have to keep checking the thermometer all the time, the probe and the computer can do it for us." Suzy said, "We can collect data even when we aren't here, then look at it later!" Heather suggested, "Could we set it up to see what happens to the temperature in the room tonight?" "Sure," Ms. Winter replied. "Why don't you all predict what the graph will look like tomorrow morning, then I'll show you how to set up the computer to collect our data."

The next morning, Ms. Winter's students could hardly wait to see how the temperature changed in their classroom the night before.

Use Spreadsheets to Organize and Analyze Data

Spreadsheets can facilitate and extend the organization and analysis of real data taken by students. A **spreadsheet** is a computer program for organizing data in rows and columns, then manipulating it in various ways through the use of mathematics. **Graphing software** contained within spreadsheet programs enables students to display data in different types of graphs. This software tool is especially useful in processing directly measured data if probes are not being used for data collected from Internet databases.

One of the most commonly used spreadsheet programs is Microsoft® Excel. Its inclusion in Microsoft® Office packages has made it available on many home and school computers. This powerful program can be used successfully by teachers and students alike with proper training.

Another spreadsheet and graphing program, Inspire Data, appropriate for grades 4 and higher, applies research-based strategies of visual learning to data literacy. It is designed to inspire students to discover meaning as they collect and explore data in a dynamic inquiry process. Using data they have collected or from databases included with the program, students formulate questions and make connections between data and its visual representations to interpret information, solve problems, and draw conclusions. This helps students develop deeper content knowledge and stronger critical thinking skills.

Communicate Through Multimedia Presentations

Multimedia software programs such as PowerPoint, Kid Pix, and Kidspiration enliven presentations, reports, and projects for both teachers and students. With these multimedia programs, users can build colorful and creative slides and combine them into the desired presentation product (Lee & Patterson, 1997). Program users have access to prebuilt graphic templates, word processing and drawing tools, built-in graphics, and high-quality clip art. Kid Pix includes movie clips as well. All three programs enable the user to insert items from other sources, including the Internet.

Teachers can create motivating slide shows that capture students' attention for instruction and model how students can present their own ideas through technology. In science instruction that follows the 5-E model, teachers might use a graphics presentation program to

- add catchy, animated graphics to the engage phase;
- list directions for the explore phase and project them onto a screen for students to view and follow;
- build concept maps and augment invention of new concepts and ideas in the explain phase;
- assist students in the elaborate phase to develop understanding by linking invented concepts to previous activities and to new investigations; and
- present tests, rubrics, and other assessment items to students in the evaluate phase of instruction.

Using teacher-developed slide shows as models, students might construct reports of their investigations and prepare interesting presentations for the class. The very act of creating products with a multimedia program forces students to clarify, extend, and refine their ideas and thus helps them in constructing understanding.

Additionally, teachers and students might use a multimedia program to create single slides to illustrate a point, to create theme files, to construct and print displays for bulletin boards and projects, to design and produce safety and lab procedure posters, or to create announcement flyers to post in the classroom or send home to parents.

Earlier in the book, concept maps were introduced as effective tools for planning, teaching, and assessing science lessons. Inspiration®, a program designed for learners in sixth grade and up, can be used to create graphic organizers such as concept maps and expand topics into writing. For younger students, Kidspiration® provides an easy way to apply the proven principles of visual learning. Students build graphic organizers by combining pictures, text, and spoken words to represent thoughts and information. For more information about both of these programs, visit http://www.Inspiration.com.

For more information about Inspire Data, visit http://www.inspiration.com

Go to the Homework and Exercises section in Chapter 8 of MyEducationLab and view the videos for this chapter, *Technology and Science Learning, Parts 1* and *2*. In these videos we see teachers and students in third and fifth grades using a variety of educational technologies, including PowerPoint presentations and the Internet, to enhance students' understanding. We return to the videos on water wheels, recycling, and explaining moon phases with a focus on the educational technology tools that are used in the lessons.

So far in this chapter, we have looked mostly at isolated uses of educational technology in teaching. Refer to the science and social studies lessons presented in Chapter 9 on weather and on river ecology for sample technology-supported lessons that can address standards from science and other disciplines.

Successfully using technology in science and other classes requires that classroom technology resources be managed effectively.

Managing Educational Technology in the Science Classroom

The success of using computers to enhance science learning of your students depends on a number of considerations.

Using Different Arrangements of Computers in Your School

Educational technology resources in schools are usually arranged in one or more of these ways: (1) technology resources may be housed in a centralized computer center or lab with computers for every student in the class, (2) classrooms may have only a single computer, or (3) classrooms may be equipped with several computers.

The One-Computer Classroom. If you have one computer in your classroom, like Dotty in the video case study described previously in this chapter, you may have a problem (Brown, 1998). How are you going to use the computer? Will it be used primarily for presentation by the teacher, or as a tool for students in creating projects? How often will students use the computer? Will you encourage cooperative learning with the computer?

Fortunately, there is advice available for the teacher in a one-computer classroom. Dockterman (1997) has compiled some good ideas in his *Great Teaching in the One Computer Classroom*. Kahn (1998) has also written a versatile and practical guide, *Ideas and Strategies for the One-Computer Classroom*, which provides many suggestions for teachers. Additionally, *Learning and Leading with Technology (L&L)*, a journal of the International Society for Technology in Education, includes a periodic section on teaching in the one-computer classroom.

In the October 1998 issue of *L&L*, Cindy Brown suggested that an important use of a single computer in a classroom is for teacher and student presentations. If you use the computer for instructional presentations, your computer will need to be connected to a large-screen monitor or liquid crystal display (LCD) projection system. You or your students work at the computer, and images are displayed on-screen for the entire class to view. Interaction can take place as students view the screen and discuss what they see.

According to Brown (1998), another important way to use a single computer in a classroom is as a learning center. Mary Ellen Swadley, an innovative sixth-grade teacher of science, mathematics, and social studies, uses the computer as one of several ongoing learning stations for her two classes of about 20 students. Each class meets for a 3-hour block of time. Students work in the learning stations—on science, math, or social studies content—in small cooperative groups. All computer activities are related to the topic being taught in the class. For example, students may engage in *The Great Ocean Rescue* as part of a study of oceans, or they might use a multimedia package to develop a report or prepare a presentation on a topic being learned.

Every child in Ms. Swadley's classes uses the computer at least 20 minutes each day as a member of a cooperative group. Additionally, students might work on the computer on their own at different times during the day, including before and after school. Although

Ms. Swadley started her adventure into educational technology with only one computer in her classroom, she has found creative ways to add five more.

More Than One Computer. It is possible that you will have more than one computer in a multimedia arrangement in your self-contained classroom. Here are some guidelines for setting up and managing computers and other electronic technology equipment for a class of 20 to 25 students:

1. Use a variety of educational technologies to accommodate the range of learning styles and backgrounds of your students (e.g., texts, videos, hands-on materials, computers, computer-based laboratory systems, software, and Internet connections).
2. Arrange tables so students can work in cooperative learning groups.
3. Consider setting up the following learning stations for groups of four students: a listening station, video station, hands-on materials station, word processing station, computer-based laboratory station, and writing station. Figure 8-2 presents a suggested floor plan for a science/technology-oriented classroom incorporating these stations.

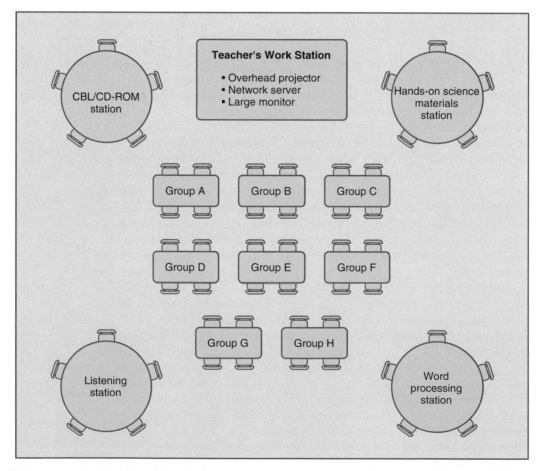

Figure 8-2   Technology-oriented self-contained science classroom.
Source: Based on *Designs for Elementary School Science and Health* (p. 50), A cooperative project of biological Science Curriculum Study (BSCS) and International Business Machines (IBM),© 1989, Colorado Springs, Co. Reprinted by permission.

4. Equip the teacher's workstation with a computer with Internet access, an LCD projection system or large-screen monitor, an electronic writing board, and a printer.
5. Consider establishing these types of computer stations in your classroom:
   - Student computer workstation with multimedia presentation software and Internet capability for data collection and sending science e-mail and bulletin board/newsgroup correspondence
   - Computer-based lab systems for student-conducted science activities
   - A videocassette, DVD, and CD-ROM station for viewing and using in the videos and software
6. Arrange to lock the computers when they are not used. Many schools engrave the name of the school on all components and bolt them to tables or portable carts.
7. Arrange your classroom schedule so that students who are responsible can use the computers on a sign-up basis when they have completed their other classroom responsibilities. You will find that computers are popular and can positively motivate students to complete assignments. Encourage this.
8. Periodically assess technology literacy content and skills with simple tests, and introduce your students to new software as it becomes available.

You should set up computer learning stations where students can work on learning software, word processing, and multimedia presentations. These would be similar to the learning centers described earlier in the text where collections of materials are arranged for students to work on individually or in small groups. Follow these guidelines:

1. Locate your computer learning stations so you can see them from anyplace in your classroom.
2. Post specific directions related to the station for easy reference.
3. Select two or three students who have used computers, and train them to be peer computer experts. They will have to know the hardware and software in your room, how to operate the computer, and how to positively help their classmates. Post the names of these students and assign them specific times when each one will be available for help.
4. Set up a schedule so students can sign up for computer time at the computer station. Include some open or free times. Your schedule should record time spent on the computer by each student, so you can ensure that everyone gets computer time.

Schoolwide Computer/Multimedia Center or Lab. Some elementary and middle schools set up computer or technology centers or labs for class-sized groups. Classes are scheduled into the technology center, and either an educational technology specialist conducts computer lessons or individual teachers work with their own classes there. It is often quite difficult to connect educational technology to the ongoing curriculum with centralized technology centers.

Selecting Science Software and Internet Sites

Computer programs and Internet sites vary greatly in suitability for use with elementary and middle school students. Many programs are designed to supplement or be an integral part of science programs and textbooks. You may be called on to suggest which software your school should buy in the coming years or to screen and select websites for student use. In the selection process, start with your instructional objectives, not the mass of available software and websites. First decide what you want to do with educational technology; then it is relatively easy to determine what hardware and software you will need.

Here are some questions to guide you in selecting and evaluating software for your elementary and middle school science program:

1. Does the program support your instructional objectives?
2. Does the software provide a better way to teach this content or skill than some other instructional approach?
3. Is the program well designed and easy to use?
4. Is the program design flexible?
5. Is the menu complete?
6. Is the program content accurate and at an appropriate developmental level for your students?
7. Does the program offer a complete learning package, including a teacher's guide that suggests integration into your science curriculum?
8. Are follow-up or enrichment science activities or demonstrations offered?
9. Is the reading level appropriate for your students?
10. Are the graphics correct, attractive, and appropriate?
11. Is there a program purchase warranty?
12. Has the software been reviewed or recommended?

There are a multitude of appropriate and inappropriate sites available on the Internet. Here are some questions to ask when selecting Internet sites for student use (Gray, 1997):

1. Do the instructional objectives and content of the site provide a high degree of correlation to your science curriculum and to national, state, and local standards?
2. Does the site's use of unique Web features, such as communication and information access, promote a significantly broader and deeper understanding of ideas, concepts, and theories than more traditional instructional materials?
3. Does the online resource facilitate person-to-person interactivity and increased understanding through the use of telecommunications?
4. Are learners able to link to additional online resources that provide related information?
5. Is the site rich in content and aesthetically pleasing? Is text easy to read, and do graphics enhance the basic instructional design of the site?
6. Is the online resource well structured and easy for students to work with?
7. Is the site without cultural, gender, or racial bias in content and format?

Another important issue related to Internet use is the determination of the information's credibility. Everyone can learn to detect dubious assertions, strategies that are particularly applicable to assessing scientific claims and information students may encounter on the Internet. Students can detect less credible information by looking for the following signs:

- Premises of arguments are not explicit.
- Evidence does not lead logically to conclusions.
- Fact and opinion are not clearly distinguished.
- Celebrity is quoted as authority.
- Specific references are vague or missing.
- Graphs are misleading.
- Measures taken to guard against distortion in self-reports are not described.
- Percentages are given without stating total sample size (Kreuger & Sutton, 2001).

According to Kreuger and Sutton (2001), scientifically literate students will respond appropriately to the barrage of information that technology provides. Separating sense from nonsense is a critical response skill that must be developed in all students.

In some cases, you will be able to download free software or programs from Internet sites. You can also join online discussion groups to find out what other teachers think of the programs, websites, or materials you are considering for your classroom. Some descriptions list schools where computer-based materials and learning models have been field-tested or reviewed. In addition, some software companies offer previews of their products and encourage teachers to return products that do not meet their needs. Be sure to explore the programs, packages, and approaches that can help you and your students take advantage of information technology.

Acceptable Use Policies for the Internet

Soholt (1999) has cautioned that "the Internet is wide open. There are sites which no child should see" (p. 43). You need to protect your students and yourself. Thus, every school should have acceptable use policies in place for children and the Internet. These policies should relate to such things as e-mail use, responses to requests for information by different sites, actions students should take when they confront an inappropriate image or site, and times when students can use the Internet. Figure 8-3 shows an acceptable use policy for one school.

Internet Standards at Sandia Elementary

The following standards must be adhered to by all students and staff at Sandia Elementary. Violation of **any** of these standards will result in immediate suspension of Internet privileges. Continued and habitual violations will result in permanent suspension of Internet privileges.

1. Students and staff must have on file a signed Acceptable Use Policy in order to use any network services at Sandia Elementary, including e-mail and Internet access.
2. Students may not have individual e-mail accounts. All accounts will be in the teacher's name.
3. Students must have specific permission from their teacher to conduct a search on the Internet.
4. Students may not add "Bookmarks" without specific permission from a teacher.
5. Students may not give the following information out on the Internet without prior permission of their teacher.
   * your last name
   * a picture of yourself or any other students
   * your home address
   * your telephone number
   * any personal information asked for by someone you do not know
6. If you ever find an inappropriate site or image, immediately hit the back key and contact an adult.
7. If you ever feel uncomfortable about a certain site or message, contact an adult immediately.
8. No chat rooms!
9. There will be no Internet or e-mail access when a substitute teacher is in the room.

Figure 8-3 A school policy for acceptable Internet use.
Source: Using Technology Effectively in Your Classroom (p. 44), by Gordon Soholt, 1999, Bellevue, WA: Bureau of Education and Research , P.O. Box 96058, Bellevue, WA 98009.

Take the Plunge—Join the Information Age

Change is taking place so rapidly in the educational technology field that it is easy to feel overwhelmed by all the new products and resources. Fortunately, help is available. A number of professional magazines review computer-based materials and provide articles that guide you through the technology maze. The NSTA journals *Science and Children* and *The Science Teacher* regularly feature articles related to educational technology. *Learning and Leading with Technology* and *Multimedia Schools* are devoted specifically to the what, how, where, and how well of incorporating technology into teaching and learning. In addition, the Eisenhower National Clearinghouse for Mathematics and Science Education (http://www.goENC.com) offers an online catalog that provides extensive information about available curriculum resources, including prices.

Computers and other electronic multimedia technology open many vistas for teaching science in the elementary and middle schools. Consider them another tool in your teaching arsenal. Be curious, but critical. Attend instructional technology workshops, conferences, and exhibitions. Keep up with the latest advances in educational technology by reading widely. Most importantly, take the plunge and find out why students are so enthusiastic about computers and other electronic technologies. Learn to share their enthusiasm.

SUMMARY

• A variety of technology tools and resources are available to enhance inquiry learning and instruction in elementary and middle school classrooms.

• Each phase of inquiry science activities can be enriched with Internet sources. Using the Internet can be beneficial, but you must also use caution and should establish an Internet use policy. Follow the suggested guidelines for evaluating software and Internet sites for your elementary and middle school science programs. There are also many sources for learning what other teachers think of specific resources.

• Other electronic resources available for teaching and learning science include computer-based lab systems, CD-ROMs and DVDs, databases, digital cameras, liquid crystal display (LCD) projection systems, interactive TV, and the Internet.

• This chapter is only introductory, opening up for you the many possibilities of using technology to enhance learning and motivation in your science classroom. Take advantage of the multiple opportunities available to foster your technological literacy.

ONLINE PROFESSIONAL DEVELOPMENT

Pre- and post-tests to assess your knowledge of chapter content, along with exercises to enhance your understanding, can be found on MyEducationLab at www.myeducationlab.com.

Video Guides

Video clips on MyEducationLab selected for this chapter include *Technology and Science Learning—Parts 1* and *2.*

Accessing the Videos

1. Go to the Homework and Exercises section in Chapter 8 of MyEducationLab to select and view videos for this chapter.

2. Videos might be viewed individually, by small groups of colleagues, or by the whole class.

3. As you watch each video, use the **Questions for Reflection** to guide your thoughts and note taking for personal use and group discussion.

4. Discuss your answers to the questions about each video with classmates.

Video: Technology and Science Learning—Parts 1 and 2

Overview

In these videos we see teachers and students at third and fifth grades using a variety of educational technologies, including PowerPoint presentations and the Internet, to enhance students' understanding. We return to the videos on water wheels, recycling, and explaining moon phases with a focus on the educational technology tools that are used in the lessons.

Questions for Reflection

1. What examples of the use of PowerPoint do you see in the lesson on recycling?

2. What does the teacher say is the advantage of using PowerPoint presentations in science lessons?

3. What examples of the use of the Internet in the moon phase lessons do you see? (The NASA photos of the moon used by the class are among the many Gizmos found at http://www.explorelearning.com.)

4. According to one of the teachers, Cindy Shofner, how does the 2-D model of moon phases found on the Internet help students connect the 3-D model to what they actually saw in their moon observations?

9

S*tudent achievement in science and in other school subjects such as social studies, language arts, and technology is enhanced by coordinaton between and among the science program and other programs. . . . As an example, . . . a coordinated social studies and science unit is natural. Oral and written communication skills are developed when students record, summarize, and communicate the results of inquiry. . . . Science requires the use of mathematics in the collection and treatment of data and in the reasoning used to develop concepts, laws, and theories.*

(National Research Council, 1996, p. 214)

Connecting Science with Other Subjects

ALTHOUGH THE CURRICULUM AND THE SCHOOL DAY are often neatly divided into separate subjects, real-world approaches to problems and issues cut across disciplinary lines. Scientists, for example, use mathematics as a tool to explore, represent, and explain patterns in data from investigations. They draw on their language and literacy skills as they read scientific literature, formulate problems, write proposals, plan investigations, record data, and communicate findings and conclusions to others. Furthermore, scientists as well as other citizens enter into discussions and make decisions about societal problems and issues arising from the applications of science and technology. In the real world, then, science, mathematics, reading, writing, social studies, and other disciplines are not isolated from one another, but connected.

Just as scientists use mathematics and language arts as tools, children should have opportunities to apply and enhance their mathematics, reading, and writing skills while investigating the natural world. This heightens the relevance of mathematics and language arts, enhances their usefulness, and promotes greater learning in science. Similarly, in their studies of both science and social studies, children should have the opportunity to examine the cause-and-effect relationships among science, technology, and societal change. Students might, for example, identify the impact of new technologies on communities around the world or study and offer solutions to environmental problems in the local community or other communities.

In this chapter, we help you confront and begin to develop answers to questions about curriculum connections between science and other subjects. As you study the chapter, consider the following questions:

- *How can mathematics and science be connected in practical instructional activities so that knowledge, understanding, and skills in both subjects are enhanced?*

- *How can reading and writing be used in the service of science learning? How can science be used to promote and improve children's abilities to read and write?*

- *How do events and issues studied in social studies connect to science and technology?*

- *How can science, social studies, mathematics, reading, writing, and other subjects be integrated to promote learning of the essential knowledge and skills of each of these subjects?*

Let us start by examining connections between science and mathematics.

NSES You can review the *National Science Education Standards* online. Go to http://www.nap.edu/readingroom/books/nses/html. For an overview of the *Principles and Standards for School Mathematics*, go to http://nctm.org/standards/overview.htm

Connecting Science and Mathematics

Mathematics has been called the language of science. It is the ultimate human method for exploring, representing, and expressing patterns. Thus, mathematics is an indispensable tool used to investigate, discover, model, and communicate the order and patterns found in the real world (Activities That Integrate Mathematics and Science, 1999).

Both the *National Science Education Standards* (National Research Council, 1996) and the *Principles and Standards for School Mathematics* (National Council of Teachers of Mathematics, 2000) emphasize that students must learn to view mathematics as a practical subject that can be applied to real-world situations and to problems arising in other disciplines. Science is a natural place for students to develop this view of mathematics.

Table 9-1 shows the array of mathematical concepts, operations, and skills that can be emphasized in both mathematics and science classes in elementary and middle schools. Figure 9-1 depicts a connections model for science and mathematics, which graphically relates the mathematical ideas of Table 9-1 to scientific inquiry. In the following sections, we will expand on the connections model and show you a variety of ways that mathematical ideas can be used and enhanced in scientific inquiry.

TABLE 9-1   WAYS OF APPLYING MATHEMATICS IN SCIENTIFIC INQUIRY

I. Quantifying the Real World	• Identifying variables • Counting objects and events • Estimating number and size • Measuring all sorts of things using standard and nonstandard units
II. Organizing and Interpreting Data	• Depicting data in pictures and diagrams • Constructing data tables • Constructing different kinds of graphs: bar graphs, histograms, line graphs • Searching for and expressing patterns in graphs, including linear, proportional, geometirc, and other relationships
III. Using Patterns and Relationships	• Using patterns and relationships from tables and graphs in explaining events and making predictions • Using ratios, rates, proportionalities, and formulas in explaining events and making predictions
IV. Operating on Numbers	• Adding, subtracting, multiplying, dividing • Using fractions, decimals, and percentages • Calculating averages • Estimating probabilities • Calculating products, ratios, and rates • Recognizing equalities and inequalities • Constructing proportionalities

Sources: Adapted from *Curriculum and Evaluation Standards for School Mathematics*, National Council of Teachers of Mathematics, 1989, Weston, VA: NCTM; and an analysis of the Third International Mathematics and Science Study (TIMSS) in *Splintered Vision: An Investigation of U.S. Science and Mathematics Education*, by William H. Smith, Curits C. McKnight, and Senta Raizen, 1997, Boston: Kluwer Academic Publishers.

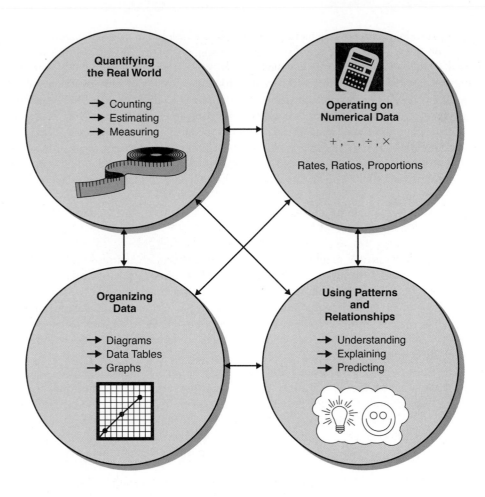

Figure 9-1 A connections model for science and mathematics.
Sources: Principles and Standards for School Mathematics, National Council of Teachers of Mathematics, 2000, Weston, VA: NCTM; *Splintered Vision: An Investigation of U.S. Science and Mathematics Education,* by William H. Smith, Curtis C. McKnight, and Senta Raizen, 1997, Boston: Kluwer Academic Publishers.

Quantifying the Real World

Expressing and thinking about the real world in terms of numbers is the first step in connecting science and mathematics (see Figure 9-1). By examining how infants respond to different stimulus situations, researchers have shown that number concepts are used to organize physical arrays and repetitive events as early as 5 to 7 months of age, if the arrays or events vary from two to four. From as early as 5 months, children can use concepts of addition and subtraction to recognize when objects have been added to or subtracted from a small array (Bransford, Brown, & Cocking, 1999, p. 89).

NSES

Program Standard C

The science program should be coordinated with the mathematics program to enhance student use and understanding of mathematics in the study of science and to improve student understanding of mathematics.

The development of mathematics concepts is often rooted in physical experiences. In school, children quantify the world through counting, estimating, and measuring all kinds of real-world variables that they encounter in the process of investigating. Children may *count* the number of seeds found in different fruits or the number of pennies added as cargo to a clay boat. They may *estimate* weights and volumes in determining whether objects might float or sink. And they may *measure* the weights of pendulum bobs, lengths of stems of growing plants, or time for an antacid powder or tablet to dissolve in water. Furthermore, they may add weights, subtract the weight of a container from the total weight to find the weight of the contents, multiply lengths and widths to find areas, and divide distances by time to find rates. All of these mathematical operations help children begin to quantify objects and events.

As an example of elementary and middle school students quantifying the world, consider the task of measurement.

Measuring. Measuring is emphasized in both science and mathematics standards. When children engage in problem-solving activities in either subject, they need skills for measuring length, volume, weight, time, temperature, and other variables. Measuring is founded on the processes of observing and comparing. "Children naturally make comparisons" (National Science Resources Center, 1996, p. 3). They stand back to back to see who is taller, line up their feet to see whose are longer, and match their bodies to different-sized clothing to see what will fit.

The need to make comparisons leads to the use of units of measurement to compare things that are not side by side. At first, children may use nonstandard units to make comparisons. For example, they stretch their own arms, use their own bodies, or use handy objects like pencils or plastic spoons as nonstandard units to measure length. However, nonstandard units have a major disadvantage. Because spoons and pencils, as well as children's arm spans and bodies, vary in length, it is often difficult to use them to consistently compare objects that cannot be held side by side.

By second grade, children use standard units—centimeters, seconds, grams, and degrees Celsius or Fahrenheit—marked on different kinds of scales to measure in their investigations. Standard units enable consistent descriptions and comparisons of measured objects.

A glossary containing definitions of important terms used in this chapter can be found on MyEducationLab.

Mathematics standards were first developed in 1989 and updated in 2000. Check out the newest version of the measurement standards at http://standards.nctm.org/document/appendix/meas.htm.

Mathematics Standards for Measurement

Throughout programs in grades pre-K through 8, the study of measurement should enable students to

- understand measurable attributes of objects and the units, systems, and processes of measurement, and
- apply appropriate techniques, tools, and formulas to determine measurements.

For example, in grades pre-K through 2, students should

- recognize the attributes of length, volume, weight, area, and time;
- compare and order objects according to these attributes;
- understand how to measure using nonstandard and standard units; and
- select and use an appropriate unit and tool for the attribute being measured.

Reference: *Principles and Standards for School Mathematics*. National Council of Teachers of Mathematics, 2000.

As an example of measuring, we will examine length.

The logic of length measurement is deceptively complex. It encompasses such ideas as the conservation of length, the notion of standard units, unit iteration (counting the number of standard units in a length), and knowledge of how to use standard measuring instruments, such as rulers. According to research by Clements (1999), however, children do not have to master all of these logical complexities to learn to measure the lengths of objects using a ruler, if the teacher provides appropriate scaffolding.

When length measurements are set within the contexts of real-world investigations and a *need to know* is established, even young children can learn to use rulers successfully. Learning to use a ruler, even by rote, provides a framework for children to begin to understand the logical complexities of length measurement.

Real-world measurements often present a challenge to children. For example, measuring the length of plant roots in germination bags (as discussed in Chapter 2) can be difficult because the roots are not straight, but curved and twisted. A simple ruler cannot be used to directly measure the roots. Children must invent ways to measure them with nonstandard measuring devices, perhaps by laying a curving string along the roots, then straightening out the string and measuring it with a ruler.

The process of measuring length in science contexts provides children an opportunity to rehearse, and consequently enlarge, their measurement knowledge. Practice and rehearsal are important concepts in learning theory. *Practice* means to do something over and over again the same way to improve a performance (Ormrod, 2007). What is learned in practice is a specific skill applicable in a specific context. As discussed in Chapter 3, *rehearsal*, in contrast, takes place "when people do something again in similar but not identical ways to reinforce what they have learned while adding something new" (Lowery, 1998, p. 28). When using measurement and other mathematics skills in science, children not only practice what they have already encountered in mathematics classes, but add something new to it. Mathematics schemas are expanded with the new additions from science activities. Children's mathematics skills are then less likely to be bound to specific tasks and are more likely to be transferable and useful in a variety of ways.

A number of innovative elementary science programs emphasize connections between mathematics and science, including AIMS (Activities That Integrate Mathematics and Science), GEMS (Great Explorations in Mathematics and Science), FOSS (Full Option Science System), and Science and Technology for Children (STC). STC has produced a series of very good lessons for first grade classes on comparing and measuring length. Through the 16 lessons of the STC unit *Comparing and Measuring* (National Science Resources Center, 1996), children begin to understand that

- comparing involves observing similarities and differences;
- one way to make comparisons is by matching;
- a common starting line is required to make fair comparisons;
- using beginning and ending points and placing units end to end are important factors when measuring;
- nonstandard units of measure can be used in comparing; and
- standard units of measure produce more consistent results than nonstandard units (p. 2).

Addresses for AIMS, FOSS, GEMS, STC, and other exemplary science programs are provided in Appendix F.

Science, Mathematics, and the Metric System. The metric system, termed the International System of Units (SI), is used exclusively in science. It is also used exclusively in daily life in all English-speaking countries except the United States. Although use of units such as feet and pounds is customary in the United States, the need for SI units has already affected machine tools, packaging, and temperature measurements. Competition with the rest of the world will continue to accelerate the use of SI in business, science, and government.

The metric system is convenient because it is based on the mathematics of place value and uses decimals rather than fractions. Thus, the metric system is often easier to use than U.S. customary units. It is easier for children to add 4.5 cm and 4.2 cm, for example, than to add 1¾ and 1⅗ inches.

American children must continue to learn and be familiar with both metric and customary units, but programs should de-emphasize the memorization and use of conversion factors between the two systems. When a student measures something 6.5 cm long, for example, accept that as a description of its length. Do not ask how many inches it is. Students' concepts of a unit of length will be just as good without knowing the exact equivalent in the U.S. standard unit system.

More on metric and customary units can be found in Appendix B.

Organizing and Interpreting Data

In science activities, once data have been obtained through measurements, they must be organized and interpreted. Organizing data into diagrams, tables, and graphs is another key step in scientific inquiry portrayed in Table 9-1 and Figure 9-1. Data tables display numerical data in column form. Graphs provide visual displays of data. Putting data obtained from scientific investigations into tables and graphs better enables students to

Chapter 8 on educational technology provides a discussion of the use of graphing programs to facilitate the construction of charts and graphs from investigative data.

- relate their data to their investigative procedures;
- make comparisons among data;
- see relationships and patterns; and
- communicate their data to other people.

A data table is one communication medium that links math and science.

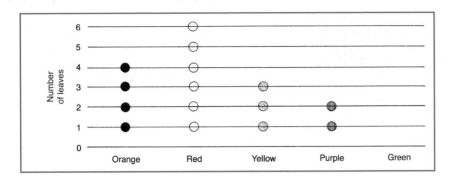

Figure 9-2 Bar graph of collected fall leaves of different colors.

Using Graphs to Organize and Interpret Data. The FOSS K–6 science program developed at the Lawrence Hall of Science provides many opportunities for children to construct and interpret graphs (Full Option Science Sysem, 1991). In the FOSS program, graphs are prepared at three levels of abstraction:

- *Concrete:* organizes real objects to facilitate comparisons and reveal patterns
- *Representational:* uses organization of pictorial representations to reveal relationship
- *Symbolic:* uses numbers and data points to reveal relationships and facilitate interpretation

There are different types of graphs. The graphs most often used in scientific applications in elementary and middle schools are bar graphs, histograms, and line graphs. Each of these was discussed in Chapter 2, but we will supplement that discussion here.

Bar graphs vividly show differences between groups in data collected. Bar graphs can be used, for example, to show the number of children in a class with each different type of eye or hair color. Comparisons of the number of students in each group are easy to see because of the relative lengths of the bars.

A bar graph at the *representational* level is shown in Figure 9-2. This graph depicts the number of leaves of different colors collected by children. The left side, or *vertical axis* of the graph, shows the number of leaves. The bottom line, or *horizontal axis*, shows leaf color. Students stack gummed dots of the appropriate color, creating a series of dots representing the number of leaves collected. Thus, this graph shows that four orange, six red, three yellow, and two purple leaves have been collected.

Histograms display the number of times a number event occurs in a large set. Histograms differ from bar graphs in that the *x* axis on a bar graph simply names a category, while the *x* axis on a histogram is a number line representing a variable. An example of a histogram of the number of unshelled peanuts of different lengths in a group of peanuts is shown in Figure 2-4.

Line graphs are more advanced; students from about grade 4 can learn to construct and interpret them. With line graphs, your students can graphically show numerical data that are continuous. A line graph typically displays visually the changes in a *responding* or *dependent variable* in an investigation corresponding to changes in the values of a *manipulated* or *independent variable*. Figure 9-3 shows an example of a line graph depicting the bounce height versus the drop height of golf balls. In collecting data for the graph,

Figure 9-3 A line graph depicting the bounce height versus the drop height of a golf ball.
Graph made with "Data Explorer" software © 1998 Sunburst Technology Company. Information from "Data Explorer," used with permission of and copyright 1998 by Sunburst Technology Company. All rights reserved.

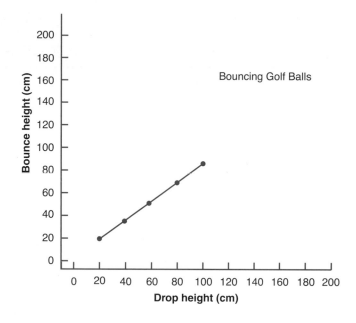

children varied the drop height of a golf ball systematically and recorded the rebound height of the ball for each drop height. Criteria for line graphs are given in Figure 9-4.

It is scientific convention to plot the manipulated or independent variable on the horizontal (x) axis and to plot the responding or dependent variable on the vertical (y) axis. The mnemonic DRY MIX is helpful for remembering this convention:

*The **D**ependent or **R**esponding variable is plotted on the **Y** axis.*

*The **M**anipulated or **I**ndependent variable is plotted on the **X** axis.*

Study the line graph in Figure 9-3 to see how the graphing conventions of Figure 9-4 are applied. For example, if students are studying bouncing golf balls, the vertical axis shows bounce height (the responding variable in centimeters) and the horizontal axis shows drop height (the manipulated variable, also in centimeters). Using the whiteboard, chalk board, or overhead, show your students how to place a point on the graph to represent the data, as well as how to draw smooth, best-fit lines indicating the pattern or relationship of the data.

Figure 9-4 Criteria for constructing line graphs in science.

1. The manipulated variable is graphed on the horizontal axis, or x axis.
2. The responding variable is graphed on the vertical axis, or y axis.
3. The name of each variable is placed along the appropriate axis.
4. The unit of measurement of each variable is included along with its label.
5. The axes are uniformly scaled and numerals are placed at regular intervals along each axis.
6. The graph is given a descriptive title.
7. Data points are plotted on the graph.
8. A smooth line, either straight or curving, is drawn through or near each point on the graph to show the best-fit pattern of the data.

Students should understand that in using mathematics in scientific investigations, they will "encounter all the anomalies of authentic problems—inconsistencies, outliers, and errors—which they might not encounter with contrived textbook data" (National Research Council, 1996, pp. 214, 218). Thus, if certain data points do not fall on a projected trend line, students should consider whether the points might be anomalies or errors and retake that data.

In connecting mathematics and science, it is important that students not only construct tables and graphs but also interpret them.

Using Patterns and Relationships

Science and mathematics can also be connected through finding mathematical patterns and relationships and using them in interpreting physical situations (see Table 9-1 and Figure 9-1). Patterns and relationships found in tables and graphs enable students to

- make predictions from collected data;
- formulate and test possible relationships between variables in the science/mathematics activities performed;
- construct hypotheses about possible patterns of change in their obtained data; and
- draw conclusions and inferences from data (Curcio, 1989).

Let us look at some examples of using charts and graphs to make interpretations in science.

Making Predictions from Graphs Predicting is an excellent way for students to use their data and for you to assess student understanding. Predictions can be made, for example, from the bouncing ball graph in Figure 9-3.

After some time investigating the bouncing ball and constructing graphs (as described in the previous section), ask students to predict what they think the rebound height will be for, say, a 200 cm drop height. To do this, students should first extend the graph line, making sure that it follows the pattern of the graphed data. Next, they should locate the 200 cm point on the x axis and draw a vertical line straight up from it until it intersects the graph line. Students can then read across to the y axis to predict the rebound height for a ball dropped from 200 cm. With appropriate safety precautions, teams should check their predictions by dropping the ball from the new height and measuring the rebound height.

For golf balls, children should find that their measured rebound height for a 200 cm or greater drop height is very close to their predicted rebound height. Interestingly, this is not the case for Ping-Pong balls. Why do you think this is so? The answer has to do with the air resistance experienced by the very light Ping-Pong balls.

Another investigation that can promote data collection and graphical analysis concerns the swing time for pendulums.

Swingers The Full Option Science System (1990) has provided an interesting activity on pendulums, in which collected data are displayed on a concrete line graph. In the activity, students are given long strings and directed to attach a small weight to one end of each string. Students then trim each string to a specific length, such as 13 cm, 15 cm, 17 cm, 18 cm, 20 cm, and so on. The students determine the number of swings in 15 seconds for their particular pendulum lengths. Next, they hang their pendulums from pushpins arranged along a number line to uniformly display the number of swings in 15 seconds for different

Recall from Chapter 2 that a prediction is a forecast of an outcome based on knowledge of patterns or trends. A line graph visually displays the pattern of the relationship between two variables.

Figure 9-5 A concrete line graph depicting the number of swings pendulums of different length take in 15 seconds. Adapted from FOSS® (Full Option Science System®) Variables, Investigation 1: swingers. © The Regents of the University of California and published by Delta Education. Adapted with permission.

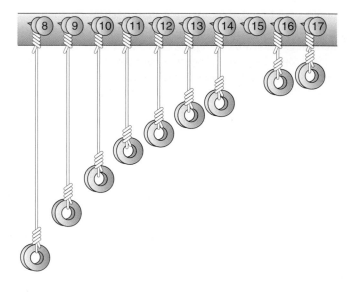

An interesting research study investigating how students with special needs and regular education students form generalizations from pendulum data is described in Chapter 10.

length pendulums. The strings have been cut so that there are whole numbers of swings in 15 seconds, for example 13 swings in 15 seconds.

When all of the data have been collected and the pendulums hung from the number line, the pendulum strings are seen to form a gentle curve (see Figure 9-5). The curve shows a relationship that can be detected and expressed by students: The longest length pendulums have the fewest number of swings in 15 seconds, and the shortest pendulums have the most swings in 15 seconds. That is, the longer the pendulum length, the fewer the number of swings in 15 seconds.

As part of the pendulum swingers activity, the students are given a swing rate for which swing data have not been collected, for example, 15 swings in 15 seconds or 6 swings in 15 seconds. They are asked to use their graph to predict the length of the pendulum that would produce that swing rate. In making predictions, the students simply hold a new string up to the graph and fix the new string length so that it will continue the gentle curve pattern established. Students then test their predictions by counting the number of swings in 15 seconds for their new pendulums to see if the length they chose produces the desired swing rate.

Operating on Numerical Data

Table 9-1 and Figure 9-1 show that operating on numerical data is another way to connect mathematics and science. Numbers obtained in scientific investigations through counting and measurement processes often need to be operated on mathematically. Lengths may need to be *added*, and weights of containers may need to be *subtracted* from total weights to determine the weights of contents. Areas might be calculated through *multiplication*; ratios, such as densities, and rates, such as speeds, must be obtained through *division*; averages must be determined through *addition* and *division* operations; and so on. Understanding mathematical operations on numbers is essential for students in understanding concepts in prealgebra and algebra.

Children encounter mathematical relationships from a very early age, for example, when pulling a wagon uphill. From experience, the child might predict that more force will be needed to pull a wagon up a steeper hill. An upper elementary or middle school student may take data on the required force to pull a cart up planes of different angles of inclination, put the data in a chart of ordered pairs, and graph the data.

At upper middle school grades, the student may search for an equation to model the mathematical relationship. Once an equation is developed, it may be manipulated through algebraic and arithmetic operations to predict the exact amount of force required to move an object of a given weight up inclined planes of different heights. The equation is connected back to the real world through the graphs, tables, measurements, verbal descriptions, and physical manipulations that serve to represent the mathematical relationship at different levels of thought. Historically, one of Galileo's great contributions to modern science was his pioneering use of mathematics to describe physical situations (Sobel, 2000). By using mathematics to summarize (or model) past experiences and to analyze real-world situations, students demonstrate true mathematical understanding.

Mathematics of the Balance. Children experience balancing from very early ages. For example, young children physically balance themselves as they walk on narrow rails, play on seesaws, or learn to ride a bicycle. Children's actions reveal the ways they think about balancing. When they start to fall to one side when walking on balance boards, they shift their weight to the other side by extending an arm or leg. A lighter child might balance a heavier child on a seesaw by sitting further out toward the end of the seesaw board. These actions show that young children are implicitly using mathematical ideas in understanding and adapting to physical reality. The seeds of mathematical thinking are present in the children's mental and physical actions.

In one FOSS (Lowery, 1998) investigation of balancing, students attempt to balance a cardboard cutout figure on the end of a finger. Children quickly discover several ways to balance the figure. They are then challenged to place clothespins at different points on the figure (to shift its center of gravity) and to discover new ways to balance it. Children solve the problem by finding a balance point that enables the weights to be distributed around it.

Qualitative Thinking About the Balance. The NSES and the NCTM standards emphasize the importance of the qualitative dimensions of children's mathematical learning. When children think qualitatively, they compare and make judgments about whether variables are equal, or one is greater or less than another, without regard to exact numbers or measurements. According to the mathematics standards,

> The mathematical ideas that children acquire in grades K–4 form the basis for all further study of mathematics. Although quantitative considerations have frequently dominated discussions in recent years, *qualitative* considerations have greater significance. (NCTM, 1989, p. 16. Emphasis added)

Children's success with quantitative thinking and problem-solving activities in mathematics and science programs at later grade levels depends largely on the qualitative foundations established in the earlier years of school.

Inhelder and Piaget (1958) have carried out a detailed study of children's mathematical thinking about the balance. Around ages 8 or 9, at the concrete operational level, balance is seen to be a function of four variable factors working together:

- weight on one side
- distance of that weight from the middle
- weight on the other side
- distance of the other weight from the middle

The Invicta Math-Balance, sold by various science education equipment companies, is an excellent tool for studying balancing from kindergarten through middle school. Addresses for science education equipment companies are given in Appendix C.

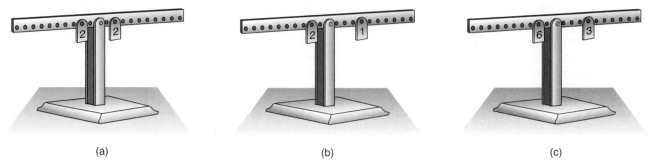

(a)   (b)   (c)

Figure 9-6 (a) Qualitative Rule #1: Equal weights at equal distances will balance. (b) Qualitative Rule #2: Heavier weights close in can balance lighter weights farther out. (c) Quantitative Rule: When the product of the weight and distance on one side of the pivot is equal to the product of weight and distance on the other side, the balance bar will be horizontal.

Through discovery activities and teacher instruction, these four variables can be coordinated into rules, though the rules are qualitative or nonnumerical at this stage. Two main rules are learned initially:

- Equal weights at equal distances will balance [see Figure 9-6(a)].
- Heavier weights close in can balance lighter weights further out [see Figure 9-6(b)].

The first rule is a symmetry rule. Children predict that, for an equal-arm balance, if weights are equal and distances are equal, the crossbar will balance. Younger children may implicitly know the symmetry rule, but they tend to focus on either the weights *or* the positions, not both at the same time. Thus, younger children may take incomplete data and fail to apply the symmetry rule appropriately. Children in third or fourth grade who are at the concrete operational level can consider the weights and distances simultaneously and use the symmetry rule to consistently predict balance.

The second balance rule, placing heavier weights closer to the center, is also a qualitative rule. It involves a nonnumerical combination of weights and distances. In making qualitative comparisons using the rule, children may note, for example, that one weight is considerably heavier than the other. If the two weights are to balance, the first one must be much closer to the central pivot-point than the second one.

The children's qualitative rules govern their trial-and-error learning as they add and take off weights and move them to different positions. This reversible and flexible way of thinking about qualitative relationships makes complex thought about numerical operations truly possible.

Quantitative Thinking About the Balance.   Around fifth or sixth grade, many children can extend their qualitative rules through using exact numbers to represent weights and distances. When one side of a balance beam has more weights, the young mathematical scientist goes beyond qualitative questions about more and less and asks such questions as:

- How much heavier is it? How much farther out is it?
- What is the proportion? Is it twice as much or three times as much?

If the weight on one side is twice as much, for example, then to compensate, either the weight or the distance on the other side has to be twice as much for balance. If this type of thinking is to be useful, it must build on the qualitative thinking at an earlier level.

At some point in the formal operational stage, the student begins to understand the use of formal mathematics to coordinate the four numerical variables. The quantitative rule of the balance can then be understood and applied [see Figure 9-6(c)]. Stated in the form of an equation, the quantitative rule of the balance is:

$$WL \times DL = WR \times DR$$

where W = weight, D = distance, L = left side, and R = right side of the balance. Thus, the product of the weight and distance on one side is equal to the product of weight and distance on the other side. Try the equation for yourself using Figure 9-6(a), (b), and (c). The products of the weights and distances on the left side will equal the products on the right side for each of these three cases.

This equation summarizes experiences at the qualitative level; for example, heavy weights must be placed closer to the pivot for balance. The quantitative rule, however, tells the child exactly how much closer to the pivot the heavier weight would need to be for balance.

The principle governing equal-arm balances also governs the operation of levers. Using a small force far out from a fulcrum, a person can lift a heavy load that is closer to the fulcrum. Using the equation, students can predict how much force is needed to lift a load of a given weight when the distances involved are known. By using mathematics to summarize (or model) past experiences and to analyze real-world situations students develop and demonstrate true mathematical understanding.

Balances and other hands-on materials provide students opportunities to personally bridge from the concrete world to the abstract world of mathematics. In so doing, students must talk about concrete objects and their actions on them, find qualitative ways to represent their thinking, and eventually construct ways of coordinating numerical variables that describe the real world. When they learn to think about mathematics and its applications in this way, students are better prepared to negotiate the complex ideas of advanced mathematics and science in later grades.

There are many more opportunities for you to integrate mathematics into your science program. To augment your own creativity, examine the abundance of excellent lessons in contemporary nationally funded science programs and on the Internet that connect science and mathematics. For exemplary activities, see FOSS (Full Option Science System) and STC (Science and Technology for Children). The URLs for the websites for these and other programs are given in Appendix F.

Next, we will discuss connections between science and language arts.

Connecting Science and Literacy

Teachers of all subjects should be engaged in language instruction. As stated in the *Standards for the English Language Arts* (International Reading Association, 1996),

> Language is the most powerful, most readily available tool we have for representing the world. . . . Language is not only a means of communication, it is a primary instrument of thought. . . . Encouraging and enabling students to use language effectively is certainly one of society's most important tasks. (p. 12)

Literacy instruction in schools generally includes four areas: reading, writing, speaking, and listening. These critical elements of language learning occur in all curricular areas and should not be separated from substantive content in science, mathematics, social studies, and other subjects. An emphasis on literacy across the curriculum is a natural way for students to learn and use language skills to communicate and reason in specific domains, as well as in their everyday lives.

A teacher of science can do many things to help students enhance their language abilities and, at the same time, enrich their science learning. The elements of literacy are valuable for

students in doing science and should be promoted through science instruction as well as in language arts classes. For example, in helping students develop language and thinking processes, teachers of both science and language arts are called on to

- develop, extend, and refine the knowledge base of students;
- assist students to organize knowledge into useful schemas or networks;
- learn vocabulary that is related to topics being studied;
- provide students with opportunities to use reading, listening, and viewing behaviors; and
- supply many opportunities for practice and rehearsal in communicating through writing, speaking, and representing things visually (Ormrod, 2007).

Let us focus first on reading. How can science and reading be connected for students?

Science and Reading

A helpful collection of articles on the why and how to use science texts in instruction can be found in *Science Learning: Processes and Implications* (Santa & Alvermann, 1991). This volume, with contributions from reading and science specialists, is sponsored by the International Reading Association.

Santa and Alvermann (1991) noted, "Science and reading teachers have very similar goals for their students. Foremost is the pursuit of meaning" (p. vi). In science, students construct meaning from the natural world; in reading, they construct meaning from text. Although investigative processes in science and comprehension processes in reading are quite different, processing strategies remain at the heart of both disciplines. Both science and reading teachers want their students to be able to describe events, make inferences, interpret information, draw conclusions, and make and test predictions (Padilla, Muth, & Padilla, 1991; Tompkins, 2006).

Contemporary learning theories in both science and reading follow a constructivist view. In the traditional view of reading, meaning resided in the text; the reader's task was to ferret it out. In the constructivist view, the reader creates meaning based on the text, and her or his existing knowledge about its content, language, and structure (Tompkins, 2006).

A key element in the construction of meaning from text by students is their existing or prior knowledge.

An instructional tool often used to teach reading, a K–W–L chart can help you assess students' prior knowledge before beginning a new topic of study. (K–What Do You Know? W–What Do You Want to Learn? L–What Did You Learn?)

Prior Knowledge and Comprehending Science Text. Science text materials, whether in activity guides, laboratory manuals, or textbooks, are notoriously difficult for students at every level to read. In successfully comprehending a topic presented in science texts, a student's existing knowledge must be extensive, accurate, and consistent with the information presented in the text. Finley (1991) has suggested that teachers must make sure that readers have sufficient prior knowledge of terms, facts, concepts, and relationships to understand an assigned text selection. Thus, it makes sense to follow the dictum suggested in Chapter 4: *investigation first; reading later* (Lowery, 1998).

Students need extensive and repetitive experiences with hands-on, minds-on activities to develop connected, accurate, and useful knowledge. It is this type of knowledge that students must be able to draw on in reading science books.

Access to Prior Knowledge. To be able to comprehend written information, students must have prior existing knowledge, access what they know, and apply it appropriately. Students differ in the degree to which they use potentially available knowledge to learn and understand (Brown, Bransford, Ferrara, & Campione, 1983). Science teachers should scaffold learning to assist students in accessing and using what they know in comprehending text material.

Finley (1991) and others have suggested various ways that science teachers can help students draw on and use their existing knowledge. Teachers can help students assess prior knowledge by having them

- write initial descriptions and explanations of phenomena;
- construct concept maps of what they know;
- draw pictures and labeled diagrams of events, accompanied by written explanations; and
- present their ideas to the class so that alternative descriptions and explanations might be considered.

All of these examples portray the student as an active learner, both in acquiring new knowledge and in accessing it in reading. In addition to helping students acquire and use prior knowledge, teachers can help students approach reading more strategically.

Strategies for Comprehending Science Textbooks. Teachers should assist students in prereading, reading, and postreading strategies to help them make sense of what they read (Yopp & Yopp, 2006).

Prereading Strategies. In beginning a reading assignment in science, students should be clear about what they are expected to learn from the text. The teacher might begin by having students make predictions about the text content before reading (Padak & Davidson, 1991; Tompkins, 2006). When making predictions about text, children might first examine the illustrations and pictures given in the text. They close the text and make their predictions about words that might appear in it.

For example, in a selection on butterflies, children might predict from a butterfly illustration and their prior knowledge that caterpillars would be a word in the text (Yopp & Yopp, 2006). This prereading process helps students think about the relationships between the text information and their own prior knowledge.

In a case study reported by Padak and Davidson (1991), students who learned to predict text content before reading were able to read for a wider variety of purposes than before. Rather than reading simply to answer the teacher's questions or questions in the passage, they read to learn more about science concepts, to verify predictions that they or others had made, and to connect text presentations to their own prior knowledge.

Using Strategies During Reading.   Students should be taught to use comprehension-monitoring strategies during reading. Comprehension-monitoring strategies include such tasks as raising questions about the text, clarifying terms, identifying main ideas and supporting statements, paraphrasing and summarizing text meanings, and making and verifying inferences and predictions about text meaning. Such strategies are not easily learned from direct instruction or from teacher modeling, because the learner tends to be a passive observer in both cases (Brown et al., 1983).

King (1994) has adapted *reciprocal reading* procedures to science teaching and learning. In King's adaptation, two children work cooperatively in reading a science text, with the children alternating in the roles of dialogue leader and student. King has used prompt cards to successfully teach fourth- and fifth-grade children to deliberately ask themselves and one another questions to access prior science knowledge, comprehend what they have read, and make connections in constructing science explanations. A sample prompt card, which students may keep in front of them during the process of reading for understanding, is shown in Figure 9-7.

Postreading Strategies.   Discussion of the text is an important way to help students check on their comprehension. In discussion, go beyond asking factual questions about what was read. Rather, you should focus on helping students:

- Link text ideas with their prior knowledge and experience.
- Make connections between main ideas and supporting details.
- Recognize and think about text statements that conflict with their own ideas.
- Work to resolve conceptual confusion.
- Use concepts presented in text to explain other real-world phenomena (Roth, 1991).

These prereading, reading, and postreading strategies help readers pay attention to how they create meaning based on the text, their own existing content knowledge, and their knowledge about language.

Next, we will examine ways science and writing can be connected.

DIRECTIONS:

Discuss the lesson with each other.

Ask each other questions.
Answer each other's questions by giving explanations.

Comprehension questions
    Describe . . . in your own words.
    What does . . . mean?
    Why is . . . important?

Connection questions
    Explain why . . .
    Explain how . . .
    How are . . . and . . . similar?
    What is the difference between . . . and . . . ?
    How could . . . be used to . . . ?
    What would happen if . . . ?
    How does . . . tie in with . . . that we learned before?

Figure 9-7   (a) A sample prompt card for interactive reading procedures.   (b) Prompt card given to students to facilitate understanding of science texts.

From "Guiding Knowledge Construction in the Classroom: Effects of Teaching Children How to Question and How to Explain," by Allison King, 1994, *American Educational Research Journal*, *31*(2), pp. 338–368. Copyright 1994 by American Educational Research Association. Reprinted with permission.

Writing in Science

The writers of the *Standards for the English Language Arts* (International Reading Association, 1996) assert that

> Reading and writing are intertwined. . . . Just as students need an array of strategies to comprehend . . . text written by others, so too do they need to apply an array of strategies as they write. (p. 34)

To build these strategies, students need frequent opportunities to write on different topics and for different purposes. Science provides students with many opportunities to write.

Writing in science forces students to consider their audience, clarify their questions, organize and present their data more clearly, and form more secure links among data, prior knowledge, and conclusions. Organizing and presenting their findings and conclusions to others helps students make new information their own and connect it to their prior understandings. Furthermore, according to the *National Science Education Standards*,

> Oral and written communication skills are developed in science when students record, summarize and communicate the results of inquiry. . . . Coordination suggests that these skills receive attention in the language arts program as well as the science program. (National Research Council, 1996, 214).

Writing might take place in journals or on prepared investigation sheets. Observation journals, sometimes referred to as *science notebooks*, provide an opportunity for students from primary grades through middle school to enhance both their science learning and writing approaches (Santa & Havens, 1991). Journal writing in science might also routinely include labeled illustrations as well as narrative descriptions and explanations. Journals may contain observations of a demonstration, personal explanations of a discrepant event, data collected through investigations, reactions to a film or oral presentation, and personal notes from reading an assignment. Journals allow students to write informally and personally explore content.

Connecting Science and Social Studies

Making connections between science and social studies helps students create a more complete picture of the world. While science emphasizes how the natural world works, social studies addresses the multiple roles of humans as they adapt to their surroundings and reorganize ways they relate to each other.

Social studies cuts across and combines several disciplines. According to the National Council for the Social Studies (1994),

> Social studies is the integrated study of the social sciences and humanities to promote civic competence. Within the school program, social studies provides coordinated, systematic study drawing upon such disciplines as anthropology, archaeology, economics, geography, history, law, philosophy, political science, psychology, religion, and sociology, as well as appropriate content from the humanities, mathematics, and natural sciences. The primary purpose of social studies is to help young people develop the ability to make informed and reasoned decisions for the public good as citizens of a culturally diverse, democratic society in an interdependent world. (p. 3)

Interactions between science and technology play a vital part in helping students understand their relationship to the world around them.

Go to the Homework and Exercises section in Chapter 9 of MyEducationLab and view the videos for this chapter, entitled *Science and Literacy: Parts 1* and *2*. In these videos, we return to the excerpts on goldfish (grade 1), recycling (grade 3), particles (grade 3), and pin-hole cameras (grade 5). The focus this time around is on children's writing and drawing as they keep records of what they notice and what they wonder about.

Go to the Homework and Exercises section in Chapter 9 of MyEducationLab, access the artifact called *Variables*, and study a student's reaction in his journal to a control of variables problem.

The national social studies standards can be found on the National Council for Social Studies (NCSS) website at http://www.socialstudies.org.

Plan Lessons Around Science/Technology/Society Themes

One of the 10 themes of the NCSS standards is science, technology, and society. This theme is also found in various state-level frameworks for social studies, which draw on the standards. In one state (Texas Education Agency, 1999), for example, social studies standards include a strand for each grade level called Science, Technology, and Society. Throughout the elementary and middle school grades, students are challenged to understand how science and technology have affected human life past and present. Appropriate to their levels of development, students are expected to

- describe how science and technology have changed transportation, communication, medicine, agriculture, industry, and recreation;
- explain how science and technology have changed the ways people meet their basic needs;
- analyze environmental changes brought about by scientific discoveries and technological innovations;
- give examples of the contributions of scientists and inventors that have shaped society;
- explain how resources, belief systems, economic factors, and political decisions have affected the use of technology from place to place, culture to culture, and society to society; and
- make predictions about future social, economic, and environmental consequences that may result from future scientific discoveries and technological innovations.

In state-level frameworks for both science and social studies, student expectations are often closely related. Both types of frameworks call for students at different grade levels to study common topics such as the use of natural resources, the history of science and scientists, the effects of physical processes on the environment, and the societal impact of energy usage. Social studies processes shared with science include representation, problem solving, decision making, data collection, data interpretation, and critical thinking.

Weather: A Science and Social Studies Lesson for Grade 3

Investigating weather provides an excellent way to merge social studies and science expectations. The following lesson on weather combines ideas from a number of sources to illustrate connections between science and social studies.

In the lesson, students work in groups to design and construct wind socks to determine what directon the wind is blowing and rain gauges to measure the amount of rainfall in a period of time. They also use thermometers to measure the outside temperature. In using these weather instruments, students have to determine what readings to take and when to take them. This lesson is included in the Annenberg video, *Bring It All Together: Processing for Meaning During Inquiry*, which is featured in the Chapter 3 Online Professional Development section.

Each day, students take data and record their data in writing on data record sheets or in their science notebooks. Through group and class discussion, students reflect on and synthesize their data to describe the local weather. In connecting to social studies, students work in groups to access Internet weather data and record the weather in different geographic regions, such as Argentina, Cambodia, Australia, Mexico, Canada, Portugal, South Africa, and Russia. Web information available to students includes physical and weather maps of each region and pictures that give identity to each area. A compendium of web resources for weather worldwide can be found on the Franklin Institute website at http://www.2.fi.edu/.

In order to apply weather information in decision making, each student describes how people in each region dress for their local weather conditions. The students write daily journal entries about the weather, the people, and unique features of the region.

As the lesson progresses each day, students develop both science and social studies concepts by exploring how humans collect weather data and how they deal with the physical processes related to weather and climate. Students also use current events to determine how weather affects the way people live. Further, students develop essential computer skills as they become weather watchers.

In concluding the lesson, students answer questions such as: *What weather instruments are used to measure weather conditions? How can weather data best be recorded? How does the weather change? How is weather different in various regions? Why is weather important to us? Why is it helpful to predict the weather?* These questions get to the heart of social studies and science because they lead students to understand the characteristics of weather, the instruments and processes real scientists use to describe and explain weather, the effects weather has on humans, and the many ways humans cope with constantly changing weather phenomena.

A River Ran Wild: A Science and Social Studies Lesson for Grades 3–5

An example of connecting science and social studies at grades 3–5 centers on a study of the book *A River Ran Wild* by Lynne Cherry (1992). The goal of this learning experience is to guide students in understanding that the history of a given environment can reveal how humans have affected an ecosystem in both responsible and irresponsible ways. In this study, students expand their understanding of the environment and its relationship to humans by merging the theme of science, technology, and society with other social studies themes, including people, places, and environment, time, continuity, and change, civic ideals and practices, and culture.

The class is divided into five groups, with each group assigned to answer one of these five guiding questions:

1. In what ways have humans historically affected particular ecosystems?
2. How do cultural beliefs and practices affect the quality of the environment?
3. What physical and human factors cause an environment to change over time?
4. How can humans help change a polluted environment?
5. How can industry exist and progress within an ecologically sound environment?

Each group researches their question and illustrates their answer by making posters or creating a multimedia presentation. The presentations include the portion of *A River Ran Wild* that deals with their question as well as answers from two other sources such as the Internet, resource books, newspaper articles, or interviews.

After students have presented their answers to the first five questions, a sixth question is posed for all students:

6. What do people in my community do to preserve our environment?

A community expert is enlisted to guide the students in answering this question. Before the expert comes to class, students write a letter summarizing what they have learned from the class presentations. This informs the expert about the students' background knowledge and also gives the students an opportunity to demonstrate understanding of all the issues raised in the guiding questions. The expert not only talks to students and answers their questions but also may arrange field trips or other appropriate means for students to

For some creative ideas about using community resources to extend this study, see Lois R. Stanley (1995), "A River Runs Through Science Learning: Tap Community Resources to Create an Integrated Science and Social Studies Unit," *Science and Children, 52*(4), 12–15, 58.

attain information. As a culminating activity, once students have answered the sixth question, they develop a rubric for an ecologically balanced community and rank their community on the basis of the rubric. Where there are problems, students may write a request to state, county, or city officials asking them to address the situations. Where there are environmentally sound practices, students write letters thanking the people who are responsible for creating a safe environment for all living things.

Through their encounter with *A River Ran Wild* and by being engaged in the lesson's procedures, students meet the expectations outlined in the national standards and grow as informed, environmentally aware, and responsible citizens.

The lessons about weather and *A River Ran Wild* illustrate how science and social studies fit together well for effective student understanding of the earth and its systems. Students benefit when teachers merge science and social studies concepts, processes, and approaches to learning on appropriate occasions and in a manner that fosters learning the essential elements of both science and social studies.

The Environment and Native American Culture: A Science/Social Studies Lesson for Upper Grades

You can view the video on *Case Studies in Science Education: Donna* on the Annenberg website. Instructions for accessing Annenberg videos are given in the Online Professional Development section of Chapter 1.

Donna, a fifth-grade teacher featured in the Annenberg video *Case Study in Science Education: Donna*, has integrated the curriculum for her students around the themes of the environment and Native American cultural heritage. In Donna's classroom, 25% of the students are Native American, while another 25% are Hispanic. One of Donna's main goals for her students is that they all "feel they have a very important heritage . . . all people have contributed to the body of knowledge we call science."

As part of a study of native plants and animals, Donna asks students to study and retell Native American myths and folktales. She emphasizes that these myths and folktales are not true stories, but they incorporate various accurate observations about nature. Donna wants her students to understand that the observations expressed in the myths often have scientific understandings at their foundation. The students share the stories with their class members using various means, including narratives, plays, and puppet shows.

The students take field trips to two ancient Native American sites and participate in an ongoing archaeological dig, using their mathematics skills to document the precise location of artifacts they discover. They also write stories that reveal their ideas about why people living in the area centuries ago might have abandoned their settlements.

In a culminating activity, students complete a chart identifying elements that are common to different cultures, such as food, shelter, medicine, and transportation. Then they construct shoe-box middens in which they have buried household items that represent their own "clan." Middens are exchanged between groups, who "excavate" the shoe-box middens to study the past as evidenced by the artifacts.

SUMMARY

• National standards in every discipline support connections between subjects in the school curriculum. There are important connections to be made between science and mathematics, language arts, social studies, and other school subjects.

• Connections between science and mathematics can center on four main themes: quantifying the world, organizing and interpreting data, using patterns and relationships, and operating on numbers.

• Children begin to quantify the world through counting, estimating, and measuring all kinds of real-world variables that they encounter in the process of investigating. Measuring should be emphasized in both science and mathematics. When children encounter measurement in problem-solving activities in science, they go beyond practice to engage in rehearsal. Through rehearsal, they not only develop skills, they add something to them.

• Organizing data into diagrams, tables, and graphs is a key step in scientific inquiry. The types of graphs most often used in elementary and middle schools are bar graphs, histograms, and line graphs. Putting data obtained from scientific investigations into tables and graphs better enables students to relate data to their investigative procedures, make comparisons among data, see relationships and patterns, and communicate their data to other people.

• Science and mathematics can also be connected through using mathematical patterns and relationships in interpreting physical situations. Patterns and relationships found in tables and graphs enable students to make predictions, formulate and test hypotheses, and draw conclusions and inferences from data.

• Operating on numerical data is another way to connect mathematics and science. Understanding mathematical operations on numbers obtained from investigations is an essential prerequisite for understanding the use of functions in prealgebra and algebra, and in high school science courses. In science and mathematics, quantitative treatments of data should be preceded by qualitative, nonnumerical investigations.

• Connecting science to reading and writing is critically important in the elementary and middle school classroom. Science teachers can help students succeed in reading through helping them acquire necessary prior knowledge, guiding them in using comprehensive strategies, and following up after science reading assignments. There are also many opportunities in science for learners to use and improve their writing skills as they communicate their inquiries to others.

• Science, technology, and society themes are common to science and social studies standards. Lessons built around such topics as weather and the environment show how science and social studies can be linked. There are many opportunities for students to connect these two disciplines as they embark on re-creations of this fantastic voyage of discovery.

ONLINE PROFESSIONAL DEVELOPMENT

Pre- and post-tests to assess your knowledge of chapter content, along with exercises to enhance your understanding, can be found on MyEducationLab at www.myeducationlab.com.

Video Guides

Video clips on MyEducationLab selected for this chapter include: *Science and Literacy—Parts 1 and 2*.

Accessing the Videos

1. Go to the Homework and Exercises section in Chapter 9 of MyEducationLab to select and view videos for this chapter.
2. Videos might be viewed individually, by small groups of colleagues, or by the whole class.
3. As you watch each video, use the **Questions for Reflection** to guide your thoughts and note taking for personal use and group discussion.
4. Discuss your answers to the questions about each video with classmates.

Video: Science and Literacy—Parts 1 and 2

Overview

In these videos, we return to the excerpts on goldfish (grade 1), recycling (grade 3), particles (grade 3), and pin-hole cameras (grade 5). The focus this time around is on children's writing and drawing as they keep records of what they notice and what they wonder about.

Questions for Reflection

1. What kinds of records do you see children using in the classroom excerpts? How do the children blend writing and drawing in keeping observational records?
2. What does the teacher do to guide the children's writing about what they notice about goldfish?
3. How is the I Notice/I Wonder chart used in the goldfish and recycling lessons?
4. In the goldfish excerpt, how does the teacher use children's literature to promote student understanding?
5. There is no audio in the first part of the particles lesson, but what do you infer about the teacher's goals in using the vocabulary cards?
6. How does the teacher in the recycling lesson use PowerPoint?

10

T*he increasing diversity of the school age population, coupled with differential science performance among student demographic groups, makes the goal of "science for all" a national challenge.*

(Lee, 2002, p. 23)

Science for All Learners

YOUR ELEMENTARY OR MIDDLE SCHOOL SCIENCE CLASSROOM will include a diverse group of students. In addition to general education students, you will be responsible for teaching students with disabilities, students from different cultural and linguistic backgrounds, and students with special gifts and talents. The *National Science Education Standards* emphasize that science must be for all students: All students—regardless of race, gender, cultural or ethnic background, disabilities, aspirations, or interest and motivation in science—should have the opportunity to attain high levels of scientific literacy (National Research Council, 1996, p. 20). This principle is one of equity and excellence. It challenges science teachers to meet the needs of all students, requiring them to recognize the diversity of students and to prepare science experiences to address these differences.

All children are unique. They will achieve understanding in different ways and at different depths as they explore answers to questions about the natural world (National Research Council, 1996, p. 20). Some children have special learning needs. You may need to adapt science activities for students who have disabilities, or you may need to work much more closely with them to scaffold learning. Students who are English Language Learners (ELLs) may need special instructional strategies, or they may need to work with other students who can help them access material more readily. Gifted and talented students may challenge you to find ways to lead them to ever-deeper understanding.

Whatever adaptations you need to make, you will want to consider the following questions to help you plan for the diverse backgrounds and abilities of your students:

- *Who are the students with special learning needs? What are likely to be the learning challenges and special needs of individual students in your science classroom?*

- *What are the goals of science for students with special learning needs?*

- *What special modifications in materials, equipment, instruction, and assessment strategies should be made in science for students with special learning needs?*

- *How can you meet the learning needs of students in your science classroom who are gifted and talented?*

- *What are the learning challenges and special needs of ELL students in your science classroom? What is sheltered instruction? How can you best help students acquire science knowledge and skills and learn English at the same time?*

NSES You can review the *National Science Education Standards* online. Go to http://www.nap.edu/readingroom/books/nses/html.

The following sections will help you begin to build a bank of resources from which you can draw as you teach science in an inclusive classroom.

Students with Special Learning Needs

Who are the learners with special needs who will likely be included in your classroom? Although we run the risk of losing sight of individual values and differences when we categorize students, it is useful with the enormous numbers of students in public education to group diverse learners into these categories (Mastropieri & Scruggs, 2004):

- Students with disabilities
- Gifted and talented student
- Students with linguistically and culturally diverse backgrounds

Although students in each of these groups may exhibit special learning needs, federal legislation addresses educational modification for only the first category—students with disabilities. Various states have passed laws relating to the identification and education of students in other categories. However, in many cases funding for accommodations is inadequate or not provided.

Grouping students according to their special learning needs can mask an essential truth: All of us are unique. Even within the same culture, community, or family, we are all different. Your students will have varying intellectual abilities and learning styles, diverse language and cultural backgrounds, and physical, social, and emotional differences. All will enter your classroom having experienced life differently. Thus, their understanding of the world will be different. The varied experiences, background knowledge, and abilities of your students should influence how you plan for and teach science.

Common Standards, Common Assessments, Diverse Pathways

Although different learning pathways and modifications in teaching approaches may be necessary for individuals and special groups, the goals of science instruction are the same for all learners. The *National Science Education Standards* (National Research Council, 1996) state that

> The understandings and abilities described in the content standards are for all students; they do not represent different expectations for different groups of students. (pp. 221–222)

The standards assert that all students should be expected to achieve the same science knowledge and inquiry standards, though learning approaches and levels of achievement may vary.

The No Child Left Behind Act of 2001 requires adherence to this principle. Although there will be modifications in materials, instruction, and testing conditions, students with disabilities and students who are learning English must take the same statewide assessments and be included in statistical analyses.

Planning for individual student needs in science requires knowing the general characteristics of students with different disabilities. The Individuals with Disabilities Education Act (IDEA) recognizes about a dozen disabilities. Data from the National Center for Education Statistics (http://www.nces.ed.gov) indicate that in 2003–2004, students with disabilities represented 13.7% of the public school student population. Approximately 6.6 million students with identified disabilities require special education services.

Statistics from the National Center for Education Statistics indicate that in 2003–2004, 42.7% of students with disabilities were categorized as having specific learn-

NSES *"Teachers of science guide and facilitate learning; recognizing and responding to student diversity and encouraging all students to participate fully in science learning."*
(*National Science Education Standards*, Teaching Standard B)

A glossary containing definitions of important terms used in this chapter can be found on MyEducationLab.

ing disabilities. Four categories of disabilities—specific learning disabilities, speech or language impairments, mental retardation, or emotional disturbance—account for 80.7% of all students with disabilities. Statistics from the center indicate that in 2003–2004, 49.9% of students with disabilities spent at least 80% of the school day in regular education classrooms, a figure that was up noticeably from the 31% of 1988–1989.

IDEA, which governs the education of students with disabilities, directs that all students have the right to a full, free public education in the *least restrictive environment*. This means that schools are required to educate students with disabilities with nondisabled students to the maximum extent appropriate for the students with disabilities.

Making Modifications for Students with Special Learning Needs

There are a variety of considerations to remember as you plan learning experiences, make modifications, and implement instruction for students with disabilities.

Use Individualized Education Plans (IEPS). Some students with disabilities will enter your classroom with an IEP (individualized education plan) in place. You should view the IEP as a dynamic, working document intended to improve student learning, rather than a set of legalities to be fulfilled. Recorded on each IEP are learning goals and objectives designed for an individual student. Once a student with special needs has been assigned to your class, you will want to review her IEP goals and objectives to see what science activities or experiences will help to meet these goals. For example, one goal in an IEP might read: *Develop communication skills and interactions with peers.*

Science teachers can help to meet this individual learning goal by including the student in a cooperative learning group. Within this group students may be asked to engage in an inquiry activity that requires meaningful student interaction to discover and communicate findings revealed by the data. The student with a disability could be required to communicate her understanding of the phenomena she observes to her peers, and together they could determine how to report these findings.

Even though the IEP lists general goals to advance the education and socialization of the student with special needs, you should develop specific science objectives that will move the student from what she knows to learning new concepts and inquiry strategies called for in state and district standards and curriculum frameworks. Just as you would strive to do this for nondisabled students, based on their abilities, so you would do this for your students with disabilities. Ascertain their areas of interest and the conceptions they have of science knowledge, and plan instruction for them accordingly.

The following sections provide concrete ideas for working with students who have varied cognitive differences, students with emotional or behavioral disorders, students with orthopedic disabilities, students who are blind or have low vision, and students who are deaf or hard of hearing.

Science for Students with Specific Learning Disabilities

Defined by IDEA, the term *specific learning disability* means a disorder in one or more of the basic psychological processes involved in understanding or in using language, spoken or written. A disorder may manifest itself in imperfect ability to listen, think, speak, read, write, spell, reason, or do mathematical calculations.

Students with learning disabilities (LD) are commonly in the normal range of intelligence. Sometimes, in fact, they are gifted intellectually. However, students with learning

Since the passage of IDEA in 1997, schools have been striving toward the inclusion of students with physical, mental, sensory, and emotional challenges in the classroom. Still, students with disabilities too often experience barriers to science learning. The NSTA Position Statement on Students with Disabilities identifies some of these barriers and makes recommendations about how teachers and administrators can address them (available online at http://www.nsta.org/about/positions.aspx).

NSES *"Teachers of science guide and facilitate learning; recognizing and responding to student diversity and encouraging all students to participate fully in science learning."* (*National Science Education Standards*, Teaching Standard B)

A very useful and well-organized compilation of strategies for teaching science to students with learning disabilities and other disorders is available online. Go to http://www.as.wvu.edu/~scidis/sitemap.html.

disabilities are generally achieving below their current grade level, or are several grade levels below where they should be, in one or more basic academic skill areas such as reading, written language, or math.

What Teaching Approaches in Science Are Most Appropriate for Students with LD? Students with learning disabilities are a heterogeneous group and can have overlapping problems. This makes it difficult to classify their learning discrepancies and prescribe learning activities and approaches for them. However, research and practical experience support some general strategies to enhance science instruction. These include the use of

- activities-based science;
- intensive scaffolding;
- learning strategies;
- visual presentations and multimedia in general; and
- mnemonics and graphic organizers.

Working cooperatively with their general education peers assists students with exceptionalities to learn science effectively.

Select an Inquiry Approach. Tom Scruggs and Margo Mastropieri, a husband-wife team at George Mason University, have conducted a variety of research studies to investigate the most appropriate methods of teaching science to students with special needs. With two colleagues (Scruggs, Mastropieri, Bakken, & Brigham, 1993), they carried out a controlled investigation comparing textbook and activities-based, inquiry approaches to teaching science to students with learning disabilities.

In the study, 26 seventh- and eighth-grade students with LD received instruction on two science topics—(1) rocks and minerals and (2) electricity and magnetism. All students received instruction through an activities approach on one of the topics and a textbook approach on the other. Lessons for the activities-based approach were from FOSS (Full Option Science System) modules. For example, in exploring electricity and magnetism, students constructed and investigated circuits, switches, an electromagnet, and a telegraph.

Interestingly, these modules on electricity and magnetism were designed for much lower grade levels (grades 3 and 4). Many science activities can be adapted to the grade level you are teaching.

In the activities approach, teachers first presented problems to be investigated by students (the *engage,* phase of the 5-E model). Students then performed activities in small groups of three to five students (*explore*). The lesson was concluded with a whole class session, in which the activities were summarized and discussed (*explain*). FOSS materials were available for students to use in describing and recording their observations.

Lessons for the textbook approach paralleled the activities approach in content. In the textbook approach, teachers presented information, and students read text materials and examined pictures (such as pictures of circuits, switches, electromagnets, or telegraphs). The children engaged in independent and guided practice activities using worksheets.

Both approaches were well structured and involved daily review, active engagement by students, formative evaluation of student products, and questioning. Teachers in the activity approach raised questions and guided students to raise questions about what happened and why, but generally refrained from directly answering them. Instead, they encouraged and challenged students to answer questions for themselves. Questions in the textbook approach were most often directed toward promoting student attention and prompting direct recall of information provided.

Tests were given individually to students in both conditions for the lessons covering the two science topics. The tests emphasized recall of what students did in the science lesson, recall of facts and vocabulary, and application of concepts, principles, and procedures. Students were also asked four questions related to their enjoyment of the two approaches.

Results strongly favored the activities-based approach to science. Students in the activities approach scored significantly higher on the tests at the end of instruction. Additionally, almost all of the students enjoyed the activities approach more. Scruggs and colleagues (1993) concluded:

> Results of the present investigation suggest that activity-based, inquiry-oriented approaches, when appropriately structured, may facilitate the acquisition of content knowledge of students with LD. . . . In the present context, when students were taught by experiential, more indirect methods, they learned more, remembered more, and enjoyed learning more than when they were taught by more direct instructional methods. (pp. 10–11)

Fradd and Lee (1999) have suggested that, rather than debate about whether a textbook or inquiry approach is best, it may be more fruitful to consider how to use the two approaches in a complementary way to meet students' needs.

Use Questioning to Guide Active Thinking.   An advantage of inquiry science for diverse learners, according to Mastropieri (Brownell & Thomas, 1998) is that it facilitates the efforts of classroom teachers to make appropriate modifications to accommodate different learning needs.

One modification teachers often make is to provide more scaffolding assistance to certain learners. Consider this example in which a teacher uses questioning to provide support for a group of seventh grade students with learning disabilities and mild mental retardation to help them draw conclusions from their observations. The students have participated in an activity in which white flowers were placed in water containing food dye and were observed over a period of time:

> *Teacher:* . . . *What do you think happened? I have a flower in blue water and a flower in green*
>   *water, a white flower, right? Ken, what is the color of this flower?*
> *Ken: Blue.*
> *Sam: White.*
> *Teacher: White and blue. Julie, what color is this flower? (designating the second flower)*
> *Julie: Green.*
> *Teacher: White and green. How did I get the colors there? How did I get the colors there, Shawn?*
> *Shawn: That's from a stain in there like . . .*
> *Teacher: A stain? What do you think? Ken, how did this blue get here?*
> *Ken: . . . Oh, you watered it with food coloring.*
> *Teacher: But I didn't put any up here, did I?*
> *Ken: You put it in the dirt.*
> *Teacher: But there's no dirt.*
> *Ken: Oh.*
> *Teacher: OK, Jimmy, what do you think?*
> *Jimmy: It went all the way up to here.*
> *Teacher: Went all the way through water? The what, Mary?*
> *Mary: A stem.*
> *Teacher: The stem. It went all the way through the stem, you're right. (Scruggs, & Magnuson,*
>   *1999, p. 243)*

This example shows us how difficult it can be for some students to generalize from real-world experiences and form new science concepts. The students in the example did not initially generalize from their observations that water was transferred through the plants along stems. The children answered the teacher's questions only through a highly structured questioning approach.

Use Scaffolding to Enhance Understanding.   How well, compared to their general education peers, can special education students form generalizations from their science experiences? How much coaching will general education students and special education students need to make generalizations? These were questions addressed in an informative study by Mastropieri, Scruggs, and Butcher (1993).

A total of 54 junior high students participated in the study, including 20 general education students, 18 students with LD, and 16 students with mental retardation (MR). Students were seen individually by a teacher-examiner. Each student was shown a pendulum and taught how to count the number of complete back-and-forth swings the pendulum made in 10 seconds. Then, the pendulum was set in motion and the student counted the number of swings while the teacher-examiner kept the time.

The first pendulum made 10 swings in 10 seconds. The examiner recorded the number of swings on a sticker below the pendulum. The student and examiner then took data on three more pendulums. The number of swings each pendulum made in 10 seconds was recorded on a sticker below the appropriate pendulum. When the four pendulums were displayed together, the labeled number of swings read, from left to right, 10, 6, 12, and 8. The corresponding lengths of the pendulums, from left to right, were second longest, fourth longest (shortest), longest, and third longest.

Inductive reasoning is the process of generalizing, or drawing general rules based on a number of specific observations. In the 5-E approach to science teaching, students are often required to generalize during the explain phase from data taken during the explore phase of instruction. The task of students in the pendulum study was to generalize from observations of four instances that the longer a pendulum, the fewer number of complete back-and-forth swings it makes in 10 seconds.

Participants in the study were provided a graded series of five prompts as needed to assist them to make the correct generalization about pendulum length and rate of swing. Here are the prompts:

1. The examiner asked, "Thinking about these pendulums, can you think of a general rule about pendulums?" If the student was not successful, the examiner went to the next prompt.
2. Students were asked to compare the number of swings in 10 seconds for the shortest and longest pendulums and then make a generalization.
3. Students were asked to sequence all of the pendulums from the shortest to the longest, compare the number of swings in 10 seconds for the pendulums, and then form a generalization.
4. The teacher pointed out that when the pendulums were sequenced, the strings got longer and the rates got smaller; based on this direct information, students were then asked to form a generalization.
5. Finally, if needed, the examiner gave the generalization, saying, "Isn't it that, as the string gets longer, the number of swings they make get smaller?" The examiner then demonstrated the rule until the students expressed understanding.

The number of prompts needed for a student to be successful on the task was taken as a measure of inductive reasoning. As shown in Table 10-1, the results indicated that 75% of the nondisabled students were successful after the first prompt and 100% were successful by the fourth prompt. For students with LD, 50% were successful with the first prompt, while 72% were successful after the fourth prompt. For students with mild mental retardation, no students were successful with one prompt, while only 19% were successful after four prompts.

**TABLE 10-1   CUMULATIVE PERCENTAGE OF STUDENTS
MAKING CORRECT INDUCTION OF THE PENDULUM PROBLEM
IN RESPONSE TO NUMBER OF PROMPTS**

Number of Prompts	Nondisabled	Learning Disabled	Mild Mental Retardation
1	75%	50%	0%
2	95%	61%	6%
3	95%	67%	12%
4	100%	72%	19%
5	100%	100%	100%

Source: From "How Effective Is Inquiry Learning for Students with Mild Disabilities?" by M. A. Mastropieri, T. E. Scruggs, and K. Butcher, 1993, *The Journal of Special Education, 31*(2), pp. 199–211. Copyright 1993 by PRO-ED, Inc. Reprinted with permission.

Additionally, students were asked to apply the rule to a new pendulum problem. The students were shown a new pendulum intermediate in length between the 8-swing pendulum and the 10-swing pendulum and asked how many swings it would make in 10 seconds. On this application problem, 90% of the nondisabled students, 50% of students with LD, and none of the students with MR provided the correct answer.

According to Mastropieri and colleagues (1993), general education junior high school students may readily make generalizations from data, with only a moderate amount of scaffolding assistance. Students with LD may also succeed on an induction task, but may need more assistance. "On the other hand," the investigators concluded, "the very low performance of students with MR on this task suggests (but does not prove) that inquiry-based teaching methods and tasks that are appropriate for normally achieving students may not be developmentally appropriate for similarly aged students with MR" (Mastropieri et al., 1993, p. 208). But this certainly doesn't imply that students with MR are better off with a text-based approach!

Teach Learning Strategies. Successful students develop many skills and strategies that they use when integrating, remembering, and using information. However, students with special needs may require explicit instruction in the use of these strategies.

Dr. Edwin Ellis (2002), a professor at the University of Alabama, advocates "watering up" rather than "watering down" instruction. He has developed a teaching/learning model referred to as Makes Sense Strategies (MSS). The MSS model is an approach to teaching based on three fundamental instructional principles:

1. Students learn better when they are actively engaged in processing new information in meaningful ways.
2. Increasing the learn-ability of information or skills is preferable to dumbing it down.
3. Students should not waste time learning trivia.

Approaches to instruction based on these principles can result in more effective learning by students with LD.

One important strategy in learning is *elaboration*. Elaboration of an idea occurs when one transforms an idea without losing the essence of its meaning. Ellis (2002) notes that students with LD often lack the language-based cognitive skills necessary to engage in effective elaboration but can be taught to use elaboration strategies. In teaching students

An informative article by Professor Ellis on teaching/learning strategies is available on the Internet. Access the article at http:// www.ldonline. org/article/5742.

with or without LD to elaborate, teach them how to create a visual image of an idea, how to paraphrase and summarize information about an idea, how to raise a series of questions about the idea, and how to use the idea in drawing inferences and forming predictions.

Another important strategy in learning is reflection. Acording to Ellis (2002), reflection is a powerful tool for developing deep knowledge structures, but promoting it can be considerably more challenging than creating situations that require students to memorize answers for tests. Important reflective processes for learning and performing include activating background knowledge, forecasting, anticipating and predicting, establishing goals, relating ideas, and recognizing manifestations of ideas as they appear in other forms and how ideas might be applied in various contexts.

Students with LD may have particular difficulties in collecting, organizing, and using data skills that are critical in science inquiry. Thus, they may benefit from explicit instruction on how to record data and how to construct and interpret charts and graphs.

Cawley and Foley (2002) have emphasized the importance of teaching students with exceptionalities the inherent relationships involved in data tables. Help your students learn to recognize relationships by involving them in connecting data to measurement procedures, describing data, filling in blank spaces in data tables, and using data to make predictions of new measurements.

In the pendulum data interpretation study described previously, for example, students with LD benefited from prompts related to examining the data, arranging it in order to form a concrete graph, and interpreting the graph to form a generalization about pendulum length and time for 10 swings. Nondisabled students in general did not need these prompts, presumably because they had learned to analyze data on their own. Students with LD may need to be provided explicit instruction in constructing and working with tables, charts, and graphs.

To teach students with disabilities to use charting and graphing strategies (Mastropieri & Scruggs, 2004), prefamiliarize them with graph paper and various types of charts and graphs, such as bar graphs, histograms, and line graphs. Use concrete examples in your instruction. For example, create a class bar graph based upon students' favorite foods, colors, or television shows. Talk with the class about what might be learned from the graph. Is each person's favorite displayed? Is there a "class favorite"? Use pictures of the objects being graphed to help reinforce what the graph represents.

Consider grouping students with and without disabilities together and allow them to record and graph data cooperatively. Peers may be able to assist with some of the more difficult components of the task. As students work together, take time to teach specific cooperative skills, such as turn taking and listening. In teaching cooperative skills, use explicit instruction procedures, such as modeling, pointing out examples and nonexamples, role playing, and providing feedback. In this way, students with and without exceptionalities can learn to actively and successfully be part of cooperative learning groups.

Procedural facilitators, such as "think sheets" and semantic maps, can assist students with special needs in the use of learning strategies. Procedural facilitators assist performance by reminding students of options, strategies, and questions to ask themselves as they attempt to learn and solve problems. Students with and without disabilities may also benefit from metacognitive training to better monitor and regulate their own learning efforts (Mastropieri & Scruggs, 2004).

Teach Mnemonics. Students with LD often have difficulty with short-term memory. One of the strategies identified for assisting students with LD is mnemonics. In their research, Mastropieri and Scruggs (1993) found the use of mnemonics very effective with students

Figure 10-1 Pegword mnemonic strategy for classes of levers.
Source: From *A Practical Guide for Teaching Science with Special Needs in Inclusive Settings* (p. 154), by M. A. Mastropieri and T. E. Scruggs, 1993, Austin, TX: PRO-ED. Copyright © 1993 by Purdue Research Foundation. Reprinted with permission of author.

who have LD. Figure 10-1 is an example of a mnemonic strategy. In this example, a pegword strategy (rhyming words) helps students remember the three classes of levers. The figure of an oar is an example of a first-class lever because it has the fulcrum at the middle and the force and load or resistance at opposite ends. To remember that an oar is an example of a first-class lever, students were given a picture of an oar with a package of buns (pegword for one) at the fulcrum. To remember that a wheelbarrow is an example of a second-class lever (with the fulcrum at one end and the force at the other), a picture of a wheelbarrow on a shoe (pegword for two) was depicted. Finally, a rake was used as an example of a third-class lever (with the fulcrum at one end and the force at the middle), to provide a picture of a rake leaning against a tree (pegword for three).

Use Graphic Organizers. A variety of graphic organizers are available to aid students with LD in visualizing how to order or sequence conceptual ideas. Figure 10-2 is one example. In using this graphic organizer, students fill in the blank spaces about the phases of the water cycle as the information is presented or as they engage in relevant activities.

Activities-based approaches are quite appropriate for students with LD, but may not be the most beneficial method for teaching science to students with mental retardation. Let us examine the characteristics of students with MR and approaches to science that may be more beneficial for them.

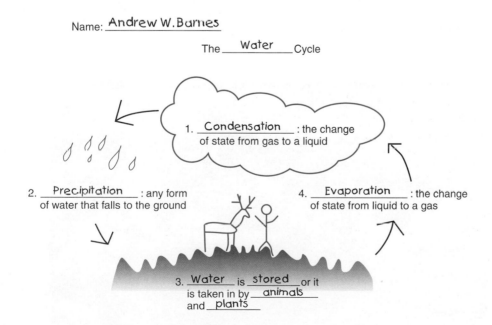

Figure 10-2 Graphic organizer modified for a student with a disability.
Source: From *The Inclusive Classroom: Strategies for Effective Instruction* (p. 514), by M. A. Mastropieri and T. E. Scruggs, 2000. Upper Saddle River, NJ: Merril/Prentice Hall. Copyright © 2000 by Merrill, an imprint of Prentice-Hall, Inc. Reprinted by permission of Pearson Education, Inc. Upper Saddle River, NJ.

Science for Students with Mental Retardation

Students with mental retardation show greater cognitive discrepancies than students with learning disabilities. To improve functioning of persons with MR, science teachers might provide learning experiences that promote self-care, home living, community use, communication, self-direction (problem-solving and decision-making skills), and functional academics as appropriate. Still, unless you emphasize and teach to the science standards that all students are expected to master, they will not be prepared to pass the state science test.

Research indicates that students with mild MR learn concepts better when they are guided to construct them through questioning than when the information was presented directly to them. Additionally, a study of the thinking of fourth-grade students with mild disabilities during an ecology unit indicated that they can actively engage in such processes as observing, describing, comparing, recording, and predicting—with appropriate assistance (Scruggs & Mastropieri, 1994).

Science for Students with Emotional/Behavioral Disorders

According to IDEA, students with emotional/behavioral disorders (EBD) exhibit one or more of these characteristics:

- an inability to learn not due to intellectual, sensory, or health factors;
- an inability to exhibit appropriate behavior under ordinary circumstances;
- an inability to maintain relationships with peers or teachers;
- an inappropriate effect such as depression or anxiety; and/or
- an inappropriate manifestation of physical symptoms or fears in response to school or personal difficulties (Turnbull, Turnbull, Shank, & Smith, 2004, p. 80).

An excellent compilation of strategies for teaching science to students with behavioral disorders is available online. Go to http://www.as.wvu.edu/~scidis/sitemap.html.

Because students with EBD may be included in your classroom, a few words of wisdom may be helpful. Consider that labels often get in the way of seeing these students as children. Even as they are aggressive, antisocial, or disruptive, you could also identify them as smart, good soccer players, lively, helpful, creative, tenacious, and daring. Picture the student(s) in your class exhibiting these positive characteristics and choose carefully the words you use to describe them. Finally, as you review the strategies in this section that will

Working cooperatively with their general education peers assists students with exceptionalities to learn science effectively.

help you work with students who have EBD, note that your utmost concern is to provide a safe and supportive environment for all of your students.

Behavior Modification. A behavior management strategy called *behavioral modification*, which was described in Chapter 5, is one approach that systematically applies behaviorist principles to classroom practices and therapeutic settings. Hundreds of research studies reveal that behavior modification improves not only classroom behaviors but academic performance as well (Ormrod, 2007). Behavior modification is often effective when other techniques are not, because (1) students know exactly what is expected of them; (2) through the gradual process of shaping, students attempt to learn new behaviors only when they are truly ready to acquire them; and (3) students find that learning new behaviors usually leads to success.

These four steps are routinely used in behavioral modification:

1. Identify problem behavior to be modified.
2. Log behavior with regard to how often and under what conditions it occurs.
3. Reinforce desired behavior(s) by initiating a system that reinforces or rewards appropriate, positive behavior.
4. Determine the type of positive reward or reinforcer to use: manipulatives (computer games, interactive videos, games); visuals (videos, CD-ROMs); physical (extra gym or recess privileges, dance); social (praise, attention, status); tactile (art time); edibles (food and drink); auditory (music as choices of audiotapes or CDs); and others selected by students. Positive (or negative) reinforcers can vary.

Science for Students with Visual Impairments

You may have students with visual impairments in your classroom from time to time. The severity of the disability determines further classification. Students with low vision might need special aids or instruction to read ordinary print. Those who are functionally blind typically use Braille for efficient reading and writing. Those who who are totally blind do not receive meaningful input through the visual sense. These individuals use tactile and auditory means to learn about their environment.

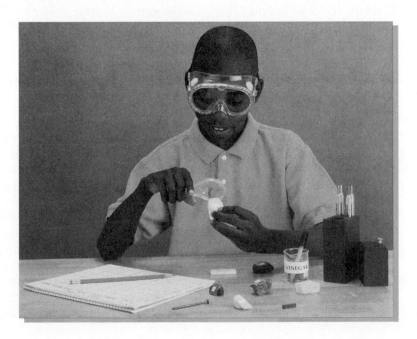

Inquiry science programs help schools to meet the needs, interests, and expectations of students.

Adapting Learning Materials. One of your main tasks if you have a student with visual impairments is to figure out how to adapt classroom materials to make them accessible. Textbooks, blackboards, whiteboards, handouts, and science instruments are not generally accessible for students with visual impairments. Thus, you may need to create alternative formats for printed materials (handouts and textbooks) and computer-based materials, and you may even have to adapt science instruments or tools. Currently, using alternative formats remains an imperfect process, but audiotapes, enlarged print, Braille, and some computer text are somewhat viable.

You may want to find out how to access printed science materials in Braille or prepare grades in Braille that you can affix to lab reports, papers, or quizzes. Students' needs will be identified on their IEP, and school or district specialists in special education should be able to assist you. In addition, there is now software that can produce synthetic speech from text and other software that can convert speech into text. Technological advances such as these offer students who are blind greater levels of independence.

Activities like those developed by the Center for Multisensory Learning, Lawrence Hall of Science, Berkeley, California, are especially appropriate. The materials published by the Lawrence Hall of Science for students with visual or physical disabilities are called SAVI/SELPH. SAVI represents Science Activities for the Visually Impaired, and SELPH represents Science Enrichment for Learners with Physical Handicaps. These programs have been combined and reworked into a single program, mostly for upper elementary school and beyond, but nine modules are adapted for primary grade students.

SAVI/SELPH consists of sets of activity folios, with a section overview, background, purpose, materials, anticipating (what to do before starting), doing the activity, and follow-up. For an example of a running summary of how the program developers provided metric measurement activities for visually impaired students, see Figure 10-3.

In addition to SAVI/SELPH, other curriculum developers have created science materials for students who are blind or have low vision, such as Adapting Science Materials for the Blind (ASMB).

Science for Students with Hearing Impairments

Students who have impaired hearing range in their hearing ability from hard of hearing (use of amplification) to total deafness. Because there are substantial differences between aided and unaided hearing (Turnbull et al., 2004), there is no consensus about how to refer to people with hearing impairments. A people-first approach—persons who are deaf—will be used in this section.

Language and Concept Development. One of the major problems of persons who are deaf is language development. Just as incidental learning accounts for the lack of certain kinds of prior knowledge for persons who are blind, persons who are deaf generally struggle with language development. Thus, psychosocial development—an interaction with the world through language—is a key need for students who are deaf or hard of hearing. Sign language, lip reading, and the reading of body and facial movements help these students with communication. However, without intervention, there are increasing gaps in vocabulary, concept formation, and the ability to understand and produce complex sentences for people who are deaf. Without intervention, both language and intellectual development may be affected.

Hands-on activities can help show students differences in the meanings of words. Begin with familiar objects from the students' everyday environment. Stress handling the objects during language/concept development. Introduce other words related to the properties of objects, such as color, size, and texture. Engage older students in activities to observe chemical changes. This process follows the constructivist learning cycle in which

Science Education in the Balance

During the past spring and fall, SAVI answered the cry for metric measurement activities for visually impaired students with the SAVI **Measurement Module.** The six hands-on activities contained in this module introduce youngsters to standard units of metric measurement.

To develop the concept of *mass,* we needed a measuring tool that would be suitable for use by the visually impaired. We finally decided to use a balance instead of a spring scale or other device and this decision resulted in some unexpected dividends for the project.

We looked at a lot of balances before we made the decision and even built a few of our own. Finally, we chose a simple, vacuum-formed model that is commercially available at a reasonable price. Then, we went to work on it!

First, we cut the bottoms of the two balance pans so that a paper or plastic cup could be dropped securely into the hole and then removed easily. Then, we added a tactile balance indicator. These slight modifications made it possible for blind students to determine weight to an accuracy of one gram!

The removable cup was the breakthrough we need to make accurate weighing easy for visually impaired students. Both the weights (20 g, 10 g, 5 g, 1 g plastic pieces) and the objects or substances to be weighed automatically centered in the cups, thus eliminating discrepancies due to the position of objects in the cups. An object, substance, or liquid can be removed from the balance—cup and *all;* a new cup can then be inserted and a new material weighed. There's no more trouble "getting all the powder out," or "transferring the beans"; the objects stay in the cups.

The students use the balances to verify that 50 ml of water (measured with a modified SAVI syringe) weigh 50 g, thereby establishing the relationship between volume and mass.

Since its introduction, the SAVI balance has crept into other modules. The forthcoming **Kitchen Interactions Module** will feature an activity that focuses on the concept of *density.* Density is defined operationally using the SAVI balance: equal volumes of two different liquids are compared on the balance and the heavier one is identified as the denser liquid.

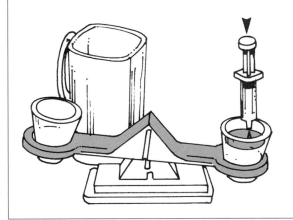

Figure 10-3 Science activity for students with visual impairments.
Source: Reprinted by permission of The Center for Mutisensory Learning, Lawrence Hall of Science, University of California, Berkeley, CA 94720.

the learner manipulates materials and then the teacher introduces or "invents" words for the scientific concepts.

In addition, use pictures, drawings, models, text, and closed-captioned TV programming or videotapes for your students who are deaf.

Science for Gifted and Talented Students

Ten-year-old Alan developed an unlikely interest in Einstein's theory of relativity. Alan's teacher invited a college professor to the classroom to talk about the theory with the boy. The child said to the professor, "I understand that Einstein described the universe in terms of four variables, but I can only think of three of them." As they discussed the problem, the professor told Alan that at age 16, Einstein set this puzzle for himself: *What would happen if I traveled along at the speed of light and held up a mirror to my face? What would I see?* The professor explained that Einstein needed the three variables of space and an additional variable of time to eventually answer this question at age 26. Somehow, this information helped Alan to bring together a variety of things he had read and thought about. He then took up the explanation, laying out Einstein's problem and solution in such an insightful way that the astounded professor began to understand them more deeply himself.

Students such as Alan provide a different kind of challenge for teachers. These students have above average intelligence and possess unusual skills, interests, talents, and attitudes about learning. Words such as *creativity*, *vitality*, *potential*, *motivation*, and *joy* tend to describe their approach to learning (Armstrong, 1998). Such students are identified as having special gifts or talents.

As a teacher, you will quickly learn that there is no typicality associated with students who are gifted, but most have general intellect, specific academic ability, creative and productive thinking, leadership ability, or abilities in visual and performing arts that stand out from their classmates. Students who are gifted or talented love to participate in many activities and usually enjoy being challenged with meaningful enrichment activities. The following suggestions may prove useful.

Make Real Inclusion a Goal

Make gifted and talented students in your classroom feel welcome and accepted. Previously, these students were accelerated to higher or special pullout classes. Currently, greater emphasis is placed on inclusion, incorporating changes in science content and activities to introduce higher levels of abstract and independent thinking and problem-solving skills. Your challenge is to help your gifted and talented students modify, adapt, and learn how to discover new skills and concepts for themselves.

Most highly motivated, bright students need little encouragement. For those who do, try these suggestions:

- Provide recognition for their efforts, but be wary of gifted students with know-it-all tendencies. Encourage cooperative efforts.
- Challenge students to come up with questions they think are difficult and then work in small groups to find answers to the questions.
- Encourage student-initiated projects and alternative activities sometimes in lieu of standard kinds of class activities.
- Introduce elementary and middle grade students to research methods.
- Encourage students to use a variety of media to express themselves in creative ways such as drawing, creative writing, drama, and role playing.
- Help students organize and publish a classroom or school science magazine.

A caution is in order: Students who are gifted must also acquire basic knowledge, understandings, and procedures, even as they are given more freedom to move in their own directions.

Stimulate Gifted Students by the Way You Teach

Your teaching methods can encourage students who are gifted and talented. In our society, students' thinking is often trained to focus on the right answer, which sometimes discourages them from taking risks in academic situations. Students may be confused or feel threatened with failure when they are faced with tasks in which there are either no clear answers or a variety of correct answers. Be sure to use some of these techniques to encourage them:

1. Use a series of questions rather than giving information.
2. Use hypothetical questions beginning with "What if . . . ?"
3. Ask students to develop open-ended situations where no one answer is correct.

4. In science tasks involving mathematics, where specific answers are usually required, encourage students to estimate their answers.

5. Instead of information, emphasize concepts, principles, relationships, and generalizations.

6. Provide opportunities and assignments that rely on independent reading and research as appropriate. Ask students to report on their research and experimentation; this helps them acquire a sense of sharing knowledge.

7. Provide students multiple opportunities to learn how to use technology to research information and gather data from a variety of global resources.

8. Challenge students to engage in, and perhaps design or originate, more open-ended, hands-on inquiry activities.
   - Start by working with the entire class or a group. Later, when routines are established, invite individuals to explore on their own.
   - Keep the experimentation within the limits of time, talents, and available apparatus. Explore these limitations before suggesting problems.
   - Be alert to the open-endedness of this type of exploration. Expect questions to arise such as, "Suppose we vary the experiment in this way. What will happen?"
   - Do not assume that the gifted student will have a sustained interest in the problem. You must continually check on progress.

Connecting science and mathematics is important for all students, particularly gifted students. Challenge them to go beyond describing what happens and why and to explore *how much* or what *quantitative relationships* exist between variables. Ask students to quantify their findings, and encourage them to use graphing when communicating their findings.

Learn with and from Your Gifted and Talented Students. Most elementary school teachers have not majored in science and therefore find that some of their students know more about certain areas of science than they do. Feeling somewhat incompetent with science should not stop you from encouraging gifted and talented students to do more advanced work than the rest of the class. Students enjoy seeing their teachers get excited about the results of their work. Facilitate the academic environment of students who are gifted by posing challenging questions and offering constructive feedback. Also, identify community people who are available to work with gifted and talented students in a mentor program. Be sure to provide some guidance to those who are knowledgeable in their fields but do not know how to motivate and teach students.

Remember that for all their knowledge and abilities, gifted students are still elementary or middle school students whose social, emotional, and physical development mirrors the development of their peers. They need your mature adult guidance, professional training, and practical experience. They will seek caring and emotionally stable adults. That's you!

Science for Students from Linguistically and Culturally Diverse Backgrounds

Our nation's motto is *e pluribus unum*, "out of many, one." Nowhere in our society is the rich mosaic of people that embodies the United States better represented than in our schools. Meeting the needs of children from diverse backgrounds in our classrooms has become an important issue in education.

Many students from diverse ethnic backgrounds are in the process of acquiring the U.S. mainstream language, culture, and discourse patterns in schools. For many of these students, a language other than English is spoken at home.

TABLE 10-2 PERCENTAGE OF PUBLIC ELEMENTARY AND SECONDARY STUDENTS BY RACE/ETHNICITY FOR THE 2005–2006 SCHOOL YEAR	
Race/Ethnicity	**Percent**
White, non-Hispanic	57.1
Black, non-Hispanic	17.2
Hispanic	19.8
Asian/Pacific Islander	4.6
American Indian/Alaska Native	1.2

Source: National Center for Education Statistics (http://nces.ed.gov/pubs2007).

Hispanic students make up the large majority of the English Language Learners (ELLs) or limited-English-proficient (LEP) students in American schools. Statistics change continually, but according to the National Center for Educational Statistics, in the 2005–2006 school year, Hispanic students made up 19.8% of the nearly 49 million students enrolled in public elementary and secondary schools (see Table 10-2). Statistics from the 1999 U.S. census indicate that 57% of Hispanic students in grades K–12 spoke mostly English at home, 25% spoke mostly Spanish, and 17% spoke English and Spanish equally. This translates to more than 4 million Hispanic students who are encountering English as a second language in U.S. public schools. Providing equal educational opportunities to students who are not proficient in English is a special challenge.

Inquiry science programs, with their emphasis on exploring, investigating, and manipulating concrete materials, are especially valuable for students who wrestle with the development of a new language, customs, friendships, and less advantageous community environments. Providing inquiry activities equalizes the opportunity for success because success is not generally dependent on the students' ability to read a textbook, answer questions from the textbook, or complete worksheets that depend on students' understanding of what they have read. Hands-on, inquiry activities help all students span the gap between their past experiences and the development of language within their immediate environment.

English Language Learners and Inquiry Science

Learning language is much more than learning vocabulary. Language learning is a complex process of developing relationships among ideas, terms, and meanings (Lee & Fradd, 1998). A great deal of language can be learned in the context of science and other subjects. Context enables children to build on what they already know to infer the meaning of new words and verbal constructs. According to Lapp (2001, p. 2), "For children who are learning science by means of an inquiry-centered approach, classroom investigations and the activities surrounding them can provide context. These experiences can be springboards for growth in verbal fluency and literacy."

In learning science through inquiry approaches, students have opportunities to develop verbal fluency as they talk about what they are doing, record their observations, summarize their findings, and create written explanations that draw on their understanding of science concepts. They also read science articles and books, write essays and stories, and do library and Internet research to complement their classroom work (Lapp, 2001).

View the NSTA position statements on multicultural science education and other issues at http://www.nsta.org/about/positions.aspx#list.

Language is only one of the internal learning systems students need to learn science and other subjects. Students also need knowledge of facts, concepts, and principles and knowledge of how to apply them in making sense of problem situations (Bransford, Brown, & Cocking, 1999). Inquiry science can help students learn how to construct understanding through teaching them the scientists' approach to solving problems—an approach that has proved successful in every culture.

One method of teaching science and English to ELL students is called **sheltered instruction**. Sheltered instruction involves a minimum dependency on language for concept development. Freeman and Freeman (1998) have presented well-thought-out general strategies for using sheltered instruction with ELL students. Lee and Fradd (1998) and Fradd and Lee (1999) have discussed the uses of sheltering within inquiry science lessons. Many of these strategies are also useful for teaching science to all students.

Following is a presentation of using sheltered instruction for ELL students within the context of the 5-E model of inquiry.

Sheltered Instruction and the 5-E Model of Inquiry

With minimum dependency on language, sheltered instruction focuses on concept development and nonlanguage cues and prompts. Sheltered instruction methods are organized in this section under Preparation and All 5-E Phases: engage, explore, explain, elaborate, and evaluate.

Preparation. Critical to effective sheltered instruction is the preparation of targeted learning objectives. In addition to science objectives, language objectives should be developed in alignment with state language proficiency benchmarks or language arts standards (Lee & Fradd, 1998).

All 5-E Phases. Sheltering teachers are careful to integrate listening, speaking, reading and writing skills into science lessons. ELLs are called upon to process, manipulate, and display large amounts of new material at a rapid pace in a foreign language. Visual aids, allowances for processing time, and opportunities for clarification provide support in this demanding process. Sheltered lessons guide the learning of content information, including inquiry strategies, in ways that ELLs can comprehend.

During all phases of 5-E lesson teachers should modify their speech and use concrete referents so that ELLs can grasp important science questions, facts, concepts, principles, and procedures. In modifying their speech, teachers should:

- speak clearly and slowly;
- employ pauses, short sentences, simple syntax, few pronouns, and idioms;
- use redundancy and discourse markers, keywords, and outlines;
- provide examples and descriptions, not definitions; and
- use visuals, hands-on resources, gestures, and graphic organizers.

Successful students develop many skills and strategies that they use when integrating, remembering, and using information. Successful sheltering teachers explicitly teach learning strategies that enable ELLs and other students to develop a toolkit for accomplishing difficult learning tasks. Such strategies might include how to relate new science terms to observed objects, organisms, and events; how to access and use prior knowledge as a context for new learning; how to record new terms and their meanings in science journals; and how to keep initiating questions in mind as inquiry proceeds.

Sheltering teachers also provide ample opportunities at each phase for students to interact with others in English around tasks that are meaningful to them. Teachers should:

- facilitate frequent pair and small-group activities focused on meaningful tasks;
- model and assign tasks requiring turn taking, questioning, supporting/disagreeing, and clarification; and
- model and discuss ways of communicating respect.

Engage.   Use simple words and simple sentences. Use body language or concrete objects while you explain what you are saying. Ask clear questions designed to elicit students' current conceptions. Their answers will help you know about previous related experience your students have had.

Explore.   During this phase students are often involved in small group activities and are observing and manipulating objects and/or organisms. Sheltering teachers strive to make the goals of the activities clear to all of their students. Cooperative group strategies with assigned tasks can supply structure that can help students stay focused on the investigation. Small group discussions give students opportunities to practice taking turns, asking and answering questions is a reduced risk environment, respectfully supporting and/or disagreeing with peers and clarifying their thinking. As appropriate for the age level of your students, challenge all class members to keep journals in English.

Explain.   Sheltering teachers encourage ELLs to contribute to the class discussion about their findings from the explore phase. Summarize what has been presented at frequent intervals. Print the key points on the board, display them with a projector, or refer to a wall chart. As new science terms are introduced in the context of the experiences of the explore phase, post the words on your "word wall," pronounce them clearly, and have your students repeat the pronunciation together.

Elaborate.   Sheltering teachers provide opportunities for students to apply their new knowledge to new tasks that involve concepts and skills students have learned. English language learners have opportunities in the classroom to practice and apply the language skills and content knowledge they have acquired.

Trying out new knowledge and practicing new skills in a safe environment, supported by teacher and peer feedback, leads to mastery. Students can reflect on and adjust their performance, initially with assistance and ultimately independently.

Evaluate.   Formative and summative assessments of science understandings and English language usage are used. In this way of learning, teaching and assessment are integrated into an ongoing process that provides feedback to students and informs future instruction.

In conjunction with formative and summative assessments, teachers might gather information for evaluative decision making through:

- conferences
- take-home reflections
- oral retelling
- learning logs
- graphic organizers

Use a scoring guide or performance rubric aligned with learning objectives to collect evidence of content learning.

Go to the Homework and Exercises section in Chapter 10 of MyEducationLab and select the Article *Teacher Skills to Support English Language Learners*. Short and Echeverria have written an informative article on using sheltered instruction with English Language Learners. The article effectively refines and extends the discussion of sheltered instruction given in this chapter.

Perhaps the best way to include ELL students in your classroom is to view these students as an asset to the learning of all students. ELL students can contribute language enrichment for native English-speaking students and abundant occasions for cross-cultural teaching and learning.

Students from Culturally Diverse Backgrounds and Inquiry Science

Meeting the needs of students from diverse cultural backgrounds has become an important issue in education (Lee, 2002). The National Science Teachers Association recognizes and appreciates the strength and beauty of cultural pluralism. In its 2000 Position Statement on Multicultural Science Education, NSTA asserted that

- children from all cultures are to have equitable access to quality science education experiences that enhance success and provide the knowledge and opportunities required for them to become successful participants in our democratic society;
- curricular content must incorporate the contributions of many cultures to our knowledge of science; and
- science teachers are knowledgeable about and use culturally related ways of learning and instructional practices.

Additionally, science teachers have the responsibility to expose culturally diverse children to career opportunities in science, technology, and engineering.

The NSTA statement on multicultural science education calls for you to become knowledgeable about the learning styles of your students from diverse cultures and how their cultures aid or hinder their science learning. The prior cultural experiences of some students may actually interfere with inquiry science. For example, newly arrived students may experience difficulties with scientific inquiry in school because they have not been previously encouraged to ask questions or devise plans for investigation. Students from cultures that respect authority may be more receptive to teachers directing and telling them than to inquiry, exploration, and seeking alternative ways (Lee & Fradd, 1998).

Students unfamiliar with more exploratory approaches to learning may need explicit instruction to acquire the skills for effective participation. Fradd and Lee (1999) suggested, "With teachers' encouragement, students learning English can also learn to pose questions, devise plans, test hypotheses, collect and analyze data, engage in science discourse, and construct theories and explanations" (p. 15).

In teaching science, you should employ a wide range of content and teaching strategies to meet the learning needs and interests of students with special needs and those from different cultural backgrounds. You should also build on and broaden the prior knowledge of students by deepening their learning experiences.

SUMMARY

- The *National Science Education Standards* emphasize that science is for all students. Students come to your classroom with a wide range of learning abilities and styles, diverse cultural backgrounds, and physical, social, and emotional differences. Some have a limited proficiency using the English language, and all have had different sensory experiences and prior knowledge. It is your challenge to provide worthwhile science learning activities for every student.
- The Individuals with Disabilities Education Act (IDEA) mandates that individuals with disabilities from birth to age 21 have the right to a full, free public education in the least restrictive environment. This has led to the current trend of

inclusion, which means that all students, including those with a wide range of disabilities (physical, social, and cognitive), are in regular classrooms for the entire school day.

• Practical teaching and learning techniques provide for the needs of students who have learning disabilities, are mentally retarded, have emotional disturbances, have orthopedic disabilities, or have sensory impairments. More important than the individual means by which you can adapt instruction is your attitude and expectations for working with each of these students to provide a sensitive and supportive learning community.

• Gifted and talented students present different kinds of challenges for teachers. Students who have unusual talents or are intellectually gifted can benefit from doing rel-atively unstructured explorations, engaging in enrichment activities such as studying abstract topics to integrate connections, and observing how math and science are connected.

• A National Science Teachers Association position paper recognizes and advocates a quality science education for students from diverse cultural and linguistic backgrounds. This challenges all science teachers to employ a wide range of science content and teaching methods to meet the learning needs and interests of students with different cultural backgrounds. Hands-on science teaching and learning activities have many benefits for students from diverse backgrounds, especially those with limited English proficiency.

ONLINE PROFESSIONAL DEVELOPMENT

Pre- and post-tests to assess your knowledge of chapter content, along with exercises to enhance your understanding, can be found on MyEducationLab at www.myeducationlab.com.

Video Guides

The video clip on MyEducationLab selected for this chapter is *Dual Language Classrooms: Science in English and Spanish.*

Accessing the Video

1. Go to the Homework and Exercises section in Chapter 10 of MyEducationLab to select and view videos for this chapter.
2. Videos might be viewed individually, by small groups of colleagues, or by the whole class.
3. As you watch each video, use the **Questions for Reflection** to guide your thoughts and note taking for personal use and group discussion.
4. Discuss your answers to the questions about each video with classmates.

Video: Dual Language Classrooms: Science in English and Spanish

Overview

Two teachers discuss the concept of dual language classrooms. We see the two teachers working together to guide an investigation on skimmers, with one teacher delivering instruction in English and the other teacher delivering instruction in Spanish.

Questions for Reflection

1. What are the respective roles of the English language teacher and the Spanish language teacher in guiding the investigation?
2. How effective for students do you think this method of instruction is?
3. What is the evidence that the dual language lessons were effective?

REFERENCES

Activities That Integrate Mathematics and Science. (1999). *AIMS programs and product catalog*. Fresno, CA: AIMS Education Foundation.

American Association for the Advancement of Science (1993). *Benchmarks for science literacy*. New York: Oxford University Press.

American Association for the Advancement of Science. (2007). *Atlas of science literacy*, Volume 2. Copublished by AAAS Project 2061 and the National Science Teachers Association.

American Association for the Advancement of Science. (2001). *Atlas of science literacy*. Copublished by AAAS Project 2061 and the National Science Teachers Association.

Anderson, C. W. (1987). Strategic teaching in science. In B. F. Jones et al. (Eds.), *Strategic teaching and learning: Cognitive instruction in the content areas*. Alexandria, VA: Association for Supervision and Curriculum Development.

Annenberg/CPB (Corporation for Public Broadcasting). (1997). *Case studies in science education: Rachel*. Washington, D.C.: Annenberg/CPB Foundation.

Annenberg Foundation. (1997). *Annenberg video case studies in science education, Linda*. South Burlington, VT: Annenberg Foundation.

Annenberg/CPB (Corporation for Public Broadcasting). (1997). *Case studies in science education: Jean*. Annenberg/CPB Foundation.

Armstrong, T. (1998). *Awakening genius in the classroom*. Alexandria, VA: Association for Supervision and Curriculum Development.

Baron, E. B. (1992). Discipline strategies for teachers. *Fastback, 344*. Bloomington, IN: Phi Delta Kappa Educational Foundation.

Biological Sciences Curriculum Study. (1989). *New designs for elementary school science and health: A cooperative project of Biological Sciences Curriculum Study (BSCS) and International Business Machines (IBM)*. Dubuque, IA: Kendall/Hunt.

Bitner, N., Wadlington, E., Austin, S., Partridge, E., & Bitner, J. (1999). The virtual trip. *Learning and Leading with Technology, 26*(6), 6–9, 25.

Blosser, P. (1991). *How to ask the right questions*. Arlington, VA: National Science Teachers Association.

Bransford, J. D., Brown, A. L., & Cocking, R. R. (Eds.). (1999). *How people learn: Brain, mind, experience, and school*. Washington, DC: National Academy Press (also available at http://www.nap.edu).

Brown, A. L., & Campione, J. (1994). Guided discovery in a community of learners. In K. McGilly (Ed.), *Classroom lessons: Integrating cognitive theory and classroom practice*. Cambridge, MA: The MIT Press.

Brown, A. L., & Campione, J. C. (1998). Designing a community of young learners: Theoretical and practical lessons. In N. L. Lambert & B. L. McCombs (Eds.), *How students learn: Reforming schools through learner-centered education*. Washington, DC: American Psychological Association.

Brown, A. L., Bransford, J. D., Ferrara, R., & Campione, J. C. (1983). Learning, remembering, and understanding. In J. H. Flavell & E. M. Markman (Eds.), *Carmichael's manual of child psychology* (Vol. 3). New York: Wiley.

Brown, A. L., Bransford, J., Ferrara, R., & Campione, J. (1983). Learning, remembering, and understanding. In J. N. Flavell & E. M. Markman (Eds.), *Handbook of child psychology* (Vol. 3, 4th ed., pp. 79–166). New York: Wiley.

Brown, C. A. (1998). Presentation software and the single computer. *Learning and Leading with Technology, 26*(2), 18–21.

Brownell, M. T., & Thomas, C. W. (1998). An interview with Margo Mastropieri: Quality science instruction for students with disabilities. *Intervention in School and Clinic, 34*(2), 118–122.

Bybee, R. W., Buchwald, C. E., Crissman, S., Heil, D. R., Kuerbis, P. J., Matsumoto, C., & McInerney, J. P. (1989). *Science and technology education for the elementary years: Frameworks for curriculum and instruction*. Washington, DC: National Center for Improving Science Education.

Caniglia, J. (1997). The heat is on! Using the calculator-based laboratory to integrate math, science, and technology. *Learning and Leading with Technology, 25*(1), 22–27.

Carin, A. A., & Sund, R. B. (1978). *Creative questioning and sensitive listening techniques: A self-guided approach*. Upper Saddle River, NJ: Merrill/Prentice Hall.

Carina Software (2006). *Voyager 4*. San Ramon, CA.

Carter, L., Sumrall, W., & Curry, K. (2006). Say cheese! Digital collections in the classroom. *Science and Children, 43*(8), 19–23.

Cawley, J. F., & Foley, T. E. (2002). Connecting math and science for all students. *Teaching Exceptional Children, 34*(4), 14–19.

Champagne, A. L., & Kouba, V. L. (2000). Writing to inquire: Written products as performance measures. In J. J. Mintzes, J. H. Wandersee, & J. D. Novak (Eds.), *Assessing science understanding: A human constructivist view* (pp. 223–248). New York: Academic Press.

Chan, A., Doran, R., & Lenhardt, C. (1999). Learning from the TIMSS. *The Science Teacher, 66*(1), 18–22.

Cherry, L. (1992). *A river ran wild*. New York: Harcourt Brace Jovanovich.

Clements, D. (1999). Teaching length measurement: Research challenges. *School Science and Mathematics, 99*(1), 5–11.

Curcio, F. R. (1989). *Developing graph comprehension: Elementary and middle school activities*. Reston, VA: National Council of Teachers of Mathematics.

Dockterman, D. (1997). *Great teaching in the one computer classroom*. Watertown, MA: Tom Snyder Productions.

Duschl, R. S., Schweingruber, H. A., & Shouse A.W. (2007). *Taking science to school: Learning and teaching science in grades K–8*. Washington, DC: National Academies Press.

Ebenezer, J., & Lau, E. (1999). *Science on the Internet: A resource for K–12 teachers*. Upper Saddle River, NJ: Merrill/Prentice Hall.

Edmondson, K. M. (1999). Assessing science understanding through concept maps. In J. J. Mintzes, J. H. Wandersee, & J. D. Novak (Eds.), *Assessing science understanding: A human constructivist view* (pp. 223–248). New York: Academic Press.

Ellis, E. S. (2002). Watering Up the Curriculum for Adolescents with Learning Disabilities, Part II: Goals for the Affective Dimension. *LD Online*. Retrieved June 2007, from http://www.ldonline.org/articles/5742.

Finley, F. N. (1991). Why children have trouble learning from science texts. In C. M. Santa & D. E. Alvermann (Eds.), *Science learning: Processes and applications* (pp. 22–27). Newark, DE: International Reading Association.

Fradd, S. H., & Lee, O. (1999). Teachers' roles in promoting science inquiry with students from diverse language backgrounds. *Educational Researcher, 28*(6), 14–20.

Freeman, D., & Freeman, Y. (1998). *Sheltered English instruction* (ERIC Digest).

Full Option Science System. (1990). *Swingers*. Berkeley, CA: Lawrence Hall of Science.

Full Option Science System. (1991). *Graphs in the elementary science program*. Berkeley, CA: Lawrence Hall of Science.

Full Option Science System. (2000). *Overview: Physics of sound*. Nashua, NH: Delta Education.

Fulton, L., & Campbell, B. (2004, November–December). Student-centered notebooks. *Science and Children, 42*(3), 26–29.

Furtak, E. M., & Ruiz-Primo, M. A. (2005, January). Questioning cycle: Making students' thinking explicit during scientific inquiry. *Science Scope,* 22–25.

Gerlovich, J.A. (1996). Developments in laboratory safety. In J. Rhoton and P. Bowers (Eds.). *Issues in science education*. Arlington, VA: National Science Teachers Association.

Grahame, K. (1981). *The wind in the willows* (E. Shepard, Illus.). New York: Charles Scribner & Sons.

Gray, T. (1997). ED's Oasis (Guidelines for evaluating educational web sites). *Learning and Leading with Technology, 25*(1), 44–45.

Hand, B., & Keys, C. W. (1999). Inquiry investigation: A new approach to laboratory reports. *The Science Teacher, 66*(4), 27–29.

Harlen, W., & Jelly, S. (1990). *Developing science in the primary classroom*. Portsmouth, NH: Heinemann.

Haury, D. L. (1993). Teaching science through inquiry. *ERIC CSMEE Digest* (March Ed 359 048).

Hodge, J., & Brocker, S. (1997). *Animals of the oceans: Whales*. Hauppauge, N.Y.: Barron's.

Hogan, K., & Pressley, M. (1997). Scaffolding scientific competencies within classroom communities of inquiry. In K. Hogan & M. Pressley (Eds.), *Scaffolding student learning: Instructional approaches and issues*. Cambridge, MA: Brookline Books.

Hunter, M. (1984). Knowing, teaching, and supervising. In P. A. Hosford (Ed.), *Using what we know about teaching* (pp. 169–192). Alexandria, VA: Association for Supervision and Curriculum Development.

Inhelder, B., and Piaget, J. (1958). *The growth of logical thinking from childhood to adolescence*. New York: Basic Books.

International Reading Association. (1996). *Standards for the English language arts* (a project of the International Reading Association and the National Council of Teachers of English). Newark, DE: Author.

Jarolimek, J., & Foster, C. D., Sr. (1997). *Teaching and learning in the elementary school* (6th ed.). Upper Saddle River, NJ: Merrill/Prentice Hall.

Jones, M. G., & Carter, G. (1997). Small groups and shared constructions. In J. J. Mintzes, J. H. Wandersee, & J. D. Novak (Eds.), *Teaching science for understanding: A human constructivist view*. New York: Academic Press.

Judson, H. F. (1980). *The search for solutions*. New York: Holt, Rinehart & Winston.

Karplus, R., & Thier, H. (1974). *SCIS teacher's handbook*. Berkeley, CA: Science Curriculum Improvement Study.

Kentucky Department of Education. (n.d.). *Designing a performance assessment*. Frankfort, KY: Author.

King, A. (1994). Guiding knowledge construction in the classroom: Effects of teaching children how to question and how to explain. *American Educational Research Journal, 31*(2), 338–368.

Klahr, D., & Nigam, M. (2004). The equivalence of learning paths in early science instruction: Effects of direct instruction and discovery learning. *Psychological Science*.

Klentschy, M., (2005). Science notebook essentials: A guide to effective notebook components. *Science and Children, 43*(3), 24–27.

Koch, J. (1999). *Science stories: Teachers and children as science learners*. Boston: Houghton Mifflin.

Kreuger, A., & Sutton, J. (Eds.). (2001). Instructional technology in science. In *EDThoughts: What we know about science teaching and learning* (pp. 69–79). Aurora, CO: Mid-continent Research for Education and Learning.

Kwan, T., & Texley, J. (2002). *Exploring safely: A guide for elementary teachers*. Arlington, VA: NSTA Press.

Kwan, T., & Texley, J. (2003). *Inquiring safely: A guide for middle school teachers*. Arlington, VA: NSTA Press.

Lapp, D. (2001). Bridging the gap. *Science Link (Newsletter of the National Science Resources Center), 12*(1), 2.

Lee, J. R., & Patterson, W. R. (1997). It's show time! Six hints for PowerPoint presentations. *Learning and Leading with Technology, 24*(5), 6–11.

Lee, O. (2002). Promoting scientific inquiry with elementary students from diverse cultures and languages. In W. C. Secada (Ed.), *Review of research in education* (Vol. 26, pp. 23–69). Washington, DC: American Educational Research Association.

Lee, O., & Fradd, S. H. (1998). Science for all, including students from non-English-language backgrounds. *Educational Researcher, 27*(4), 12–19.

Loucks-Horsley, S., Hewson, P., Love, N., & Stiles, K. (1998). *Designing professional development for teachers of science and mathematics*. Thousand Oaks, CA: Corwin Press.

Lowery, L. (1998, November). How new science curriculums reflect brain research. *Educational Leadership,* 26–30.

Lowery, L. (1998a). How new science curriculums reflect brain research. *Educational Leadership,* November, 26–30.

Lowery, L. F. (1998b). Classroom arrangements and teaching. *FOSS Newsletter, 11,* 6–9.

Lowery, L. F. (Ed.). (1997). *Pathways to the science standards: Elementary school edition.* Arlington, VA: National Science Teachers Association.

Malone, L., Palmer, A., & Voigt, C. (2002). *Mapping our world: GIS lessons for educators.* Redlands, CA: ESRI Press.

Maslow, A. H. (1987). *Motivation and personality* (3rd ed.). New York: Harper and Row.

Mastropieri, M. A., & Scruggs, T. E. (1993). *A practical guide for teaching science to students with special needs in inclusive settings* (p. 154). Austin, TX: PRO-ED.

Mastropieri, M. A., & Scruggs, T. E. (2004). *The inclusive classroom: Strategies for effective instruction.* Upper Saddle River, NJ: Merrill/Prentice Hall.

Mastropieri, M. A., Scruggs, T. E., & Butcher, K. (1993). How effective is inquiry learning for students with mild disabilities? *Journal of Special Education, 31*(2), 199–211.

Mechling, K. R., & Oliver, D. L. (1983). *Handbook I: Science teaches basic skills.* Arlington, VA: National Science Teachers Association.

Meng, E., & Doran, R. L. (1993). *Improving instruction and learning through evaluation: Elementary school science.* Columbus, OH: ERIC Clearinghouse for Science, Mathematics, and Environmental Education.

Minnesota Mathematics and Science Teaching Project. (1970). *Overview: Minnesota mathematics and science teaching project.* Minneapolis: Minnemast Project, University of Minnesota.

Mintzes, J., Wandersee, J., & Novak, J. (1998). *Teaching science for understanding: A human constructivist view.* San Diego, CA: Academic Press.

Nachmias, R., & Linn, M. C. (1987). Evaluations of science laboratory data: The role of computer presented information. *Journal of Research in Science Teaching, 24*(5), 491–506.

National Academies of Science. (2006). *Rising above the gathering storm.* Washington, DC: National Academy Press.

National Aquarium in Baltimore. (1997). *Living in water: An Aquatic science curriculum.* Dubuque, IA: Kendall/Hunt.

National Council for the Social Studies. (1994). *Expectations of excellence: Curriculum standards for the social studies.* Washington, DC: Author.

National Council of Teachers of Mathematics. (1989). *Curriculum and evaluation standards for school mathematics.* Weston, VA: Author.

National Council of Teachers of Mathematics. (2000). *Principles and standards for school mathematics.* Weston, VA: Author.

National Gardening Association. (1992). *GrowLab: Activities for growing minds.* Burlington, VT: Author.

National Research Council. (1996). *National science education standards.* Washington, DC: National Academy Press.

National Research Council. (2000). *Inquiry and the national science education standards: A guide for teaching and learning.* Washington, DC: National Academies Press.

National Research Council. (2001). *Classroom assessment and the national science education standards.* Washington, DC: National Academy Press.

National Science Resources Center. (1996). *Science and technology for children: Comparing and measuring.* Burlington, NC: Carolina Biological Supply.

National Science Teachers Association (2000). Safety and school science instruction: A position statement. Arlington, VA: National Science Teachers Association (Available online at http://www.nsta.org/about/positions/safety.aspx)

Novak, J. (1995). Concept mapping: A strategy for organizing knowledge. In S. Glynn & R. Duit (Eds.), *Learning science in the schools: Research reforming practice.* Mahwah, NJ: Erlbaum.

Ormrod, J. (2004). *Human learning.* Upper Saddle River, NJ: Merrill/Prentice Hall.

Ormrod, J. (2007). *Human learning, 5th ed.* Upper Saddle River, NJ: Merrill/Prentice Hall.

Ostlund, K., & Mercier, S. (1999). *Rising to the challenge of the national science education standards: The process of science inquiry.* Squaw Valley, CA: S&K Associates.

Padak, N. D., & Davidson, J. L. (1991). Instructional activities for comprehending science text. In C. M. Santa & D. E. Alvermann (Eds.), *Science learning: Processes and applications* (pp. 76–85). Newark, DE: International Reading Association.

Padilla, M. J., Muth, K. D., & Padilla, R. K. (1991). Science and reading: Many process skills in common? In C. M. Santa & D. E. Alvermann (Eds.), *Science learning: Processes and applications* (pp. 14–19). Newark, DE: International Reading Association.

Passow, M. (1996). Storm studies. *The Science Teacher, 63*(3), 21–23.

Paulu, N., & Martin, M. (1991). *Helping your child learn science.* Washington, DC: U.S. Department of Education, Office of Educational Research and Improvement.

Piaget, J. in Gruber, H.E. & Voneche, J.J. (1977). *The Essential Piaget.* New York: Basic Books.

Price, C. L. (1989). Microcomputer applications in science. *Journal of Science Education, 1*(2), 30–33.

Reynolds, K., & Barba, R. (1996). *Technology for the teaching and learning of science.* Needham Heights, MA: Allyn & Bacon.

Rezba, R. J., Sprague, C., Fiel, R. L., & Funk, H. J. (2003). *Learning and assessing science process skills.* Dubuque, IA: Kendall/Hunt.

Rock, B. N., Blackwell, T. R., Miller, D., & Hardison, A. (1997). The GLOBE program: A model for international environmental education. In K. C. Cohen (Ed.), *Internet links for science education: Student-scientist partnerships.* New York: Plenum Press.

Rosenshine, B. (1997). Advances in research on instruction. In J. Lloyd, E. Kameanui, & D. Chard (Eds.), *Issues in educating students with disabilities* (pp. 197–221). Mahwah, NJ: Lawrence Erlbaum.

Roth, K. (1991). Reading science texts for conceptual change. In C. M. Santa & D. V. Alverson (Eds.), *Science learning: Processes and applications.* Newark, DE: International Reading Association.

Roth, K. (1993). *What does it mean to understand science? Changing perspectives from a teacher and her students.* East Lansing: Center for the Learning and Teaching of Elementary Subjects, Institute for Research on Teaching, Michigan State University.

Rowe, M. B. (1973). *Teaching science as continuous inquiry.* New York: McGraw-Hill.

Rowe, M. B. (1987). Wait-time: Slowing down may be a way of speeding up. *American Educator, 11*(1), 38–47.

Rowe, M. B. (1996). Mounting and maintaining an elementary science program: What supervisors can learn from research. In J. Rhoton & P. Bowers (Eds.), *Issues in science education* (pp. 162–166). Arlington, VA: National Science Teachers Association.

Rutherford, F. J., & Ahlgren, A. (1989). *Science for all Americans.* New York: Oxford University Press.

Santa, C. M., & Havens, L. T. (1991). Learning through writing. In C. M. Santa & D. E. Alvermann (Eds.), *Science learning: Processes and applications* (pp. 122–133). Newark, DE: International Reading Association.

Santa, C. M., & Alvermann, D. E. (Eds.). (1991). *Science learning: Processes and applications.* Newark, DE: International Reading Association.

Scruggs, T. E., & Mastropieri, M. A. (1994). The construction of scientific knowledge by students with mild disabilities. *Journal of Special Education, 28*(3), 307–321.

Scruggs, T. E., Mastropieri, M. A., Bakken, J. P., & Brigham, F. J. (1993). Reading versus doing: The relative effects of textbook-based and inquiry-oriented approaches to science learning in special education classrooms. *Journal of Special Education, 27*(1), 1–15.

Shapiro, B. (1994). *What children bring to light: A constructivist perspective on children's learning in science.* New York: Teachers College Press.

Shepardson, D. P., & Britsch, S. J. (2001). Tools for assessing and teaching science in elementary and middle schools. In D. P. Shepardson (Ed.), *Assessment in science: A guide to professional development and classroom practice* (pp. 119–147). Boston: Kluwer.

Sobel, D. (2000). *Galileo's daughter.* New York: Penguin Books.

Soholt, G. (1999). *Using technology effectively in your classroom* (p. 44). Bellevue, WA: Bureau of Education & Research.

Stahly, L. L., Krockover, G. H., & Shepardson, D. P. (1999). Third grade students' ideas about the lunar phases. *Journal of Research in Science Teaching, 36*(2), 159–177.

Stokes, N. C., & Hull, M. M. (2002, May). Every drop counts! *The Science Teacher, 69*(5), 40–44.

Stull, A. T. (1998). *Education on the Internet: A student's guide* (adapted for Merrill Education by R. J. Ryder). Upper Saddle River, NJ: Merrill/Prentice Hall.

TERC. (1993). *Hands-on elementary science project leader's manual.* Cambridge, MA: TERC Communications.

Texas A&M Center for Mathematics and Science Education. (2006). *Texas science initiative meta-analysis of national research regarding science teaching: Executive summary.* Austin: Texas Education Agency (available online at http://72.14.209.104/search?q=cache:AWfRsosvXPIJ:www3.science.tamu.edu/cmse/tsi/ExecutiveSum).

Texas A&M Center for Mathematics and Science Education (2005). *Effective research-based science instruction.* Austin: Texas Education Agency (available online at http://72.14.209.104/search?q=cache:q4rfHv7MDMYJ:www3.science.tamu.edu/cmse/tsi/).

Texas Education Agency. (1999). *Texas social studies framework, kindergarten–grade 12.* Austin, TX: Author.

Tompkins, G. E. (2006). *Literacy for the 21st century,* 4th ed. Upper Saddle River, NJ: Pearson/Merrill.

Trowbridge, L., & Bybee, R. (1996). *Teaching secondary school science* (6th ed.). Upper Saddle River, NJ: Merrill/Prentice Hall.

Turnbull, A., Turnbull, R., Shank, M., & Smith, S. J. (2004). *Exceptional lives: Special education in today's schools* (4th ed.). Upper Saddle River, NJ: Merrill/Prentice Hall.

U.S. Department of Education. (1996). *Planning excellence: A study of U.S. eighth-grade mathematics and science teaching, learning, curriculum, and achievement in international context.* Washington, DC: U.S. Department of Education, Office of Educational Research and Improvement.

U.S. Department of Education. (1997). *Introduction to TIMSS: The third international mathematics and science study.* Washington, DC: U.S. Department of Education, Office of Educational Research and Improvement.

Vasquez, J. A. (1990). Teaching to the distinctive traits of minority students. *The Clearing House, 63,* 299–304.

Vitale, M. R., & Romance, N. R. (2000). Portfolios in science assessment: A knowledge-based model for classroom practice. In J. J. Mintzes, J. H. Wandersee, & J. D. Novak (Eds.), *Assessing science understanding: A human constructivist view* (pp. 167–196). New York: Academic Press.

Vygotsky, L. S. (1962). *Thought and language.* Cambridge, MA: The MIT Press.

Watson, S., and Marshall, J. (1995). Effects of cooperative incentives and heterogeneous arrangements on achievement and interaction of cooperative learning groups in a college life science course. *Journal of Research in Science Teaching, 32,* 291–299.

Weiss, I. R., & Pasley, J. D. (2004, February). What is high-quality instruction? *Educational Leadership, 45:* 24–29.

Wiggins, G., & McTighe, J. (1998). *Understanding by design.* Alexandria, VA: Association for Supervision and Curriculum Development.

Wilson, M. R., & Berthenthal, M. W. (2006). *Systems for state science assessment.* Washington, DC: National Academies Press.

Wiske, M. S. (Ed.). (1998). *Teaching for understanding.* San Francisco: Jossey-Bass.

Wolfinger, D. M. (2000). *Science in the elementary and middle school.* New York: Longman.

Yopp, H. K., & Yopp, R. H. (2006, November). Primary students and informational texts, *Science and Children, 44*(3), 22–25.

Activities for Teaching Science as Inquiry

SECTION I
Teaching Inquiry Science Activities

NSES *Inquiry is a set of interrelated processes by which scientists and students pose questions about the natural world and investigate phenomena; in doing so, students acquire knowledge and develop a rich understanding of concepts, principles, models, and theories. Inquiry is a critical component of a science program at all grade levels and in every domain of science. (National Research Council, 1996, p. 214)*

Terrariums offer a wonderful opportunity for children to investigate the world by questioning and hypothesizing, describing and classifying, manipulating and experimenting, explaining and predicting. Sharon Olson began a series of terrarium lessons with her second graders by asking: *What might you find on a forest floor?* As the class discussed this question, Ms. Olson held up the different materials the students suggested (soil, sand, leaves, seeds, fruit, plants, water, twigs, grass, and so on). She then told the students these were some of the things they would put in a container to make a home for living things. For the next few days, small groups of students built and investigated their own terrariums (Hosoume & Barber, 1994). Using readily available containers, such as large, plastic soda bottles (Ingram, 1993), the children arranged soil in the bottom of the containers, planted plants, sprinkled seeds, added moisture, and introduced earthworms and pill bugs to their new homes. With Ms. Olson's assistance, they asked questions about these organisms and planned and conducted investigations. They also organized the data of observations and used it as evidence to answer their questions. Throughout the terrarium lessons, the teacher observed and assessed the children's inquiry abilities and developing knowedge of the habitats and needs of living organisms.

This scenario draws on activities described in this book. Here, you will find directions for more than 140 inquiry activities in physical science, life science, and earth and space science designed for elementary and middle school students. The activities presented here are consistent with and reflect the *National Science Education Standards* and the standards of most states. They do not comprise a comprehensive science curriculum, but they do represent a large number of examples that will

1. help you connect science in the classroom to national and state science standards in a practical way;
2. provide concrete suggestions for teaching science as inquiry; and
3. provide a bank of activities that you can draw on in teaching science as inquiry.

You do not have to be a science specialist to engage your students in these activities, merely curious and willing to learn along with them.

Let us look more closely at what it means to teach science as inquiry.

When Scientists and Students Inquire

Science is an attempt to understand the natural world. Doing science can be as simple as one individual conducting field studies or as complex as hundreds of people across the world working together on a major scientific problem. Whatever the circumstances or level of complexity, scientists are likely to work from some common assumptions, have some common goals, and use some common procedures. When scientists inquire, they

- ask questions about objects, events, and systems;
- employ a variety of equipment and tools to make observations and measurements in order to obtain data and seek evidence to answer their questions;
- use scientific concepts and principles along with clear reasoning to develop tentative explanations that make sense of collected evidence;
- make predictions to test explanations;
- blend logic and imagination;
- reach conclusions or *not* (American Association for the Advancement of Science, 1993; National Research Council, 1996; Rutherford & Ahlgren, 1990).

Although what scientists do is a model for science instruction, because of developmental differences children may not be able to engage in inquiry as scientists do in professional communities. Thus, elementary and middle school science instruction occurs in a simplified form that enables children to participate with understanding (Lee, 2002).

The key to accommodating scientific inquiry to the level of children is the teacher, who plans, guides, scaffolds, questions, informs, and explains—all in the context of children's hands-on engagement with the objects, organisms, and activities of the real world.

Phases of Inquiry Instruction: The 5-E Model

Inquiry instruction can be thought of in terms of five main components or tasks: *engage*, *explore*, *explain*, *elaborate*, and *evaluate*. You may recognize these five instructional phases as the components of the *5-E model of instruction*.

Engage

Inquiry is initiated at the engage phase. In this phase, teachers probe prior knowledge and conceptions (and misconceptions) of learners and help them generate a question to be investigated. Ideally, inquiry in the classroom should begin with authentic questions developed by students from their own experiences with objects, organisms, and events in the environment (American Association for the Advancement of Science, 1993).

In classroom practice, teachers must be prepared to provide guidance in forming questions that can be investigated scientifically. Students learn from teachers how to ask good questions. Teachers can maintain the spirit of inquiry by focusing on questions that can be answered by collecting observational data, using available knowledge of science, and applying processes of reasoning (National Research Council, 1996).

Explore

The essence of science is to use whatever methods fit to gather evidence that can be used in making sense of the natural world. Scientists and children can use various types of investigations in doing science. Different types of questions call for different forms of investigation.

In the early grades, investigations are largely based on systematic description and classification of material objects and organisms (Lowery, 1997), as in the terrarium lessons. Young children's natural curiosity motivates them to explore the world by manipulating and observing, comparing and contrasting, and sorting simple objects in their environment.

By grade 4 or 5, children begin to engage in experimental inquiry—posing questions, collecting information through experiments, and arriving at logical conclusions. Controlled experiments or fair tests can be important parts of experimental investigations, especially in the upper elementary and middle grades. In controlled investigations, students manipulate one variable at a time, determine its effect on a responding variable, and control all other relevant variables. Carefully guided variations of experiments might also be introduced at earlier grades.

As students engage in these inquiry activities, they develop simple skills such as how to observe, measure, cut, connect, switch, pour, tie, hold, and hook. Beginning with simple instruments, they learn to use rulers, thermometers, watches, spring scales, and balance beams to measure important variables. Students learn to use magnifying lenses and microscopes to see finer details of objects and organisms. They may also begin to use computers and calculators in investigations (National Research Council, 2000).

Explain

This phase of inquiry involves the interpretation of collected data. To interpret is to go beyond the data given and to construct inferences, make predictions, and build explanations that make sense of the world. Interpretations use reasoning processes to coordinate scientific knowledge and observational evidence in order to answer initiating questions.

In children's inquiry, teachers should refrain as much as possible from supplying information and providing explanations that children could attain on their own. Nevertheless, it is often necessary for teachers to directly teach terms and concepts, experimental procedures, and scientific principles. Although inquiry teachers may use expository methods to teach principles, the instruction always builds on children's recent activities, and what is learned is applied to new situations to assist students in comprehending it.

Elaborate

If understanding is to be a result of inquiry, students must have opportunities to transfer or apply their new knowledge to new issues and problems (Bransford, Brown, & Cocking, 1999). In the elaborate phase of inquiry instruction, students identify additional questions to investigate, collect pertinent evidence, and connect their newly constructed knowledge to the evidence through such processes as classifying, relating, inferring, predicting, and explaining. Students communicate their investigations to one another and critique and analyze their work and the work of others. By applying their new knowledge in investigating new situations, students continually build understanding.

Evaluate

Evaluation in inquiry teaching involves use of assessment data to discover what students are learning (or not learning) and to provide feedback to modify lesson plans and teaching methods where needed. Continuous assessment through asking key questions, observing and judging the performances and products of students, and administering assessment tasks of various designs will help you probe your students' understanding, consider how misconceptions and alternative theories are affecting their learning, and determine how they are able to apply what they know in new situations. This informaton will provide you the basis for decision making about next steps in instruction.

Characteristics of Inquiry Classrooms

At every step of inquiry instruction, learning takes place within classrooms characterized by student discourse, cooperative group activities, continuing assessment, and teacher scaffolding.

Discourse

Children love to talk about their experiences. Inquiry science provides a rich context in which to develop language and thought (Rowe, 1973). Confronted with puzzling phenomena and given some freedom to investigate, children work hard at expressing their experiences through language.

Just as communication among scientists is central in the construction of scientific knowledge, students learn by talking among themselves and writing about and formally presenting their ideas. Oral and written discourse focuses the attention of students on *what* they know, *how* they know it, and *how* their knowledge connects to the knowledge of other people, to other subjects, and to the world beyond the classroom (National Research Council, 1996).

Teachers make students' ideas more meaningful by commenting and elaborating on them and asking students to clarify, expand, and justify their own emerging conceptions and those of others. Conversational partnerships with the teacher and classmates allow students to build on and use the thinking processes of others to support their own efforts to think in more flexible and mature ways.

Cooperative learning groups play a vital role in the learning community.

Cooperative Groups

Glenn Seaborg, 1951 Nobel Prize winner in chemistry and formerly the principal investigator for GEMS (Great Explorations in Math and Science) at the Lawrence Hall of Science, reminds us that cooperation is the norm in science:

> In the case of all great "discoveries" it must be remembered that science is a group process. When we devise experiments and research today, we do so on the basis of an enormous body of knowledge contributed by people from all over the world over thousands of years. . . . Research effort is above all a team effort. (Seaborg, 1991)

In the context of inquiry instruction, cooperative learning is an important process that asks students to work together and support one another's learning. It entails students working collaboratively in small groups to

* consider a problem or assignment together;
* share limited supplies and science equipment;

- verbalize what they know and what they want to find out;
- plan investigations;
- collect and compare the data;
- consider the multiple viewpoints of group members; and
- propose group solutions to the problem.

Setting Up Cooperative Learning Groups (CLGs). Initially, you should assign students to teams because they tend to gravitate to friends only. For primary grade students or older students who have not worked previously in CLGs, it is best to start with two students. As students acquire basic cooperative group skills, combine two groups of two as a working team. Generally, CLG teams of three or four are recommended once your classroom is comfortable and knowledgeable about the process.

When you form groups, you will want to integrate students with various abilities, disabilities, and cultural backgrounds. To initiate conversation and encourage team cohesion, provide time for each team to choose its own name. Once you have established a cooperative group routine, keep teams together for 3 to 6 weeks so teammates have time to learn to work with each other. After 3 to 6 weeks, change team membership, so students get to work with other students and to experience the differences in team dynamics.

A specific job is assigned to each CLG team member. The names and functions are quite similar in all CLGs. The following are from Robert Jones's (1990) *Inquiry Task Group Management System:*

- *Principal investigator.* In charge of team operations including checking assignments, ensuring that all team members can participate in activities, and leading group discussions. The principal investigator is also the one group member who communicates with the teacher when questions arise. This enables a more orderly atmosphere and limits the number of questions to which the teacher must respond. Often groups can solve their own problems without consulting the teacher.
- *Materials manager.* Gets, inventories, and distributes materials to the team.
- *Recorder/reporter.* Collects and records data on lab sheets and reports results to whole class orally or in writing on class summary chart posted on chalkboard.
- *Maintenance director.* With the assistance of other team members, cleans up and returns materials and equipment to their appropriate storage space or container. Directs the disposal of used materials and is responsible for team members' safety.

Staff members at research institutions, hospitals, and other entities routinely wear name badges indicating job responsibilities. This is a good practice for inquiry team members as well. *Job badges* (see examples in Figures I-1 and I-2) or ID badges will make it easier for students to remember their responsibilities and for you to spot students who should not be straying away from their group's space. Younger students will especially enjoy displaying an ID badge. Their importance in professional communities may have to be established with older students.

Continuing Assessment

Three assumptions underlie inquiry teaching:

1. Clear standards and indicators (assessment criteria) must be written;
2. Teachers must provide high-quality opportunites for students to achieve standards, including both conceptual understandings and inquiry abilities;
3. Students must demonstrate understandings and abilities through well-designed assessments.

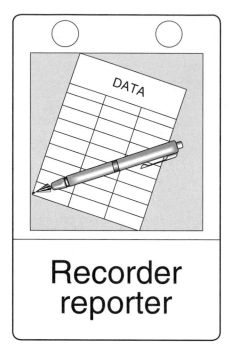

Figure I-1 Cooperative learning group
(CLG) job badge.
Source: Reprinted by permission from Robert M. Jones,
*Teaming Up! The Inquiry Task Group Management System
User's Guide.* LaPorte, TX: ITGROUP, December 1990, 55.

Figure I-2 Cooperative learning group
(CLG) job badge.
Source: Reprinted by permission from Robert M. Jones,
*Teaming Up! The Inquiry Task Group Management System
User's Guide.* LaPorte, TX: ITGROUP, December 1990, 43.

An assessment strategy involving formative and summative assessment is especially compatible with inquiry instruction.

Formative and Summative Assessment. In formative assessment, informal observations, formal performance tasks, and written work are used during the inquiry lessons to assess students' developing understanding of concepts, principles, theories, and explanations to determine the level and growth of inquiry abilities. For example, through formative assessment, teachers seek to determine:

- What information do students know about an activity before they begin?
- Do students understand that data collected must relate to observations of the real world and provide a basis for predictions, inferences, and explanations?
- Do students use their data to make predictions? How well were students able to provide reasons for their predictions? Are the reasons plausible?
- Are students providing plausible explanations for their observations? Are the students' reasons becoming more detailed? Do students provide more than one reason for their explanations? What do students do to test their predictions and explanations?
- What should they do next to enable students to achieve the planned objectives.

For summative assessment, teachers use application or transfer tasks to determine conceptual understanding. These tasks might be built around the task used in the elaborate phase of inquiry lessons. Be sure to key both formative and summative assessments to standards and objectives. Performance tasks, written tests, and final work products might be used in summative assessment. Scores or grades representing what students know and are able to do can be assigned based on such assignments.

Assessments should always have a clear purpose. The purpose of formative and summative strategies is the continuous improvement of learning and instruction. It is important that both formative and summative assessments are aligned to standards and objectives.

An assessment tool called *performance assessment* is especially compatible with assessing inquiry science learning.

Performance Assessment. Performance assessment is a technique of assessing learning through performance tasks that can be observed or work products that can be examined. Student performances might include measuring, observing, collecting and organizing data, constructing a graph, making a visual or audio presentation, participating in group discussion, presenting an oral defense of work, or presenting a how-to explanation of a procedure. Products presented for assessment could include data tables, graphs, models, reports, and oral or written explanations and problem solutions. Detailed scoring guides, such as checklists and rubrics, are developed and used with performance tasks to judge performance.

Performance assessment techniques make it possible to gather data on the processes of learning rather than just the outcomes, and to assess *how* students know rather than merely what they know. Performance assessments are often embedded in daily instruction, rather than administered at the end of the week or after a series of lessons.

Student participation is a key component of successful assessment and evaluation systems. If students are to participate successfully in inquiry, they need to be clear about the objectives and criteria for good work, assess their own efforts in light of the criteria, and share responsibility in making judgments and taking action (Atkin, Black, & Coffey, 2001).

Ongoing, formative assessment provides a basis for teacher scaffolding of student understanding.

Scaffolding

In *scaffolding* student learning, the teacher supplies enough external support for students to be successful with the various inquiry tasks. The teacher might help learners at various steps in the inquiry process as they formulate the focus question for an investigation, plan and carry out procedures for data collection, and make sense of the data and answer the question posed. The younger the children and the less experience they have with scientific inquiry, the more scaffolding assistance they will probably need and the more structured the inquiry lessons will need to be. Due largely to language and cultural differences, English Language Learners (ELLs) profit from careful teacher scaffolding.

To scaffold the learning process for students, inquiry teachers might provide suggestions, questions, prompts, or hints. They might also guide students to clarify, elaborate, or justify their investigation procedures and findings. Teachers might even choose to provide necessary terms, concepts, and principles to students through formal, direct instruction. Textbooks, videos, the Internet, and other means might also be used to help students develop knowledge needed to support understanding.

An important skill in the art of teaching is to know when to scaffold a student's learning and when to allow it to take its own course. Just as scaffolds in a building project are designed to be taken down when the building walls are strong, scaffolding support in teaching should be gradually removed or "faded" (Ormrod, 1999) as students develop science knowledge and inquiry processes. In the long run, students should develop their own self-regulated strategies to guide learning.

The PALS (Performance Assessment Links in Science) website has collected many excellent performance assessment examples from the World Wide Web. Peruse the site at http://pals.sri.com/index.html.

About the Science Activities in This Book

This book presents for your use a wealth of physical science, life science, and earth and space science activities. Through engaging in these activities, children develop a better understanding of science and how the world works. At the same time, they develop their abilities to inquire—to ask questions about the world around them, to investigate and gather data, and to use their observations as evidence to construct reasonable explanations for the questions posed (see Figure I-3). Furthermore, they develop an understanding of the nature of scientific inquiry (see Figure I-4).

The activities in this book should not be thought of as complete lesson plans; building lesson plans and sequences is something that teachers should do for themselves. Rather, the activities are just that—activities that can be incorporated into lesson plans.

To assist and guide you in the lesson planning process, relevant *Standards and Concepts and Principles That Support the Standards* are given for each activity or for groups of activities on common science topics. Targeted student *Objectives* for building understanding and connecting activities to *Standards* are given. *Relevant Safety Precautions* and *Materials* needed are also provided.

All students should develop abilities to:
- ask questions about objects, organisms, and events in the environment;
- plan and conduct simple investigations;
- use appropriate tools and techniques to gather and interpret data;
- use evidence and scientific knowledge to develop explanations; and
- communicate investigations, data, and explanations to others.

Figure I-3   NSES science as inquiry standards.
Source: Based on the *National Science Education Standards.*

All students should understand:
- Scientific investigations involve asking and answering a question about the world.
- Scientists use different kinds of investigations depending on the questions they are trying to answer.
- Simple instruments, such as magnifiers, thermometers, and rulers, provide more information than scientists obtain using only their senses.
- Scientists develop explanations using observations (evidence) and what they already know about the world (scientific knowledge).
- Scientists make their investigations and results public.
- Scientists review, repeat, and ask questions about the results of other scientists' work.

Figure I-4   NSES standards for understanding the nature of scientific inquiry.
Source: Based on the *National Science Education Standards.*

Using the Science Activities in This Book

The science activities in this book should be thought of as "bare bones" outlines that must be "fleshed out" through lesson planning and instruction. For example, engage activities presented here provide only questions to focus inquiry. You must add activities that arouse motivation and interest and elicit information on students' relevant prior knowledge to expand the basic structure of the engage phase.

Each activity in the book is organized according to the 5-E model of instruction. The activities focus primarily on the first three Es of the instructional model: engage, explore, and explain. In addition, examples of elaborate and evaluate activities are given in some of the activities, which can serve as models as you develop your own elaborate and evaluate activities. Activities that help students understand the nature of science and scientific inquiry are occasionally given within the content of a 5-E activity.

Although the activities in this book may be used individually, most of them are arranged sequentially in clusters to provide a comprehensive view of the phenomena, concepts, and principles of each topic.

Getting Started with Inquiry Science

Following are some suggestions for using the activities in this book for your own classroom inquiry lessons.

Step 1: Preparation

- Organize students into cooperative groups.
- Organize materials needed by teams in small boxes or bags, or on trays.
- Try out activities before they are introduced to students. By trying out activities beforehand, you can anticipate questions and ensure that the activity will work. Finding out in the middle of a lesson that you do not have enough materials or cannot get the equipment to work properly can discourage you or your students.

Step 2: Engage

At the engage phase, you should present an initiating activity that leads to a question students can investigate. The initiating activity should also enhance motivation and interest and provide you with an understanding of the prior knowledge students bring to a lesson. Insofar as possible, you should build on students' prior knowledge at every phase of inquiry.

Remember to:

- Keep the engage portion of the lesson brief and open-ended.
- Ask or help students ask a specific key question that can be investigated.
- Ask questions or use demonstratons and hands-on activities to find out students' prior knowledge and conceptions or misconceptions.
- Tell students they will be exploring this and other related questions.
- Review general and specific safety procedures with students (see Figure I-5).
- Introduce or review pertinent activity information and cooperative group procedures such as, "When we begin, move quickly and quietly into your team. Stay with your team at all times. Speak softly, listen and respond to one another, and take turns. Concentrate on your assigned job."

Safety guidelines for students:

* Always follow the safety procedures outlined by the teacher.
* Never put any materials in your mouth.
* Avoid touching your face, mouth, ears, or eyes while working with chemicals, plants, or animals.
* Always wash your hands immediately after using materials, especially chemicals or animals.
* Always be careful when using sharp or pointed tools. Always make sure that you protect your eyes and those of your neighbors.
* Wear American National Standards Institute approved safety goggles (with Z87 printed on the goggles) whenever activities are done in which there is a potential risk to eye safety.
* Report all accidents, even small ones, to your teacher.
* Follow directions and ask questions if you're unsure of what to do.
* Behave responsibly during science investigations.

Safety guidelines for teachers:

* Examine each of the science activities carefully for possible safety hazards. Eliminate or be prepared to address all anticipated problems.
* Be particularly alert to potential hazards related to children handling and caring for animals. Instruct children in the proper care and handling of classroom pets, fish, or other live organisms used as part of science activities.
* Consider eliminating all activities using open flames. Use hot plates as heat sources, but make sure that the hot plates are not in an area where children might touch them.
* Consider eliminating activities in which students are required to taste substances.

Additional safety suggestions are given in Appendix A.

Figure I-5   Guidelines for safety.

Step 3: Distribution of Science Materials

Do not begin distributing materials until step 2 is completed. Then, have the materials managers collect science materials from the central materials station and deliver them to their team station. This step can make or break the best-planned activity. Make certain that materials managers are reliable and know the specifics of their jobs before they begin.

Step 4: Explore

* Guide students as they consider what data they should collect and what they will do to collect the data.
* As each team begins its work, move from team to team to ensure the proper distribution of materials has occurred and that teams have necessary materials and are proceeding safely. Also check that students understand their goal during the exploration session, how they will collect and record data, why they will do it that way, and how that data connects to the initiating question. Depending on the amount of

scaffolding needed, students might develop their own plan for investigation or they might follow suggestions or a structure provided by their teacher.

- Be careful that you do not give away the "answer" during the explore phase. If students ask questions, respond with a question that will guide them in their exploration. Tell students very little about what can be expected to happen. You want students to make observations, discuss what they observe, and have a chance to make predictions and/or inferences from their observations. Otherwise, they are likely to discover exactly what you have told them they will discover. Part of the joy of exploring is not knowing what to expect!

- Resist presenting science vocabulary during the engage and explore phases. Do not give students the vocabulary words that will describe what they observe before they do the activity. Let students engage in the inquiry and experience the phenomena they observe. It is after exploration that science vocabulary will have more meaning for students.

Step 5: Explain

- Instruct reporter/recorders to report team results to the whole class. In some cases it will be appropriate to post team data on a class summary chart, visible to all. Conduct a discussion of the reported results of the groups. Then ask for students' conceptions of ideas learned and discuss the similarities and discrepancies of team data.

- As students exchange their ideas, listen to how they have conceptualized what they think. Often, they will have developed erroneous beliefs about how something "works." Misconceptions are difficult to change. Simply pointing out alternative and naive conceptions will not generally change what students believe. You can employ several strategies to help students confront and reconsider their alternative conceptions:
  a. Ask questions that challenge students' current beliefs.
  b. Present phenomena that students cannot adequately explain within their existing perspectives.
  c. Engage students in discussions of the pros and cons of various explanations.
  d. Point out explicitly the differences between students' beliefs and "reality."
  e. Show how the correct explanation of an event or phenomenon is more plausible or makes more sense than anything students themselves can offer (Ormrod, 2004; Roth & Anderson, 1988).

- Although the child must do the interpretation work, teachers must be ready to assist in the process. During the explain phase of inquiry, it is appropriate for teachers to supply vocabulary terms, invent relevant concepts and principles, and give hints and even complete explanations to children. But always follow this principle: *Tell only after student explorations.*

Step 6: Elaborate

Suggest questions and activities that allow students to apply what they have learned to new and novel situations. Principal investigators then lead their teams in inquiring into the new questions. Follow up with appropriate class discussion. Also, have students extend their learning with readings, Internet research, or other individualized reinforcement of concepts and principles being learned.

Step 7: Evaluate

Use ongoing, formative assessments at every phase of the lesson as a basis for scaffolding and continued improvement of instruction and learning. All assessments should be directly related to lesson objectives. Vary your methods for assessing understanding of individual team members and the group as a whole. Watching and listening to students, asking them questions, and using performance tasks and traditional assessment items could be used as a basis for evaluation.

Step 8: Team Cleanup

Maintenance directors, with the assistance of team members, should arrange materials so they can be easily reused, return all supplies to designated areas, and ensure that work areas are cleaned. This step might occur at other transition points in the lesson as well, particularly after explore or elaborate. Note that cleanup is a team effort.

The most important element in these inquiry activities is that students can discover the joy and wonder of science. And so can you. Have fun!

REFERENCES

American Association for the Advancement of Science. (1993). *Benchmarks for science literacy*. New York: Oxford University Press.

Atkin, J. M., Black, P., & Coffey, J. (Eds.). (2001). *Classroom assessment and the national science education standards*. Washington, DC: National Academy Press.

Bransford, J. D., Brown, A. L., & Cocking, R. R. (Eds.). (1999). *How people learn: Brain, mind, experience, and school*. Washington, DC: National Academy Press.

Hosoume, K., & Barber, J. (1994). *Terrarium habitats*. Berkeley: Great Explorations in Math and Science (GEMS), Lawrence Hall of Science, University of California.

Ingram, M. (1993). *Bottle biology*. Madison: Bottle Biology Project, Department of Plant Pathology, College of Agricultural and Life Sciences, University of Wisconsin.

Jones, R. M. (1990). *Teaming up! The inquiry task group management system user's guide*. LaPorte, TX: ITGROUP.

Lee, O. (2002). Promoting scientific inquiry with elementary students from diverse cultures and languages. In W. C. Secada (Ed.), *Review of research in education* (Vol. 26, pp. 23–69). Washington, DC: American Education Research Association.

Lowery, L. F. (Ed.). (1997). *Pathways to the science standards: Elementary school edition*. Arlington, VA: National Science Teachers Association.

National Research Council. (1996). *National science education standards*. Washington, DC: National Academy Press.

National Research Council. (2000). *Inquiry and the national science education standards: A guide for teaching and learning*. Washington DC: National Academy Press.

Ormrod, J. (1999). *Human learning* (3rd ed.) Upper Saddle River, NJ: Merrill/Prentice Hall.

Ormrod, J. (2004). *Human learning* (4th ed.) Upper Saddle River, NJ: Merrill/Prentice Hall.

Roth, K., & Anderson, C. (1988). Promoting conceptual change learning from science textbooks. In P. Ramsden (Ed.), *Improving learning: New perspectives*. London: Kogan Page.

Rowe, M. B. (1973). *Teaching science as continuous inquiry*. New York: McGraw-Hill.

Rutherford, F. J., & Ahlgren, A. (1990). *Science for all Americans*. New York: Oxford University Press.

Seaborg, G. T. (1991, Fall/Winter). Some thoughts on discovery. *GEMS Network News*. Berkeley: Lawrence Hall of Science, University of California, p. 5.

Trowbridge, L., & Bybee, R. (2000). *Teaching secondary school science* (7th ed.). Upper Saddle River, NJ: Merrill/Prentice Hall.

SECTION II
Physical Science Activities

I. PROPERTIES OF MATTER

The simple activities on properties of matter included here enable children to exercise their natural curiosity as they manipulate, observe, and classify common objects and materials in their environment and continue to form explanations of the world. Consistent with the *National Science Education Standards*, topics studied include describing and classifying properties of material objects and the nature of solids, liquids, and gases (air).

Science Standards on Properties of Matter

Students should develop an understanding of

- properties of objects and materials (K–4).
- changes of properties in matter (5–8).

Concepts and Principles That Support the Standards

- Objects have many observable properties (K–4).
- Objects are made of one or more materials (K–4).
- Properties can be used to separate or sort a group of objects or materials (K–4).
- Materials can exist in different states—solids, liquids, and gases (K–4).

A. PROPERTIES OF MATERIAL OBJECTS

▶ *Science Background*

All material objects may be described by their unique properties. By dynamically investigating and classifying properties of different objects, children can function much as research scientists do.

Objectives

1. Define *property* as a characteristic of an object—something you can see, touch, hear, smell, or taste.
2. Develop descriptions and classifications of objects based on their properties.
3. Use description and classification to identify the most significant properties of buttons and how different properties of buttons might be related.

Materials

For each group:

- Collection of 20 to 30 buttons differing in many ways, including color, shape, number of holes, etc.
- One small tray to hold buttons or other objects to be observed and grouped
- Button bingo cards

Safety Precautions

- Caution the students not to put the buttons or other small objects in their mouths, ears, nostrils, or eyes.

1. HOW ARE BUTTONS ALIKE AND DIFFERENT? (K–2)

ENGAGE

a. With the children in a large group, hold up an object, such as a ball. Ask: *What can you tell me about this object? Yes, it is a ball, but what else can you tell me about it? What can you observe about it, using your senses? What is its shape, its color, its texture?* Then hold up a large button. Ask: *Can you use your senses to observe this?* When children recognize that they can make observations about the button, too, tell them: In your groups you will make observations in order to play a game with lots of buttons.

EXPLORE

b. Organize children into cooperative groups. Give each small group of children about 20 different buttons on a tray. Observe the buttons and describe them to one another. Using a gamelike format similar to "I Spy," allow each child to describe a button in sufficient detail (without touching it or otherwise designating it) for the other children in the small group to pick it out. They might describe the button's color, its shape, its texture, the number of holes it has, and other properties.

EXPLAIN

c. Gather children as a whole class and ask: *What words did you use to describe the buttons you observed?* On the board, under the heading *Properties*, make a list of the words suggested by the children.

   Discuss with the children the various words that can be used to describe the object. Tell the children that, in science, the term *property* refers to a characteristic of an object or material—things you can observe with your senses. Discuss other uses of the word *property* with the children if they bring them up; be sure to emphasize the way this word is used in science.[1]

---

[1]For a delightful introduction to properties of buttons, see *The Button Box* by Margarette S. Reid (illustrated by Sarah Chamberlain), New York: Dutton Children's Books, 1990.

ELABORATE

d. Ask: *What are buttons for? How are buttons used?* Answers might relate to the function of buttons to fasten garments or the ornamental nature of buttons. Encourage children to find buttons on their clothing or on other children's clothing. You might want to have some extra clothing with buttons on it available for students to examine, as well as books or pictures that show buttons in use. *What properties of buttons relate to how they work? What properties of buttons relate to their ornamental use?* Encourage students to discuss these questions in their small groups, then have groups share their ideas in a whole-class discussion.

EVALUATE

e. Tell each student to select one button. Challenge them to list five properties of their button. Do this orally with very young children. If the class is already writing words, ask students to write the properties on a card with their name written on it and a hole punched in it. Provide 30 cm long pieces of string, wire, or dental floss for students to use to attach their button to their cards. The following rubric could be used to evaluate student's understanding of the term *property*:

Exemplary—successfully lists five properties of the button
Proficient—successfully lists three or four properties of the button
Developing—successfully lists one or two properties of the button
None—unable to list any of the button's properties[1]

2. WHAT ARE SOME DIFFERENT WAYS YOU CAN GROUP BUTTONS? (K–2)

ENGAGE

a. Ask: *How can you group your buttons? How many different ways can you find to group them?*

EXPLORE

b. Tell the children to sort their buttons into groups based on the properties of the buttons. For example, children might make groups of red buttons, blue buttons, green buttons, and multicolored buttons.

c. As children sort their buttons, circulate among them and ask such questions as: *How are the buttons in this group alike? How are they different from one another?*

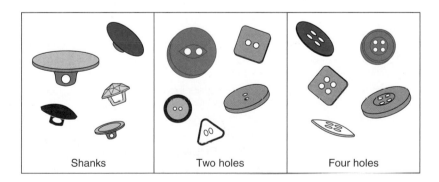

| Shanks | Two holes | Four holes |

d. Let two cooperative groups come together. Members of one group should study the button classification system of the other group and try to identify the basis of the classification.

EXPLAIN

e. Ask: *How did you sort the buttons? How many different ways was your group able to sort your buttons? Is one way "best"?* Lead the students to the idea that objects can be classified according to various properties and that there is not just one way to sort objects as long as the sorter can explain the property used for sorting.

f. Show the children how to classify their buttons according to two properties. For example, in the first stage of classification they may get a class of all red buttons. In the second stage of classification, they may group the red buttons into two groups, such as round and not round. Thus, they end up with a group of red buttons that are round and a group of red buttons that are not round.

Nature of Scientific Inquiry

g. Tell students that scientists classify (sort, group) trees, leaves, minerals, and other objects and organisms. Ask: *Why do scientists classify things? What is the purpose of classification?* Through discussion, bring out the advantage that through classification, we can simplify our thinking by dealing with a few groups rather than many individual elements.

ELABORATE

h. Let student groups practice multistage classification as you monitor their work. Ask questions like: *How did you sort the buttons first? How did you sort this subgroup of buttons?*

i. For additional practice, prepare several different 9-square (3 by 3) button bingo cards, with button properties named in each square. As in the diagram, include single properties such as red, round, two-holed, wooden, and cloth. Also include some multiple-property squares, such as red and round, or two-holed and plastic. Write different properties of buttons in each square of button bingo cards, as in the diagram.

RED	RED AND ROUND	NOT RED
CLOTH	ROUND	WOODEN
NOT ROUND	TWO HOLES AND PLASTIC	TWO HOLES

SAMPLE BUTTON BINGO CARD

Pass a button bingo card facedown to each pair of children. Give each pair several bingo tokens. Draw buttons from a bag of buttons. Call on children to name different properties of each button you draw. Instruct the children that they are to place a token in each square on their cards that contains a property named. Circulate among the children and interact with them about their understanding of the meaning of properties and classification. If you use a competitive group structure, winners might be the children who are able to correctly place three tokens in a row, column, or diagonally, or the children who are able to place the most tokens on their button bingo card.

EVALUATE

j. Use a digital camera to take pictures of different groupings of buttons. Number the pictures and put them in a slide show for the class to see. For each picture students should write or orally explain the property by which the buttons in the slide were sorted. If the picture shows a multistage classification, they should explain the classification steps that might have been used. Students' understanding of classification can be assessed based on their explanations.

 ## B. PROPERTIES OF LIQUIDS

▶ *Science Background*

Students can conduct simple investigations with water that can be explained through use of an abstract, mental model. In the model of water developed through the activities in this section, water consists of tiny particles or droplets. These particles of water are attracted to each other. Scientists refer to this force of attraction as *bonding*. For children, water drops are *sticky* or *grabby*.

As they develop new understandings of liquids, students also continue to develop their abilities to inquire and their understandings of the nature of scientific inquiry.

 NSES   **Science Standards**

Students should develop an understanding of

• properties of objects and materials (K–4).

Concepts and Principles That Support the Standards

• Objects have many observable properties (K–4).
• Materials can exist in different states—solids, liquids, and gases (K–4).

Objectives

1. Use simple apparatus and tools to gather data and extend the senses.
2. Describe the behavior of water and other liquids under various conditions.
3. Describe and explain the bonding model of liquid particles.
4. Use observational evidence and the model of the bonding of liquid particles to explain the behavior of water and other liquids under different conditions.
5. Set up simple controlled experiment "fair tests" to explore the behavior of water and other liquids.

Materials

Each group will need the following materials:

- Two 30 ml medicine cups
- Beaker for water
- Magnifying lens
- Two medicine droppers (use identical droppers for the whole class)
- 15 cm squares of aluminum foil, wax paper, and plastic wrap
- 30–45 small paper clips

For the teacher:

- Small container of liquid dishwashing soap
- Toothpicks

Safety Precautions

- Caution the students not to taste any liquid substances, unless approved by a responsible adult.
- When children work with water, provide table coverings, such as newspapers, and plenty of paper towels to absorb spills. Clean up spills promptly.

1. HOW MUCH WATER CAN HEAP UP IN A CUP? (2–4)

ENGAGE

a. Pouring water from the beaker, students should fill the medicine cup completely full of water until some overflows. When the children's cups seem completely filled, ask: *How many drops of water from a medicine dropper do you think you can add to your filled cup before it overflows?* Tell the children to make a prediction and record it before they carry out the activity.

EXPLORE

b. Tell your students to hold the medicine dropper about 2 cm above the cup as in the diagram. Slowly drop water into the cup, counting the number of drops needed for the water to overflow. As they count drops, students should observe the shape of the surface of water in the cup and what happens to water drops as they are added to the cup. Instruct them to bend down so that they are eye level with the top of the cup when they observe it.

EXPLAIN

c. Let students chart their predictions and actual counts on the chalkboard or a transparency. Note and discuss variations in the data. If you think there is too much variation among groups, you might ask the groups to repeat their investigation under more common procedures.

Ask: How many drops did you add before the water spilled over the edge of the cup? How does your tested result compare with your prediction? How would you describe the shape of the water above the rim of the cup? What happens to each drop of water as it hits the surface of water in the cup? What happens to the last drop added to the cup, the one that makes the water overflow?

Encourage each group to contribute to the discussion of their drop data and their observations.

d. *Ask: What keeps the water from overflowing as water drops are added?*

As children discuss possible answers to this question, begin to develop a mental model of water, with water consisting of particles or drops that are all attracted to one another. Lead children to understand that water heaps up in medicine cups and does not overflow because water particles bond to, stick to, or grab on to one another. This simple model of liquids anticipates and lays a foundation for the introduction of atomic and molecular forces in later grades. If the children mention atoms and molecules of water (H_2O), listen but do not pursue the idea at this time. Rather, continue to focus on the notion that water is made up of tiny droplets that attract one another.

ELABORATE

e. As an extension, ask: *How many drops of water do you think you can place on the surface of a clean penny? Can you add more drops to the head or tail of a penny?*

Lead children to make and record predictions, and then to design and conduct investigations to answer their questions. Chart the results on the board and discuss the results.

EVALUATE

f. To get an idea of your student's mastery level for Objective 5, apply the following rubric to the procedures they develop and use in their groups as you informally monitor their work on the second question.

Exemplary: In addition to the standards for Proficient, multiple trials are used.

Proficient: Except for side of penny, all variables are kept constant (i.e., height of dropper above the penny, angle the dropper is held).

Developing: Students talk about the importance of holding variables constant, but don't actually do it when conducting the experiment.

None: Students proceed without a plan, just add drops to pennies without regard to variables that might affect the outcome.

2. HOW MANY PAPER CLIPS CAN YOU ADD TO A CUP OF WATER? (2–4)

ENGAGE

a. Using the beaker, students should fill the 30 ml cup completely full of water again. *Ask: How many paper clips do you think you can add to the water in the cup before it flows over the rim?* Tell the children to make and test a prediction.

EXPLORE   b. Tell students to gently slide small paper clips one at a time into the water in the cup and count the number of paper clips needed to make the water flow over the rim. Remind them to record their data. Tell them to repeat this activity two more times. Students should discuss what happened in their group while other groups finish collecting data.

EXPLAIN   c. Ask each group to chart results on the board, then discuss similarities and differences. Ask: *How do your predictions compare with actual results? Why do you think you were asked to do three trials in your group? Why do you think so many paper clips could be added to the cup before the water overflowed?* Students should explain that the water did not overflow at first because of the attractive forces between water droplets. Even though putting in more paper clips made the water level rise, the water's surface was still "sticking together" as in the previous investigation.

Nature of Scientific Inquiry   d. As children carry out these investigations of water, occasionally emphasize to them that they are *doing* science and *being* scientists. They are asking questions, gathering evidence, building a model of water drops, and using their model to construct explanations of what they see. Point out that scientists don't do an experiment one time before drawing a conclusion. They conduct many trials.

....

3. CAN YOU GET A PAPER CLIP TO "FLOAT" ON TOP OF WATER? WHY DOES THE PAPER CLIP NOT SINK? (2–4)

ENGAGE   a. Ask: *What can you do to make a paper clip "float" on the surface of water? If you push the paper clip down, will it bob back up?*

EXPLORE   b. Allow students to try to make a paper clip stay on the top of water in a medicine cup or glass. To accomplish this task, bend a second paper clip so that a cradle is formed (see diagram). Place the other paper clip on the cradle and lower it into the water as in the diagram. The paper clip should stay suspended on top of the water.

Use wire cradle to place another
paper clip on water.

EXPLAIN

c. Ask: *Why does the paper clip stay suspended on the top of the water?* (Some students may suggest that it's floating, but it really isn't.) *Did the paper clip stay on the top of the water every time you put it in the cup? Why?* Tell students that to explain why the paper clip stayed on top of the water, we must connect observations to our model of water. Lead students to understand that because of the attractive forces among water drops, the surface of the water acts like a skin. The paper clip does not float in the water, like boats do, but is supported by water's skinlike effect. The paper clip rides on the top of the water's skin. If you push the paper clip down in the water, it breaks the skin and goes to the bottom of the container and will not bob back up. Scientists refer to the skinlike effect of water as *surface tension*.

ELABORATE

d. Show some images of water striders and other organisms that are walking on the surface of water. Ask: *How do some bugs walk on water?* (Students may suggest surface tension or floating.) Explain that similar to the paper clip, a water strider is able to walk on the "skin" at the surface of the water. Challenge students to find other objects or organisms that stay on the surface of water because of water tension.

4. WHAT DOES SOAP DO TO THE SKINLIKE EFFECT OF WATER? (2–4)

ENGAGE

a. Ask: *How can we break or overcome the skinlike effect on the surface of water?*

EXPLORE

b. Tell students to use a beaker to fill the 30 ml cup completely full of water again. Tell them to add drops of water to the cup until it is about ready to flow over the rim. Take two toothpicks. Dip one of the toothpicks in a container of liquid dishwashing soap. Go from group to group, touching the end of the clean toothpick and then the soapy end of the other toothpick to the surface of the water in the cups.

EXPLAIN

c. Ask: *What did you see happen?* (The water flowed over the rim of the cup.) *What do you think was on the second toothpick? Why do you think the water flowed over the rim of the cup when it was touched with the soapy toothpick? Why did we use two toothpicks, a clean one and a soapy one?* (This is a controlled experiment. Using two toothpicks, a clean one and a soapy one, shows that it was not the toothpick, but what was on it that caused the water to overflow.)

d. Through discussion, lead the students to apply the model of water drops, adding the idea that soap tends to break the bonds that water drops have for one another. When the bonds are broken, the weight of the water causes it to flow over the rim of the cup.

5. WHAT HAPPENS TO WATER DROPS ON DIFFERENT SURFACES? (2–4)

ENGAGE

a. Ask: *Do water drops look and act the same on different kinds of surfaces? How could we investigate to find out?*

b. Provide each group small squares (about 15 cm by 15 cm) of wax paper, aluminum foil, and plastic wrap. Tell students to use a medicine dropper to place three or four drops of water on the wax paper. Ask: *How would you describe the shape of the water drops?*

c. Tell students to push the drops of water around with a pencil point. Ask: *What happens to the drop when you push on it with a pencil point? What happens when you push several drops near each other?*

d. Tell them to investigate and compare what water drops look like and what they do on each of the three surfaces—wax paper, aluminum foil, and plastic wrap (see diagram). Provide magnifying lenses to enhance student observations.

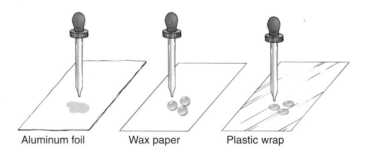

Aluminum foil   Wax paper   Plastic wrap

Ask: *What is the smallest size drop you can make? What is the largest size drop you can make? On which of the three surfaces does water heap up the most? spread out the most? What is the shape of water drops on wax paper? on aluminum foil? on plastic wrap?*

e. Ask: *What did you find out? Why do you think the drops were heaped up on wax paper and spread out on aluminum foil?*

Using *evidence* from the children's investigations, invent (directly teach) the terms *cohesion* and *adhesion*. The bonding of a material to the same kind of material is known as **cohesion**. Water drops cohere to one another. The attraction of one material for another material is called **adhesion**. Adhesive tape bonds to different kinds of material, such as skin. Add the notions of cohesion and adhesion to the model of water drops bonding to one another.

Help children understand that the adhesive attraction between water and aluminum foil is greater than the adhesive attraction between water and wax paper. Thus, water drops can bead up more on wax paper because they do not have to overcome a great adhesive force for the surface.

ELABORATE

f. Ask: *Do you think it would be easier to use a toothpick to lead a drop of paper around on wax paper or on aluminum foil? Why do you think so? Try it and see. What differences do you observe for the two surfaces? Why do you think these differences happen?*

Guide children to plan and conduct an investigation and to use their data to answer these questions. With your assistance, children should reason that because there is greater adhesion (greater stickiness) between aluminum foil and water than between wax paper and water, it is harder to lead a drop of water around on aluminum foil than on wax paper. The aluminum foil grabs on to the drop more than the wax paper does.

EVALUATE

g. To determine if the students can apply the two terms introduced in this lesson, have them respond to the following items.

　1. Cohesion describes how well a liquid. . .

　2. Adhesion describes how well a liquid. . .

You put a drop of water on each of three surfaces. The following drawing shows how the drops look when viewed from the side.

Drops on Different Surfaces

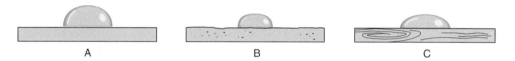

A　　　　　　　　　B　　　　　　　　　C

　3. To which surface does water have the greatest adhesion? How do you know?

　4. On which of the surfaces shown previously would it be easiest to lead around a drop of water with a toothpick? Why?

You put a drop of three different liquids onto the same surface. The following drawing shows how the drops look when viewed from the side.

Different Liquids on Same Surface

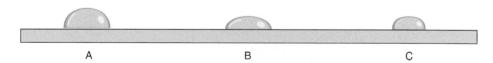

A　　　　　　　　　B　　　　　　　　　C

　5. Which liquid has the greatest cohesion? How do you know?

　6. Which of the drops shown in the previous figure would be the easiest to lead around with a toothpick on this surface? Why?

6. WHEN THE SURFACES ARE SLANTED, WILL WATER DROPS RUN DOWN FASTER ON WAX PAPER, PLASTIC WRAP, OR ALUMINUM FOIL? (3–5)

ENGAGE

a. Ask: *When the surfaces are slanted, on which surface will water drops slide or roll down fastest? What could you do to find out?*

EXPLORE

b. Help students plan a *controlled experiment (fair test)* to determine on which surface the water drops run down more quickly (see the diagram). They might, for example, control the slant of the surface and vary the type of surface (aluminum foil, plastic wrap, or wax paper).

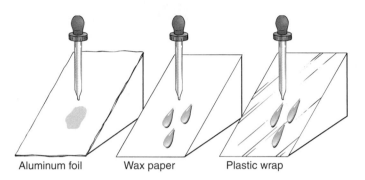

Aluminum foil   Wax paper   Plastic wrap

EXPLAIN

c. Ask: *What were your results? Why do you think the water drops ran more quickly down the wax paper ramp?* With your assistance, children should explain that water drops do not adhere or stick to wax paper as much as they do to aluminum foil and plastic wrap. Thus, the water drops ran down the wax paper ramp more quickly.

Nature of Scientific Inquiry

d. Ask: *What is a fair test or controlled investigation? What question are we trying to answer in the water drop race? Why is the water drop race fair? What is controlled in the investigation? What is deliberately changed or manipulated? Why do scientists use controlled investigations?*

   Discuss the meaning of fair tests or controlled investigations with the children. The question of which type of surface the water drops will roll or slide down fastest is answered through a fair test. The test is fair if none of the surfaces has an unfair advantage, such as being more slanted than the other surfaces. Scientists use fair tests in order to keep clear which variable is making a difference in an investigation.

e. Ask: *What does it mean to explain something? How do scientists develop explanations? How do they know their explanations are correct?*

   Through discussion, lead children to understand that to explain an event means to use observations and science knowledge to show that the event is reasonable and could be expected to occur. Explain that scientific explanations are tentative ideas about the way things are. They can be altered with new observations and new scientific knowledge.

7. WHY DO SEVERAL STREAMS OF WATER COHERE INTO ONE STREAM? (2–4)

ENGAGE

a. About 2 cm apart as shown in the diagram, puncture four very small holes in a horizontal line about 2 cm from the bottom of a 1 gallon plastic jug. Put masking tape over the holes.

   Note: Do not make the holes too large. Also, be sure the holes are very close together. Ask: *What do you think will happen when water is poured into this container and the masking tape is removed? How many jets of water will you get coming out of the holes in the bottom of the plastic jug?*

EXPLORE

b. This activity might be conducted as a teacher demonstration with students assisting. Hold the jug over a sink or large tub, pour water into the jug, and remove the tape. Ask: *What do you observe?*

Tell students to pinch the four jets of water together just as if they were going to pinch someone. Repeat this procedure several times to see if it always works the same way.

EXPLAIN

c. Ask: *What do you observe? Why do you think this happened?*

Lead students to use the water drop model and the concept of cohesion (the bonding of water drops) to explain why the four streams of water cohered into one stream.

 ## C. PROPERTIES OF OOBLECK

▶ *Science Background*

Investigating and describing the properties of oobleck can be a fascinating task for students grades 1–8. Oobleck is the name given to a special mixture of cornstarch, water, and food coloring that has some unique properties. The substance flows like liquid when you pour it, but keeps its shape like a solid when you hit it hard and fast.

You may have recognized the name *oobleck* from the Dr. Seuss children's book, *Bartholomew and the Oobleck*. Other books that treat this strange substance or its variations include *Horrible Harry and the Green Slime* by Suzy Kline and *The Slimy Book* by Babette Cole.

NSES Science Standards

All students should develop an understanding of

• properties of objects and materials (K–4).
• changes in properties in matter (5–8).

Concepts and Principles That Support the Standards

• Objects have many observable properties (K–4).
• Materials can exist in different states—solid, liquid, and gas (K–4).

Objectives

1. Conduct simple investigations to determine the properties of oobleck.
2. Describe properties of oobleck and compare them with various properties of solids and liquids.
3. Explain how their investigations of oobleck are like what scientists do when they investigate.

Materials

- Four boxes cornstarch
- Plastic bowls
- Water
- Post-It Notes

▶ *Preparation*

Pour 4¼ cups of water into a large bowl and add four boxes of cornstarch and another 2½ cups of water. Swirl and tip the bowl to level the mixture, mix it well with a large spoon or your hands, and then set the bowl aside.

Safety Precautions

- Oobleck is strange but is safe to handle.
- However, oobleck can be quite messy. Have plenty of newspaper around for children to use as a work surface. Impress on the children that part of doing science is to maintain a clean, orderly laboratory for investigating. Thus, they must be actively responsible for the cleanliness of their own work area.
- To protect their clothing, let the children wear large shirts over their regular clothes, as in art. Or give the children "lab coats" made of plastic grocery sacks with armholes and a neck hole cut in the bottom.
- Do not put oobleck down the sink as it will clog the drain. If oobleck falls on the floor, scoop most of it up and mop up the remainder with a damp sponge. If it falls on a carpet area, scoop up what you can, then vacuum after it dries.

1. WHAT ARE THE PROPERTIES OF OOBLECK? (1–6)

ENGAGE

a. Ask the class if they remember what *property* means in science. If they are are not sure, remind the children that a *property* is a characteristic of something that can be seen, heard, smelled, or felt by the senses or detected by instruments, such as magnifying lenses, that extend the senses. Tell the children that you have a very strange substance that you will call oobleck, after the Dr. Seuss story, *Bartholomew and the Oobleck*. Ask: *What are the properties of oobleck? What can you do to find out?*

EXPLORE

b. Tell children they are to play the role of scientists in investigating the properties of this strange substance. Each group will get a sample of oobleck and a pad of Post-It notes. Instruct them to write down as many properties of oobleck as they can discover, one property per Post-It note. (Suggest that they write darkly with large letters so that the property can be read from across the room.)

c. Pour about a cup of oobleck into each plastic bowl, give a bowl to each cooperative group, and encourage each group to explore this strange substance and record their findings. Some properties children might observe include:

> *It is gooey, sticky, and white; you can squeeze it into a ball but when you release the pressure it seems to melt into a puddle; it is soft when you move your hand through it slowly, and hard when you move your hand fast; it dries out when left on paper for more than 10 seconds.*

When they can think of no more properties to write down, ask each group to sort its pile of Post-Its according to the importance of the property observed. Have them put a star on the two notes they think have the most important properties written on them.

EXPLAIN

d. Ask cooperative group reporters to read one property their group has found and post it on a chart for all to see. If any other groups have that property, they should add it to the chart at this time. Moving from group to group, continue until all properties have been posted. Discuss which of the properties the children think are most important or distinctive for oobleck and why they picked those properties.

e. Show the children a solid object and a liquid in a container.
Ask: *Do these two things have the same properties?* (No) *Are these things the same state of matter?* (No, one's a liquid and one's a solid) *Which is a liquid? How do you know?* (Because of the way it acts; its properties) *What are the main properties of liquids?* (Flowing easily and taking the shape of its container) *Which is a solid? How do you know?* (Because of the way it acts; its properties) *What are the main properties of solids?* (Maintaining its shape) Discuss whether oobleck is best classified as a liquid or a solid. Discuss whether oobleck should be called a solid or a liquid—or do we need a third category? Consider using a graphic organizer such as a three-column chart or a Venn diagram to support this discussion.

Nature of Scientific Inquiry

f. Ask the students to identify and list the ways they acted like scientists during their investigation of oobleck. In their lists they might include *asked questions, talked, searched, planned, used magnifying lenses, experimented, recorded, explained, discussed, argued, defined, criticized, changed ideas, decided, asked more questions.*

Discuss with students how what they did fits within these more formal statements in the NSES Inquiry Standards (see Figure I-3).

Ask students to give specific examples of what they did that is like one or more of these processes of scientists.

 ## D. PROPERTIES OF WHITE POWDERS

▶ *Science Background*

Investigating the physical and chemical properties of materials forms the basis for an exciting inquiry for children. This set of activities involves the study of four common white powders: granulated sugar, table salt, baking soda, and cornstarch. At first, it seems hard to distinguish among the powders; they appear to have closely similar properties. But when observed through a magnifier, powders are found to be quite distinctive. Further, chemical tests reveal that the white powders react differently from one another when drops of water, iodine, and vinegar are added to them.

NSES

Science Standards

All students should develop an understanding of

- properties of objects and materials (K–4).
- changes in properties in matter (5–8).

Concepts and Principles That Support the Standards

- Objects have many observable properties (K–4).
- Materials can exist in different states—solid, liquid, and gas (K–4).
- Substances react chemically in characteristic ways with other substances (5–8).

Objectives

1. Use simple tools and instruments that extend the senses to gather data.
2. Carry out chemical indicator tests to determine how different powders react with water, iodine, and vinegar.
3. Accurately record and analyze data.
4. Use data to draw conclusions.

Materials

For each pair of students:

- Small quantities of salt, granulated sugar, baking soda, cornstarch, and flour
- Medicine droppers
- Plastic spoons
- Zip-lock bag (large enough to hold recording chart)
- Magnifying lenses
- Safety goggles
- Small containers of water, vinegar, and iodine
- Copies of recording chart

Safety Precautions

- Students should wear safety goggles for these investigations with powders.
- Caution children not to taste any of the powders or liquids and to wash their hands after they test each powder.
- Do not put powders in the sink as they may clog drains.

1. WHAT ARE THE DISTINGUISHING PROPERTIES OF COMMON WHITE POWDERS? (3–6)

ENGAGE

a. Ask: *How are sugar and salt different? How are they alike? If you have several white powders, how can you tell them apart?*

Tell the students they will be observing some powders with a magnifier and doing chemical tests, acting like scientists (e.g., forensic chemists) to see what happens when different indicators (water, vinegar, and iodine) are added to different powders.

Prepare data tables like the one in the diagram. Give each team two data tables. Instruct the students to place one of the data table sheets into the plastic bag and seal it, for use as a lab tray. Show the students how to enter data on the other data table.

Explain that the data table provides a record of observations and experiments that we can refer to later. If necessary, remind students how to use a magnifying lens to extend the sense of sight.

DATA TABLE FOR INVESTIGATING WHITE POWDERS

Observations	Powder 1 Granulated Sugar	Powder 2 Table Salt	Powder 3 Baking Soda	Powder 4 Cornstarch
Visual (Magnifying Glass)				
Water Test				
Iodine Test				
Vinegar Test				

Using a Magnifier

To observe an object through a magnifier or magnifying lens, hold the magnifier close to the object, look through the magnifier at the object, then lift the magnifier toward your eye, stopping when the object begins to blur.

Many science classrooms have magnifiers with three lenses. The large lens usually provides a twofold magnification, the medium-sized lens provides a sixfold magnification, and the small lens an eightfold magnification. To provide increased magnification, two or even three magnifiers can be fitted together and used as a single magnifier.

EXPLORE

    b. *Visual observation.* Instruct students to use a magnifying lens to visually observe each powder and to write down their observations on the data table.

    c. Show students how to use the data table/investigation tray to guide their investigations. Data will be recorded on the other data table.

    d. *Water tests.* Students should place a small spoonful of each powder in the water test row on the lab tray (plastic bag with record sheet inside). They should then add several drops of water and mix with a toothpick to see what happens. Observations should be recorded in the data tables.

    e. *Iodine tests.* Instruct students to place a small spoonful of each powder in the iodine test row of the lab tray. Then, they should add a drop or two of iodine to each powder and write down the results in their data tables. Caution the students to be careful. Iodine can stain hands and clothing.

    f. *Vinegar tests.* Students should place a small spoonful of each powder in each vinegar test row of the lab tray. They should then add a drop or two of vinegar to each powder and write down the results in their data tables.

EXPLAIN

    g. *Compare.* Discuss the properties of the four powders that have been revealed through the different chemical tests. Help students to compare the results of their tests with the master chart of properties of white powders shown in the diagram. If necessary, ask students to repeat tests to see what happens.

PROPERTIES OF WHITE POWDERS

Observations	Powder 1 Granulated Sugar	Powder 2 Table Salt	Powder 3 Baking Soda	Powder 4 Cornstarch
Visual (Magnifying Glass)	White crystals	White box-shaped crystals	Fine white powder	Fine yellowish white powder
Water Test	Dissolves in water	Dissolves in water	Turns milky water	Makes water cloudy
Iodine Test	Turns yellow with iodine	No reaction with iodine	Turns yellow orange with iodine	Turns red, ends black with iodine
Vinegar Test	Dissolves in vinegar	No reaction with vinegar	Fizzes with vinegar	Gets thick, then hard with vinegar

ELABORATE

    h. Ask: *If you had a mixture of powders, how could you find out what is in the mixture?*

        Give each pair of students small samples of a mixture of two white powders, flour, and one of the original white powders. Be sure to keep track of which mixture each group gets.

        Ask: *What powders are these?* Challenge children to determine if each powder is one they have encountered previously, and if so, which one. (Children would not have studied the properties of flour.) Ask: *What is the evidence for your conclusions?*

i. Clean Up. Students should throw away plastic bags and toothpicks, return powders and test supplies to teacher-designated spot, clean and dry anything dirty, including their hands. Caution students not to put any of the powders in the sink since they can clog drains.[2]

EVALUATE

j. Let students present and discuss their procedures and their conclusions. Ask students to explain the basis for their conclusions. Use the following checklist as an assessment tool to monitor the quality of the presentations.
    - ☐ Explained their procedure clearly.
    - ☐ Conducted tests with the mixture in the same way as with single powders previously.
    - ☐ Referred to data table of properties of single powders.
    - ☐ Used that data as evidence of conclusion.
    - ☐ Stated conclusion clearly.
    - ☐ Recognized that the other powder in the mixture must be a powder not yet studied.
    - ☐ Correctly identified the powder that they had previously studied that was in their mixture.

Nature of Scientific Inquiry

k. Discuss with the children how their activities in these investigations are like those of scientists. Ask: *What are some of the ways you have acted as scientists in this investigation of powders?* Common activities of children and scientists might include asking questions, talking, searching, planning, using magnifying lenses, experimenting, recording, explaining, discussing, arguing, defining, criticizing, exchanging ideas, deciding, asking more questions.

 E. PROPERTIES OF AIR

▶ *Science Background*

Although we cannot see, taste, smell, hear, or feel air (if we reach out our hand to grab it), we know that air is a real substance because of the way it interacts with objects that we can see.

Through the following activities, discussion, and expository teaching, you will help the students begin to develop an understanding of these principles about air:

▶ *Principles About Air*

1. Air, like solids and liquids, is a real material substance (made up of particles too small to see).
2. Bubbles in water indicate the presence of air.
3. Air exerts pressure; it can press or push on things.

---

[2]More information on these activities on white powders can be found at these Internet sites: http://www.csulb.edu/~lhenriqu/mysterypowder.htm, http://etc.sccoe.k12.ca.us/i98/ii98units/cross/mystery/text/powders.html, http://eduref.org/cgi~bin/printlessons.cgi/virtual/lessons/science/chemistry/chm0200.html.

4. We live at the bottom of an ocean of air that exerts a great pressure on all things on the surface of the earth.
5. Objects tend to be moved from regions of high air pressure toward regions of low air pressure.

Together, these principles can be used to explain evidence gathered about a wide variety of phenomena.

 Science Standards

All students should develop an understanding of

- properties of objects and materials (K–4).
- changes in properties of matter (5–8).

Concepts and Principles That Support the Standards

- Materials can exist in different states—solid, liquid, and gas (K–4).
- Objects (such as gases) have many different properties (K–4).
- The position and motion of objects can be changed by pushing or pulling. The size of the change is related to the strength of the push or pull (K–4).
- Unbalanced forces will cause changes in the speed or direction of an object's motion (5–8).

Objectives

1. Investigate and describe natural events related to air and air pressure.
2. Demonstrate and describe evidence for each of the principles about air and air pressure.
3. Use observational evidence and the principles about air to explain what happens in various investigations and phenomena.

Materials

- Large syringes
- Soda straws
- Several medicine droppers
- Containers for water

▶ *Teaching Suggestions*

We suggest that you use Activities 1–5 as teacher demonstrations in inventing, developing, and applying principles about air. Emphasize that these principles are based on evidence and are useful in explaining phenomena and predicting outcomes. The demonstrations might then be made available later to your students, perhaps at learning stations.

1. IS AIR A REAL MATERIAL SUBSTANCE LIKE SOLIDS AND LIQUIDS? (1–4)

ENGAGE

a. Show the children three sealed plastic food storage bags, one filled with a solid (such as sand), a second with water, and a third with air. Ask: *What is in each bag?*

After children discuss the contents of each bag, ask: *How do you know what is in each bag?*

Some children may say that air is in the third bag. Ask: *Since you cannot see, hear, feel (if you place your hand in the bag), smell (if you open the bag), or taste what's in the bag, how do you know that air is really in the bag?*

Water   Air   Sand

EXPLORE

b. As a demonstration, partially submerge the bag of air in a clear container of water. Use scissors to clip one of the submerged corners of the plastic bag or use a push pin to poke a hole in the plastic bag below the water's surface. Ask: *What do you observe?* (Bubbles in the water)

EXPLAIN

c. Ask: *How can you explain what you see?* Use this activity to introduce and develop Principles 1 and 2 about air. Lead students to note that although we cannot see air, evidence for the existence of air comes from many activities, such as activities with medicine droppers and plastic syringes.

Discuss the meaning of the term *evidence* (observations that we can use to support conclusions). Use the term in story form, such as:

> *Two boys came out of the house and noticed that the driveway was wet. One boy said, "It has rained." The other boy said, "No. My Dad washes his car every Saturday."*

What *evidence* might have supported the first boy's conclusion? What was the implied conclusion of the second boy? What evidence might have supported the second boy's conclusion?

ELABORATE

d. Ask: *What other evidence can you think of to show that air is a real material substance?* Through discussion, help your students come up with many examples involving interactions with air, such as wind, rustling of leaves in a tree, paper airplanes, kites, balloons, your breath on a cold morning, or a dropped sheet of paper floating down to the floor.

2. DOES AIR TAKE UP SPACE? (1–4)

ENGAGE

a. Ask: *Can air and water be in the same space at the same time?*

EXPLORE

b. Push an "empty" glass straight down into a container of water. Ask: *What do you observe?*

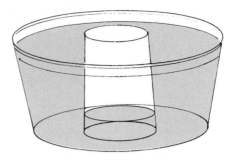

c. Tilt the glass while it is underwater. Ask: *What do you observe?*

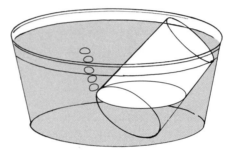

EXPLAIN

d. *How can you explain why the water did not come into the glass?* Through discussion, lead students to apply the principle that air is a real material substance. Air keeps the water from coming into the glass. Although the glass looks empty, we infer that it contains air.

e. Ask: *Why were bubbles seen in the water when the glass was tilted?*
Through discussion and direct instruction, help students use Principle 2 to explain that bubbles show that air is escaping into the water from the glass.

3. HOW CAN AIR KEEP WATER OUT OF A CONTAINER? (1–4)

ENGAGE

a. Will water enter a glass pushed mouth-down into a container of water?

EXPLORE

b. Crumple up a paper towel in the bottom of a dry, empty glass. Push the glass mouth down into a large container of water so that it is completely submerged. Ask: *What do you observe?*

EXPLAIN

c. Ask: *Why do you think that the paper towel remains dry?* Help students use Principle 1 to explain what they see in this demonstration. Air is a real material substance that keeps water from coming up into the glass and wetting the paper towel. Tell the students that large, air-filled, inverted containers, called **diving bells**, have been used in underwater work for centuries. Ask: *Why does water not come into a diving bell when it is submerged?*

ELABORATE
d. Push an empty glass mouth down into a large container of water until it is completely submerged. Tilt the glass so that it fills with water. Ask: *How can you use a straw to replace the water in the glass with air? When you have emptied the glass of its water using the straw, how can you use the straw to replace the air in the glass with water again?*

   Your students will need Principle 1 to explain their observations. Air is a real material substance. When air is blown into the glass through the straw, it replaces the water in the glass. When the air is removed through the straw, the water comes back in.

4. HOW CAN YOU USE A SYRINGE TO FEEL AIR PRESSURE? (3–5)

ENGAGE
a. Hold up a syringe and pull back on the plunger. Ask: *What is in the syringe?* (Air) *What evidence would support your answer?* (If you put the tip into water, bubbles come out when you push the plunger.)
b. In this activity you will make more observations about air in the plunger.

EXPLORE
c. Distribute small- to medium-sized plungers to the students. Tell them to try the following activity, then demonstrate for them. With the plunger pulled out part of the way, plug the opening of the syringe with your finger. Try to push the plunger in. Ask: *What do you observe?*

EXPLAIN
d. Ask: *Why do you think the plunger of the syringe is so hard to push in?* Use Principle 1 to help students understand that when you push in on the plunger, the air presses back. This demonstration is another type of evidence that air is a real material substance. The demonstration also shows that air can exert pressure. Building on this experience and the children's discussion of it, teach (invent) Principle 3.

5. HOW DOES A DRINKING STRAW WORK? (3–5)

ENGAGE
a. Ask: *What do you have to do to drink water with a straw?*

EXPLORE
b. Have the students work in pairs. Give each student a clear drinking straw and clean paper cup containing fresh water. Have them take turns drinking water through their straw as their partner observes. Ask: *What did you see happen? What did you do to get water up the straw and into your mouth?*

EXPLAIN
c. Ask: *Why do you think the water rose into the straw?* Your students will likely say that the water was "sucked" into the straw. Help the students understand that, even though the term is commonly used, *suction* is a misconception; liquid is not pulled into the straw by suction.

   Lead the children to understand that when you expand your lungs, some air comes out of the straw and enters your lungs. There is then less air in the straw and it exerts less pressure. According to Principle 4, the outside air pressure is now greater than the pressure in the straw. According to Principle 5, the atmosphere (remember, we live at the bottom of an ocean of air) then pushes liquid up into the straw.

ELABORATE

d. Ask: *What do you do to get water to come into a medicine dropper?* (You dip the tube of the medicine dropper in water, squeeze the bulb, release it, and water comes into the medicine dropper tube.) *What happens to the air in the medicine dropper tube when you squeeze it?* (Some air comes out of the tube.)

e. Ask: *In what ways might a medicine dropper be like a drinking straw?* Help students to see that the two systems are similar. When you reduce the pressure in either system, the pressure of the atmosphere surrounding us pushes down on the surface of the water, forcing some liquid up into the dropper or straw.

Nature of Scientific Inquiry

f. Ask: *What do scientists do when they explain something?* Through discussion, lead students to understand that when scientists explain an event, they connect observations and scientific concepts and principles in a reasonable way to make sense of the observations. When scientists propose an explanation, they use scientific knowledge and observational evidence to support their explanation. Children should check their explanations against scientific knowledge, experiences, and observations of others.

EVALUATE

g. Refill the students' paper cups from part b of this investigation with water. Using a straight pin, walk around the room and put a tiny hole in each drinking straw above the water line. Challenge the class to drink their water through their straw as before. Ask students to answer the following questions in their science notebooks: *What do you observe?* (When I try to get water to come into my mouth as I usually do, nothing happens.) *Why do you think this happens?* (Because of the hole. Air comes in through the hole so I can't lower the pressure of the air at the top of the straw. Therefore the water isn't pushed up by the water pressure on the rest of the water.) *What evidence supports your explanation?* (My straw worked before the hole, but didn't work after the hole. Or if I cover the hole in my straw tightly, I can use it again to bring water from the glass to my mouth.)

II. MOTION AND FORCES

Forces are needed to change the motion of an object—to start it moving or stop it, to speed it up or slow it down. There are many different kinds of forces in the physical world, such as frictional forces, mechanical forces exerted by simple machines, gravitational forces, magnetic forces, static electric forces, and the bonding forces between water molecules. A force may be direct, as when we push on a lever arm, or it may be indirect, as when a magnet pulls on a piece of iron from a distance.

The study of simple forces in grades K–7 provides concrete experiences on which a more comprehensive study of forces and motion may be based in secondary grades.

 NSES **Science Standards**

All students should develop an understanding of

- the position and motion of objects (K–4).
- motions and forces (5–8).

NSES   Concepts and Principles That Support the Standards

- The position and motion of objects can be changed by pushing or pulling (K–4).
- The size of the change is related to the strength of the push or pull (K–4).
- Unbalanced forces will cause changes in the speed or direction of an object's motion (5–8).
- Changes in systems can be quantified through measurement (5–8).
- Mathematics is essential for accurately measuring change (5–8).
- Rate involves comparing one measured quantity with another measured quantity (5–8).

 # A. FRICTIONAL FORCES

▶ *Science Background*

Friction is the result of an interaction between a moving object and the surface on which it moves. Students' everyday experience is that friction causes all moving objects to slow down and stop if they are not being continuously powered. Through experiences in which friction is reduced (by a lubricant or through the use of wheels), students can begin to see that a moving object with no friction would continue to move indefinitely.

Objectives

1. Design and conduct an investigation to demonstrate the friction present as an object moves across a level surface.
2. Ask questions about friction and describe frictional effects as an interaction between an object and a surface.
3. Explain how wheels and lubricants can reduce friction.

Materials

- Screw hook
- Block of wood
- Rubber bands
- Ruler
- Sheets of coarse sandpaper
- Five or six round pencils

1. WHAT IS FRICTION? HOW CAN FRICTION BE REDUCED? (3–6)

ENGAGE

a. Ask: *How can you measure the effects of friction?*

EXPLORE

b. Students should carry out these investigation procedures in cooperative groups.
   1. Turn the screw hook into the end of a block of wood. Attach a rubber band (or a spring scale) to the hook.
   2. With the rubber band on your finger, lift the block into the air and measure the stretch with a ruler, as in diagram (a). Design a data table and record your measurement in it.

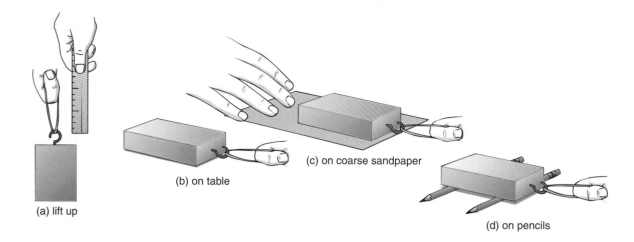

(a) lift up

(b) on table

(c) on coarse sandpaper

(d) on pencils

3. Position the block on a table with the rubber band extended, as in diagram (b). Now drag the block on the table and measure the rubber band's stretch once the block begins to move. Record your measurements.

4. Repeat the procedure in step 3, this time with sandpaper beneath the block, as in diagram (c).

EXPLAIN

c. Invite students to present their procedures and findings. During the discussion ask: *What change did you observe in the stretch of the rubber band when the block is dragged on the table and on sandpaper?* (It stretched more on the sandpaper.) *How does the surface on which the block slides affect the force to move it?* (The rougher the surface, the more force it takes to move the block.) *What is the cause of the increase in force needed to move the object on sandpaper?* (There is more friction.) *What is friction?* Introduce the concept of friction. **Friction** is a force opposing motion that results when two surfaces slide across one another.

ELABORATE

d. Now place two round pencils underneath the block and drag it across the table, as in diagram (d). Measure the stretch of the rubber band just after the block begins to move. Once each group has tried this several times, ask: *What happens to the stretch of the rubber band this time?* (It is less.) *Why?* (The pencils are rolling, reducing the friction.) *In what way do rollers (wheels) help objects to move?* Explain that rollers (wheels) reduce friction.

EVALUATE

e. As an assesment of the student's abilities to understand and apply their knowledge about the concept of friction, ask them to answer these questions in their science notebook:

1. Your teacher needs help rearranging her new classroom. She asks you to push her desk from the front of the room to the back of the room. You don't want to have to push very hard. *Which kind of floor covering do you hope there is in the classroom: A. Smooth, polished cement; B. Thick carpeting; or C. Rough concrete?* (Surface A) *Why did you select this surface?* (There would probably be less friction since it is smoother.) *What does friction have to do with your choice?* (If the friction between the desk and the floor covering is low, I won't have to push as hard.)

2. In your investigation today, how does the stretch of the rubber band relate to the force of friction between the block and the surface on which it is sliding? (The greater the friction between the block and the surface on which it is sliding, the greater the stretch of the rubber band.)

B. EQUAL-ARM BALANCES

▶ *Science Background*

An equal-arm balance is a system consisting of a crossbar pivoted in the center and weights that can be placed at different positions on each side of the bar, as is shown in the diagram. The amount of each weight and its distance from the central pivot point are the relevant factors in determining balance.

Objectives

1. Use these qualitative rules to predict and explain balance on an equal-arm balance:
   Symmetry rule. Equal weights at equal distances will balance [see diagram (a)].
   Relational rule. Heavier weights close in can balance lighter weights farther out [see diagram (b) and diagram (c)].
2. Demonstrate and explain that balance occurs when the product of weights and distances on one side of the pivot equals the product of weights and distances on the other side of the pivot.

Materials

• Equal-arm balance for each pair of students

(Plastic equal-arm balances, often referred to as "math balances," are sold by Delta Education and other equipment companies. Addresses for equipment companies are given in Appendix E.)

....

1. WHAT FACTORS AFFECT THE EQUILIBRIUM OF AN EQUAL-ARM BALANCE? (3–6)

ENGAGE

a. Ask: *What affects the balance of an equal-arm balance scale? How can you predict accurately whether a balance will be level?*

EXPLORE

b. Distribute balances to your students. Give the children the following balance problems, one at a time. Allow ample time for students to work on each problem and discuss their findings, before giving the next one. Be noncommittal about patterns they may discover.

   1. Place two weights at the second peg from the center on the left side of the balance. Leaving the left side always the same, find at least three different ways to balance the crossbar by adding weights to a peg on the other side. (You can use as many weights as necessary, but be sure to add weights to only one peg at a time on the right side, not to two or three pegs.) Use drawings, words, or data columns to show what you did. Tell your teacher what you did to balance the crossbar.
   2. Start with two weights on the left side at the third peg from the center. Find at least four ways to balance the crossbar. (Remember, you can use as many weights as necessary, but be sure to add weights to only one peg on the right side, not to two or three pegs.) Write down what you did and show your work to your teacher.

3. Start with four weights at the third peg on the left side. How many ways can you find to balance the crossbar? (Remember to add weights from only one peg at a time on the other side.)

4. Set up your own combinations of weights and distances on one side of the balance and use your developing knowledge to predict what might be done to the other side to produce balance.

EXPLAIN

c. Ask: *What did you do to balance the crossbar? Can you find patterns in the different ways you found to balance the crossbar? How can you test to determine if the pattern you found is a general one, applying in all cases?*

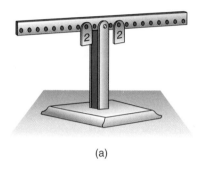

(a)

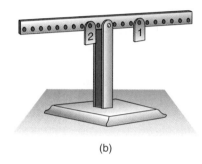

(b)

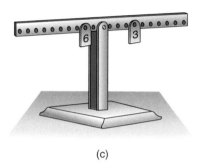

(c)

d. Through discussion, lead your students to understand the following balance patterns or rules:

Symmetry rule. Equal weights at equal distances will balance [see diagram (a)].
Relational rule. Heavier weights close in can balance lighter weights farther out [see diagram (b) and diagram (c)].

Both of these rules are qualitative or nonnumerical rules. They are understood by children from ages 8 or 9, but they may not be stated explicitly.

ELABORATE

e. At some point, older students (from ages 10 or 11) may understand the use of formal mathematics to coordinate weights and distances. Challenge students to work with their data from step *b* to find a mathematical rule for the balance, a rule involving doing something with the actual numbers.

The mathematical rule for the balance is:

$$(W_L) \times (D_L) = (W_R) \times (D_R)$$

where W = weights, D = distances, L = left side, and R = right side of the balance. Thus, the product of the weight and distance on one side is equal to the product of weight and distance on the other side.

Lead older children to try this rule for themselves, using the data from different trials. If the crossbar is balanced, the products of the weights and distances on the left side will always equal the products on the right side for each of these three cases.

Interestingly, this rule applies even if weights are placed on more than one peg on each side. Then, the sum of the weights multiplied by their distances on one side must equal the sum of the weights multiplied by their distances on the other side.

EVALUATE

f. Use these or similar multiple-choice items to assess the students' understanding of the principles related to equal-arm balances.

For students in grades 3 or 4 who only explored the balance qualitatively:

1. If one blue weight is near the pivot on the left side of the balance and one blue weight is near the end of the beam on the right side of the balance:
   A. The beam will be level (balanced).
   B. The right side of the beam will be lower than the left side of the beam.
   C. The left side of the beam will be lower than the right side of the beam.

2. If three blue weights are at the end of the left side of the beam and two blue weights are at the end of the right side of the beam:
   A. The beam will be level (balanced).
   B. The right side of the beam will be lower than the left side of the beam.
   C. The left side of the beam will be lower than the right side of the beam

3. Which of the following is NOT a true statement about the balance?
   A. Equal weights at equal distances will balance.
   B. Equal weights at different distances will not balance.
   C. A heavier weight far out can balance a lighter weight close in.
   D. A lighter weight far out can balance a heavier weight close in.
   E. Different weights at equal distances will not balance.

For students in grades 5 or 6 who investigated the balance quantitatively:

4. On the right side of the balance beam there is a 10 gram weight on the second peg from the pivot point. Where should you put a 5 gram weight to make the beam balance?
   A. On the second peg from the pivot point on the left side of the balance beam.
   B. On the fourth peg from the pivot point on the left side of the balance beam.
   C. On the fifth peg from the pivot point on the left side of the balance beam.
   D. On the 10th peg from the pivot point on the left side of the balance beam.

5. The right side of the balance beam has a 5 gram weight on the 10th peg from the pivot. The left side of the balance beam has a 10 gram weight on the sixth peg from the pivot. Which statement best describes the position of the balance beam?
   A. It is level.
   B. The right side is up.
   C. The left side is up.

Answer Key: (1. B; 2. C; 3. D; 4. B; 5. B)

 ## C. LEVERS

▶ *Science Background*

The rules governing equal-arm balances are important in science because they also apply to the operation of levers. A lever system has a crossbar, pivoted at a fulcrum. Using a small effort force far out from a fulcrum, a person can lift a heavy load that is nearer the fulcrum. At the lower grades, students can use the symmetry and relational rules of the equal-arm balance to explain and predict actions of a lever. Middle school students might use the balance equation to predict how much force is needed to lift a load of a given weight when the distances involved are known.

Objectives

1. Identify the fulcrum, effort force, and load/resistance of different kinds of levers.
2. Explain how a lever is like an equal-arm balance.
3. Demonstrate and explain that a small effort force far from the fulcrum can lift or move a large load near the fulcrum.

Materials

• Heavy box or other heavy object
• Half-meter stick or 50 cm board

1. WHAT IS A LEVER? HOW COULD YOU USE ONE? (2–6)

ENGAGE

a. Tell students a story about two girls who were climbing a mountain. A rock slide deposited a boulder, trapping the leg of one of the girls. The boulder was too heavy to lift directly. Ask: *What might her companion do to lift the boulder enough so that the girl could get her leg free?*

EXPLORE

b. Lead students to consider getting a tree limb, finding something to use as a fulcrum (pivot), and then using the tree limb to lift the boulder enough for the girl to get her leg free. Model the situation in the classroom using a heavy box to represent the boulder, a half-meter stick for the lever arm, and a book as the pivot.

EXPLAIN

c. Introduce the terms *load, force,* and *resistance* as they relate to levers. Ask: *Where was the load (or resistance) for this lever? Where was the fulcrum? Where was the force applied?*

Lead students to understand that a lever can be used to lift a heavy load, if the force on the lever is much farther from the fulcrum than the load is.

2. HOW IS A LEVER LIKE A BALANCE? (3–6)

ENGAGE

a. Make sure that students have studied the equal-arm balance, following procedures similar to those in the previous section of these activities. Ask: *How is a lever like an equal-arm balance?* Ask the students to identify the fulcrum, effort, and resistance on a balance and on a lever.

EXPLORE

b. Instruct the students to design an investigation to determine how much effort they must exert at different distances on one side of the balance/lever to lift weights at specific positions on the other side. For example, using the balance as a lever, they might place a load of 8 weights at a distance of 10 units from the fulcrum and note that the farther from the pivot/fulcrum they apply the effort force, the easier it is to lift the load.

EXPLAIN

c. Encourage students to discuss their procedures and conclusions. Through this activity, students should realize that a great amount of effort force is needed to move a heavy load when the effort force is much nearer to the fulcrum than is the load.

ELABORATE

d. Ask: *How does the balance and lever principle apply to a seesaw?*

If possible, take your students to a playground seesaw. Or make a classroom seesaw by placing a solid 2 inch by 6 inch board about 6 to 8 feet long on another board under it to act as a pivot. Let the children investigate how a smaller child far out from the pivot of the seesaw can balance a larger child nearer to the fulcrum.

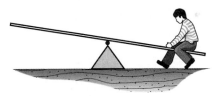

1. If two children are the same weight, where should they sit on a seesaw to make it balance?
   A. Both should sit on board on the same side of the pivot.
   B. One should sit close to the pivot on one side and the other one should sit far away from the pivot on the other side.
   C. They should sit equal distances from the pivot, one on each side of the seesaw.
2. If Joe and Bill are sitting at opposite ends of the seesaw board and Joe's end of the board is on the ground, what do you know about the weights of these students?
   A. Bill weighs more than Joe.
   B. Joe weighs more than Bill.
   C. Joe and Bill each weigh the same amount.
   D. Joe and Bill have gained weight since the beginning of the year.
3. Elizabeth, a first grader, wants to seesaw with her father. Where should they sit so they can make the seesaw go up and down?
   A. Elizabeth should sit on one end of the board and her father should sit on the other end of the board.
   B. Elizabeth should sit near the fulcrum and her father should sit near the end of the board on the other side.
   C. Elizabeth should sit near one end of the board and her father should sit near the fulcrum on the other side.
   D. Elizabeth should sit on her father's lap.

Answers (1. C; 2. B; 3. C)

D. INCLINED PLANES

▶ *Science Background*

An inclined plane or ramp can be used as a simple type of machine to reduce the force needed to move an object up to a given height.

Objectives

1. Describe and demonstrate how an inclined plane can be used to reduce the force needed to move an object up to a given height.
2. Name and describe examples of inclined planes in everyday life.

Materials

- Smooth board, 4 feet long
- Block with screw eye in one end or a rubber band wrapped around it
- Spring scale

---

1. WHAT IS AN INCLINED PLANE? HOW CAN YOU USE IT? (3–6)

ENGAGE

a. Ask: *What happens to the force needed to move an object up an inclined plane when the angle of the plane is increased?*

EXPLORE

b. Lead students to plan and conduct an investigation similar to this one.
   1. Use the spring scale to find the weight of the block by lifting it straight up, as shown in the diagram. Repeat this several times and find the average reading on the scale. Record the average weight.
   2. Take the 4-foot board and place two or three books under one end so that the end of the board is raised about 10 cm. Place the block with the screw eye in it on the inclined board as shown in the diagram. Slip the hook of the spring scale through the eye of the block.

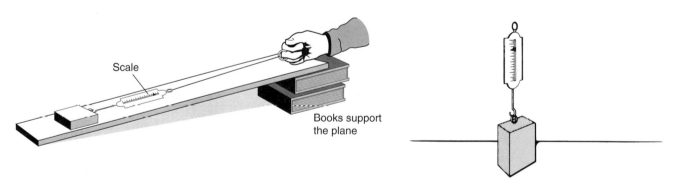

Scale

Books support the plane

   3. Slowly and evenly pull the scale and block up the board.
   4. Record the amount of force needed to pull the block up the board and the height of the plane. Do this several times and record your observations. Using the data obtained, determine the average force required to pull the weight.
      Ask: *How much force is required to pull the block up each plane? Is the force to move the block up the plane greater than, equal to, or less than the weight of the block? Why?*
   5. Repeat the activity, but this time make the inclined plane steeper by changing the number of support books so that the end of the board is about 20 cm high.
   6. Again, find the average force needed to pull the weight up the board.

EXPLAIN

c. Ask: *How do the forces to move the block up the two inclined planes compare? How is the force needed different when lifting the block straight up than when pulling the block up the board? Why?*

Guide students to understand that inclined planes are used for moving objects that are too heavy to lift directly. An inclined plane is a simple type of machine. Because of the slant of the plane, a smaller force is needed to move an object up an inclined plane than to lift it straight up the same height.

Ask: *What generalization can you make about the amount of force required to move a block as an inclined plane becomes steeper? What is the advantage of having a long inclined plane rather than a short inclined plane if both planes are the same height?*

ELABORATE

d. Ask: *Why do roads not go straight up and down mountains?*
Which of the following examples is an inclined plane?

wheelchair ramp	stairway
hill	vertical cliff
gangplank	head of an ax

Ask: *Where are there examples of inclined planes in the school or on the school campus?*

EVALUATE

e. To assess students' understanding of inclined planes, ask students to respond to this application question.

1. You have a very heavy box to move to the top of a wall. To use the least force to accomplish this task, you should:
   a. Use a smooth board about five times as long as the wall is high as an inclined plane, and push the box up the board to the top of the wall.
   b. Use a smooth board about three times as long as the wall is high as an inclined plane, and push the box up the board to the top of the wall.
   c. Use a smooth board about two times as long as the wall is high as an inclined plane, and push the box up the board to the top of the wall.
   d. Don't bother finding a board; just lift the box onto the top of the wall.

 E. PULLEYS

▶ *Science Background*

A pulley also can be used as a simple type of machine to reduce the force needed to lift an object.

Objectives

1. Describe and demonstrate how pulleys can be used to reduce the force needed to lift an object to a given height.
2. Name and describe examples of pulleys in everyday life.

Materials

- Ring stand and clamp for attaching pulleys (or other pulley support)
- Two single pulleys
- String for the pulley
- Spring scale
- 100 g weight
- 50 g weight
- Meterstick

1. WHAT IS A PULLEY, AND HOW CAN YOU USE IT? (3–6)

ENGAGE
    a. Ask: *What is a pulley? How do pulleys work? How can pulleys help us lift heavy objects?*

EXPLORE
    b. Lead students to conduct this investigation.

1. Obtain a ring stand and a clamp for attaching a pulley (or find another suitable support for the pulley), a single pulley, some string, a spring scale, and a 100 g weight. Assemble your equipment as shown in the diagram.
Ask: *How much do you think you will have to pull on the scale to raise the 100 g weight?*

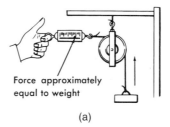

Force approximately
equal to weight

(a)

2. Pull on the scale and raise the 100 g weight. Record the force needed to raise the weight.
3. Repeat this activity several times and record each measurement.
Ask: *What do you think will happen when you use two pulleys to raise the 100 g weight?*
4. In addition to the equipment you have, obtain a second pulley and a 50 g weight. Assemble your equipment as shown in the diagram.

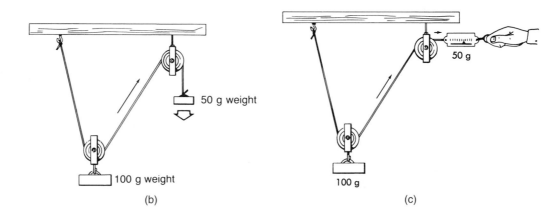

50 g weight

100 g weight
(b)

50 g

100 g
(c)

5. Pull the 50 g weight with the spring balance and record your observations.
6. Remove the 50 g weight and attach the spring scale to the free end of the string, as shown in the following diagram.
Ask: *How much force do you think the scale will show when you raise the 100 g weight?*
7. Raise the weight by pulling on the scale. Ask: *How much is the reading on the scale when you raise the weight?* Repeat the activity several times and record each measurement. Ask: *Why is there an advantage in using this type of pulley system?*

EXPLAIN

c. Ask: *From your investigation, what can you generalize about pulley systems?* Get input from the students. They might first suggest that more pulleys reduce the amount of force needed to lift a heavy weight. Actually, it is not the number of pulleys, but the number of ropes or strings pulling against the resisting weight that makes a difference. In diagram (a), one string pulls upward and the force needed to lift the block is the same as the weight of the block. In diagram (b), two strings pull upward against the load/block and the force needed to lift the load is one-half its weight.

ELABORATE

d. Challenge each group to design a pulley system to lift a piano weighing 300 pounds. Draw a sketch of that pulley system and explain why your group chose that design.

EVALUATE

e. Each group will present their design to the class. They should display and explain their diagram, and give reasons why they think their design is best.

f. The rubric that follows is designed to assess students' understanding of how pulleys change the force needed to lift heavy objects. Distribute this rubric to the students to guide their work and then use it to evaluate their presentations.

Exemplary:
- Includes all of the bullets in the Proficient Level.
- Includes an accurate estimate of the amount of force needed to lift the piano with their pulley system.

Proficient:
- Diagram is neat and legible, and major parts of the system are labeled.
- Explanation of the diagram is clear and relates accurately to the diagram.
- The reasons for their design are clearly stated and based on an accurate understanding of how pulleys make lifting easier.

Developing:
- Only one or two of the three bullets from the Proficient Level are achieved.

Very Little:
- None of the three bullets from the Proficient Level is achieved.

2. HOW CAN A PULLEY ARRANGEMENT HELP YOU USE A SMALL FORCE TO OVERPOWER A LARGE FORCE? (4–6)

Materials

- Two 1¾ inch dowel rods, about 36 inches long
- 20 feet of ½ inch nylon rope

Safety Precautions

Since a large force will be involved, make sure the dowel rods are short and very strong. Safe dowel rods can be cut from a shovel handle purchased from a hardware or building supply store.

ENGAGE

a. Ask: *How can we design a pulley system out of dowel rods and a rope so that a small force can overcome a very large force?*

EXPLORE

b. Tie a strong loop in one end of the rope and loop it over one of the dowel rods. With one person holding one dowel rod in both hands and a second person holding the other dowel rod in both hands, pass the rope back and forth over the dowel rods about four times as in the illustration.

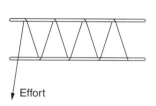

Effort

c. Select four large volunteers and let them hold on to the ends of the dowel rods, with two against two in a tug-of-war. Let a smaller person pull on the free end of the rope.

EXPLAIN

d. Ask: *What happens? Why?* (The force of the smaller person draws the two larger persons together. The rods and rope make up a pulley system with several pulleys. If the rope is looped four times over the rods, there are eight ropes pulling on a dowel. The smaller person will have to pull with one-eighth of the force of the four students trying to hold the rods apart. The effect of this pulley system is dramatic.)

F. BERNOULLI'S PRINCIPLE

▶ *Science Background*

When air rushes over a surface, it has the effect of reducing the air pressure on that surface. This cause-and-effect relationship is called Bernoulli's principle, for Daniel Bernoulli (1700–1782), an important Swiss mathematical scientist who first described the relationship.

Objectives

1. State Bernoulli's principle and use it to analyze a rushing air situation.
2. Use Bernoulli's principle to explain what happens in various rushing air demonstrations.

Materials
- Notebook paper
- Drinking straw

....

1. WHAT IS BERNOULLI'S PRINCIPLE? HOW CAN YOU USE A PIECE OF PAPER TO INVESTIGATE IT? (4–6)

ENGAGE

a. Conduct this demonstration for students.
  1. Obtain a piece of paper.
  2. Make a fold 3 cm wide along one of the sides of the paper. Make another 3 cm wide fold on the opposite side as indicated in the diagram.
  3. Place the paper on a flat surface, with the folds acting as legs to hold the paper up. Ask: *What do you think will happen if I blow through a straw under this folded paper?*
  4. Using a drinking straw, blow a stream of air under the paper.

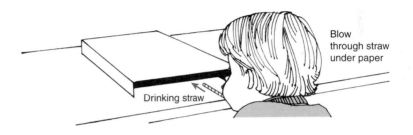

Blow through straw under paper

Drinking straw

EXPLORE

b. Provide paper and straws to students and allow them to repeat the demonstration.

EXPLAIN

c. Ask: *What do you notice about the way the paper moves?* (The center of the paper moves down.)

How did the air move under the paper when you blew under it? (The air was moving in a stream under the paper.)

What can you infer about why the paper went down in the center? Guide students to understand that air pressure pushed the paper down.

Would the air pressure be greater on the top of the paper or on the bottom of the paper? Help students understand that the air pressure would be greater on the top if the paper was pushed down by the air pressure.

Why is the air pressure lower on the bottom of the paper? Invent Bernoulli's principle: When air rushes over a surface, the air pressure on that surface is reduced. Make sure that the students can use Bernoulli's principle, along with their observational evidence, to explain the example.

....

2. HOW WILL A PIECE OF PAPER MOVE WHEN YOU BLOW ACROSS THE TOP OF IT? (3–6)

ENGAGE

a. Ask: *If you were to hold a strip of paper by each corner and blow across the top of the paper, what would happen to the paper? Why do you think so?*

EXPLORE

b. Assist students to conduct this investigation.
   1. Obtain a strip of paper about 5 cm by 27 cm.
   2. Along the 5 cm side, hold the upper left corner of the strip with your left hand and the upper right corner with your right hand.
   3. Blow hard across the top of the paper (see diagram).

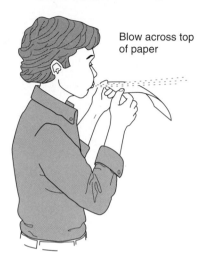

Blow across top
of paper

EXPLAIN

c. Ask: *What happens to the paper while you are blowing across it?* (It moves upward.)
   Why does the paper move in this direction? Where does the air move faster, over the top of the paper or the bottom of the paper? Why do you think so?
   Lead students to apply Bernoulli's principle to explain why the paper strip moves upward. The air pressure was reduced as air rushed over the top of the paper. The greater air pressure under the paper pushed the paper upward, overcoming the gravitational forces that tend to bend the paper downward.

ELABORATE

d. Discuss these questions with the class:
   1. *Why is it unwise to stand close to the edge of a platform as a moving train is coming?*
   2. *How does Bernoulli's principle apply to flying planes?*
      If a plane is moving fast enough, the upward pressure on the wings is enough to support the weight of the plane. The plane must keep moving to stay aloft. If the plane's engines cut out in midair, it would glide down immediately.
   3. Look at the following diagram of an airplane wing. *Is the air moving faster at A or B? Why?*

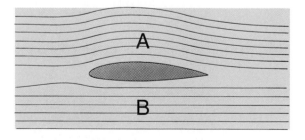

   4. *How do wing slopes vary and why?*

3. WHAT WILL HAPPEN TO A WAD OF PAPER PLACED IN THE OPENING OF A POP BOTTLE IF YOU BLOW ACROSS THE BOTTLE OPENING? (3–6)

ENGAGE

a. Ask: *Using what you know about the effects of rushing air on air pressure, what do you think will happen to a wad of paper placed in the opening of a pop bottle if you blow across the bottle opening? Will the paper go into the bottle or come out of the bottle? Make a prediction. Explain your reasoning.*

EXPLORE

b. Guide students to conduct this investigation.
   1. Wad a small piece of paper so it is about the size of a pea (about 0.5 cm diameter).
   2. Lay the pop bottle on its side.
   3. Place the small wad of paper in the opening of the bottle, next to the edge of the opening. (See diagram.)

Blow across opening of bottle

   4. Blow across the opening in front of the bottle. Make sure you bend down so that you are level with the bottle.

EXPLAIN

c. Ask: *What happens to the wad of paper?* (It moves out of the bottle.)
   Why is the wad of paper forced to do that?
   What do you infer about the air pressure in the bottle and the air pressure at the opening of the bottle when you blow across it? (Air pressure in the bottle is greater.)

G. PENDULUMS

▶ *Science Background*

Students typically identify three variable factors that might affect the rate of swing of a pendulum: the weight of the pendulum bob, the angle at which it is released, and the length of the pendulum string. Determining which factors are indeed relevant requires that students conduct controlled investigations in which one factor at a time is varied and its effect on the rate of swing of the pendulum is determined, while the other two variables are controlled or left unchanged.

Surprisingly, only the length affects the rate of swing. Varying the weight of the pendulum bob or the angle at which the pendulum is released has no effect on its rate of swing.

Objectives

1. Demonstrate procedures for measuring the rate of a pendulum's swing.
2. Design controlled experiments to test hypotheses about factors that might affect the speed of a pendulum.
3. Record, analyze, and draw accurate conclusions from data.

Materials

Watch with a second hand for each group, or clock with a second hand for the whole class

- Paper clips
- Pennies
- Ball of string
- Tongue depressors or pencils (to support the pendulums)
- Masking tape (to tape the pendulum support to a desk)

▶ *Preparation*

- Tie paper clips to one end of several pieces of long string and insert one or more pennies into each paper clip to make the pendulum bobs (as in the drawing). Wedge the string into the slit of a tongue depressor as in the drawing. Students can adjust the length of string as needed by sliding it along the notch of the tongue depressor.

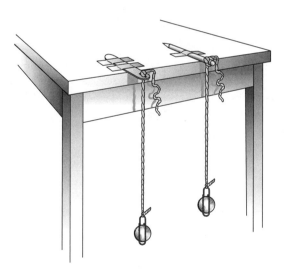

- Determine where teams of students can set up pendulums that can swing freely. To support the pendulums, students should tape or hold the tongue depressor or the pencil securely on the edge of a table.

....

1. WHAT FACTORS MIGHT AFFECT THE RATE OF SWING OF A PENDULUM? (5–8)

ENGAGE

a. Show students a pendulum using pennies as the pendulum bob and a tongue depressor or pencil as the support. Ask: *Do all pendulums swing at the same rate, or do some swing slower or faster? How can you measure how fast a pendulum swings?*

EXPLORE

b. Provide each cooperative group with the materials to make a pendulum similar to the one you demonstrated. Lead the students to count the number of swings of their pendulum in 15 seconds. Explain that this is called the rate of swing of the pendulum. Define a swing as one complete back-and-forth cycle.)

Ask: *How can you get a pendulum to swing faster or slower (more or fewer swings in 15 seconds)?* Challenge the students to identify the things about their pendulum that they could possibly change.

c. After some discussion, ask students to focus on these three separate, measurable *variables* that might make a pendulum swing faster or slower:

1. Length of the pendulum
2. Weight or number of pennies that make up the pendulum bob
3. Angle at which the pendulum is released

d. Instruct students to write down a separate question about each variable (e.g., *How does the rate change when the weight of the pendulum bob is changed?*). Then tell them to design and conduct controlled experiments to answer the questions they have asked.

e. Monitor students' experiments and provide assistance with the procedures, logic, and data interpretation for controlled experiments. Ask the students to record what they do and what they find out.

f. When students have had ample time to explore, help the class to standardize the way they measure weight, length, angle, and rate (number of back-and-forth swings in 15 seconds). At this time you should be ready to introduce the use of a data table like the one illustrated to help students organize their investigations, keep track of their data, and interpret their data to form conclusions.

PENDULUM DATA TABLE

Does length affect the rate of swing of a pendulum?		Does weight affect the rate of swing of a pendulum?		Does the release angle affect the rate of swing of a pendulum?	
What variable did you manipulate?		What variable did you manipulate?		What variable did you manipulate?	
What variables did you control?		What variables did you control?		What variables did you control?	
What responding variable did you measure?		What responding variable did you measure?		What responding variable did you measure?	
Length of Pendulum	Rate (number of swings in 15 seconds)	Weight of Pendulum (number of pennies)	Rate (number of swings in 15 seconds)	Angle of Pendulum Release	Rate (number of swings in 15 seconds)
20 cm		1		small	
40 cm		2		medium	
60 cm		3		large	
What can you conclude about length and rate of swing?		What can you conclude about weight and rate of swing?		What can you conclude about the angle of release and rate of swing?	

This data table is not only a place for students to record measurements so they can remember them but also a "think sheet" that facilitates the planning and conducting of investigations, guides the students in recognizing relationships, and assists them in drawing conclusions.

EXPLAIN

g. Instruct students to use their data to answer their questions about the factors that affect the rate of a pendulum.

    If students have changed more than one variable at a time (for example, changing length and weight together), discuss with them the importance of experimental design. Ask: *Why must you change only one variable at a time when investigating? Why must other variables be kept constant?* (So you can be sure which of the variables really made a difference)

ELABORATE

h. Challenge students to notice pendulums in the world around them or find examples of pendulums in books or magazines or on the Internet. Grandfather clocks, swings, and trapezes are all forms of pendulums.

EVALUATE

i. Assessment task for cooperative learning groups:
   * Instruct students to create a pendulum that swings from one extreme to the other in one second (7.5 complete back-and-forth swings in 15 seconds). They should record the steps they followed to achieve their goal.
   * Use the following rubric to assess levels of group performance in solving the task.

   Exemplary:
   * Includes all of the bullets from the Proficient Level.

   * The pendulum's rate is exactly 7.5 complete back-and-forth swings in 15 seconds.

   Proficient:
   * The steps they followed were clearly described.
   * They only varied the length of the string, since they knew that the mass of the bob and the angle of release do not affect the rate of the pendulum's swing.
   * They referred to their data table from previous trials to estimate a reasonable string length to try.
   * The pendulum's rate is between 7 and 8 complete back-and-forth swings in 15 seconds.

   Developing:
   * One or two of the bullets from the Proficient Level were not observed.

   Little Understanding:
   * No more than two of the bullets from the Proficient Level were observed.

j. Assessment task for individuals:
   * Ask students to explain in writing: *How would you adjust a grandfather clock that was running too fast? too slow?* (Students should realize that the pendulum must be lengthened for the clock to slow down and shortened for the clock to run faster.)

III. SOUND

Sound is an important part of our lives, enabling us to communicate with one another, be alert to different situations, and enjoy music and the sounds of the world around us. The simple activities included here enable children to begin to understand the basic physics of sound. Consistent with the *National Science Education Standards*, topics studied include sources of sounds, the way sounds travel, and detectors of sound.

NSES Science Standards

All students should develop an understanding of

- position and motion of objects (sound) (K–4).

Concepts and Principles That Support the Standards

- Sound is produced by vibrating objects (K–4).
- The pitch of a sound can be varied by changing the rate of vibration (K–4).
- Sound is a form of energy (5–8).
- Energy is transferred in many ways (5–8).
- Most change involves energy transfer (5–8).
- Vibrations in materials set up wavelike disturbances that spread away from the source. Sound waves and earthquake waves are examples. These and other waves move at different speeds in different materials (*Benchmarks for Science Literacy*, 6–8).

A. SOURCES OF SOUND

▶ *Science Background*

Sounds are produced when objects vibrate or move back and forth rapidly. An object that produces sound is called a *sound source*. Many different objects can generate sounds. For example, musical instruments produce sound when some part of them is made to vibrate.

Characteristics such as pitch and loudness allow us to distinguish one sound from another. Pitch is determined by the frequency, or rate, of a vibration of sound.

Objectives

1. Define *vibration* as the back-and-forth movement of an object.
2. Demonstrate, describe, and explain the generation of sound by various vibrating sources.
3. Define *pitch* as how high or low a sound is. Demonstrate, describe, and explain how the pitch of a sound may be varied.
4. Define *loudness* as the amount, amplitude, or intensity of sound. Demonstrate, describe, and explain how the loudness of a sound may be increased.

1. HOW ARE DIFFERENT SOUNDS PRODUCED? (2–4)

Materials
- Craft sticks (15 cm in length)

ENGAGE
a. Ask: *How can you use a craft stick to create sounds?*

EXPLORE
b. Instruct students to hold a 15 cm craft stick firmly against a desk with one hand. With the other hand, they should pluck the overhanging part of the stick, causing it to vibrate. Remind the students to observe carefully while carrying out this procedure.

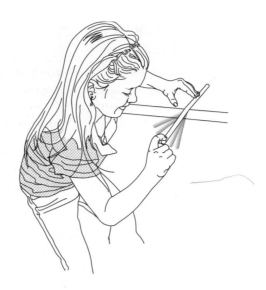

EXPLAIN

c. Ask: *What did you hear?* (A sound) *What did you see?* (Part of the craft stick was moving up and down.) *What did you feel?* (Possibly, the end of the craft stick moving up and down) *What is meant by vibration?* (A rapid back and forth motion) *Which part of the craft stick vibrates and produces sound? Were all the sounds produced by the craft sticks the same?* (No, not exactly) *How were they different?* (They were different notes, some high, some lower. Some children may mention the term *pitch* to describe this difference.)

Ask: *What is meant by the pitch of a sound? How can you change the pitch of a vibrating craft stick?*

ELABORATE

d. Challenge students to produce a high-pitched sound by vibrating the stick and to produce a low-pitched sound by vibrating the stick. Then have them try to make pitches that fall in between. Remind students to observe carefully and to pay attention to what they are changing about the craft stick. Then let them discuss their findings.

e. Ask: *What did you do to change the pitch of the vibrating craft stick?* (Change the amount of the craft stick hanging over the edge of the desk.) *How did you make your lowest pitch?* (Hold the craft stick so that most of it hangs over the edge of the desk.) *How did you make your highest pitch?* (Hold the craft stick so that only a little of it hangs over the edge of the desk.) *Does the craft stick vibrate faster or slower when more of it hangs over the edge of a desk?* (It vibrates slower when more of it hangs over the edge of the desk.) *How is the speed of vibration related to the pitch of the sound produced?* (The faster the vibration, the higher the pitch of the sound produced.) Consider asking students to demonstrate their ideas with the craft sticks to support the answers to these questions.

EVALUATE

f. To check for understanding of the relationship among length of vibrating object, speed of vibration, and pitch of the sound produced, have the students respond to the following assessment items.

1. Compete the following table to describe the relationships among variables in this investigation. The words to choose from are:
Fast, High, Long, Low, Short, Slow

Length of craft stick hanging over the edge of the table	Speed of vibration	Pitch of the sound produced

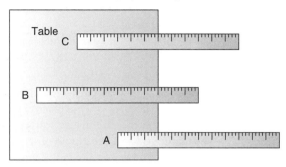

Rulers hanging over edge of table.

2. Which of the rulers shown in the drawing would produce the lowest pitched sound when plucked? (A)

3. Which of the rulers shown in the drawing would vibrate the fastest when plucked? (B)

2. HOW IS SOUND PRODUCED BY A TUNING FORK? (2–4)

Materials

- Tuning forks
- Wood blocks
- Container of water

Safety Precautions

To protect tuning forks from damage, strike them only against a wood surface or the sole of your shoe or with a rubber mallet to produce vibrations and sounds.

ENGAGE

a. Ask: *What is a tuning fork? How does a tuning fork produce sounds?*

EXPLORE

b. Instruct students to observe while you conduct this demonstration:
   1. Hold the tuning fork by its stem.
   2. Strike a wood block or sole of your shoe crisply with the tip of one of the fork tines.
   3. Bring the fork near your ear and listen. Strike the fork again and lightly touch the tip of one of the fork tines to the surface of the water in a container.

EXPLAIN   c. Ask: *What vibrates in producing sound from a tuning fork? What is your evidence that the fork tines are vibrating?*

....

3. HOW IS SOUND PRODUCED BY A DRUM? (2–4)

Materials
- Cylindrical container
- Puffed rice or wheat cereal
- Large balloon or sheet rubber
- Strong rubber band
- Drumstick or pencil with eraser

ENGAGE   a. Ask: *What vibrates in a drum to produce sound?*

EXPLORE   b. Stretch a large balloon or piece of sheet rubber over the open end of a cylindrical container, such as an oatmeal container. Place a rubber band around that end to hold the rubber sheet securely in place. This makes a simple drum. Sprinkle puffed rice or wheat cereal on the drumhead. Tell students to tap the drumhead softly with a drumstick or eraser end of a pencil and observe what happens. Then tell them to hit the drumhead harder and watch the cereal and observe the sound produced.

EXPLAIN   c. Ask: *What part of a drum vibrates to produce sound? What is your evidence? What is meant by loudness? How do you vary the loudness of a drum?*

....

4. HOW IS SOUND PRODUCED BY A BANJO? (2–4)

Materials
- Rubber bands of varying lengths and thicknesses
- Small, open box or plastic cup

ENGAGE   a. Ask: *What vibrates to produce sound in a stringed musical instrument, such as a banjo?*

EXPLORE   b. Tell students to make banjos by stretching rubber bands of varying lengths and thicknesses over a small box or plastic cup. Pluck the rubber bands to produce sounds.

EXPLAIN   c. Ask: *What part of a rubber band banjo vibrates to produce sound? What is your evidence?*
                         d. Ask: *What do you think might affect the pitch of the sound from a banjo?* Instruct students to investigate how the pitch of a sound is varied on a rubber band banjo by varying the tension and thickness of the rubber bands. Ask: *What variables can you change to vary the pitch of a rubber band banjo?* (Length, thickness, and tension of the rubber bands) *How do you vary the loudness of the banjo?*

ELABORATE   e. Ask: *How can you vary the pitch of the sound produced by a stringed musical instrument, such as a guitar or ukulele?* Allow students to observe how strings of differing thickness and different lengths produce different pitches in guitars, ukuleles, or other stringed instruments. Demonstrate how the tension of a string can be varied to produce high- and low-pitched sounds with a guitar or other stringed instrument.

TEACHING BACKGROUND

Each time a guitar player plucks a guitar string, it starts to vibrate. The rate of vibration determines the pitch of the string. Guitars have strings of differing thickness. Thinner strings vibrate more quickly and produce higher-pitched sounds than thicker ones. Strings under greater tension also vibrate more quickly and produce higher pitches than strings under less tension. The musician uses the tuning knobs on the guitar to adjust the tension of the strings. As she increases the tension of a string, that string vibrates more rapidly and the pitch gets higher. As she decreases the tension of a string, the string vibrates more slowly and the pitch gets lower.

Source: Full Option Science System, *Physics of Sound.* Lawrence Hall of Science, University of California, Berkeley.

EVALUATE

f. Challenge students to create a stringed instrument on which they can play a scale of eight ascending notes (eight notes in a row, each with a higher pitch). Each student will explain his or her stringed instrument to the class, then play a scale. Give the following rubric to the students to aid in their preparation, then use it to evaluate their instruments and presentations. Total possible score is 35. If you want an approximate grade on a 100-point scale, just multiply the score from the rubric by 3. A student who was judged Exemplary in all categories would have a grade of 105. A student who was judged Proficient in all categories would have a grade of 84. A student who was judged Developing in all categories would have a grade of 42.

Criteria	Exemplary (5 Points)	Proficient (4 Points)	Developing (2 Points)
Appearance	Very attractive; shows much effort and care in construction	Looks OK; some effort and care in construction is evident	Sloppy; shows little effort; careless construction
Sturdiness	Very sturdy; looks like it will withstand repeated use	Somewhat sturdy; didn't fall apart before or during performance, but looks like it might	Not sturdy; falls apart before or during performance
Safety	Completely safe, all potential safety issues addressed	Seems safe, if instrument used properly	Obvious that someone could be harmed during the use of this instrument
Explanation	Tells (in an interesting, organized manner) their name, name of their instrument, what is vibrating, and how different pitches are produced	Presents most information described in Exemplary; but presentation not very enthusiastic or interesting; or presentation is unorganized	Not informative, not interesting, unprepared, or silly

(continues)

Criteria	Exemplary (5 Points)	Proficient (4 Points)	Developing (2 Points)
Speaking Skills	Presenter speaks clearly and at a proper volume for audience to hear; uses good eye contact; and holds instrument so it is visible to all	One of the desired elements from Exemplary not achieved	Two or more of the desired elements from Exemplary not achieved
Playing of Scale	All 8 notes of scale are played in order from low pitch to high pitch and are all "in key"	8 different pitches are played, they are in order from low pitch to high pitch, but they are not "in key"	Instrument produces fewer than 8 pitches or scale not played in order
Volume of Instrument	All notes produced can be easily heard throughout the classroom	Most notes produced can be heard in the classroom	Can't hear many notes, too quiet

5. HOW CAN YOU MAKE A DRINKING STRAW FLUTE? (2–4)

Materials
- Drinking straws
- Scissors

ENGAGE

a. Ask: *What is a flute? How is sound produced in a flute? How can you vary the pitch of a sound produced by a flute?*

EXPLORE

b. Give each student a drinking straw. Have students use scissors to cut a V-shape at the end of the straw and pinch it closed to produce a reed.

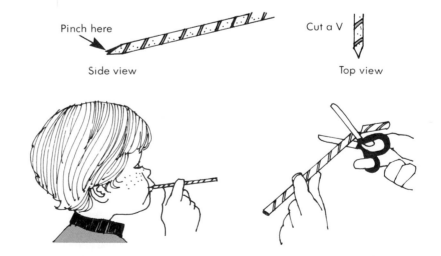

Pinch here — Side view

Cut a V — Top view

Have students blow on the V cut into the straw flute to produce a sound. (*Note:* They will need to experiment to get the proper lip vibration.) Now, have students cut the straw into different lengths and blow on the straw flute to get different pitches.

EXPLAIN

c. As you circulate among students, or when you return to a whole class structure, ask: *What part of a straw flute vibrates to produce a sound? What can you vary to change the pitch of a straw flute?*

ELABORATE

d. *How do you think clarinets, oboes, and saxophones produce sounds? How could we find out?* Provide the opportunity to do library and/or internet research about how these woodwind instruments make sounds.

6. HOW CAN YOU MAKE A BOTTLE PIPE ORGAN? WHAT AFFECTS THE PITCH OF THE SOUND PRODUCED BY A BOTTLE? (2–4)

Materials

For each cooperative group:

- 8 identical glass or plastic soda or water bottles
  Or a test-tube rack with 8 identical test-tubes

- Water

ENGAGE

a. Blow across a bottle that is about three-fourths full of water so that a sound is produced from the bottle. Ask: *How could you vary the pitch of the sound coming from the bottle?*

EXPLORE

b. Fill eight identical bottles with varying amounts of water. Blow across the open ends of the bottles. Explore the sounds they produce. Arrange the bottles to play an ascending scale (pitches that get higher one after another).

EXPLAIN

c. Ask: *What part of a bottle vibrates to produce sound?* (The air) *How is the air in the pop bottle made to vibrate?* (By blowing over the opening in the bottle) *What can you vary to change the pitch of a pop bottle?* (Change the amount of water in the bottle) *How do you think pipe organs and horns produce sounds?* (The air inside them vibrates.)

TEACHING BACKGROUND

In a pipe organ, air is blown across the bottom opening of a metal pipe. The air in the pipe then vibrates to produce a sound. The pitch of the sound depends on the length and thickness of the pipe. Shorter pipes produce higher-pitched sounds.

When a musician blows air into the mouthpiece of a horn, the air in the open column of the horn vibrates and produces sounds. The pitch of the sound produced in a horn depends on the length and volume of the air column.

ELABORATE

d. Challenge student groups to play a simple tune using their bottle organs.

B. TRANSFER OF SOUND

▶ *Science Background*

Sound moves away from a source through a material medium. Air, water, and solids are all good media for carrying sound. Sounds travel through media in waves that are analogous to waves in water. Sound cannot travel through a vacuum because there are no particles to vibrate and carry the sound waves. When sound waves bounce off some solid object in the distance, they return to the source as echoes.

Objectives

1. Define *medium* as the material substance through which sound travels from a vibrating source to a receiver.
2. Demonstrate and describe how sound travels through solid, liquid, and gas media.
3. Describe how sound travels through different media in waves that are analogous to water waves.
4. Demonstrate and describe ways that sound can be directed and amplified.
5. Describe and explain echoes as the reflection of sound waves.

1. DOES SOUND TRAVEL THROUGH AIR, SOLIDS, AND LIQUIDS? (2–4)

Materials

- Lengths of garden hose
- Metersticks
- Pieces of metal or rocks
- Bucket

ENGAGE

a. Ask: *How does sound travel? Does sound travel through all kinds of materials? Can sound travel through the air in a garden hose? Does sound travel through solids? Does sound travel through water?*

EXPLORE

b. Have students listen to sounds through straight and curving lengths of garden hose. Make sure all of the water is drained out of the hose.
c. Have students work in pairs. One student should hold a meterstick to her ear. The partner should scratch the other end of the stick with a pencil. Repeat the activity with the meterstick held away from the ear a few centimeters.

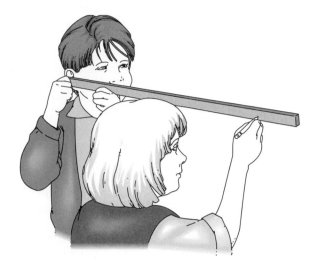

d. Obtain a large bucket of water. Ask students to take two pieces of metal or two rocks and hit them together under the water. Then, tell them to hit the objects together out of water.

EXPLAIN

e. Ask: *How does the garden hose demonstration show that sound travels through air?*
   What do you hear through the meterstick? How do you think the sound of the pencil travels through the meterstick?
   What did you hear when you hit the objects together underwater? Was the sound louder or softer when you hit the objects together out of the water?
   Which seemed to be a better conductor of sound: the solid meterstick, air, or water?

 ## C. RECEIVERS OF SOUND

▶ *Science Background*

Receivers are instruments that detect sound. Sound is one of the many forms of energy. Our ears are marvelously designed receivers of sound that are tuned to keep us in touch with much of our environment.

Objectives

1. Explain how the outer ear and an ear trumpet are similar in gathering incoming sound signals.
2. Explain that in receiving sound, a detector in the receiver is set in vibration by the incoming sound signals.
3. Identify and describe the operation of the sound detectors in the human ear and a stethoscope.

....

1. HOW CAN SOUNDS BE HEARD BETTER? (2–4)

Materials

- Stethoscope
- Ear trumpet
- Listening tube

ENGAGE

a. Ask: *What part of your body detects sounds? How is your ear specially designed to receive and detect sounds?*

EXPLORE

b. Roll a piece of poster board into a cylinder and fasten it on both ends with paper fasteners. Have students use the listening tube to listen to faint sounds.

c. To make an ear trumpet, curl a fan-shaped piece of cardboard into a cone. Fasten the cone with three brass fasteners. Ask students to place the small end of the ear trumpet to their ears and listen to the faint whispers of partners some distance away from them.

d. Ask students to tap their fingers together and listen to the sound. Have them tap their fingers together again and listen to the sound through a stethoscope. Then, have them tap their fingers underwater and listen to the sound without and with a stethoscope.

Safety Precautions

- Help students to clean earpieces of stethoscopes with alcohol and cotton swabs before and after using them.
- Caution students not to damage the diaphragm of a stethoscope by striking it against hard objects.
- Only use listening tubes, ear trumpets, and stethoscopes to listen to faint sounds. Since these listening devices make sounds louder, listening to loud sounds with them may damage your ears.

EXPLAIN

e. Ask: *How do listening tubes enable sounds to be heard better?*

How does the ear trumpet enhance hearing? How is an ear trumpet similar to the outer ear?

How does the stethoscope work? How does a stethoscope enable you to hear soft sounds better?

In what ways do the rolled cylinder, the ear trumpet, and the stethoscope extend the sense of hearing?

Teaching Background

A sound receiver must be able to detect sound pulses that reach it. The ear is a sound receiver. The outer part of the ear collects sound much like the large end of an ear trumpet when it is used as a listening tube. When sound energy strikes the eardrum, the resulting vibrations initiate the hearing process.

A stethoscope has a diaphragm that vibrates when sound strikes it. Faint sounds can be detected by the diaphragm. The sounds are then conducted from the diaphragm down the air-filled tubes to the ear. In a similar way, a telephone mouthpiece has a diaphragm that vibrates when sound energy strikes it. In a telephone, the vibrations in the diaphragm are converted electromagnetically to electrical energy. Electrical energy is then conducted from one telephone along telephone wires or from a series of towers to another telephone where the diaphram in the earpiece vibrates because of the electrical signals it receives.

D. SOUND CHALLENGES: HOMEMADE TELEPHONES

NSES **Science and Technology Standards**

Students should develop

- abilities of technological design, including the ability to
  a. identify a simple problem of human adaptation in the environment;
  b. propose a solution;
  c. implement proposed solutions;
  d. evaluate a product or design; and
  e. communicate a problem, design, and solution (K–4).

Objectives

1. Construct homemade telephones.
2. Explain the operation of a homemade telephone, using the concepts of vibrating source, conducting material, and receiver.
3. Design and carry out investigations to determine the best type of materials for a homemade telephone.
4. Demonstrate abilities of technological design.

1. CAN SOUND TRAVEL THROUGH A STRING? (2–4)

Materials
- Spoon
- String

ENGAGE
a. Ask: *Can sound travel through a long string?*

EXPLORE
b. Loop a length of string around a spoon. Try to tie the spoon at about the middle of the string. Hold the two ends of the string in your ears. Bend over so the spoon hangs freely. Have your partner gently strike the spoon with another spoon.

EXPLAIN
c. Ask: *What do you observe? What is your evidence that the string is a conductor of sound?*

2. HOW CAN YOU MAKE A DEMONSTRATION TELEPHONE? (2–4)

Materials
- String, wire, or nylon fishing line
- Cups of various kinds (Styrofoam, waxed cardboard, plastic, large, small)
- Nail, paper clips, toothpicks

ENGAGE
a. Ask: *How can you design a "telephone" that will enable you to communicate across some distance using a string as a medium?*

EXPLORE

b. Show students how to construct a homemade telephone using plastic cups. In advance, use a small nail to punch a hole in the bottom of each cup. Tell pairs of students to cut a 20 foot (6 or 7 meter) length of string and thread the ends into cups. Tell them to tie a paper clip around each end to hold the string firmly in place inside the cup. Instruct them to try out their homemade telephones with their partners.

EXPLAIN

c. Ask: *What is the original source of sound for your telephones? What is set in vibration in the mouthpiece of the telephone? What is the conductor of sound? How is the sound detected at the other end of the telephone?*

ELABORATE

d. Challenge students to improve the quality of their homemade telephones by investigating the effects of different string or wire media, different types of cups, and different ways to hold the string or wire against the bottom of the cups. Tell students to come up with standard ways to test their telephones so they can decide which parts are most effective. If you have a microphone probe to use with CBL software, this would be a great time to introduce that technology.

TEACHING BACKGROUND

A homemade telephone is a human-constructed product that connects well to scientific principles. Many concepts introduced in the activities on sound are used in this activity. The voice of one partner sets particles of air in vibration. The cup/mouthpiece of the string telephone is then set in vibration. The sound energy produced by the vibrating cup is conducted along the string to the other cup. Thus, the second cup is set in vibration. This vibrating cup sets the air in vibration, producing sound. The sound is then carried to the ear. Designing, constructing, and evaluating homemade telephones provides a good introduction to the technological design cycle.

▶ *Evaluate*

To demonstrate mastery of Objective 2, ask each pair of students to create a labeled drawing and brief explanation of the homemade telephone they constructed that they think worked best.

Distribute the following checklist to guide their work then use it to evaluate their products.

Your explanation of your best homemade telephone should:

☐ Fit on one page.
☐ Include first and last name of both partners.
☐ Include a neat sketch of your homemade telephone in use.
☐ Label the following parts of your homemade telephone on the sketch: vibrating source, conducting material, and receiver.
☐ Indicate the length of the conducting material (in centimeters).
☐ Identify the materials used to make each part of your homemade phone.
☐ Include a description of how your phone works.
☐ Include an explanation of why this phone was the best one you designed.

IV. TEMPERATURE AND HEAT

▶ *Science Background*

Heat, like light, sound, and electricity, is a form of energy. Energy is one of the few concepts in science that children talk about accurately before they can define it. Children's ideas about energy—getting "quick energy" from a candy bar or turning off lights so as not to "waste energy"—may be imprecise but are reasonably close to the concept of energy that we want children to learn (*Benchmarks for Science Literacy*, American Association for the Advancement of Science, 1993).

Technically, energy is the ability to do work. More intuitively, something has energy if it can bring about a change in another object or in itself. Heat can bring about many changes. For example, it can change the state of a substance from liquid to gas (evaporation) or from solid to liquid (melting); it can change the temperature of a substance; it can cause most things to expand; and it can change the rate of a reaction, such as how fast a substance dissolves.

 Science Standards

All students should develop an understanding of

- light, heat, electricity, and magnetism (K–4).
- transfer of energy (5–8).

Concepts and Principles That Support the Standards

- Heat can be produced in many ways, such as burning, rubbing, or mixing one substance with another (K–4).
- Energy is a property of many substances and is associated with heat (5–8).
- Energy is transferred in many ways (5–8).
- Heat moves in predictable ways, flowing from warmer objects to cooler ones, until both reach the same temperature (5–8).

Objectives

1. Name and describe sources of heat and activities that produce heat.
2. Design, conduct, and interpret experiments to determine the effects of the color of a material on the amount of radiated heat absorbed by the material.
3. Design and conduct experiments to determine the final temperature of water mixtures.
4. Explain that heat flows from warmer substances to cooler substances until an equilibrium temperature is reached.

1. WHAT MAKES THINGS GET HOTTER? (3–5)

Materials

- 6 inch piece of wire coat hanger
- Mineral oil
- Brass button

- Wool cloth
- Piece of metal
- Pencil eraser
- Notebook paper

ENGAGE

a. Hold up the piece of wire coat hanger. Ask the class: "*If you touched this, how do you think it would feel?*" If its temperature is not mentioned, lead them to also consider that property. Let several students feel the wire before you start and report their observations, especially about temperature, to the class. Bend a 6 inch piece of wire hanger back and forth 10 times as shown. Let the students quickly touch the wire at the point where you bent it.

   Ask: *How does the wire feel now?* (The wire got hotter.) *What do you think will happen if I bend the wire more times, for example, 20, 25, 30, 35 times?* (Each time the wire gets hotter.)

Safety Precautions

Try out this activity first to find out how many bends will make the wire too hot for students to safely touch.

EXPLORE

b. In cooperative groups, have students explore actions that cause materials to heat up. For example, rub your hands together very fast and hard, or rub a brass button on a piece of wool, metal on paper, or a pencil eraser on paper and quickly touch it to your upper lip or the tip of your nose (sensitive parts of your body).

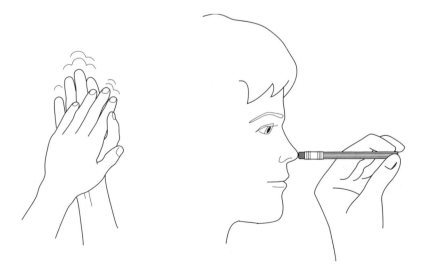

c. Have groups each complete an *I Notice/I Wonder* chart about their observations and the questions they generate.

If temperature probes and CBL software is available for student use, students could use this technology to make their observations quantitative rather than just qualitative.

EXPLAIN

d. Ask: *What did you observe in each case? How was heat produced in these activities?* Guide students to understand that bending things and rubbing things produces heat.

ELABORATE

e. Try rubbing your hands together again, but put a few drops of oil or water on your hands first. Ask: *How do you think the second rubbing will feel different from the first rubbing?*
Ask: *What did you observe? Why do you think it happened?*

....

2. HOW CAN YOU HEAT UP THE SAND IN A JAR? (5–8)

Materials

- Baby food jar with screw top or small plastic food storage container with secure lid
- Sand
- Thick towel
- Thermometer or temperature probes with CBL software on computers

ENGAGE

a. Hold up a baby food jar three-fourths full of sand. Ask: *What do you think will happen to the sand in a baby food jar if you shake it many times?* Hint: *Think back to the previous activity.*

EXPLORE

b. For each cooperative group, fill a baby food jar three-fourths full of sand, screw on the jar top, and then wrap it with a thick towel. Each person should take a turn doing the following things:
   1. Measure the initial temperature of the sand, then shake the sand vigorously for 5 minutes.
   2. Measure the temperature of the sand.
   3. Write your findings on a record sheet like the one shown.

Person	Minutes of Shaking	Temperature in °C
1	5	
2	10	
3	15	
4	20	
5	25	

4. Pass the jar to the next person.
5. When everyone has had a turn, compare the temperature of the sand from the first to the last reading.
6. How were they different? (The temperature was higher after each shaking.)
7. Set up a graph like the one shown, then graph the data from the record sheets.

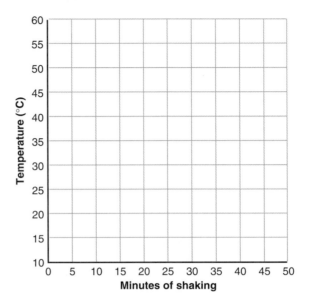

EXPLAIN

c. Ask: *What did you observe? What do your data indicate? What was the source of the heat energy in the sand?* Explain that shaking something is a form of energy (mechanical energy; kinetic energy). Heat is also a form of energy. When you shook the sand, the energy of the sand's motion was transferred to heat energy when the sand grains struck one another and the container. The heat energy in the sand caused its temperature to go up.

3. WHAT IS THE EFFECT OF HEAT ON AIR IN A CONTAINER? (1–4)

Materials

For each group:

• Liquid soap solution in a wide-mouthed container or pie pan
• Ice water in a deep container
• Test tube, medicine vial, small juice can

ENGAGE

a. Ask: *What can we do to change the shape of a soap bubble on the mouth of a container?*

EXPLORE

b. Squirt some liquid soap into a large container of water with a wide opening at the top. Stir the water. Dip the open end of a test tube, medicine vial, or small juice can into the soapy water so that a soap film forms across the end of the container. Challenge students to get the soap film to expand. One way to get the soap film to expand is for

students to wrap their hands around the container (without squeezing) so that their hands cover as much of the container as possible.
  Ask: *What do you observe?*

c. Get a soap bubble on a small container, such as a test tube or medicine vial. Put the container in the container of ice water. Ask: *What happens to the soap bubble?*

EXPLAIN

d. Ask: *Were you able to change the shape of the soap film? How? Why did the soap bubble expand when you held the container in your hands? Why did the soap bubble go down into the container when you placed the container in ice?*

Through their explorations, the students should note that when they hold the container in their hands, the air in the container is heated and the soap film expands, becomes dome-shaped, and eventually pops. Lead students to understand this principle about heat and air pressure:

Air expands (takes up a greater volume) when it is heated. Thus, air in a closed container exerts more pressure on its container when it is heated. Air contracts (takes up a smaller volume) when it is cooled. Thus, air in a closed container exerts less pressure on its container when it is cooled.

ELABORATE

e. Obtain a large can, such as a vegetable can from the school cafeteria. Dip the open end of the can into soap solution in order to form a soap film over the open end of the large can. Let several students wrap their hands around it to see if they can get the soap film to expand. Ask children to describe what they see and to explain why it happens.

EVALUATE

f. To assess if students can apply the principles they have been investigating to a new situation, have them answer the following question.

  1. You blow up a red balloon so that it is 40 cm around its widest part. Then you put the balloon into the freezer for an hour. What do you predict will be true about the balloon immediately after it is taken out of the freezer compared to before it was placed in the freezer?

For each pair of answers below, circle the answer you predict to be true.

The balloon will be blue.	The balloon will be red.
The air in the balloon will be colder.	The air in the balloon will be warmer.
The balloon will be larger.	The balloon will be smaller.
The balloon's circumference will be less than 40 cm.	The balloon's circumference will be more than 40 cm.
The air in the balloon is exerting more pressure on the balloon.	The air in the balloon is exerting less pressure on the balloon.

Then write an explanation of why you expect the changes you have circled.

4. WHAT AFFECTS THE TEMPERATURE CHANGE OF WATER HEATED IN SUNLIGHT? (5–8)

Materials

- Three tin cans of same size
- Small can of shiny white paint
- Small can of dull black paint
- Two small paintbrushes
- Styrofoam covers for cans
- Three thermometers or temperature probes with CBL software
- Lamp with 150 to 300 watt bulb (to use in place of sunlight)

ENGAGE

a. Ask: *If something is left in sunlight, does its color affect how hot it gets? How could you investigate to find out?*

EXPLORE

b. Guide students to plan and conduct a controlled experiment to determine the effect of color on heating in sunlight. These activities may be done in cooperative groups or as a whole class demonstration. Based on the experience of your class with inquiry you might give them the following instructions (structured inquiry) or allow them to design their own investigation to answer the question.

1. Obtain three identical-sized cans and remove all labels. Paint one can dull black and another can shiny white; leave the third can unpainted, shiny metal.
2. Fill each can with the same amount of regular tap water.
3. Put a Styrofoam cover on each can and insert a thermometer through each cover.
4. Set the cans in direct sunlight or at equal distances from a 150 to 300 watt light bulb. (See diagram.)
5. Prepare a table for data collection and record the temperature of the water in each can at 1-minute intervals. (Do not move the thermometers when you record the temperature each time.)

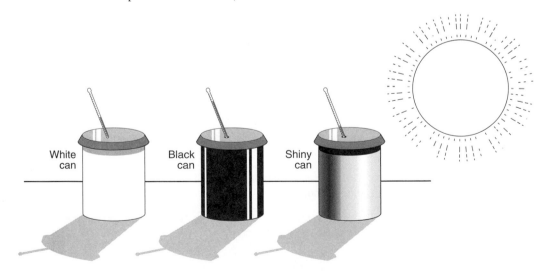

White can   Black can   Shiny can

EXPLAIN

c. Ask: *What happens to the water temperature in the three different cans after being in the sun or near light bulbs for a while? If they are different temperatures, how would you explain that?* Explain that heat energy is transferred from the sun to earth. Lead students to understand that the shiny surface of the unpainted can and the shiny white paint reflect radiant energy, whereas the dull black paint absorbs most of the radiant energy which then heats the water.

ELABORATE

d. Ask: *How would you relate the unequal heating in the tin cans to different land and water surfaces of the earth?* Guide students to understand that dark patches of ground absorb more radiant energy than do shiny water surfaces or lighter-colored land surfaces. The unequal heating of the earth contributes to climate and weather changes.

e. Ask: *What color space suits do astronauts wear? Why?*

EVALUATE

f. Use the following item to check student understanding about this concept.

1. You are planning to camp in a sunny area during the summer. You want to be able to stay cool in your tent during the hottest part of the day. All of the tents are identical except for their color. What color tent do you want? Why? (Students should select a white or very light colored tent, so that most of the sun's rays are reflected rather than absorbed. This tent should remain cool longer than a dark tent.)

5. WHAT AFFECTS THE FINAL TEMPERATURE OF A WATER MIXTURE? (3–6)

Materials

* Styrofoam cups (at least 250 ml)
* Graduated cylinders or measuring cups
* Thermometers or temperature probes with CBL software
* Stirring spoons

ENGAGE

a. Ask: *What happens to the temperature of bath water when you add hot water to cold water? Does the amount of hot water and cold water matter? How could you predict the new temperature when hot and cold water are mixed?*

EXPLORE

b. Tell students to plan an investigation to determine the final temperature when hot and cold water are mixed. Students could plan and conduct the following activity in cooperative groups:

1. Pour the following volumes of water at the indicated temperatures into separate Styrofoam cups:
    * 100 ml of hot water
    * 100 ml of cold water
    * 50 ml of hot water
    * 50 ml of cold water
    * 150 ml of hot water
    * 150 ml of cold water

2. Measure and record the temperature of the 100 ml samples of water in a copy of the prepared data table (see illustration). If possible, make all temperature measurements in degrees Celsius.
3. In a third cup, carefully mix and stir the two 100 ml samples of water.
4. Measure and record the final temperature.
5. Repeat steps 2, 3, and 4 for the following mixtures:
   * 150 ml of hot water and 50 ml of cold water
   * 150 ml of cold water and 50 ml of warm water
c. Instruct cooperative group recorders to record their data on the class master data table.

TEMPERATURE OF WATER MIXTURES			
	Amount of Water in Each Container	Initial Temperature of Water	Final Temperature of Mixture
Mixture 1	100 ml		
	100 ml		
Mixture 2	150 ml		
	50 ml		
Mixture 3	50 ml		
	150 ml		
Mystery Mixture			Predicted _____
			Measured _____

EXPLAIN

d. Ask: *What patterns do you see in the class data? In what ways do these patterns help you predict the final temperature of the mixtures?* Lead students to notice that if the volumes of two samples of water are the same, the final temperature will be halfway between the two initial temperatures. If the volumes of the two samples are different, the final temperature will be nearer the initial temperature of the larger sample.

ELABORATE

e. Tell students you are going to give them a new water mixing problem, but they will need to predict the final temperature before they mix the water samples and take data.
f. Prepare a large container of cold water at near freezing temperature (but with no ice). Prepare another large container of water at room temperature. Give materials managers a cup of cold water and a cup of room temperature water.
g. Instruct groups they are going to mix 175 ml of cold water with 50 ml of warm water. Ask groups to make a prediction of the final temperature and then to conduct the investigation. Predictions do not need to be exact. For example, a group may just predict that the final temperature will be halfway between the temperatures of the two samples or very near the temperature of the larger sample.
h. Instruct recorders to record the predicted and final temperatures of their mixtures on a class chart. Invite students to present and discuss their predictions, the basis of the predictions, and the final temperatures obtained.

Explain that the final temperature of a mixture depends on both the initial temperatures and volumes of the samples. When a large volume of water is mixed with a smaller volume of water, the final temperature will be nearer the initial temperature of the large volume. There are actually mathematical ratios here that can be dealt with at upper grades.

Nature of Scientific Inquiry

i. Ask: *What have you done in this investigation that is like what scientists do?*

Lead students to understand that they have formulated a problem, planned and conducted an investigation, used a thermometer and graduated cylinder to collect data, recorded data in a table, interpreted the data and formed an explanation for experimental results, and tested the explanations through a prediction. These are some of the things scientists do.

EVALUATE

j. Use the following item to check student understanding of the principle presented in this lesson:

1. The water that comes from your cold faucet is 10°C. The water that comes from your hot faucet is 72°C. If you mix equal parts of water from each faucet in the bathtub, what will be the initial temperature of your bath water? How do you know? (41°—Since I put in equal amounts of the two temperatures of water, the resulting temperature is halfway between the two temperatures.)

V. LIGHT

▶ *Science Background*

Visible light is a form of energy. In empty space, light travels at a speed of 186,000 miles per second.

Because our eyes are light detectors, light is an especially important part of our lives, enabling us to see the world around us. We see objects when light that is either emitted or reflected from an object reaches our eyes. Further, light is the energy source for photosynthesis and the growth of plants that sustain both human and animal life. Thus, light is at least indirectly essential for most forms of life.

 Science Standards

All students should develop an understanding of

- light, heat, electricity, and magnetism (K–4).

Concepts and Principles That Support the Standards

- Light can be reflected by a mirror, refracted by a lens, or absorbed by an object (K–4).
- Light travels in straight lines until it strikes an object (K–4).

A. SOURCES AND RECEIVERS OF LIGHT

Objectives

1. Distinguish between sources and reflectors of light.
2. Identify and describe human-constructed sources of light (e.g., lightbulbs) and natural sources of light (e.g., the sun).
3. Explain that our eyes are detectors of light and that we can "see" an object only if light is emitted or reflected from the object.
4. Identify materials that are transparent, translucent, and opaque, and explain what we "see" when each of these materials is placed over an object.

1. HOW DO WE SEE THINGS? (1–5)

Materials

- Flashlights
- Shoe boxes
- Assorted small objects

Safety Precautions

As they study light, impress on students the importance of protecting their eyes at all times. Students should never look directly into the sun or any other bright light source. Also, they should never look into a laser light source or shine a laser toward someone else.

ENGAGE

a. Darken the room completely and write this statement on the chalkboard: "We cannot see without light." Tell students to read what you have written. Illuminate the sentence with a flashlight and tell students to read it. Ask: *Why did the words on the chalkboard appear? Is light needed in order for us to see?*

EXPLORE

b. Cut two small holes in a shoe box, one for students to look into the box and the other to illuminate the inside of the box with a flashlight. Place an object in the box, cover the flashlight hole, and put the top on the box. Tell students to look into the box and describe the object. Illuminate the object with the flashlight and tell students to describe the object again.

c. Build a small electric circuit consisting of a bulb in a bulb holder, a battery in a battery holder, a switch, and wires. Place the circuit inside another shoe box with only one hole cut in the end of it. Arrange the circuit so the switch is outside the box and place the top on the box. Tell students to look into the box and describe the objects in it. Tell them to activate the switch and describe the objects again.

EXPLAIN

d. Ask: *How did light enable you to see the statement on the chalkboard? How did the flashlight enable you to see the object in the shoe box?* Lead students to understand that the eye is a receiver of light, like the ear is a receiver of sound. We see things only when light from them reaches our eyes. *Why were you able to see the bulb in the box?* (Light coming from the bulb reached our eyes and enabled us to see it.) Explain that there are natural sources of light, such as a flame, and artificial, human-constructed sources of light, such as the lightbulb.

ELABORATE

e. Tell the student groups that they have 5 minutes to make a list of the objects/things they can see in the classroom or outside now. When the 5 minutes are up, encourage them to discuss in their small groups: *What enables you to see these objects?* Then have them indicate which of the things on their list produce their own light and which only reflect light. Have a whole class discussion about their conclusions.

f. Ask: *Why are you able to see the sun?* (It produces light.) *Why are you able to see the moon?* (It reflects light from the sun.)

EVALUATE

g. To assess student understanding about the effect of light on what we see, ask students to respond to the following.

1. Imagine you are exploring a cave when your yellow flashlight goes out. No one else in your group has a source of light. No light is entering the cave from outside. It is completely dark.

   Which of the following statements best describes what you see in the the dark cave?
   A. I can't see my flashlight at all, even after my eyes are adjusted to the dark cave.
   B. After my eyes are adjusted to the dark cave, I can see my yellow flashlight.
   C. After my eyes are adjusted to the dark cave, I can see my flashlight but I can't see its yellow color.
   D. After my eyes are adjusted to the dark cave, I can only see a faint outline of my flashlight.

2. Explain why you selected the answer you did.

....

2. WHY CAN WE SEE CLEARLY THROUGH SOME MATERIALS AND NOT OTHERS? (K–2)

Materials

- Transparent materials (clear plastic wrap, clear glass)
- Translucent materials (wax paper, cloudy plastic, tissue paper)
- Opaque materials (cardboard, aluminum foil, wood)

ENGAGE

a. Allow students to examine a small object placed underneath a sheet of wax paper or a piece of cloudy plastic. Ask: *What do you see? Why is the object not easily seen?*

EXPLORE

b. Give each group of students some samples of transparent, translucent, and opaque materials. Ask the students to place one kind of material at a time over a printed page. For each material, have students fill in a chart with one of these choices: (1) can see through it easily; (2) can see through it but not very clearly; (3) cannot see through it.

EXPLAIN

c. Ask: *Through which of the materials could you see the print on the page easily? Through which of the materials could you tell there was print on the page but it could not be seen clearly? Through which of the materials was it impossible to see the print on the page?* List the student responses in three columns on the board. Introduce the terms *transparent, translucent,* and *opaque* by adding them as headings to the three column chart on the board. Guide students to understand that light is transmitted through transparent media, such as air, water, and glass, so the print was clearly visible. Translucent materials transmit some light, so the print was not so clear. Opaque materials do not transmit any of the light energy striking them, so the print was not possible to see.

ELABORATE

d. Using the same materials as before, let the students look through them at the lights on the ceiling of the classroom. Ask: *In terms of how much light comes through, what is the difference between the transparent, translucent, and opaque materials?*

e. Have them classify other objects/materials in the room according to their ability to transmit light as transparent, translucent, or opaque.

EVALUATE

f. To check student understanding about this concept, ask them to complete this chart in their science notebook.

Type of material		Translucent	
How much light is transmitted	Nearly all		
Example			Aluminum foil

B. HOW LIGHT TRAVELS

▶ *Science Background*

Light travels in straight lines until it is absorbed, reflected, or refracted by an object. Unlike sound, light cannot ordinarily bend around corners. Evidence that light travels in straight lines is apparent in our daily lives: beams of sunlight streaming through windows, not being able to see around corners, looking straight at objects to see them. The inverted image that is formed on the screen of a pin-hole camera is also evidence that light travels in straight lines.

Objectives

1. Demonstrate that light travels in straight lines unless it is absorbed, refracted, or reflected by an object.
2. Construct a pin-hole camera and demonstrate how it works to form an image.
3. Describe the pathway of light as it passes through a hole in the end of a pin-hole camera and forms an inverted image on a wax paper screen in the camera.
4. Investigate how the size and number of holes affects the image produced in a pin-hole camera.

1. WHAT TYPE OF PATH DOES LIGHT TAKE AS IT TRAVELS? (3–6)

Materials
- Flashlight or projector
- Index cards
- Hole puncher or pointed object (pencil)
- Modeling clay
- Wax paper

ENGAGE

a. Tell a child to stand behind a barrier or just outside the classroom so that she can be heard but not seen. Instruct the child to speak softly. Ask: *Can you hear her talking? Can you see her? Why can you hear someone talking when the person is out of sight?*

EXPLORE

b. Holding three or four index cards together, punch a 1/4 inch (7 mm) hole in the center of each card. Stand each card up in a lump of modeling clay. Instruct students to space the cards about 30 cm apart and to arrange them in such a way that light from a flashlight passes through the center hole in each of the cards.

EXPLAIN

c. Ask: *What must you do to the holes in the index cards if light is to pass through them? Do you think that light travels along a straight or curved pathway? What is your evidence, or why do you think so? Can light travel around an opaque object? Can sound travel around an opaque object? How can you test your inference about how sound travels?*

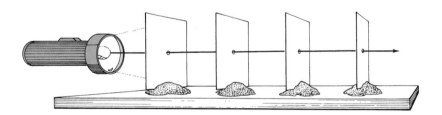

▶ *Science Background*

A pin-hole camera can be used to illustrate what happens in a regular camera. In a pin-hole camera, light passes through a small hole in the end of a box and forms an inverted image on a wax paper screen. In a real camera, light is focused by a lens and forms an inverted image on a strip of film.

2. HOW CAN YOU MAKE A PINHOLE CAMERA? (3–6)

Materials

For each student:

- Two plastic cups, opaque (16 oz) or two cardboard tubes
- Two rubber bands
- Scissors
- Recording sheets
    - Difference in image
    - Difference in number and arrangement of holes
    - Difference in size of hole

For each cooperative group:

- Aluminum foil
- Wax paper
- Masking tape
- Push pin
- Paper clip, large
- Nail
- Pencil

For whole class:

- Overhead projector
- Construction paper

DIFFERENCE IN IMAGE

Appearance of Arrow on Screen	Appearance of Arrow on Wax Paper in Pinhole Viewer
↑	
→	
←	
↓	

Describe how the image on the wax paper compares with the image on the screen.

What does the pinhole viewer seem to do to the image?

DIFFERENCE IN NUMBER AND ARRANGEMENT OF HOLES

Number of Holes	Appearance of Holes in Aluminum Foil	Prediction of Image on Wax Paper	Actual Image on Wax Paper
1			
2			
3			
4			

Describe how the number of holes in the aluminum foil affects the image produced.

Describe how the arrangement of holes in the aluminum foil affects the image produced.

DIFFERENCE IN SIZE OF HOLE

Hole Size	Prediction of Image on Wax Paper	Actual Image on Wax Paper
• Pin Hole		
● Paperclip Hole		
● Nail Hole		
● Pencil Hole		

Describe how the size of the hole affects the image produced.

ENGAGE

a. Ask: *What are cameras used for?* (To create images of objects around us) Today each of you will build a pinhole camera, like this one. (Hold up a completed pinhole camera.) Then you will explore how changing the hole affects the image produced.

EXPLORE

b. Have students follow these directions to construct their pinhole cameras. It may be helpful to demonstrate pinhole camera construction for the class.
   1. Cut the bases off of both plastic cups.
   2. Cut a circle of wax paper and a circle of aluminum foil about 3 cm larger than the mouth of the cup.
   3. Place the circle of wax paper on the mouth of one of the cups. Use a rubberband and some tape to hold the wax paper in place.
   4. Hold the other cup so that the mouths of the two cups are together with the wax paper in between. Tape the cups together.
   5. Place the circle of aluminum foil over one of the open ends of one of the cups. Secure it in place with a rubber band and tape.
   6. Use the push pin to poke a small hole in the center of the aluminum foil.

c. Cut a large arrow from the center of the construction paper. Place the construction paper with the arrow-shaped hole on the overhead projector so that a large, bright arrow pointing upward appears on the screen or wall.

d. Encourage the students to hold their pinhole cameras with the aluminum foil end toward the bright arrow, then look into the open end. Ask: *What do you see on the wax paper screen in your pinhole camera? How does it compare to the bright arrow on the wall?*

Tell students to record their observations on the first row of the chart on the Difference in Image sheet by drawing what they see on the wax paper in the pinhole viewer.

e. Shift the orientation of the construction paper so the bright arrow on the screen or wall appears to point toward the right. Have students look into their pinhole viewers, then record the appearance of this arrow on the wax paper in the viewer. Reorient the construction paper two more times, first projecting a left-pointing arrow, then a downward-pointing arrow.

f. Have the students answer the questions at the bottom of the Difference in Image sheet: *Describe how the image on the wax paper compares with the image on the screen. What does the pin-hole viewer seem to do to the image?*

EXPLAIN

g. Encourage students to share and discuss their observations and the answers to their questions. The consensus should be that the arrow on the wax paper in the pinhole camera is smaller, not as bright, and the other way around, flipped, or backwards compared to the arrow on the wall.

h. Introduce the term *inverted* meaning "reversed in position."

i. Ask: *How does the image on the screen provide more evidence that light travels in straight lines?* Draw this figure below on the board. Ask: *Where does the ray of light from the top point of the arrow land on the wax paper, after it goes through the pinhole?* (On the bottom) *Where does the ray of light from the base of the arrow land on the wax paper, after it goes through the pinhole?* (On the top) Lead students to the conclusion that if the light travels in straight lines through the pinhole, then the image on the wax paper is inverted compared to the bright arrow on the wall. Remind students that there are rays coming from all lit parts of the arrow, not just the ends, and as they pass through the pinhole, the inverted image forms on the wax paper.

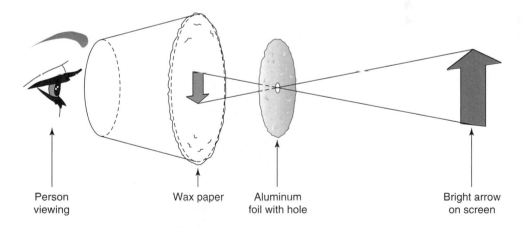

| Person viewing | Wax paper | Aluminum foil with hole | Bright arrow on screen |

ELABORATE

j. Ask: *What would happen to the image on the wax paper in the pinhole camera if the number or arrangement of the holes in the aluminum foil was changed?* Point out that the record sheet titled Difference in Number and Arrangement of Holes includes a chart on which they can record the appearance of the holes in the foil, their predictions of the image on wax paper, and their observations of the image on wax paper. Mention that the last three rows are left open for them to decide the number and arrangement of the holes. Tell the class that the bright arrow on the wall will stay

in the pointing-upward position for all of their observations. Suggest that cooperation and sharing of pinhole viewers can reduce the replacement of aluminum foil,
then allow them to investigate.

k. For an additional surprise, if students don't try rotating their pinhole cameras as they
are observing with multiple holes, suggest that they try that.

l. Have students summarize their findings by responding to the two items at the bottom
of the record sheet: *Describe how the number of holes in the aluminum foil affects the image produced. Describe how the arrangement of holes in the aluminum foil affects the image
produced.*

m. Encourage groups to share their observations and summaries with the class. Ask:
Explain why you saw what you did on the wax paper during this investigation.

n. Ask: *What would happen to the image on the wax paper in the pin-hole camera if the size of
the hole in the aluminum foil was changed?* Point out that the record sheet titled Difference in Size of Hole includes a chart on which they can record the size of the hole in
the foil, their predictions of the image on wax paper, and their observations of the image on wax paper. Mention that the last two rows are left open for them to try other
sizes of holes. Provide groups with additional aluminum foil and suggest that one person make the hole shown on the first row, another make the hole for the second row,
etc. Tell the class that the bright arrow on the wall will stay in the pointing-upward
position for all of their observations, then encourage them to investigate.

o. Have students summarize their findings by responding to the item at the bottom of the
record sheet: Describe how the size of the hole affects the image produced.

p. Encourage groups to share their observations and summary with the class. Ask: *Explain
why you saw what you did on the wax paper during this investigation.*

EVALUATE

q. Ask students to respond to these items in their science notebooks.

　　1. You use your pinhole camera to look at a brightly lit EXIT sign. What will the image on the wax paper in the pinhole camera look like?

　　　A. **EXIT**

　　　B. **EXIT** (inverted)

　　　C. **TIX∃** (mirrored)

　　　D. **∃XIT** (rotated)

　　2. Explain why the appearance of the image on the wax paper in the pin-hole camera provides evidence that light travels in a straight line. You may use words
and/or drawings.

C. LIGHT REFRACTION

▶ *Science Background*

Light ordinarily travels in straight lines, but it bends or refracts when it passes at an angle into a clear material, such as glass, plastic, or water. Lenses use the property of refraction to form images of objects. A magnifying lens bends the light coming from an object so that we see the object larger than it actually is. A lens can also be used to form an image of an object on a screen.

Objectives

1. Describe the refraction or bending of light rays passing through water, clear plastic, or glass.
2. Use knowledge of refraction to explain different light phenomena.
3. Define *magnifying power* and relate it to the curvature of a lens.
4. Define *image* and describe the image of an object formed on a screen.

1. WHAT IS REFRACTION? (3–6)

Materials

For the teacher:

* Glass
* Pencil

For each group:

* Flashlight
* Black rubber or plastic comb
* Two cylindrical jars of different diameters

ENGAGE

a. Place a pencil in a glass of water so that half of it is in water and half of it out of water. Ask: *What do you see? Why does the pencil seem distorted?*

EXPLORE

b. Provide each group with a flashlight, a comb, and two cylindrical jars of different diameters. Show them how to form rays of light by laying the flashlight on a white poster board and shining the flashlight through the comb. Instruct students to follow these directions:
   1. Fill a jar almost full of water, place it in the path of the rays, and observe what happens.
   2. Repeat the procedure with the other jar.
   3. Record your observations. Include any differences you observed.

EXPLAIN

c. In a large group, invite students to discuss their procedures and observations.
   Ask: *What did you observe? What differences did you observe in the effects of the two jars? Which jar, the larger or smaller diameter one, bent the light rays more and caused them to converge nearer to the jar?* Lead students to recognize that the smaller jar, which had the greater curvature of its surface, caused the most bending of the light rays.
   Explain that light rays are bent when they pass into and out of a clear material, such as water, plastic, or glass. The bending of light rays is called *refraction.*

Ask: *Why do you think the pencil appeared distorted in the glass of water?* Lead the students to understand that the water bent or refracted the light rays coming from the pencil, causing it to appear distorted.

....

2. WHAT IS A MAGNIFIER? HOW DOES IT WORK? (3–6)

Materials

For each group:

- Two or more cylindrical, glass jars or jugs of different diameters
- Magnifying lenses, including at least two lenses of different magnifying power
- Clear plastic sheets, such as transparency sheets (sandwich bags might be substituted)
- Dropper

ENGAGE

a. Obtain two cylindrical, glass jars of different diameters. Fill them with water within a few centimeters of the top. Allow students to look through each jar of water at some small writing. You can place the jars on a tray and carry them around the room for all students to see. Ask: *What do you see? Do you see the same thing through each jar? Which jar makes things appear larger? Why do you think the jars of water magnify? What other things will magnify?*

EXPLORE

b. Arrange students in small groups of three or four. Provide each group a clear plastic sheet, a dropper, and a small container of water. Tell students to place different-sized drops of water on the plastic sheet and to look through the drops at some very small writing. Ask: *What do you see through drops of different sizes? Do different-sized drops magnify differently?* (*Note:* Very small drops provide greater magnification.) Tell students to record their observations on a record sheet or in their science journals.

c. Provide at least two magnifiers of different magnifying power to each group. If necessary, show students how to use the magnifiers. Lead students to examine writing and different objects through each of the magnifying lenses. Lead students to compare the magnifying lenses. Ask: *How are your magnifying lenses different? What makes lenses have different magnifying power?*

EXPLAIN

d. Invite students to share their observations.

Explain that what your students see through a lens is called an *image*. Lenses fool our eyes; we think the light comes from the image, when it really comes from the object and only appears to come from the image. The lens bends or *refracts* the light, making it appear to come from the image.

Define the *magnifying power* of a lens as the number of times bigger it can make an object appear or how many times bigger the image is than the object. Ask: *Which jar had a greater magnifying power?* (The smaller one) *Which water drop had a greater magnifying power?* (The smaller one) *Why do you think this is so?* Guide students to understand that the smaller jar and smaller water drops have a greater curvature. Light is refracted or bent more when the surface at which refraction is occurring is curved more. The magnifying power of a magnifier depends on how much the surface of the magnifier is curved. The greater the curvature, the greater the magnifying power.

e. Ask: *Which magnifying lens had a greater magnifying power? Did that lens have a greater curvature?* If lenses are of the same diameter, the lens with greater curvature will be the one that is thicker in the middle.

ELABORATE

f. Challenge students to measure the magnifying power of each of their magnifying lenses. This might be done by examining a millimeter scale through a lens to determine the number of times bigger an image appears than the object.[3]

EVALUATE

g. To check students' understanding of the relationship between lens shape and magnification, have them answer the following question.
   1. Which of these lenses (viewed from the edge) would you expect to have the greatest magnifying power?

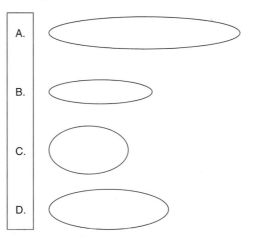

   2. Why did you select the lens that you did?

3. WHAT DO LENSES DO IN CAMERAS? (3–6)

Materials

For the class:

* Lamp with 40 to 75 watt bulb

For each group:

* At least two lenses of different magnifying power

ENGAGE

a. Ask: *Where have you seen lenses? What things have lenses in them?* List students' answers on the board. Students might suggest eyeglasses, contact lenses, the eye, microscopes, telescopes, projectors, binoculars, cameras, and other instruments.
   Ask: *What do lenses do in cameras? How do they work?*

---

[3]Adapted and modified from *More than Magnifiers*, one of more than 75 teacher's guides in the Great Explorations in Math and Science (GEMS) series, available from the Lawrence Hall of Science, University of California at Berkeley. For more information, visit the website at http://www.lhsgems.org.

EXPLORE

b. Arrange students in groups. Provide two lenses of different magnifying power to each group. Show students how to support a lens vertically by taping it to the bottom of a Styrofoam cup. Remove the shade from the lamp and place the lamp in the room so that all groups have an unobstructed view of it.

Provide these instructions to students:

1. Tape each of the two lenses to the bottom of cups. Label the cups and lenses A and B.
2. Place lens A, supported by a cup, on the table so that it faces the lamp.
3. Fold a white sheet of paper along two opposite edges so it will stand up.
4. Place the sheet of paper behind the lens and move it back and forth until you see an image of the lamp on the paper.

5. Measure and record the distance from the lens to the image on the paper.
6. Ask: *Is the image inverted or right side up?* (Inverted) *Is the image of the lamp larger or smaller than the lamp itself?* (Smaller) Record your answers on a record sheet or in your science journal.
7. Repeat the procedures for lens B. Is the image formed on the paper inverted or right side up? Is the image larger or smaller than the lamp?
8. Which lens, A or B, formed a larger image? For which lens, A or B, was the lens closer to the paper screen?

EXPLAIN

c. In a large group, invite students to discuss their procedures and observations.

Ask: *Why do you think the images formed of the lamp were inverted?* Draw the following diagram to show how light rays from the top of the lamp are bent or refracted by the lens and converge so that the lamp is upside down.

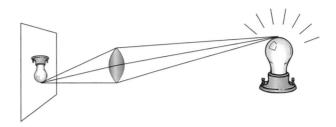

d. Ask: *How are lenses used in cameras? What do the lenses do? Do you think the images formed in cameras are right side up or upside down? Are they larger or smaller than the object forming the image?*

Draw on the board the illustration of a camera and lens showing an image formed on a film. Explain that some of the light coming from the bulb strikes the lens. The light is bent and converges on the film so that the image is small and upside down. The film is coated with a light-sensitive chemical. When the film is developed, the image of the bulb is clearly seen.[4]

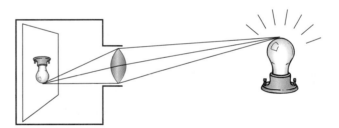

 ## D. LIGHT REFLECTION

▶ *Science Background*

Reflection, the bouncing of light rays, follows a pattern that can be discovered through investigations. Light reflects from a smooth, plane surface in such a way that the angle at which it strikes the surface is equal to the angle at which it reflects from the surface. Mirrors are excellent examples of reflecting surfaces. As a consequence of reflection, images can be seen in mirrors. In a flat, plane mirror, an image is symmetric with the object forming the image, but the image is reversed.

Objectives

1. Describe the reflection of light off reflecting surfaces.
2. Describe images in mirrors as symmetric with objects, but reversed.

[4]Adapted and modified from *More than Magnifiers*, one of more than 75 teacher's guides in the Great Explorations in Math and Science (GEMS) series, available from the Lawrence Hall of Science, University of California at Berkeley. For more information, visit the website at http://www.lhsgems.org.

1. WHAT ARE IMAGES IN MIRRORS LIKE? WHAT IS MEANT BY MIRROR SYMMETRY? (1–4)

Materials

For each cooperative group:

* Mirrors
* Set of pictures of butterflies, flowers, and other things that might show symmetry and of things that do not show symmetry (same set of pictures for each group)

ENGAGE

a. Ask: *When you look at something in a mirror, does it look exactly like the object when it is viewed directly? How could we find out?*

EXPLORE

b. Ask: *Do these pictures look the same in the mirror as when you view them directly?* Allow the students time to try it to find out. As you monitor their work, point out that the view in the mirror should be identical to the direct view, not upside down or switched around.

c. Challenge groups to sort the pictures into two groups: those that can look the same in the mirror as when viewed directly and those that cannot. Encourage them to look at the similarities of the pictures within each group. Ask: *What is special about the pictures in the group that can look the same in the mirror as when viewed directly?*

EXPLAIN

d. Ask: *What did you find out? Did all the pictures look the same in the mirror as when viewed directly?* (no) *How did they look in the mirror?* (upside down, backwards, switched, etc.) *Which pictures could look the same in the mirror and when viewed directly? Did you have to do anything to make them look the same?* (Put mirror in certain position; turn the picture a certain way) *How are the pictures in the group that look the same in the mirror and when viewed directly different from the pictures in the other group?* Lead students to realize that the image of an object is reversed in a mirror.

e. Introduce the term *symmetry* to describe a picture or shape that can look the same when viewed in a mirror as when viewed directly. Show how a symmetric picture can be completed.

f. Use one of the symmetric pictures from the students' collections and a mirror to introduce the term *axis of symmetry*.
   1. Find an axis (line) you think divides the picture in half so that if folded along that line, the two parts would match.
   2. Place a plane mirror along that axis.
   3. Look at the image of one-half of the picture in the mirror and compare it with the other half of the picture.

ELABORATE

g. Challenge groups to identify the axes of symmetry on the pictures they decided were symmetrical. Monitor their progress and clarify questions as you informally visit each group.

h. Provide students an activity sheet with all of the letters of the alphabet displayed in block lettering. Tell students to use a mirror to identify all of the axes of symmetry for each letter. For example, ask: *Does the letter* **A** *have an axis of symmetry? How many axes of symmetry can you find for an* **H**? Discuss with the students the axis or axes of symmetry of each letter of the alphabet.

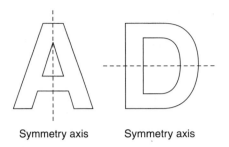

Symmetry axis   Symmetry axis

EVALUATE

i. To assess student understanding of the concepts of mirror images and symmetry, have them complete the following items.
  1. When you look in a mirror, do you see yourself as others see you when they are looking at you directly? Why or why not?

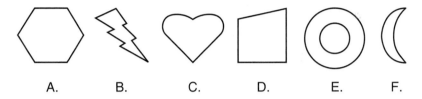

A.   B.   C.   D.   E.   F.

  2. Which of the figures above could look the same in a mirror as when viewed directly. (A, C, E, F)
  3. Which of the figures above are not symmetric? (B, D)
  4. Which of the figures above have only one axis of symmetry? (C, F)

2. HOW DOES LIGHT REFLECT FROM A MIRROR? (3–6)

Materials

For each cooperative group:

* Light-ray source (flashlight, cardboard, scissors or knife, transparent tape)
* Mirror
* Rubber band
* Wood block
* Pencils or markers
* White poster board or large sheet of white paper

▶ *Preparation*

Make a light-ray source by obtaining a stiff cardboard shield about the diameter of a flashlight, cutting a slit in the shield, and attaching the shield over the lens of a strong flashlight with transparent tape. A light ray is formed when light from the flashlight passes through the slit.

ENGAGE

a. Ask: *When you look in a mirror, do you always see yourself?*
      Hold a mirror facing the class. Adjust it so everyone might see themselves or another student's face. *Ask: Do you see yourself in the mirror?* (Only students directly in front of the mirror should say yes.) Ask a student who is looking into the mirror at an

angle: *What or who do you see in the mirror?* (Someone or something on the other side of the classroom) After some discussion, ask: *What is the pattern of who sees what in the mirror?*

EXPLORE

b. In each cooperative group lay the light-ray source on a white poster board so you can see the light ray on the board. Attach a small, plane mirror to a block of wood with a rubber band. Put the mirror in the path of light. Tell children to mark a spot on the poster board and to orient the mirror so that the reflected ray hits the spot. Instruct the students to initially use trial and error to align the mirror so that the reflected light ray hits the desired spot. Gradually, the students should make and test predictions of how the mirror should be aligned to direct the reflected light ray to the spot.

EXPLAIN

c. Ask: *How does light reflect from a mirror? What pattern did you detect about how light reflects? How did you know how to align a mirror to make a reflected light ray hit a desired spot?* Lead students to understand that the angle formed between a reflected light ray and a mirror is the same as the angle between the incoming light ray and the mirror.

ELABORATE

d. Have students explore the rays and mirror positions again to check if the statement that "the angle between the reflected light ray and a mirror is the same as the angle between the incoming light ray and the mirror" is indeed true. Suggest that they place the edge of an index card against the reflective surface of the mirror. Then shine a light ray toward the mirror. Draw lines on the index card showing the incoming and reflected rays. By folding the index card at the point the light ray hit the mirror, students can check if the lines drawn on the card touch when folded. This would confirm that the angles with the edge were the same. If students know how to use a protractor, they can use it to compare the angles the rays made with the edge of the index card.

EVALUATE

e. To assess student understanding of the way a light beam would reflect from a plane mirror, have students respond to this item:

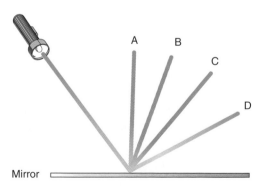

1. In this illustration, which line represents the reflected ray? How do you know?

E. LIGHT AND COLOR

▶ *Science Background*

Color is a response of the human eye to different frequencies of visible light. The visible color spectrum includes red, orange, yellow, green, blue, indigo, and violet. White light is a combination of all colors. An object appears black when all colors of visible light are absorbed by it. The color of an opaque object depends on the colors reflected by it. A red rubber ball, for instance, will appear red because it reflects mostly red and absorbs other colors of light. The color of a transparent or translucent object depends on the colors that are transmitted by it. For example, a green glass bottle on a sunny window sill will appear green because it transmits mostly green light and absorbs other colors of light.

1. WHAT IS WHITE LIGHT? (3–6)

Materials

- Prism
- Sheet of heavy, white cardboard
- Scissors
- Felt markers or crayons
- String
- Flashlights
- Colored filters (red, green, blue) for flashlights (these can be cut from colored clear plastic report covers)

ENGAGE

a. Obtain a prism. Place the prism in the path of a strong beam of light as indicated in the diagram.

Ask: *What do you see? What happened to the white light when it passed through the glass prism? What colors do you see?*

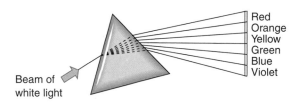

EXPLORE

b. This part of the activity can be done in small groups or as a whole group investigation.

Put a different colored filter on each of three flashlights. Darken the room for the best effect. Shine each of the flashlights on three different places on a white sheet of paper. Draw and color (or label) a picture to show how the paper looks.

c. Shine two of the flashlights so their beams overlap on the paper. Draw and color (or label) a picture to show how the paper looks.

Repeat this step with all possible pairs of colors (red-blue; blue-green; green-red).

d. Shine all three flashlights so their beams all overlap on the paper. Draw and color (or label) a picture to show how the paper looks.

EXPLAIN

e. Ask: *What did the prism do to the light?* (It separated white light into different colors.) *What does that tell you about the composition of white light?* (It is made up of different colors of light.)

f. Ask: *What happened when you mixed colored light beams from flashlights?* (A different color appeared.) Have students share what color was produced by each pair of overlapped colored light beams and what colors were produced when all three colored light beams were overlapped. Creating Venn diagrams based on student observations on the board might be helpful during this discussion. The class should agree that when these three colors of light were mixed, white light was produced. This supports the idea that white light is a combination of different colors of light.

ELABORATE

g. Introduce another way of mixing colors of light. Challenge students to construct spinning color wheels by following these directions:
    1. Cut out a circle about 10 cm in diameter from stiff cardboard.
    2. Divide the circle into three pie-shaped sections.
    3. Use red, green, and blue felt markers or crayons to color each section a different color.

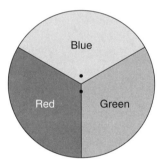

    4. Punch two small holes about a centimeter apart in the center of the cardboard circle.
    5. Pass a string about 60 cm long through the two holes; tie the free ends of the string forming a loop.
    6. Hold the loop by the ends and turn the cardboard color wheel many times, twisting the string as you go.
    7. Pull the two ends of the string suddenly and watch the color wheel spin. What do you see? What colors do you observe as the color wheel is spinning?

h. Encourage students to share their observations with the class. Expected comments include: *The wedges of color seem to disappear. The whole wheel looks white when it spins.* Ask: *What did the color wheel do to the light?* (It combined different colors to form a white color.) Ask: *Why do you think this happened?* Lead students to the idea that red, green, and blue light were reflecting from the wheel, and when it was spinning fast, our eyes couldn't see the sections separately so the reflected light mixed together so it looked white.

i. To further extend the lesson, let different groups color their color wheel sections differently. Have groups compare what they see with different color wheels.

j. Invite student groups to report on their procedures and findings related to their color wheels.

EVALUATE

k. To assess student understanding about the composition of white light have the class respond to the following question in their science notebook.
  1. What evidence have you seen that white light is made up of many colors?
l. Use the following rubric to evaluate student responses to the question.

Exemplary:
- Clearly explains all three examples presented in the lesson.
  - White light separated into colors by a prism.
  - Colored beams mix to create white light.
  - Spinning color wheel.

Proficient:
- Clearly explains two of the examples presented in the lesson.

Developing:
- Clearly explains only one of the examples presented in the lesson.

Lacks Understanding:
- None of the examples presented in the lesson are suggested as evidence.

VI. MAGNETISM

▶ *Science Background*

The *National Science Education Standards* emphasize that, through the study of its history and nature, students should begin to understand science as a human endeavor. The study of magnetism is a good place for students to examine the long history of science and technology. As you guide students in learning about magnetism, provide them with interesting information about the history of the topic and make appropriate biographies and other books and resources available to them.

Four hundred years ago, William Gilbert, an English physician, wrote a book titled *On the Loadstone and Magnetic Bodies*. It was the first important work in physical science published in England. Gilbert's book provides the first written account of numerous experiments on magnetism, experiments that can be readily carried out in elementary and middle school science today. Gilbert argued for a new method of knowing, dedicating his book to those "ingenuous minds, who not only in books, but in things themselves look for knowledge."

 Science Standards

All students should develop an understanding of

- light, heat, electricity, and magnetism (K–4).

Concepts and Principles That Support the Standards

- Magnets attract each other and certain kinds of other materials (K–4).
- Magnets can be used to make things move without touching them (K–2).

A. MAGNETS AND MAGNETIC MATERIALS

Objectives

1. Identify materials that interact with magnets.
2. State that magnets come in many sizes and shapes.
3. Demonstrate that only some metal objects (those that contain iron) stick to magnets.
4. Demonstrate that magnetism will act through most materials.

....

1. HOW DOES A MAGNET INTERACT WITH DIFFERENT OBJECTS? (1–4)

Materials

For each group:

- Assortment of magnets, including bar magnets, U-shaped magnets, ring magnets, disc magnets, and other magnets
- Bag of assorted materials that are attracted to magnets (objects containing iron, such as paper clips and most screws and nails) and materials that are not attracted to magnets (such as wood, plastic, and paper objects, and non-iron metallic objects, such as aluminum nails, most soda cans, pennies, and brass fasteners)

Safety Precautions

- Keep computer disks, audio- and videocassettes, and credit cards away from magnets, as magnets can destroy information on them. Also, keep magnets away from computer and television screens and antique watches, as magnetism can damage them.
- Magnets must be treated with care so as not to destroy their magnetic effects. Magnets can be destroyed by dropping them, extreme heat, or storing two magnets of the same type together.

ENGAGE

a. Give each student a magnet. Without pointing out what it is or calling it a magnet, tell students to find out how the object interacts with the things within reach of their seats. Explain that when things interact, they do something to one another. Ask: *Did this object interact with anything you could reach from your seat? What?* Describe the interactions. Many possible interactions may be observed, but the key one is that some objects stick to a magnet.

EXPLORE

b. Ask: *What kinds of things will stick to this object?*

Give each small group of students a bag of materials, some of which are attracted to magnets and some which are not. Instruct students to sort the objects into two piles, according to which objects they predict will stick to the object they were given earlier and which will not. When groups have made their predictions, have them use the magnets to test each object.

EXPLAIN

c. Ask: *How accurate were your predictions? Were you surprised by any objects you tested?* (Students might mention the aluminum nail or the brass fastener.) *Are there any metal objects in the things-that-don't-stick pile? What do you think is the difference between the metal objects in the "will stick" and "won't stick" piles?*

d. Ask: *Does anyone know the name of the object they have been using to test the objects in the bag?* (A magnet) *What have you discovered that magnets do? Are all magnets the same?* (No, they come in different shapes and sizes, but the same things stick to all of them.)

> ### TEACHING BACKGROUND
>
> Iron is the only common kind of metal that magnets attract. Magnets will not stick to such metals as aluminum, copper, and brass. Magnets stick to steel because steel is mostly iron.

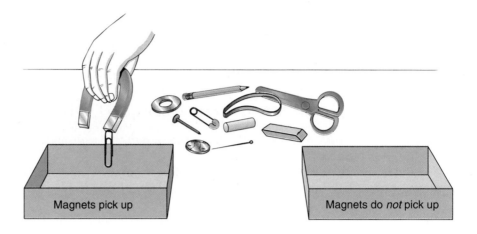

Magnets pick up | Magnets do *not* pick up

ELABORATE

e. Ask students to explore the room to determine which objects interact with magnets. Place "NO MAGNETS HERE!!" signs on computers, computer and television screens, computer disks, and audio- and videocassettes. Caution students not to bring magnets near these objects, because magnets can damage them.

EVALUATE

f. To check for understanding about which objects are attracted to magnets, ask students to answer the following questions in their science notebook:
1. *Which objects in the room contain iron?*
2. *What is your evidence?*
3. *Did some objects, such as painted objects, turn out to contain iron when you thought they would not?*

2. CAN MAGNETS INTERACT WITH OBJECTS THROUGH DIFFERENT MATERIALS? (1–4)

Materials

- Magnets
- Paper clips

ENGAGE

a. Ask: *Will magnets work through paper and other materials? How do you know? How could you find out?*

EXPLORE

b. Ask students to investigate if a magnet will attract a paper clip through different materials. Students should try a sheet of paper, cardboard, plastic tumblers, glass jars, aluminum foil, a tin can, and a sheet of steel, such as the walls of a filing cabinet.

EXPLAIN   c. Ask: *What kinds of things did you find that magnetic forces act through?*

ELABORATE   d. Challenge students to investigate how many pages of a book magnets can act through. Ask: *Does it matter which magnet you are using?*

> **TEACHING BACKGROUND**
>
> Magnetic forces act through most materials, although the magnetic interaction decreases with the thickness of the materials.

B. MAGNETIC INTERACTIONS

Objectives
1. Define the terms *force*, *attract*, and *repel*, and apply them to the interactions between two magnets.
2. Demonstrate procedures for mapping magnetic fields.
3. State in their own words the meanings of the terms *pole*, *north-seeking* or *north pole* and *south-seeking* or *south pole*.
4. Demonstrate a procedure for identifying the north and south poles of magnets.
5. State and demonstrate that like poles of magnets repel and unlike poles attract.

1. WHAT HAPPENS WHEN TWO MAGNETS INTERACT? (2–4)

Materials   For each group:

- Three or four ring magnets
- A pencil

ENGAGE   a. Ask: *How do two magnets interact with each other?*

EXPLORE   b. Give each pair or small group of students three or four ring-shaped magnets. Ask the students to find out what happens when magnets interact. Suggest that they record their observations and new questions on an I Notice/I Wonder chart.

c. Allow time for exploration. If necessary, challenge students to try

- using one magnet to move another magnet without the two magnets touching; and

- placing several ring magnets over a pencil in different ways to see what happens.

EXPLAIN

d. Ask: *What did you do to test how the magnets interact? What did you find out about how the two magnets interact?* Building on the children's activities, use discussion and expository teaching to help them understand the terms *attract*, *repel*, and *force* to describe magnetic interactions.

- When two magnets or a magnet and an object pull or stick together, we say they attract.

- When two magnets push apart, we say they repel.

- A force is a push or a pull. We can see some forces, such as when you push someone in a swing. Some forces, such as magnetic forces, are invisible and act without direct contact between objects.

- Magnets can attract or repel each other. When two magnets come together, there is a force of attraction. When two magnets push apart, there is a force of repulsion.

Ask: *What did you wonder about as you explored?* Collect the questions by writing them on the board or on chart paper.

ELABORATE

e. Tell students: In your group, select one of the questions you still wonder about. Design an investigation that will help you answer that question. Carry out your investigation. Then prepare a poster showing what you found out.

EVALUATE

f. Give each group a copy of the rubric so they have a clear idea of the expectations for their poster.

Rubric

Exemplary: Poster —
- Includes all components of Proficient
- Is very neat, easy to read, and well organized

Proficient: Poster includes —
- Clear statement of the question being investigated
- Clear statement of your procedure
- Clear statement of what you found out
- Correct use of the terms *attract*, *repel*, and *force*

Developing: Poster includes —
- At least two of the components of Proficient

Needs Improvement: Poster includes —
- Fewer than two of the components of Proficient

2. HOW DO THE ENDS (POLES) OF TWO BAR MAGNETS INTERACT WITH EACH OTHER? (2–6)

Materials
- Bar magnets
- Masking tape
- Red and blue crayons

ENGAGE

a. Ask: *How do bar magnets interact with each other? How could we find out?*

EXPLORE

b. Place masking tape over the ends of bar magnets so the N-pole and S-pole designations are obscured. Provide each group with three identical bar magnets with taped ends. Ask: *Can you find a way to determine which ends of the magnets are the same?* Give the class plenty of time to explore.

EXPLAIN

c. Ask: *What did you find out?* The students should arrive at the idea that if the ends of two magnets are the same, then they interact in the same way with the end of the third magnet. For example, if the ends of two magnets both attract one end of a third magnet, the ends of the first two magnets are the same. Tell children to use red and blue crayons to designate the like ends of the three magnets. (*Note:* Do not introduce the terms *magnetic pole* and *north* and *south magnetic poles* yet. They will be introduced through later investigations.)

d. Ask: *Now that you know which ends of the magnets are like and which are unlike, can you find a pattern or rule in how like and unlike ends of magnets interact?*

   Through exploration, discussion, and expository teaching of new concepts, make sure that students understand this rule:
   - When two magnets are brought together, like ends repel (push one another apart), while unlike ends attract (pull one another together).

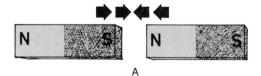
A

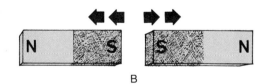
B

ELABORATE

e. Ask the students to try out their rule with other types of magnets, such as ring-shaped or horseshoe magnets.

EVALUATE

f. To check for student understanding about the interaction of the ends of magnets, have them answer the following items:
   Fill in the blanks, so that the following sentences are true.
   1. When like ends of magnets are brought close together, they _____.
   2. When unlike ends of magnets are brought close together, they _____.

3. WHAT ARE MAGNETIC FORCE LINES? (2–6)

Materials
- Magnets
- Iron filings
- Food storage bags

▶ *Preparation*

Sprinkle iron filings into a large, transparent, food storage bag so that a thin layer covers about three-fourths of the area of one side of each bag. Prepare a bag for each cooperative group of students.

ENGAGE
a. Ask: *How will a magnet interact with the material in this storage bag?*

EXPLORE
b. Ask students to explore what happens when a magnet touches or is brought near a bag containing iron filings. Give students these instructions:
- Spread an iron filings bag out flat on your desk. Tap the bag lightly so that the iron filings are evenly distributed. Slide a bar magnet under the bag. Tap the bag again so that the iron filings move about. (See the diagram.)

- Draw a diagram of the magnet's field as shown by the iron filings.

- Investigate the field around two magnets placed end to end a few centimeters apart so that the magnets attract. Draw a diagram showing the reaction of the iron filings.

- Investigate the field around two magnets placed end to end a few centimeters apart so that the magnets repel. Draw a diagram showing the reaction of the iron filings.

EXPLAIN
c. Ask: *What did you observe about the magnetic field around a single bar magnet? What did you observe about the magnetic field for attracting bar magnets? What did you observe about the magnetic field for repelling bar magnets?*
d. Explain that all magnets have two regions where the magnetic interaction with other magnets or magnetic materials is strongest. These regions are called *poles*. Point out that the concentration of iron filings is greatest at the poles of the magnets.

4. HOW DOES A MAGNET INTERACT WITH THE EARTH? WHAT ARE NORTH-SEEKING AND SOUTH-SEEKING POLES OF A MAGNET? (4–8)

Materials
- Ring magnets
- Bar magnets
- String
- Compasses

ENGAGE

a. Ask: *How can you use a magnet to tell directions?*

EXPLORE

b. Suspend a bar magnet by a string from a nonmagnetic support as in the diagram. Note the directions the ends of the bar magnet point. Compare the directions pointed to by the bar magnet and the directions indicated by a compass. How does the bar magnet interact with a second bar magnet? (See the following diagram.)

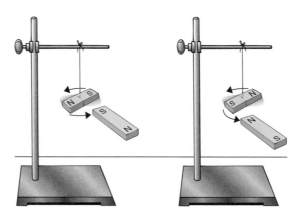

EXPLAIN

c. Ask: *What happens to the suspended bar magnet?* Lead students to compare the directions pointed to by the magnet and the directions indicated by the compass.

- One end of the magnet points toward the north (as indicated by the compass) and is called a north-seeking pole, or simply a north pole. The other pole of the magnet is a south-seeking pole or south pole.

- Our suspended magnet acts like a compass. The main part of a compass is a small permanent magnet attached to a pivot at the bottom of the compass.

- North and south are defined geographically by the rotational axis of the earth and astronomically by observations of the fixed North Star. The projection onto earth of a line drawn between us and our North Star, Polaris, will be within a degree of true, geographic north.

- The earth's magnetic poles are nearly a thousand miles from the geographic poles. Thus, a compass may point several degrees away from true north.

5. HOW CAN YOU MAKE A COMPASS? (4–8)

Materials

For each group:

- Steel needle
- Bar magnet
- Cork
- Plastic bowl of water

ENGAGE

a. Ask: *How can you make a compass?*

EXPLORE

b. Obtain a steel needle, a magnet, a cork (substitute a flat piece of Styrofoam), and a plastic bowl with a few centimeters of water in it. Holding the magnet in one hand and the needle in the other, stroke the needle about 25 times in one direction with the magnet.

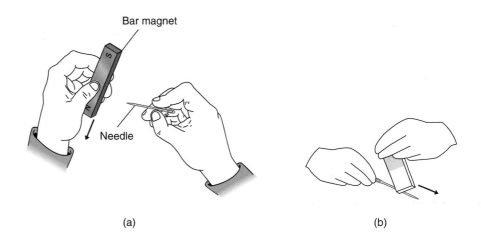

(a)   (b)

c. Float the cork in the water, and lay the needle on it.
    Ask: *What happens to the needle and the cork?* Rotate the needle and cork 90 degrees and then release it. *What happens to the needle-cork system when you release it?*

d. Bring the magnet near the needle on the cork. Ask: *What happens to the needle and cork now?*

EXPLAIN

e. Ask: *What is your evidence that stroking the needle magnetized it? What made the needle move when it was first placed on the cork? How is this like a compass? How can you make a compass? Which pole of the needle is the N-pole? What is your evidence?*

VII. ELECTRICITY

 ## A. STATIC ELECTRICITY

▶ *Science Background*

More than 2,000 years ago, the Greeks were aware that when amber, a resinous substance, was rubbed with a cloth, the amber was able to attract small bits of straw. The Greek word for amber is *electron*, so the phenomenon came to be called *electricity*.

Benjamin Franklin, the American statesman and scientist, investigated electric phenomena in the 1700s. Franklin found that things could be not only attracted by electric forces but also repelled. Franklin proposed that the attracting and repelling forces of static electricity resulted from two kinds of electrical "fluids," which he called positive and negative fluids.

Static electricity is understood today in terms of these concepts and principles:

1. There are two kinds of electric charges in all materials: positive charges and negative charges.
2. In ordinary substances, positive charges and negative charges are balanced. These substances are electrically neutral.
3. When some materials are rubbed together, the friction causes the materials to acquire electrical charges.
4. Two electrically charged substances can interact.
5. An electrically charged substance can interact with a neutral substance by a process called *induction*.

NSES   **Science Standards**

All students should develop an understanding of:

- light, heat, electricity, and magnetism (K–4).

Concepts and Principles That Support the Standards

- The position or motion of an object can be changed by pushing or pulling (K–4).
- The size of the change is related to the strength of the push or pull (K–4).
- Without touching them, a material that has been electrically charged pulls on all other materials and may either push or pull other charged materials (*Benchmarks*, 3–5).

Objectives

1. Describe electrostatic investigations and identify materials that can interact electrostatically.
2. Describe ways electrostatic interactions are different from magnetic interactions.
3. Explain in their own words what is meant by electrical charge and how objects become electrically charged.

4. State and demonstrate evidence for the electrostatic force rule: Like charged bodies repel; unlike charged bodies attract.
5. Demonstrate and explain what is meant by electrostatic induction.
6. Apply the model of electrostatic interaction to explain evidence from electrostatic investigations.

1. HOW CAN YOU DEMONSTRATE STATIC ELECTRIC FORCES? (3–6)

Materials

- Plastic or acetate sheet
- Plastic rulers
- Hard rubber comb or resin rod
- Wool cloth
- Balloons
- Paper towels
- Paper clips
- Flour
- Salt
- Thread
- Bits of paper

ENGAGE

a. Have students rub a clear acetate sheet with a rough paper towel. (Coarse paper towels from restrooms work well.) Instruct them to bring the rubbed acetate near a pile of tiny bits of torn paper and observe what happens.

EXPLORE

b. Investigate to see what other materials interact with the acetate sheet. Try such materials as paper clips, bits of aluminum foil, flour, salt, cotton and nylon thread, and wood shavings from a pencil sharpener.

c. Rub a hard rubber comb or resin rod with a wool cloth. Try to pick up flour with the rubbed comb or rod.

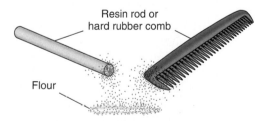

Resin rod or
hard rubber comb

Flour

d. Tie a 1 meter string around the mouth of an inflated balloon. Vigorously rub the inflated balloon with a piece of wool. Investigate to determine what materials interact with the balloon.

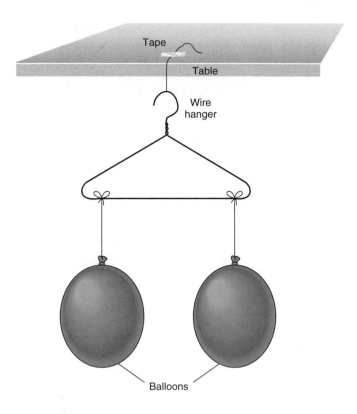

Tape

Table

Wire hanger

Balloons

e. Inflate a second balloon. Tie a 1 meter string around the mouth of the balloon. Vigorously rub the two balloons with wool. Suspend the two balloons by their strings from a support as in the diagram and investigate how they interact with each other.

EXPLAIN

f. Ask: *What happened when you rubbed the clear acetate sheet and moved it near the new materials? If the new materials moved, what must they have experienced?* (a force)

g. Ask: *What happened when you rubbed the comb or rod with a wool cloth and then moved it toward flour?*

h. Ask: *What did your rubbed balloon attract? Why do you think it happened? In what ways is this investigation similar to your previous investigation? Which materials did the ruler pick up? What materials did the balloon attract?*

i. Ask: *What happened when the two rubbed balloons were brought near one another? What kind of force did you observe, attraction or repulsion?*

j. Introduce the notions of positive and negative electric charges and electrical forces. Help the students relate each part of the explanation to some part of their investigation.

 ## B. CURRENT ELECTRICITY

▶ *Science Background*

Current electricity refers to a movement of electrical charge along a conducting path. Electrical energy is produced in a battery and converted to heat, light, or motion in an electrical component such as a lightbulb or a motor. For energy to be transferred to an electrical component, there must be a complete conducting path—a complete circuit—from the

battery along conducting wires through the electrical component and back to the battery along conducting wires.

If two or more electrical components are aligned so that current flows from one to the next, the circuit is a series circuit. If the components are arranged so that each is in an independent circuit, then the circuit is a parallel circuit. A switch is a device that breaks or opens a circuit so that it is not a continuous path and current cannot flow through it.

 Science Standards

All students should develop an understanding of

- light, heat, electricity, and magnetism (K–4).

Concepts and Principles That Support the Standards

- Electricity in circuits can produce light, heat, sound, and mechanical motion (K–4).
- Electrical circuits require a complete conducting loop through which an electric current can pass (K–4).
- Electrical circuits provide a means of transferring electrical energy to produce heat, light, sound, mechanical motion, and chemical changes (5–8).

Objectives

1. Demonstrate and explain through words and drawings how to make a bulb light in various ways, given one or two batteries, one or two bulbs, and one or two wires.
2. State, explain, and demonstrate the complete circuit rule:

   For a bulb to light,
   - the bulb must be touched on the side and the bottom;
   - the battery must be touched on both ends; and
   - there must be a complete circuit or continuous path along the wires and through the battery and bulb.
3. Explain in their own words what a conductor is and how to test a material to determine if it is an electrical conductor.
4. Identify and construct series circuits and use the complete circuit rule to explain why the other bulbs in a series circuit go out when one bulb is removed from its holder.
5. Identify and construct parallel circuits and use the complete circuit rule to explain why the other bulbs in a parallel circuit stay lit when one bulb is removed from its holder.
6. Demonstrate a switch and use the complete circuit rule to explain how it works.

1. HOW CAN YOU CONSTRUCT A CIRCUIT IN WHICH A BULB LIGHTS? (3–6)

Materials

For each student, at least:

- One flashlight bulb
- One battery (1.5 volt D-cell)
- One 15–25 cm wire

(Students initially need their own materials but will later combine materials with one or more other students.)

Safety Precautions

Discussing safe habits to use with electricity is a must.

- Caution children not to experiment with anything but 1.5 volt flashlight batteries (D-cells) and flashlight bulbs. There is no danger of electrical shock from these batteries.
- Children should wear safety goggles to protect their eyes from the sharp ends of the copper wires used in the activities.
- Tell children that if their wire gets hot, they should do something different with the connections of the wire(s).
- Children should never experiment with the electricity from wall sockets or from car batteries.
- Do not use electrical appliances near water; for example, do not use a hair dryer near a water-filled sink.
- When you pull an electrical cord out of a wall socket, grasp it by the plug and pull firmly.

ENGAGE

a. Tell a story about some hikers who lost their flashlight in a dark cave. One hiker had an extra battery, another had an extra bulb, and a third had a wire. *Can you help them light the bulb so they can get out of the cave?*

EXPLORE

b. Give each child a small flashlight bulb, a length of wire, and a 1.5 volt D-cell. (*Note:* A 1.5 volt D-cell is commonly referred to as a battery, although batteries actually have multiple cells.) Ask: *Can you make the bulb light?* Let the children work to light the bulb. Some children may take 20 minutes or longer to light the bulb. Resist the temptation to step in and "teach" them how to light the bulb. Encourage them to keep trying on their own. As they succeed, the children develop confidence in their own abilities to learn about electrical circuits.

As each child lights the bulb, ask: *Can you find another way to light the bulb?* Students may experiment by placing the bulb on its side or on the other end of the battery. If two or more children want to cooperate at this point, let them. More hands may be helpful. Be accepting and reinforcing of the children's efforts.

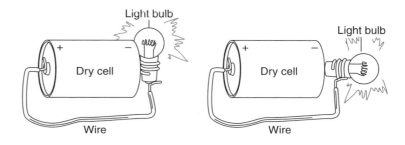

c. Ask children, individually, to draw pictures of what they did to light the bulb with one battery and one wire. Look at the children's drawings carefully to see if they have observed that the electrical path (circuit) is a continuous or complete one.

EXPLAIN

d. Ask the children to explain their drawings to you and to one another. Look at the drawings carefully to see if the wires touch the bulb on the bottom and the side.
   Ask: *What two places must you touch a bulb for it to light? Where must the battery be touched?*
   Referring to actual circuits and drawings, children should state, explain, and write the complete circuit rule:
   For a bulb to light,
   • the bulb must be touched on the side and the bottom;

   • the battery must be touched on both ends; and

   • there must be a continuous path through the battery, bulb, and wires.

ELABORATE

e. Give each pair of children a second wire. Ask: *Can you make the bulb light using two wires?* Children may simply twist the two wires together and make one wire of them. If so, ask: *Can you use two wires to light the bulb without the bulb touching the battery?* Also ask them to draw a picture of what they did to light the bulb using two wires, with the bulb not touching the battery.

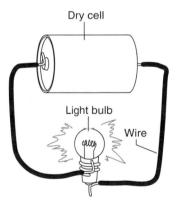

Dry cell

Light bulb

Wire

EVALUATE

f. As a self-evaluation of their understanding of how to light a bulb with just one battery and one wire, ask each child to do Prediction Sheet 1. For each frame the students should ask themselves: *Will the bulb light?* and then write *Yes* or *No* in the frame to record their prediction. After making predictions for all the frames, students should test their predictions by setting up a circuit like the one shown to try it and see. When all the children have completed the prediction sheet and checked it, go back over it with them. Ask: *Will this one light? Why won't it light? What could you do to get it to light?*

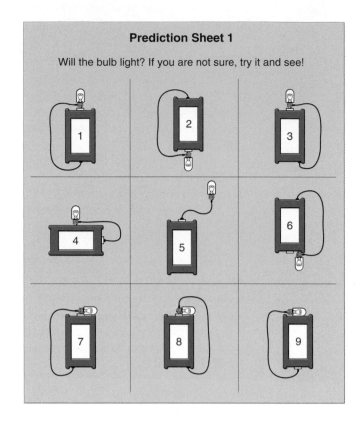

Prediction Sheet 1

Will the bulb light? If you are not sure, try it and see!

2. WHAT HAPPENS WHEN THERE IS MORE THAN ONE BULB OR BATTERY IN A CIRCUIT? (3–6)

Materials

- Batteries, bulbs, wires
- Bulb holders
- Battery holders

ENGAGE

a. Ask: *What happens when you try two bulbs? Try two batteries. Can you use three batteries and two bulbs? Does the orientation of the batteries matter? How could you find out?*

EXPLORE

b. Let children explore and discover. As they try different arrangements, have them complete an I Notice/I Wonder chart to record their observations and questions.

c. As the children try different arrangements, the need for "bulb holders" and "battery holders" arises. Give the children bulb holders and battery holders and demonstrate how to use them.

d. Children may discover that when batteries are placed end-to-end (in series), a positive terminal of one battery must be connected to the negative terminal of an adjacent battery.

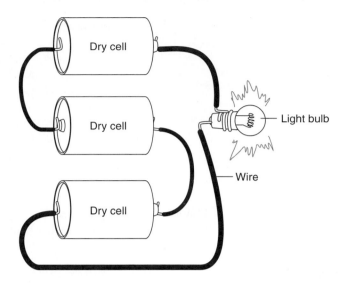

Dry cell

Dry cell

Light bulb

Dry cell

Wire

Safety Precautions   Do not allow children to experiment with more than three batteries. More batteries can result in burned-out bulbs. Remind students that if the wires become hot, the bulbs will not light, and they should immediately disconnect the wires from the batteries.

EXPLAIN   e. Encourage children to share and discuss the information on their I Notice/I Wonder charts with the class. If conversation lags, ask: *Who tried one battery and three bulbs? What did you notice? Did this make you wonder anything? What? Did everyone that tried this notice the same thing?*

f. Ask: *Can you trace the complete circuit path for each circuit you have built?* Help children see that the bulb holder is constructed so that one part of it is connected to the metal side of a bulb and another part is connected to the bottom base of the bulb. The terminals of the bulb holder are then connected to the battery. The bulb holder is doing the same thing the children were doing with their hands when they made the bulb light. The bulb holders provide a complete circuit path for the electricity.

3. WHAT IS A SERIES CIRCUIT? (3–6)

Materials   • Batteries, bulbs, wires
             • Bulb holders

ENGAGE   a. Show the children the accompanying circuit illustration. Ask them to build the circuit using their materials.

Bulb and bulb holder

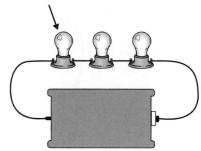

EXPLORE

b. Ask: *What will happen to the other bulbs in a series circuit if one of the bulbs is removed from its holder? Try it and see.* (The other bulbs will go out.)

EXPLAIN

c. Ask: *What happened? Why did the other bulbs go out?* The children should tell you that the continuous path was broken when the bulb was removed.

Tell the children that electricians, scientists, and engineers call this circuit a *series circuit* because the bulbs are lined up in a series and electricity flows from bulb to bulb.

4. WHAT IS A PARALLEL CIRCUIT? (3–6)

ENGAGE

a. Show the children the accompanying circuit illustration and ask them to build it.

Bulb and bulb holder

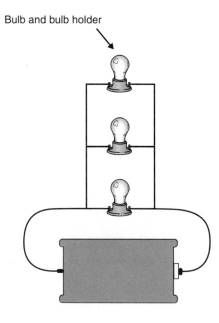

EXPLORE
    b. Ask: *What will happen to the other bulbs if one of the bulbs is removed from its bulb holder? Try it and see.* (The other bulbs remain lit.)

EXPLAIN
    c. Ask: *What happened to the other bulbs when you removed one? Why did it happen?* The students should observe and explain that the other bulbs stay lit because it is still part of a continuous path with the battery.

        This circuit is called a *parallel circuit* because there are parallel paths through the bulbs for the electricity. Each bulb is part of an independent circuit with the battery.

    d. Ask: *How are the electrical circuits in the classroom wired, series or parallel? If one light burns out, will the others light?* Through discussion, lead children to understand that electrical circuits in the classroom are wired in parallel. If the lights in the room are off, the TV or computers will still work. If one light bulb (or bank of lights) is out, the others still work.

        You might discuss strings of Christmas tree or holiday lights at this point. Most strings of lights sold today are wired in parallel. If one bulb burns out, the others still light. If the bulbs were in series, if one bulb burned out, none of the others would light. You would have to test each one of them to determine which one needed to be replaced.

....

5. WHAT ARE CONDUCTORS AND NONCONDUCTORS? (3–6)

Materials
- Batteries
- Bulbs
- Wires
- Bulb holders
- Battery holders
- Diverse array of conducting and nonconducting materials made from paper, cloth, wood, plastic, and metals of different kinds

ENGAGE
    a. Hold up a battery, a bulb, and a wire. Then put down the wire. Ask: *If I didn't have a wire, could I complete this circuit so the bulb would light?*

EXPLORE
    b. Make available to each cooperative group a diverse array of conducting and nonconducting materials. Instruct students to use the test circuit illustrated to find out which materials could be substituted for the wire and which materials could not. Place the test object (made of metal, cloth, wood, plastic, etc.) between the bare ends of the two pieces of wire. If the bulb lights, then electricity flows easily through that material, so it could be substituted for a wire. If the bulb does not light, then electricity does not flow easily through the material, so it would not be a good substitute for a wire.

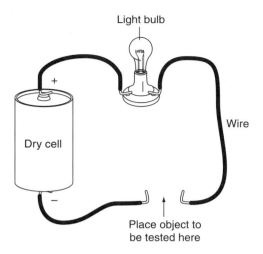

Light bulb

Wire

Dry cell

+

−

Place object to
be tested here

c. Design and use a data table in which to record your findings.

EXPLAIN

d. Ask students to share their findings with the rest of the class. They will probably report that the bulb lit when they tested some of the materials and did not light when they tested other materials. As students describe their findings, summarize the class data on the board using a T-chart with the headings *Bulb Lights* and *Bulb Does Not Light*.

e. Through discussion lead children to understand that some materials will conduct electricity. Others will not. Materials that conduct electricity well are called *conductors*. If conductors are substituted for wires, the circuit would be complete and the bulb would light. Materials that do not conduct electricity well are called *insulators* or *nonconductors*. If insulators or nonconductors are substituted for wires, the circuit would not be complete and the bulb would not light.

f. Ask: *What types of materials are good conductors of electricity?* (Metals) *How do you know?* (The bulb lights when metals are tested.) *Can you tell which of the metals you tested is the best conductor? How? What types of materials are good insulators of electricity?* (nonmetals) *How do you know?* (The bulb does not light when nonmetals are tested.)

EVALUATE

g. To assess student understanding about conductors and insulators of electricity, have students respond to the following items:

1. How can you determine if a material is a good conductor or a good insulator of electricity?

2. Predict which of these items is a good conductor of electricity. (Display or give each student a new collection of conductors and insulators to consider. Do not give students the testing device. They are only to make predictions.)

3. What evidence from this investigation supports your prediction?

6. WHAT IS A SWITCH AND HOW DOES IT WORK? (3–6)

Materials

- Heavy cardboard
- Brass paper fasteners
- Paper clips

ENGAGE

a. Ask: *What does a switch do? How does a switch work? How can you make a switch?*

EXPLORE

b. Ask your students to make an electrical "switch" using a 10 cm by 10 cm piece of corrugated cardboard, two brass paper fasteners, and a paper clip, as in the illustration. Tell them to connect the switch into an electric circuit as shown.

EXPLAIN

c. Ask: *What happens when the switch is open (with the paper clip not touching the second fastener)? What happens when the switch is closed (with the paper clip touching the second fastener)?*

The children should note that when the switch is closed, a complete circuit is formed and the bulb lights. When the switch is open, the circuit is broken and the bulb does not light. Take time for children to identify and talk about the electrical switches in the classroom.

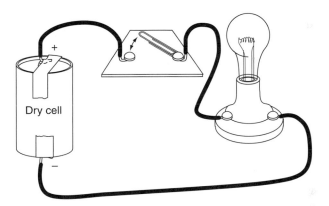

Dry cell

 C. ELECTROMAGNETS

▶ *Science Background*

All magnetism is the result of moving electrical charges. When current flows in a wire, a magnetic field is set up. If the wire is placed over a compass, the magnetic field of the wire interacts with the magnetic field of the compass needle, causing it to deflect. Since the earth's magnetic field also affects the compass needle strongly, the needle may deflect only a small amount. More coils of wire increase the magnetic effects of the current. When the current is less, which occurs when a bulb is wired into the circuit, the resulting magnetic field produced will also be less.

NSES Science Standards

All students should develop an understanding of

• light, heat, electricity, and magnetism (K–4).

Concepts and Principles That Support the Standards

• Electricity in circuits can produce heat, light, sound, and magnetic effects (K–4).
• Electric currents and magnets can exert a force on each other (*Benchmarks*, 6–8).

Objectives

1. Describe interactions between compass needles and current-carrying wires.
2. Construct an electromagnet.
3. Design and conduct an experiment to determine the effects of variables such as the type of core, number of loops of wire, and amount of current on the strength of an electromagnet.
4. Explain the cause of electromagnetic effects.

Materials

- Batteries
- Bulbs
- Wires (various materials and gauges)
- Iron nails or rivets
- Other rods to use as a core (wood dowel, plastic rod, pencil, etc.)
- Switches
- Paper clips

1. HOW DO COMPASS NEEDLES INTERACT WITH CURRENT-CARRYING WIRES? (4–6)

ENGAGE

a. *How does a current-carrying wire interact with a magnetic compass?*

EXPLORE

b. Instruct students to take a 50 cm length of wire and stretch it out on a table. Lay a compass over the wire as in the diagram. Orient the wire so the compass needle is perpendicular to the wire. Connect one end of the wire to one of the terminals of a D-cell. Quickly touch the other end of the wire to the other terminal of the D-cell and then disconnect it. Observe what happens to the compass needle. Move the wire so it points in different directions. Quickly connect and disconnect the wire to the D-cell.

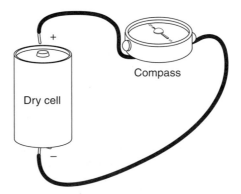

Compass

Dry cell

Safety Precautions

Since there is no light bulb or other resisting component in the circuit in this investigation, it is a "short" circuit. You must connect and disconnect the short circuit quickly so that the wire does not get too hot and the D-cell is not drained of electrical energy.

EXPLAIN

c. Ask: *What did you observe in this investigation?* (The compass needle moved.) *Why do you think this happened? What is your evidence that the electric current in the wire produced some magnetism?*

ELABORATE

d. Tell students to obtain a wire about 50 cm long and to wrap five loops of the wire around a compass as in the diagram. Leave the ends of the wire long enough to connect to a D-cell. Quickly connect and disconnect the wire to a single D-cell. Ask: *What did you observe?* (The compass needle deflected more than before.)

e. *Why do you think this happened? What evidence can you state that a magnetic interaction took place? Was the effect stronger or weaker than in the first investigation? What is your evidence that the electric current in the loops of wire produced some magnetism?*

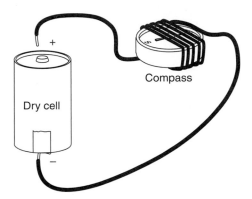

2. WHAT IS AN ELECTROMAGNET, AND HOW CAN YOU MAKE ONE? (3–6)

ENGAGE

a. Show children an electromagnet. Demonstrate how it can attract small objects like paper clips. Ask: *How can we make an electromagnet?*

EXPLORE

b. Give students these directions:
   1. Obtain a D-cell, a large iron nail or rivet, a 50 cm length of insulated (enameled) copper wire, some iron filings in a plastic bag, and some paper clips.
   2. Wrap the nail around the wire about 15 times as shown in the diagram.
   3. Place the nail on the bag of iron filings.
   4. Scrape the insulation off the two ends of the wire. Connect one end of the wire to one of the terminals of the D-cell.
   5. Holding the other end of the wire along the insulated portion, touch the bare end of the wire to the other terminal of the D-cell for only a few seconds. Move the nail around on the plastic bag and observe how it interacts with the iron filings.
   6. Repeat the activities using paper clips rather than iron filings to observe electromagnetic effects.

Safety Precautions

Do not let the wire and terminal remain in contact for more than a few seconds because

- intense heat builds up, and you could get a burn through the insulation; and
- the electrical energy in the battery will be used up quickly.

EXPLAIN

c. Ask: *What happens to the iron filings and the paper clip when the circuit is completed (or when the wire is touched to the battery)? What happens to the iron filings and the paper clip when the circuit is broken (or when the wire is removed from the battery)? What is the evidence that the nail became a magnet temporarily?*

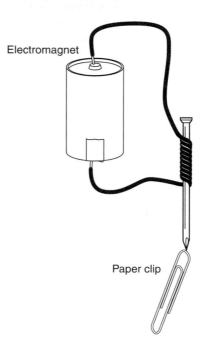

Electromagnet

Paper clip

d. Explain that when a loop of wire is placed around an iron object and current runs through the wire, the system becomes an electromagnet. The electromagnetic effect is suddenly reduced when current no longer runs through the wire.

3. HOW CAN YOU INCREASE THE STRENGTH OF AN ELECTROMAGNET? (3–6)

ENGAGE

a. Hold up the electromagnet from the previous activity. Ask: *How could you measure the strength of an electromagnet?* (By seeing how much mass it can pick up) *How could you change the strength of an electromagnet?* (Change or vary a component of the system.) *What are the possible variables in an electromagnet?* (Number of coils of wire, the way in which the coils are wrapped, core material, diameter of core, length of core, number of batteries, etc.)

Safety Precautions

Remember to only leave the wires from the electromagnet connected to the battery for a short time, as they will become hot. Do not use more than three batteries to power your electromagnet, because the increased voltage will cause the wires to get very hot very quickly.

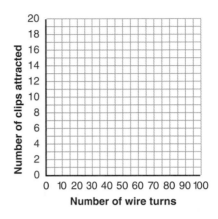

EXPLORE

b. Tell students to design and conduct a controlled experiment to determine how the number of coils of wire around the core affects the strength of the electromagnet. State the question you are investigating, and state a hypothesis. Measure the strength of the electromagnet by how long a chain of paper clips it can pick up. Create a data table on which to record your findings. Instruct students to display their data in a graph like the one shown here.

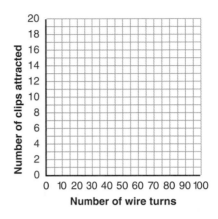

EXPLAIN

c. Ask: *What is the responding variable in this experiment?* (Number of paper clips lifted) *What is the manipulated variable in the experiment?* (Number of coils of wire around the core) *What variables have you controlled in this experiment?* (Type of wire, number of batteries, length of wire, core material, length of core, diameter of coil)

d. Have each group report their results to the class and post their graphs. Ask: *What similarities do you notice in the data?* (Slope of the line on the graph) *What relationship did you find between the number of coils and the strength of the electromagnet?* (The greater the number of coils, the greater the strength of the electromagnet.)

ELABORATE

e. Ask: *Do you think other variables might affect the strength of an electromagnet?* Have each group select another variable that they think might affect the strength of an electromagnet. Encourage each group to select a different variable to investigate. Have each group: develop a research question; state a hypothesis; design and conduct a controlled experiment to test the hypothesis; record data and graph it as before; and write a conclusion that describes the relationship between the manipulated and responding variables.

f. Have each group present its research question, hypothesis, procedure, results, and conclusion. Encourage discussion and questions. Lead the class to identify which of the variables studied affected the strength of the electromagnet. Have them give evidence from their data that supports their selection.

EVALUATE

g. To assess student understanding about the variables in this experiment, have students answer the following questions:
   1. What was the manipulated variable in your last experiment?
   2. What was the responding variable in your last experiment?
   3. What variables were controlled in your last experiment?

h. To assess student understanding about the variables that affect the strength of an electromagnet, have students answer the following questions:

4. Based on the data collected by you and your classmates, which variable has the most effect on the strength of an electromagnet?

5. Did any other variables have an effect on the strength of an electromagnet? If so, list them in order of the amount of the effect each variable has, from greatest effect to least effect.

6. What evidence did you use to answer question 5?

7. Describe how you would build the strongest possible electromagnet?

NOTES:

Information, recipes, and activities related to oobleck are excerpted from the GEMS teacher's guide, *Oobleck: What Do Scientists Do?* by Cary L. Sneider (Lawrence Hall of Science, University of California at Berkeley).

William Gilbert's book on magnetism is readily available as part of Volume 28 of the Great Books Series published by the Encyclopedia Britannica and found in many libraries.

Some of the concepts and activities in this section are adapted from a FOSS (Full Option Science System) grade 3–4 unit on Magnetism and Electricity.

Moisture in the air can interfere with electrostatic effects. Thus, electrostatic investigations are best done on a cool, dry day.

SECTION III
Life Science Activities

Life is a complex, exciting, and mysterious subject for inquiry. Students should have the opportunity to develop a deep and personal appreciation for the variety and wonder of life. Children are naturally curious about the diversity of life around them. Studying characteristics of plants and animals and of their habitats provides a good context for students to develop inquiry skills. Investigations in life science might involve:

1. asking different kinds of questions that suggest different kinds of scientific investigations;
2. observing and describing plants and animals;
3. classifying plants and animals (insects, fish, birds, mammals) according to their properties;
4. investigating plant and animal life cycles;
5. planning and carrying out investigations that show the function of different parts/structures of plants and animals;
6. investigating how different habitats or environments enable the needs of plants and animals to be met; and
7. investigating how the activities of people bring about changes in the environment.

As students learn more and more about plants, animals, and the environment, they become better prepared to assume responsibility for the well-being of living things on our planet.

Investigation Journals. Life science activities provide an excellent context for students to learn how to keep good records of investigations. Records may be kept in student observation journals, or you may want students to keep their records on pages you prepare.

Here is a sample prepared form for student investigation journals and examples of a child's journal entries from a seed germination experiment.

My Investigation Journal	

1. **Key Question**	• *Is moisture needed for seeds to sprout?*
2. **My Investigation**	• *We put a sponge in a bowl of water and sprinkled grass seeds on it. We put grass seeds on a dry sponge. We watched the seeds for several days.*
3. **My Prediction**	• *I think the dry seeds won't grow but the moist ones will.*
4. **What Happened**	

Day	What I Observed on the Wet Sponge	What I Observed on the Dry Sponge
1	• *Nothing is happening.*	• *Nothing is happening.*
2	• *Nothing.*	• *Nothing.*
3	• *Some sprouts are coming up on the moist sponge.*	• *Nothing.*
6	• *There was lots of grass on the moist sponge but nothing growing on the dry one.*	• *Nothing.*

5. **What I Concluded**	• *Seeds need moisture to sprout.*

I. CHARACTERISTICS OF ORGANISMS

Children can begin to appreciate the astounding variety of living things on our planet as they investigate seeds, plants, insects, and birds.

 ## A. SEEDS

▶ *Science Background*

Amazingly, seeds contain the ingredients of life. A living seed may lie dormant for years until it is awakened by just the right conditions. To begin the **germination** or sprouting process, seeds need moisture, air, and moderate temperatures.

   Seeds typically have very hard **seed coats** that keep water from penetrating them. Thus, they will germinate more quickly after being soaked or scarified to allow water inside the seeds. Within every viable seed lives a tiny **embryo plant**, complete with leaf, stem, and root parts. When the seed begins to germinate, a temporary food supply, stored within the **cotyledons** of the seeds, nourishes the growing embryo. Eventually, as the leaves develop, the plant obtains its energy for growth and survival from sunlight through the process of **photosynthesis**.

NSES   **Science Standards**

All students should develop an understanding of

- characteristics of organisms (K–4).
- structure and function in living systems (5–8).
- life cycles of organisms (K–4).
- organisms and their environments (K–4).

NSES Concepts and Principles That Support the Standards

- Some animals and plants are alike in the way they look and the things they do, and others are very different from one another (K–2).
- A great variety of living things can be sorted into groups in many ways using various features to decide which living things belong to which group (3–5).
- Features used for grouping depend on the purpose of the grouping (3–5).
- Organisms have basic needs. Plants require air, water, nutrients, and light (K–4).
- Organisms can survive only in environments in which their basic needs are met (K–4).
- Each plant or animal has different structures that serve different functions in growth, survival, and reproduction (K–4).
- Plants and animals have life cycles that include being born, developing into adults, reproducing, and eventually dying. The details of this life cycle are different for different organisms (K–4).
- All animals depend on plants (K–4).
- Some animals eat plants for food (K–4).

Objectives

1. Recognize the wide variation in seeds.
2. Name the part of a plant where seeds are found.
3. Identify and describe different parts/structures of seeds (seed coats, cotyledons, embryo plants) and describe the functions of each.
4. Define *germination* and describe the sequence of events in the germination of a seed.
5. Ask questions about seeds that can be answered through investigations.
6. Design and carry out descriptive, classificatory, and experimental investigations to gather information for answering questions about seeds.
7. Use simple equipment and tools to gather data and extend the senses.
8. Through investigations, identify basic conditions for seed germination: air, water, and moderate temperature.
9. Use evidence from investigations and science knowledge to answer questions about seeds, construct explanations, and make predictions.

1. WHAT IS INSIDE A BEAN POD? (K–4)

Materials

- Bean pods
- Plastic knives
- Paper plates
- Paper
- Crayons, markers, or colored pencils
- Pea pods

ENGAGE

a. Distribute two bean pods to each small group. Ask: *What are these? What are their properties? What do you predict will be inside of them?*

EXPLORE

b. Encourage students to use all of their senses, except taste, to observe the outside of their objects. They should observe color, texture, size, shape, and other features. Ask students to record their findings using drawings and words.

c. Distribute a plastic knife to each group. Provide instructions on safe use of the plastic knife. Challenge students to use the knives to open their objects.

d. Encourage students to use all of their senses, except taste, to observe the inside of their objects. They should observe color, texture, size, shape, and other features. Ask students to record their findings using drawings and words.

EXPLAIN

e. Ask: *What observations did you make? What did you find inside? What are the properties of what is inside? Were both of your objects the same? Why or why not?* List the students' observations on the board. Encourage discussion about their findings. If the students don't use the terms *pod* and *seed*, introduce them. Tell students that the pod is the part of the bean plant that holds the seeds. Have them label the pod and seeds on their drawings.

f. Explain that although in everyday language we call bean pods *vegetables*, in scientific terms they are *fruits*. Scientifically, a plant part that contains seeds is called a *fruit*. The special name of the fruit of a bean or pea plant is pod. Tell students that they will study more about fruits in future lessons.

ELABORATE

g. Distribute two pea pods to each small group. Just as they did with the bean pods, students should observe and record about the outside of the pods.

h. Then students should open the pods. Ask them to observe and record about the inside of the pods. Tell them to label the pod and the seeds on their new drawing.

i. Lead a discussion of their findings. Ask: *What did you observe about the outside and inside of the pea pods?*

j. Ask: *How are the pea pods like the bean pods? How are they different?* Draw a Venn diagram (two partially overlapping circles) on the board on which to record student ideas. Label one circle *Bean Pods*. Label the other circle *Pea Pods*. As ideas are suggested, if there are ways the pods are alike, write them in the intersection of the circles. If suggestions are ways one type of pod is different from the other, write the idea in the nonoverlapped part of the appropriately labeled circle.

k. When all ideas have been added, review how the Venn diagram is a good way to record ideas when you find ways things are alike and different.

EVALUATE

l. Formatively evaluate students' observation and recording skills during the explore and elaborate phases of the lesson. The following checklists may be helpful to guide and organize the data you collect about your students' skills.

Observation Skills
☐ Takes time to carefully examine objects.
☐ Makes use of several senses in exploring objects.
☐ Identifies obvious ways objects are alike and different.
☐ Identifies detailed ways objects are alike and different.

Recording Skills
☐ Uses words.
☐ Uses phrases.
☐ Uses complete sentences.
☐ Uses drawings.
☐ Uses words and drawings together (labeled drawings or drawings with related descriptions).
☐ Drawings bear a resemblance to the objects that were observed.

☐ Realistic color is used in drawings.
☐ Size of drawing is similar to size of the real thing.
☐ Drawings are either an enlarged or reduced version of the objects, and they enable relative size comparison of objects observed.
☐ Drawings include much detail.

2. WHERE ARE SEEDS FOUND? HOW ARE SEEDS ALIKE AND DIFFERENT? (K–2)

Materials
- Paper plates
- Plastic knives
- Variety of fresh fruits (Children might be encouraged to bring a fruit from home. Tomatoes, apples, corn on the cob, apples, cherries, cantaloupes, bean and pea pods, and bell peppers make interesting fruits for children to observe.)

ENGAGE

a. Ask: *Are there seeds in each of these fruits? How many seeds are in each of the fruits? How can we find out?*

EXPLORE

b. Distribute paper plates and several fruits to each group. Tell children to use their plastic knives to cut their fruits open. They should find and observe the seeds in each one.

EXPLAIN

c. Ask: *Did you find seeds in your fruit? How many seeds did you find? What are the properties of the seeds? How are they alike? How are they different?*

ELABORATE

d. Tell the students to take turns sorting the seeds on the paper plates. Ask: *How have you sorted the seeds?* Allow groups to describe and explain how they sorted the seeds. Lead students to compare and contrast the different ways they have sorted the seeds and to discuss the best ways to sort them.

EVALUATE

e. To check for understanding about where seeds are found and how they are alike and different, have students respond to these questions.
   1. Draw pictures to show where the seeds were in two of the fruits you observed.
   2. How are seeds alike?
   3. How are seeds different?

3. HOW DO SEED PODS VARY? (3–6)

Materials
- Large number of pea pods
- Paper plates

ENGAGE

a. Ask: *Do all pea pods have the same number of peas?*

EXPLORE

b. Give two pea pods to each pair of students. Tell students to open the pods, count the number of peas in each pod, and put the peas and pods on their paper plates.

EXPLAIN

c. Ask: *Who found the most peas in their pods?* Record this number on the chalkboard. Also ask: *Who found the least number of peas in their pods?* Record this number on the board. Let each group report the number of peas they found in their pods.

d. Construct a histogram showing the numbers of peas in the different pods. Have one student from each pair come to the chalkboard and place an *x* above the numbers that correspond to the number of peas in each of their two pods. Ask: *What does the graph (histogram) show? What does it tell about peas and pods? If you open another pea pod, what might be the most likely number of peas in the pod? Why do you think so?* Discuss the notion of predictions and how predictions are based on collected evidence.

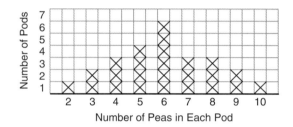

e. Give each pair another pea pod, and tell them to make predictions about the number of peas in each pod. Tell them to open the pea pods to test their predictions. Ask: *How accurate were your predictions? Why were your predictions so accurate (or so inaccurate)?*

ELABORATE

f. Ask: *Do you think there is a relationship between the number of peas in a pod and the length of the pod? How would you investigate to find out?* Carry out an investigation to see if the number of peas in a pod is related to the length (in centimeters) of the pod. Display class data in a line graph (number of peas in a pod on the *y*-axis; length of the pod in centimeters on the *x*-axis). Use the graph to make predictions about the number of peas in pods of different lengths.

Nature of Scientific Inquiry

g. Discuss how scientists use mathematics and how science can enable students to put mathematical skills, such as graphing, to work. Discuss the use of graphs to display data from investigations and to make predictions.

EVALUATE

h. To check students' ability to construct and analyze graphs, have them complete the following activity.

Another class collected data about bean pods. Their data table follows:

Bean Pod	Number of Seeds	Length of Pod (cm)
1	6	9
2	7	11
3	6	11
4	7	10
5	6	7
6	7	12
7	5	9
8	7	10
9	7	11
10	6	11
11	6	9
12	7	10
13	5	9

1. Construct a histogram showing the number of beans in different pods.
2. What does your histogram tell you about the beans and pods?
3. If the students opened another bean pod, what is the most likely number of beans it would contain? Why?
4. Construct a line graph (length of pod in centimeters on the *x*-axis; number of seeds in pod on the *y*-axis). Be sure to title your graph and label your axes.
5. Is there a relationship between the length of the pod and the number of beans in it? If so, describe the relationship.

4. WHAT ARE THE PROPERTIES OF SEEDS? (K–4)

Materials

- Assortment of seeds, perhaps from old seed packets
- Magnifying lens

ENGAGE

a. Give each group an assortment of 10 to 15 seeds. Ask: *How are the seeds alike? How are they different? How many different kinds of seeds do you have? What are the properties of each seed?*

EXPLORE

b. Students should be encouraged to notice and talk about the color, shape, size, and texture of each kind of seed. Provide magnifying lenses to each group to better observe details.

For very young children, include other small objects with the seed assortments, such as marbles, small pebbles (gravel), jelly beans, and other small pieces of candy. As children observe and talk about their collection, discuss what is living and what is not living. Caution children not to place small objects in their mouths, noses, or ears.

c. Invite students within small groups to play "I'm thinking of . . ." with their assortment of seeds. One child describes a particular seed or a type of seed and the other children try to figure out which one is being described.

EXPLAIN

d. Ask: *What characteristics do seeds seem to have in common? What makes a seed a seed? How can you tell a seed from a nonseed?*

5. WHAT DOES THE INSIDE OF A SEED LOOK LIKE? (K–4)

Materials
- Lima bean seeds
- Magnifying lenses

ENGAGE

a. Ask: *What do you think the inside of a seed looks like?* Discuss possibilities.

EXPLORE

b. Give each pair or group of students four lima bean seeds, one-half cup of water, and a magnifying lens. Have them place two seeds in the water for 24 hours and observe them regularly. After 24 hours, ask: *How have the seeds in the water changed? How are the soaked seeds different from the unsoaked seeds?* (They are larger.) *Why are the soaked seeds larger?* (They have soaked up water.)

c. Ask: *What do you think was happening inside the seed?* Have students carefully peel the outer coat from one of the seeds and examine it with the magnifying lens. Show students how to pull the coatless seed in half with a fingernail. Ask: *What does the inside of the seed look like? What are the distinctive parts of a seed?* Tell students to draw a picture of the inside of the seed.

EXPLAIN

d. Ask students to compare their drawings with the illustration.

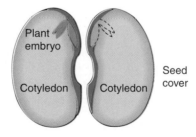

e. Provide names for the main parts of the bean seed: *seed coat* or cover; *cotyledon* or the meaty, pulpy part of the seed; and the *embryo*, with its embryo leaves, stem, and root.

6. HOW MUCH WATER CAN A BEAN SEED SOAK UP? (2–6)

Materials
- Unsoaked lima bean seeds
- Lima bean seeds that have been soaked overnight
- Balances
- 1 g weights
- Plastic containers

ENGAGE

a. Ask: *If the seeds are soaking up water, how can we find out how much water they are holding?* Through discussion, arrive at the possibility of weighing the seeds before and after they have been soaked to gather data on how much water seeds can soak up.

EXPLORE

b. Provide each group 10 unsoaked bean seeds and a plastic container. Tell students to use a balance to find the mass of their 10 bean seeds and to record their measurements in the data table:

DATA TABLE

Mass of 10 soaked bean seeds _____

Mass of 10 unsoaked bean seeds _____

How much water did the bean seeds soak up? _____

c. Instruct students to add water to the container to a level of about 1 cm above the bean seeds. Set the bean seeds aside for 24–48 hours to soak up water. Allow students to add water to their containers if necessary during this time. After the bean seeds have soaked, students should pour off the excess water and use a balance to determine the mass of the soaked seeds and to record this measurement in the data table.

EXPLAIN

d. Ask: *How much water did the bean seeds absorb?* Lead students to subtract the before-soaking measurement from the after-soaking measurement to determine how much water the seeds soaked up. Enter the difference in the data table.

e. Ask: *How does the amount of water soaked up compare to the initial mass of the bean seeds? Is it larger, much larger, smaller, much smaller, or about the same? Why do you think water is important in the sprouting of the dry seeds?*

Nature of Scientific Inquiry

f. Explain that scientists use mathematics in all aspects of scientific inquiry. Ask: *How did we use mathematics in this activity?* (Measuring, putting data in a table, subtracting, comparing) Discuss that one value of mathematics is using it to answer questions in science. *Mathematics is the language of science.*

7. WHAT HAPPENS TO SEEDS WHEN THEY GERMINATE? (K–4)

Materials
- A quart size plastic storage bag for each child
- Paper towels
- Stapler
- Lima bean seeds
- Ruler

ENGAGE

a. Ask: *What are some things we do with seeds?* When students suggest that we plant them, ask: *What happens to seeds when they are planted?* Explain that if we plant the seeds in the soil, we cannot see what happens to them underground. Tell them we will place the seeds in a plastic bag and observe what happens for a few days.

EXPLORE

b. Give each child a quart size plastic storage bag. Show students how to line the inside of the bag with a paper towel. Place eight or nine staples along the bottom portion of the bag about 4 to 5 cm from the bottom. Place five lima bean seeds above the staples inside the bag, as in the illustration. Gently pour water into the bag, being careful not to dislodge the seeds (the water should bulge slightly at the bottom of the bag to about a finger's thickness). There should be enough water to keep the seeds moist, but the seeds should not rest in water. Some of the seeds will germinate within 24–48 hours. Others may take longer.

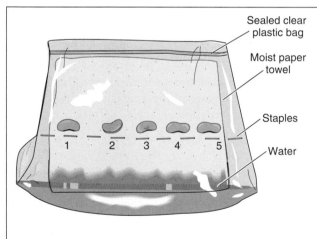

Sealed clear plastic bag

Moist paper towel

Staples

Water

- Line a quart size sealable, trans-parent storage bag with a moist paper towel.
- Place nine staples across the bag about 4 to 5 cm from the bottom, as shown in the diagram.
- Position five seeds to be germinated above the staples.
- The seeds may be presoaked for about 24 hours.
- Gently pour water from a small container into the bag, being careful not to dislodge the seeds (the water should bulge slightly at the bottom of the bag to about a finger's thickness).

The water will soak the paper towel and keep the seeds moist. The staples keep the seeds from lying in the water at the bottom of the bag. The transparent bag allows the seeds and roots to be observed.

c. Children should observe their germinating seeds and developing plants regularly for 2 weeks or more, recording daily in their investigation journals or on a prepared chart any changes in color, length, shape, texture, special features, and so on. To make the growth sequence clear, ask students to make drawings of changes they observe for one of their germinating bean seeds.

d. This investigation is a good one to promote careful measurement. Tell students to use a ruler to measure the length of the stem and root each day and to record the measurements in a chart. The chart should show length in centimeters for each day observed. The measurement data can then be displayed in a graph, which provides a picture of growth.

At lower grade levels, rather than measuring with a ruler, students can cut a green strip of paper to the length of the stem and a brown strip of paper to the length of the root. If the strips of paper are attached to a time line, such as a calendar, with the green strip above the line and the brown strip below, a visual display of growth over 2 or 3 weeks can be seen.

EXPLAIN

e. From their observational data, you want children to discover the sequence of growth changes for the beans from day to day—to learn that the root appears first and grows downward, that the stem is connected to the root and grows upward carrying the cotyledon with it, and that leaves grow on the stems.

f. In addition to observing the sequence of growth, students should also learn to recognize the seed coat, cotyledons, and embryo plant of seeds, and the root, stems, and leaves of the developing plants. Provide the names of these seed and plant parts.

ELABORATE

g. Have students add labels for seed and plant parts to the sequential drawings they have recorded.

EVALUATE

h. A good opportunity for peer assessment is available at the end of the elaborate phase. Students can exchange their recorded data with a peer and check for such things as correct placement of labels; neat, detailed drawings; and meaningful comments. A class discussion to select the criteria to assess creates focus for the analysis of each other's work. Students could write comments about their partner's work or just talk to their partner about his or her work.

i. To evaluate student awareness of the changes that occur during the germination process, have them write a description of how their seed changed into a seedling over time.

8. WHAT IS THE FUNCTION OF EACH SEED PART IN THE GROWTH OF THE SEEDLING? (3–6)

Materials

- Transparent storage bags
- Paper towels
- Soaked bean seeds

ENGAGE

    a. Ask: *What are the parts of a seed? How do different parts of a seed change during germination? Which part of the seed do you think grows into a plant? How could we investigate to find out?* Lead children to observe that a lima bean seed has two cotyledons (it is a dicot), with the embryo embedded in one of them. Lead them to consider trying to germinate a cotyledon by itself, an embryo plant and cotyledon, an embryo plant by itself, and a whole lima bean, and to observe what happens.

EXPLORE

    b. Assist children to set up a germination bag (as in Activity 7) containing
       1. one cotyledon by itself;
       2. one cotyledon with an embedded embryo plant;
       3. an embryo plant by itself; and
       4. a whole lima bean.
    Allow the students to observe their germination bags for several days, keeping records on their observations. *Note:* Open the bags daily for 15 minutes to prevent mold formation. Add just enough water to keep the paper towel slightly moist.

EXPLAIN

    c. Ask: *Which of the seed parts, if any, started to grow? Why do you think that is so? Which parts did not grow at all? What do you conclude from your investigation about what seed parts are necessary for seed germination and growth into a plant?* (Only the whole seed and the one cotyledon and embryo produced growth.) *What do you think the role of the embryo was in sprouting? What do you think the role of the cotyledon was? Why do seeds not germinate (sprout) if the embryo is removed? Why do seeds not germinate if the cotyledon is removed?*

9. WHAT CONDITIONS ARE NEEDED FOR SEEDS TO GERMINATE OR SPROUT? (3–6)

Materials

- Lima bean seeds
- Radish seeds
- Transparent storage bags
- Paper towels
- Stapler

ENGAGE

    a. Ask: *What do seeds need to germinate?*

EXPLORE

    b. Ask: *How could we find out?* Lead children to suggest an investigation to determine if light is needed for seed germination. In the investigation, the same kinds of seeds are placed in two germination bags. One bag is placed in a well-lit place; the other in a very dark place. Ask: *What is the manipulated variable?* (The amount of light) *What is the responding variable?* (The germination of the seeds) *What variables should be controlled?* Emphasize that to be a controlled investigation, the moisture in each bag and its temperature have to be the same.

    c. Let groups of children set up the investigation and observe the seeds for about 2 weeks, being careful not to expose the dark seeds to light. Tell students to keep their observational records in a chart like the one illustrated.

Seed name and amount	Date planted	Germination date		Germination conditions	Number of seeds germinated
		Predicted	Actual		

EXPLAIN

d. Ask: *What did you observe? What do you conclude?* (Light is not necessary for seed germination. After all, seeds germinate underground in the dark.)

ELABORATE

e. Ask: *Are there other factors that affect the germination of seeds? How could we determine the range of temperatures that seeds can tolerate and still sprout?* Lead the students to plan a controlled investigation using two germination bags, with one bag placed in the refrigerator and one in a warm, dark place. Discuss the responding variable (growth), the manipulated variable (temperature), and the variables to be controlled (amount of light, kinds of seeds, amount of water, etc.). Ask: *If one bag is placed in a refrigerator, why would the other one need to be in a "dark" place?*

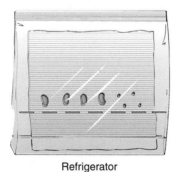
Refrigerator

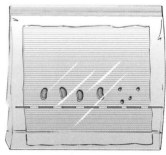
Dark cabinet

f. Tell students to place four lima bean seeds and four radish seeds in two separate plastic germination bags. Have students carry out the controlled investigation they planned. Put one bag in a cool, dark place (e.g., inside a refrigerator) and one bag in a warm, dark place (e.g., inside a cabinet). Make sure the two bags have the same amount of moisture and light.

g. Instruct students to observe the two bags regularly for about 2 weeks and to record their observations in their chart (like the one in the previous illustration). *Note:* Open the bags daily for about 15 minutes to prevent the formation of mold. Also, keep the paper towels just slightly moist.

EVALUATE

h. Ask students to respond in writing to the following questions at the end of the observation period, as an assessment of their understanding of their experiment, its results, and the conclusions that can be drawn from it.
   1. What question were you investigating?
   2. How were the conditions for the two bags different?

3. How do the seeds in the two bags compare?
4. What do you think is the effect of temperature on germination (sprouting)? Why do you think so? What is your evidence?

10. WHAT SEEDS DO WE EAT? (K–4)

ENGAGE

a. Ask: *What seeds or seed products do we eat?*

EXPLORE

b. Hold a classroom "seed feast." Provide a variety of seeds for children to eat. Consider some of the seeds and seed products in the accompanying chart for the seed feast.

Safety Precautions

Make sure children are not allergic to any food you provide for them to eat, such as peanuts.

EXPLAIN

c. Using the chart, conduct a discussion of the various seeds and seed products we eat. Emphasize that rather than the cotyledons providing food for the seeds to germinate and begin growth, they are providing food energy for our survival and growth.

SEEDS AND SEED PRODUCTS WE EAT

Food	Seed or Seed Product
Peas	seeds (and fruit)
Beans	seeds (and fruit)
Corn	seeds
Rice	seeds
Peanuts	seeds
Sunflower seeds	seeds
Chocolate	made from seeds of cacao plant
Coffee	made from seeds of coffee plant
Vanilla	made from seeds of orchid
Cumin (spice)	made from cumin seeds
Flour	made from wheat, barley, or other grass seeds
Pretzels	made from flour
Bread	made from flour
Tortillas	made from flour or corn
Breakfast cereals	made from the seeds of grasses including wheat, rye, oats, and barley

Source: Adapted from National Gardening Association, 1990. *GrowLab.* National Gardening Association, Burlington, VT.

ELABORATE

d. As a take-home activity, have the students keep a mini-journal about the seeds they eat for a week. Have a discussion with the class to identify the kinds of information that should be included in their journal. Draft a letter to parents describing the project.

EVALUATE

e. Create a checklist, to be included with the parent letter, that students can use to self-evaluate their work. Use the same checklist to assist in your evaluation of the final products.
f. Post the mini-journals so students can view and have discussions about the different kinds of seeds their classmates eat. This is a form of informal peer assessment.

B. PLANTS

▶ *Science Background*

Biologists classify organisms on the basis of their structures and behaviors. Most easily observed organisms can be classified as plants or animals. Each type of plant or animal has different structures that serve different functions in growth, survival, and reproduction. All organisms have basic needs. Plants need light, air, water, and nutrients. Animals need air, water, and nutrients. Plants and animals can survive only in environments in which their needs are met. Roots absorb water and nutrients through small root hairs. Water and nutrients are carried from the roots to the leaves through small tubes, called *capillaries*, that are inside the stem. Plants get their energy for survival and growth directly from sunlight through a process called *photosynthesis*. Animals live by consuming the energy-rich foods initially synthesized by plants.[1]

 Science Standards

All students should develop an understanding of

- characteristics of organisms (K–4).
- structure and function in living systems (5–8).
- life cycles of organisms (K–4).
- organisms and their environments (K–4).

Concepts and Principles That Support the Standards

- Some animals and plants are alike in the way they look and the things they do, and others are very different from one another (K–2).
- A great variety of living things can be sorted into groups in many ways using various features to decide which things belong to which group (3–5).
- Features used for grouping depend on the purpose of the grouping (3–5).
- Each plant or animal has different structures that serve different functions in growth, survival, and reproduction (K–4).

Objectives

1. Recognize and discuss the wide variation in plant life.
2. Identify and describe different parts/structures of plants (roots, stems, leaves) and describe the functions of each.
3. Observe and describe the life cycles of plants.
4. Ask questions about plants that can be answered through investigations.
5. Design and carry out descriptive, classificatory, and explanatory investigations to gather information for answering questions about plants.
6. Use simple equipment and tools to gather data and extend the senses.
7. Through investigations, identify basic needs of plants: air, water, nutrients, and light.
8. Use evidence from investigations and science knowledge to answer questions about plant life, construct explanations, and make predictions.

---

[1]Adapted from National Research Council, 1996. *National Science Education Standards.*

....

1. WHAT IS A TREE LIKE? (K–2)

Materials
- Paper
- Crayons or markers
- String
- Scissors
- Glue or tape

ENGAGE

a. Have students draw a picture of a tree. Give them between 5 and 10 minutes to complete their drawing. Post all of the drawings so the class can see them. Ask: *How are the drawings of trees different? How are they alike?*

EXPLORE

b. Assign groups to trees in or near the school yard. Have students feel the surface of their assigned tree and describe how it feels. Have them make a rubbing of the bark using the same color as the bark. Have them use string to measure the trunk. Encourage students to smell the bark.

EXPLAIN

c. Ask: *What was your group's tree like? What did it look like? How did it smell? How did it differ from other trees?* Compare rubbings. Ask: *What do the rubbings show? Why do some rubbings look different? Why do some rubbings look the same?* Compare the lengths of the strings that were used to measure the trunks of the groups' trees. Ask: *Which group studied the tree with the widest trunk? Narrowest trunk? How do you know?* Discuss children's findings with them.

ELABORATE

d. Have each student create a poster about the tree he or she studied during the explore stage of the lesson. The poster should include a drawing of the tree, the rubbing of its bark, the distance around the tree, and a brief description of the tree. Posters can be placed beside their initial tree drawing to show how much students have learned.

EVALUATE

e. Informal assessment of the change in students conceptual understanding of trees is possible by comparing students' initial drawing with their posters.

....

2. HOW DO THE CHARACTERISTICS OF LEAVES VARY? (K–2)

Materials
- Assortment of leaves
- Magazines
- Newspapers
- Colored paper
- Paintbrushes
- Poster paint

ENGAGE

a. Ask: *What are leaves like? What are the similarities in leaves from different trees? What are the differences in the leaves from different trees?*

b. Invite students to collect a variety of fallen leaves and bring them to class.

Safety Precautions   Stress collecting fallen leaves only. Do not allow students to pick from living trees and plants.

EXPLORE   c. Instruct students to spread the leaves out and compare them. Ask: *How are the leaves alike? How are they different? How do the leaves differ in shape? size? color? number of points? arrangement of veins? How do they differ in other ways? Why do you think the leaves vary so much from one another?*

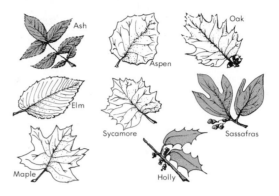

d. Tell the students to place the leaves in groups according to color, shape, size, or some other characteristic.

EXPLAIN   e. Ask: *How many groups did you form?* Then tell them to rearrange the leaves according to other characteristics. Ask: *How many groups did you form?*

. . . .

3. HOW CAN SOME PLANTS GROW WITHOUT SEEDS? (K–2)

Materials
- Small tumblers (preferably clear plastic)
- Small sweet potatoes, white potatoes, and carrot tops (with some leaves)
- Toothpicks
- Cuttings from coleus, philodendron, ivy, and other houseplants

ENGAGE   a. Ask: *What is needed for new plants to grow? How can we get new plants to grow without planting them in soil?*

EXPLORE   b. Put three toothpicks each in a sweet potato, white potato, and carrot, as shown in the diagram. Place them in small tumblers of water. Take cuttings of houseplants and place them in small tumblers of water. Put all the tumblers in a well-lit place and make sure the water levels are maintained so that the water always touches the plants. Have students observe, measure, and record the changes in the plants, such as root development, height, and number of leaves.

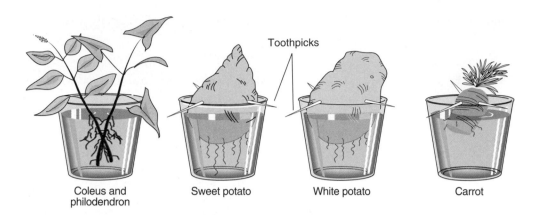

Coleus and philodendron   Sweet potato   White potato   Carrot

EXPLAIN

c. Ask: *Do new plants come only from seeds? What is your evidence?*

d. Ask: *What do plants need to grow?* Explain to students that plants require air, water, nutrients, and light. Plants can survive only in environments in which these basic needs are met. Ask: *How do you think these basic needs of plants are met when they are growing in water?*

....

4. WHAT ARE ROOTS LIKE? (K–5)

Materials

- Lima bean plants and radish plants growing in a germination bag
- Magnifying lenses
- Small, healthy coleus, geranium, or petunia plants
- Potting soil
- Planting containers (such as clean, empty milk cartons)

ENGAGE

a. Ask: *What do the roots of a young plant look like? What could you do to find out?*

EXPLORE

b. Lead students to answer this question through their observations of the roots of bean plants and radish plants growing in a germination bag. Instruct students to use a magnifying lens and to record their observations, including drawings, of the structure of roots.

c. Continue the observation of the roots of plants for several days. Require students to make daily records of their observations in their journals.

EXPLAIN

d. After several days of observation, ask: *What do you notice about the roots? How are the roots of the bean plant and radish plant similar? How are they different? What are the small, fuzzlike projections coming from the roots?* (Root hairs)

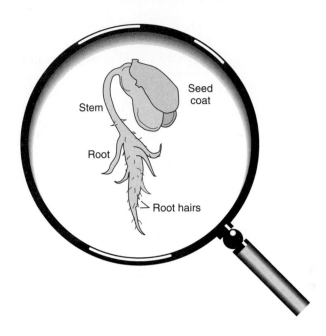

ELABORATE

e. Permit students to grow other seeds in order to compare and contrast roots from other types of young plants. Allow time for students to discuss their findings about their new roots and relate their discoveries to the bean and radish roots they examined previously.

EVALUATE

f. Challenge students to use a Venn diagram or some other graphic organizer to summarize the similarities and differences among the roots of the three young plants they observed. The detail they include should provide evidence of their observation and comparison skills.

5. WHAT IS THE FUNCTION OF ROOTS? (K–5)

ENGAGE

a. Ask: *What do you think is the function of the roots and the root hairs? What could you do to investigate to find out?* Lead students to suggest that functions of roots may be to absorb water and nutrients for plant growth and to provide support for plants. Ask: *How might you investigate these hypotheses?*

EXPLORE

b. Obtain two similar coleus, petunia, or geranium plants and remove all the roots from one plant. Fill the bottom half of two milk cartons or other planting containers with soil. Place the plant without roots down on top of the soil. Release the plant and observe what happens. Ask: *How might roots have helped this plant?* Explain that one function of the roots is to provide support for plants.

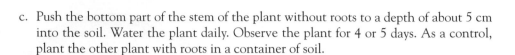

c. Push the bottom part of the stem of the plant without roots to a depth of about 5 cm into the soil. Water the plant daily. Observe the plant for 4 or 5 days. As a control, plant the other plant with roots in a container of soil.

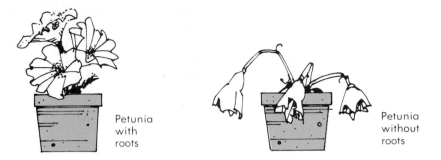

Petunia with roots

Petunia without roots

EXPLAIN

d. Ask: *What did you observe about the two plants? Why do you think this happens?* Explain that one function of the root hairs is to absorb water and nutrients for the plant. Because the root hairs are critical to the life of the plant, it is important that they not be damaged when a plant is pulled up or transplanted.

　　Gently pull the plant without roots from the soil. If this plant has developed new roots, discuss the function of the newly developed roots.

ELABORATE

e. Ask: *Why do you think some roots grow comparatively shallow and others grow deep? What are some ways people use the roots of plants?* Permit students to use library and Internet resources to find information to help them answer these questions.

EVALUATE

f. To assess student understanding about the function of roots, have each student complete this chart based on this investigation.

Function of Root	Evidence

6. DO PLANTS GET WATER THROUGH ROOTS OR LEAVES? (K–5)

ENGAGE

a. Ask: *Do plants get water through their roots or leaves? What could we do to find out?*

EXPLORE

b. To gather evidence to answer this key question, lead children to set up a controlled investigation like the one illustrated. This investigation involves two plants. Water is added to the soil of one plant so that it can reach the roots. Water is sprinkled on the leaves of the second plant, with a plastic bib keeping the water from reaching the soil and roots. All other conditions are controlled.

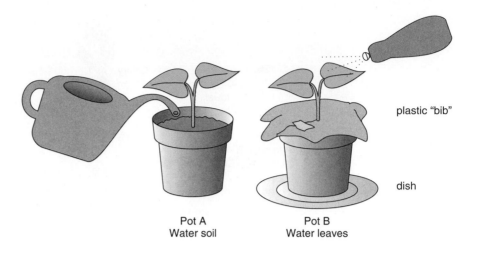

plastic "bib"

dish

Pot A
Water soil

Pot B
Water leaves

c. Tell the children to keep daily records of their observations.

EXPLAIN

d. After about 2 weeks, lead a discussion of the children's findings. Ask: *What did you do in the investigation? What did you observe? How did your findings compare with your predictions? What can you infer about the role of leaves in taking in water? Did you actually see roots taking in water? What makes you confident in your inference that water is taken in by roots? What factors might have affected the results of your investigation?* (For example, watering might have damaged the leaves.)[2]

7. WHAT IS THE FUNCTION OF A STEM? (K–5)

Materials

- Carnations
- Geranium or celery stem
- Red and blue food coloring
- Drinking glass or clear plastic cup
- Paper towel

Preparation

Place the stem of a white carnation in a cup containing water with blue food coloring. Leave the carnation in the water until it has turned blue.

ENGAGE

a. Ask: *Why is this carnation blue? Aren't carnations usually white? Do you think I planted a blue carnation seed? How does water get from the roots of a plant to the leaves? How do you think a florist produces blue carnations? If you wanted to change a white carnation into a blue carnation, what would you do? How could you find out if your idea was correct?*

---

[2]Adapted from National Gardening Association, 1990. *GrowLab: Activities for Growing Minds.* National Gardening Association, 180 Flynn Avenue, Burlington, Vermont 05401.

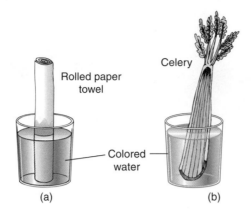

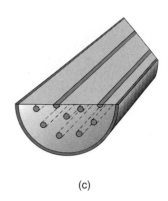

(a)	(b)	(c)

Rolled paper towel

Celery

Colored water

EXPLORE

b. Fill a cup with water, tint with food coloring, and add a rolled paper towel, as in diagram (a).

Ask: *What do you see happening to the paper towel? Why do you think this happens? How could this work in plants?*

c. Tell children to put some water in the drinking glass and add the food coloring. Cut a small slice off the bottom of the celery stem. Set the stem into the glass of colored water as in diagram (b). Allow it to sit in a sunny area for 2 hours. At the end of this period, cut open the stem. See diagram (c).

EXPLAIN

d. Ask: *What has happened to the celery stem? What parts of the stem appear to contain the colored water? How do you know? What can you conclude about the function of a stem?*

ELABORATE

e. Ask: *What do you think might happen if you put half of a split stem in one color of water and the other half in another color of water? Try it and see.*

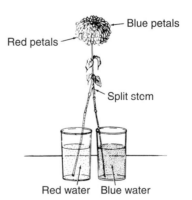

Blue petals

Red petals

Split stem

Red water   Blue water

f. Ask: *What do you think might happen to the upward movement of water in a stem when the plant is in the dark or out of sunlight? How could you find out?*

EVALUATE

g. Use the following multiple-choice item to check student knowledge of the function of stems.

Stems:

    A. Hold the entire plant in place.
    B. Get water from the soil.
    C. Transport water to the upper parts of a plant.
    D. Determine the color of the flower.

---

8. HOW MUCH WATER IS ENOUGH FOR HEALTHY PLANT GROWTH? (3–6)

Materials

- Young bean or radish plants
- Milk cartons or plastic cups
- Graduated cylinder or measuring cup

ENGAGE

a. Ask: *How much water do you need each day? How much water do you think a plant needs to grow in a healthy way? How could you find out?*

EXPLORE

b. Guide students to design an investigation to determine how much water a plant needs to grow. Tell them each group will have three similar plants to test and we will decide together how to make our experiment a "fair test." Ask: *What should be different for each of your three pots?* (how much we water it) *What should be kept the same for each of your three pots?* (Size of pot, where we put it, kind of soil, etc.) *What should be observed?* (The way the plant looks, color of leaves, number of leaves, height, etc.) *When should we observe? How long will the experiment last?* Based on class consensus, develop a procedure for all groups to follow. For example, students might decide to label each group's cups A, B, C. Then water daily as follows: cup A—0 ml water; cup B—20 ml water; cup C—40 ml water. All other variables will be controlled.

EXPLAIN

c. At the end of the observation period defined by the class, ask: *How do the conditions of the plants differ? Which one seems healthiest? What are the indications of health?*

---

9. HOW MUCH FERTILIZER IS ENOUGH FOR HEALTHY PLANT GROWTH? (3–6)

Materials

- Young bean or radish plants
- Milk cartons or plastic cups
- Fertilizer
- Graduated cylinder or measuring cup

ENGAGE

a. Ask: *How much fertilizer do plants need?*

EXPLORE

b. Guide children to plan and set up an investigation similar to that in the illustration to determine how much fertilizer is enough for plants.

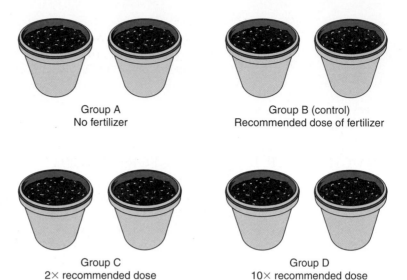

Group A
No fertilizer

Group B (control)
Recommended dose of fertilizer

Group C
2× recommended dose

Group D
10× recommended dose

c. Lead students to observe the plants and make records in their observation journals. They might observe, measure, and compare the height of each plant, leaf color, number of leaves, and leaf size.

EXPLAIN

d. Ask: *How do the conditions of the plants differ? Which one seems healthiest? What do you conclude about the amount of fertilizer a plant needs? What does fertilizer supply for plants?*

▶ *Teaching Background*

Plants require **mineral nutrients** for growth, repair, and proper functioning. Mineral nutrients are formed by the breakdown of rocks and found in soil. Mineral nutrients can also be supplied by fertilizers applied by humans. Humans ordinarily obtain minerals by eating plants or animals. Nutrients can also be obtained from supplements.[3]

10. WHAT IS THE EFFECT OF LIGHT ON PLANT GROWTH? (3–6)

Materials

- Germinated bean seeds
- Sunny window or light source
- Ruler
- Potting soil
- Clean milk carton
- Shoe box with cover

ENGAGE

a. Ask: *What effect does light have on the way a plant grows? What do you think might happen to a plant if the amount of light from a light source is very limited? What do you think might happen if a plant is placed near a window? What could you do to find out?*

[3]Adapted from National Gardening Association, 1990. *GrowLab: Activities for Growing Minds*. National Gardening Association, 180 Flynn Avenue, Burlington, Vermont 05401.

EXPLORE

b. Plant four bean plants 2 cm deep in moist soil in a clean milk carton.
c. Place the milk carton in a shoe box that has only a single, 2 cm hole cut in the middle of one end. Cover the box and turn the opening toward bright sunlight or a strong lamp, as shown in the diagram.

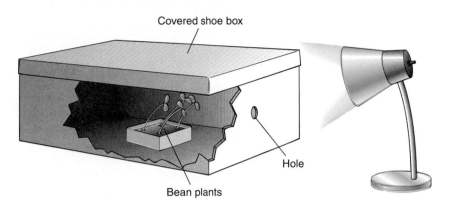

Covered shoe box

Hole

Bean plants

d. Lift the cover every 2 days and see how the bean plants are growing. Record observations. Add water as needed.

EXPLAIN

e. Ask: *What is happening to the stems and leaves? Why do you think they are growing as they are? What do you think might happen if you turned the milk carton with the plants completely around in the shoe box?*
f. Try it and observe what happens in 2 days.

▶ *Teaching Background*

Students should see that the beans grow toward the opening in the shoe box. When turned around, they reverse their direction of growth toward the opening again. The stems and leaves of plants turn toward the light because of phototropism. This adaptation causes the cells on the dark side of stems to grow more rapidly than the cells on the lit side. This causes the leaves to turn to the light, allowing the plant to produce more food by photosynthesis than it would if the leaves were not turned to the light.

11. HOW DOES LIGHT AFFECT PLANTS? (K–2)

Materials

• Two similar healthy plants growing in separate similar pots.
• Water
• Crayons or markers

ENGAGE

a. Show students two similar healthy plants growing in separate similar pots. Ask: *Do these two plants appear to be the same? How do you know? Do plants need light in order to grow and stay healthy? How could we use these two plants to find out?*

EXPLORE

b. Lead students to suggest that one plant should be put in a dark place, and the other plant should be put in a place that it gets sunlight. Point out that the plants are about the same now and that their pots are the same, too. Ask: *Is there anything else that should be kept the same to make this experiment a fair test?* If students don't suggest that they each be watered the same amount, lead them to that idea.

c. Have students record their first observation of the plants in their investigation journal or on a chart that you provide. Tell students that they will observe the plants each week for the next 3 weeks. Each time they will draw and write about how the plants look.

EXPLAIN

d. After each weekly observation, ask: *What do you see? Why do you think this happened?*

e. In addition, after the last observation, ask: *Do you think plants need light to grow and stay healthy? How do you know?*

12. DO LEAVES GIVE OFF MOISTURE? (3–5)

Materials
- Two clear plastic bags
- Two small, identical geranium plants
- Plastic ties
- Magnifying lenses

ENGAGE

a. Ask: *Do leaves contain moisture?*

EXPLORE

b. Instruct students to do this activity:
 1. Place a clear plastic bag over one geranium and tie the bag around the stem, just above the soil level.
 2. Wave a second plastic bag through the air and tie it as well, as illustrated in the diagram.
 3. Put both plastic bags in direct sunlight for at least 3 hours.
 4. After at least 3 hours, observe both plastic bags. Notice any differences.

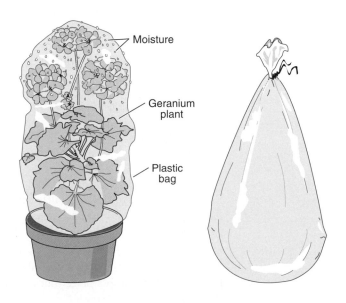

Moisture

Geranium plant

Plastic bag

EXPLAIN

c. Ask:

- *What do you see forming near the top of the plant in the plastic bag? Where do you think the moisture came from?* (From the leaves of the plant)

- *What is your evidence that the moisture came from the leaves and not the soil?* (The plastic bag was tied off above the soil line.)

- *How is the plastic bag without the plant different after 3 hours? Why do you think this happened? Why do you think the empty plastic bag was used in this activity?*

- *What makes this investigation a controlled experiment?* (Two identical bags containing air are used, one with a plant and one without a plant. The condition varied—the manipulated variable—is whether or not a bag has a plant. The outcome or responding variable is the production of moisture.)

▶ *Teaching Background*

Moisture is formed in the plastic bag with the plant because leaves give off water in a process called *transpiration*. The purpose of tying off the bag at the stem was to prevent moisture evaporating from the soil from entering the bag. The "empty" clear plastic bag is the control.

13. WHAT IS THE EFFECT OF GRAVITY ON THE GROWTH OF ROOTS AND STEMS? (5–8)

Materials

- Young, growing bean plants
- Paper towels
- Two pieces of glass or thick plastic to place growing plants between
- Craft sticks or tongue depressors
- Small pebbles
- Tape

ENGAGE

a. Ask: *What do you think might happen to roots of a plant if they were planted facing up or sideways rather than facing down? What do you think might happen to roots if something were in their way? What could we do to find out? What do you think would happen to the stems of plants that are planted upside down or sideways?*

EXPLORE

b. Lead students to design an investigation in which the plant is planted upside down so that the growth of roots and stems can be observed.

This investigation might be done as a class demonstration. Place four young bean plants between two moist paper towels. Put the paper towels with the seedlings between two pieces of glass or rigid, clear plastic. Put small pebbles under each root. Place the applicator sticks or tongue depressors between the pieces of glass or clear plastic, and tape as shown in the diagram.

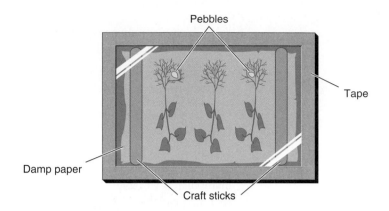

Pebbles

Tape

Damp paper

Craft sticks

c. Stand the glass so the roots point up and the stems point down. Instruct the students to observe the plant growth for several days and record their observations.

EXPLAIN

d. Ask: *What did you observe about the roots? What did you observe about the stems? Why do you think this happened?* Through discussion, lead students to conclude that roots grow downward under the influence of gravity and that they grow around objects in the soil. Stems grow upward.

▶ *Teaching Background*

The roots will grow down (toward the earth), and the stems will grow up (away from the earth). The plant responses that cause this are called **tropisms.** **Geotropism** forces roots down as auxins (plant hormones) are concentrated by gravity along the bottom cells of stems and root tips. The bottom cells in the stem are stimulated by the hormones to grow faster than cells higher up; they get longer and curl upward. Root cells are more sensitive to these hormones than are stem cells, so the root cells inhibit cell growth. Root top cells elongate faster, and root tips curve downward.

C. INSECTS

▶ *Science Background*

Insects are the most successful group of animals on earth. Insects dominate the planet in terms of number of individuals and species. There are more kinds of insects than all other kinds of animals put together. All insects have six legs and three body parts: the head, thorax, and abdomen. Insects that may be familiar to children include dragonflies, crickets, lice, beetles, butterflies, flies, fleas, and ants.

Insects change in form through a process called *metamorphosis* as they grow and mature. Some insects progress from egg, to larva, to a pupal stage, and then to adults. Other insects look pretty much like adults when they hatch from eggs.[4]

---

[4]Adapted from FOSS (Full Option Science System), 1995. *Insects.* Lawrence Hall of Science, Berkeley, CA. (Published by Delta Education, Nashua, NH.)

NSES Science Standards

All students should develop an understanding of
- characteristics of organisms (K–4).
- structure and function in living systems (5–8).
- life cycles of organisms (K–4).
- organisms and their environments (K–4).

Concepts and Principles That Support the Standards

- Plants and animals have life cycles that include being born, developing into adults, reproducing, and eventually dying. The details of this life cycle are different for different organisms (K–4).
- Organisms have basic needs. Animals need air, water, and food (K–4).
- Organisms can survive only in environments in which their basic needs are met (K–4).
- Each plant or animal has different structures that serve different functions in growth, survival, and reproduction (K–4).

Objectives

1. Recognize the wide variation in insects.
2. Identify and describe different parts/structures of insects.
3. Define *metamorphosis* and name the stages in the metamorphosis of a mealworm.
4. Describe the sequence of stages in the development of a mealworm.
5. Ask questions about ants that can be answered through investigations.
6. Design and carry out descriptive investigations to gather information and answer questions about ants.

1. WHAT STAGES DO MEALWORMS GO THROUGH? (K–5)

Materials

- Jars with covers (clear plastic, if possible)
- Mealworms (from pet shop)
- Branmeal, or other cereal flakes
- Magnifying lenses
- Spoons
- Pictures or drawings of mealworms at different times during their life cycle (These can be made during the explore phase of the lesson.)
- Tape or glue

ENGAGE

a. Ask: *What are the stages people go through as they grow and change? Do insects, like mealworms, go through stages too? How could we find out?*

EXPLORE

b. Obtain some mealworms from a pet store or commercial supplier (see Appendix C). Introduce the mealworms and challenge students to predict how the mealworms will change over time. Using spoons, you or the students can transfer several mealworms and some bran or cereal flakes into a jar or other container with a lid. Provide a container for each student or group of two or three students. Punch several small holes in the lids for air.

c. Have students observe the mealworms several times a week and record on a chart or log any observed changes in appearance (color, length, stage, etc.) or behavior.

EXPLAIN

d. Using their charts or logs as a reference, students should discuss how the mealworms have changed over time. Ask: *What happened to the mealworms? Did they all change in the same way? Did they all change at the same time? Which stage do you think is the adult? Why do you think that?*

e. Introduce the term *metamorphosis* for this type of change during an organism's life cycle. Using pictures of mealworms at different stages of growth, discuss how these living things grow. Point out that when people grow, they change but not in such extreme ways as a metamorphosing insect. Human children, teenagers, and adults look a lot like each other, while mealworm larvae, pupae, and adults don't look much alike at all. Help students make a table comparing the stages of mealworms' lives with humans', like the one shown.

Stages	
People	*Mealworms*
Child	Larva
Teenager	Pupa
Adult	Adult

f. In addition, guide students to make a diagram, similar to the one shown, and include photos or drawings to visualize the stages of mealworm metamorphosis.

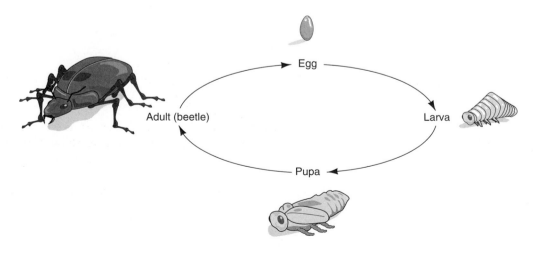

ELABORATE

g. Have students use print and online resources to learn about the life cycles of other insects. Students should report back to their class about their findings. Ask: *Are all insect life cycles just like the mealworm's life cycle? If not, how are they different?*

EVALUATE

h. To assess student knowledge about the series of changes that occur during mealworm metamorphosis, prepare cards with drawings or photographs of mealworms during their life cycle. (You could take these pictures with a digital microscope or camera during the explore phase of the investigation.) Give each child a set of cards. Have them put them in order to represent the mealworm's life cycle. Ask them to label parts of the mealworm life cycle using terms they learned during this lesson. Finally, ask them to explain why they arranged the cards in the way they did.

2. HOW DO ANTS LIVE? (K–2)

Materials

- Widemouthed glass jar (commercial mayonnaise or pickle jar) with screw top punctured with very small holes
- Empty washed soup can
- Soil to fill the jar two-thirds full
- Small sponge
- Pan large enough to hold the widemouthed glass jar
- Sheet of black construction paper
- Crumbs and bits of food such as bread, cake, sugar, and seeds
- Colony of ants (from pet shop or science materials supplier)

Safety Precautions

- Caution children not to handle the ants. As a defense, ants bite and sting. Sometimes after biting an enemy, ants will spray a chemical into the open wound.
- Use ants from a pet store or science materials supplier, so that you don't disrupt a natural colony and to avoid accidentally bringing fire ants or other dangerous types of ants into the classroom.

ENGAGE

a. Ask: *What do ants look like? Are all ants alike, or are there different kinds of ants? Where do ants make their homes?* Lead children to draw pictures of ants and to describe and explain their pictures.

EXPLORE

b. Set up an ant colony following these directions:
   1. Place the soup can in the center of the widemouthed glass jar as in the diagram.
   2. Fill the jar two-thirds full of soil.
   3. Punch several airholes in the screw cover.
   4. Place a sheet of black construction paper around the outside of the jar.
   5. Add a small sponge with water. Add crumbs and bits of food (bread, cake, sugar, and seeds).
   6. Add ants.
   7. Place a cloth over the top of the jar and screw the jar lid in place.
   8. Place the jar in a pan of water.

EXPLAIN

c. Ask: *What effect will a sheet of black paper placed around the jar have on the ants?* (This simulates the dark underground so ants will tunnel close to the sides of the glass jar.) *Why place the soup can in the center of the jar with soil around it?* (So ants will not burrow into the center but will tunnel out to the jar's sides and be more visible.) *What is the purpose of placing the jar in a pan of water?* (So the ants cannot escape.)

ELABORATE

d. Guide children to observe ants, including observing with magnifying lenses. Instruct students to make records, including drawings, of what ants look like and what the ants do. Students should observe body characteristics such as are shown in the diagram.[5]

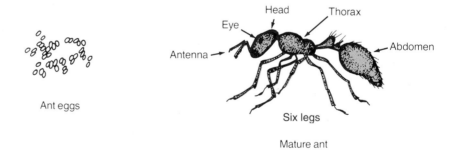

Ant eggs

Mature ant

e. Your class should also keep an I Notice-I Wonder chart about the ants and their colony. Over time, children can confirm or find evidence against the things others noticed and can design investigations to address the *I Wonder* questions generated by the class.

---

[5]Adapted and modified from *Ant Homes Under the Ground*, one of more than 75 teacher's guides in the Great Explorations in Math and Science (GEMS) series, available from the Lawrence Hall of Science, Berkeley, CA. (For more information, visit the website at http://www.lhsgems.org.)

EVALUATE

    f. Formatively assess students' curiosity as they investigate the ant colony over time. Use the following indicators, which become more sophisticated as you move down the list, as a checklist to record your observations about your students.[6]

Students:

☐ Give some attention to new things happening in the ant colony, but are easily distracted and ask few questions.

☐ Show interest in new things happening in the ant colony by asking "what" questions.

☐ Explore the ant colony and ask questions about it in response to invitations to do so.

☐ Examine the ant colony carefully and ask "how" and "why" questions as well as "what" questions.

☐ Explore and investigate things about the ant colony to answer their own questions.

☐ Spontaneously seek information about ants and their colonies from books or other sources to satisfy their own curiosity.

D. BIRDS

▶ *Science Background*

Birds are familiar animals in the child's environment. Birds differ in a variety of ways. Children can observe many different characteristics of birds, such as colors and sizes. Birds sing different songs, eat different kinds of food, and make different kinds of nests where they care for their young. The male bird may have a more colorful plumage than the female. Some birds change color with the season. Some birds migrate. Birds need trees and shrubs for protection from their predators, including small mammals, humans, and even other birds.

 NSES   **Science Standards**

All students should develop an understanding of

- characteristics of organisms (K–4).
- structure and function in living systems (5–8).
- organisms and their environments (K–4).

Concepts and Principles That Support the Standards

- Some animals and plants are alike in the way they look and the things they do, and others are very different from one another (K–2).
- A great variety of living things can be sorted into groups in many ways using various features to decide which things belong to which group (3–5).
- Organisms have basic needs. Animals need air, water, and food (K–4).
- Organisms can survive only in environments in which their basic needs are met (K–4).

---

[6]Adapted from Harlen, W. (2000). *Teaching, learning and assessing science 5-12* (3rd ed.). Thousand Oaks, CA: Sage Publications.

Objectives	1. Recognize the wide variation in birds. 2. Identify and describe different characteristics of birds. 3. Ask questions about birds that can be answered through investigations. 4. Design and carry out descriptive and classificatory investigations to gather information for answering questions about birds.

1. WHAT DO YOU KNOW ABOUT THE BIRDS AROUND YOU? (K–6)

Materials

- Bird book (showing local birds)
- Pictures of birds
- Bird feeders (commercial or made in class)

ENGAGE

a. Lead children in a discussion of what they know about birds.
   Ask:
   How are all birds alike? How do birds differ from each other?
   Where do some birds go during the winter?
   What kinds of homes do birds live in?
   What do birds do that is different from what other animals do?
   What kinds of foods do birds eat?
   What are the names of some local birds?
   What do these birds look like?

EXPLORE

b. If the natural environment lends itself to observing birds, have students observe birds on the way to and from school, or take a class field trip to a local area, park, or zoo. In a city, you will probably see sparrows or pigeons, jays in picnic areas, ducks in ponds, geese on golf courses, and seagulls at the seashore. In addition, you may want to provide pictures of different birds, nests, and eggs for students to handle, observe, and discuss.

EXPLAIN

c. Ask: *What birds did you see? How did you know which birds you saw? How were the types of birds different from each other? In what ways were all the birds you observed the same?*

d. Record students' responses to this question on the board: *How could we attract birds to our school grounds?* Ask: *Where could we make a good bird observing area?* (Tree and shrub shelter that is free from predators and visible from the classroom)

ELABORATE

e. Set up a bird observing area.
   1. With your students, survey your school grounds and pick the best spot for a bird feeding and observing area.
   2. Find out what kinds of birds are common in your area, what their food preferences are, how they eat (on the ground or from feeders), and any other information that will enhance observations. Discuss and provide information to children about common birds in your area, what they prefer to eat, and how they eat. Encourage them to find and use additional resources in the library or online.
   3. Develop investigatable questions that observational data from your bird feeding and observing areas could help to answer. Let small groups of students select a question for investigation, then carry it out.

EVALUATE

f. Allow children to present their findings from their investigation. Their oral report should address:

- the question they were investigating,
- their hypothesis,
- their observational procedures,
- their data, presented in a way that is easy to understand (table and/or graph), and
- their conclusions.

The group should also be prepared to answer questions from their classmates and their teacher.

2. HOW DO BIRD BONES DIFFER FROM MAMMAL BONES? (3–6)

Materials

- Beef and chicken bones (one of each for every two students). If possible, these should be cut in half so the inside of the bone is visible.
- Wing bones of chickens (or any other bird)

Safety Precautions

Be sure that students wash hands thoroughly after handling the bones.

ENGAGE

a. Ask: *In what ways do birds behave differently than mammals? How would you expect bird bones to differ from the bones of mammals?*

EXPLORE

b. Allow students to help furnish beef and chicken bones.
   1. Obtain a cut chicken bone, a cut beef bone, and a wing bone of a chicken.
   2. Ask: *How did you know which bone was from a chicken and which was from a cow?*
   3. Examine the centers of the two bones and record how the structure of the beef bone differs from that of the chicken bone.
   4. Look at the chicken wing bone. Ask: *How does its structure compare with the arm bones of a person?*

EXPLAIN

c. Ask: *What advantages do you think bones of birds and mammals have for them? What are some other structural differences between birds and mammals?*

II. ORGANISMS AND THEIR ENVIRONMENTS

Organisms have basic needs. Animals need air, water, and food. Plants require air, water, nutrients, and light. Organisms can survive only in environments in which their basic needs are met.

 ### A. AQUARIUM HABITATS

▶ *Science Background*

An aquarium is a wonderful context for studying aquatic life. Many environmental factors are important to life in aquarium habitats, including temperature, water transparency, nutrients, and concentrations of dissolved gases (oxygen and carbon dioxide).

Both plants and animals use oxygen and give off carbon dioxide through respiration. Plants also use carbon dioxide and give off oxygen in the process of photosynthesis. During daylight hours, aquatic plants produce more oxygen than plants and animals consume in respiration. At night, both plants and animals use accumulated oxygen.

When carbon dioxide dissolves in water, it makes the water acidic. Bromothymol blue (BTB) is a chemical indicator that can be used to monitor acid concentration in aquariums. BTB changes color, depending on the acidity of the water. A few drops of BTB in a container of water that is neutral produces a pale blue. If the water is acidic, its color shifts to green or yellow when BTB is added. If the water is basic, the color turns to deep blue.

 NSES   **Science Standards**

All students should develop an understanding of

- organisms and their environments (K–4).

Concepts and Principles That Support the Standards

- Organisms have basic needs. Animals need air, water, and food. Plants require air, water, nutrients, and light. Organisms can survive only in environments in which their basic needs are met (K–4).
- An organism's patterns of behavior are related to the nature of that organism's environment, including the kinds and numbers of other organisms present, the availability of food and resources, and the physical characteristics of the environment (K–4).
- When the environment changes, some plants and animals survive and reproduce, and others die or move to new locations (K–4).

Objectives

1. Define *habitat* and *ecosystem*.
2. Identify and describe the parts of an aquarium habitat and describe how the parts of this system interact.
3. Construct an aquarium habitat.
4. Ask questions and design and carry out investigations about components and interactions within ecosystems.

1. HOW CAN WE CONSTRUCT AN AQUARIUM HABITAT? (1–5)

Materials

- A 6 liter, clear plastic basin (used as the aquarium)
- Five small aquatic plants (approximately 10 cm in height)
- Freshwater fantailed guppy
- Two water snails

Prepare

a. Ask: *What is an aquarium? What lives in an aquarium? What are some of the things fish, plants, and other organisms need in order to survive in an aquarium? How must an aquarium be constructed and maintained to support living things?*

Construct

b. It is preferable for each group of students to have their own aquarium. Teachers should guide and work with students to construct and maintain a freshwater aquarium, following these instructions:

1. *Container.* Obtain a 4 to 6 liter (1 to 1.5 gallons), rectangular clear plastic container with strong walls. The container should have a large surface area to allow gas exchange with the atmosphere, but should not be too shallow. Wash the container well with water, but not soap.

2. *Sand.* Obtain a supply of coarse white sand. Rinse the sand in a bucket to remove debris. Add white sand to a depth of about 4 cm to the bottom of the aquarium container.

3. *Water.* Age tap water in an open container for 24 to 48 hours to allow chlorine in the water to escape. You may choose to use bottled spring water (but not distilled water). Gently pour the water into the container, perhaps over clean paper to prevent disturbing the sand.

4. *Plants.* Obtain water plants from a pond or purchase them from a science supply company or a local pet shop (see Appendix B). Root about two sprigs of waterweed (elodea) and two sprigs of eelgrass in the sand. Add some duckweed as a floating plant. Overplanting is better for your aquarium than underplanting. Allow 1 to 2 weeks for the plants to become acclimated to the water before adding animals.

5. *Fish.* Purchase small fish from a pet store or obtain some free from an aquarium hobbyist. Obtain male and female guppies or goldfish. Place the plastic bag containing the fish in your aquarium water for a few hours for the water temperatures in the bag and the aquarium to become equal. Use a dip net to add three to four fish to the aquarium. A rule of thumb is not to have more than 1 cm of fish (excluding tail) per liter of water. Dispose of the plastic container and water the fish came in.

6. *Snails.* Add several small pond snails to your aquarium.

7. *Care.* Add a plastic lid to your aquarium. Lift the corners of the lid to allow exchange of gases between the water and the atmosphere. Thus, you will not need a pump for aeration. Keep a supply of aged tap water available to replace evaporated water as necessary, keeping the water in the aquarium at a predetermined level.

8. *Temperature.* Place your aquarium in the room so that it can get light, but not direct sunlight. Too much light will promote the growth of algae (which can, if you desire, be observed and studied by students). The aquarium should be maintained at room temperature (70° to 78°F or 21° to 25°C). A gooseneck lamp with a 60 to 75 watt bulb can be used to warm the water if necessary. Adjust the lamp so the bulb is a few centimeters above the water, until the temperature is maintained at the desired level. Check with your principal about school regulations concerning leaving the lamp on over the weekend.

9. *Food.* Feed the fish a small amount (a pinch) of commercial fish food every other day (or as instructed on the package). Do not overfeed. Uneaten food will decay, polluting the water. Fish can go as long as 2 weeks without food. Fish may supplement their diet by eating from the water plants. Snails do not require any special food. They eat water plants or the debris that collects on the bottom of the aquarium.

c. Two alternative containers for aquariums are shown in the following illustrations.

Food jar
aquarium

Soda bottle
aquarium

2. WHAT CAN WE OBSERVE IN AN AQUARIUM? (1–3)

Materials
- Aquarium
- Plants
- Fish
- Snails
- Magnifying lenses

ENGAGE

a. Ask: *What happens to the living things within an aquarium? How can we find out?*

EXPLORE

b. Let the children assist you in preparing one aquarium for each group of four students, following the instructions in Activity 1. Tell each group to observe their aquarium closely. Provide magnifying lenses to assist the students in their observations. Encourage them to talk freely about what they see. While the students are observing, move from group to group and listen to their discourse and questions. Do not answer their questions yet, but use them to help you plan class discussion.

c. Instruct the children to make records in their investigation journals of what they observe. Students might write about what they see and make labeled drawings with crayons, markers, pens, and pencils. Let children use their own terminology in their journals at first, gradually introducing (inventing) technical terms to supplement descriptions.

EXPLAIN

d. Take time on a regular basis to discuss with students what they are observing, changes they have noted, and questions they may have raised. Gather the students in a large group and ask such questions as: *What did you observe? Did anyone observe anything else? What is on the bottom of the aquarium?* (Sand)

e. Explain that a **habitat** is a place where an animal or plant naturally lives or grows. A habitat provides the food, shelter, moisture, light, air, and protection the plants or animals need to survive. Ask: *Think of the aquarium as a habitat for fish; what components of the aquarium habitat support the fish and snails that live there?*

ELABORATE

f. Ask: *What do you wonder about fish and snails?* Lead the children to ask questions that can be answered through further observations or investigations. Children might ask such questions as: *What do the fish and snails eat? How much do they eat? Do the snails have mouths? What are those feelers on the snails?* (Tentacles) *What do they do?* (They contain the snails' eyes.) *What do the snails eat?* (Algae) *Do the fish and snails sleep? Can they see me? What makes the water green? Will the fish have babies? Which is the mother fish and which is the daddy fish?* (The male guppies are more brightly colored than the females, and the females give birth to the baby guppies.) *What is the black stuff on the bottom of the aquarium?* (Detritus; waste products from fish)

g. Do not answer the children's questions yet. Post their questions in the room for them to see, think about, and answer through further observation and investigation. Encourage them to observe carefully to try to answer the questions they have posed. Students should add to their journals and drawings regularly.

▶ *Teaching Background*

Encourage children to look for changes in their aquariums. Point out that they will need their records to help them determine what is new in their aquariums.

- Children might observe clumps of transparent spheres on plants and the aquarium sides. These are eggs laid by the snails. Baby snails will hatch from the eggs. Mark the location of snail eggs on the outside of the aquarium with a marking pen. Ask students to observe the clumps regularly. Eventually, a small, black spot will appear in each sphere, becoming larger each day. After a week or two a small snail will hatch.

- If you are keeping guppies in your aquariums, children might also observe the birth of baby guppies. Female guppies carry their eggs in their bodies and deliver their young live. Children might note, with much amazement, that the baby guppies are eaten by the adults. To keep the young from being devoured, use a fish net to transfer the adults to another aquarium.

EVALUATE

h. Use concept maps as a formative evaluation tool throughout the year. Have students construct a concept map about their aquarium shortly after it is set up. Then periodically, have them add new learning to their concept map throughout the year. If you want to be able to see what they add at different times during the year, provide transparencies or tracing paper so that new additions will be on separate sheets.

i. Alternatively, develop a rubric for their aquarium work in their investigation journals. Share the rubric with the students so they know your expectations for their work. Better yet, involve the students in the development of the rubric. Then use the rubric periodically to formatively assess learning and to guide feedback to the students on their work.

B. TERRARIUM HABITATS

▶ *Science Background*

A terrarium is a habitat for plants and small animals, such as earthworms, pill bugs, and frogs. Terrariums must include everything a plant or animal needs to survive.

> **NSES** **Science Standards**
>
> All students should develop an understanding of
>
> • organisms and their environments (K–4).
>
> **Concepts and Principles That Support the Standards**
>
> • Organisms have basic needs. Animals need air, water, and food. Plants require air, water, nutrients, and light. Organisms can survive only in environments in which their basic needs are met (K–4).
> • An organism's patterns of behavior are related to the nature of that organism's environment, including the kinds and numbers of other organisms present, the availability of food and resources, and the physical characteristics of the environment (K–4).
> • When the environment changes, some plants and animals survive and reproduce, and others die or move to new locations (K–4).

Objectives

1. Define habitat and ecosystem.
2. Identify and describe the parts of a terrarium habitat and describe how the parts in each system interact.
3. Construct a terrarium habitat.
4. Ask questions and design and carry out investigations about components and interactions within ecosystems.

1. WHAT IS IN SOIL? (K–5)

Materials

- Soil
- Magnifying lenses
- Plastic spoons

ENGAGE

a. Show the class some soil. Ask: What is this? *Where do you find soil? What do you think is in soil?*

EXPLORE

b. Instruct materials managers to pick up materials. Tell students to use the spoon to spread out their soil on a piece of white paper. Ask: *What do you observe about the soil?* Challenge students to use all of their senses, except taste, and a magnifier to observe the soil and to record at least three observations using each sense. To enhance the smell of soil, tell students to spray a bit of moisture on it.

EXPLAIN

c. Ask: *What did you observe? What was in your soil sample? With which senses was it easier to make observations?*

ELABORATE

d. Challenge each group to sort their soil into components (different sizes of particles, pieces of living things, etc.). They can then estimate what part of the soil is composed of each of the components they have identified. Then each group should construct a pie chart or a bar graph to show the relative amounts or weights of the components in their soil sample.

EVALUATE

e. To check student understanding about the composition of soil, have students complete the following writing prompt:
1. Soil is made up of. . .
   Apply the following rubric to assess students' written responses.
Exemplary—Response includes:
   * ideas from Proficient response and mentions evidence for including these ideas.
Proficient—Response includes:
   * Soil is a mixture of different sized particles.
   * Some particles are small pieces of rock.
   * Some particles came from living things.
Developing—Response includes:
   * Only two of the points from Proficient
Lacks Concept—Response includes:
   * Only one or none of the points from Proficient

2. WHAT IS AN EARTHWORM LIKE? (K–5)

Materials
   * Earthworms
   * Magnifying lenses

ENGAGE

a. Ask: *What are earthworms like? How do they move? Where do they live? What do they eat? How could we find the answers to these questions?*

EXPLORE

b. Distribute an earthworm in a clear plastic cup to each group. Ask: *What do you observe about the earthworm?* Encourage students to use magnifying lenses to see details of the earthworms. If students wish, allow them to gently feel the earthworms or to hold them in their hands. Use the spoons to gently move the earthworms and see how they respond. Tell students to draw pictures of the earthworms in their investigation journals.

EXPLAIN

c. Ask: *What did you observe about the earthworm? What were its characteristics? Did your earthworm have eyes and ears? How do you think it senses things, finds food, and finds its way around? What did your earthworm tend to eat? What did it do?*

▶ *Teaching Background*

Worms are segmented and have bristles on each segment. Worms have no eyes or ears, but their pointed head and round body is sensitive to vibrations and chemicals. Earthworms absorb water and oxygen through their skin. Remind students to keep an earthworm moist at all times when observing or it can dry out and die.

Earthworms prefer to eat dried leaves and other organic matter, but will eat soil and extract the decomposing nutrients if nothing else is available. A worm's waste or casings contain nutrients that enrich the soil and provide the necessary nutrients for plant growth. An earthworm's tunneling mixes and aerates the soil.[7]

3. HOW CAN WE BUILD A TERRARIUM ENVIRONMENT FOR EARTHWORMS? (1–3)

Materials

- Container for the terrarium (e.g., glass or plastic tanks, storage boxes, deli salad containers, fish bowls, plastic bottles, or jars)
- Soil
- Sand
- Small plants
- Birdseed or grass seeds
- Spray bottle for water
- Litter (twigs, bark, and leaves)
- Earthworms (obtained from digging in moist soil, from bait shop, or from commercial supplier—see Appendix C)

Safety Precautions

Collect soil from clean areas so that it is free from contaminants; wash your hands and have students wash their hands thoroughly after handling soil.

Prepare

a. Show the class a terrarium or a picture of one. Ask: *Do you think earthworms could survive in a container like this? Why?*
b. Explain that a **terrarium** is any enclosed container that has been set up to house plants and small animals. Terrariums must contain all the components the plants and animals need to survive.

Construct

c. Assist your students to construct a terrarium for each cooperative group in your classroom. To build a terrarium, follow these instructions:
  1. Obtain a container for your terrarium.
  2. Clean the container with water and rinse it well.
  3. Mix three parts soil with one part sand and fill the terrarium container one-third full of the mixture.
  4. Make small holes in the soil and plant two or three small plants in the holes. Cover the roots with soil and firmly press soil on all sides of the stems. Sprinkle some seeds over the soil.
  5. Add litter—twigs, bark, and leaves.
  6. Add moisture with a spray bottle. Limit the amount of moisture in a terrarium to about four squirts of water. *Caution:* Do not overwater the terrarium during this investigation.
  7. Carefully place an earthworm and a dry leaf for the earthworm to eat in the terrarium.

---

[7]Adapted from GEMS (Great Explorations in Math and Science), 1994. *Terrarium Habitats.* Lawrence Hall of Science, Berkeley, CA.

8. Place a lid on the terrarium and put it in a cool place where it can get natural light, but no direct sunlight.
9. Your terrarium should need no more than about two squirts of water per week.[8]

....

4. WHAT CAN WE OBSERVE IN A TERRARIUM FOR EARTHWORMS? (1–3)

Materials

• Terrarium for earthworms (constructed in previous activity)
• Magnifying lenses
• Spray bottle for water
• Investigation journals

ENGAGE

a. Ask: *What happens to the living and nonliving things within a terrarium for earthworms over time? How can we find out?*

EXPLORE

b. Allow small groups of students to observe and discuss their terrariums regularly for several weeks. Provide magnifying lenses to assist students in making detailed observations. While the students are observing, move from group to group and listen to their discourse and questions. Do not answer their questions. Instead, challenge them to think of ways they could find answers on their own. If groups seem stuck, ask a focusing question to restart their observations, such as: *What are the earthworms doing? How have the plants in your terrarium changed? Is there any moisture in your terrarium? How do you know?*

c. Remind students to use their investigation journals to document their work. Students might use I Notice / I Wonder charts, write about what they observe, and/or make labeled drawings. Let children use their own terminology in their journals during the explore phase. Technical terms will be introduced later.

EXPLAIN

d. In a whole-class setting, ask: *What changes have taken place in your terrarium? What do the earthworms do? What evidence do you have about what earthworms eat? What happened to the plants? What happened to the seeds? Was there moisture in your terrarium? What evidence supports your answer?*

e. Ask: *What is a habitat?* Explain that a **habitat** is a place where an animal or plant naturally lives or grows. A habitat provides the food, shelter, moisture, light, air, and protection that the plants or animals need to survive. Your terrarium is a habitat for plants and earthworms. Ask: *How are the needs of earthworms met by the terrarium habitat? What other habitats do you observe regularly? What is the habitat for birds? fish? deer? humans?*

ELABORATE

f. Encourage groups to select several new questions they have about what's happening in their terrariums. Challenge them to collect data through observation that would provide evidence leading to answers to their questions.

---

[8]Adapted from GEMS (Great Explorations in Math and Science), 1994. *Terrarium Habitats.* Lawrence Hall of Science, Berkeley, CA.

g. Allow small groups to continue to monitor changes and collect data about their terrarium. Encourage groups to share findings with the class, throughout the school year.

EVALUATE

h. Have students draw a concept map to represent their knowledge about the components of their terrarium and the interactions among them. Examining the number of components identified, the details included, and the interrelationships shown by links provides data about the students' understanding of the concepts.

5. HOW CAN WE BUILD A DESERT TERRARIUM? (3–5)

Materials
- Terrarium container
- Cactus plant
- Twig
- Bottle cap
- Desert animal, such as a lizard or horned toad

Prepare

a. Ask: *What is a desert terrarium? What animals and plants might live there? How can we build desert terrariums?*

Construct

b. A desert terrarium can be built out of a large mayonnaise jar, soda bottle, or other container, as in the illustrations.
   1. Select and clean a container for the terrarium.
   2. Place about 2 cups of sand onto the bottom of the jar or bottle.
   3. Place a small cactus plant, a twig, and a small bottle cap filled with water in the terrarium.
   4. Place a small desert animal, such as a lizard or horned toad, in the desert terrarium habitat.
   5. Place the terrarium so that it receives sunlight every day.
   6. Feed the animals live mealworms. These can be obtained from a local pet shop.
   7. Keep the bottle cap filled with water.
   8. Spray one or two squirts of water into the terrarium every 2 weeks, only if the terrarium is dry.

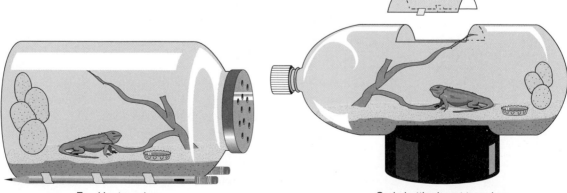

Food jar terrarium　　　　　　Soda bottle desert terrarium

6. WHAT CAN WE OBSERVE IN A DESERT TERRARIUM? (3–5)

Materials
- Desert terrarium (constructed in previous activity)
- Magnifiying lenses
- Investigation journals

ENGAGE

a. Ask: *What happens to the living and nonliving things within a desert terrarium over time? How can we find out?*

EXPLORE

b. Over several weeks, allow small groups of students to regularly observe and discuss how the desert animals interact with their terrarium habitat. Provide magnifying lenses to assist students in making detailed observations. During observation times, move from group to group and listen to their discourse and questions. Do not answer their questions. Instead, challenge them to think of ways they could find answers on their own. If groups seem stuck, ask a focusing question to restart their observations, such as: *How are the living things interacting with each other? with the nonliving things in the terrarium?*

c. Remind students to use their investigation journals to document their work. Students might use I Notice/I Wonder charts, write about what they observe, and/or make labeled drawings. Let students use their own terminology in their journals during the explore phase. Technical terms will be introduced later.

EXPLAIN

d. Ask: *What natural habitat is this terrarium modeling? How do the living things in the terrarium have their needs met? What interactions have you observed between the organisms in the terrarium and the nonliving things in their environment?*

ELABORATE

e. Provide time for students to do library or Internet research about other organisms that live in a desert habitat.

EVALUATE

f. Have each student produce an educational poster about the organism they have researched. Posters should include: the name of the organism; a picture or drawing of the organism; a concise description of the organism; a description of the organism's habitat; the organism's range (where it can be found on the earth); and its interrelationship to other organisms in its environment (what it eats, what eats it, etc.).

g. Assess the posters based on the presence of all of the required components, the quality of information in the components, and how well others can learn from it. You might want to involve the class in the development of a rubric for this product.

7. HOW CAN WE BUILD A WETLAND TERRARIUM? (3–5)

Materials
- Terrarium container with lid
- Gravel
- Ferns, mosses, lichens, and liverworts
- Small water turtle or frog

Prepare

a. Ask: *What is a wetland terrarium? What animals and plants might live there? How can we build wetland terrariums?*

Construct

b. A wetland terrarium can be built in a large mayonnaise jar or other container, as in the illustration.

1. Select and clean a container for the terrarium.
2. Spread gravel out on the bottom of the jar so it will be concentrated toward the back of the jar, as shown in the diagram.
3. Place ferns, mosses, lichens, and liverworts over the gravel.
4. Pour some water in the jar. (Do not put in so much that it covers the back portion of the arrangement.)
5. Place a dried twig in the jar.
6. Place a small water turtle or frog in the jar.
7. Cover the jar with the punctured lid.
8. Feed the turtle or frog insects or turtle food every other day.
9. Place the terrarium in an area where light is weak.

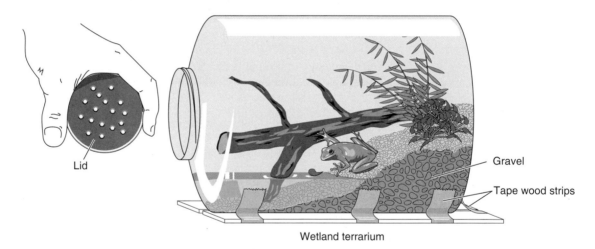

Lid

Gravel

Tape wood strips

Wetland terrarium

8. WHAT CAN WE OBSERVE IN A WETLAND TERRARIUM? (3–5)

Materials

- Wetland terrarium (constructed in previous activity)
- Magnifiying lenses
- Investigation journals

ENGAGE

a. Ask: *What happens to the living and nonliving things within a wetland terrarium over time? How can we find out?*

EXPLORE

b. Allow students time to regularly observe and keep records on how the wetland animal interacts with its terrarium habitat over several weeks.

EXPLAIN

    c. Ask: *What natural habitat is this terrarium modeling? How do the living things in the terrarium have their needs met? What interactions have you observed between the organisms in the terrarium and the nonliving things in their environment?*

ELABORATE

    d. The questions generated by your students' wonderings and those that follow can drive focused observational investigations related to the wetland terrariums or lead to library and/or Internet research.

       Ask:
       What kinds of conditions does the turtle, frog, or lizard need to survive in its particular habitat?
       What kinds of conditions do the wetland plants require to grow well?
       What kinds of food does the turtle, frog, or lizard eat?
       What do you think would happen to the turtle if you left it in the desert habitat or to the lizard if you put it in the wetland habitat?
       What other kinds of environments or habitats could you make?
       What does the environment have to do with the kinds of organisms found in it?
       What might happen to a fern plant if it were transplanted to a desert region?
       What might happen to a penguin if it were taken to live in a desert?
       What would humans need to survive in an arctic region?

EVALUATE

    e. Have students complete the following chart for the wetland terrarium habitats they constructed and observed, describing the food, water, shelter, and other conditions you provided for the organisms living there.

NAME OF HABITAT:	
Habitat Living Conditions	Description
Food	
Shelter	
Air	
Temperature	
Climate	
Water	
Others	

    f. If the class has constructed other terrariums or aquariums modeling other habitats, students could complete charts for all of them, then write a brief report comparing and contrasting those habitats.

III. STRUCTURES AND FUNCTIONS OF HUMAN SYSTEMS

Each plant or animal has different structures that serve different functions in growth, survival, and reproduction. For example, animals, including humans, have body structures for respiration, protection from disease, and digestion of food. Warm-blooded animals have structures for regulating temperature. Humans have distinct body structures for walking, holding, seeing, and talking.

A. THE HUMAN SYSTEM FOR RESPIRATION

▶ *Science Background*

Humans, like other animals, need oxygen to survive. Oxygen is taken in through breathing. Breathing is controlled by movement of the diaphragm. When the diaphragm moves down, air is forced into the lungs. When the diaphragm moves up in the rib cage, air is forced out of the lungs. Gases and water vapor are exhaled from the lungs. When a person exercises, breathing rate increases. Breathing increases because more carbon dioxide is produced. Carbon dioxide causes the diaphragm to involuntarily work more rapidly. Lung capacity varies from person to person and can be increased by aerobic training.

NSES   **Science Standards**

All students should develop an understanding of

- characteristics of organisms (K–4).
- structure and function in living systems (5–8).

Concepts and Principles That Support the Standarads

- Living systems at all levels of organization demonstrate the complementary nature of structure and function (5–8).
- The human organism has systems for digestion, respiration, reproduction, circulation, excretion, movement, control and coordination, and protection from disease. These systems interact with one another (5–8).

Objectives

1. Define *system* and apply the term to human systems.
2. Ask questions and design and carry out investigations to answer questions about structure and function in the human respiratory system.
3. Describe the form and function of the human system for respiration.

---

1. IS THE AIR WE BREATHE IN THE SAME AS THE AIR WE BREATHE OUT? (5–8)

Materials

- Three plastic cups
- Turkey baster or large syringe
- Plastic drinking straws
- Calcium hydroxide tablets (limewater tablets; obtain from a drugstore or science materials supplier)

ENGAGE

a. Ask: *Is there a difference in the composition of the air around us and the air we exhale? How could we find out?*

EXPLORE

b. This investigation can be done as a teacher demonstration or by students in cooperative groups:

1. Obtain two clear plastic cups, a turkey baster, a straw, and 100 cc of limewater made by dissolving a calcium hydroxide tablet in a large container of water. Mix half the limewater with regular water in each cup. Let the water settle.

2. Put a straw in one cup and a turkey baster or large syringe in the other. Describe how the limewater in the cups looks.

(a) Breathe in limewater   (b) Baster in limewater

3. One student should blow through a straw into one cup of limewater while the other pumps the bulb of the turkey baster into the other cup of limewater.

EXPLAIN

c. Ask:
What happens to the limewater as you blow (exhale) through the straw into the water?
Why does the water get "cloudy"?
What happens to the limewater when you squeeze the turkey baster into it?
Why do you think the limewater did not change?
Why is this a controlled experiment? What condition is varied?
What is the responding variable? What do you think is controlled?

d. Tell the class that limewater is an indicator for carbon dioxide. When carbon dioxide is bubbled through limewater, it turns milky. Ask: *Based on this information, is there more carbon dioxide in the air you breathe in (inhale) or in the air you breathe out (exhale)? What is your evidence?*

▶ *Teaching Background*

This investigation compares breathed air that is blown through a straw with regular air that is pumped from a turkey baster. The test results suggest that breathed air contains a significant amount of carbon dioxide gas. When carbon dioxide is added to limewater, the water changes to a milky color because the carbon dioxide combines with calcium hydroxide to form a white precipitate. You can see the white powder precipitate on the bottom of the cup. You can test the white powder that falls to the bottom by adding some vinegar; vinegar will cause calcium or carbonate to foam. Regular air may also contain carbon dioxide, but not enough to detect by this procedure.

2. WHAT MAKES YOU BREATHE FASTER? (3–8)

Materials
- Stopwatch
- Mirror

ENGAGE

a. Ask: *How many times a minute do you breathe? How do you know? How would you go about finding out?*

EXPLORE

b. This activity should be done in groups of three: one student does the activity, the second student counts the number of breaths, and the third student is the timekeeper. At the completion of each activity, the students should rotate in their tasks until all have completed the activity. Explain that students should count the number of exhaled breaths in a time interval. Students may use a mirror to see the exhaled breaths.
  1. Student 1 should breathe normally. Student 2 should count the number of exhaled breaths in 15 seconds. Student 3 should use a stopwatch to start the count at an inhale phase and stop the count after 15 seconds.
  2. Have the student being tested run in place for 1 minute and then repeat step 1.
  3. Use this table for recording your data.

	Breaths/15 seconds			
	Student 1	Student 2	Student 3	Average
At rest				
After running in place for 1 minute				

4. When "At rest" and "After running in place for 1 minute" data have been collected for each student in the group. Calculate the group average for each experimental condition.
5. Graph your group's average data using the axes shown here.

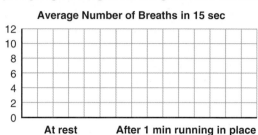

Average Number of Breaths in 15 sec

Average Number of Breaths in 15 sec

12
10
8
6
4
2
0

At rest   After 1 min running in place

EXPLAIN

c. Have groups present and post their graphs so the entire class can compare their findings. Ask: *What is the average number of times per minute a person in this class breathes at rest? . . . after running in place for 1 minute? How could we find out?* (Average the group results for each experimental condition.) *Why do you think exercise makes a person breathe faster?*

· ·

3. HOW CAN WE MAKE A MODEL OF LUNGS? (3–8)

Materials

For each group:

- Plastic cup
- Drinking straw
- Small plastic bag
- Small balloon
- Rubber band
- Scissors

ENGAGE

a. Ask: *How do your lungs work to inhale and exhale gases?*

Construct

b. Guide students to conduct this activity. You may wish to punch a hole in the plastic cups (see step 3) before students begin the activity. The heated tip of an ice pick will pierce the plastic easily.
1. Obtain a plastic drinking straw, a small plastic bag, two rubber bands, a clear plastic cup, a small balloon, and scissors.
2. Cut the straw in half.
3. In the bottom of the cup, punch a hole the same width as the straw.

4. Stretch and blow up the balloon a few times.
5. Using a tightly wound rubber band, attach the balloon to the straw. Be sure the balloon does not come off when you blow into the straw and the rubber band does not crush the straw.
6. Push the free end of the straw through the cup's hole and pull until the balloon is in the middle of the cup. Seal the area around the hole and straw with modeling clay.
7. Place the open end of the cup into the small plastic bag and fold the bag around the cup, securing it tightly with a rubber band or masking tape. The plastic bag should be loose, not stretched taut, across the cup's opening.

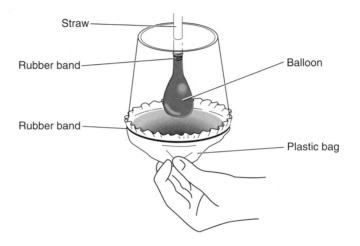

EXPLORE

8. Ask: *What do you think might happen to the balloon if you pull down on the plastic bag at the bottom of the cup?*
9. Pull down on the plastic bag. Record your observation. Ask: *What do you think might happen if you push up on the plastic bag?*
10. Push up on the plastic bag. Record your observation.

EXPLAIN

c. Ask: *What changes did you observe in the system? Why do these changes happen? Where in your body do you have something that works like this?*

Referring to a model or illustration of the chest cavity, guide students to identify the parts of the body used in breathing and describe how they function. Ask: *How is this physical model like the lungs?*

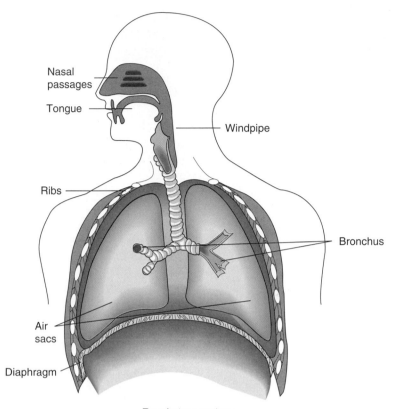

Respiratory system

 B. THE HUMAN SYSTEM FOR REGULATING TEMPERATURE

▶ *Science Background*

Normal body temperature is 98.6°F. To maintain this temperature, the body converts food energy to heat energy. When the environment is very warm or through exercise, the temperature of the body may exceed the normal level. The body then cools itself through perspiring. When perspiration evaporates from the body, the body is cooled.

NSES   **Science Standards**

All students should develop an understanding of

- structure and function in living systems (5–8).

Concepts and Principles That Support the Standards

- All organisms must be able to obtain and use resources, grow, reproduce, and maintain stable internal conditions while living in a constantly changing external environment (5–8).
- Regulation of an organism's internal environment involves sensing the internal environment and changing physiological activities to keep conditions within the range required to survive (5–8).

Objectives   1. Describe and explain how the evaporation of perspiration cools the body.

1. HOW DOES YOUR BODY COOL ITSELF? (K–5)

Materials
- Two old socks (wool or cotton are best) for each student
- Electric fan

ENGAGE   a. Using a medicine dropper, place a few drops of water on the back of the hand of each student. Tell the students to gently blow across the water drop. Ask: *What happened to the water drop?* (It disappeared—evaporated.) *How did your hand feel?* (It got cooler.)
Ask: *How does your body use evaporation to cool itself?*

EXPLORE   b. Have students place a dry sock on one hand and a wet sock on the other hand. To improve the cooling effect, use a fan to blow air over the students' hands.

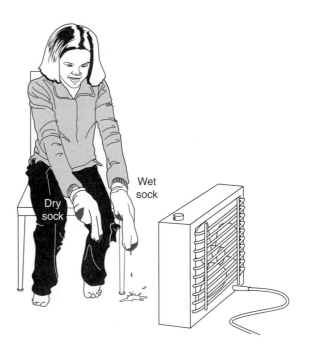

EXPLAIN   c. Invite students to share their findings from the explore phase. Ask: *Which hand felt cooler, the one with the wet sock or the one with the dry sock? Why?* Explain that evaporation is a cooling process. When water evaporates, the surface from which it evaporated gets cooler.
Ask: *What is the role of the moisture in cooling? What do you think happens when perspiration evaporates? Why does a fan cool us even on a hot day? Why do you feel cool on a hot summer day when you come out of the water after swimming?*

ELABORATE

d. Encourage students to develop a question that can be investigated related to evaporative cooling, then plan and carry out an experiment to help answer that question. If temperature probes and CBL software are available, familiarize students with their use as they may provide more accurate temperature data than simple laboratory thermometers. In addition, temperature probes enable students to look at real-time graphs showing cooling trends rather than first collecting data and then graphing it manually.

EVALUATE

e. To assess student understanding of why the human body perspires, administer this multiple choice item:

    1. When we are hot, our body perspires because:
        A. when liquids evaporate, they cause cooling.
        B. heat causes the pores in our skin open.
        C. we need to stay hydrated (drink lots of water) in hot weather.
        D. cells in our body are melting due to the heat.

 ## C. FOOD AND THE HUMAN SYSTEM FOR DIGESTION

▶ *Science Background*

Food provides energy and nutrients for growth, development, and normal functioning. Good nutrition is essential for good health. Foods contain starches, sugars, fats, and proteins the body needs. During digestion, our body breaks down starches into glucose, a type of sugar, and the glucose then supplies energy for our muscles. Rice, corn, and potatoes are major sources of starch. Glucose itself is another major source of energy. Grapes, raisins, and bananas are natural sources of glucose. Soft drinks are another source of glucose. Fatty foods, such as fried foods, candy bars, cookies, and chips, can supply a great deal of energy per gram, but if the energy is not used, it is stored as fat within the body. During digestion, proteins are broken down into amino acids, substances our bodies need to build and repair tissues.

Specific chemical and physical tests can be conducted to determine which nutrients are in foods. Iodine can be used to **test** for starches. Tes-Tape can be used to test for glucose. Brown paper can be used to test for fats. Protein test papers (Coomassie blue test papers), purchased from a scientific supply company, can be used to test for proteins.

NSES

Science Standards

All students should develop an understanding of

- structure and function in living systems (5–8).
- regulation and behavior (5–8).

Concepts and Principles That Support the Standards

- The human organism has systems for digestion, respiration, reproduction, circulation, excretion, movement, control and coordination, and protection from disease (5–8).
- Behavior is one kind of response an organism can make to an internal or environmental stimulus (5–8).
- Behavioral response is a set of actions determined in part by heredity and in part from experience (5–8).

1. HOW MUCH WATER IS IN OUR FOODS? (5–8)

Materials
- Blunt plastic knives
- Scale for weighing
- Lettuce, tomatoes, apples, oranges
- Hand juicer
- Paper plates
- Small paper cups
- Thick white bread
- Bread toaster

ENGAGE

a. Display a collection of foods. Ask: *How much water is in our foods? How could we find out?*

EXPLORE

b. As a class or in cooperative groups, guide students to carry out these activities:
1. Weigh each of the foods individually on a scale and record their weights in the "before" column of the chart.

WATER CONTENT CHART

Weight of Food in Grams or Paper Clips			
Food	Before	After	Weight of Water in Food
Lettuce			
Tomato			
Orange			
Apple			
Bread			

2. Using a hand juicer, squeeze out all of the juice from the tomato. Weigh the tomato pulp (without the juice) and record the weight in the after column.
3. Spread the lettuce leaves out on paper plates to dry overnight. The next day, weigh the lettuce leaves and record their weight in the after column.
4. Repeat the previous step for the apple and the orange.
5. Toast the bread in the toaster, weigh the bread, and record the number in the after column.
6. Calculate the fractions of water in each food by dividing the weight of water in the food by the original weight of the food.

EXPLAIN

    c. Ask: *What changes did you note in the foods? Why do you think the weight of each food changed? Which food initially had the highest fraction of water? Which food had the lowest fraction of water?*

ELABORATE

    d. Ask: *What foods can you think of that are eaten in both fresh and dried form?* (grapes/raisins, plums/prunes, and so on) *What would you do to investigate what happens to raisins or prunes when they are soaked in water?* (Try it and see.)

▶ *Teaching Background*

Although water is not one of the basic nutrients, we must have it every day. We could not live without it. Besides drinking liquids, here are some common foods and the percentages of water by weight we get when we eat them. Students' test results may not agree with these. Even after students treat the various foods, they still will likely contain some water.

Lettuce	95%	Carrot	90%
Yogurt	90%	Apple	85%
Pizza	50%	Bread	35%

EVALUATE

    e. To assess if your students have grasped the general concept that our foods contain a lot of water, have them respond to the following:

      1. Which of the following statements about water in food do you agree with most?
        A. Most of the foods we eat contain very little water.
        B. Most of the foods we eat are more than 25% water by weight.
        C. Most of the foods we eat are made only of water.

      2. Give evidence that supports your choice.

2. WHAT IS STARCH, AND HOW CAN WE TEST FOR IT? (5–8)

Materials

- Paper plates
- Dropper
- Thin slices of banana, apple, potato, white bread, cheese, egg white, butter
- Cracker
- Cornstarch
- Iodine solution
- Granulated sugar

ENGAGE

    a. Ask: *Which of these foods contains starch? How might we find out?*

Safety Precautions

Iodine solution is poisonous, may cause burns if it is too strong, and can stain clothing. It must not be eaten. Because iodine is poisonous, do *not* eat any of the tested foods or give them to pets. Dispose of them properly.

EXPLORE

b. Assist cooperative groups to carry out this investigation.
   1. On a paper plate, arrange and label each food sample as shown in the illustration.

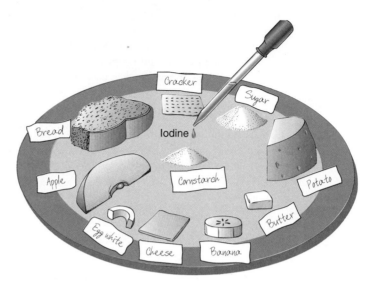

   2. Look at the colors of each food and record them on a chart.
   3. Place a drop of iodine solution on each sample of food.
   4. Look at the color of each food where the iodine drop touched it.

EXPLAIN

c. Ask: *How have some of the food colors changed? Which foods have something in common after getting an iodine drop?*

   Explain that the chemical iodine can be used to test foods for starches. When iodine is placed on a starchy food, the food turns varying shades of purple-black in relation to the amount of starch present in it.

   Ask: *If starch turns purple-black in iodine, which of your sample foods would you say contain starch? Which do not have starch?*

   As you've seen, some foods contain starch. Starch is a nutrient that provides energy for cells to use.

▶ *Teaching Background*

Starch provides energy for cells to use. Major sources of starch are rice, corn, and potatoes. Like most starchy foods, these foods also contain vitamins and minerals. During digestion, the body breaks down starch into glucose, and the glucose provides energy for cells.

   Some starchy foods are also high in fiber, indigestible material that helps move matter through the digestive tract. Fruits, vegetables, and whole grains are some sources of fiber.

   Because they contain large amounts of starch, rice and flour turn purple-black when iodine is added. Certain vegetables and fruits contain little starch and may turn only a very faint purple-black during an iodine test.[9]

---

[9]Adapted from Science and Technology for Children (STC), 1994. *Food Chemistry*. Carolina Biological Supply Co., Burlington, NC.

3. WHAT ARE FATS, AND HOW DO WE TEST FOR THEM? (5–8)

Materials

- Paper plates
- Water
- Butter
- Vegetable oil
- Samples of common snack foods: peanuts, bread, margarine, celery, carrots, mayonnaise, lettuce, bacon, corn or potato chips, pretzels, cheese, cookies, cake, apple, whole milk, yogurt, chocolate
- Brown paper bags or brown paper towels cut into 5 cm squares (enough so that there is one square for each food sample)
- Source of light: sunlight or lamp
- Dropper

ENGAGE

a. Ask: *Do some foods contain fats? Which ones? How could we test to see if foods contain fat?*

EXPLORE

b. Assist students to carry out this test in cooperative groups:
   1. Put several drops of water on one square of brown paper, as in diagram (a). On a second square, put drops of oil as in diagram (b).

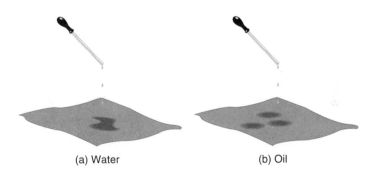

(a) Water   (b) Oil

   2. Fats feel slippery when rubbed between the fingers.
      Ask: *How does the water stain feel? How does the oil stain feel?*
   3. Ask: *How do the two stains look? What do you think will happen to the two stains after 10 minutes?*
   4. After 10 minutes, check the two squares of paper.

EXPLAIN

c. Ask: *What happened to each stain? Where did the water stain go? How do the oil stains look?*
   Explain that the water evaporated, but the oil stains remained shiny. This is the spot test for fats. Explain that fats leave greasy spots on brown paper. Tell students that like starches, fats are a nutrient that supply energy for the body.

ELABORATE

d. Have groups of students conduct their own spot tests using the samples of snack foods.
   1. Get a paper plate containing samples of snack foods, squares of brown paper, and a copy of the lab sheet shown in the diagram.

FAT SPOT TEST LAB SHEET		
Food Samples	Predicted Fat	Contains Fat
Peanuts		
Bread		
Margarine		
Celery		
Carrots		
Mayonnaise		
Lettuce		
Bacon		
Corn/Potato chips		
Pretzels		
Cheese		
Cookies		
Cake		
Apple		
Whole milk		
Yogurt		
Chocolate		

2. Mark an **X** in the "predicted fat" column for foods you think contain fat.
3. Firmly rub each food sample 10 times on a separate square of brown paper, and label the paper with the food's name.
4. After 10 minutes, hold each paper square up to a source of light as in the illustration.

Safety Precautions   It is all right to use illumination from a window as a source of light, but caution children not to look directly into the sun.

5. Mark an **X** in the "contains fat" column of your chart for each food that left a greasy spot.

e. Ask: *How did your predictions compare with your findings? How would you summarize your test findings as to which foods contained fat?*

f. Discuss with students the importance of reading food labels for ingredients. Also discuss how they might select foods with less fat.

Ask: *Why might it be healthier to eat such foods as skim milk, low-fat cottage cheese, and nonfat ice cream? How could we have a party, serving good-tasting foods, and still cut down on the amount of fat we eat?*

▶ *Teaching Background*

Some foods have a lot of fat, and others have little or no fat. Fats that are thick (solid) at room temperature usually come from animals like cows, pigs, and sheep. These fats are called **saturated fats**. Fats that are soft (semisolid) at room temperature usually are made from animals (e.g., lard and butter) or are manufactured (e.g., margarine). Fats that are liquid at room temperature usually come from plants (e.g., peanut oil, olive oil, corn oil).

EVALUATE

g. To check student understanding about the presence of fat in food, have them respond to the following writing prompt:

1. You have been given a sample of food that you do not recognize. Before you eat it, you want to know if it contains fat. *What would you do to find out?*

4. WHAT IS GLUCOSE, AND HOW DO WE TEST FOR IT? (5–8)

Materials

- Tes-Tape (get in drugstore)
- Bananas (fairly ripe)
- Milk
- Different kinds of apples (McIntosh, Delicious, Rome)
- Granular sugar, moistened with water
- Oranges
- Maple syrup
- Honey
- Paper plates
- Small paper cups

Preparation

For efficiency in distribution, the teacher or designated students should prepare the following beforehand for each group of two to four students: paper plate containing cut samples of foods and small cups with very small samples of honey, milk, and maple syrup; 1 inch Tes-Tape strip for each food to be tested; data collection sheet.

ENGAGE

a. Ask: *What is glucose? How can we test foods for glucose?*

EXPLORE

b. Guide cooperative groups of students to conduct this investigation:
1. Get a paper plate that contains food samples, Tes-Tape strips, and a data collection sheet.
2. Assign one group member to each of the following tasks: tester, observer, and recorder.
3. The tester should number each food, then write the numerals 1 through 10 on separate Tes-Tape strips.
4. Using the appropriately numbered strip that corresponds to the food being tested, the tester should touch a 1 inch strip of the Tes-Tape to each food separately, until the strip is wet, and hand the Tes-Tape to the observer.

5. The observer should look at the wet end of the Tes-Tape to see what color it is.
6. The observer gives the following information to the recorder:
   a. Number of the sample Tes-Tape strip
   b. Name of the food sample
   c. Color of the wet end of the Tes-Tape strip
7. The students should repeat the preceding procedures with all of the food samples.
8. As each food is tested, the recorder notes on the Tes-Tape data collection sheet the data that the observer provides. The recorder attaches each Tes-Tape strip in the appropriate place on the data table.

TES-TAPE SUGAR TEST DATA COLLECTION SHEET		
Food Samples	Tape Color After Test	Tape Strip
Orange		
Banana, ripe		
Banana, green		
Maple syrup		
Milk		
Honey		
McIntosh apple		
Yellow Delicious apple		
Rome apple		
Granulated sugar		

EXPLAIN

c. Explain that glucose is one kind of sugar. Many foods contain glucose. Glucose is a major source of energy for our bodies. Explain to students that they used Tes-Tape to test different foods for glucose. Tes-Tape is a special chemically treated paper designed for use by people who have diabetes.

d. Ask:

From the data collected, which foods contain glucose? What evidence do you have to support this?

From the changes in the Tes-Tape color, which foods appear to have the most glucose? the least?

Which foods, if any, did not change the color of the Tes-Tape? Why do you think this happened?

ELABORATE

e. Have students bring in labels from food packages, read the ingredients list, and list all the forms of sugar each food contains, such as honey, brown sugar syrup, sweeteners, corn sugar, corn sweeteners, molasses, invert sugar, sucrose, fructose, dextrose, maltose, lactose, and so on.

Find out the amounts of sugar (both labeled and "hidden") in the common foods you eat. For example, soft drinks can contain about 8 teaspoons per 12 ounces, and many breakfast cereals contain about 2½ teaspoons (10 g) of sugar plus 3 teaspoons (13 g) of other carbohydrates for a total of 5½ teaspoons (23 g) per 1 ounce serving.

Ask:

What do you think might happen if you tested artificial sweeteners (saccharin, aspartame, etc.) with Tes-Tape?

Why would it be healthier to eat fresh fruit as a snack rather than cakes, candy, and soft drinks, even though all of these contain sugar?

► *Teaching Background*

There are several types of sugars, including sucrose, lactose, fructose, and glucose. Glucose is a major source of energy for the body. Starches consist of long linked chains of glucose. Much of the glucose the body needs comes from the breakdown of starches. Natural sources of glucose include apples, grapes, raisins, and bananas. Soft drinks are another source of glucose. Sweets ordinarily contain other types of sugars.[10]

EVALUATE

f. To check student understanding about the presence of glucose in food, have them respond to the following writing prompt:
  1. You have been given a sample of food that you do not recognize. Before you eat it, you want to know if it contains glucose. What would you do to find out?

5. HOW CAN YOU DETERMINE WHICH SODA HAS MORE SUGAR? (5–8)

Materials

* Three pairs of 12 ounce cans of soft drinks, unopened, assorted flavors and brands (each pair should contain one diet and one regular of same flavor and brand)
* Aquarium or large transparent tub filled with water
* Scale for weighing

ENGAGE

a. Ask: *What would happen if we placed a can of diet cola and regular cola in a container of water?*

EXPLORE

b. Place a can of regular cola and a can of diet cola in an aquarium filled with water. Ask: *What did you observe?* (The regular can of cola sinks, but, surprisingly, the can of diet cola floats.)

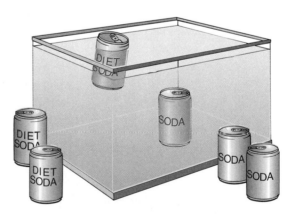

EXPLAIN

c. Ask: *What happened? Why do you think the can of diet cola floated while the can of regular cola sank?*

When students suggest that the can of diet cola was lighter, ask: *How could we test this hypothesis?*

---

[10]Adapted from Science and Technology for Children (STC), 1994. *Food Chemistry*. Carolina Biological Supply Co., Burlington, NC.

ELABORATE

d. Instruct students to
1. weigh each of the six cans of diet and regular soft drinks;
2. record the weights in a table like the one illustrated;
3. test each of the six cans to determine if it floats or sinks; and
4. record their observations about floating or sinking in the table.

SUGAR CONTENT OF DIET AND REGULAR SOFT DRINKS

Pair	Brand	Diet Weight	Regular Weight	Float or Sink?
1				Diet
				Regular
2				Diet
				Regular
3				Diet
				Regular

e. Ask: *What did you determine in your tests? Did your data support the hypothesis that the cans of regular soft drinks were heavier than the cans of diet soft drinks?*

f. Ask: *Why do you think a can of diet cola is lighter than a can of regular cola of the same brand and flavor?* When students suggest that the cans of regular soft drink contain more liquid than the cans of diet soft drink, lead them to examine labels to compare the volumes of liquid in the regular and diet soft drink cans. Students might also open the cans and measure the volume using a graduated cylinder.

If students do not suggest it, also ask them to compare the ingredients of the regular and diet soft drinks. The weight of a diet soft drink is usually about 10 to 15 g less than the weight of a regular soft drink. The difference is usually sugar or corn syrup.

6. WHAT ARE PROTEINS, AND HOW DO WE TEST FOR THEM? (5–8)

Materials

For each group:

- Six Coomassie blue protein test strips in a clean envelope
- Test tray
- Forceps
- Petri dish
- Toothpicks
- Paper towels

(Protein test strips and other materials are available from Carolina Biological Supply—see Appendix C for address.)

For the class:

- Half liter (1 pint) white vinegar
- Half liter (1 pint) rubbing alcohol

- 1 liter plastic bottle to mix and store developing solution
- Medicine droppers
- Plastic spoons
- One carton skim milk, 237 ml (one-half pint)
- Unshelled peanuts
- Rice grains

Preparation

To test for proteins, students immerse a Coomassie blue test strip in a liquid or food, and then place the test strip in a developing solution for several minutes. To prepare the developing solution, mix together half a liter of white vinegar and half a liter of rubbing alcohol in a 1 liter plastic mixing bottle. Close the bottle and store the developing solution.

ENGAGE

a. Ask: *What nutrients have we tested for so far?* [Starch, fat, and glucose (sugar)] *What do you know about proteins? What foods contain proteins? How can we test liquids and foods for proteins?*

EXPLORE

b. Hold up a strip of protein test paper. Handle the test strip only with forceps so as not to contaminate it with your hands. Explain to students that the strip contains a special chemical—Coomassie blue—that reacts to proteins. During testing, the paper must be developed in a special solution. When developed, the color of the paper will stay deep blue if the protein content of the food being tested is high; the blue color will fade if there is a medium amount of protein in the food; and the blue color will disappear if the food contains little or no protein.

c. To test liquids or foods for proteins, have students follow these directions:
   1. Put three drops of milk in section 1 of the test tray.
   2. Put three drops of water in section 2 of the test tray.
   3. Using a spoon, put a few grains of rice in section 3 of the test tray. Put two or three drops of tap water on the rice and stir for about a minute with a toothpick.
   4. Shell a peanut (without touching the nut itself) and place it in section 4 of the test tray. Use a plastic spoon to crush the peanut. Add two or three drops of water and stir with a new toothpick.
   5. Using a spoon, put a small amount of crushed granola bar in section 5 of the test tray. Add two or three drops of water and stir with a new toothpick.
   6. Obtain six test strips and number them 1 to 6 on the white end of the strips. Be careful not to touch the test strips. Holding a test strip by its white end with forceps, immerse the blue end in the liquid or food just long enough to wet the strip—test strip 1 in the milk, test strip 2 in water, test strip 3 in the moistened rice, test strip 4 in the moistened peanut, and test strip 5 in the moistened granola bar. Place test strip 6 in the empty section 6 of the test tray as a control. Use clean toothpicks to make sure each food is in contact with the test paper. Be sure the white end of each test strip is not in contact with the liquid or food being tested.

7. Leave the test strips in the tray sections just long enough to wet the strips. Using forceps, remove each of the numbered test strips from the tray sections and place them on a paper towel. Use clean toothpicks to clean any food particles from them and use a paper towel to blot off any excess liquid.

8. Ask your teacher to pour a little developing solution in the bottom of your petri dish. Using forceps, transfer each of the test strips to the developing solution. Make sure the blue tip of the test strip is immersed.

9. Leave the test strips in the developing solution for about 5 minutes. Keep stirring the solution with a toothpick.

10. After 5 minutes, remove the protein test papers from the developing solution and place them on a paper towel.

11. Note and record the color of each test strip in the following chart. Based on the color observed, determine the protein content of each food—high, medium, or low.

PROTEIN TEST RESULTS

Liquid or Food	Color of Protein Test Strip	Protein Content (High, Medium, or Low)
1. Milk		
2. Tap water		
3. Rice		
4. Peanut		
5. Granola bar		
6. Control		

EXPLAIN

d. In a class-sized group, invite students to discuss their procedures and share their results.

Ask: *What happened to the protein test strips in each liquid or food? Which food or liquids were high in proteins? Which had a medium protein content? Which foods had a low amount or no proteins?* Share the following master chart of protein test results with students.

PROTEIN TEST RESULTS

Liquid or Food	Color of Protein Test Strip	Protein Content (High, Medium, or Low)
1. Milk	Remains blue	High
2. Tap water	Blue disappears	Low
3. Rice	Blue disappears	Low
4. Peanut	Remains blue	High
5. Granola bar	Blue almost disappears	Medium
6. Control	Blue disappears	Low or none

▶ *Teaching Background*

Protein is one group of food nutrients that the body uses for building tissues and repairing broken-down cells. Proteins are vital for children's proper physical and mental growth and development. Because protein cannot be made by or stored in the body, it must be eaten regularly to promote the repair of used body cells. Eggs, cheese, meat, fish, and legumes are some foods that contain large proportions of protein.

In a protein test, the chemical Coomassie blue actually binds to protein. Because of this chemical reaction, the protein and Coomassie blue will remain on the test paper after it has been in the developing solution. In the absence of protein, the Coomassie blue will dissolve in the developing solution.[11]

---

[11]Activities on proteins adapted from Science and Technology for Children (STC), 1994. *Food Chemistry*. Carolina Biological Supply Co., Burlington, NC. (Reprinted with permission from the National Science Resources Center, Washington, DC.)

7. WHAT IS VITAMIN C, AND HOW DO WE TEST FOR IT? (5–8)

Materials

To make vitamin C indicator liquid for the class:

- Teaspoon
- Cornstarch
- Measuring cup
- Water
- Pan
- Hot plate
- Empty plastic gallon jug
- Iodine

For each group:

- Ruler
- Six clean baby food jars
- Variety of at least six different juices that are canned, frozen, or fresh (e.g., orange, apple, grape, pineapple, etc.)
- Six droppers
- Six wooden stirrers

Preparation

A simple vitamin C indicator liquid can be made ahead of time and will keep for several days. You will know when it is time to dispose of it, because it will lighten from its optimum color of royal blue to a very pale blue. To make 1 gallon of vitamin C indicator:

1. Boil 1½ teaspoons (6 ml) of cornstarch in 1 cup (250 ml) of water for 2 minutes.
2. Put 10 full droppers of the cornstarch mixture into a gallon jug of water, use a clean dropper to add 1 dropper full of iodine, cover the jug, and shake it until you have a uniform blue color.

ENGAGE

a. Ask: *What do you know about vitamin C? How can we test foods for vitamin C?*

EXPLORE

b. Instruct students to follow these directions to test foods for vitamin C:
   1. Using your ruler to measure, pour 1 cm of vitamin C indicator liquid into each of six clean baby food jars. Label each jar with the name of the juice you will test for vitamin C.
   2. Using a clean dropper for each juice, add one kind of juice to each jar of indicator liquid, one drop at a time, and count the number of drops. (See the diagram.) Stir the liquid indicator with a clean wooden stirrer as you add drops.
   3. When the indicator is no longer blue, the test is finished.
   4. Record the number of drops of each juice needed to clear up the blue vitamin C indicator liquid.

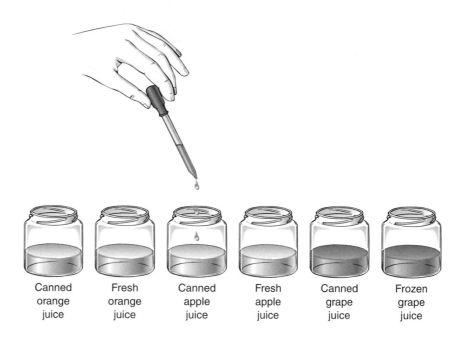

Canned orange juice   Fresh orange juice   Canned apple juice   Fresh apple juice   Canned grape juice   Frozen grape juice

EXPLAIN

c. Invite students to discuss their procedures and results.

   Ask: *Which juice(s) caused the blue color to disappear with the least number of drops? Which juice(s) caused the blue color to disappear with the most drops?*

d. Tell students that we tested for vitamin C by testing how it reacts with a special mixture of cornstarch, iodine, and water. Explain that the fewer drops of juice needed to make the blue color disappear, the more vitamin C that juice contains.

   Explain that scientists have discovered more than 26 vitamins our bodies need. The lack of one vitamin could result in a vitamin deficiency disease. Vitamin C is probably the best known vitamin. It is found in citrus fruits, tomatoes, raw cabbage, strawberries, and cantaloupe.

   Ask: *From these tests, which juice(s) had the most vitamin C? the least vitamin C? How do you know?*

ELABORATE

e. Ask: *How do you think the following conditions could affect the vitamin C content of foods: heat, sunlight, air, age of food, and so on? How could you design experiments to test these variables?* If time permits, allow student groups to carry out their experiments and report their findings to the class.

EVALUATE

f. You could use these investigations to formatively assess students' ability to plan and conduct investigations through observations of their work. The following indicators, based on Wynne Harlen's work on process skill indicators,[12] are listed in order of sophistication and can be used to judge students' performance level for these process skills.

---

[12] Adapted from Harlen, W. (2000). *Teaching, learning and assessing science 5-12* (3rd ed.). Thousand Oaks, CA: Sage Publications.

Indicators for Planning and Conducting Investigations

Students:

☐ Start with a useful general approach even if details are lacking or need further thought.
☐ Have some ideas of which variable should be changed, or what things should be compared.
☐ Do not change those variables that must be kept constant to have a fair test.
☐ Have some idea before they start the investigation of what they must look for to get results.
☐ Choose a realistic way to measure or compare things to get results.
☐ Take steps to ensure that their results are as accurate as possible.

8. HOW MUCH OF EACH NUTRIENT DOES YOUR BODY NEED, AND HOW CAN YOU FIND OUT WHAT IS IN EACH FOOD? (5–8)

Materials

• Food labels from a large variety of packaged foods. Collect food labels yourself, and ask students to collect and bring in empty food packages or labels from the packages. You will need at least one food label for each pair of students.

ENGAGE

a. Ask: *Can you think of another way, besides testing, to determine the nutritional content of foods?* If students do not suggest reading food labels, raise the idea.

EXPLORE

b. Pass out food labels and a copy of the food label record sheet to pairs of students. Ask: *What kind of information is given on the food labels?* Allow students time (10 to 15 minutes) to discuss the information given on the food labels and how it relates to the tests they have completed previously.

Nutrition Facts

Serving Size 2/3 cup (55g)
Servings Per Container 12

Amount Per Serving

Calories 210
   Calories from Fat 25

% Daily Value*

Total Fat 3g	**5%**
Saturated Fat 1g	**4%**
Polyunsaturated Fat 0.5g	
Monounsaturated Fat 1.5g	
Cholesterol 0mg	**0%**
Sodium 140mg	**6%**
Potassium 190mg	**5%**
Total Carbohydrate 44g	**15%**
Other Carbohydrate 23g	
Dietary Fiber 3g	**13%**
Sugars 18g	
Protein 5g	
Vitamin A	0%
Vitamin C	0%
Calcium	2%
Iron	6%
Thiamine	10%
Phosphorus	10%
Magnesium	10%

* Percent Daily Values are based on a 2000 calorie diet. Your daily values may be higher or lower depending on your calorie needs.

	Calories	2,000	2,500
Total Fat	Less than	65g	80g
Sat Fat	Less than	20g	25g
Cholesterol	Less than	300g	300g
Sodium	Less than	2400mg	2400mg
Potassium		3500mg	3500mg
Total Carbo		300g	300g
Dietary Fiber		25g	30g

Calories per gram:
Fat 9   •   Carbohydrate 4   •   Protein 4

EXPLAIN

c. Explain that starch and sugar are carbohydrates. The labels give the total amount of carbohydrates in one serving of the food, but not the specific amounts of starch or sugar. Also explain that people who study nutrients (called **nutritionists**) suggest the average amount of each nutrient a person should consume. This amount is called the *recommended daily allowance*, or RDA. Answer questions students might have, for example, about serving sizes or grams and milligrams.

ELABORATE

d. Tell students to examine the food labels and record on their record sheet the information given about carbohydrates (starch and sugar), fats, proteins, calcium, and vitamin C (the type of vitamin they have tested).

Food Label Record Sheet

Name of Food _____

Serving Size _____

Nutrient	Weight per Serving	Percentage of U.S.RDA
Carbohydrates		
Fats		
Proteins		
Minerals-calcium		
Vitamins-vitamin C		

e. Bring pairs of students together in groups of six. Ask students to compare the nutrition facts from their food labels and record sheets and to complete the food group facts chart illustrated:

FOOD GROUP FACTS CHART

Calories	Food highest in calories per serving:	Food lowest in calories per serving:
Carbohydrates	Food highest in carbohydrates per serving:	Food lowest in carbohydrates per serving:
Fats	Food highest in fats per serving:	Food lowest in fats per serving:
Proteins	Food highest in proteins per serving:	Food lowest in proteins per serving:
Calcium	Food highest in calcium per serving:	Food lowest in calcium per serving:
Vitamin C	Food highest in vitamin C per serving:	Food lowest in vitamin C per serving:

f. Assemble the class as a whole and discuss which kinds of food are high and low in basic nutrients.

9. HOW CAN STUDENTS PLAN A HEALTHY DAILY MENU FOR THEMSELVES? (5–8)

▶ *Teaching Background*

The U.S. Department of Agriculture (USDA) has replaced the Food Pyramid used for many years with an interactive website, called MyPyramid, found at http://MyPyramid.gov. This imaginative innovation can be valuable and fun for children and adults. Before teaching this lesson, you should explore the website for yourself. You will want, especially, to locate the MyPyramid Plan web page and find your own healthy eating plan.

Materials

- Computers connected to the Internet (ideally, one computer for each team of four students)

ENGAGE

a. Ask: *How can you plan a health daily menu for yourself?*

Tell students that from research findings and conclusions, nutritionists recommend the amount of each food group, including grains, vegetables, fruits, milk, and meat and beans, that people should include in their daily diets.

EXPLORE

b. Direct teams of students working at computers to the MyPyramid website, at http://MyPyramid.gov. Allow some time for students to explore the website. Tell students to locate the My Pyramid Plan web page and fill in the requested information. The computer will then display a My Pyramid Plan for recommended daily food requirements, based on the information submitted.

c. Tell students to fill in the following My Pyramid Plan chart to show their own daily requirements.

MY PYRAMID PLAN DAILY FOOD GROUP REQUIREMENTS

Food Group	Recommended Daily Amount	Estimated Food Group Amounts in Yesterday's Menu (breakfast, lunch, and dinner)	Goals for Tomorrow
Grains			
Vegetables			
Fruits			
Milk			
Meat and Beans			

d. Ask students to locate the Meal Tracking Worksheet on the website, access and review it, and then follow these steps.

1. Working individually, students should write down their breakfast, lunch, and dinner menus for yesterday or a typical day.

2. Using the My Pyramid Worksheet (Meal Tracking Worksheet), estimate the total amount of grains, vegetables, fruits, milk products, and meat and cheese they ate on that day.
3. Set food goals for themselves for tomorrow.
4. Determine breakfast, lunch, and dinner menus that will help them meet their food group goals.

EXPLAIN

e. Allow teams of students to present their findings and menu goals to the class as a whole. Provide ample time for presentations, discussion, and questions from other students. Ask: *How close are the daily food choices in yesterday's menu to the recommendations of the pyramid?*

IV
Earth and Space Science Activities

Earth is the home planet of human beings, the only planet in the universe known to support life. Life is possible on the earth largely because of a set of linked factors, including the earth's position within the solar system, its size and mass, its structure and resources, its range of temperatures, its atmosphere, and its abundance of water.

Students in grades K–8 can begin to develop understanding of the earth as a set of closely interrelated systems by studying the geological structure of the earth; the atmosphere, climate, and weather of the earth; the earth's oceans; and the earth in the solar system.

I. STRUCTURE OF THE EARTH

Children explore the complexities of the earth as they study the properties of rocks and minerals, the crystalline structure of minerals, and the structure of the earth's surface.

A. PROPERTIES OF ROCKS AND MINERALS

▶ *Science Background*

A mineral is a solid element or compound that has a specific composition and a crystalline structure. There are many different minerals in and on the earth—for example, talc, calcite, quartz, fluorite, and diamond. Minerals can be distinguished by such properties as hardness, texture, luster, streak color, cleavage, density, crystalline structure, and chemical properties.

Rocks are composed of minerals. Waves, wind, water, and ice cause erosion, transport, and deposit of earth materials. Sediments of sand and smaller particles are gradually buried and are cemented together with dissolved minerals to form solid rock. Rocks buried deep enough may be re-formed by pressure and heat, melting and recrystallizing into different kinds of rock. Layers of rock deep within the earth may be forced upward to become land surfaces and even mountains. Eventually, this new rock will erode under the relentless, dynamic processes of the earth.[1]

---

[1]American Association for the Advancement of Science. 1993. *Benchmarks for Science Literacy* (New York: Oxford University Press); F. J. Rutherford & A. Ahlgren, 1990. *Science for All Americans* (New York: Oxford University Press).

Science Standards

All students should develop an understanding of

- properties of the earth's systems (K–4).
- structure of the earth's systems (5–8).

Concepts and Principles That Support the Standards

- The earth's materials are solid rocks and soils, water, and gases of the atmosphere (K–4).
- The varied materials have different physical and chemical properties (K–4).

Objectives

1. Describe properties of rocks and minerals, including texture, luster, color, cleavage, hardness, density, and crystalline structure.
2. Perform tests to determine the hardness of minerals and rocks.
3. Construct charts of the properties of a variety of minerals and rocks, and use the charts to identify specific minerals and rocks.

1. WHAT ARE ROCKS AND MINERALS LIKE? (2–5)

Materials

- Kits of rock samples, including such rocks as basalt, granite, limestone, marble, pumice, sandstone, shale, and slate
- Kits of mineral samples, including such minerals as feldspar, calcite, fluorite, gypsum, graphite, hematite, hornblende, magnetite, mica, and quartz

(Kits of rocks and minerals can be obtained from scientific supply houses such as Delta Education or Carolina Biological. For addresses, see Appendix C.)

ENGAGE

a. Ask: *Where do you find different kinds of rocks?* (At home, on the school campus, on the way to school) *How are the different rocks alike? How are they different? Where do you think the rocks originally came from?*

EXPLORE

b. Initially refer to both rocks and minerals as "rocks." Provide each small group with a mixture of samples of several different rocks. For example, select large and small samples of calcite, quartz, feldspar, talc, granite, sandstone, and magnetite. Let each student in the cooperative groups examine each rock. Ask the groups to discuss what is the same and what is different about the rocks. Students often describe rocks in imaginative detail: "This rock weighs three and a half crayons. This rock is shiny and has little ripples. This one is shaped like a loaf of bread and you can stand it on its end."

EXPLAIN

c. Ask: *What were some of the property words you used to describe the rocks?* (Words related to color, texture, relative shininess, relative weight, shape, etc.)
d. Explain that rocks can be described in terms of properties, such as shape, size, color, weight, or texture. All rocks are made of materials called *minerals* that have properties that may be identified by testing. Mineral properties include color, odor, streak, luster,

hardness, and magnetism. Rocks are made up of one or more minerals, so all of the specimens we looked at are rocks, even though some of them were made of just one mineral.

ELABORATE

e. Select four rocks that are similar in color, such as four black rocks. Place the rocks on a tray so that each student in the group can observe them. Tell each student to write down descriptions of the four rocks, without letting the other students in the group know which rocks they are describing. Ask them to take turns reading their description of one rock, while the other students try to determine which rock is being described.

EVALUATE

f. You can assess a student's level of development for the process skill of observing by comparing these indicators with evidence you observe in the classroom. As you progress down this list, when you reach a statement that you would answer negatively based on your observation of the student or when you reach a statement that is difficult to answer yes or no, you have found the student's level of development for the process skill of observing. By looking further down the list, you can see the next steps for the student's learning about how to observe. The list that appears below is adapted from the Exploratorium's Institute for Inquiry and based on Wynne Harlen's work.[2] The student:

1. can identify obvious differences and similarities between the rock samples.
2. makes use of several senses in exploring the rock samples.
3. identifies differences in detail between the rock samples.
4. identifies ways rock samples are similar, even if the ways they are different are more obvious.
5. uses his/her senses appropriately and use hand lenses or microscopes to see details on rock samples.
6. can distinguish from many observations of rock samples, those that are relevant to the task they are doing.

2. WHAT IS MEANT BY THE STREAK OF A MINERAL, AND HOW CAN WE TEST FOR IT? (2–5)

Materials

- Kits of mineral samples, including such minerals as feldspar, calcite, fluorite, gypsum, graphite, hematite, hornblende, magnetite, mica, and quartz (with identifing numbers 1–12 on the samples (e.g., in each kit the feldspar sample is labeled 1, etc.)
- Copies of Mineral Properties Chart
- Streak plates
- Colored pencils or crayons

ENGAGE

a. Display a set of minerals. Ask: *What are some ways these minerals are different from each other?* When color is mentioned, explain that in this investigation they will record information about the property of color for each of the minerals in their kit. Tell them

---

[2]Adapted from Chapter 9 of *Teaching, Learning and Assessing Science 5–12* by Wynne Harlen (Sage, 2000).

they will also test each mineral by scratching it on a streak plate, then record information about the color of the streak produced by each mineral.

EXPLORE

b. Provide each small group with a mineral kit and two streak plates.

c. Demonstrate how one stroke of the mineral across the porcelain plate will usually produce a streak.

d. Have the students begin a mineral properties chart as in the illustration. Children should start with a blank chart and fill in all parts, including the labeling of each column as they make observations and tests of each mineral in this and future activities. Use observed color and streak color as the first two properties on the chart.

MINERAL PROPERTIES CHART

Number of Mineral	Observed Color	Streak Color	Feel	Hardness	Luster		
1	green to white	grayish					
2			soapy	softer than a penny			
3					metallic		
4					dull		
5							
6							
7							
8							
9							
10							
11							
12							

e. Provide time for the groups to observe each rock to determine its color and record their findings in the Observed Color column, and to test each rock by scratching it on the streak plate, then record their findings in the Streak column on the chart.

EXPLAIN

f. Have groups share their data with the class. Discuss the ways each group's data was alike and different and the possible reasons for that. Point out differences in details of the descriptions presented by the groups. Ask: *In what ways might these details be helpful in identifying another sample that was the same mineral as one you have tested? Are there any ways the details might not be helpful?*

Ask: *Does just looking at the color a mineral give you enough information to identify it?* (not really) *Were there more than one black mineral sample in your kit?* (Yes) *Did the streak test help in any way to tell the black minerals apart?* (The streaks of the black minerals aren't the same so they help tell the black samples apart.)

g. Explain that color was probably one of the first properties you used to describe the minerals. However, *observable color* of a mineral is not a conclusive clue to its identity, because different samples of the same mineral may have different colors. The color of the powdered form of the mineral is more consistent than its observable color. Geologists obtain powdered forms of minerals by wiping them across a *streak plate*. That mineral property, called *streak*, is described in terms of the color of the streak of powdered mineral that is left on the streak plate.

Nature of Science

Ask: *Why should we record descriptions of rocks and minerals in a chart?* Explain that building a chart of mineral properties is a way to organize data. Charts of mineral properties help us to summarize observations and identify unknown minerals. Other ways to organize data and information include data tables, graphs, and classification systems. Scientists use all of these ways to display data in order to make it easier to analyze or make sense of.

ELABORATE

h. Distribute colored pencils and/or crayons to each group. Instruct the groups to look at the observable colors and streaks of their minerals again. This time they should use colored pencils or crayons to record their findings on their chart.

EVALUATE

i. During the Explore and Elaborate stages, interact with cooperative groups to formatively assess their color and streak descriptions of different minerals. The following checklist might be helpful in monitoring and record keeping:

☐ Data table is organized and appropriately labeled.
☐ Data are entered in correct cells of the data table.
☐ Color and streak are described in detail with words.
☐ Color and streak are represented by coloring.

3. HOW CAN MINERALS BE IDENTIFIED BY THE WAY THEY FEEL? (2–5)

Materials

- Kits of mineral samples, including such minerals as feldspar, calcite, fluorite, gypsum, graphite, hematite, hornblende, magnetite, mica, and quartz
- Mineral Properties Charts

ENGAGE

a. Ask: *How can the way a mineral feels be used to identify the mineral? What are some words that describe the way a mineral feels?* (Smooth, rough, rounded edges, and soapy.)

EXPLORE

b. Have students feel each mineral and record their descriptions in their charts. Encourage them to use as much detail as possible in their descriptions.

EXPLAIN

c. Bring the whole class together to discuss their findings. Write the descriptive words they have used on the board. Look for synonyms, and identify subtle differences in meaning among them. Work with the class to develop an operational definition of the "feel" of a mineral.

ELABORATE

d. Have students work with a partner. One partner should close their eyes or be blind-folded. The other partner should hand the non-seeing partner each mineral sample to describe by touch and write down the description the non-seeing partner suggested. Then the partners should switch roles, and repeat the activity.

    The partners should look over the lists that they made and discuss similarities and differences in the words used. Encourage them to also discuss if it was easier to make detailed observations with their sense of touch when their sense of sight could not be used.

EVALUATE

e. Check students' Mineral Properties Charts to formatively assess their ability to include detail about how minerals feel in their descriptions and drawings.

....

4. WHAT IS MEANT BY THE HARDNESS OF A MINERAL, AND HOW CAN WE TEST FOR IT? (2–5)

Materials

- Kits of mineral samples, including such minerals as feldspar, calcite, fluorite, gypsum, graphite, hematite, hornblende, magnetite, mica, and quartz
- Pennies
- Steel nails
- Mineral Properties Charts

ENGAGE

a. Ask: *Are the minerals in your kit equally hard? Which one seems hardest? Which one seems softest? How can you tell?*

EXPLORE

b. Demonstrate how to use a penny to gently scratch a soft mineral and a nail to gently scratch a mineral of medium hardness. Explain that students will classify minerals as *soft*, *medium*, and *hard* using a copper penny and a steel nail as standards:

- A soft mineral can be scratched by a penny.
- A mineral of medium hardness can be scratched by a nail, but not by a penny.
- A hard mineral cannot be scratched by a nail.

To prevent damage to minerals, encourage students to scratch gently.

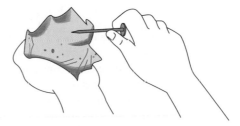

c. Have students test the hardness of each mineral in their charts. Tell students to add a "hardness" column to the mineral properties chart and to record the hardness of each mineral.

EXPLAIN

d. In a large group, ask students to report the results of their hardness tests. Work toward agreement in hardness test results, that is, they are classified as soft, medium, or hard based on the criteria given previously. Students may have to retest some mineral samples in order to reach consensus.

ELABORATE

e. You've classifed the minerals in your set into three groups soft, medium, and hard. Ask: *How could you put the minerals in order from hardest to softest?* Lead students to suggest that we could scratch two minerals together gently.

Explain that the relative hardness of a mineral can be determined by a scratch test. The harder of two minerals will scratch the softer.

EVALUATE

f. To assess student understanding of the mineral property called hardness, have students respond to the following writing prompts in their science notebook.
   1. Mineral hardness is . . .
   2. I found the hardness of the minerals in my kit by . . . .

5. WHAT IS MEANT BY LUSTER, AND HOW CAN IT BE USED IN IDENTIFYING MINERALS? (2–5)

Materials

- Kits of mineral samples, including such minerals as feldspar, calcite, fluorite, gypsum, graphite, hematite, hornblende, magnetite, mica, and quartz
- Mineral Properties Charts
- Penlights or flashlights
- Overhead projector (optional)

ENGAGE

a. Hold a shiny mineral sample in the beam of light coming from an overhead projector or a flashlight, rotate it so it sparkles when viewed by the class. Ask: *What are some words you can use to describe the way light reflects from the surface of this mineral?*

EXPLORE

b. Have students hold each of their minerals up to the light or shine a flashlight on each one and describe in their own words the way each mineral looks in the light. Tell them to record their descriptions in their science notebooks.

EXPLAIN

c. In a large group, ask students to report their results. Write the words they use to describe luster on the board. Discuss the descriptive words (adjectives) that were used.

d. Tell students that *luster* refers to the way a mineral's surface reflects light. Explain that some minerals have a metal-like luster and are called *metallic*. Other minerals are *nonmetallic*. Some terms you could use to describe the nonmetallic luster of a mineral might be *dull, glassy, waxy, pearly,* and *shiny*. Write the italicized words on the board for future reference. Revisit the student's words and see if any of them are synonyms for the terms geologists typically use to describe luster.

Find examples of things in the room, other than mineral samples, that have lusters that could be described with the terms listed above and use them for examples of the meanings of these terms.

ELABORATE

e. Have students label the next column of their Mineral Properties Chart, Luster. Instruct them to select the most appropriate scientific term describing luster for each of the mineral samples and write that term in the correct cell on the chart.

EVALUATE

f. To assess student understanding of the mineral property called luster, have students respond to the following writing prompts in their science notebook.
1. A mineral's luster is a description of . . .
2. I found the luster of the minerals in my kit by . . .

6. HOW CAN THE TRANSMISSION OF LIGHT THROUGH A MINERAL BE USED TO IDENTIFY THE MINERAL? (2–5)

Materials

- Kits of mineral samples, including such minerals as feldspar, calcite, fluorite, gypsum, graphite, hematite, hornblende, magnetite, mica, and quartz
- Mineral Properties Charts
- Flashlights or penlights
- Overhead projector (optional)
- Clear plastic wrap or a blank transparency for the overhead
- Wax paper
- Aluminum foil

ENGAGE

a. Hold common transparent (e.g., clear plastic), translucent (e.g., wax paper), and opaque (e.g., aluminum foil) materials to the lens of an overhead projector or flashlight. Ask: *How do these materials differ in the way they transmit light? Do the minerals in our kits also transmit light differently?*

EXPLORE

b. Have students shine a flashlight on each mineral and look to see how much light is transmitted. Students should record their findings for each of the numbered minerals in their science notebooks.

EXPLAIN

c. In a large group, ask students to report their findings. Then introduce the terms scientists use to describe materials that tranmit different amounts of light. Explain that materials can be *transparent*, with a lot of light shining through them; *translucent*, with a little light shining through; or *opaque*, with no light shining through. Ask: *How can the amount of light a mineral transmits help us in identifying it?* (Different minerals transmit different amounts of light.)

ELABORATE

d. Have students label the next column of their Mineral Properties Chart, Light Transmission. Instruct them to select the most appropriate scientific term describing light transmission for each of the mineral samples and write that term in the correct cell on the chart.

EVALUATE

e. To assess student understanding of the mineral property called light transmission have students respond to the following writing prompts in their science notebook.
1. A mineral's light transmission is a description of . . .
2. I found the light transmission of the minerals in my kit by . . .

7. WHAT CAN THE SHAPE OF A MINERAL TELL US? (2–5)

Materials

- Kits of mineral samples, including such minerals as feldspar, calcite, fluorite, gypsum, graphite, hematite, hornblende, magnetite, mica, and quartz
- Mineral Properties Charts
- Models of various geometric solids—cube, tetrahedon, sphere, etc. (as found in math kits)

ENGAGE

a. Display the models of geometric solids you have collected. Ask: *How are these shapes different? Do you know what any of these shapes are called? Do any of your minerals seem to have a characteristic shape?*

EXPLORE

b. Have students describe and sketch the shape of each mineral in their science notebooks. Circulate among cooperative groups to formatively assess the descriptions of shape entered in the chart. This will let you know what concepts should be addressed during the explain phase of the lesson. Work with individuals and small groups to suggest procedures and answer questions related to the shape property.

EXPLAIN

c. In a large group, ask students to report their findings. Then introduce the terms scientists use to describe the shapes of mineral samples. Tell students that the shape of a mineral is often a clue to its crystal-like structure. The shape of minerals might be described as like a cube, like a tilted box (e.g., calcite), having crystals, having masses that are not fully crystals, having thin layers (e.g., biotite), or having no special shape.

ELABORATE

d. Have students label the next column of their Mineral Properties Chart, Shape. Instruct them to use a term that was discussed to describe the shape for each of the mineral samples and write that term in the correct cell on the chart.

EVALUATE

e. Check students' Mineral Properties Charts to formatively assess their ability to include detail about mineral shape in their descriptions and drawings.

8. WHAT SPECIAL PROPERTIES DO DIFFERENT MINERALS HAVE? (2–5)

Materials

- Kits of mineral samples, including such minerals as feldspar, calcite, fluorite, gypsum, graphite, hematite, hornblende, magnetite, mica, and quartz
- Mineral Properties Charts
- Paper clips
- Conductivity testers (made from a battery, battery holder, bulb, bulb holder, and three wires)

ENGAGE

a. Ask: *Do any of your mineral samples attract iron or steel objects? How could you find out?* (Test if paper clips are attracted to any of the mineral samples.) *Do any of your mineral samples conduct electricity? How could you find out?* (Test them with the conductivity testers we used in our electricity unit.)

EXPLORE

b. Give each group several paper clips and a conductivity tester or the materials to construct one. Have students label the next column on their Mineral Properties Charts, *Magnetic*, and label the following column, *Conducts Electricity*. As they test each mineral for these properties students should write *Yes* or *No* in the appropriate cell on their Mineral Properties Chart to indicate if each mineral sample is magnetic (attracts the paper clips) and if each mineral sample conducts electricity (the bulb lights in the circuit tester when the mineral sample is placed between the ends of the two wires).

EXPLAIN

c. Bring the class together to share their findings about these two special mineral properties. Ask: *Did each group find the same mineral sample(s) were magnetic? Did each group find the same mineral sample(s) were conductors of electricity?* If not, have students complete the elaborate phase of this activity.

ELABORATE

d. Have groups re-test their samples to provide evidence for their data. Let other groups observe each other's evidence. If the results for a mineral are different from the group, discuss strategies for determining the reason for the surprising result, they apply those strategies.

EVALUATE

e. To assess student understanding of these two special mineral properties, have students respond to the following writing prompts in their science notebook.
   1. If a mineral is magnetic, it . . .
   2. If a mineral conducts electricity, it . . .

9. HOW CAN YOU IDENTIFY AN UNKNOWN MINERAL? (2–5)

Materials

- Kits of mineral samples, including such minerals as feldspar, calcite, fluorite, gypsum, graphite, hematite, hornblende, magnetite, mica, and quartz
- Mineral Properties Charts
- Streak plates
- Pennies
- Iron nails
- Paper clips
- Conductivity testers
- Flashlights or penlights

ENGAGE

a. Ask: *How can you use your mineral properties chart to identify a mineral sample?*

EXPLORE

b. Give students one or more of minerals 1–12 with the identifying number labels removed. Have students use their mineral properties charts to identify each mineral.

EXPLAIN

c. Ask: *What have you concluded about the identity of your unknown samples? How did you use observation, testing, and your charts to identify the unknown samples?*

ELABORATE

d. Provide students with a master chart of mineral properties. Instead of having letters related to the mineral sample properties, this chart lists the names of minerals and their properties. Have them label the next column on their Mineral Properties Chart, Mineral's Name. Challenge students to compare their data with the information on the master chart to figure out the names of each of the samples they have been testing.

e. Encourage students to use library and Internet resources to look up additional information and deepen their understanding about the minerals they have been investigating.

EVALUATE

f. As a self-assessment, if discrepancies between their chart and the master chart occur with any of the minerals, encourage students to make some fresh observations.

g. As a summative assessment, give each student four mineral samples labeled A, B, C, D. One sample should be a mineral not included on students' charts; the other three samples should be minerals that are included on their charts. Allow each student to use his or her completed Mineral Property Chart to determine the name of three of the minerals and to identify the one the student cannot name because it is new. On a sheet of paper, students should write their name and list the letters A, B, C, D. Beside each letter the name of a mineral or the word *new* should be written.

B. THE STRUCTURE OF MINERALS: CRYSTALS AND CRYSTAL FORMATION

▶ *Science Background*

Crystals are nonliving substances that form into rocklike bodies of various shapes. Crystals grow in size when more layers of the same substance are added on; the basic crystal shape, however, remains the same. The size of crystals is determined by differences in the rate of crystallization and in the length of time crystals have to form. If crystals are disturbed in the forming process, they will break apart into hundreds of microscopic pieces. Crystalline form is important in determining some of the properties of substances.

 NSES

Science Standards

All students should develop an understanding of

- properties of the earth's systems (K–4).
- structure of the earth's systems (5–8).

Concepts and Principles That Support the Standards

- Earth materials are solid rocks and soils, water, and gases of the atmosphere (K–4).
- The varied materials have different physical and chemical properties (K–4).

Objectives

1. Demonstrate and describe different kinds of investigations to grow crystals.
2. Describe how crystal size is affected by conditions during formation.
3. Distinguish between and describe the formation of stalactites and stalagmites.

1. HOW CAN SALT CRYSTALS BE GROWN? (3–6)

Materials
- Salt
- Tablespoon
- Jar lid
- Small glass
- Magnifying lens
- Water

ENGAGE

a. Guide students to examine a grain of salt through a magnifying lens. If a video microscope is available, use it to show the class salt grains under higher magnification by displaying the image on a TV or computer monitor or projecting it onto a screen. Ask: *What do you see? What does a salt grain look like? What are crystals? How are crystals formed?*

EXPLORE

b. Guide students to conduct these activities within their cooperative groups and to record the answers to the questions below in their science notebooks:

   1. Obtain a tablespoon of salt, a jar lid, and a small glass of water. Mix the salt into the glass of water. Stir the water well. Let the solution stand for a few minutes until it becomes clear.
   Ask: *What happens to the salt?*

   2. Very gently pour some of the salt solution into the jar lid. Put a piece of string in the solution, letting one end hang out, as in diagram (a). Let the solution stand for several days where the lid will not be disturbed.
   Ask: *What do you predict will happen to the salt solution?*

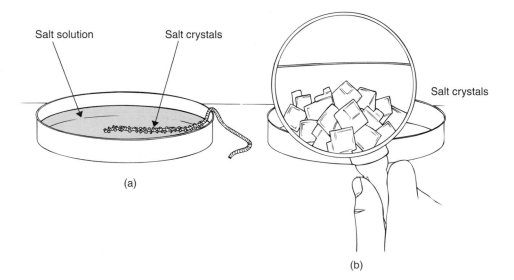

   3. After several days have passed, use your magnifying lens to look at the materials in the lid. Lift the string out of the jar lid. Examine the string with your magnifying lens. Describe what you see with the hand lens. See diagram (b).

EXPLAIN

c. Bring students together for a whole class discussion about their findings. Have each group describe and show their results to the class. Ask: *How are the materials in the lid different from your original salt solution? Why do you now have a solid when you started out with a liquid? What name could you give to the formations in the lid?*

d. Explain to the students that the salt dissolved in the water. When the salt water stood for several days, the water evaporated, leaving behind crystals of salt. Crystals are non-living substances found in nature that are formed in various geometrical shapes.

2. HOW CAN SUGAR CRYSTALS BE GROWN? (3–6)

Materials

- Tablespoon
- Jar lid
- Granulated sugar
- Small glass
- Water

ENGAGE

a. Instruct students to examine grains of sugar through a magnifying lens. If a video microscope is available, use it to show the class salt grains under higher magnification by displaying the image on a TV or computer monitor or projecting it onto a screen. Ask: *What do you observe? How are sugar grains different from salt grains? How can we grow crystals of sugar?*

EXPLORE

b. Students should conduct these activities in their cooperative groups and record the answers to the questions below in their science notebooks:

1. Obtain a tablespoon of sugar, a jar lid, and a small glass of water. Be sure the tablespoon is clean. Mix a tablespoon of sugar into the glass of water. Stir the water well. Let the solution stand for a few minutes until it becomes clear. Ask: *What happens to the sugar? How is the sugar solution similar in appearance to the salt solution?*

2. Very gently pour some of the sugar solution into the lid and let the solution stand undisturbed for several days. Ask: *What do you think might happen to the sugar solution?*

3. After several days have passed, use your magnifying lens to look at the materials in your lid.

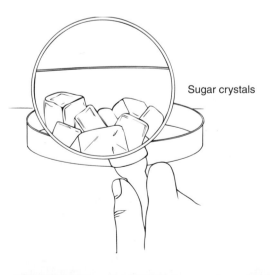

Sugar crystals

EXPLAIN

c. Bring students together for a whole class discussion about their findings. Have each group describe and show their results to the class. Ask: *How are the materials in this lid different from your original sugar solution? How are the materials in this lid different from the salt crystals? How are they alike? What happened to the sugar solution?*

d. Explain that when the sugar water stood for several days, the water evaporated, leaving behind sugar crystals.

3. WHAT ARE STALACTITES AND STALAGMITES, AND HOW ARE THEY FORMED? (3–6)

Materials

- Paper towel
- Epsom salt
- Spoon
- 30 cm (1 ft) of thick string
- Large tin can
- Two small jars or clear plastic cups
- Two heavy washers

ENGAGE

a. Display a picture of the inside of a cavern showing stalactites and stalagmites. Ask: *Where do you think this picture was taken? How are rock formations like these formed?*

EXPLORE

b. Allow students to carry out this investigation in cooperative groups:

1. Fill the large tin can about three-quarters full of water. Add Epsom salt one spoonful at a time, stirring vigorously after each addition, until no more will dissolve.

Note: Epsom salt crystals will fall to the bottom of the can when no more will dissolve.

2. Fill the two small jars or plastic cups with the Epsom salt solution and place the containers 5 cm (2 in.) apart on the paper towel. Tie a heavy washer to each end of the string. Place one washer in each of the small jars or paper cups.

Note: Arrange the string in the cups so that you have at least 5 cm between the string and the paper towel.

3. Observe the jars or cups, the paper towel, the string, and the washer daily. Record the observations on a record sheet or in your science journals.

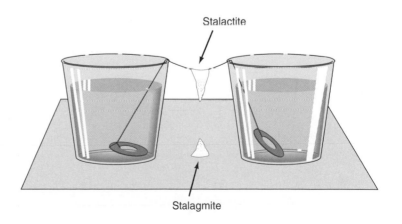

Stalactite

Stalagmite

EXPLAIN

c. Bring the whole class together to discuss the results of the investigation. Ask: *What did you observe? What is the substance deposited on the string and on the paper towel? How did they get there? What is your evidence?*

d. Help students learn the difference between stalactites and stalagmites. Point out that the deposits that hang down are called **stalactites** (*c* for ceiling), while those that point up are called **stalagmites** (*g* for ground).

Ask: *Is the crystal formed on the string like a stalactite or a stalagmite? Why do you think so? Is the crystal formed on the paper towel like a stalactite or a stalagmite? Why do you think so?*

Nature of Science

e. Children sometimes fail to understand the link between causes and effects because they think of an investigation in terms of its component parts rather than its interactions. Scientists use the notion of *system* to help them think in terms of components and interactions. Explain that a system is a collection of components that interact to perform some function. Examples of systems are a school system and the city water system.

Thinking of an investigation as a **system** made up of parts that interact with one another can help to broaden children's thinking. Ask: *What are the components of our investigation system?* (Containers, Epsom salt, water, string, washers, paper towels) *How does each component interact with other components? What is your evidence?*

By observing small systems, we can draw inferences about what happens in larger systems of the world. Ask: *How is what we observed like what might happen in a cavern in the earth?*

ELABORATE

f. Encourage students to learn more about rock features in caverns and caves through library and Internet research. Each research group could prepare an educational brochure or commercial encouraging travel to a specific underground attraction. Through their research they will probably find that other underground features exist, including columns and helectites.

EVALUATE

g. Before research begins, have the class help you develop a rubric describing the criteria and expectations for the brochures and commercials. These rubrics will guide student work and serve as a scoring guide when you assess their final products.

Stalactites and stalagmites in Mammoth Cave, Mammoth Cave National Park, Kentucky.

C. STRUCTURE OF THE EARTH'S SURFACE

▶ *Science Background*

The earth's surface is always changing. Waves, wind, water, and ice shape and reshape the earth's land surface by eroding rock and soil in some areas and depositing it in other areas, sometimes forming seasonal layers. Smaller rocks come from the breaking and weathering of bedrock and larger rocks. Soil is made partly from weathered rock, partly from plant and animal remains. Soil also contains many living organisms.[3]

 NSES   Science Standards

All students should develop an understanding of

- properties of the earth's systems (K–4).
- structure of the earth's systems (5–8).

[3]American Association for the Advancement of Science, 1993. *Benchmarks for Science Literacy* (New York: Oxford University Press).

Concepts and Principles That Support the Standards

- Soils have properties of color and texture, capacity to retain water, and ability to support the growth of many kinds of plants (K–4).
- Soils consist of weathered rocks and decomposed organic material from dead plants, animals, and bacteria. Soils are often found in layers, with each having a different chemical composition and texture (5–8).
- The surface of the earth changes. Some changes are due to slow processes, such as erosion and weathering, and some changes are due to rapid processes, such as landslides, volcanic eruptions, and earthquakes (K–4).

Objectives

1. Describe how germinating seeds and plants can naturally break up rocks and soil.
2. Demonstrate a procedure for determining the composition of soils.
3. Describe what might be found in soils.
4. Demonstrate a procedure to illustrate how the earth's surface forms layers.
5. Demonstrate, describe, and explain a procedure to illustrate how layers in the earth's surface might be observed.

1. HOW CAN LIVING THINGS PRODUCE FORCES THAT CAN CHANGE THE EARTH'S SURFACE? (K–4)

Materials

- Two plastic vials or medicine bottles with snap lids
- Dry bean seeds
- Water

ENGAGE

a. Display a large rock. Ask: *How could this rock be broken?* List students' suggestions on chart paper for use later in the lesson.

EXPLORE

b. Fill both of the vials or medicine bottles with as many dry beans as will fit. Add as much water as you can to one vial of beans. Snap the lids on both vials.
    Ask: *What do you think might happen to the two vials?*

A Water   **B** No water

c. Observe both vials the next day.

EXPLAIN

d. Bring the class together for discussion. Ask: *What do you observe? Why do you think it happened?* Lead students to understand that in the container with water, the beans expanded and lifted the lid off. In the vial without water, there was no observable change.

e. Refer back to the chart developed during the engage phase of the lesson. Lead students to realize that all ideas on the list are related to force. Remind students that force is needed to make something move. Ask: *Was there force involved when the lid came off one of our containers? How do you know?*

Ask: *How could the force of germinating seeds and growing plants produce changes in the earth's surface?* Help students infer that swelling and growing plants change the land by breaking up rocks and soil just as the swelling beans lifted the vial's lid off.

ELABORATE

f. Ask students to find places on the school grounds or on concrete walks where plants grow through and crack rocks like this:

EVALUATE

g. Have students draw and write in their science notebooks about their observations during the explore and elaborate phases of the lesson. By looking over this work, you can formatively assess their observation and recording skills.

h. To assess their understanding of the concept that growing plants can affect the earth's surface, display the rock used during the engage phase of the lesson, then ask children to respond to the following questions:
   1. Could a plant break this rock?
   2. Why or why not?
   3. What evidence supports your answer?

2. WHAT IS IN SOIL? (3–6)

Materials

- Soil (from backyard)
- Alum
- Clear plastic vial with lid

ENGAGE

a. Ask: *What is in soil? How can we find out?*

EXPLORE

b. To observe different kinds of materials in backyard soil:
   1. Add about 1 inch of soil to a clear plastic vial with a lid (approximately 1 inch in diameter and 3 inches high).
   2. Add a pinch of alum to the soil. Tell the students that alum is a chemical used in making pickles. It is safe, but caution the students not to taste it.
   3. Fill the vial to the top with water, cover it, and shake it vigorously.
   4. Place the vial on the table and leave it there for the duration of the investigation.
   5. After several minutes, observe and record observations. The alum acts as a dispersing agent, helping the soil particles to break into smaller parts and settle out into layers. Students should observe sand at the bottom of the vial, silt above the sand, clay above the silt, water, and organic matter floating on the water.

Soil + alum + water

EXPLAIN

c. Ask: *From the results of your investigation, what do you conclude is in soil? Which particles do you think are larger: sand, clay, or silt? Why do you think so?*

ELABORATE

d. Ask: *How could you find out how much of each kind of material their is in soil?* Lead students to suggest measuring the layers that were formed during the Explore section of the lesson. Then provide rulers so they can measure the layers in their vial. Suggest that they display their finding using either a bar or pie graph. Then allow each group to share their findings with the class.

EVALUATE

e. Challenge each student to produce a visual representation of soil and its contents. Before they start, have them suggest critera and expectations for this product, leading to a rubric that will guide them in their work and that you will use for assessing their products.[4]

---

[4]Adapted from GEMS (Great Explorations in Math and Science), 1994. *Terrarium Habitats*. Lawrence Hall of Science, Berkeley, CA.

3. WHAT IS CORE SAMPLING, AND HOW CAN WE USE IT TO INFER LAYERS IN THE EARTH'S CRUST? (3–6)

Materials

- Cupcakes
- Clear plastic straws
- Plastic knives

Preparation

In this activity, straws will be used to take core samples of layered cupcakes. Layered cupcakes may be made by the teacher or a parent volunteer as follows:

1. Use either different flavors or white batter mixed with food coloring.
2. Put batter in four layers in foil or paper cups.
3. Bake the cupcakes. Add frosting if desired.

ENGAGE

a. Show students a cupcake. Ask: *What do you think is inside the cupcake? How could we find out without eating it or cutting into it? How can scientists learn what's underground?*

EXPLORE

b. Provide groups of students one cupcake on a paper plate, five clear plastic straws cut into thirds, a plastic knife, drawing paper, and markers. Do *not* remove the foil or paper cup from the cupcake.
c. Instruct students to draw what they think the inside of the cupcake looks like.
d. Show and tell students how to take side "core samples," as in diagram (a):
   1. Carefully insert a straw into the side of the cupcake, rotate slightly, remove, and place sample on paper plate.
   2. Repeat with another straw.
e. Instruct students to take two side core samples of their cupcake. Ask: *Can you determine what the entire cupcake looks like with these two core samples? If not, what must you do?*
f. Instruct students to take three samples by inserting the straw straight down into the cupcake, as in diagram (b).

Core samples of cupcake

(a)   (b)   (c)

g. Compare these samples with those taken from the side, as in diagram (c).

h. Ask: *How are they different? Based on your core samples, what do you infer is inside the cupcake?* Instruct students to make drawings of what they now think the inside of the cupcake looks like.

EXPLAIN

i. Post the student drawings completed in step h of the lesson. Ask: *On what data did you base your drawing? How sure are you of the accuracy of your drawing? Why?*

j. Provide students this background information:

Geologists study the earth and use many devices to discover what is under the surface. Core sampling is done by putting hollow drilling tubes into the ground and extracting a sample of what the tubes went through.

k. Ask how does your straw sampling of the cupcake compare and contrast with core sampling done by geologists?

ELABORATE

l. Ask: *How could you find out what the inside of your cupcake looks like?* Tell students to use the plastic knives to cut down and separate the cupcakes into halves. Have them draw what the inside of the cup cake actually looks like. Ask: *How do your direct observations compare with your inferences and your drawings? Can geologists check the inferences they make from their core samples, the way you checked the inside of your cupcake? Why or why not?*

EVALUATE

m. To assess student understanding about the use of data from core sampling, show students pictures of cores from a different cupcake. Challenge them to draw what the inside of the cupcake looks like when sliced vertically through the center and horizontally through the center, based on the data. Then ask them to expain why they drew the inside of this cupcake the way they did.[5]

II. ATMOSPHERE, WEATHER, AND CLIMATE OF THE EARTH

Our spherical earth consists mostly of rock, with three-fourths of the planet covered by a thin layer of water and the entire planet blanketed by a thin layer of air called the *atmosphere*. Weather (in the short run) and climate (in the long run) involve the transfer of heat energy from the sun in and out of the atmosphere. The earth has a variety of climatic patterns, which consist of different conditions of temperature, precipitation, humidity, wind, air pressure, and other atmospheric phenomena. Water continuously circulates in and out of the atmosphere—evaporating from the surface, rising and cooling, condensing into clouds and then rain or snow, and falling again to the surface. The water cycle plays an important part in determining climatic patterns.

Children can begin to understand the atmosphere, water cycle, weather, and climate by engaging in inquiry activities related to evaporation and condensation, and observing and recording the weather on a regular basis. Emphasis should be on developing observation and description skills and forming explanations based on observable evidence.[6]

---

[5]Cupcake Geology activity in the Mesa Public Schools Curriculum Unit "Earthquakes" by JoAnne Vasquez.

[6]Adapted from *Science for All Americans, Benchmarks for Science Literacy,* and the *National Science Education Standards.*

A. THE WATER CYCLE

▶ *Science Background*

In the **water cycle**, water evaporates into the air as **water vapor**. As the air becomes laden with water vapor, the **relative humidity** of the air increases. When warm, moist air cools, it condenses as liquid water on available surfaces such as an iced tea glass, a bathroom mirror, or dust particles in the air.

 Science Standards

All students should develop an understanding of

- changes in the earth and sky (K–4).
- structure of the earth's systems (5–8).

Concepts and Principles That Support the Standards

- Water, which covers the majority of the earth's surface, circulates through the crust, oceans, and atmosphere in what is known as the *water cycle* (5–8).
- Water evaporates from the earth's surface, rises and cools as it moves to higher elevations, condenses as rain or snow, and falls to the surface where it collects in lakes, oceans, soil, and rocks underground (5–8).

Objectives

1. Observe and describe the disappearance of water that is left uncovered.
2. Define *evaporation* and explain that evaporated water has not disappeared but has changed into water vapor (a gaseous state) and has gone into the air.
3. Use the cohesive bond model of water developed in previous activities to explain what happens when a liquid evaporates.
4. Explain how interactions between a liquid and its environment may affect evaporation.
5. Define *condensation* and *dew point*.
6. Describe and demonstrate the conditions for condensation.
7. Construct and explain a model of the water cycle.

1. HOW MUCH WATER EVAPORATES FROM AN OPEN AQUARIUM, AND WHERE DOES IT GO? (K–4)

Materials

- Aquarium or other large, open container
- Measuring cup or graduated cylinder
- Water
- Masking tape or marking pen

Safety Precautions

When children work with water, cover their work tables, perhaps with newspapers. Have plenty of paper towels on hand to clean up water spills.

ENGAGE

a. Direct children's attention to the aquarium. Ask: Does the amount of water in the aquarium stay the same? How could we find out?

EXPLORE

b. Assist students to conduct this investigation:

1. Using masking tape or marking pens, mark the beginning water level of a class-room aquarium.

2. Check the water levels each morning. Using a measuring cup, add enough water to the aquarium to bring the water level back up to the original marks you made. Be sure the water added to the aquarium sits in a large open container for at least 24 hours so that chemicals such as chlorine will dissipate and the new water won't harm the fish.

3. Keep a record of how much water was added each day over a period of a week or two.

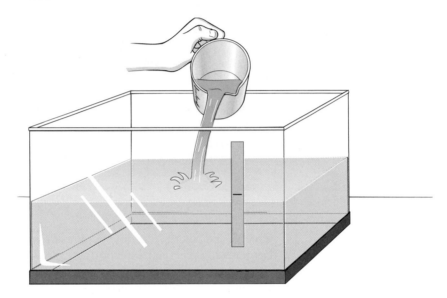

EXPLAIN

c. Remind the class that several weeks ago we asked the question: *Does the amount of water in the aquarium stay the same?* Ask: *What did we find out?* Discuss the record of how much water was added each day with the class. Ask: *Why did we need to add water? Was the amount of water we needed to add the same each day? Why or why not?*

d. Ask: *Where do you think the water that was missing from the aquarium went?* List students' suggestions on chart paper. They might suggest the following:

• The missing water soaked into the sand.
• The fish drank it.
• The custodian spilled it.
• It went into the air.

ELABORATE

e. Challenge the children to design fair tests (controlled investigations) to check their ideas. Depending on the age and experience of your class, you may want to do these investigations one at a time with the whole class or you may have groups working on different investigations simultaneously. In kindergarten, the plans will probably be formulated in a whole class discussion scaffolded with many strategic questions by the teacher. In higher grades, student groups might be expected to design their own investigation. Be sure children share their plans with you before they begin their investigation.

f. Remind students that in a controlled investigation, all variables are kept the same except one. Some summarized plans that represent controlled investigations follow:
    1. To test if the water soaked into the sand, observe two aquariums with water and fish, one with and one without sand.
    2. To test if the fish drank the water, compare one container with fish and one without. Both containers should be identical in every other way except one has no fish.
    3. To test if the water went into the air, observe one container covered and one uncovered.

g. After the investigations are complete, ask: *What did you observe in your investigations? What can you conclude?* Discuss with the students how they can interpret the data from each of their experiments. For example, explain that the amount of the missing water was the same in aquariums with and without sand, so the water must not have soaked into the sand. There was a difference in the missing water only in the experiment in which one aquarium was covered and the other was not covered. Therefore, the cover must have prevented water from going into the air.

Discuss with the children how these experiments provide evidence that the water went into the air. Explain that the missing water does not just disappear; it changes into water vapor (a gaseous state) and goes into the air. Tell them that scientists call this process *evaporation*.[7]

EVALUATION

h. If student groups planned and conducted their own investigations, you could formatively assess their skill in planning and conducting investigations by applying indicators for assessing the development of process skills. The following indicators have been adapted from Wynne Harlen's work.[8] The indicators in the following checklist are arranged sequentially so the level of the process skills increases from the beginning to the end of the list.

Students:

☐ develop a plan that is general but still useful (lacking detail or needing further thought.

☐ have an idea of the variable to be changed (the independent or manipulated variable) or what things should be compared.

☐ keep constant those variables (the controlled variables) that must be kept the same for a fair test.

☐ have some idea ahead of time what they will compare or measure (the dependent or responding variable) to find a result.

☐ select a realistic way of measuring or comparing things (the dependent or responding variable) to find a result.

☐ use procedures that ensure reasonably accurate results.

---

[7]Adapted from a variation of an SCIS activity developed by Herbert Thier.
[8]Adapted from Chapter 9 of *Teaching, Learning and Assessing Science 5–12* by Wynne Harlen (Sage, 2000).

2. HOW CAN YOU PROMOTE THE EVAPORATION OF WATER? (3–6)

Materials

- Various containers of various depths and sizes of openings
- Medicine droppers
- Construction paper
- Lamps with 60 watt bulb
- Water
- Straws

Safety Precautions

Caution the children not to touch the light bulb and electrical connections. For safety reasons, you may choose to demonstrate that water evaporates more quickly when it is heated.

ENGAGE

a. Ask: *What can you do to speed up the evaporation of water?*

EXPLORE

b. Form small groups of 3 or 4 students. Each group should have all of the materials listed previously. Tell the students to use these materials to try out different things that might speed up the evaporation of a drop of water on construction paper. Let them know that they will only have 20 minutes to explore.

c. In their science notebooks, students should create an I Notice/I Wonder chart. Throughout the exploration phase they should record things they observed (noticed) and questions (wonders) that come to mind as they explore the interactions of these materials with water.

EXPLAIN

d. Bring the class together to discuss their findings. Draw an I Notice/I Wonder chart on the board, then use it to consolidate the class's ideas. Ask the students to identfy the variables they changed to try to speed up evaporation, such as fanning, blowing, heating, being in the light, and spreading out the drop (surface area).

e. On a sticky note each student should write his or her name and list in order of preference the three variables he or she is interested in investigating. Then students should stick their notes on the board under the first variable on their list. The teacher can move notes around if needed to form workable cooperative groups for the next part of the lesson. As long as the teacher moves students to one of their choices, even if they don't get their first choice, the students still have input into the decision.

ELABORATE

f. In their new groups, ask students to develop a question that can be investigated relating to the variable their group has chosen. Remind them that it is important to only change one variable, so that they have a fair test (controlled experiment). Each group should share its question with the class for a discussion to determine if all of the suggested questions can be investigated. If necessary, the class can help reword any questions so they can be investigated.

　　　In their new groups, students develop the procedure for their investigation. Once the teacher approves their plan, they may begin their investigation.

　　　After experimenting, collecting data, analyzing it, and drawing conclusions, students should prepare and present a summary of their findings for the class.

EVALUATE

g. To assess student understanding of how different variables affect the speed of evaporation, challenge students to develop a plan for a system to evaporate a liter of water as quickly as possible. The plans should include a description of the system, the purpose of each of its parts, an explanation of why it was designed this way, supported by evidence from the class's prior investigations, and a labeled sketch of the system.

3. HOW FAST DOES WATER IN A WET SPONGE EVAPORATE? (3–6)

Materials

- Meterstick or wire coat hanger
- Paper clips
- Sponge
- Masking tape or marking pens

ENGAGE

a. Ask: *How can we determine the rate of evaporation of water in a wet sponge?*

EXPLORE

b. Assist students to set up and conduct this investigation:
   1. Using a meterstick or wire coat hanger and paper clips, build either of the balances shown.

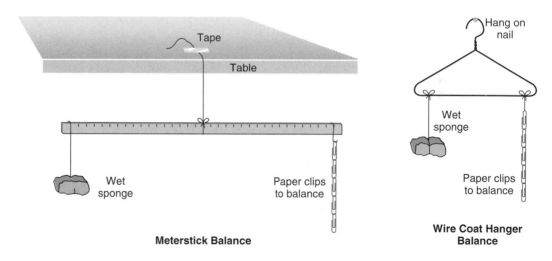

Meterstick Balance

Wire Coat Hanger Balance

   2. Soak a piece of sponge until it is very wet, but not dripping. Hang the sponge with an S-shaped paper clip or string to one end of the balance. Add paper clips to the other end until the balance is level. Ask: *How many clips did it take?*
   3. Every 15 minutes, check to see if the balance is level. Ask: *What do you see happening after several observations? Why do you think the paper clip end of the balance is lower?*
   4. Keep a written record of what happens.
   5. At each 15-minute observation, take off and record how many paper clips must be removed to keep the balance level.

6. When the sponge is dry, take your written observations and plot a line graph with the data. Set up your graph like the one that follows.

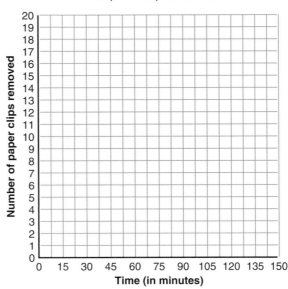

Graph of Evaporation Data

EXPLAIN

c. Bring the class together to compare the result from each group. Ask: *What were you measuring? How did you measure it? What does the graph tell you about the rate of evaporation of the water in a wet sponge?*

ELABORATE

d. Ask: *What are some variables that might affect how quickly the water in the sponge evaporates? How could you set up an experiment to test the effect of these variables on evaporation?*
e. Some variables that might affect the rate of evaporation are type of liquid (water vs. alcohol), temperature of the liquid (hot vs. cold), air temperature (hot vs. cold), wind velocity (no wind, moderate wind, strong wind), and relative humidity (dry day vs. moist day). Guide students in designing investigations, gathering data, and recording and graphing the results in the same way as they did previously.
f. Ask: *What did you observe in your investigations? What do you conclude?*

EVALUATE

g. To assess student understanding of variables that affect evaporation, have students respond to this writing prompt:
   How do your findings from your investigation relate to each of these situations?
   • Water evaporates faster from your hands when you vigorously rub them together.

   • A blow dryer can be used to dry your hair faster.

   • Your hair dries faster on a dry day than on a wet one.

   • A wet towel dries faster if it is spread out rather than crumpled in a ball.

4. WHAT IS CONDENSATION? HOW DOES IT OCCUR? (3–6)

Materials
- Clean, empty vegetable or fruit cans
- Water
- Ice

ENGAGE

a. Hold up a cold soda can. Drops of water will probably appear on the outside surface of the can. Ask: *What do you see on the outside of this soda can? Where do you think these droplets came from?*

EXPLORE

b. Provide each group two identical, empty vegetable cans. Give students these instructions:
 1. Add the same amount of water to each can so that they are about three-fourths full.
 2. Place ice in one of the cans so that the water is almost to the top of the can.
 3. Stir the water in each can.
 4. Observe the outside of each can.

EXPLAIN

c. Ask: *What happened to the outside of each can as you stirred the water?* (Moisture collected on the outside of the container with ice water.) *What conditions were necessary for the water to appear on the outside of the can?* (The can had to be cool.) *Where did the water come from?*

d. If students suggest that cold water soaked through the can, ask: *How could we test this hypothesis?*

 Hint: You might put food dye in the water and then observe to see if any of the food coloring actually soaked through the can.

 Ask: *People often say that a glass of ice water is sweating; why is this explanation incorrect?*

e. Provide this explanation of condensation:

 When water evaporates, it goes into the air as water vapor. If moisture-laden air comes into contact with a surface that is cool enough, then water vapor condenses (changes from a gas to a liquid) from the air and collects on the cool surface.

ELABORATE

f. Ask: *What is the source of the warm, moist air in each of these examples of condensation? What is the surface on which water condenses in each case?* Allow students to use library and Internet resources to confirm their answers.

- Formation of clouds. (Warm, moist air in the atmosphere rises and cools. As the water vapor cools, it condenses on dust particles.)
- Dew. (Warm, moist air is cooled as it mixes with cooler air near the surface of the earth. As the water vapor cools, it condenses on the grass and other surfaces.)

- Vapor trails. (Warm, moist air from the exhaust of a jet mixes with cooler air high in the atmosphere. As the water vapor cools, it condenses on dust particles in the atmosphere.)
- Moisture on bathroom mirrors after a hot shower. (Warm, moist air produced during the hot shower condenses on the cooler bathroom mirror.)

EVALUATE

g. To check student understanding about the concept of condensation, ask students to use the Frayer model, a graphic organizer that helps students develop their vocabularies.

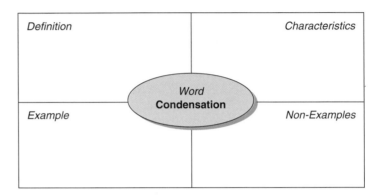

5. HOW CAN EVAPORATION AND CONDENSATION BE USED TO DESALINATE SALT WATER? (3–5)

Materials

- Salt
- Water
- Tablespoon
- Small weight (rock)
- Large sheet of black construction paper
- Large clear plastic bowl
- Plastic wrap
- Large rubber band
- Small glass custard cup

ENGAGE

a. Ask: *How can evaporation and condensation be used to remove the salt from salt water?*

EXPLORE

b. This activity may be done individually or in groups of two to four:
1. Pour 3 tablespoons of salt into a large clear plastic bowl, add water to a depth of about 2 to 3 cm, and stir until all the salt is dissolved.
2. Place the small glass cup in the water in the center of the bowl, as in the diagram.
3. Cover the large bowl with plastic wrap and fasten the wrap with a large rubber band.
4. Place a weight (small pebble) on top of the plastic wrap directly above the custard dish, as shown in the diagram.

5. *Caution:* Make certain that the plastic wrap sticks tightly to the sides of the bowl and that the large rubber band keeps it sealed when the pebble is placed on the wrap.
6. Carefully place the bowls in direct sunlight on a sheet of black construction paper, making sure the custard cup is directly under the weight pushing down on the plastic wrap.

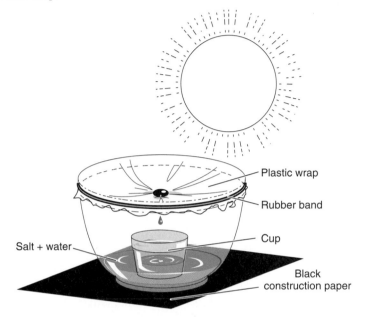

7. Record your observations every day in your observation journal.
8. After about a week, take off the plastic wrap and taste the water in the custard cup.

c. Bring the class together to discuss the changes they observed over the week. Ask:

Why do you think you were told to cover the salt water with plastic wrap? (To keep the water in the system)

Why do you think you were told to put the bowl on black construction paper? (To absorb sunlight and warm the system)

How does the water in the custard cup taste? (Like pure water)

Where did the water in the custard cup come from? (It condensed on the plastic wrap, then dripped into the custard cup.)

What happened to your salt solution? (Its surface got gradually lower in the bowl.)

Where did the water in the bowl go? (It evaporated into the air above the bowl and under the plastic wrap, then condensed on the plastic wrap and dripped into the custard cup.)

What is left in the bottom of the large bowl? (Depending on how much water is left, either salt crystals or very salty water)

▶ *Science Background*

Water in a saline solution absorbs the sun's energy and evaporates, leaving the salt behind. The water vapor contains no salt, so when it condenses on the cool surface of the plastic wrap and drips from the lowest point, only water falls into the cup. This system for removing salt from salt water is called a solar still.

6. WHAT IS THE TEMPERATURE AT WHICH CONDENSATION TAKES PLACE? (3–6)

Materials
- Clean, empty cans
- Ice
- Thermometers

ENGAGE

a. Ask: *How can we find out how cold a surface has to be before water vapor condenses on it?*

EXPLORE

b. Give students these instructions:
   1. Fill an empty can about three-fourths full of tap water at room temperature.
   2. Place a thermometer in the water and read the temperature.
   3. Add about one-fourth can of ice to the water.
   4. Stir the ice and water and read the temperature every 2 minutes.
   5. Carefully observe the outside of the can. At the first sign of condensation, read the temperature of the cold water. Wiping the outside of the can occasionally with a brown paper towel will aid in determining when condensation first forms on the can.

EXPLAIN

c. Instruct groups to record on the board the temperature at which condensation first occurred. Note discrepancies among the data collected. According to the *Benchmarks for Science Literacy*, when students arrive at very different measurements of the same thing, "it is usually a good idea to make some fresh observations instead of just arguing about who is right" (American Association for the Advancement of Science, 1993, *Benchmarks For Science Literacy*. New York: Oxford University Press, p. 10).

d. Explain that the temperature at which condensation will form on a cool surface is called the *dew point*. The dew point depends on the relative humidity of the air—that is, on the relative amount of moisture already in the air.

B. WEATHER

▶ *Science Background*

The components of weather are temperature, precipitation, humidity, wind, air pressure, clouds, and other atmospheric phenomena. These weather conditions can be readily observed and recorded by children. By keeping a weather journal during the year, students can discover weather patterns and trends, though they may not be consistent. Younger students can draw daily weather pictures of what they see; older students can make charts and graphs from the data they collect using simple weather instruments.

Science Standards

All students should develop an understanding of

- properties of the earth's systems (K–4).
- structure of the earth's systems (5–8).

Concepts and Principles That Support the Standards

- Water circulates through the crust, oceans, and atmosphere in what is known as the water cycle (5–8).
- The atmosphere is a mixture of gases that include water vapor (5–8).
- Clouds, formed by the condensation of water vapor, affect weather and climate (5–8).
- Global patterns of atmospheric movement influence local weather (5–8).

Objectives

1. Name and measure such components of weather as temperature, wind direction and speed, air pressure, and precipitation.
2. Describe patterns and trends in local weather conditions.
3. Construct a variety of weather instruments.
4. Name and describe different types of clouds, and explain how clouds are formed.

1. HOW CAN WE DESCRIBE THE WEATHER? (K–3)

Materials

- Thermometers

ENGAGE

a. Ask: *What is our weather like today?* Record the words students use to describe the weather (*cold, hot, warm, muggy, cloudy, rainy, windy,* etc.).

EXPLORE

b. Ask: *If we wanted to compare the weather today with the weather on another day, what would we record about today's weather?* Most children see weather forecasts on television. They are beginning to learn that weather controls much of their lives, from the clothes they wear to the games they play. Through discussion, lead children to consider these variables related to weather: temperature, cloud cover, wind, humidity, and rain or snow (precipitation).

c. Construct a bulletin board depicting a large weather chart similar to the one shown. Encourage children to make daily observations of weather conditions and to make entries on the class weather chart.

Day Date	MON	TUES	WED	THURS	FRI	MON	TUES	WED	THURS	FRI	MON	TUES	WED	THURS	FRI
Temperature															
Clouds	◯	◯	◯	◯	◯	◯	◯	◯	◯	◯	◯	◯	◯	◯	◯
Wind	|	|	|	|	|	|	|	|	|	|	|	|	|	|	|
Other	▯	▯	▯	▯	▯	▯	▯	▯	▯	▯	▯	▯	▯	▯	▯
Student's Name															

EXPLAIN

    d. Examine the weather chart with the children. Discuss the kinds of things children might do that would be affected by the weather. If they play outside, what would they wear: warm clothes, rain gear? Discuss the weather conditions for several days in a row.

    e. Ask: *What patterns in the weather do you see? How has the temperature changed from day to day? How is the weather today different from last summer? last winter?* Count the number of cool days, warm days, cloudy days, clear days, rainy days, and dry days to help find patterns in the weather.

ELABORATE

    f. Ask: *What is the weather like in other regions? How would weather conditions affect life in other regions?* Using the Internet, find and chart daily weather conditions in other regions and countries around the globe.

2. HOW DOES TEMPERATURE VARY FROM PLACE TO PLACE AND DURING THE DAY? (2–4)

Materials

    • Thermometers

ENGAGE

    a. Ask: *How does the temperature vary from place to place? Is the temperature the same inside and outside the classroom? Is the temperature the same everywhere on the school grounds? Is the temperature the same in the shade and the sun? How could we find out?*

EXPLORE

    b. Guide students to measure and compare the temperature at various locations: near the floor and near the ceiling of the classroom, inside and outside the classroom, in the sun and in the shade, and at different places on the school grounds.

EXPLAIN

c. Have students share their findings with the class. Discuss the differences in the temperatures at different locations and the possible reasons for these differences.

ELABORATE

d. Ask: *Is the temperature the same throughout the day?* Allow students to measure the outside temperature every hour. Discuss the temperature differences that are observed.

EVALUATE

e. To assess student understanding about the reasons for different temperatures at different places and at different parts of the day, ask students to respond to the following multiple choice questions and give reasons for their answers:

1. Where would you expect it to be cooler on a sunny day?
    A. in the shade
    B. in the sun

2. On a sunny day, when would you expect the outside temperature to be highest?
    A. early in the morning
    B. mid-morning
    C. noon
    D. late afternoon
    E. just before sunset

3. HOW CAN YOU MAKE A WIND VANE, AND HOW IS IT USED TO DETERMINE WIND DIRECTION? (3–6)

Materials

- Scissors
- Construction paper
- Drinking straw
- Pencil with eraser
- Straight pin
- Glass bead
- Empty thread spool
- A 30 cm square piece of corrugated cardboard
- Electric fan

ENGAGE

a. Ask: *How can you tell the direction the wind is blowing?*

Construct

b. To make a wind vane, follow these directions:
    1. Cut an arrow-shaped point and tail fin from construction paper, as shown in the diagram.
    2. Attach the point and tail fin to the straw by cutting notches in both ends of the straw and gluing the cutouts in place.
    3. Attach the straw to a pencil by sticking the straight pin through the middle of the straw, through a glass bead, and into the pencil eraser. Make sure the straw can swing easily in all directions and is balanced.

    Note: Move the pin in the straw until it balances with arrow and tail attached.

4. Glue the empty thread spool to the center of the corrugated cardboard. Mark north, south, east, and west on the cardboard as shown in the diagram.
5. When the glue has dried, push the pencil into the hole of the spool and check to see that the straw moves easily. You now have a wind vane.

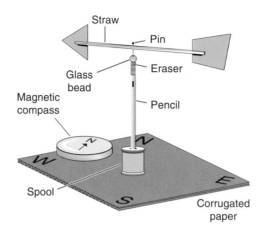

EXPLORE

c. Turn on the fan to produce a breeze so that you can test your wind vane. Notice what happens when you place your wind vane in the air flow 2 to 3 meters from the fan.

EXPLAIN

d. Ask: *What do you see happening to the arrow?* (It turns.) *Why do you think the arrow turns this way?* (The tail of the arrow is larger than its point so the tail gets pushed away from the wind source.) *From which direction is the wind blowing?* (From the direction of the fan) *How do you know?* (The arrow on the wind vane is pointing toward the fan.)

   The arrow will swing around until the point faces the direction from which the wind is blowing. This direction then becomes the wind's name. Ask: *How would you name this wind?* (It would be called a "fan wind," because it comes from the direction of the fan.)

ELABORATE

e. Carefully take your wind vane outdoors and line up the north label on your wind vane with the north on a magnetic compass. If the wind is strong, tape the cardboard to a horizontal surface or weight it down with something heavy.
f. Ask: *What do you see happening to the arrow?* (It turns to point into the wind.) *From which direction is the wind blowing?* (Answers will vary but should be the compass direction toward which the arrow points.) *How do you know?* (The arrow points toward the direction from which the wind blows.) *What would you name this wind?* (It would be named for the compass direction the arrow points.)
g. Ask: *Does the wind always blow from the same direction? How could we find out?*
h. Keep a record of wind observations three times a day for 1 week. Make sure to record the data on a chart.
   After 1 week, do you detect
   any pattern of winds during the day?
   any pattern of winds from day to day?
   any prevailing or consistent direction from which the wind blows?
   any correlation between wind direction and weather conditions, such as temperatures, humidity, clouds, and so on?

i. Check local TV weather and newspapers for wind direction. *How do your data compare? If they differ, why do you think so?*

EVALUATE

j. To assess student understanding about how to use a wind vane to determine wind direction, ask students to respond to the following related items.
   The arrow of the wind vane is pointing to the west.

   1. From what direction is the wind blowing?
      A. North
      B. South
      C. East
      D. West

   2. What should this wind be called?
      A. a north wind
      B. a south wind
      C. an east wind
      D. a west wind

   3. Why did you select that name?
      A. Because winds are named for compass directions
      B. Because winds are named for the direction from which they are blowing
      C. Because winds are named for the direction toward which they are blowing

▶ *Science Background*

Wind, or moving air, brings about changing weather conditions. A **wind vane** is an instrument that shows the direction from which the wind is blowing. Winds are named for the direction from which they blow. For example, a north wind is blowing from the north to the south. An **anemometer** is an instrument that measures wind speed.

4. HOW CAN YOU MEASURE HOW FAST THE WIND BLOWS? HOW DOES WIND SPEED VARY WITH LOCATION AND TIME? (3–6)

Materials
- Long sewing needle
- Red marking pen
- 30 cm of monofilament nylon line
- Protractor
- Ping-Pong ball
- Bubble level (hardware store)
- Glue
- Tongue depressor
- Cardboard

Preparation

For teachers only: Thread a sewing needle with a 30 cm monofilament line, push the needle through the Ping-Pong ball, and knot and glue the end of the line to the Ping-Pong ball.

Safety Precautions

Use caution when pushing the needle through the Ping-Pong ball.

ENGAGE

a. Ask: *How can we measure how fast the wind blows?*

CONSTRUCT

b. Either the teacher or students should follow these directions to make an anemometer:
   1. Glue the other end of the line that is attached to the Ping-Pong ball to the center of a protractor. With the marking pen, color the line red.
   2. Glue a bubble level to the protractor as shown in the diagram.
   3. Glue a tongue depressor to the protractor as a handle. You now have an anemometer to measure wind speed.
   4. When the glue is dry, turn on the fan to produce a breeze so that you can test your anemometer.

EXPLORE

c. To take readings of the wind's speed, follow these directions:
   1. In the wind, hold the protractor level using the tongue depressor handle.
   2. Keep the protractor level by making sure the bubble is centered in the bubble level.
   3. Observe any swing of the Ping-Pong ball and string and see what angle the string makes on the protractor. For instance, in the diagram the string moved to approximately 65 degrees.

Bubble level

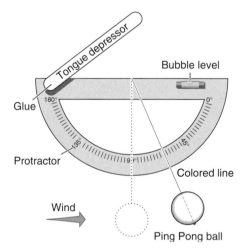

d. Explore how the angle of the string holding the Ping-Pong ball changes when you hold your anemometer different distances from the fan and in different positions in the breeze coming from it. Record your findings on a data table.

EXPLAIN

e. Invite students to describe their anemometers and explain how they work. Have them share their findings. Ask: *Where do your think the wind speed was greatest?* (Answers will vary.) *What evidence do you have to support your answer?* (It was where the Ping-Pong ball blew up at the greatest angle.) What have you measured? (angle of the string) *How do you think the angle of the string relates to the wind speed?* (The smaller the angle on the protractor crossed by the string, the greater the wind speed.)

f. Explain that the following table relates the wind speed to the angle of the string on the anemometer. Have students use the table to determine the wind speeds at the places they collected data in the fan's breeze.

PROTRACTOR ANEMOMETER WIND SPEEDS			
String Angle	**Wind Speed (Miles per Hour)**	**String Angle**	**Wind Speed (Miles per Hour)**
90°	0	50°	18.0
85°	5.8	45°	19.6
80°	8.2	40°	21.9
75°	10.1	35°	23.4
70°	11.8	30°	25.8
65°	13.4	25°	28.7
60°	14.9	20°	32.5
55°	16.4		

ELABORATE

g. At different times over the next few days, use your anemometer in various spots on your school grounds and then refer to the chart to find the wind speed.

After you have tested the wind speed in different places on your school grounds, record the data on a chart like this one.

Date	
Time	
Protractor angle	
Wind speed	
Wind direction	

h. Guide students to use their charts to answer these questions:
Where does the wind blow the fastest on your school grounds?
Does wind blow faster at ground level or at higher levels?
Is there a place where wind blows faster, such as between two buildings or at a corner of two wings of a building? Why?

EVALUATE

i. To assess student understanding of how to determine wind speed with the anemometer, have students respond to the following item.

1. Max is holding his anemometer at 5:00 p.m. outside of his house. The string crosses the protractor at the 80° mark. Based on the table, what is the approximate wind speed?
A. 5 miles per hour
B. 8 miles per hour
C. 32 miles per hour
D. 80 miles per hour

5. HOW CAN YOU MEASURE RELATIVE HUMIDITY AND HUMIDITY CHANGES? (3–6)

Materials
- Two thermometers
- Wide cotton shoelace
- Small dish of water
- Empty milk carton
- Thread
- Piece of cardboard

ENGAGE

a. Ask: What is humidity? How can it be measured?

Construct

b. Give students these instructions:
1. Obtain an empty milk carton, two identical thermometers, a cotton shoelace, and some thread. *Note:* The two thermometers should register the same temperature before the shoelace is placed over one of them; otherwise, the difference in readings must be considered a constant that is part of all computations.
2. Cut a 10 cm section from the cotton shoelace and slip the section over the bulb of one of the thermometers. Tie the shoelace section with thread above and below the bulb to hold the shoelace in place. Thread the other end of the 10 cm section through a hole in the milk carton and allow it to rest in water inside the milk carton.
3. Attach both thermometers to the milk carton as shown in the diagram.

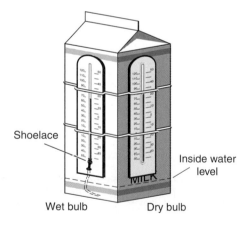

Shoelace

Inside water level

Wet bulb   Dry bulb

EXPLORE

c. Ask: *What do you think might happen to the thermometer with the wet shoelace? Why do you think so?*
d. When their shoelace is wet, tell students to fan it with a piece of cardboard for 1 minute. Then have them check the temperature readings of the two thermometers.

EXPLAIN

e. Tell the class that they have built **hygrometers**— instruments that measure the relative humidity in the atmosphere.
f. Have each student group post their results on a class chart for all to see. Discuss the data. Ask: *How do you account for the difference in readings between the thermometer with the shoelace (called the "wet bulb") and the one without the shoelace (called the "dry bulb")?*

g. Explain that when the shoelace is wet, the evaporation of the water results in a cooling of the wet-bulb thermometer, whereas the dry-bulb thermometer continues to read the temperature of the air around it. Ask: *Why do you think you were asked to fan the wet-bulb thermometer?*

h. Demonstrate how to use the relative humidity table provided. To locate the relative humidity on the table, find the temperature of the dry-bulb thermometer on the y-axis (vertical axis) and the difference between the readings of the two thermometers on the x-axis (horizontal axis). The example described after the following table shows a dry-bulb temperature of 76°F, a difference of 8°F (wet-bulb, 68°F), and a relative humidity of 67%.

FINDING RELATIVE HUMIDITY IN PERCENT

Difference in degrees between wet-bulb and dry bulb thermometers

Air temperature (reading of dry-bulb thermometer) in degrees fahrenheit

	1	2	3	4	5	6	7	8	9	10	11	12	13	14	15	16	17	18	19	20	21	22	23	24	25	26	27	28	29	30
30°	89	78	68	57	47	37	27	17	8																					
32°	90	79	69	60	50	41	31	22	13	4																				
34°	90	81	72	62	53	44	35	27	18	9	1																			
36°	91	82	73	65	56	48	39	31	23	14	6																			
38°	91	83	75	67	59	51	43	35	27	19	12	4																		
40°	92	84	76	68	61	53	46	38	31	23	16	9	2																	
42°	92	85	77	70	62	55	48	41	34	28	21	14	7																	
44°	93	85	78	71	64	57	51	44	37	31	24	18	12	5																
46°	93	86	79	72	65	59	53	46	40	34	28	22	16	10	4															
48°	93	87	80	73	67	60	54	48	42	36	31	25	19	14	8	3														
50°	93	87	81	74	68	62	56	50	44	39	33	28	22	17	12	7	2													
52°	94	88	81	75	69	63	58	52	46	41	36	30	25	20	15	10	6													
54°	94	88	82	76	70	65	59	54	48	43	38	33	28	23	18	14	9	5												
56°	94	88	82	77	71	66	61	55	50	45	40	35	31	26	21	17	12	8	4											
58°	94	89	83	77	72	67	62	57	52	47	42	38	33	28	24	20	15	11	7	3										
60°	94	89	84	78	73	68	63	58	53	49	44	40	35	31	27	22	18	14	10	6	2									
62°	94	89	84	79	74	69	64	60	55	50	46	41	37	33	29	25	21	17	13	9	6	2								
64°	95	90	85	79	75	70	66	61	56	52	48	43	39	35	31	27	23	20	16	12	9	5	2							
66°	95	90	85	80	76	71	66	62	58	53	49	45	41	37	33	29	26	22	18	15	11	8	5	1						
68°	95	90	85	81	76	72	67	63	59	55	51	47	43	39	35	31	28	24	21	17	14	11	8	4	1					
70°	95	90	86	81	77	72	68	64	60	56	52	48	44	40	37	33	30	26	23	20	17	13	10	7	4	1				
72°	95	91	86	82	78	73	69	65	61	57	53	49	46	42	39	35	32	28	25	22	19	16	13	10	7	4	1			
74°	95	91	86	82	78	74	70	66	62	58	54	51	47	44	40	37	34	30	27	24	21	18	15	12	9	7	4	1		
76°	96	91	87	83	78	74	70	67	63	59	55	52	48	45	42	38	35	32	29	26	23	20	17	14	12	9	6	4	1	
78°	96	91	87	83	79	75	71	67	64	60	57	53	50	46	43	40	37	34	31	28	25	22	19	16	14	11	9	6	4	1
80°	96	91	87	83	79	76	72	68	64	61	57	54	51	47	44	41	38	35	32	29	27	24	21	18	16	13	11	8	6	4
82°	96	91	87	83	79	76	72	69	65	62	58	55	52	49	46	43	40	37	34	31	28	25	23	20	18	15	13	10	8	6
84°	96	92	88	84	80	77	73	70	66	63	59	56	53	50	47	44	41	38	35	32	30	27	25	22	20	17	15	12	10	8
86°	96	92	88	84	80	77	73	70	66	63	60	57	54	51	48	45	42	39	37	34	31	29	26	24	21	19	17	14	12	10
88°	96	92	88	85	81	78	74	71	67	64	61	58	55	52	49	46	43	41	38	35	33	30	28	25	23	21	18	16	14	12
90°	96	92	88	85	81	78	74	71	68	64	61	58	56	53	50	47	44	42	39	37	34	32	29	27	24	22	20	18	16	14

Example:
Temperature of dry-bulb thermometer 76°
Temperature of wet-bulb thermometer 68°
The difference is 8°

Find 76° in the dry-bulb column and 8° in the difference column. Where these two columns meet, you read the relative humidity. In this case, it is 67%.

ELABORATE

i. Take readings on your hygrometer every day for 2 weeks and record your findings. Also try readings in different places.

j. Discuss the data groups have collected. Ask: *What patterns have you discovered? Using your hygrometer, can you predict which days are better for drying clothes outside?*

k. Use library and Internet resources to find the answer to this question: *How is relative humidity used by weather forecasters to predict weather?*

EVALUATE

1. To check student understanding about how to use the hygrometer and the Finding Relative Humidity in Percent chart to measure relative humidity, have students answer the following items.

   1. On the hygrometer the wet-bulb thermometer reads 66°F and the dry-bulb thermometer reads 84°F. What is the relative humidity?
      A. 18%
      B. 38%
      C. 66%
      D. 84%

   2. *Explain how you determined the relative humidity from the data given in the previous problem.*

▶ *Science Background*

Air contains moisture (from evaporated water from the ground, rivers, lakes, and oceans). Air pressure and temperature affect the amount of moisture air can hold at any given time. Relative humidity is the amount of water vapor actually contained in volume of air divided by the maximum amount that could be contained in the same volume.

III. THE EARTH'S OCEANS

Our earth has been called *the water planet*. Children are naturally drawn to water. "Whether they are playing in a pond, chasing waves at the beach, or splashing in a rain puddle on a city street, children are entranced by water" (Valerie Chase, 1997, *Living in Water*. Baltimore: National Aquarium in Baltimore, p. 1).

The earth's water is found in oceans, lakes, rivers, ponds, and streams; in ground water systems; and in ice and water vapor forms. Water circulates through the crust, atmosphere, and oceans of the earth in the *water cycle*. Rain falling on land collects in rivers and lakes, soil, and porous layers of rock, and much of it flows back to the oceans.

More than 97% of all the water on the earth is salt water in ocean basins. Oceans, as well as the land, are contained within the crust of the earth. Oceans cover 71% of the earth's surface, with land covering 29%. There are four oceans on the earth: Pacific Ocean, Atlantic Ocean, Indian Ocean, and Arctic Ocean. The Antarctic Ocean is included with the Pacific, Atlantic, and Indian Oceans. Seas, gulfs, and bays are all parts of oceans that are partially enclosed by land.

Plants and animals survive in the ocean, on the ocean floor and ocean trenches, or on rocky shores, because they have adapted to the conditions of these tremendously different habitats. For example, plants and animals on the seashore must resist battering ocean waves or find security in crevices and fissures. Most of the animals on sandy shores live below the surface. A sandy beach may appear lifeless, but when the tide rolls in, the inhabitants spring into action and an astounding variety of life is revealed.

NSES Science Standards

All students should develop an understanding of

• structure of the earth's systems (5–8).

NSES   Concepts and Principles That Support the Standards

- In the course of the water cycle, water evaporates from the earth's surface, rises and cools as it moves to higher elevations, condenses as rain or snow, and falls to the surface where it collects in lakes, oceans, soils, and underground (5–8).
- Water is a solvent. As it passes through the water cycle, it dissolves minerals and gases and carries them to the oceans (5–8).
- Oceans have a major effect on climate, because water in the ocean holds a large amount of heat (5–8).

Objectives

1. Demonstrate that the water pressure in a body of water increases with depth.
2. Demonstrate and explain that the buoyant force of salt water is greater than the buoyant force of fresh water.
3. Compare the surface area of the earth that is ocean with that which is land.
4. Compare the amount of water in the oceans with the total amount of water in the earth system.
5. Identify a variety of foods that contain nutrients from ocean organisms.
6. Describe and explain the effects of pollution on life in water.

1. WHAT PART OF THE EARTH'S SURFACE IS COVERED BY OCEANS? (3–6)

Materials

- Inflatable globe (preferably showing natural land features rather than political boundaries)

ENGAGE

a. Hold up the inflatable globe. Ask: *What is this globe a model of?* (Earth) *How is it like the real earth and how is it different? What is shown on the globe's surface?* (Land and oceans) *About how much of the earth is covered by oceans? How could we use the globe to find out?*

EXPLORE

b. Tell the class we need to collect data by using a sampling method. Help the students follow these steps:
   1. Show the class a two-column table with the headings "Ocean" and "Land."
   2. Select a student to be the record keeper.
   3. Instruct one student to toss the inflatable globe to another student.
   4. The person who catches the globe will look to see if his or her right thumb is on an ocean or land part of the globe's surface and report this information to the record keeper.
   5. The record keeper will make a tally mark in the appropriate column on the table.
   6. Then the inflatable globe should be tossed to another student and the process repeated.
   7. Continue for a total of 100 tosses.

EXPLAIN

c. Ask: *How many times out of 100 tosses was the catcher's right thumb on an ocean area?* (Approximately 70 times) *How many times out of 100 tosses was the catcher's right thumb on a land area?* (Approximately 30 times)

d. Ask: *Why do you think the catcher's right thumb was on an ocean area more often than on a land area?* (Because more of the surface of the inflatable globe is ocean area so there is more chance of the catcher's right thumb being on an ocean.) Discuss the term *percent* with the class. *What percent of the times was the catcher's thumb on an ocean area?* (The answer should be close to 70%.) *What percent of the times was the catcher's thumb on a land area?* (Answer should be close to 30%.)

ELABORATE   e. Challenge the class to find out what percent of the earth's surface is covered by oceans using their textbook or other references. (70%) Ask the class to explain how well and why this sampling technique worked to estimate the relative amount of land and ocean on the earth's surface.

2. WHAT PART OF THE EARTH'S WATER IS IN THE OCEANS? (3–8)

Materials
- Six 2-liter bottles
- Graduated cylinders
- Permanent marker
- Colored water

ENGAGE   a. Ask: *What part of the earth's water is in the oceans? How could we make a model to show this?*

EXPLORE   b. Conduct this teacher demonstration:
        1. Show the class a 2-liter bottle labeled "All Earth's Water" filled with 2,000 ml of colored water. Tell them this represents all the water on the earth.
        2. Then display five other 2-liter bottles containing the following volumes of colored water on a table in front of a sheet of chart paper: Bottle A, 1,944 ml; Bottle B, 1,750 ml; Bottle C, 1,400 ml; Bottle D, 1,000 ml; Bottle E, 700 ml.
        3. Tell the students that one of these bottles represents the amount of water in the earth's oceans.
        4. Ask students to vote for the one they think represents the water in the earth's oceans by writing the letter of their choice on a Post-It note. Have the students stick their Post-It in a column above the bottle that matches the letter they chose.

EXPLAIN   c. Tell the class they have just created a histogram of their ideas. Ask: *Which bottle do most of you think represents the water in the earth's oceans? How do you know? How could we find out which bottle best represents the amount of water in the earth's oceans?*
     d. Ask groups of students to decide what information they would need and how they would make the bottle that represents the water in the earth's oceans. After they have had some discussion time, provide the information that 97.2% of the earth's water is in the oceans. You might also reveal that the bottle labeled "All Earth's Water" contains 2,000 ml of colored water.

ELABORATE   e. Allow groups to use colored water, graduated cylinders, and a 2-liter bottle to create a model that represents the amount of water in the oceans.

f. Encourage groups to compare their completed model with the "All Earth's Water" bottle. Ask each group to explain to the class how they decided how much water to put in the bottle and how they carried out their idea.

g. Based on the models constructed by the groups, ask them to vote again (this time by a show of hands) for the lettered bottle that they think best represents the amount of water in the earth's oceans. (They should select bottle A.) Ask: *Are you surprised by how much of the earth's water is in the oceans? Do you think that the oceans are an important part of our planet? Why?*

h. Ask students to list the places that water is found in the earth's system. Answers might include lakes, rivers, ponds, oceans, puddles, in the soil, underground, in the air as water vapor, in clouds as water droplets, frozen in ice caps and glaciers, and so on. Challenge them to find out how much of the earth's water is found in each and to create a visual representation of their findings. They might make a model or a circle graph.[9]

EVALUATE

i. The products from the elaborate phase of the lesson could be assessed with the help of the following rubric.

Criteria	Developing	Proficient	Exemplary
Accuracy of data	Some data is inaccurate	All data is accurate	All data is accurate and sources for data are listed
Places water is found	Less than 8 places are listed with data	At least 8 places are listed with data	More than 8 places are listed with data
Visual representation	Graph or model does not show correct proportions or is not labeled to show what parts of the graph or model represent each water place	Model, circle graph, or bar graph shows relative proportions of water in different places	Meets Proficient expectations and includes % of water on earth for each place

3. DO OBJECTS FLOAT DIFFERENTLY IN SALT WATER THAN IN FRESH WATER? (4–6)

Materials

- Two raw eggs
- Two clear glass containers
- Box of kosher or pickling salt, which can be purchased in many supermarkets. When dissolved in water, this salt produces a clear solution. Table salt can be substituted, but it makes a cloudy rather than a clear solution
- Large container for mixing concentrated salt water

[9]Information relating to this investigation is available at http://www.sea.edu/12lessonplans/K12WatersEarth.htm.

Preparation

For this teacher demonstration, you will need a mixture of concentrated salt water for one container and an equal amount of fresh water for the other container. To prepare for the demonstration, follow these steps:

1. Prepare the salt water by mixing one part salt with four parts cool water in a large container. For example, if you use 300 ml cups (10 oz), add half a cup of salt to 2 cups of water. Stir the salt-water mixture thoroughly until the salt dissolves.
2. Pour concentrated salt water into one container and put an equal amount of fresh water in the other container.

ENGAGE

a. Show the students the two containers of water without discussing their contents. Ask: *Do you think an egg will float in water?*

EXPLORE

b. Put an egg in each container. Have students record their observations and questions on an I Notice / I Wonder chart in their science notebooks.

EXPLAIN

c. Ask: *What did you observe?* Discuss students' observations with them. Ask: *Why do you think the egg floated in one container of water and sank in the other one?* Through questioning and discussion, lead students to understand that salt water is denser than fresh water. The denser salt water was able to support the egg. Ask: *Would it be easier for you to float in a fresh water lake or in the ocean? Why?*

ELABORATE

d. Ask: *How much salt will need to be added to fresh water to increase its density so that it will support an egg?*
e. Place an egg in the fresh water. Add salt a spoonful at a time, stirring the water, until the egg rises and floats. Count the number of spoonfuls of salt needed. Measure the volume of salt added and compare it to the original volume of the water.[10]

4. WHAT AFFECTS THE PRESSURE OF A STREAM OF WATER? (3–5)

Materials

- Plastic gallon milk jug
- Water
- Nail or pencil

ENGAGE

a. Ask: *If the side of a plastic milk jug were punctured with very small holes (one above another) and the jug were then filled with water, what do you think would happen to the water? How would the water pour out of the holes?*

---

[10]For additional information on this activity, see Science and Technology for Children (STC), 1995. *Floating and Sinking: Teacher's Guide.* Carolina Biological Supply Co., Burlington, NC.

EXPLORE

b. Prepare and perform this teacher demonstration for students:
   1. Obtain a clean, plastic, 1-gallon milk jug.
   2. About 4 cm from the bottom of the milk jug, puncture a very small hole with a pencil or nail. Puncture three additional small holes 1 cm apart, vertically, above the first hole as in the diagram. Put masking tape over the holes.
      Note: Do not make the holes too large.

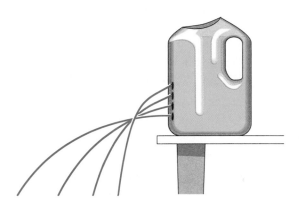

   3. Fill the container half full with water. Hold the plastic jug over a sink, large basin, or tub, and remove the masking tape as shown.
c. Ask: *What do you notice about the way the water comes out of the holes? Which stream went the greatest distance? Which stream went the least distance?*

EXPLAIN

d. Ask: *Why do you think the water comes out of the holes like this?*
e. Ask: *If the jug were filled closer to the top with water, do you think there would be a difference in the way the water comes out?* Tape over the holes, refill the jug until the water is within a centimeter of the top, and remove the tape. Ask: *What do you notice about the way the water comes out of the holes? What difference did you notice in the way the water came from the holes of the jug when there was less water and when there was more water in it?*
f. Ask: *What can you conclude about how water pressure varies with depth?*

ELABORATE

g. Ask: *What results do you think you would get if you used a quart, half-gallon, or 2-gallon container? Try it and record your findings.*

5. WHAT FOODS CONTAIN PRODUCTS FROM THE OCEAN? (4–6)

Materials

- Food product labels
- Grocery store advertisements
- Sorting mats and transparency with a Venn diagram as shown

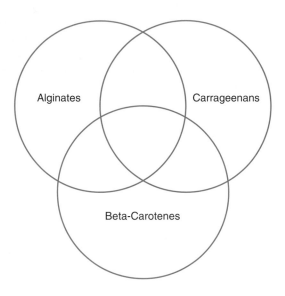

Preparation

Several weeks before this lesson, ask your students and colleagues to collect the ingredient lists from the following products they might use at home: brownie mix, cheese, chocolate milk, coffee creamer, cottage cheese, egg substitute, evaporated milk, frozen foods and desserts, frozen yogurt, ice cream, infant formula, margarine, mayonnaise, multiple vitamins, pet food, pudding, relishes, salad dressing, sauces and gravies, sour cream, toothpaste, whipped topping, whipping cream, and yogurt. Provide a box for collection of the labels and containers in your classroom.

ENGAGE

a. Distribute the grocery store advertisements to the class and encourage them to look them over. Ask: *Do you eat anything that comes from the ocean?* (Students will probably suggest fish, shrimp, clams, etc.) *What do these products eat?* (Students will probably say other smaller animals in the ocean.) *Are there plants in the ocean?* (Students will probably say seaweed or algae.) *Do some of the animals in the ocean eat the ocean plants? Do you eat any of the ocean plants?* (Some students may know that seaweed is used to wrap sushi.)

EXPLORE

b. Guide students to collect data following these procedures:
   1. With students working in small groups (four students per group is best), distribute to each group at least 10 ingredient lists from different products from the collection box. The groups do not need to have the same assortment of ingredient lists.
   2. Provide each group with a copy of the Venn diagram. Give the students a few minutes to look at their materials. Suggest that they use the Venn diagram to organize their ingredient lists based on the presence of alginates, carrageenans, and beta-carotenes.
   3. If students need assistance, display the transparency of the Venn diagram on the overhead projector and model the procedure. Ask a student to read an ingredient list to look for any or all of these ingredients. Then write the name of the product in the appropriate segment of the Venn diagram. Do several more examples if necessary.
   4. Each group should write the names of each of the products for which they have an ingredients list on their Venn diagram. If you want them to include more product names, they can switch label sets with another group.

EXPLAIN

c. Ask the groups to share their findings with the class. Have them describe what the product names in each segment of the Venn diagram have in common.

d. Ask if anyone knows what these ingredients are. Then tell the students that each of these ingredients comes from seaweeds, which are large forms of marine algae that grow in coastal waters around the world. The three terms on the Venn diagram refer to compounds extracted from each of the three main kinds of marine algae: brown, red, and green. Alginates come from brown algae. They make water-based products thicker, creamier, and more stable. In ice cream, they prevent the formation of ice crystals. Carrageenans come from red algae. They are used in stabilizing and gelling foods, cosmetics, pharmaceuticals, and industrial products. Beta-carotene comes from green algae. It is a natural pigment that is used as yellow-orange food coloring and may help prevent certain types of cancers.

ELABORATE

e. Challenge students to find other products that contain these ingredients in their pantries or at the grocery store. Bring samples of edible seaweed such as nori, kombu, dulse, and kelp to class for students to observe. Explain that these marine algae are used in many Asian cuisines, often as wrappers for rice, meat, and vegetables (sushi). Using proper sanitation precautions, offer samples of the edible seaweed to students who wish to try it.[11]

6. WHAT ARE SOME EFFECTS OF WATER POLLUTION? (3–8)

Materials

- For each group, four quart-sized or 2-liter clear containers (plastic soda bottles, food jars with covers, etc.)
- Tap water aged for 3 to 4 days
- Soil and/or gravel from an aquarium or pond
- Water with algae and other aquatic microorganisms from a freshwater aquarium or a pond
- Measuring cups and spoons
- Plant fertilizer
- Hand lenses for each group
- Liquid laundry detergent (not green)
- Motor oil
- Vinegar

Preparation

Two weeks in advance of conducting this activity, four jars should be set up by you and designated student helpers for each cooperative group of students:

1. Fill four containers one-third full with aged tap water, add 4 cm of pond soil or aquarium gravel, and then fill the rest of the jar with pond water and algae.
2. Add 1 teaspoon of plant fertilizer to each jar, stir well, and loosely screw on the jar covers.
3. Put the jars near the window in good, indirect light or under a strong artificial light.
4. Label the jars A, B, C, and D.

---

[11] Adapted from two Internet lessons: "There Are Algae in Your House!" from the Ocean Planet website of the Smithsonian (http://oceancolor.gsfc.nasa.gov/seaWIFS) and "Is There Seaweed/Algae in Your Food?" from Neptune's website (http://pao.cnmoc.navy.mil/educate/Neptune/lesson/social/algae.htm).

ENGAGE

a. Ask: *What things do people do, sometimes unknowingly, that result in water pollution? How can water pollution affect water environments in ways that are detrimental to the organisms that live in or depend on the water?*

EXPLORE

b. Guide students to conduct this investigation:

1. Provide each group of students the four jars that were set up 2 weeks earlier. The jars contain pond water, algae, pond soil or aquarium gravel, and fertilizer.
2. Instruct the groups to observe and describe on their record sheets how each jar looks. Make sure students use hand lenses.

RECORDING OBSERVATIONS		
Date _____ Observers'/Recorders' Names _____		
Jar	Observation Before Additive	Observation After Additive
A		
B		
C		
D		

3. Students should add 2 tablespoons of detergent to jar A, enough motor oil to cover the surface of jar B, and 1/4 to 1/2 cup (250 ml) of vinegar to jar C. Jar D will not have any additive and will be the control. See the diagram.

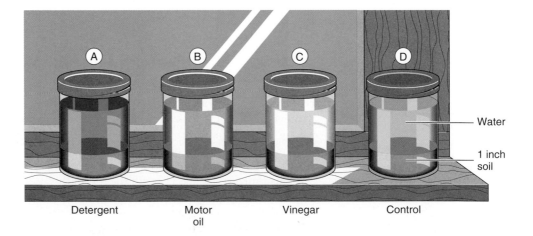

Detergent   Motor oil   Vinegar   Control

4. Students should loosely cover the jars and return them to the light as before.
5. Ask: *What do you think might happen in each of the jars?*
6. Provide time for students to observe and record their observations two to three times a week. After 4 weeks, groups should summarize their observations.

EXPLAIN

c. Ask: *What changes did each jar go through? Why do you think jars A, B, and C went through such changes?*

ELABORATE

d. Guide students to related readings in texts or online that provide further information about the effects of these pollutants on water and on organisms exposed to the polluted water.

e. Ask:
How could you apply these findings?
How might you set up activities to try to reverse the effects of the pollutants used in jars A, B, and C?
Where in everyday life do we see the effects of water pollution like that in jars A, B, and C? How could these effects be prevented?

7. HOW CAN WE TRY TO REVERSE THE EFFECTS OF AN OIL SPILL? (3–8)

Materials

- Aluminum pan
- Motor oil
- Feathers
- Paper towels
- Dishwashing liquid
- Four hard-boiled eggs
- Paper plate
- Very large rubber band
- Turkey baster

ENGAGE

a. Ask:
How difficult do you think it is to clean up an oil spill? How do you think it could be done?
What is the most effective way to clean up an oil spill?
What devastating effects does an oil spill have on the environment?

EXPLORE

b. Fill an aluminum pan half full of water, cover the water surface with motor oil, and use it for the following parts of the activity.

c. Feathers in an oil–water mix. Leave feathers in the oil–water mix for several minutes. Remove the feathers. Ask: *How do you think we might remove oil from the feathers?* Try wiping the feathers with paper towels. Ask: *Did wiping with paper towels remove all the oil?* Try cleaning the feathers with dishwashing liquid. Ask: *Which method of cleaning the oil off the feathers was better? What other ways might we try to remove the oil from feathers?* Try them.

d. Eggs in an oil–water mix. Put four hard-boiled eggs (with shells on) into the oil–water mix and then remove one egg at a time after each of these intervals: 15 minutes, 30 minutes, 60 minutes, and 120 minutes. Ask: *What happens to the eggs?* Try removing the oil from the eggs with the methods you used for the feathers. After cleaning the oil off the eggs, crack and remove the shells. Ask: *Did the oil get inside the egg that was in the oil for 15 minutes? the one for 30 minutes? the one for 60 minutes? the one for 120 minutes?* Record your findings. Ask: *If oil did get into the egg, can it be removed?*

e. Removing or containing oil. Using the following materials, how might you remove or keep the oil from spreading: paper towel, dishwashing liquid, turkey baster, large rubber band? Lay a paper towel on the surface of the oil and let it stay for 3 minutes. Remove the paper towel and put it on the paper plate. Ask: *What do you see happening to the paper towel and oil?* Add more motor oil, if needed, and spread a very large rubber band on the top of the oil. Ask: *What happens to the oil?* Using the turkey baster, try to remove the oil. Ask: *What happens to the oil?* Replace the oil into the pan of water. Add several drops of dishwashing liquid. Ask: *What happens to the oil?* Ask: *Which method was best for removing the oil? Which method was best for keeping the oil together in one place?*

EXPLAIN

f. Ask: *What possible problems and adverse effects might result when chemicals are used to remove oil from animals in a real oil spill? How might an oil spill in Alaska affect people in the continental United States? Sometimes oil spills are purposely set on fire. What adverse effects might this have on the environment?* Lead students to understand that oil spills adversely affect land and water plants and animals directly by coating them with oil, often leading to their deaths. In addition, an oil spill affects future plant and animal life by destroying eggs and interfering with plant reproduction. Sometimes, the procedures used to reverse oil spills can interfere with environmental interrelationships, especially when chemicals are used.

Additional Activities Related to Oceans

Scientific study of the oceans bridges many science disciplines. Marine biologists monitor animals and plants that live in ocean habitats. Some chemists investigate mineral content and salinity levels of oceans. Physical oceanographers study wave and tidal action. Meteorologists observe weather systems affected by ocean currents. Therefore, many of the activities from previous sections could be included in a study of the oceans.

- Activities on the water cycle, such as "How Much Water Evaporates from an Open Aquarium, and Where Does It Go?" (p. A-219), "How Can You Promote the Evaporation of Water?" (p. A-222), and "What Is Condensation? How Does It Occur?" (p. A-225) can contribute to an understanding of how water circulates between land, the atmosphere, and bodies of water.
- Activities on aquariums, including "How Can We Construct an Aquarium Habitat?" (p. A-158), "What Can We Observe in an Aquarium?" (p. A-160), and "What Environmental Factors Affect Life in an Aquarium Habitat?" (p. A-181) involve simulations of marine environments.
- "How Can Salt Crystals Be Grown?" (p. A-209) could help to explain formation of sea salt and the increased salinity of some tidal pools. "How Can Evaporation and Condensation Be Used to Desalinate Salt Water?" (p. A-226) further explores the nature of salt water.

IV. VIEWING THE SKY FROM EARTH

 ## A. POSITIONS AND MOTIONS OF THE SUN, MOON, AND STARS

▶ *Science Background*

Beyond the earth's atmosphere, other objects are visible in the earth's sky. The brightest and most noticeable of these is our sun, the star at the center of our solar system. Energy from the sun heats both the ocean and land, drives the process of photosynthesis enabling plants to produce food, and illuminates our world during the daytime. Our moon appears about the size of the sun in our sky, though it does not shine as brightly. Rather than producing its own light, the moon is visible because of reflected sunlight. Other planets in our solar system are also visible in the earth's sky. Mercury, Venus, Mars, Jupiter, and Saturn appear at times in the night sky, looking like bright, non-twinkling stars.

Objects in our sky appear to move because the earth rotates on its axis once every 24 hours, the period known as 1 day. Though it appears that the sun, moon, planets, and most of the stars rise in the east and set in the west, it is really the earth's turning that is responsible for this apparent motion. Polaris, the North Star, because of its unique location directly above the earth's north pole, appears to remain stationary in the sky for viewers in the northern hemisphere.

NSES

Science Standards

As a result of their science activities, all students should develop an understanding of

- objects in the sky (K–4).
- changes in the earth and sky (K–4).
- the earth in the solar system (5–8).

Concepts and Principles That Support the Standards

- The sun, moon, and stars all have properties, locations, and movements that can be observed and described (K–4).
- The sun has a pattern of movement through the sky. It appears to move across the sky in the same way every day, but its path slowly changes during the season (K–4).

Objectives

1. Observe and describe properties, locations, and movements of the sun, moon, and stars in the sky.
2. Describe the apparent daily motion of the sun across the sky and discuss how this motion varies during the year.
3. Compare and contrast the apparent motion of the sun across the sky with the apparent motion of the moon across the sky.
4. Observe, describe, and name the moon's phases as they change during the month, and explain why this happens.
5. Use compass directions and angles to describe the position of objects in the sky.

1. WHAT CAUSES SHADOWS? (K–2)

Materials

- Overhead projector
- Projection screen or blank wall

ENGAGE

a. Ask: *How are shadows formed?*

EXPLORE

    b. Turn on the overhead projector so that it illuminates the projection screen or blank wall. Select several students to stand between the projector and the screen (facing the screen). Ask: *What do you see on the screen?* (Shadows) *What causes these shadows?*

    c. Ask: *What is necessary for a shadow to form? If we didn't have the light from the overhead or the students standing here, would there be a shadow on the screen? How could we find out?* Students may suggest having the volunteer students move out of the light or turning off the overhead. Try these things and any other suggestions from students.

EXPLAIN

    d. Ask: *When were shadows produced? What did they look like? What two things must you have to create a shadow?* Lead the children to the realization that in order to have a shadow, there must be a light source and an object to block the light. Encourage them to develop an operational definition of a shadow as dark area caused by the blocking of light.

2. HOW CAN SHADOWS BE CHANGED? (K–2)

Materials

- Flashlight
- Two large sheets of white paper
- Scissors
- Plastic funnel
- Pencil or crayon

ENGAGE

    a. Ask: *Are shadows of the same object always the same size and shape?* Encourage students to share their ideas.

EXPLORE

    b. Working with a partner, students should put a funnel on a large sheet of white paper. Suggest that they use the flashlight to make a shadow of the funnel on the paper. Encourage them to try shining the flashlight from different positions. Ask: *How does the shadow change?*

    c. Suggest that students do the following to record the size and shape of two shadows. One student should shine the flashlight on the funnel while the other one traces and cuts the shadow shape out with the scissors, in this sequence:

        1. First, while holding the flashlight low and to the side, trace and cut out the shadow of the funnel. Label it "low."

        2. Next, switch roles with your partner. Put a new piece of white paper under the funnel, hold the flashlight high, and then trace and cut out the shadow of the funnel. Label it "high."

        3. Compare the size and shape of the two cutout shadows.

EXPLAIN

d. Ask: *Are both of your shadow shapes the same?* (No) *How are they different?* (They are different sizes and shapes.) *Which one is longer?* (The one labeled "low" is longer.) *Which one is shorter?* (The one labeled "high" is shorter.) *What caused the difference in shapes?* (The position of the light source.) Try to lead the students to the conclusion that the position of the light source affects the shadow's size and shape. When the light source is low, shining on the object from the side, the shadow is long and when the light source is high, shining down on the object from above, the shadow is short.

ELABORATE

e. Ask: *What happens to the shadow if you move the light source in an arc from one side of the object, over it, and to the other side of the object?* This simulates the apparent motion of the sun in the sky and provides background experience for future activities.

EVALUATE

f. To see if students understand the relationship between the position of a light source and the length and direction of the shadow of a wooden block on a table, have students match the following statements:

Position of light source
1. Light is directly above the block.

2. Light is on the table on the right side of the block.
3. Light is above the table to the right side of the block.
4. Light is on the table on the left side of the block.
5. Light is above the table to the left side of the block.

Length and direction of shadow
A. Very long shadow to the left of the block.

B. Very long shadow to the right of the block.

C. Medium-long shadow to the right of the block.

D. No shadow, or very short shadow all around the block.

E. Medium-long shadow to the left of the block.

3. HOW DO SHADOWS CAUSED BY THE SUN CHANGE DURING THE DAY? (K–4)

Materials

- Flagpole or fence post
- Sidewalk chalk
- Paint stirrers (to use as stakes in the lawn)

ENGAGE

a. Ask: *Do you think that shadows outdoors change during the day? How might we find out?*

EXPLORE

b. On a sunny day, take the class outside to the flagpole or a fence post early in the morning. Ask: *Does the flagpole or fence post have a shadow? How could we mark the position of this shadow?*

c. Show the students the sidewalk chalk and paint stirrers if they need a hint. Have the students identify the "end" of the shadow, that is, the part cast by the top of the flagpole or the fence post. If the end of the shadow falls on concrete, sidewalk chalk can be used to mark its position. If the end of the shadow falls on grass, a paint stirrer can be used as a stake to mark its position. Record the time of the observation either in chalk on the concrete or with pencil on the paint stirrer. Throughout the day, about once each hour if possible, return to the flagpole or fence post with the class to mark the shadow's current position.

EXPLAIN

d. After making the final afternoon observation, ask: *What did you find out about how the shadow changed during the day?* (It started out long on that side, then got shorter, then got longer on the other side.) *Why do you think the shadow changed in this way?* (Because the sun seemed to move across the sky.) *How did the position of the sun change during our observations today?* (Indicating directions, lead students to understand that it started out low over there in the morning, moved higher in the sky around noon, then kept moving that way in the afternoon.) Develop the concept that the sun appeared to move from east to west in the sky during the day and that caused the size, shape, and direction of the shadow to change over time.

ELABORATE

e. Ask: *Do you think the flagpole or fence post shadow will change the same way tomorrow? next week? next month? How could we find out?* Assist the students in continuing their investigation of shadow positions throughout the school year and help them look for patterns in their findings.

EVALUATE

f. To check student understanding about how shadows change throughout the day have them fill in the blanks in the following story.

Early in the morning the sun is low in the _____.
When I am outside early on a sunny morning my shadow is _____ and points toward the _____.
During the morning the _____ rises higher in the sky.
My shadow gets _____.
My shadow is _____ at noon when the sun is almost _____.
During the afternoon my shadow becomes _____.
In the evening the sun is low in the _____.
My shadow is _____ and points toward the _____.

4. HOW CAN SHADOWS TELL YOU WHEN IT IS LOCAL NOON? (4–6)

Materials

For each small group of students

- Long nail
- Hammer
- Sheets of white paper (8.5 × 11 inches)
- Rectangular board big enough to hold the paper
- Pencil
- Clock or watch
- Metric ruler

ENGAGE

a. Ask: *On a sunny day, at what time are shadows the shortest? How could we find out? How does the position of the sun in the sky relate to the length of the shadow cast by an object?*

EXPLORE

b. Put a piece of paper in the middle of the board. Hammer the nail into the board and paper as shown, making sure the nail will not easily come out of the board.

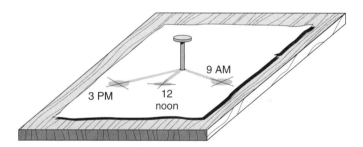

c. Late in the morning about 10:30, place the board where it will get sunlight until about 2:00 in the afternoon. Do not move the board during your observations. Every half hour or at shorter intervals, draw an X at the end of the shadow cast by the nail. Beside the X, note the time of each observation.

d. Upon returning to the classroom, carefully measure the distance between each X and the nail to the nearest millimeter. Create a data table that shows the time of the observation and the length of the corresponding shadow. Construct a line graph to represent these data. The manipulated or independent variable, "time of observation," should be plotted on the *x*-axis; the responding or dependent variable, "shadow length," should be plotted on the *y*-axis.

EXPLAIN

c. Ask: *Did the shadow length change during your observation period? When was it shortest? When would you expect to have the shortest shadow?* (When the sun was highest in the sky) Explain that "local noon" occurs when the sun is at its highest point above the horizon for a given day. Local noon does occur in the middle of the day at a given location, but because time zones cover large geographic areas, local noon probably does not occur exactly at 12:00 noon according to your accurately set clock. Daylight savings time, which shifts the time by 1 hour during certain months of the year, also affects the clock time that local noon occurs. Ask: *Is local noon exactly at 12:00 noon on the clock at our location? How do you know?*

ELABORATE

f. Ask: *Do you think local noon will occur at the same time tomorrow at this location? How could we find out? How could you modify your observations to be more certain of the actual time of local noon? Do you expect students in other towns to find the same time for local noon at their location? Why or why not? How could you find out?* (Students might suggest sharing data electronically with schools in other geographic areas.)

5. WHY IS THERE DAY AND NIGHT? (2–4)

Materials

- Styrofoam ball (about the size of a baseball)
- Craft stick and brad for each small group
- Lamp with a bright bulb (at least 100 watts)
- Globe
- Room that can be darkened
- Small lump of sticky tack

ENGAGE

a. Ask: *What do you think causes day and night? Does every place on earth have daytime or nighttime at the same time?*

EXPLORE

b. Distribute a ball, craft stick, and brad to each small group. Demonstrate how to assemble these parts as shown.

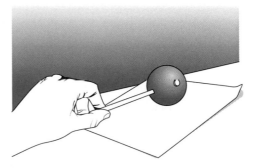

c. Have the students hold the ball by the craft stick. Then darken the room lights and turn on the bright light. Tell students to discover what they can about the way the ball is lit and record observations about their ball. The following questions might guide their thinking: *How much of the ball is lit up? Is the brad in the lit part? If not, what can you do to the ball to move the brad to the lit part? If you became tiny and were on the brad on the lit side of the ball, would you be able to see the bright light bulb? If you were tiny and were on the brad on the unlit side of the ball, would you be able to see the bright light bulb?*

EXPLAIN

    d. Ask the class to share their observations of the balls in the bright light.

    e. Show the globe to the class. Ask: *What is the globe a model of?* (Earth) *How is the globe like the earth? How is it different?* Place the lamp several meters from the globe and darken the room. Then, turn on the bright bulb. Ask: *What do you think the bright bulb is a model of?* (The sun) *How is the bright bulb like the sun? How is it different? Is the entire globe lit by the bright light? How much of it is lit?* (One half) *Which half?* (the half toward the bright light) *How does this model now show day and night?* (The lit side of the earth is having daytime, and the unlit side is having nighttime.) *What happens when I turn the globe?* (The places that are lit change.) *Are the same places on the earth having daytime when the globe is turned?* (No)

    f. Stick the small lump of sticky tack on the globe to mark the location of your school. Ask: *Is it day or night where the sticky tack is? What could I do to the globe so that the sticky tack is having daytime, then nighttime, then daytime, and so on?*

    g. Slowly spin the globe on its axis in a counterclockwise direction as viewed from above the north pole. As the sticky tack moves from darkness into the light, explain to the students that this is sunrise for the people at that location. When the sticky tack is in the center of the lit side of the globe, with the light shining directly onto it, it is noon for the people at that location. When the sticky tack moves from the lit to the unlit area, it is sunset. When the sticky tack is in the center of the unlit area, on the side of the earth away from the sun, it is midnight.

EVALUATE

    h. Check for student understanding of why we have day and night by having students respond to the following multiple-choice item:

        1. We have day and night because:
            A. The earth turns once on its axis each day.
            B. The sun travels around the earth once each day.
            C. The earth travels around the sun once each day.
            D. The sun turns on and off, it shines during the day but is dark during the night.

6. HOW DOES THE APPEARANCE OF THE MOON'S SHAPE CHANGE OVER TIME? (2–4)

Materials

  • Black construction paper
  • Soft white chalk

ENGAGE

    a. Distribute materials to the students. Give them 5 minutes to draw the shape of the moon. Post the pictures for all to see. Ask: *Are all the drawings the same shape?* (No) Sort them so that similar shapes are grouped together. Ask representatives from each group to tell why they drew the moon the way they did. Ask: *Can everyone's drawing be correct even if they are different shapes?* (Yes) *How can this be?* (The moon doesn't always appear the same shape.) *How could we find out how the appearance of the moon's shape changes over time?* (Hopefully, someone will suggest observing and recording the moon's appearance in the sky for a week or so.)

EXPLORE

b. Have the students take home a large sheet of black construction paper and some white chalk, then observe the moon daily for a week. They should divide their paper into eight equal rectangles as shown.

Moon Calendar by Suzy	11/5	11/6	11/7
11/8	11/9	11/10	11/11

Students can use the first rectangle for the title and their name and the remaining seven spaces for their daily observations. It is best to begin this assignment several days after new moon when fair weather is expected—the waxing crescent moon should be visible in the western sky shortly after sunset. Assuming it is clear, the moon should be visible in the evening sky for the next week. If there is an overcast night, students should indicate on their chart that the sky was cloudy.

EXPLAIN

c. At the end of the observation period, students should bring their moon calendars to class to share and compare. Ask: *How did the moon's shape seem to change during the week?* Have them see if everyone's observations supported the same conclusions. Ask: *Did more of the moon appear to be illuminated each night?* Tell the students that the apparent shape of the moon is known as its phase. Use a chart like this to introduce the names of the phases. Challenge the students to identify which phases they observed.

New moon	Waxing crescent	First quarter	Waxing (Gibbous)
Full moon	Waning (Gibbous)	Last quarter	Waning crescent

Phases of the Moon as Seen From the Earth

ELABORATE

d. Ask students to predict what the moon will look like for the next few days, then make observations to check their predictions.

An ongoing Moonwatch Bulletin Board[12] could be maintained in your classroom. Each night, have three students draw the shape of the moon on an index

[12]For additional details on moon watches, see G. Robert Moore, "Revisiting Science Concepts," *Science and Children* 32(3), November/December 1994, 31–32, 60.

card. Have the three students compare their drawings and arrive at one drawing that represents their observations. Post the drawing on the appropriate month/date cell on the bulletin board calendar. As a pattern develops, have the class predict the next day's moon phase.

7. WHY DOES IT APPEAR THAT THERE ARE PHASES OF THE MOON? (4–6)

Materials

- Styrofoam ball (about the size of a baseball) and a craft stick for each student
- Lamp with a bright bulb (at least 100 watts)
- A room that can be darkened

ENGAGE

a. Ask: *What are moon phases? Why does the moon have phases?*

EXPLORE

b. Use some simple objects to create a model that shows the cause of the moon's phases as viewed from the earth. In this model a styrofoam ball represents the moon, a bright lightbulb represents the sun, and your head represents the earth. Your eyes will see the view of the moon phase from the earth.

c. Insert the craft stick into the styrofoam ball to act as a handle. Hold the moon ball in your left hand with your arm outstretched. Ask: *How much of the moon ball can you see at one time?* Darken the room. Ask: *Is it easy to see the moon ball? Is any part of it illuminated?* Turn on the bright lightbulb to represent the sun. Look at the moon ball from several angles. Ask: *Is part of it illuminated now? How much of the moon ball is illuminated at the same time?* Describe the location of the lit part in relation to the bright light.

d. The moon orbits around the earth each month. To simulate this in your model, stand facing the bright light, hold the moon ball in your left hand so that the moon ball appears to be a little to the left of the lightbulb. Ask: *Is a lit area visible on the moon ball when it is in this position?* Describe it. (The right edge of the moon ball is illuminated in a narrow crescent shape.) Slowly turn to your left, keeping your arm holding the moon ball outstretched. Watch how the illuminated part of the moon ball varies as its position changes. If the moon ball goes into the shadow cast by your head, just lift the moon ball a little higher so the light can reach it. Move the moon ball around its orbit several times. Look for patterns in the way it is illuminated.

EXPLAIN

e. Have a class discussion about the questions posed in the explore phase of the lesson. Lead the students to an understanding of the following concepts.
1. The moon does not produce its own light; it reflects light from the sun.
2. Half of the moon, that half facing the sun, is illuminated at any given time.
3. We can only see half of the moon's surface at any given time, the half that is facing the earth.
4. Depending on the relative positions of the earth, sun, and moon, only part of the illuminated moon's surface may be facing the earth, so we see phases of the moon.

ELABORATE

f. Have the students complete an illustration showing the apparent moon phase when the moon is at various positions in its orbit around the earth. This illustration is really a two-dimensional model to explain why the moon appears to have phases. A completed illustration might look something like the following diagram.

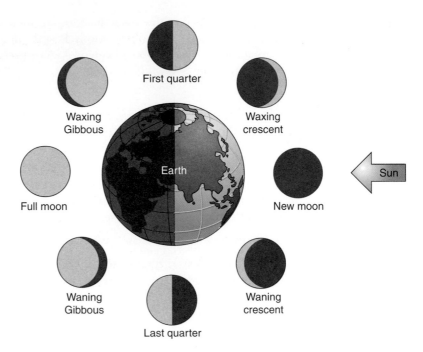

EVALUATE

g. To assess student understanding about why the moon has phases, have students answer the following questions.

   1. If the moon is full, it will rise in the east as the sun
     A. rises in the East.
     B. sets in the East.
     C. rises in the West.
     D. sets in the West.

   2. If the moon is between the earth and the sun, its phase will be:
     A. new.
     B. crescent.
     C. gibbous.
     D. full.

   3. Which of the following statements best describes why the moon has phases when viewed from the earth?
     A. The earth's shadow creates the moon's phases.
     B. How much of the illuminated half moon we see from the earth depends on the relative position of the earth, moon, and sun.
     C. Different parts of the moon emit light at different times of the month.
     D. Clouds in the earth's atmoshere block parts of the moon from our view.

8. HOW CAN WE DESCRIBE POSITIONS OF OBJECTS IN THE SKY? (4–6)

Materials

- Cardinal direction signs
- Ten index cards each labeled with a large number from 1 to 10
- Masking tape or sticky tack
- Adding machine tape
- "Handy Angle Measurements" sheet

Preparation

Post cardinal directions—north, south, east, and west—on the classroom walls. Post the 10 index cards at various locations on the walls and ceiling of the classroom. Put a strip of adding machine tape all the way around the room at the students' seated eye level. This represents the horizon.

ENGAGE

a. Ask: *How could you explain to someone where to look for a particular object in the sky? What kinds of measurements and units might be helpful?* Ask several students to describe the location of something in the classroom. Discuss alternative approaches.

EXPLORE

b. Point out the cardinal directions signs posted in the room. Distribute copies of the "Handy Angle Measurements" sheet shown. Demonstrate how to extend your arm, and discuss the angles represented by the different parts of the hand. Mention that the adding machine tape around the room represents the horizon, the starting point for their angle measurements. Ask the students to try to measure the angle from the horizon line to the point straight overhead using an outstretched arm and clenched fist. It should take approximately nine fists, since the angle from the horizon to the point overhead (zenith) is 90 degrees and each fist represents about 10 degrees.

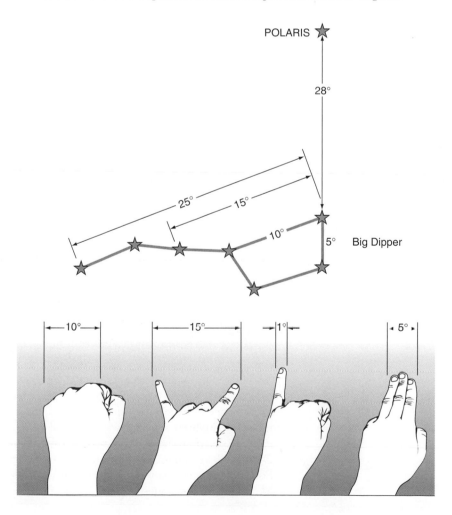

c. Have the students number from 1 to 10 on a sheet of paper. Ask them to use cardinal directions and angle measurements to describe the position of each index card number posted in the room, from their seat.

Note: Because the cards are relatively close to the observers, the observing position will affect the results. Do not expect students in different parts of the room to have the same direction and angle measurement for each card.

EXPLAIN

d. Ask: *How were you able to describe the positions of the index cards?* (By finding the direction to look and measuring how high above the horizon with my outstretched hand)

> *Could you use this same technique to describe the position of objects in the sky? What would you need to know to be successful?* (Cardinal directions)

Safety Precautions

Caution students to never look directly at the sun. The sun is very bright. Looking at it could cause blindness. Only use this technique to describe the location of the moon, stars, planets, and so on.

ELABORATE

e. Apply this measuring technique to describing the position of the moon in the sky. Find out how the moon moves across the sky during the night. Determine the cardinal directions around your observation point. A compass, street map, or locating Polaris (the North Star) should help.

f. Record your observations in a data table like the one shown.

Time of Observation	Direction	Angle Above the Horizon
7:30 p.m.		
8:00 p.m.		
8:30 p.m.		
9:00 p.m.		
9:30 p.m.		
10:00 p.m.		

Observe and record the position of the moon at half-hour intervals. Describe how the moon moves during the night. Develop an investigation to determine how the position of the moon at a given hour changes from night to night. Ask: *What did you find?*

g. If you live in the northern hemisphere, you can determine your latitude by measuring the position of Polaris above the horizon. Polaris is the end star in the handle of the Little Dipper. The pointer stars of the Big Dipper are helpful in finding Polaris. Polaris is *not* the brightest star in the sky. To find it, face the northern horizon. Look for the patterns shown in the Handy Angle Measurement diagram. The orientation of the Big Dipper will vary, but its pointer stars always point toward Polaris. Decide which star is Polaris. Determine how many degrees it is above the horizon using the Handy Angle Measurement technique. That number of degrees should be the same as the latitude of your observation position. Note the position of Polaris relative to objects on the ground (trees, houses, etc.). Try finding Polaris several hours later. Ask: *Is it still in the same angle above the horizon? Is it still in the same place relative to the objects on the ground?*

You might notice that while Polaris is in the same location, the nearby star patterns have seemed to move in a counterclockwise direction around Polaris. Activity 5, Making a Star Clock in the GEMS (Great Explorations in Math and Science) Module *Earth, Moon, and Stars*, is a good activity related to the motion of the circumpolar constellations (those around the pole).[13]

B. MODELS OF THE SOLAR SYSTEM AND THE EARTH-MOON SYSTEM

▶ *Science Background*

Our solar system includes the sun (our star), eight planets, and numerous smaller bodies including Pluto, asteroids, and comets that orbit the sun. The four planets closest to the Sun—Mercury, Venus, Earth, and Mars—are known as the inner planets. The other four planets—Jupiter, Saturn, Uranus, and Neptune—are known as the outer planets. Pluto lost its status as a planet in 2006 when 424 astronomers at the International Astronomical Union meeting voted to change the definition of the term *planet*.

The earth-moon system is unique in the solar system. Other planets have moons, but the earth is the only planet with just one very large moon. Although much smaller than the sun, our moon appears about the same size in our sky. This is because it is much closer to the earth.

NSES   **Science Standards**

All students should develop an understanding of

• the earth in the solar system (5–8).

Concepts and Principles That Support the Standards

• The earth is the third planet from the sun in a system that includes the moon, the sun, seven other planets and their moons, and smaller objects, such as dwarf planets, asteroids, and comets (5–8).
• The sun, an average star, is the central and largest body in the solar system (5–8).
• Models can represent the real world, making abstract concepts more concrete (5–8).

Objectives

1. Demonstrate and describe a scale model of our solar system.
2. Name the planets in order of size.
3. Name the planets in order of distance from the sun.
4. Demonstrate and describe a model of the earth-moon system.

---

[13]For many good astronomy activities, see GEMS (Great Explorations in Math and Science), 1986. *Earth, Moon, and Stars*, by Cary I. Sneider. Lawrence Hall of Science, Berkeley, CA.

1. HOW SPREAD OUT ARE THE PLANETS IN OUR SOLAR SYSTEM? (3–6)

Materials

- Ten sentence strips, each labeled with one of the solar system bodies (Sun, Mercury, Venus, Earth, Mars, Jupiter, Saturn, Uranus, Neptune, Pluto)

ENGAGE

a. Ask students to draw a picture showing what they know about the orbits of the planets around the sun in our solar system. To assess students' prior knowledge, ask: *How many planets did you include? Could you name the planets? Do you think you placed the planets in the right order from the sun? Are the orbits of the planets all the same distance apart? What is a scale model? Was your drawing a scale model? Why or why not?*

EXPLORE

b. Select 10 students to represent the major bodies in the solar system. Give each of them a labeled sentence strip to hold.

Select a starting place at one edge of the playground or at the end of a very long hall. Instruct the sign holding students to follow these instructions for constructing the model solar system.

1. The "sun" stands at one end of the area.
2. Mercury takes 4 small steps from the sun.
3. Venus takes 3 small steps outward from Mercury.
4. Earth takes 2 small steps beyond Venus.
5. Mars takes 5 small steps beyond Earth.
6. Jupiter takes 34 small steps beyond Mars.
7. Saturn takes 40 small steps beyond Jupiter.
8. Uranus takes 90 small steps beyond Saturn.
9. Neptune takes 100 small steps beyond Uranus.
10. Pluto takes 88 small steps beyond Neptune.

c. Tell the class that the positions of the students with the signs represent the average distance between the planets' orbits. With the holders remaining in their places and holding up their signs, all the students should observe the spacing and think about these questions: *Which planets' orbits are closest together? Which ones are really spread out? Are the planets' orbits spaced at equal distances from the sun?*

EXPLAIN

d. Upon returning to the classroom, discuss the students' responses to the questions. Important ideas to emerge from the discussion include the following:

- The first four planets—Mercury, Venus, Earth, and Mars—do not have much distance between their orbits. These planets are known as the *inner planets*.
- The rest of the planets—Jupiter, Saturn, Uranus, and Neptune—have rather large distances between their orbits. These planets are known as the *outer planets*.
- Pluto, once considered a planet, was reclassified as a dwarf planet in 2006. Pluto's average distance from the sun is represented in the model we created on the playground.

e. Explain that the planets are not usually lined up as in our model. The model does not show the actual positions of the planets, just the relative spacing of their orbits.

EVALUATE

f. To assess student knowledge of the relative positions of the planets in our solar system, have students respond to the following items.

   1. List the planets in order by their distance from the sun.   .

   2. Which of the following statements best describes the location of the planets in our solar system?

      A. The planets are all lined up in a straight line.

      B. The planet's orbits are equal distances apart.

      C. The inner planets' orbits are closer together than the orbits of the outer planets.

      D. The planets are all the same distance from the sun.

2. HOW DO THE PLANETS IN OUR SOLAR SYSTEM COMPARE IN SIZE? (5–8)

Materials

- Butcher paper
- Pencils
- Markers
- Scissors
- Metersticks
- Metric rulers or metric tapes

ENGAGE

a. Cut out a circle with a diameter of 5.6 cm to represent Earth. Show the circle to the class. Ask: *If we made a scale model of the planets in our solar system, how big would each planet be if Earth was this big?*

EXPLORE

b. Have the class count off by sevens. Tell each of the "ones" to draw a circle to represent Mercury in this model. Each of the "twos" should draw Venus to this scale, and so on. When the models showing student's prior knowledge are cut out, ask all the "ones" to bring their Mercury circles to the front of the room. Compare the range of sizes represented and how these circles compare with the Earth circle. Ask: *What does this tell us about what these people know about the size of Mercury compared to Earth?* Repeat this procedure with each of the other number groups and their cutout planets. You will probably be able to conclude that as a class we really are not sure how the planets compare in size.

c. Tell the class that the diameter of the Earth circle in our model is 5.6 cm. Measure its diameter so they can confirm its size. Tell them that you will give each person the diameter measurement of their planet, so that they can make an accurate scale model for our solar system models. The following table includes the data:

Group Number From Counting Off	Planet	Diameter in Centimeters
Ones	Mercury	2.1
Twos	Venus	5.3
Threes	Mars	3.0
Fours	Jupiter	62.6
Fives	Saturn	52.8
Sixes	Uranus	22.4
Sevens	Neptune	21.7

It may be necessary to review the meaning of the term *diameter*—the distance across the circle through the center. If students are reminded that diameter = 2 × radius, they might realize that if they find the radius (half of the diameter) of their circle and swing the radius around a center point, they will get a circle of the proper diameter. This technique is especially useful for the big planet circles.

d. After each circle is cut out, it should be labeled with the name of the planet it represents. Students should have the diameter of their planet circle checked for accuracy by at least two other students and make any necessary corrections.

e. Encourage students to get into solar system groups of eight so that there is one model of each planet in their group. Provide each group with a 5.6 cm diameter Earth circle. Challenge the groups to use their models to make a list of the planets in order of size from smallest to largest.

EXPLAIN

f. Ask: *How did you compare the planets' sizes?* (We made scale models.) *Are our models the actual sizes of the planets?* (No. They are much smaller, but are "to scale" so they can be compared.) You may want to explain that in our model 1 cm = approximately 2,285 km. At this scale, the diameter of the sun would be approximately 6 meters. Perhaps you could draw a circle with a diameter of 6 meters on the playground so they could see how big the sun is compared to the planets. Ask: *Do our models show the actual shapes of the planets?* (No. Planets are spheres, not circles. We made a two-dimensional rather than a three-dimensional model.)

g. Ask: *What did you learn about the relative sizes of planets?* (They vary greatly in size.) *What was the order of the planets from smallest to largest diameter?* (Mercury, Mars, Venus, Earth, Neptune, Uranus, Saturn, Jupiter)

ELABORATE

h. Ask students to make up comparison questions about the relative diameters of the planets, for example: *Which planet has a diameter about half Earth's diameter?* (Mars) *How many Earth diameters would fit in one Jupiter diameter?* (11) Have them challenge each other to find the answers using the scale models as an aid.

EVALUATE

    i. To assess student knowledge of the relative sizes of the planets in our solar system, have students respond to the following items.

        1. List the planets in our solar system in order from smallest to largest.   .

        2. Which of the following statements best describes the relative sizes of the planets in our solar system?

           A. All of the planets in our solar system are about the same size.

           B. The inner planets are all much smaller than the outer planets.

           C. The further a planet is from the sun, the larger it is.

           D. The further a planet is from the sun, the smaller it is.

3. HOW COULD YOU MAKE A SCALE MODEL OF THE EARTH AND MOON? (5–8)

Materials

- Basketball
- Volleyball
- Softball
- Baseball
- Tennis ball
- Golf ball
- Ping-Pong ball
- Piece of rope 7.28 meters long
- Metric rulers

ENGAGE

    a. Hold up the basketball. Tell the class that in our model of the earth and moon, it will represent the earth. Display the other balls. Ask: *Which ball would you select to represent the size of the moon in our model?* Record responses on a histogram on the board. *What would we need to know to determine which ball best represents the size of the moon when the earth is the size of a basketball?* (The actual diameter of the earth and the moon)

EXPLORE

    b. The diameter of the earth is 12,756 km and the diameter of the moon is 3,475 km. Ask: *What information do we need to collect about the balls to select the best ball to represent the moon?* Have the students get into small groups to come up with a plan to determine which ball would represent the moon. Carry out your plan.

EXPLAIN

    c. Ask: *Which ball did your group select to be the best moon ball if the earth is the size of the basketball?* (The tennis ball is best, because the earth's diameter is about 3.7 times the diameter of the moon, and the basketball's diameter is about 3.7 times the diameter of the tennis ball.)

        Ask: *What procedures did your group use to solve this problem?* (Measured the balls, used ratios, etc.) This might be an appropriate time for a review about ratios and proportions. *What is the scale of this model?* (1 cm on this model = approximately 530 km in reality)

ELABORATE

d. Ask: *If we use the basketball to represent the earth and the tennis ball to represent the moon, how far apart should they be held to represent the actual distance between the earth and the moon?* Ask a student to hold the basketball to represent the earth. Start with the tennis ball close to the basketball and slowly walk away. Ask the students to tell you when you should stop. As different groups of students or individuals tell you the distance is right, stick a piece of tape on the wall or floor to show the distance they predicted. After all have expressed their ideas, move back close to the basketball. Give the student holding the basketball one end of the 7.28 meter rope. Slowly unwrap the rope as you retrace your steps away from the basketball. When you get to the end of the rope, hold up the tennis ball. Now the model represents the relative sizes of the earth and the moon and how far they are apart. The actual distance from the earth to the moon is approximately 384,000 km. The moon is approximately 30 earth-diameters from the earth.

Appendixes

Safety Requirements and Suggestions for Elementary and Middle School Inquiry Activities

Consult your state's classroom safety and health manual for specific state policies, requirements, and suggestions.

Safety Guidelines for Teachers

1. Review science activities carefully for possible safety hazards.
2. Eliminate or be prepared to address all anticipated hazards.
3. Consider eliminating open flames; use hot plates where possible as heat sources.
4. Be particularly aware of possible eye injuries from chemical reactions, sharp objects, small objects such as iron filings, and flying objects such as rubber bands.
5. Consider eliminating activities in which students taste substances; do not allow students to touch or inhale unknown substances.
6. Warn students of the dangers of electrical shock; use small dry cells in electrical activities; be aware of potential problems with the placement of extension cords.
7. Maintain fair, consistent, and strictly enforced discipline during science activities.
8. Instruct students in the proper care and handling of classroom pets, fish, or other live organisms used as part of science activities.
9. Instruct students to report immediately to the teacher
   * any equipment in the classroom that appears to be in an unusual or improper condition,
   * any chemical reactions that appear to be proceeding in an improper way, or
   * any personal injury or damage to clothing caused by a science activity, no matter how trivial it may appear.
10. Post appropriate safety rules for students in the classroom, review specific applicable safety rules before each activity, and provide occasional safety reminders during the activity.

Safety Rules for Students

1. Always follow the safety procedures outlined by your teacher.
2. Never put any materials in your mouth.
3. Avoid touching your face, mouth, ears, or eyes while working with chemicals, plants, or animals.
4. Always wash your hands immediately after touching materials, especially chemicals or animals.
5. Be careful when using sharp or pointed tools. Always make sure that you protect your eyes and those of your neighbors.
6. Wear American National Standards Institute approved safety goggles (with Z87 printed on the goggles) whenever activities are done in which there is a potential risk to eye safety.
7. Behave responsibly during science investigations.

REFERENCES

The University of the State of New York, *Elementary Science Syllabus*, 49, 1985, Albany, NY: The State Education Department, Division of Program Development; Ralph E. Martin, Colleen Sexton, Kay Wagner, and Jack Gerlovich, *Teaching Science for All Children*, 1994, Boston: Allyn & Bacon; Full Option Science System (FOSS) Teacher's Guides, 1994, Washington, DC, National Academies of Science.

Measuring Tools, Measuring Skills

In elementary and middle school science and mathematics, students should have many opportunities to

- use a variety of types of measuring instruments;
- measure length, area, volume, mass, and temperature; and
- make comparisons using different systems of units.

Metric Prefixes

milli = .001 (one thousandth)
centi = .01 (one hundredth)
kilo = 1000 (one thousand)

Measuring Length
Length is a linear measure.

Metric Units

millimeter = 0.001 meter (one-thousandth of a meter; the thickness of about 20 pages)
centimeter = 0.01 meter (one-hundredth of a meter; width of a little fingernail)
kilometer = 1000 meters (about 10 city blocks)

Some Conversions

1 inch = 2.54 centimeters
1 centimeter = 10 millimeters
100 centimeters = 1000 millimeters = 1 meter
1 meter = 39.37 inches = 3.28 feet
1000 meters = 1 kilometer = 0.621 mile
100 meters = 109 yards
1 yard = 3 feet

Use the ruler to convert lengths between units.

1 in. = _____ cm = _____ mm
3 in. = _____ cm = _____ mm
10 cm = _____ mm = _____ in.
140 mm = _____ cm = _____ in.

Use the ruler to measure lengths.

Length of dollar bill = _____ in. = _____ cm = _____ mm
Diameter of quarter = _____ in. = _____ cm = _____ mm
Thickness of quarter = _____ in. = _____ cm = _____ mm

Measuring Area
Area is a surface measure.

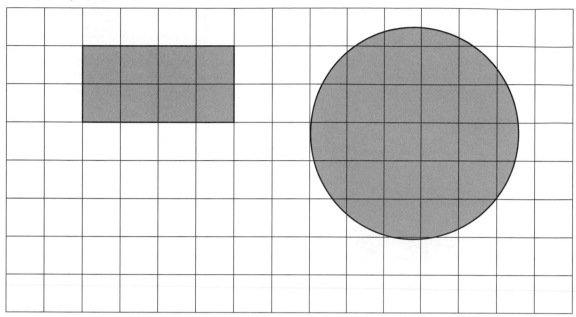

The area of each small square in the figure is 1 square centimeter = 1 cm^2.

Determine the area of the shaded rectangle

- by counting squares. _____
- by formula ($A = L \times W$). _____

Determine the area of the shaded circle

- by counting squares. _____
- by formula ($A = \pi r^2$). _____

Measuring Volume
Volume is three-dimensional.

1 cubic centimeter (cm^3 or cc) is the volume of a cube that is 1 centimeter on each side.

Some Conversions

1 cm^3 = 1 cc = 1 milliliter (ml)
1000 cm^3 = 1000 ml = 1 liter
1 liter = 1.06 quarts

Determine the volume of the large solid in the figure

- by counting unit cubes.
- by using the formula, $V = L \times W \times H$. _____

Estimate the volume of a golf ball in cubic centimeters. A golf ball has a
diameter of about 4 cm.

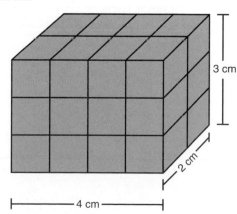

[*Answer:* Estimate how many unit cubes (1 cm³) might fit inside a golf ball if it were hollow. A good estimate of its volume might be between 25 and 40 unit cubes. By formula, the volume of a golf ball is about 33.5 cm³.]

Measuring Mass and Weight

Mass is a measure of the amount of matter in an object and, also, a measure of the inertia of an object. Mass is measured in grams, milligrams, or kilograms using a balance. Weight is a measure of the gravitational pull on an object, measured with a spring scale. Mass and weight are not the same thing, but the weight of an object can be found from its mass.

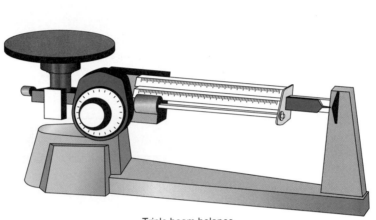

Triple beam balance

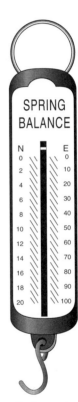

Spring scale

Some Conversions

> 1000 grams (g) = 1 kilogram (kg)
> 1 milligram = 0.001 gram (one-thousandth of a gram)
> 1 gram = 1000 milligrams (mg)
> 1 kg-mass weighs 2.2 pounds on the surface of the earth

Some Masses and Weights

> Mass of nickel = 5 g
> Mass of small child weighing about 60 pounds on earth = 27.3 kg (divide 60 by 2.2)
> Weight on moon of small child of mass 27.3 kg = 10 pounds (1/6 of weight on earth)

Food labels tell how many grams and milligrams of different substances are in a food product.

Measuring Temperature

Temperature is a measure of how hot or cold a substance is. Temperature is measured with a thermometer in degrees Celsius or degrees Fahrenheit.

Some Equivalent Temperatures: Use the Fahrenheit/Celsius thermometer to convert from one temperature unit to the other.

Boiling point of water	100°C = _____ °F
Normal body temperature	_____ °C = 98.6 °F
Room temperature	22°C = _____ °F
Freezing point of water	0°C = _____ °F
Slush of crushed ice, water, and ice cream salt	_____ °C = 10°F
A really cold day in Alaska	_____ °C = −15°F

Nutrition Facts

Serving Size 2/3 cup (55g)
Servings Per Container 12

Amount Per Serving

Calories 210
  Calories from Fat 25

% Daily Value*

Total Fat 3g	**5%**
Saturated Fat 1g	**4%**
Polyunsaturated Fat 0.5g	
Monounsaturated Fat 1.5g	
Cholesterol 0mg	**0%**
Sodium 140mg	**6%**
Potassium 190mg	**5%**
Total Carbohydrate 44g	**15%**
Other Carbohydrate 23g	
Dietary Fiber 3g	**13%**
Sugars 18g	
Protein 5g	

Vitamin A	0%
Vitamin C	0%
Calcium	2%
Iron	6%
Thiamine	10%
Phosphorus	10%
Magnesium	10%

* Percent Daily Values are based on a 2000 calorie diet. Your daily values may be higher or lower depending on your calorie needs.

	Calories	2,000	2,500
Total Fat	Less than	65g	80g
Sat Fat	Less than	20g	25g
Cholesterol	Less than	300g	300g
Sodium	Less than	2400mg	2400mg
Potassium		3500mg	3500mg
Total Carbo		300g	300g
Dietary Fiber		25g	30g

Calories per gram:

Fat 9   •   Carbohydrate 4   •   Protein 4

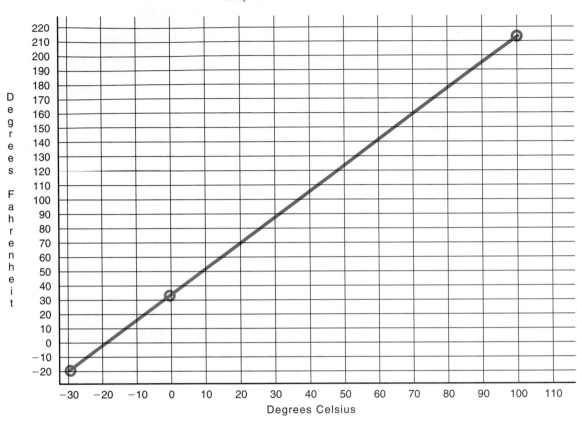

Temperature in °C and °F

Use the graph to find equivalent temperatures.

0°C = _____ °F
212°F = _____ °C
40°F = _____ °C
180°F = _____ °C
50°C = _____ °F

Selected Sources of Science Supplies, Models, Living Things, Kits, and Software

Brock Optical

Microscopes—rugged enough for small
children
E-mail: magiscope@aol.com
URL: http://www.magiscope.com

Carolina Biological Supply Company

Instructional materials for all sciences;
Science and Technology for Children
(STC) guides and materials
E-mail: carolina@carolina.com
URL: http://www.carolina.com

Delta Education

Materials, kits, and activities for hands-on
science programs, including FOSS,
SCIS 3+, and DSMIII (Delta Science
Modules)
E-mail: ecurran@delta-edu.com
URL: http://www.delta-education.com

Discovery Scope

Small, handheld microscopes
E-mail: dscopes@aol.com
URL: http://www.discoveryscope.net

Educational Innovations

Heat-sensitive paper, UV-detecting beads,
Cartesian diver, super-absorbent
polymers, and other science supplies
E-mail: info@teachersource.com
URL: http://www.teachersource.com

Educational Products, Inc.

Science fair display boards and materials
E-mail: kdavis@educationalproducts.com
URL: http://www.educationalproducts.com

ETA/Cuisenaire

Hands-on science materials
E-mail: info@etacuisenaire.com
URL: http://www.etacuisenaire.com

Fisher Science Education

Instructional materials for all sciences
E-mail: info@fisheredu.com
URL: http://www.fisheredu.com

Forestry Suppliers, Inc.

Orienteering compasses, water, soil, and
biological test kits, tree borers, soil
sieves, rock picks, weather instruments,
and other materials for interdisciplinary
science teaching
E-mail: fsi@forestry-suppliers.com
URL: http://www.forestry-suppliers.com

Ken-A-Vision Manufacturing Co., Inc.

Microscopes
E-mail: info@ken-a-vision.com
URL: http://www.ken-a-vision.com

Lab-Aids, Inc.

Single-concept hands-on kits for
chemistry, biology, environmental
science, and earth science
E-mail: customerservice@lab-aids.com
URL: http://www.lab-aids.com

Learning Technologies, Inc.

Portable planetariums and other materials
for astronomy teaching
E-mail: starlab@starlab.com
URL: http://www.starlab.com

Mountain Home Biological

Living materials, barn owl pellets, skull
sets
E-mail: mtnhome@gorge.net
URL: http://www.pelletlab.com

NASCO

Science materials and supplies
E-mail: info@enasco.com
URL: http://www.nascofa.com

National Gardening Association

GrowLab guides for kids' gardening,
professional development materials on
plant science
E-mail: MK@garden.org
URL: http://www.kidsgardening.com

NSTA Science Store

Books, posters, software, CD-ROMs
URL: http://www.nsta.org

Ohaus Corporation

Balances and measurement aids
E-mail: cs@ohaus.com
URL: http://www.ohaus.com

Pitsco LEGO Educational Division

LEGO construction kits, model hot air
balloons, educational technology
products
E-mail: pitsco@pitsco.com
URL: http://www.pitsco-legodacta.com

Rainbow Symphony, Inc.

Lesson kits for the study of light and color,
specialty optics materials, diffraction
gratings, 3-D lenses, solar eclipse safe-
viewing glasses
E-mail: kathy@rainbowsymphony.com
URL: http://www.rainbowsymphony.com

Sargent-Welch

GEMS materials, materials for all sciences
E-mail: Sarwel@Sargentwelch.com
URL: http://www.Sargentwelch.com

TOPS Learning Systems

Science lessons using simple available
materials
E-mail: tops@canby.com
URL: http://www.topsscience.org

Source: Compiled by authors from advertisements and Web searches.

Selected Science Education Periodicals for Teachers and Children

American Biology Teachers

National Association of Biology Teachers
http://www.nabt.org/

Audubon Magazine

National Audubon Society
http://www.Audubon.org/nas/

Journal of Research in Science Teaching

National Association for Research in Science Teaching
http://www.narst.org

National Geographic

National Geographic Society
http://www.nationalgeographic.com/

National Geographic Kids

National Geographic Society
http://www.nationalgeographic.com/kids/

Natural History

American Museum of Natural History
http://www.amnh.org/naturalhistory/

Ranger Rick

National Wildlife Federation
http://www.nwf.org

School Science and Mathematics

School Science and Mathematics Association
http://www.ssma.org

Science

American Association for the Advancement of Science
http://www.aaas.org

Science and Children

National Science Teachers Association
http://www.nsta.org

Science Education

John Wiley & Sons
http://www.wiley.com

Science Scope

National Science Teachers Association
http://www.nsta.org

Scientific American

http://www.sciam.com

Sky and Telescope

Sky Publishing Corp.
http://www.skyandtelescope.com

Super Science (for grades 3–6)

Scholastic
http://teacher.scholastic.com

The Science Teacher

National Science Teachers Association
http://www.nsta.org

Your Big Backyard

National Wildlife Federation
http://www.nwf.org/kidszone/

Professional Societies for Teachers of Science, Science Supervisors, and Science Educators

American Association for the Advancement of Science (AAAS)

http://www.aaas.org

American Association of Physics Teachers (AAPT)

http://www.aapt.org/

American Chemical Society (ACS)

http://www.acs.org/

Association for Educators of Teachers of Science (AETS)

http://theaste.org/

Association for Supervision and Curriculum Development (ASCD)

http://www.ascd.org/

Council for Elementary Science International (CESI)

http://unr.edu/homepage/crowther/cesi. html

International Society for Technology in Education (ISTE)

http://www.iste.org/

National Association of Biology Teachers (NABT)

http://www.nabt.org/

National Association of Geoscience Teachers (NAGT)

http://www.nagt.org/

National Geographic Society (NGS)

http://www.nationalgeographic.com

National Science Education Leadership Association (NSELA)

http://www.nsela.org

National Science Teachers Association (NSTA)

http://www.nsta.org

National Wildlife Federation (NWF)

http://www.nwf.com/

School Science and Mathematics Association (SSMA)

http://www.ssma.org

Contemporary Elementary Science Projects and Programs

Name	Grades	Contact Information	Characteristics
AIMS	K–9	AIMS Educational Foundation http://www.aimsedu.org	*Activities Integrating Math and Science* are hands-on activities that supplement science programs; available as content-themed or state-specific collections of student and teacher pages; supported by professional development workshops; strong math integration, especially in areas of organization and graphing of data.
Bottle Biology	K–8	Department of Plant Pathology, College of Agricultural and Life Sciences, University of Wisconsin, Madison Available from NSTA Science Store http://www.nsta.org	*Bottle Biology* is an ideas book for exploring environmental interactions using soda bottles and other recyclable materials. The book contains more than 20 scientific investigations using bottle constructions, including the Ecocolumn, the Predator-Prey Column, the Niche Kit, and the TerrAqua Column.
BSCS Science Tracks: Connecting Science and Literacy	K–5	Biological Science Curriculum Study, Attn: BSCS Science Tracks, 5415 Mark Dabling Blvd., Colorado Springs, CO 80918-3842 http://bscs.org Available from: Kendall/Hunt Publishing http://www.kendallhunt.com	*BSCS Science Tracks: Connecting Science and Literacy* is a comprehensive, modular, kit-based elementary science program. Developed with the help of NSF funding it features: standards-based content, teaching, and assessment; the 5-E learning cycle; guided inquiry; focus on conceptual understanding; collaboration; student journals and continuous assessment.
FOSS	K–8	Lawrence Hall of Science, University of California, Berkeley http://www.lhs.Berkeley.edu Available from: Delta Education http://www.delta-education.com	*Full Option Science System* is an inquiry-based science program, funded in part by the NSF. This comprehensive, modular, kit-based program features: developmentally appropriate materials and concepts; informative teacher guides, FOSS Readers that provide reading in the content area practice through a variety of literary genres; suggestions for science notebooking; and newly developed formative assessment tools.
GEMS	K–10	Lawrence Hall of Science, University of California, Berkeley http://www.lhs.Berkeley.edu/	*Great Explorations in Math and Science* includes more than 70 teacher guides and handbooks. Materials kits for the stand-alone and supplementary units can be purchased. Easy to use, well organized teacher guides, support teachers with limited science background. Typical units can be completed in 2 to 4 weeks.
GrowLab	K–8	National Gardening Association Burlington, VT http://kidsgardening.com	*GrowLab: Activities for Growing Minds* is an innovative curriculum guide to support plant-related instruction though indoor gardening. Activities are inquiry-based and follow GrowLab's version of the 5-E instructional model. A workshop toolkit titled, *Growing Science Inquiry,* was also developed with the support of NSF.
Insights	K–6	EDC Center for Science Education http://cse.edc.org Available from: Kendall/Hunt Publishing Company http://www.kendallhunt.com	*Insights: An Inquiry-Based Elementary School Science Curriculum* is designed to meet the needs of all children in grades K–6 while specifically addressing urban students. Insights is a core curriculum of seventeen, 6- to 8-week kit-based modules. This NSF supported program focuses on key science concepts, creative and critical thinking, problem solving through experiences in the natural environment, developing positive attitudes about science, bridging science concepts to current social and environmental events; and integration with language arts and mathematics.

Name	Grades	Contact Information	Characteristics
Peaches	Preschool	Lawrence Hall of Science, University of California, Berkeley http://www.lhs.Berkeley.edu	*Preschool Explorations for Adults*, Children, and Educators in Science consists of 10 teacher's guides for children's activities and teacher workshops. Topics include Ant Homes Under the Ground, Homes in a Pond, and Ladybugs.
SAVI/SELPH	3–8	Lawrence Hall of Science, University of California, Berkeley http://www.lhs.Berkeley.edu	*Science Activities for the Visually Impaired/Science Enrichment for Learners with Physical Handicaps* is an interdisciplinary, multi-sensory science enrichment program designed to be used with students who are blind or visually impaired, physically disabled, learning disabled, hearing impaired, or developmentally delayed. There are nine modules, each focusing on a specific content area; teacher guides to the activities; teacher preparation videos; and specially designed equipment that allow students with disabilities full access to science investigations.
SCIS 3(+)	K–6	Lawrence Hall of Science, University of California, Berkeley http://www.lhs.Berkeley.edu Available from: Delta Education http://www.delta-education.com	*Science Curriculum Improvement Study*, one of the elementary science projects developed with NSF support in response to the launch of Sputnik, is now available (after multiple revisions) as SCIS 3(+). Its modules are organized around a hierarchy of science concepts. Science process skills are integrated into the materials centered modules, which use an inductive instructional approach at the three-phase learning cycle which evolved into the 5-E instructional model.
Seeds of Science	2–5	*Seeds of Science/Roots of Reading*, Lawrence Hall of Science, University of California, Berkeley, CA 94720 seeds@berkeley.edu Available from: Delta Education http://www.delta-education.com	*Seeds of Science/Roots of Reading* is a research-based, field-tested curriculum that integrates inquiry science with content-rich literacy instruction. This developing project, funded in part by the NSF, addresses the urgent need for materials that help students make sense of the physical world while addressing foundational dimensions of literacy. The program will include 12 concept-focused, kit-based modules two text series: a collection of integrated science and literacy units, and a parallel collection of literacy units. Both series feature delightful 4-color student books that are central to each of the units.
STC	1–8	National Science Resources Center, Smithsonian Institution Available from: Carolina Biological Supply Company http://www.carolina.com	*Science and Technology for Children* is a comprehensive, modular, kit-based science program featuring inquiry-centered science education curricula that can be used by school districts to construct core instructional programs. Developed using a rigorous research and development process, STC modules provide age-appropriate opportunities for children to expand their conceptual understanding of important science concepts, acquire problem-solving and critical-thinking skills, and develop positive habits of mind toward science.
The Young Scientist Series	Preschool	Education Development Center, Inc. Available from: Redleaf Press http://www.redleafpress.org	*The Young Scientist Series* is an NSF supported science curriculum for children who are three to five years old. Each of the three teacher's guides (*Discovering Nature with Young Children, Building Structures with Young Children, and Exploring Water with Young Children*) provides background information and detailed guidance for incorporating science into preschool programs using materials typically found in an early-childhood classroom.

Index